V&R

Lutherjahrbuch

Organ der internationalen Lutherforschung

Im Auftrag der Luther-Gesellschaft herausgegeben von
Helmar Junghans
Professor i. R. an der Universität Leipzig
in Verbindung mit Dr. Michael Beyer

76. Jahrgang 2009

Luthers Ethik
Christliches Leben in ecclesia, oeconomia, politia

Luther's Ethics
in the Realms of Church, Household, Politics

Referate und Berichte
des Elften Internationalen Kongresses für Lutherforschung
Canoas/RS 21.-27. Juli 2007

Vandenhoeck & Ruprecht

Bibliografische Information der Deutschen Nationalbibliothek

Die Deutsche Nationalbibliothek verzeichnet diese Publikation in der
Deutschen Nationalbibliografie; detaillierte bibliografische Daten sind
im Internet über http://dnb.d-nb.de abrufbar.

ISBN 978-3-525-87441-7

ISSN 0342-0914

© 2010, Vandenhoeck & Ruprecht GmbH & Co. KG, Göttingen
Internet: www.v-r.de

Layout: Institut für Kirchengeschichte der Theologischen Fakultät Leipzig
Gesamtherstellung: Hubert & Co, Göttingen
Gedruckt auf alterungsbeständigem Papier

Die *Abkürzungen* der »Lutherbibliographie 2008« werden im ganzen »Lutherjahrbuch 2008«
verwendet. Den Abkürzungen für die *Lutherausgaben* liegt »Kurt Aland: Hilfsbuch zum Lu-
therstudium. 4. Aufl. Bielefeld 1996« zugrunde; StA verweist auf »Martin Luther: Studienaus-
gabe. B; L 1979 ff«; BSLK auf »Die Bekenntnisschriften der evangelisch-lutherischen Kirche/
hrsg. vom Deutschen Evangelischen Kirchenausschuß im Gedenkjahr der Augsburgischen
Konfession 1930. 2 Bde. GÖ 1930« und Nachdrucke.
Die Abkürzungen für *biblische Bücher* und die *Zeichensetzung bei Stellenangaben* folgen
dem »Novum testamentum graece« von Eberhard Nestle.
Die *Anordnung der Rezensionen* folgt der Systematik der »Lutherbibliographie«

Anschriften

der Mitarbeiter: Prof. i. R. Dr. Helmar Junghans, Gletschersteinstraße 37, D-04299 Leipzig; Prof. Dr. Robert Kolb, 801 Seminary Place, Saint Louis, MO 63105 (USA); Wissenschaftlicher Mitarbeiter Dr. Stefan Michel, Theologicum, Fürstengraben 6, D-07743 Jena. Die Anschriften der übrigen Mitarbeiter sind in dem Verzeichnis »Die Teilnehmenden des Elften Internationalen Kongresses für Lutherforschung in Canoas/RS 2007« unten Seite 285 bis 292 zu finden.

für Rezensionsexemplare: Prof. Dr. Albrecht Beutel, Evangelisch-Theologische Fakultät, Seminar für Kirchengeschichte II, Universitätstraße 13-17, D-48143 Münster.

für Sonderdrucke und Mitteilungen zur Herstellung der »Lutherbibliographie«: Theologische Fakultät, Institut für Kirchengeschichte, Abt. Spätmittelalter und Reformation, Lutherbibliographie, Otto-Schill-Straße 2, D-04109 Leipzig (Tel. 0341-9735436, FAX 0341-9735439; E-mail: Lutherjahrbuch@uni-leipzig.de);

der Geschäftsstelle der Luther-Gesellschaft in der Leucorea: Collegienstraße 62, D-06886 Lutherstadt Wittenberg (Tel.: 03491-466233; Fax: 03491-466278; E-Mail: info@luther-gesellschaft.de; www.Luther-Gesellschaft.de).

Präsident des Elften Internationalen Kongresses für Lutherforschung war Professor Dr. Gottfried Brakemeier, der den Kongress am 22. Juli 2007 in der Kapelle der Universidade Luterana do Brasil (ULBRA) eröffnete, in deren Räumen der Kongress tagte. Anstelle des am 9. Juli 2007 verstorbenen Chairman des Continuation Comitee für den Elften Internationalen Kongress für Lutherforschung, Prof. Dr. Günther Wartenberg, übernahm Prof. Dr. Scott H. Hendrix die Leitung des Kongresses. Chairman des Local Arrangements Committee war Prof. Dr. Nestor Luiz João Beck. Eine Besonderheit stellte eine Konferenzschaltung dar, mit deren Hilfe die Teilnehmer den zu einer Reise nach Canoas zu diesem Zeitpunkt nicht fähigen Prof. Dr. Robert Kolb in Saint Louis, Missouri sehen, seinen Vortrag hören und mit ihm diskutieren konnten. Am Kongress nahmen 100 Forscherinnen und Forscher aus 16 Ländern teil. Ungewöhnlich viele der Angemeldeten – 33 – sahen sich nicht in der Lage, anzureisen, weil es ihr Gesundheitszustand nicht zuließ oder die gebuchten Flugverbindungen ausfielen. Die Exkursion am 25. Juli führte nach Nova Petrópolis/RS, wo der Parque do Imigrante (Park des Einwanderers) besucht wurde.

Das Continuation Comitee zur Vorbereitung des Zwölften Internationalen Kongresses für Lutherforschung besteht aus Bischof Dr. Carl Axel Aurelius, Göteborg (Schweden); Prof. Dr. Albrecht Beutel, Münster (Deutschland); Akad. Mitarb. Michael Beyer, Leipzig (Deutschland); Prof. Dr. Mary Jane Haemig, St. Paul, MN (USA); Prof. Dr. Scott H. Hendrix, Pittsboro, NC (USA); Prof. Dr. Robert Kolb, Saint Louis, MO (USA); Prof. Dr. Volker Leppin, Jena (Deutschland); Prof. Dr. Antti Raunio, Helsinki (Finnland); Prof. Dr. Ricardo Willy Rieth, São Leopoldo, RS (Brasilien) und Professor Ph. D. Anna Vind, København (Dänemark). Es bestätigte Scott H. Hendrix als seinen Chairman für die Vorbereitung des Zwölften Internationalen Kongresses für Lutherforschung, der vom 5. bis 10. August 2012 in Helsinki unter dem Thema »Luther als Lehrer und Reformer der Universität / Luther as teacher and reformer of the university« stattfinden soll. Chairman des Local Commitees ist Prof. Dr. Risto Saarinen, Helsinki (Finnland).

Luthers Auftrag in Brasilien heute

Von Gottfried Brakemeier[1]

Es ist mir, in meiner Eigenschaft als Präsident dieses Kongresses, eine große Freude, Sie zu begrüßen und Ihnen, den Teilnehmern und Gästen, meinerseits ein herzliches Willkommen zu sagen. Dass ein internationaler Kongress für Lutherforschung den Weg nach Brasilien gefunden hat, ist einer besonderen Würdigung wert. Jahrhunderte lang hatte sich das Land gegen den Geist der Reformation abgeschottet, zunächst als portugiesische Kolonie, dann – seit Anfang des 19. Jahrhunderts – als autonome Monarchie. Der Katholizismus war Staatsreligion. Erst mit der Erklärung der Republik im Jahre 1889 wurde das Recht auf Religionsfreiheit zugestanden. Allerdings musste schon das Kaiserreich Protestanten dulden, die als Einwanderer, als Soldaten, Fachkräfte und Bauern benötigt wurden und unter denen es nicht wenige Lutheraner gab. Die ersten evangelischen Gemeinden, die sich auf brasilianischem Boden bildeten, hatten gleichwohl unter Diskriminierung und Benachteiligung zu leiden. Dem Namen Martin Luthers hing der Makel des Ketzers an, den er auch in späteren Zeiten nicht wirklich los wurde. Ich erinnere mich, dass ich noch Anfang der fünfziger Jahre des vergangenen Jahrhunderts ein Buch im Schaufenster einer Buchhandlung sah mit dem suggestiven Titel: »O Diabo, Lutero e o Protestantismo« (»Der Teufel, Luther und der Protestantismus«).

Nun, die Zeiten, in denen so etwas ernst genommen wurde, sind vorbei. Die frühere konfessionelle Isolation Brasiliens wird heute auch von Nichtlutheranern beklagt. Sie habe den gesellschaftlichen, sozialen und geistigen Fortschritt gebremst und auch sonst dem Land Nachteile gebracht. Der ökumenische Aufbruch nach dem Zweiten Vatikanischen Konzil – zusätzlich motiviert durch die Menschenrechtsverletzungen der Militärdiktatur

---

[1] Eröffnungsvortrag zum Elften Internationalen Kongress für Lutherforschung am 22. Juli 2007.

in den sechziger und siebziger Jahren – hat die Kirchen einander näher gebracht. Der Name »Martin Luther« ist für die meisten heute kein Schreckgespenst mehr, wenngleich die Schatten der Vergangenheit immer wieder auftauchen und sich in billiger Polemik gegen den Reformator äußern. Leider ist das ökumenische Klima in jüngster Zeit wieder spürbar rauer geworden. Da der Papst vor ein paar Tagen die römisch-katholische Kirche erneut zur einzigen legitimen Vertreterin der Kirche Jesu Christi erklärt hat, ist ungewiss, wie es sich weiter entwickeln wird. Der Traum von der Einheit der Christen wird sich offenbar nicht so bald erfüllen, zum Schaden der Kirche und einer pluralen Gesellschaft, in der das friedliche Zusammenleben auch mit Differenzen zu einer Überlebensfrage geworden ist.

Unter solchen Bedingungen versuchen die »Evangelische Kirche Lutherischen Bekenntnisses in Brasilien« (IECLB) und die »Evangelische Lutherische Kirche Brasiliens« (IELB) mit ihren Gemeinden und theologischen Fakultäten, neben einigen kleineren lutherischen Splittergruppen, das Vermächtnis des großen Reformators zu wahren und in Ökumene, Staat und Gesellschaft zur Geltung zu bringen. Aber sie bilden in Brasilien eine verschwindende Minderheit, die noch nicht einmal ein Prozent der Bevölkerung ausmacht. Nimmt man den Süden des Landes aus, wo die lutherische Präsenz am dichtesten ist, wird sie kaum zur Kenntnis genommen. Martin Luther ist in unserem Land ein weitgehend Unbekannter geblieben.

Ein Grund dafür war bis vor Kurzem der mangelnde Zugang zu den Schriften Luthers in der Landessprache. Wir freuen uns, dass es unseren Kirchen gelungen ist, seit 1987 eine gemeinsame Übersetzung von Luthers Werken ins Portugiesische auf den Weg zu bringen. Sie ist noch nicht abgeschlossen, liegt aber schon in neun von den insgesamt siebzehn geplanten Bänden vor. Natürlich hat es auch vorher Übersetzungen einzelner Schriften, allen voran des Kleinen Katechismus, gegeben. Aber wer nicht des Deutschen oder des Englischen bzw. des Lateinischen mächtig war, konnte sich nur begrenzt über Luthers Theologie informieren, meist aus dritter Hand. Nun ist »Übersetzung«, sofern sie über die bloße Zurkenntnisnahme hinausgeht, ein komplexer Vorgang, der sich nicht auf eine literarische Frage reduzieren lässt. Er fordert die geistige Auseinandersetzung, die Entdeckung der Bedeutung Martin Luthers für die Gegenwart, die kritische Aneignung seines Erbes. Die Kontextualisierung Luthers, das heißt seine Lösung aus ethnischen Bindungen und seine Inkulturation in der lateinamerikanischen Welt kann ohne eine solche Anstrengung nicht gelingen. So gesehen hat die brasilianische Theologie und Geisteswelt das, was man Lutherrezeption nennt, noch vor sich. Zu lange war Luther in unserem Kontext aus dem öffentlichen Gespräch ausgegrenzt.

Daher lautet die entscheidende Frage: Was hat Luther im heutigen Brasilien zu sagen? Bedeutet lutherische Konfessionalität lediglich eine weitere Variante im religiösen Spektrum des Landes? Als lutherische Christen fragen wir nach unserem Auftrag in der brasilianischen Gesellschaft, der im Grunde kein anderer sein kann als jener, den Luther für sich selbst in seiner Zeit erkannt hatte. Obwohl sich die Zeiten gewandelt haben und ein tiefer historischer Graben die Welt Luthers von der heutigen trennt, muss vorausgesetzt werden, dass die lutherische Reformation bleibende Bedeutung besitzt. Anders verlöre Kirche mit lutherischer Konfessionalität ihre Existenzgrundlage. Unter den Bedingungen eines verschärften religiösen Wettbewerbs gewinnt diese Frage höchste Brisanz. Wir müssen Rechenschaft ablegen über unseren Glauben und unser Bekenntnis. Dabei verbietet die historische Differenz von gestern und heute, Rezepte der Vergangenheit unbesehen zu übernehmen. Es darf nicht um den Buchstaben gehen. Wichtig ist der Geist, der sich allerdings des Buchstabens bedient. Wie äußert sich dieser Geist, der Martin Luther zur Reformation bewegte und der die Welt veränderte?

Es darf von der Lutherforschung erwartet werden, dass sie zur Beantwortung dieser Frage beiträgt. Gewiss, historische Forschung ist rückwärts gewandt. Sie befasst sich mit Gewesenem, in diesem Fall mit einer Persönlichkeit der Vergangenheit, und will wissen, wie es war. Die Frage nach dem Tagungsort ist insofern zweitrangig, da sich Forschungsergebnisse, die sich wissenschaftlichem Bemühen verdanken, nicht durch örtliche Gegebenheiten beeinflussen lassen dürfen. Wissenschaft weiß sich dem Kriterium der Objektivität und Allgemeingültigkeit verpflichtet. Dennoch geschieht jede Rückfrage aus aktuellem Anlass. Sie vollzieht sich keineswegs im luftleeren Raum. Im Gegenteil, jede wissenschaftliche Untersuchung ist von Interessen geleitet. Deshalb darf man hoffen, dass sich aus den Forschungsergebnissen und den Beratungen auch dieses Kongresses Impulse ergeben, die für heutige Fragestellungen wegweisend sind und lutherische Kirche auf ihrem Weg ermutigen.

Natürlich handelt es sich um globale Probleme, auf die lutherische Theologie heute zu reagieren hat. Ich denke beispielsweise an die Dringlichkeit des interreligiösen Dialogs, der nicht nur auf lokaler Ebene geführt werden kann. Die Wirklichkeiten dieser Welt sind zu eng miteinander vernetzt, als dass sie privatisiert werden könnten. Die ökologische Problematik ist dafür besonders instruktiv. Wir sind zur Verständigung und Kooperation auch über Grenzen hinweg gezwungen. Auch das Luthertum sieht sich weltweit gemeinsam herausgefordert, weshalb es auf globale Strukturen nicht verzichten kann. Ähnliches gilt für die Christenheit als Ganze, sodass Ökumene zunehmend an Bedeutung gewinnt. Dennoch dürfen regionale Besonderheiten nicht übersehen werden. Universalität und Partikularität bedingen sich gegenseitig und wollen in ihrer Polarität geachtet werden. So hat auch die brasilianische Welt ihr Proprium, ohne dass mit dieser Erkenntnis die globale Verflochtenheit der Realitäten geleugnet werden soll. Was in Brasilien geschieht, ist typisch für die Gegenwart und gleichzeitig spezifisch. Aus diesem Grund ist es nicht unrealistisch zu hoffen, dass trotz oder gerade wegen des internationalen Rahmens dieses Kongresses einige Brosamen für lutherische Existenz in Brasilien abfallen werden. Umgekehrt darf man sich ebenfalls wünschen, dass das brasilianische Umfeld die internationale Lutherforschung befruchten möge, auch wenn dieses, schon aus zeitlichen Gründen, nur bruchstückhaft zur Kenntnis genommen werden kann.

Die Beschäftigung mit Luther geschieht in unserem Lande unter den Bedingungen dessen, was man die »Erschöpfung des protestantischen Projekts für die brasilianische Gesellschaft« genannt hat. Gemeint ist, dass der Protestantismus in seiner herkömmlichen Gestalt die religiösen Erwartungen der Menschen nicht mehr erfüllt. Das Urteil erstreckt sich mutatis mutandis auch auf den traditionellen Katholizismus. Alle sogenannten »historischen Kirchen« haben in den vergangenen Jahren und Jahrzehnten empfindliche Einbußen an Mitgliedern hinnehmen müssen. Die neue religiöse Welle geht an den kirchlichen Institutionen vorbei. Das wird auch in anderen Ländern empfunden. Dogmatische Traditionen werden relativ, ja geradezu irrelevant. Man spricht von einem Traditionsabbruch, den es vorher so nicht gegeben hat und der die Kirche vor eine missionarische Aufgabe stellt, wie sie größer kaum gedacht werden kann.

Das ist auch in Brasilien nicht anders. Zwar ist die Zahl derer, die sich religionslos bezeichnen, mit zirka 7% vergleichsweise gering. Aber die Menschen verschwinden in anderen, oft schwer identifizierbaren Gruppen. Die Zukunft scheint einer charismatischen, mystischen, erfolgsorientierten Spiritualität zu gehören.

Es bestätigt sich damit auch in diesem Land die Beobachtung, dass in sogenannten postmodernen Zeiten die Religion eine andere Funktion erfüllt als früher. Sie emanzipiert sich von den sie tragenden Institutionen und wird zu einer Privatangelegenheit. Ohne in Details dieser komplexen Thematik einzusteigen, soll nur so viel gesagt werden, dass diese Bewegung in Brasilien zu erheblichen Verschiebungen in der religiösen Landschaft geführt hat und weiterhin führt. Mit ihr müssen sich auch lutherische Theologie und Kirche auseinandersetzen. Die Veränderungen in der religiösen Szene erinnern energisch daran, dass von Religion Hilfe zur Lebensgestaltung und Problembewältigung erwartet wird. Die angebliche Erschöpfung des protestantischen Projekts geht eindeutig zulasten eines Defizits von therapeutischer, diakonischer und poimenischer Qualität kirchlicher Praxis. Daher wird es erneut darauf ankommen, dem »Volk aufs Maul zu schauen« – wie Luther gesagt hat –, was auch heißen muss, die Bedürfnisse der Menschen zu erkennen und ihre Sehnsüchte und Hoffnungen zu erahnen. Nicht die Preisgabe der eigenen Identität, wohl aber Korrekturen in Wort und Tat sind von lutherischer Kirche in unserem Land gefordert. Wir wagen die These, dass lutherische Theologie von jeher praktische Theologie gewesen ist, so sehr sie sich auch um die »theoretische« Begründung des Evangeliums bemüht hat. Die Wertschätzung der Praxis, wie sie nicht nur für die Befreiungstheologie, sondern auch für evangelikal orientierte Theologie kennzeichnend ist, findet in Martin Luther eine kräftige Stütze.

Das heißt nicht, dass sich lutherische Kirche um des bloßen Markterfolgs willen den religiösen Moden ausliefern darf. Sie würde ihren reformatorischen Elan verlieren. Anpassung alleine verspricht nur kurzlebigen Erfolg und ist meist nur um den Preis des Verrats am Evangelium zu haben. Luther sah seinen Auftrag darin, die Kirche zu ihrem evangelischen Ursprung zurückzuführen. Reformation ist stets kritische Arbeit, die das Bestehende prüft und auf seinen Wert hin befragt. Es ist eine

Binsenwahrheit, dass auch in Sachen Religion nicht alles Gold ist, was glänzt. Die Ambivalenz des Religiösen treibt viele Menschen geradezu dem Nihilismus in die Arme, der jede Religion als Aberglaube ablehnt und seine schädlichen Auswirklungen anprangert. Menschen werden betrogen, verführt und bis zur Gewaltbereitschaft fanatisiert. Darf man Religion in die Beliebigkeit stellen und zur Privatsache erklären? Der Glaube ist noch immer die größte Geschichtskraft überhaupt, ein Grund, ihm größere Aufmerksamkeit zu schenken, als dies weithin geschieht. Zwar ist Brasilien bislang vor neuen Religionskriegen bzw. vor Terror im Namen der Religion bewahrt geblieben. Das erschreckende Ausmaß von Gewalt in der brasilianischen Gesellschaft hat andere Ursachen. Dennoch sind sehr fragwürdige religiöse Tendenzen zu beobachten. Sie müssen lutherische Theologie und Kirche beunruhigen und sie in ihrer »protestantischen« Rolle bestärken. Dafür zwei Beispiele:

1. Wohl noch nie war die Vermarktung von Glaubensgütern so groß wie heute. In Brasilien hat sie vor allem in der sogenannten »teologia da prosperidade«, was man mit Wohlstandstheologie übersetzen könnte, wie sie von einigen Kirchen gepredigt wird, dramatische Proportionen angenommen. Glaube muss Erfolg bringen und Profit abwerfen. Das aber geschieht nicht, ohne dass zuvor massiv in die Kirche, die dies beides verspricht und vermittelt, materiell investiert wurde. Ein solcher Diskurs wendet sich vorrangig an die Verlierer des globalen Wettbewerbs, nicht indem er das herrschende Wirtschaftssystem in Frage stellt und auf soziale Reformen drängt, sondern indem Armut, Krankheit, Arbeitslosigkeit und andere Übel auf dämonische Kräfte zurückgeführt werden, die den sozialen Aufstieg blockieren und daher ausgetrieben werden müssen. Die Verheißung von Reichtum und Glück fügt sich nahtlos einer hedonistischen Kultur ein, die den Erfolg von der Tüchtigkeit des Einzelnen abhängig macht, mit dem Unterschied, dass zum Erreichen dieses Zwecks auch religiöse Mittel angepriesen werden. Das Heil wird definitiv im Diesseits erwartet, als Gottes Segen, und zwar ohne Aufschub, sofort. Die Wohlstandskirchen sind die reichsten in unserem Land. Ihre Propaganda kennt selbstverständlich nur die Erfolgsmeldung, woher sich ihre enorme Popularität und ihre Faszination erklären. Aber nicht nur in diesen Kirchen werden Glaubensgüter gehandelt. Dass die Gnade Gottes umsonst

ist, wie Luther nicht müde wurde, zu betonen, ist dem Menschen offenbar nur schwer zu vermitteln. Für Gottes Wohltat muss doch irgendein Preis entrichtet werden! Das ist nach wie vor die herrschende Auffassung in der römisch-katholischen Volksfrömmigkeit mit ihrem Heiligenkult. Sie hat neue Nahrung gewonnen durch die Kanonisierung des »Frei Galvão«, dem ersten brasilianischen Heiligen, anlässlich des kürzlichen Besuches von Papst Benedikt XVI. in diesem Land. Das Volk sucht in der Religion die Heilung seiner Gebrechen, was im Grunde ja nicht falsch ist. Aber es meint, die Rettung aus Not durch Gelübde und deren Einlösung beschleunigen oder erzwingen zu können. Man sucht das Wunder und ist bereit, auch dafür zu zahlen. Mit Religion kann man gute Geschäfte machen. Kirchen, die sich gegen diese Wahrheit sperren, haben meistens mit finanziellen Problemen zu kämpfen. Wie kann eine Kirche, die die Rechtfertigung »sola gratia et sola fide« predigt, wirtschaftlich überleben?

Generell wird man sagen müssen, dass die Erwartungshaltung des brasilianischen Volkes gegenüber den Kirchen ausgesprochen utilitaristisch geprägt ist. Kirchenzugehörigkeit muss sich auszahlen, und sei es nur in Form der Garantie eines kirchlichen Begräbnisses. Das aber bedeutet, dass die Mitgliedschaft relativ wird. Die Menschen privilegieren diejenigen Kirchen, die ihren Bedürfnissen am besten entgegenkommen. Daher erklärt sich das, was man die »religiöse Binnenwanderung« nennen könnte. Es gibt Menschen, die haben schon alles mal probiert. Sie sind römisch-katholisch gewesen, dann in den synkretistischen Kult Umbanda abgewandert, um es darauf bei den Pfingstlern zu versuchen und schließlich auch das lutherische Angebot zu testen. Kirchentreue wird selten. Natürlich darf man ein solches Urteil nicht verallgemeinern. Aber es spiegelt eine Wirklichkeit, die sich vor allem in den Städten ausbreitet und zur Normalität zu werden droht. Damit kommt auch lutherische Kirche unter Druck. Sie hat sich auf dem Markt zu bewähren und ihr Angebot an den Mann und die Frau zu bringen. Wie würde der Rat Martin Luthers in dieser Situation aussehen?

2. Das zweite Beispiel betrifft die Art der brasilianischen Frömmigkeit. Sie ist ausgesprochen emotionaler Natur. Das ekstatische Erlebnis wird zum Kennzeichen echter Religion. Man will sich begeistern, charismatische Erfahrungen sammeln, im tiefsten der Seele gerührt werden. Entscheidend ist die Begegnung mit dem Heiligen, das Hingerissenwerden

durch die Präsenz des Göttlichen, die Erfahrung von Epiphanie. In den Gottesdiensten der Pfingstgemeinden wird davon einiges spürbar. Hier wird die Manifestation des Geistes in außergewöhnlichen Zeichen wie Glossolalie, Transe, Wunderheilungen und ähnlichen Phänomenen handgreiflich. Wie man weiß, gehören die Pfingstgemeinden hierzulande zu den am stärksten wachsenden religiösen Gruppen. Die »Taufe mit dem Geist«, wie sie es nennen, ist dafür sicherlich nicht die einzige Ursache. Den durch die sozialen Umwälzungen entwurzelten Menschen wird eine neue Heimat geboten und im gottesdienstlichen Feiern eine alternative Welt zum oft bedrückenden Alltag ermöglicht. Andere Gründe mehr könnten genannt werden. Dennoch ist nicht zu übersehen, dass pfingstlerische Spiritualität offenbar ein verbreitetes Bedürfnis des brasilianischen Volkes anspricht. Rationalität kann gegen derartige Religiosität nur wenig ausrichten.

Auch diese besondere Erscheinung von Religion gehört in den Rahmen eines größeren, ja weltweiten Trends. Man könnte ihn den Mystischen nennen, der auf Emotionen fixiert ist, der die Erfahrung schätzt und das Erlebnis sucht. Glaubensinhalte werden dabei zweitrangig. Natürlich beruht auch solche Religiosität auf bestimmten Vorstellungen wie etwa die der Existenz von dämonischen Mächten oder der Möglichkeit von Heilkräften magischer Mittel. Aber sie braucht kein eigentliches Glaubensbekenntnis. Im Grunde kann sie auf Theologie verzichten. Ökumene sucht in diesem Fall nicht den Konsens in der Lehre und in der Ethik. Hauptsache ist vielmehr, dass die Emotionen stimmen. Diese können sich sehr wohl an unterschiedlichen Gegenständen entzünden, wie etwa an der Gottesmutter Maria oder an der Meereskönigin Yemanjá, eine Gottheit afro-brasilianischer Kulte. Und doch zeigt emotionale Religiosität letztlich überall das gleiche Gesicht. Sie ist wesentlich synkretistisch, transkonfessionell, ja sogar transreligiös. Fundamentalismus gibt es in allen Religionen. Auch die charismatische Bewegung kann als Beispiel dienen. Sie hat in allen Kirchen ihre Ableger und unterscheidet sich nur unwesentlich in ihren Varianten.

Braucht lutherische Kirche zu ihrem Überleben mehr Emotion bzw. Religion? Die Frage sollte nicht vorschnell verneint werden, da sie gründlicher Überlegung bedarf. Das Christentum ist immer auch Religion gewesen, die nicht nur den Verstand, sondern auch die Seele und das Gemüt in den Glauben einbezogen hat. Das war bei Luther nicht anders, wie etwa seine herrlichen Lieder bezeugen, die noch der heutigen Gemeinde Trost spenden und Mut machen. Aber die emotionale Welle hat etwas zutiefst Problematisches. Man kann den Verdacht nicht unterdrücken, dass sie das Denken verbannt und die Vernunft unterdrückt. Sollte sie ein Mittel sein, über die Verlegenheit des Glaubens hinweg zu täuschen? Religion statt Glaube? Denn dieser steckt in einer tiefen Krise. Die Welt des 21. Jahrhunderts weiß nicht mehr, woran sie glauben darf und kann.

Papst Benedikt XVI. hat in seiner berühmten Regensburger Vorlesung auf die enge Beziehung von »fides« und »ratio« in der Tradition des Christentums verwiesen. Ohne auf Einzelheiten seines Vernunftbegriffes einzugehen, ist doch so viel zuzugestehen, dass Glaube an Jesus Christus nicht ohne Weisheit gedacht werden kann. Glaube muss einsichtig bleiben und daher den Verstand gebrauchen. Lutherische Theologie hat sich daher stets um Nüchternheit bemüht, die über der Begeisterung des Glaubens die Realitäten der Welt nicht übergeht. Hier bleibt ein Unterschied zur römisch-katholischen Kirche, die das Auge fasziniert, wofür der schon erwähnte Papstbesuch in unserem Land ein nochmaliges Beispiel war. Neben dem Papst war die lutherische Kirche in den Medien unsichtbar. Sollte sie die römisch-katholische Kirche daher um eine solche repräsentative Gestalt beneiden? Um des Evangeliums willen ist dieser Versuchung zu widerstehen. Denn der Papst ist nicht nur ein Symbol, das Frömmigkeit inspiriert, sondern ebenfalls und vor allem Inbegriff einer hierarchischen Kirche. So wie Glaube nicht nur Begeisterung und emotionale Ergriffenheit bedeutet, so darf er auch nicht mit Unterwerfung unter das Diktat der Kirche verwechselt werden. Es geht heute noch oder wiederum um evangelische Freiheit, die sich nicht zum Knecht schwärmerischer Emotionen noch religiöser Unmündigkeit machen lässt.

Mit all dem ist das ökumenische Mandat lutherischer Kirche nicht geleugnet. Denn das Bemühen um die Einheit der Kirche wäre falsch verstanden, würde es die Auseinandersetzung über strittige Fragen unterbinden. Geschwisterlichkeit muss Differenzen ertragen und austragen können, ohne dass es zu Hauen und Stechen oder gegenseitiger Exkommunikation kommt. Das gilt auch für die weitere Ökumene, welche die gesamte Menschheit umfasst. Es muss möglich sein, auf Gottes Erde in

Frieden miteinander zu leben. Eben aus diesem Grund muss mehr über den Glauben geredet werden. Religion darf sich weder in Emotionen erschöpfen noch in blindem Gehorsam gegenüber angeblich göttlichen Gesetzen und Strukturen, noch auch im unbedachten Massenkonsum religiöser Waren. Worauf wir uns im Leben und im Tod verlassen können, also was wir glauben dürfen, war schon immer die entscheidende Frage der Menschen, sowohl individuell wir kollektiv. Um darin Klarheit zu gewinnen, braucht die Welt von heute eine neue Reformation.

Sie kann nicht »gemacht«, das heißt programmiert und produziert werden. Reformation ist immer Sache des Heiligen Geistes, um den gebeten und der empfangen werden will. Aber lutherischer Kirche ist die Rolle Johannes des Täufers anvertraut, der sich zum Wegbereiter des Herrn berufen wusste. Diese Rolle sollte sie beherzt und ohne Zögern übernehmen. Dazu braucht sie ein klares Profil. Nur eine Kirche mit unmissverständlicher Identität wird in einem multireligiösen Kontext überzeugen können. Das schließt »ökumenisches Lernen« nicht aus. Man darf ruhig einmal um sich schauen, um von anderen, vor allem von den Schwesterkirchen zu lernen. Denn auch man selbst hat seine Defizite und Fehler. Wir wissen es aus persönlicher Erfahrung. Aber wenn darüber die eigene Identität verloren geht, ist der Lernprozess fehlgeschlagen. Deshalb gibt es unsere Theologischen Fakultäten, deshalb gibt es theologische Veranstaltungen in den Gemeinden und Synoden, deshalb gibt es, »last, not least« einen Internationalen Kongress für Lutherforschung wie diesen, den wir am heutigen Tag eröffnen. Möge auch er der Wegbereitung der Reformation Gottes dienen, die wir in unserem Land und sicher auch anderswo so dringend benötigen.[2]

---

2 Literaturhinweise: Walter ALTMANN: Lutero e libertação: releitura de Lutero em perspectiva latino-americana. São Leopoldo: Sinodal; São Paulo: Ática, 1994; Leonardo BOFF: A significação de Lutero para a libertação dos oprimidos. In: E a Igreja se fez povo: eclesiogênese; a Igreja que nasce da fé do povo. 2. Aufl. Petrópolis: Vozes, 1986, 164-179; REFLEXÕES EM TORNO DE LUTERO/ hrsg. von Martin Norberto Dreher. Bd. 1-3. São Leopoldo 1981, 1984, 1988; Joachim FISCHER: Luther in Brasilien. LuJ 50 (1983), 150-165; RELEITURA DA TEOLOGIA DE LUTERO EM CONTEXTOS DO TERCEIRO MUNDO/ hrsg. von Nelson Kirst. Estudos teológicos 30 (São Leopoldo 1990) Sonderheft. Einen besonderen Hinweis verdient Joachim FISCHER: Bibliografia Luterana brasileira. In: Reflexões em torno de Lutero/ hrsg. von Martin N. Dreher. Bd. 3. São Leopoldo: Sinodal, 1888, P 87-144.

Faith and Christian Living in Luther's Confession Concerning Christ's Supper (1528)

By Antti Raunio

I Introduction

Our theme, »Faith and Christian living«, is not in the focus of Luther's »Confession concerning Christ's Supper« (Von Abendmahl Christi. Bekenntnis). The Confession consists of three parts. The first and second parts contain a long discussion about the understanding of certain biblical verses which have been used in the dispute on Christ's presence in the Eucharist.[1] Its purpose is to answer to Zwingli's and Oecolampadius' arguments concerning the right understanding of the Gospel's words »He took bread, and gave thanks and broke it, and gave it to his disciples and said, Take, eat: this is my body which is given for you« and »this cup is the new testament in my blood, which is poured out for you for the forgiveness of sins«. The third part is a confession of faith, which Luther wrote as a »testament« of his central teaching. The confession may be read independently, but it also has an inner connection with the discussion concerning the Eucharist.

As Wolfgang Schwab puts it in his study on the development of Luther's theology of the sacraments, Luther expresses his appreciation of the Eucharist more vividly in some other writings than in the theological disputes.[2] Nevertheless, the Confession refers time and again to the relation between Christ's Supper and the Christian way of life.[3] And what is even

---

1 For the Reformers' interpretations of biblical passages on the Eucharist see David C. STEINMETZ: Luther in context. Grand Rapids, Michigan 2002, 72-84.

2 Wolfgang SCHWAB: Entwicklung und Gestalt der Sakramententheologie bei Martin Luther. F 1977, 299.

3 Luther's conception of the relation between the Lord's Supper and Christian life or his »Eucharistic ethics« has not received much attention in Luther research. For example Schwab: Entwicklung und Gestalt ..., 302, writes in the chapter »Lord's Supper in the

more important, the debate of the understanding of the Eucharist deals with the very foundations of Christian living. Many researchers have pointed out that the deep questions in this debate are the nature of God's word, the relation between spirit and matter and the role of creation and creatures in God's saving work. Zwingli followed the at least partly platonic ideals of Erasmian humanism in aiming toward a »spiritual and inward religion«.[4] For him the Spirit and grace are totally independent of everything material and visible whereas Luther stressed God's commitment with his material creation and especially with word, water, bread and wine, and Christ's human nature in his saving work.[5] For Luther it is important that in the Eucharist Christ's body and blood are really delivered to the recipients.

The main question of this study is, then, the relation of the delivering of Christ's body and blood with faith and Christian living. In order to fulfill the task we need to reconstruct Luther's views on the delivering of Christ's body and blood and of Christian living and its relation to faith. Because the Reformer deals with Christian living only cursorily in the »Confession concerning Christ's Supper«, I have taken leave to use other texts in addition: Luther's writings concerning the debate on the Lord's Supper, and the Large Catechism, for which the Large Confession forms an important background. The Confession will nevertheless be the main source and the other texts are used to explain thoughts that are either presupposed in the Confession or that follow from the ideas presented in it.

life of Christians« only that as Christ has received us in the Sacrament, we must also receive other human beings. Thus the Sacrament lives further in the active love of one's neighbor. For a more thorough presentation of the theme see Albrecht PETERS: Sakrament und Ethos nach Luther. LuJ 36 (1969), 41-79: Antti RAUNIO: Summe des christlichen Lebens: die Goldene Regel als Gesetz der Liebe in der Theologie Martin Luthers. MZ 2001, 345-354.

4 For Zwingli's relation to Erasmian humanism see W. P[eter] STEPHENS: The theology of Huldrych Zwingli. Oxford 1986, 9-17.

5 Kjell Ove NILSSON: Simul: das Miteinander von Göttlichem und Menschlichem in Luthers Theologie. GÖ 1966, 261-285; Leif GRANE: Vision och verklighet: en bok om Martin Luther (Vision und Wirklichkeit: ein Buch über Luther)/ übers. von Margareta Brandby-Cöster. Skellefteå 1994, 238-240; Steinmetz: Luther in context, 74f.

In what follows I will approach the relation between faith and Christian living from Luther's comments on spiritual and fleshly ways of regarding Christ and the neighbor. These statements may be considered Luther's most important remarks concerning Christian living in the Large Confession.

II Spiritual and fleshly manner of regarding Christ and the neighbor

1 Seeking what is best for others as spiritual regarding of the neighbor

Luther also calls Christian living spiritual living. He describes the spiritual way of life when he interprets II Corinthians 5, 16 f. He writes:

> »[…] the text of St. Paul irresistibly forces us to conclude that this is his meaning: Because we all have died with Christ to the world and the flesh, from now on we should no longer live or think according to the flesh, or in a fleshly manner. So we should know no one in a fleshly but only in a spiritual manner […]. Now the flesh has power only to seek its own from anyone else; it hates, envies, and does all manner of evil to its enemy, seeks pleasure, prestige, enjoyment and friendship from everyone for its own advantage, etc. This is the way men of the world regard one another. But we Christians regard no one so, for we are a new creation in Christ, and regard one another according to the Spirit, i. e. each seeks not his own advantage but what is best for others, as Paul teaches also in Romans 14 and Philippians 2.«[6]

Here Luther contrasts fleshly or worldly living and thinking with spiritual or Christian living. Fleshly living and thinking means that the flesh seeks its own from everyone else. Luther expresses the point very accurately here: he does not say that a human being seeks his own, but that the flesh seeks its own and does everything for its own advan-

---

6 WA 26, 310, 30 - 311, 24 ≙ StA 4, 73, 24 - 74, 4: »Weil wir alle mit Christo der welt vnd fleisch abgestorben sind / so sollen wir hinfurt nicht mehr nach dem fleisch odder fleischlich leben noch dencken / Vnd also niemand fleischlich / sondern allein geistlich kennen / Denn den andern fleischlich kennen / ist yhn nicht weiter kennen / denn fleisch vermag / Nu vermag fleisch nicht mehr / denn das es das seine an yderman sucht / hasset / neidet vnd thut alles vbel dem feinde / sucht aber lust / gonst / genies vnd freundschafft an yderman zu seinem nutz etcetera. Auff solche weise kennet die welt einander / Aber wir Christen kennen nu niemand also / Denn wir sind eine newe Creatur in Christo / vnd kennen einander nach dem geist / das ist / ein iglicher sucht nicht das seine / sondern was des andern ist / zu desselbigen besten / wie er auch Ro. 14. vnd Phil. 2. leret.«

tage. Then he goes on by stating that the men of the world regard each other in this fleshly way. Luther's view of fleshly and spiritual living presupposes the distinction between the old, fleshly man and the new, spiritual man.

This presupposition becomes clear when we look at Luther's explanation of the relation between flesh and spirit in his writing »That this word of Christ, ›this Is My Body‹, etc. still stands firm against the fanatics«. His theme there is the verse »Flesh is of no avail« (John 6, 63) and he argues for the view that these words do not refer to the flesh or body of Christ, but to the old, sinful man, which is born of flesh. The old Adam does not have the Spirit, which means that it is contrary to the Spirit and understands everything in a fleshly way. The flesh in this sense includes even the highest and best parts of the human nature: the intellect, reason, will, heart, and mind. If the flesh is of no avail, even all its capacities and works do not profit anything, i. e., the flesh cannot understand Christ's words correctly. All Christ's words are specifically spiritual and they have to be understood in a spiritual, not fleshly, manner.[7]

7 WA 23, 195, 17 - 197, 13: »Weil denn solchs war und unwiddersprechlich ist, das fleisch, wo es dem geist entgegen gesetzt wird, das daselbst nicht Christus leib heisst, sondern den alten Adam aus dem fleisch geboren: So ists gewislich, das auch hie Johan. vi. ›fleisch ist kein nůtze‹ nicht kan von Christus leib verstanden werden, Weil Christus daselbst fleisch gegen dem geist helt. Denn also lauten klarlich seine wort: ›Der geist macht lebendig, fleisch ist kein nůtze. Meine wort, die ich euch sage, sind geist und leben‹. Da sihestu offenberlich, das er fleisch scheidet vom geist und setzt es widder den geist, Denn er leret ja, das leben und geist sey yn seinen worten und nicht ym fleisch, Dem fleisch aber gibt er, es sey kein nůtze, Und wie solts nůtze sein, wenn widder leben noch geist drynnen ist? Ist kein leben noch geist drynnen, so mus eitel tod und sunde drinnen sein. [...]
Haben wir denn nu, das an diesem ort ›fleisch‹ nicht Christus leib heissen můge, sondern gewislich den alten Adam und das da widder den geist ist odder yhe on geist und nicht geist ist (welchs gleich so viel gilt als widder der geist), so hoffe ich, das wir armen sunder nicht so gar weyt gefeylet haben, da wir fleisch gedeutet haben, Es sey fleischlicher verstand. Denn ym fleisch, da nicht geist ist, da ist freylich das aller hőhest und beste der verstand, synn, wille, hertz und mut. Ist nu fleisch kein nůtze, so ist auch sein synn, verstand, wille und alle sein thun und vermůgen kein nůtze, und mus die meinung Christi an diesem ort die sein: Lieben jůnger, die yhr murret und last euch meine wort ergern, yhr verstehet mich nicht recht, Denn yhr fallet auff das werck: leiblich fleisch essen, und verstehets, wie mans mit zeenen zu reysset und ym leibe

The Christians are spiritual because, with Christ, they have died to the world and the flesh and they are a new creation in Christ. Since they live and think in the spiritual manner they do not seek their own advantage but what is best for others. Now Luther says that the Christians, who are new creatures, do not seek their own advantage. But were he to apply the differentiation between flesh and spirit consistently, he would say that the spirit is not seeking its own advantage. However, there may be a purpose behind Luther's change in reasoning. The reason for this is the reference of the term »own« in this context. Does Luther speak of the »own« of the old, fleshly man here, or of the new, spiritual man? Or is it so, rather, that the spiritual man does not have anything of his »own«. If this holds true, the seeking of one's own refers always to the efforts of the fleshly and sinful man. The proper meaning of »own« is crucial for the understanding because for Luther the Apostle Paul's saying »love does not seek its own« is one of the most important foundations of Christian living.

Another difficulty in this passage is that Luther seems to ignore the understanding of a Christian as simul iustus et peccator, and speak about Christians as if they were totally spiritual men, who live in a spiritual way. Of course, this is not the only occasion where Luther speaks without referring to the remaining sin in the Christians. In any case this should not be understood as a complete description of the factual condition of a Christian person. Luther does not suppose that Christians seek only what is best for others in their daily lives. When speaking about the concrete believers Luther uses the synecdoche, so that one aspect of being a Christian represents the whole being.[8] In other words we can say that the spiritual

verdewet als fleisch aus den scherren [Fleischerladen]. Das ist ein fleischlicher tödlicher verstand, Solch fleisch geb ich euch nicht so zu essen, Es mus geist hie sein, nicht fleisch, Geistlich müssen meine wort verstanden werden, vom geistlichem fleisch, Alle meine wort sind geist, drumb ist beide, fleisch und essen vnd alles davon ich rede, auch geist und geistlich zuverstehen und zubrauchen, Denn der geist macht lebendig, Fleisch ist kein nütze &c.«

8 This aspect of the biblical way of speaking is often ignored when the so-called real-ontic interpretation of Christ's presence in faith is criticized of diminishing the reality of sin in a Christian. For example Jens WOLFF: Metapher und Kreuz: Studien zu Luthers Christusbild. TÜ 2005, 573, maintains as a truism that the real-ontic understanding of the participation in Christ as well as some other interpretations underestimate the weight

way of regarding other people characterizes the believers to the extent that they are real Christians. Luther's idea of spiritual living in which one does not seek his or her own also includes the spiritual regarding of Christ. Understanding his theological conception of the term »own« presupposes examination of both the relation with God and the relation with other creatures.

2 Seeing the true life and glory in his death and suffering as spiritual regarding of Christ

In the same context Luther even writes about the fleshly and spiritual ways to regard Christ: But just as we regard our brothers in a spiritual, no longer a fleshly manner, so much the less do we regard Christ in a fleshly manner. Formerly, he means to say, when we were holy in Judaism and in the works of the law [...], we knew nothing spiritually about Christ, but what we sought was merely fleshly. For we »had hoped that he would redeem Israel« (Luke 24, 21) and would regard our holiness and glorify us according to the flesh. Now, all who regard and know Christ from a fleshly point of view are inevitably offended at him [...]. For since flesh and blood thinks no further than it sees and feels, and since it sees that Christ was crucified as a mortal man, it inevitably says, »This is the end; neither life nor salvation is to be found here; he is gone; he can help no one; he himself is lost.«

But he who is not offended at him must rise above the flesh and be raised by the Word so that he may perceive in the Spirit how Christ precisely through his suffering and death has attained true life and glory. And

of sin. This critique seems to presuppose that Christ's presence and the sinfulness of a Christian are understood in a habitual sense. This, however, has never been the point of the real-ontic understanding. The main concern has been to reject all kinds of idealistic interpretations of Luther's conception of faith and to stress Christ's ontic (»ontic« in this sense does not presuppose any specific philosophical understanding of being) real presence in the believer through faith. As Luther himself says, this means that in Christ the believer is righteous and without sin because Christ takes all his sins upon himself. In himself the believer is still a sinner and only begins to become righteous. The intentions of the real-ontic understanding introduced by Tuomo Mannermaa have been presented correctly in Bengt HÄGGLUND: Tro och verklighet: tre studier i 1900-talets teologihistoria (Glaube und Wirklichkeit: drei Studien zur Theologiegeschichte des 20. Jahrhunderts). Skellefteå 2007, 119-121.

whoever does this properly, whoever is able to do it, is a new creation in Christ, endowed with new spiritual knowledge.[9] The spiritual knowledge sees the hidden reality that is quite the opposite to its appearance.

One who regards Christ in a fleshly manner expects that Christ regards and glorifies the »holiness in the works of the law«. But also those who say that only bread and wine are offered in the Lord's Supper are regarding Christ according to the flesh. They are offended at him when he says, »This is my body.« But they who regard Christ in a spiritual manner understand that true life and glory are attained through suffering and death, not through works of law. This is spiritual knowledge which is given by the Word of God. Furthermore, spiritual knowledge is to believe and understand that the bread is not mere bread but the true body of Christ.[10] Exactly they who have this spiritual knowledge and understanding are a new creation in Christ.

In the text concerning the spiritual knowledge of Christ, Luther does not mention faith explicitly but it is clear that he speaks about the content of faith. In faith one sees the true life and glory in Christ's suffering and death, that is, one sees them beneath their counterparts. Simultaneously, even though Luther doesn't explicitly mention love, he speaks about the Christian love, agape, which does not seek its own. The spiritual man does not seek his own glory, but sees the real glory in Christ. The spiritual

---

9 WA 26, 311, 29 - 312, 19 ≙ StA 4, 74, 8-16: »Aber gleich wie wir vnser brüder geistlich vnd nicht mehr fleischlich kennen / also kennen wir auch viel weniger Christum fleischlich / Vorhin aber (wil er sagen) da wir ym Iůdentum vnd ynn des gesetzs wercken heilig waren (dahin itzt die falschen Apostel widder treiben) wusten wir nichts von Christo geistlichs / sondern eitel fleischlichs suchten wir dazumal / Denn wir hoffeten / er solt Israel erlösen Luce vltimo vnd vnser heilickeit ansehen / vnd vns nach dem fleisch herlich machen. Das war freylich Christum nach dem fleisch kennen / vnd ein rechter fleischlicher synn.«

WA 26, 312, 23-32 ≙ StA 4, 74, 20-29: »Alle nu die Christum fleischlich ansehen vnd kennen / můssen sich an yhm ergern / [...] Denn weil fleisch vnd blut nicht weiter dencket / denn es sihet vnd fulet / Vnd sihet / das Christus als ein sterblich mensch gekreutzigt wird / mus es sagen / Das ist aus / da ist widder leben noch selickeit / Der ist dahin / der kan niemand helffen / Er ist selbs verloren. Wer sich aber nicht sol an yhm ergern / der mus vber das fleisch faren / vnd durchs wort auffgericht werden / das er ym geist erkenne / wie Christus eben durch sein leiden vnd sterben / recht lebendig vnd herlich wird / Vnd wer das recht thut vnd thun kann / der ist ein newe Creatur ynn Christo / mit newem geistlichem erkentnis begabt.«

10 StA 4, 74, 29-36 ≙ WA 26, 312, 32 - 313, 20.

understanding of Christ is also the basis for the spiritual regarding of other human beings. Luther's view of Christian living may thus be described in a preliminary way as follows. One who does not seek his or her own glory from Christ does not seek his or her own advantage from other men either. Or, as we can also say, one who sees the true glory in Christ's suffering and death seeks what is best for others. Luther's conception of the spiritual regarding of Christ and fellow human beings contains the aspects of faith and love. Faith sees the true glory and life in Christ's suffering and death and love seeks the glory of Christ and what is best for others.

Luther stresses that the Word of God raises the believers above the flesh so that they perceive in the Spirit how Christ attains true life and glory through his suffering and death.[11] In fact, he allots a considerable part of the text to explaining the nature of the Divine Word. Although the discussions on the Word of God and its grammar and metaphorical nature are partly quite technical and theoretical, his aim is still practical: his purpose is to give an argument for the belief that Christ is present in the elements of the Lord's Supper and delivers his merit there to the believers. Receiving the Lord's Supper is thus essential for Christian living, regarding Christ and the neighbor in the spiritual way.

III Delivering Christ's Merit through the Word and Sacrament

1 God's Creative and Metaphorical Word

In order to understand how Christian living actualizes through the Word and Sacraments, we investigate Luther's understanding of the divine Word's nature first. Luther deals with the nature of the Word from different points of view. His starting point can be expressed for example with the words from the Sermon on the Sacrament: »If the Word of God is present, it will soon happen as the words say.«[12] One important aspect

---

11 See the text in footnote 8.

12 WA 19, 501, 3-9: »Si velimus mirari, quomodo veniat Christus in panem, virginem miremur, quomodo in ventre. Augustinus: venit adferens verbum. Hoc verbo audito statim venit Christus, et fit praegnans. Hic non aliter possum dicere quam gravidam factam per verbum. Sicut hic non potes negare per verbum tantum concepisse, sic hic, quando dicitur ›Hoc est‹, adest ex vi verborum. Si verbum adest, so ist bald da, wie die wort lautten.« See also Schwab: Entwicklung und Gestalt ..., 269f.

of this understanding of the Word of God as creative and effective is its metaphorical nature which Luther explains in the Large Confession. It is also a presupposition of the delivering of Christ's merit in the Eucharist. The main problem is, of course, the correct understanding of the words by which the Lord's Supper is instituted. Luther's intention is to show that both Zwingli and Oecolampadius are wrong in their interpretations of these words. It is well known that Zwingli had adopted the view of the Dutch humanist Cornelius Hoen († 1524), who stated that the words »this bread is my body« and »this cup is the new testament in my blood« should be understood in the sense that the bread signifies Christ's body and the wine signifies Christ's blood. For Zwingli such understanding is necessary, since Christ's body is in heaven and can't be present in the physical elements. For Luther this is a fatal misunderstanding of the biblical way of speaking. In fact, it shows that Zwingli ignores even the teaching of the common grammar. The critique against Oecolampadius deals with the same theme from a slightly different point of view. In Luther's opinion Oecolampadius has understood the biblical language incorrectly so that the new, metaphorical words are symbolizing the old meanings. For example the bread of the Supper is a symbol of Christ's physical body.

When the Bible uses a trope, it refers to a new, real thing or essence but not to any symbol of that thing. In Luther's opinion the verb »is« has to be taken literally in tropes of this kind.[13] The tropes or metaphors[14] are able to make two or many words of one word by giving them new meanings. If two or more different things are named by the same literal name, they have to possess some similarity. Then there are actually at least two words, the old and the new, and they differ through power, use and meaning even though they have the same letters.[15]

13 WA 26, 380, 32 f ≙ StA 4, 129, 30 f: »[...] alle tropi ynn der schrift / deuten das rechte newe wesen / vnd nicht das gleichnis desselbigen newen wesen.«
14 In Luther's time it was common to identify the trope with the metaphor. So does, for example, Melanchthon in his Rhetoric. See Hartmut HILGENFELD: Mittelalterlich-traditionelle Elemente in Luthers Abendmahlsschriften. ZH 1971, 161. 168. For Luther's use of the term »trope« in the Large Confession see Hilgenfeld: Mittelalterlich-traditionelle Elemente ..., 167-169, and Anna VIND: Latomus og Luther: striden om, hvorvidt enhver god gerning er synd; en teologihistorisk afhandling. København 2001, 235. (Handskrift)
15 WA 26, 272, 8 - 273, 27 ≙ StA 4, 40, 7 - 41, 4: »Gar fein ists geredt / wenn du ein gemeyn

The Bible often uses these kinds of metaphorical, new words. One example of the biblical way of speaking is Christ's words »I am the true vine«. According to Luther all the biblical metaphors are formed so that the old meaning or thing is a symbol (Gleichnis) of the new things. The metaphors refer to the new things or essences, but no longer back to the old things. The true vine is thus Christ himself, who does not signify the natural vine, but the natural vine signifies or symbolizes Christ.[16] Luther also makes a distinction between the essence of a thing and its meaning. He stresses that in all languages the word »is« speaks about the essence

wort kanst wol vernewen. Daraus man hat / das einerley wort / zwey odder vielerley wort wird / wenn es vber seine gemeyne deutunge andere newe deutunge kriegt / Als blume / ist ein ander wort / wenn es Christum heist / vnd ein anders / wenn es die natůrliche rosen vnd der gleichen heist / Item ein anders / wenn es eine gůlden / sylbern odder hőltzern rosen heist. Also wenn man von einem kargen man spricht / Er ist ein hund. Hie heist hund den kargen filtz / vnd ist aus dem alten wort ein new wort worden / nach der lere Horatij / Vnd mus nicht hie (Ist) eine deuteley sein / denn der karge bedeutet nicht einen hund. Also redet man nu ynn allen sprachen vnd vernewet die wőrter / als / wenn wir sagen / Maria ist eine morgenrődte / Christus ist eine frucht des leibes / Der teuffel ist ein Gott der wellt / Der Bapst ist Iudas / Sankt Augustin ist Paulus / Sankt Bernhard ist eine taube / Dauid ist ein holtzwůrmlin / Vnd so fort an / ist die schrifft solcher rede vol / vnd heist tropus odder Metaphora ynn der grammatica / wenn man zweyerley dingen / einerley namen gibt / vmb des willen / das ein gleichnis ynn beiden ist / Vnd ist denn de selbige name nach dem buchstaben wol einerley wort / aber potestate ac significatione plura / nach der macht / brauch / deutunge / zwey wort / ein altes vnd newes / wie Horatius sagt vnd die kinder wol wissen.«

16 WA 26, 379, 8 - 380, 26 ≙ StA 4, 129, 8-26: «Wo ein tropus odder vernewet wort wird ynn der heiligen schrifft / Da werden auch zwo deutunge / eine newe / vber die ersten alte odder vorige / wie droben gesagt ist / als / das wort / weinstock / ynn der schrifft hat zwo deutunge / ein alte und newe / Nach der alten odder ersten / heist es schlecht den strauch odder gewechse ym weinberge / Nach der newen heist es Christum / Johan. 15. […]

Nu sind die selbigen tropi ynn der schrifft also gethan / das die wort nach der alten odder ersten deutunge / zeigen das ding / so des newen gleichnis ist / Vnd nach der newen deutunge / zeigen sie das newe rechte ding odder wesen selbs / vnd nicht widderumb zurück / Als ynn diesem spruch / Ich bin der rechte weinstock / Hie ist das wort / Weinstock / ein tropus odder newe wort worden / welchs nicht kan zu růck deuten / den alten weinstock / der des newen gleichnis ist / sondern deutet fur sich / den rechten newen weinstock selbs / der nicht ein gleichnis ist / Denn Christus ist nicht ein gleichnis des weinstocks / sondern widderumb der weinstock ist ein gleichnis Christi etcetera.«

of a thing and not about its meaning.[17] To speak about the essence of a thing and to speak about its meaning are two different propositions and it is erroneous to assimilate them into one proposition. Even in the case of the new words there has to be the essence before we can ask what they signify or symbolize.[18] When the essence of a thing is defined, it becomes possible to say what it means. For example, a wooden rose is first a certain kind of rose and not only a symbol or mark of a natural rose. When this is clear, we can also say that it means or symbolizes some other rose or that it is made according to a model.[19]

Applied to the words »this is my body« of the Eucharist,[20] the metaphorical way of speaking means that the old meaning of these words is the natural body of Christ, but the new meaning is another, new body

17 WA 26, 19-27 ≙ StA 4, 132, 6-14: »Denn das ist eine gewisse regel ynn allen sprachen / Wo das woertlin ›Ist‹ ynn einer rede gefurt wird / da redet man gewislich vom wesen des selbigen dinges vnd nicht von seim deuten / Das mercke dabey / Ich neme eine hůltzin odder sylbern Rose fur mich / vnd frage / Was ist das? So antwort man mir / Es ist eine rose / Hie frage ich nicht / was es bedeute / sondern nach dem wesen was es sey / so antwortet man mir auch / was se sey vnd nicht was es bedeute / Denn es ist viel ein ander frage / wenn ich sage / Was bedeut das? Vnd wenn ich sage / Was ist das? Ist / gehet ymer auffs wesen selbs / das feylet nimer mehr.«

18 WA 26, 383, 27-35 ≙ StA 4, 132, 14-22: »Ja sprichstu / Es ist ia nicht eine rose / sondern ein holtz. Antwort / Das ist gut / Dennoch ists eine Rose / Obs nicht eine gewachsen natůrliche rose ist ym garten / dennoch ists auch wesentlich eine Rose auff seine weise / Denn es sind manchereley Rosen / als sylbern / gůlden / tůchern / papyren / steinern / hůltzen. Dennoch ist ein igliche fur sich wesentlich eine rose ynn yhrem wesen / Vnd kann nicht ein blos deuten da sein / Ia wie wolte ein deuten da sein / das nicht zuuor ein wesen hette? Was nichts ist / das deutet nichts / Was aber deutet / das mus zuuor ein wesen vnd ein gleichnis des andern wesens haben.«

19 WA 26, 383, 36 - 384, 2 ≙ StA 4, 132, 23 - 133, 1: »Darumb ist an einer hůltzen rosen /beides von einander zu scheiden / Das wesen vnd das deuten / sicut actum primum et secundum / sicut verbum substantiuum et actiuum / Nach dem wesen / ists warhafftig eine Rose / nemlich eine hůltzerne rose / Darnach / wenn das wesen also stehet / mag man denn sagen / Diese Rose bedeut odder ist nach einer andern Rosen gemacht / Denn dis sind zwo vnterschiedliche rede odder propositiones / Das ist eine Rose / vnd das bedeut eine Rose / Vnd wer ein rede draus machet / der thet so viel / als der propositionem Hypotheticam vnd Cathegoricam fur eine proposition hielte / quod est impossibile /«

20 For the metaphorical nature of the words of institution see also Wolff: Metapher und Kreuz, 557-569.

of Christ.[21] The same holds true also of Luther's conception of unity and love as the signification of the Eucharist. The bread that consists of ground grains and the wine that is made from pressed grapes are symbols of the Christian unity. Luther criticizes Oecolampadius for turning the correct order of symbols the other way round. The new words are then marks or symbols of the old things.[22] In the Bible the order is always from the marks or symbols to the real essences and the fulfilment of the symbols. This is true both of God's work and of the biblical way of speaking. The new words are formed so that there is an old word and symbol first, which then becomes the new meaning which is its real essence.[23]

The words with the new meaning are theological words that refer to such entities in which the created and the divine reality are somehow united. These new metaphorical words belong to God's way of speaking. Christ himself is using the new words and, as Luther likes to say, the divine speaking follows the grammar of the Holy Spirit. The new words are biblical words which are given in order to enable human beings to speak

21 WA 26, 381, 35 - 382, 14 ≙ StA 4, 130, 22 - 131, 8: »Aber nu der text also stehet / Das ist mein leib / vnd er wil einen tropum da machen / mus er der schrifft nach also sagen / Das wort »leib« nach der alten deutunge heist den natürlichen leib Christi / Aber nach der newen deutunge mus es einen andern newen leib Christi heissen / welchem sein natürlicher leib / ein gleichnis ist / Das were nach der schrifft weise / das wort recht vnd wol vernewet / das der newe text also stunde / Das ist mein rechter newer leib / der nicht ein gleichnis ist / gleich wie ich sage von Christo / Das ist vnser weinstock / das ist / ein newer rechter weinstock / welches gleichnis ist der alte weinstock ym weinberge.«

22 WA 26, 380, 34 - 381, 21 ≙ StA 4, 130, 1-6: »Solchs aber keret Ecolampad vmb / vnd macht ein solchen tropum odder vernewet wort / das zu rücke deutet / die gleichnis des newen wesen vnd spricht ›leib‹ solle leibs zeichen odder gleichnis heissen / ynn dem spruch / Das ist mein leib / so er doch / wo er der schrifft nach folgen wolt / viel mehr solt das wort ›leib‹ also vernewen / das es den rechten newen leib heisse / welchen der natürliche leib Christi / ein gleichnis were / Denn die Schrifft troppet nicht also zu rücke /«

23 WA 26, 382, 25 - 383, 3 ≙ StA 4, 131, 19-25: »Denn die heilige Schrifft helt sich mit reden / wie Gott sich helt mit wircken / Nu schafft Gott alle wege / das die deutung / odder gleichnis zuuor geschehen vnd darnach folge / das rechte wesen vnd erfullunge der gleichnissen / Denn also gehet das alte testament / als ein gleichnis furher / vnd folget das newe testament hernach als das rechte wesen / Eben also thut sie auch wenn sie tropos odder newe wort macht / das sie nympt das alte wort / welches die gleichnis ist / vnd gibt yhm ein newe deutunge / welche das rechte wesen ist.«

about things which exceed the capacities of human natural understanding and language. Since they provide the possibilities for speaking about spiritual things, they are the grammatical rules that regulate Christian speaking. But at the same time they have an ontological reference. In fact, these new words not only refer to the reality but they contain and give the reality that they are speaking about.[24] They are also creative and effective words which realize what they say. Already for this reason Christ's words cannot be only marks of symbols which refer to something else.

Applying a differentiation used by Zwingli, Luther speaks about two arts of divine speaking in the Confession, which he names »action-words« and »command-words«.[25] When Christ speaks action-words, what he says also takes place. The action-word is a powerful word which creates what is spoken. In the same way as God creates the sun and the moon by speaking, Christ also created something new by saying »this bread is my body« and »this cup is my blood«. These action-words were spoken when the Lord's Supper was celebrated for the first time.[26]

24 For a clear exposition of Luther's conception of the »new words and of the »theological grammar« see Reijo TYÖRINOJA: Nova vocabula et nova lingua: Luther's conception of doctrinal formulas. In: Thesaurus Lutheri: auf der Suche nach neuen Paradigmen der Luther-Forschung/ hrsg. von Tuomo Mannermaa; Anja Ghiselli; Simo Peura. Helsinki 1987, 221-236.

25 Difference between the two arts of speaking is not the same for Luther as for Zwingli. For Zwingli there is also a third way of speaking which he calls promising word. Luther doesn't speak about promising word in this context. For Zwingli's and Luther's understanding of the different ways of speaking see Rolf SCHÄFER: Zum Problem der Gegenwart Christi im Abendmahl. Zeitschrift für Theologie und Kirche 84 (1987), 202-204; Hilgenfeld: Mittelalterlich-traditionelle Elemente ..., 123-128. As Nilsson: Simul, 278, remarks, Luther rejects the distinction in the Zwinglian sense because for him God's action in his word is always creative and incarnatory. Consequently, both the command-words and the action-words are creative words.

26 WA 26, 282, 39 - 283, 7 ≙ StA 4, 51, 16-23: »Denn es sind thetel wort / die Christus auffs erste mal redet vnd leuget nicht / da er spricht / Nemet / esset / das ist mein leib etcetera eben so wol / als son vnd mond da stund / da er sprach Gen. 1. Es sey sonn vnd mond / vnd war kein lûgen wort / So ist sein wort freylich nicht ein nachwort / sondern ein machtwort / das da schaffet / was er lautet. Psalm. 33. Er spricht / so stehets da / sonderlich weil es hie am ersten gesprochen wird vnd ein thetel wort sein sol. Also haben wir das erste einige abendmal erhalten / da sie selbs auch geben vnd bekennen.

2 Divine Words and Human Speaking in the Institution of the Eucharist
The question is now how the relation between the first Lord's Supper and
the Holy Communions celebrated later by the Church should be understood. Luther explains this relation with the help of the second way of divine speaking. In addition to action-words Christ speaks command-words
as well. This means that our speaking or acting is bound with Christ's
commands. As an example Luther compares two ways of saying to a
mountain that it should be pulled up and thrown into the sea. If somebody
only said so, nothing would happen. But because Christ has combined it
with a command-word by saying »If you have faith say to this mountain,
be pulled up and thrown into the sea«, it will be done as the words say if
they are spoken according to Christ's order.[27]

When a human being speaks such words without the order of Christ,
they are mere action-words. This implies a differentiation between divine and human action-words. In fact, the English translation of Luther's
Works has chosen different words for the two cases. The latter action-word
is translated into »declarative«. The human action-words or declaratives
do not create what they say. Only when the human words are combined
with Christ's command-word, it will be done as they say.[28] This holds true
of the words which institute the Lord's Supper, baptism and absolution.[29]
Since Christ has ordered his followers to say the words »take and eat, this
bread is my body«, and »this cup is the new testament in my blood«, the
bread will be his body and the wine will be his blood. Christ's effective
order is the link between the first and all other Lord's Suppers.[30] Human

27 WA 26, 284, 5-10 ≙ StA 4, 53, 9-14: »Als Matthei .21. stehet ein thattel wort / das die Iünger
sprechen solten / Heb dich und wirff dich ynns meer / Welchs so yemand schlecht da
her redet / folgete freylich nichts draus vnd bliebe ein thetel wort / Aber da es Christus
yns heissel wort fasset vnd spricht / So yhr werdet sagen mit glauben zu diesem berge /
heb dich etcetera so mus warlich nicht mehr ein thettel wort sein / sondern geschicht
wie es lautet / so mans nach seinem befehl spricht.«

28 WA 26, 3-7 ≙ StA 4, 54, 15-19: »Wenn sie nu fragen / Wo ist die krafft / die Christus leib ym
abendmal mache / wenn wir sagen / das ist mein leib? Antwort ich / Wo ist die krafft /
das ein berg sich hebe vnd yns meer werffe / wenn wir sagen / Heb dich vns wirff dich
yns meer? freylich ist sie nicht ynn vnserm sprechen / sondern ynn Gottes heissen / der
sein heissen an vnser sprechen verbindet.«

29 StA 4, 53, 14-22.

30 StA 4, 54, 6-14: »[...] / fragen wie nu weiter / ob Christus habe vns liegen heissen / da er

words are creative words because of Christ's effective order which he has combined with the human words of doing.[31] That is why the words of institution are needed to unite the bread and Christ's body as well as the wine and Christ's blood.

IV The Presence of Christ's Person

1 Three Ways of Being and Christ's Omnipresence

Luther gives another argument for Christ's dwelling in the elements by describing three different ways how something can be present in a place. The three ways of being somewhere which Luther has learned from his philosophical teachers are called: circumscriptive or localiter, diffinitive or immeasurable, and repletive or supernatural.[32] According to Luther, Christ is able to use all these ways of being somewhere and probably some others,

> befilhet vnd vns heist diese thetel wort sprechen / Nemet / Esset / das ist mein leib / weil sie allzu mal ynn seiner person vnd als seine eigene wort gesprochen werden? Heist er vns liegen / so sehe er zu / Heist er vns aber war reden / so mus freylich sein leib da sein ym abendmal / aus krafft / nicht vnsers sprechens / sondern seines befehls / heissens vnd wirckens / Vnd also haben wir denn nicht allein das erst einig abendmal / sondern alle andere / so gehalten werden nach befelh vnd einsetzunge des Herrn Christi.«

31 WA 26, 285, 7-18 ≙ StA 4, 54, 19-30: »Item / Wo ist die krafft / das wasser aus dem fels gehet / weil Moses nichts dazu thut / denn schlegt drauff? Solt schlahen gnug sein / so wolten wir auch wol alle steine zu wasser machen / Aber dort ist Gottes heissen / vnd Mose hat nichts denn mag das thetel wort sprechen / Ich shlahe den fels / welchs ich auch wol sprechen kůnd / vnd folget dennoch kein wasser / denn das heisselwort ist bey Mose vnd nicht bey mir / Also hie auch wenn ich gleich vber alle brod spreche / das ist Christus leib / wůrde freylich nichts draus folgen / Aber wenn wir seyner einsetzunge vnd heissen nach ym abendmal sagen / das ist mein leib / So ists sein leib nicht vnsers sprechens odder thettel worts halben / sondern seines heissens halben / das er vns also zu sprechen vnd zu thun geheissen hat / vnd sein heissen vnd thun an vnser sprechen gebunden hat.»

32 For the background of these concepts in the theological tradition see Hilgenfeld: Mittelalterlich-traditionelle Elemente ..., 183-232. Thomas OSBORNE: Faith, philosophy, and the nominalist background to Luther's defense of the real presence. Journal of the history of ideas 63 (2002), 63-82, discusses Luther's understanding of the three modes of being somewhere and its relation to nominalist tradition. His conclusion is somewhat ambiguous; either Luther misunderstood the nominalist meaning of these concepts or he used them deliberately in another sense. In any case it is clear that his conception of Christ's presence in the Eucharistic elements differs from the nominalist position.

too. The first, local way refers to the »normal« situation where the place or room and the entity which is in it pass together. For example wine is in this way in a barrel or water in a glass. In the second, definitive way the entity is in a place or room so that it can't be measured. It may take only little room, but it may also take much room. For example the angels are in this way in places or areas. One angel may be in a whole house or town, but it may also be in a nut's cover. This means that the place or room has certain measures, length, breadth and depth but the entity which is in the room has no measures at all. This was the way of Christ's being when he came out of his grave and moved through the closed doors. The third, supernatural or repletive way of being somewhere belongs to God only. In this way God is everywhere and fills all places and rooms.[33]

Luther accentuates that Christ can be in a place in all these three ways because he is both God and man, and his two natures are united into one person so that they cannot be separated. Christ is thus there wherever God is in the third, supernatural way. Luther emphasizes furthermore that Christ is supernaturally present both in his divinity and humanity. If we say that God is somewhere, we have to say that the man Christ is there as well.[34] Luther stresses that the humanity of Christ cannot be God by essence, but it has to be at least personally God.[35] This differentiation presupposes the Chalcedonian solution to the Christological question. The divine and human nature in Christ do not change or lose their own essences, but they are inseparably united in Christ's person. In the Confession Luther stresses the incarnation of the Son of God and the communication idiomatum as presuppositions for Christ's omnipresence, which entails also His human nature and body.[36] Luther understands God's and Christ's presence in a definitely different way from Zwingli, who accepts the ubiquity of Christ's divine nature, but denies the omnipresence of his human nature.

According to Luther, from the fact that Christ is in God or by the Father follows that he is present as a divine and human person everywhere in the repletive way. The supernatural, repletive way of being

33 StA 4, 87, 21 - 90, 1.
34 StA 4, 91, 14-34.
35 StA 4, 103, 16-31.
36 Osborne: Faith, philosophy ..., 70.

means, however, that Christ is at the same time inside and outside, very near and far away from all creatures. The creatures cannot measure nor grasp Christ, but they are present for him so that he can measure and grasp them.[37] In the repletive way Christ is present everywhere with the Father. Human beings cannot learn to know God and Christ through this common ubiquity. The repletive presence must be differentiated from Christ's real presence in the Word and Sacraments. There God is not only in his majestic essence, but as God for you, as God's incarnated Son and Word.[38]

37 WA 26, 336, 8-19 ≙ StA 4, 96, 15 - 97, 2: »Zum dritten die Gŏttliche hymelische weise / da er mit Gott eine person ist / Nach welcher freylich alle Creaturn yhm gar viel durchleufftiger vnd gegenwertiger sein mŭssen / denn sie sind nach der andern weise / Denn so er nach der selbigen andern weise / kan also sein ynn vnd bey den Creaturn / da sie yhn nicht fulen / rŭren [berühren] / messen noch begreiffen / wie viel mehr wird er nach dieser hohen dritten weise / ynn allen Creaturn wŭndlicher sein / das sie yhn nicht messen noch begreiffen / sondern viel mehr / das er sie fur sich hat gegenwertig / misset vnd begreifft? Denn du must dis wesen Christi / so er mit Gott eine person ist / gar weit weit ausser den Creaturn setzen / so weit als Gott draussen ist / widderumb so tieff vnd nahe ynn alle Creatur setzen / als Gott drynnen ist / Denn er ist ein vnzer-trennete person mit Gotte / Wo Gott ist / da mus er auch sein / odder vnser glaube ist falsch /«

38 Nilsson: Simul, 275. Luther's speaking about »God in his essence« and »God for you« refers clearly to the Aristotelian categories of substance and relation. On the philo-sophical level Luther seems to think principally in the Aristotelian way about these categories. Using the Aristotelian categories in speaking about things doesn't imply that Luther accepts Aristotle's metaphysics as such. It is however questionable to speak about Luther's relational ontology in the sense that the philosophical concept of substance is wholly replaced by a theological one. In theology the problem is often that we are not able to know the natures of the things (res), for example, God's majestic nature or essence is unknown to human reason. God can be known only in the category of relation, namely through his Word or revelation, i. e., through Christ. This episte-mological point does not presuppose that God is only in this relation. As Luther says in his lectures on Genesis, through the revealed God the believer also learns gradually to know the hidden God. This means that through faith one learns to understand what God is in his own nature; WA 43, 460, 23-25. See Antti RAUNIO: Speculatio practica: das Betrachten Gottes als Ursprung des aktiven Lebens bei Luther. In: Caritas Dei: Beiträge zum Verständnis Luthers und der gegenwärtigen Ökumene; Festschrift für Tuomo Mannermaa zum 60. Geburtstag/ hrsg. von Oswald Bayer; Robert W. Jenson; Simo Knuuttila. Helsinki 1997, 375 f.

2 Christ's Presence in the Bread and Wine

In the bread and wine of the Lord's Supper Christ is present not only in the supernatural repletive way but also in the definitive way, which Luther even calls spiritual.[39] Because Christ is present supernaturally in his divinity and humanity in any case, we may ask, does Luther mean that the pronunciation of the words of institution according to Christ's order brings forth the definitive presence of Christ in the elements? This seems to be his understanding even though he does not say it quite directly.[40] For him it is important that Christ, who is already present everywhere, is also in an immeasurable way present for human beings in certain concrete things or elements.[41] With His Word God tells them where he is present for human beings so that they can receive him through faith.[42] However, in order to know what the faith receives in the Holy Communion, it does not suffice to say that Christ is there; we also have to ask what kind of unity he forms with these created elements.

39 WA 26, 327, 33 - 329, 26 ≙ StA 4, 88, 13 - 89, 26; Schwab: Entwicklung und Gestalt …, 265 f.
40 Schäfer: Zum Problem der Gegenwart …, 205-207. Albrecht PETERS: Realpräsenz: Luthers Zeugnis von Christi Gegenwart im Abendmahl. B 1960, 87, accentuates that the words of testament (verba testamenti) do not bring the body of Christ into the bread, but the Lord who is bodily present reveals himself in them to the communicant. However, he does not take into account the possibility that the Word brings forth the definitive, immeasurable presence. Osborne: Faith, philosophy, …, 76, also overlooks this when he states that in the Confession Concerning Christ's Supper Luther does not use the different modes of presence to distinguish between Christ's Euchristic presence and Christ's omnipresence (Osborne refers here to Christ's presence in a cabbage).
41 See Erwin METZKE: Sakrament und Metaphysik: eine Lutherstudie über das Verhältnis des christlichen Denkens zum leiblich-materiellen. In: Ders.: Coincidentia oppositorum: gesammelte Studien zur Philosophiegeschichte. Witten 1961, 199. Metzke states that in His revelation God makes his omnipresence apparent in a concrete place
42 WA 23, 151, 10 - 153, 4: »Also auch Christus: ob er gleich allenthalben da ist, lesst er sich nicht so greifen und tappen. Er kan sich wol aus schelen, das du die schale davon kriegest und den kerne nicht ergreiffest. Warumb das? Darumb, das ein anders ist, wenn Gott da ist, und wenn er dir da ist. Denn aber ist er dir da, wenn er sein wort dazu thut und bindet sich damit an und spricht: Hie soltu mich finden. […], Aber dis ist aber das rechte ›Tuto‹, das ›Das ist mein leib‹, Wenn du dis issest, so issest du meinen leib und sonst nicht. Warumb? Darumb das ich mich hie wil mit meym wort hefften, auff das du nicht mussest schwermen und mich wollen suchen an allen orten, da ich bin, […]«; see Lorenz GRÖNVIK: Die Taufe in der Theologie Martin Luthers. Åbo 1968, 31-33.

In order to explain Christ's union with bread and wine Luther differentiates between four different kinds of unions. In theology one can speak, firstly, about the essential or natural unity between the divine persons who have one divine nature, and, secondly, about the personal unity between Christ's two natures which unite themselves in one person. Thirdly, Luther deals with the unity of the angels with a different natural phenomenon, for example with fire. For this kind of unity he suggests the name union of effect.

V The Sacramental Union

1 Bread and Christ's Body and Wine and Christ's Blood as United in Sacramental Elements

But the relation between Christ's body with the bread and his blood with the wine is still a fourth kind of unity. Luther calls it a sacramental unity, since Christ's body and blood are given to believers as sacraments.[43] In all these different unions the two or sometimes more entities form one new essence or being. Luther uses the German word »Wesen« here, which can be translated both »essence« and »being«. He strongly denies the understanding that the united entities would lose their own essences even though they form the new essence. For him this kind of union between different entities is beyond human reason and the rules of logic. This means that logic teaches quite correctly that two different entities like bread and body, a dove and the Spirit, or God and man, have different natures. However, the grammar shows that it is a common way of speaking in all human languages that two different beings become one being. It is also possible and acceptable to speak about two things as one being. For Luther this is not just a way of speaking without any correspondence in the reality. On the contrary, this kind of speaking refers to the reality and for this reason one should not speak about the new beings using the logical language which keeps the beings apart. However, Luther does not want to eliminate the logical differentiation between the essences.[44] We

---

43 WA 26, 442, 8-28 ≙ StA 4, 182, 19 - 183, 12.
44 WA 26, 443, 12-32 ≙ StA 4, 184, 9-30: »Die Logica leret recht / Das brod vnd leib / taube vnd geist / Gott vnd mensch vnterschiedliche naturn sind / Aber sie solt zuuor auch

could say that the logic is still valid in the philosophical sense, but it does not suffice to describe these new beings, where two things are united into one new being. To be able to speak about them we need the theological grammar and way of speaking. This also applies to speaking about the new, spiritual man in whom Christ and his Spirit are present and who is united with Christ.

Luther says somewhat unclearly that even though bread and body are different things when they are separated from each other, they lose their difference (Unterschied) as far as they have become such a new united being. He only seems to mean that the entities are no longer separated because it is possible to speak about them as one being without their merging into one and losing their own identity. Both bread and body remain, but because of the sacramental union there is no longer ordinary bread but »flesh-bread« or »body-bread«. The one sacramental essence and one being has come from the bread and Christ's body. The same holds true likewise of the wine and Christ's blood; as sacramental being there is now »blood-wine«.[45]

die Grammatica hören zur hülffe / Welche leret also reden ynn allen sprachen / Das wo zwey vnterschiedliche wesen ynn ein wesen komen / das fasset sie auch solche zwey wesen / ynn einerley rede / Vnd wie sie die einickeit beider wesens ansihet / so redet sie auch von beiden mit einer rede / als ynn Christo / ist Gott vnd mensch ein personlich wesen / darumb redet sie von beiden wesen also / Der ist Gott / der ist mensch. Item von der tauben Iohan .1. Das ist der heilige geist / das ist eine taube. Item von den Engeln / das ist ein wind / das ist ein Engel / das ist brod / das ist mein leib / Vnd widderumb auch zu weilen ein iglichs vom andern also / Der mensch ist Gott / der Gott ist mensch / Die taube ist der heilige geist / Der heilige heist ist die taube / Der wind odder diese flamme ist de Engel / der Engel ist die flamme / Das brod ist mein leib / Mein leib ist das brod / Denn hie mus man nicht reden nach dem die wesen vnterschieden vnd zweyerley sind an yhn selbs / [...] sondern nach dem wesen der einickeit / nach dem solche vnterschiedliche wesen / einerley wesen sind worden / ein iglichs auff seine weise / Denn es ist auch ynn der warheit also / das solche vnterschiedliche naturn so zu samen komen ynn eins / warhafftig ein new einig wesen kriegen aus solcher zu samen fugung / nach welchem sie recht vnd wol einerley wesen heissen / ob wol ein iglichs fur sich sein sonderlich einig wesen hat.«

Luther's analysis of the theological language and its semantics is again an example of how he includes the philosophical concepts of substance / essence or nature in the theological way of speaking without confusing philosophy and theology.

45 WA 26, 444, 39 - 445, 15 ≙ StA 4, 186, 9-25: »Weil dann nu solche weise zu reden beyde ynn

It is, thus, according to the theological grammar, correct to point to the bread and say: this is Christ's body. Because this is not only a way of speaking but corresponds to the reality, one who sees the bread, sees the body of Christ and one who eats the bread, eats the body of Christ. Because of the sacramental union everything that is done to the bread, concerns the body of Christ as well.[46]

2 *The Composition of a Sacramental Being*

Luther also explains what kind of reality a sacramental essence or being is. First there is the Word, which embraces the remission of sins, the Spirit, grace, life and salvation. The Word unites all these with bread and wine, which were nothing without the Word. But bread and wine are also necessary, because without them Christ's body and blood could not be there. And they are needed for the presence of the New Testament which, according to St. Paul and St. Luke, is in the Lord's Supper. Without the New Testament the remission of sins would not be there, and life and salvation

der schrifft vnd allen sprachen / gemein ist / so hindert vns ym abendmal die predicatio identica nichts / [...] / denn ob gleich leib vns brod zwo vnterschiedliche naturn sind / ein igliche fur sich selbs / vnd wo sie von einander geschieden sind / freylich keine die ander ist / Doch wo sie zu samen komen / vnd ein new gantz wesen werden / da verlieren sie yhren vnterscheid / so fern solch new einig wesen betrifft / vnd wie se ein ding werden vnd sind / also heisst vnd spricht man sie denn auch fur ein ding / das nicht von nŏten ist / der zweyer eins vntergehen vnd zu nicht werden / sondern beide brod vnd leib bleibe / vnd vmb der sacramentlichen einickeit willen / recht gered wird / Das ist mein leib / mit dem wŏrtlin ›Das‹ auffs brod zu deuten / Denn es ist nu nicht mehr schelcht brod ym backofen / sondern fleischbrod odder leibs brod / das ist / ein brod mit dem leibe Christi / ein sacramentlich wesen vnd ein ding worden ist / Also auch vom wein ym becher / Das ist mein blut / mit dem wortlin ›Das‹ auff den wein gedeutet / Denn es ist nu nicht mehr schlechter wein ym kellet / sondern Blutswein / das ist ein wein / der mit dem blut Christi ynn ein sacramentlich wesen komen ist /«

46 WA 26, 442, 29-38 ≙ StA 4, 183, 13-22: »Darumb ists aller ding recht geredt / das man so auffs brod zeiget vns spricht / Das ist Christus leib / Vnd wer das brod sihet / der sihet den leib Christi / [...] / Also fort an ists recht gered / Wer dis brod angreiffet / der greiffet Christus leib an / Vnd wer dis brod isset / der isset Christus leib / wer dis brot mit zenen odder zungen zu drŭckt / der zu drŭckt mit zenen odder zungen den leib Christi / Vnd bleibt doch allwege war / das niemand Christus leib sihet / greifft / isset odder zubeisset / wie man sichtbarlich ander fleisch sihet vnd zubeisset / Denn was man dem brod thut / wird recht vnd wol dem leibe Christi zugeeignet vmb der sacramentlichen einickeit willen.«

could not be present without the forgiveness of sins. The sacramental essence may be described as follows: The words form the bread and the cup into a sacrament first and then the elements embrace Christ's body and blood. Body and blood embrace the New Testament and it embraces the forgiveness of sins which then embraces eternal life and salvation. When describing the relation of the different contents of the sacramental essence the Reformer uses constantly the German term »fassen«, which has a quite a wide spectrum of meanings. He concludes by saying: »See, the words of the Holy Communion offer and give us all this and we embrace it by faith.« Again he uses the same word »fassen«, which above was mostly translated with the verb »to embrace«, and once with the verb »to form«. What does Luther actually mean when he says that »wir fassen es mit dem Glauben«?

VI Receiving and Embracing the Sacrament

1 Receiving and Embracing Christ, the Spirit, Forgiveness of Sins, Righteousness and Eternal Life through Faith

The Lord's Supper as an object of faith where bread is Christ's body and wine is Christ's blood is one important aspect of regarding Christ in a spiritual way. For Luther, the spiritual way of regarding Christ does not exclude matter and body. On the contrary, Christ's suffering and death cannot be regarded without his body and blood. For this reason Luther says that Christ uses the sacrament for the sake of the faith.

They who regard Christ spiritually are a new creation in Christ. They understand the content of the sacrament through word and faith. Luther stresses that the words have to be proclaimed in order to let the people know what the sacrament is. But in addition Christians have embraced the sacrament. The content of the sacrament, the merit of Christ, is also delivered to those who have received the sacrament. So the faith not only understands the words, but also receives and then embraces everything that is given with bread and wine which actually are »body-bread« and »blood-wine«.[47] Here is, thus, the connection between Christ's suffering

---

47 WA 26, 78, 25 - 479, 8 ≙ StA 4, 222, 9-31: »Sankt Paulus vnd Lucas sagen. Das newe testament sey ym abendmal / vnd nicht das zeichen odder figur des newen testaments /

and death, and the individual believer. By receiving bread and wine the believer becomes Christ's body and blood which means that he becomes Christ himself in a visible and concrete way, with his materiality and humanity. With Christ's body and blood one receives also the Spirit of Christ[48] and the New Testament, through which one receives the forgiveness of sins, righteousness, salvation and eternal life.

2 Receiving the Communion of Christ's Body and the Spiritual Body of Christ

The bread that we break is the communion of Christ's body. For Luther it is undeniable that this is said about the physical bread, not about the communion of faith in the hearts. The communion or koinonia of Christ's body is a common good, which means that it is delivered to all and everyone who receives the broken bread and the blessed cup receives the body of Christ. Because the body of Christ is a common good, it is received and enjoyed by both the worthy and the unworthy. In Luther's view from this fact follows that the body of Christ has to be received and enjoyed in a physical manner. The broken bread is Christ's body to

Denn figur odder zeichen des newn testaments haben gehört yns allte testament vnter die Iuden / Vnd we bekennet / das er die figur odder zeichen des newen testaments habe / der bekennet damit / das er da newe testament noch nicht habe / [...]. Denn Christen sollen das newe testament an yhm selbs / on figur odder zeichen haben. Verborgen mügen sie es wol haben vnter frembder gestalt / Aber warhafftig vnd gegenwertig müssen sie es haben. Ist nu das newe testament ym abendmal / so mus vergebung der sunden / geist / gnade / leben vnd alle seligkeit drynnen sein / Vnd solchs alles ist yns wort gefasset / Denn wer wolt wissen / was ym abendmale were / wo es die wort nicht verkündigten? Darumb sihe / welch ein schön / gros / wunderlich ding es ist / wie es alles ynn einander henget vnd ein sacramentlich wesen ist. Die wort sind das erste / Denn on die wort were der becher vnd brod nichts / Weiter / on brod vnd becher / were der leib vnd blut Christi nicht da / On leib vnd blut Christi were das newe testament nicht da / On das newe testament / were vergebung der sunden nicht da / On vergebung der sunden / were das leben vnd seligkeit nicht da / So fassen die wort erstlich das brod vnd den becher zum sacrament / Brot vnd becher fassen den leib vnd blut Christi / Leib vnd blut Christi fassen das newe testament / Das newe testament fasset vergebung der sunden / Vergebung der sunden fasset das ewige leben vnd seligkeit. Sihe / das alle reichen vnd geben vns die wort des abendmals / vnd wir fassens mit dem glauben.«

48 WA 26, 468, 39-42 ≙ StA 4, 210, 18-20.

all who receive it, not only to those who believe that it is Christ's body. The unbelievers cannot receive Christ spiritually, but nevertheless they receive his body, not just bread.[49]

Luther would thus show that even though all who receive the Lord's Supper receive the body of Christ and become one body, they do not all belong to Christ's spiritual body. The word »body« is grammatically a new word and it refers to a new body, which is constituted by the Word of God. It is also a proper trope or metaphor in the biblical sense. This one body consists of all those who take part of the one bread.[50] However, the body of Christ, which in itself is physical, may be received in a bodily or spiritual manner. Luther does not see these two ways of receiving Christ as alternatives. In other words, we should not say that we could receive the body of Christ either bodily or spiritually. The alternatives are rather as follows: some receive Christ only in the bodily manner without the Spirit, but others receive him both bodily and spiritually. We could even say that the spiritual receiving includes the physical receiving of Christ's body. Luther explains this in his writing »That these words of Christ still hold fast«. He combines physical and spiritual eating there. Physical eating means that the body of Christ is eaten with the bread and spiritual eating means that the heart believes that it is the body which he gives for my sake and for the forgiveness of sins.[51]

Both physical and spiritual eating is needed for the salvation and eternal life of the human being. Christ has instituted both ways of eating by the word of God »take and eat, this is my body«. Not all pay attention to these words, but Christians receive them by their faith.[52] A mouth that eats Christ's body physically can neither understand the words nor know what it eats. But the heart embraces and understands the words; from them it knows what the mouth is eating and eats thus spiritually what the mouth eats physically. It is one and the same body of Christ that is eaten in two different ways. Because the mouth can't eat spiritually, the heart does this for the body. So the mouth, which is a member of the heart,

49 WA 26, 490, 19-38 ≙ StA 4, 237, 27 - 238, 13.
50 WA 26, 491, 37 - 492, 19 ≙ StA 4, 240, 3-24.
51 WA 23, 179, 10-32.
52 WA 23, 183, 5-10.

lives at last eternally because of the heart which lives eternally through the Word. The mouth takes part in the eternal life, because it eats physically the same eternal food that its heart eats spiritually. But the mouth's physical eating takes place also for the heart, which cannot do it by itself. As a result both the body and the heart become satisfied and blessed from the one meal.[53] Body and soul are thus receiving and enjoying the Lord's Supper for the sake of each other. This is one dimension of the spiritual way of life where one does not seek his or her own advantage. In Christian life the body works for the spirit and the spirit for the body.

Spiritual eating, drinking or acting does not presuppose that the object of action as such is a spirit or a spiritual thing. Even the natural physical flesh may be used in a spiritual way: »Obiectum non est semper spirituale, Sed vsus debet esse spiritualis.«[54] When the Word of God is added to something that our body is doing outwardly and in a bodily manner and it also happens through faith, it is called a spiritual action. What happens in the Word and in faith is spiritual regardless of the corporeal or spiritual nature of the object. The spirit is primarily in the use of things, not inevitably in the things themselves. The spiritual use of a thing may be, for example, seeing, hearing, speaking, touching, bringing, eating, or drinking. Serving the neighbor is also a certain kind of using.

The whole life of a Christian is spiritual so that, without any doubt, one who eats the body of Christ physically in faith also eats the same body in this physical eating spiritually and lives and wanders spiritually. Also, the fruits and works of the Spirit such as the feeding and strengthening of the new man or the soul[55], love, joy, patience and the like are spiritual because they are born of the Spirit.[56]

Christ's body or flesh which is received in the Supper is of a quite special nature. It is in fact flesh, but not in the sense which the Scripture calls »fleshly« as contrary to the Spirit. Christ's flesh does not belong together with the verse »flesh is of no avail«, but it should be understood in the light of the verse »That which is born of the Spirit is spirit.« His flesh is specifically born

53 WA 23, 181, 7-15; 191, 10-28.
54 WA 23, 183, 34 - 185, 6.
55 WA 30 I, 25, 1-4.
56 WA 23, 193, 22-28.

of the Holy Spirit as the Creed and the Scripture say. Christ is the only man of whom the Scripture says that his flesh is born of the Spirit. Christ's body or flesh is thus wholly compatible with the Spirit. Christ is also the Spirit's bodily dwelling place, and through him the Spirit comes into all others.[57] Consequently, eating Christ's spiritual body both by the body through the mouth and by the soul through faith is the source of a Christian's spiritual life.

3 The Transforming Power of Christ's Spiritual Body

Because the flesh of Christ is the only spiritual flesh for all born of the Spirit, it is also a spiritual food. And since it is a spiritual food, it is an eternal meal which cannot perish. It is also the true, living and eternal food which makes alive and sustains all who eat of it. But all who do not eat of it must die. The eternal and imperishable food is so powerful that it transforms the fleshly and mortal person who eats it into what it is itself and makes her like itself, namely spiritual, alive, and eternal.[58] In other words, this spiritual food feeds the new man, who needs continuous strengthening in the battle against the fleshly and furious old Adam. As we see, Luther adheres clearly to the patristic understanding of the Eucharist as a medicament of immortal and eternal life.

Since Christ's flesh is a spiritual flesh, the eating of it brings forth only spirit. Since the human body has been given the hope of the resurrection of the dead and of everlasting life, it must also become spiritual.

---

57 WA 23, 193, 36 - 195, 5; 201, 13-28.

58 WA 23, 203, 14-30: »Ist nu Christus fleisch aus allem fleisch ausgesondert und allein ein geistlich fleisch fur allen, nicht aus fleisch, sondern aus geist geboren, so ists auch eine geistliche speyse. Ists eine geistliche speyse, so ists ein ewige speyse, die nicht vergehen kann, Wie er selbst sagt Johan. vi. ›Wirckt die speyse, die nicht vergenglich ist, welche euch des menschen son geben wird [J 6, 27]‹, Und abermal ›Ich bin das lebendig brod vom hymel komen [J 6, 41]‹. Item ›wer mich isset, der lebt ewiglich [J 6, 51]‹. Und so fort an durchs gantze Capitel leret er, wie sein fleisch sey die rechte lebendige ewige speyse, die da lebendig mache und behalte alle die sie essen, Und wer sie nicht isset, der musse sterben &c. Warumb das? Darumb: sein fleisch ist nicht aus fleisch noch fleischlich, sondern geistlich, darumb kan es nicht verzeret, verdewet, verwandelt werden, denn es ist unvergenglich wie alles was aus dem geist ist, Und ist eine speise gar und gantz ander art denn die vergengliche speise. Vergengliche speise verwandelt sich ynn den leib, der sie isset, Diese speise widderumb wandelt den, der sie isset, ynn sich und macht yhn yhr selbs gleich, geistlich, lebendig und ewig, wie sie ist, als er sagt: ›Dis ist das brod vom hymel / das der wellt leben gibt‹.«

This happens when the body eats the spiritual food physically; this food digests the body's flesh and transforms it so that it too becomes spiritual. It will also become blessed and live eternally. In fact, the Christians who eat Christ's flesh physically by their mouth and spiritually by their heart are thus already transformed out of fleshly, sinful and mortal to spiritual, holy and living men. But their spiritual way of being is still hidden in faith and hope; only in the Last Day will it be apparent.[59]

VII The right use of Christ's suffering and merit

1 Delivering of Christ's merit through the Eucharist

From the point of view of Christian living the central theme in the Large Confession is the right use of Christ's suffering and merit. We could also consider the right use or the presuppositions of the right use of Christ's passion the main issue of the whole Confession. The correct use of Christ's suffering presupposes namely that the suffering is delivered and given to human beings and received by them. The giving and delivering of his suffering takes place through the Word and sacraments. Especially the Lord's Supper is about the usus passionis, the use of Christ's suffering.[60]

---

59 WA 23, 205, 9-25: »Sondern also: wird Christus fleisch geessen, so wird nichts denn geist draus, denn es ist ein geistlich fleisch und lesst sich nicht verwandeln, sondern verwandelt und gibt den geist dem, der es isset. Weil denn der arme maden sack, unser leib, auch die hoffnung hat der aufferstehung von todten und des ewigen lebens, so mus er auch geistlich werden und alles was fleischlich an yhm ist, verdewen und verzeren. Das thut aber diese geistliche speise: wenn er die isset leiblich, so verdewet sie sein fleisch und verwandelt yhn, das er auch geistlich, das ist ewiglich lebendig und selig werde, wie Paulus .i. Corin. xv. [1 K 15, 44] sagt: ›Es wird der leib geistlich aufferstehen‹. Denn ynn diesem essen gehets also zu, das ich ein grob exempel gebe, als wenn der wolff ein schaff fresse, und das schaff were so ein starcke speise, das es den wolff verwandelt und macht ein schaff draus. Also wir, so wir Christus fleisch essen leiblich und geistlich, ist die speise so starck, das sie uns ynn sich wandelt und aus fleischlichen sundlichen sterblichen menschen geistliche heilige lebendige menschen macht, wie wir denn auch bereid sind, aber doch verborgen ym glauben und hoffnung, Und ist noch nicht offenbar, Am Jüngsten tage werden wirs sehen.«

60 WA 26, 296, 30 - 297, 9 ≙ StA 4, 63, 30 - 64, 3: »Desselbigen gleichen hab ich ia vleissig geschrieben widder die hymlischen Propheten / wie die geschicht vnd brauch des leidens Christi nicht ein ding sey / factum et applicatio facti / seu factum et vsus facti / Denn

In his sermon on the Eucharist (1526) Luther stresses that we should know and preach two things about the Lord's Supper: First, that there is the work or thing which one believes, and second, that there is the faith itself or the correct use of the content of faith. The first, namely the Sacrament itself, is called obiectum fidei and it is outside the human heart and visible to the human eye. The sacrament as object of faith contains the visible elements and the belief that Christ's body and blood are truly in bread and wine. Faith, then, is inwardly in the human heart and its issue is the heart's relation with the outward sacrament.[61] Faith is the correct use of the Sacrament and of Christ's suffering which is delivered by it.

In the Large Confession Luther gives the arguments for the continuous using of Christ's suffering and death in the life of Christians. Even here Luther's way of speaking is not exclusive: it is clear from the context that Christ's suffering and death should not be separated from his resurrection.

For Luther's argumentation it is essential to differentiate between Christ's merit and the delivering of his merit. Christ has once suffered on the cross and so he has deserved the forgiveness of sins. The suffering, death and resurrection which have deserved the forgiveness are together the merit of Christ. This merit Christ delivers to human beings continuously through certain means wherever he is present. Luther thus presupposes that Christ himself is present in these means by which he delivers his merit. The delivering of Christ's merit takes place by preaching repentance and through baptism, the Spirit, reading of the Scripture, faith, and the eating of bread and wine, but it can be done even by other means if Christ wants it so.[62] Luther's purpose here is not to explain in detail how

Christus leiden ist wol nůr ein mal am creutz geschehen / Aber wem were das nůtz / wo es nicht ausgeteilet / angelegt vnd ynn brauch bracht wurde? Wie sols aber ynn brauch komen vnd aus geteilet werden / on durchs wort und sacrament?« WA 26, 297, 12-14 ≙ WA StA 4, 64, 6 f: »Sehen nicht / das ym abendmal vsus passionis et non factum passionis gehandelt wird /«

61 WA 19, 482, 15-25.
62 WA 26, 23-27 ≙ StA 4, 62, 17-20: »Der blinde tolle geist / weis nicht / das meritum Christi vnd distributio meriti zwey ding sind / Vnd mengets ynn einander wie ein vnfletige saw. Christus hat ein mal der sunden vergebung am creutz verdienet / vnd vns erworben / Aber die selbigen teylet er aus / wo er ist / alle stunde vnd an allen ŏrten.« In »Wider den himmlischen Propheten, von den Bildern und Sakrament« Luther makes the distinction

Christ's merits are delivered, but to stress that one has to differentiate between Christ's merit on the cross and its delivery through different means everywhere where Christ is present. He thus criticizes Zwingli who does not differentiate between these two aspects. Elsewhere he gives a more systematic and consistent description of the delivery of Christ's merit.

Luther emphasizes that Christ is not only on the cross and forgives the sins there. Christ is eternally on the cross because of our sins, but at the same time he is also in other articles of faith and forgives sins there as well.[63] Luther would say that Christ's presence and delivering of the forgiveness of sins is contained in every article of the Christian faith, not only in the article of crucifixion. This statement is an example of Luther's conception of the relation between the life, work and person of Christ and the theological language. Even though Luther differentiates between Christ's merit on the Cross and the delivering of his merit to the believers, he does not separate Christ from his merit. Christ is present wherever he delivers his merit and in this delivering he also gives himself. Articles of faith in which Christ is present are not only theological propositions but also real, concrete events of the history of creation and redemption. As such they are words in God's continuous speaking. Like the Gospel, all articles of faith contain and give Christ and his work or merit.[64]

In the »Sermon on Sacrament of the body and blood of Christr against the fanatics« Luther combines Christ's self-giving in the proclaimed Gospel and in the Eucharist explicitly. The created material voice brings Christ to the heart of a believer. When she believes truly so that her heart

between the deserving of the forgiveness of sins on the Cross and its delivering and donating through Word and Sacraments. There he opposes Karlstad's understanding of the Eucharist as mental remembering and experiential tasting of Christ's suffering; WA 18, 202, 1 - 203, 38. See Jari JOLKKONEN: Uskon ja rakkauden sakramentti: opin ja käytännön suhde Martti Lutherin ehtoollisteologiassa (The sacrament of faith and love: doctrine and practice in Martin Luther's theology of the Eucharist). Helsinki 2004, 305-307.

63 WA 26, 293, 32 - 294, 4 ≙ StA 4, 62, 12-16: »Also wollen wir aus Christo nichts machen / denn einen solchen / der ewiglich am creutz leide fur vnser sunde / auff das wir nicht widder den gleuben handeln / so wir ynn andern artickeln gleuben / das Christus da sey / vnd sunde vergebe / welchs dieser geist allein am creutz haben wil.«

64 About Luther's conception of the nature of doctrine and the creeds and their relation with the Gospel see Eeva MARTIKAINEN: Doctrina: Studien zu Luthers Lehrbegriff. Helsinki 1992, 60-71.

lays hold of the Word and holds fast within it that voice, she has the true Christ in her heart. All other believers have received the same Christ in their hearts as well. Christ is in their hearts in the same way as he is at the right hand of the Father. Christ's sitting at the right hand of God does not refer to any specific location but to the fact that he is present with the Father everywhere and rules over all creatures, sin, death, life, the world, devils and angels. When a person believes this, Christ is in her heart and her heart is truly with Christ in heaven.[65] According to Luther it is not possible to know how this comes about, but the heart is able to feel Christ's presence through the experience of faith. Certainly the experience of Christ's presence in faith should not be understood as any kind of presupposition for remission of sins and salvation. The theme that Luther is dealing with here is how Christ delivers himself and his merit, that is, salvation, through the Word.[66]

If Christ is able to come in the human heart and spirit and to live in the soul, it should not be difficult for him to reach the material things. The heart is certainly much more subtle than the material thing. Consequently, as Christ makes himself present in the heart through the Word and faith, so he unites himself through the Word with bread and wine so that they may be received in a material way. He has first included himself in the Word and through the Word he includes himself in the bread.[67] Christ is present in the elements of the Eucharist in order to grant his merit to the whole human being who consists of body and soul.

---

65 WA 19, 489, 24 - 490, 3.
66 WA 19, 489, 9-21: » Item ich predige das Euangelion von Christo und mit der leiblichen stim bringe ich dir Christum yns hertz, das du yhn ynn dich bildest. Wenn du nu recht glewbist, das dein hertz das wort fasset und die stim drinne hafftet, so sage mir, was hastu ym hertzen? Da mustu sagen, du habest den warhafftigen Christum, nicht das er also darin sitze, als einer auff einem stul sitzet, sondern wie er ist zur rechten des vaters. Wie das zugehet, kanstu nicht wissen, dein hertz fület yhn aber wol, das er gewislich da ist, durch die erfarung des glaubens. Kan ich nun abermal mit einem wort solchs ausrichten, das der einige Christus durch die stim ynn so viel hertzen kompt und ein iglicher, der die prediget horet und annimpt, fasset yhn gantz ym hertzen; Denn er lesset sich nicht stucklich zu teilen und wird doch gentzlich ausgebreitet ynn alle glewbigen, Also das ein hertz nicht weniger, und tausent hertzen nicht mehr kriegen denn den einigen Christum, [...].«
67 WA 19, 492, 30 - 493, 26.

2 The Triune God's Self-giving through the Creatures and the Right Use of the Divine Gifts

This self-giving of Christ is exactly the core idea of the well-known and often cited summary which Luther presents at the end of his Large Confession. There he describes how the Triune God, Father, Son and Holy Spirit, totally gives himself to human beings. With himself God gives everything that he is and that he has.[68] In the Large Catechism Luther summarizes the whole Creed by stating that it tells what the Triune God does for human beings and grants to them. For the understanding of Christian living it is important that he completes the thought presented in the Confession by saying that God gives himself to us completely, with all his gifts and his power, to help us keep the Ten Commandments.[69] The aim of God's self-giving is also Christian living according to God's Commandments.

In the Large Confession Luther's aim is Christian living as well. The viewpoint, however, is not the fulfillment of the Commandments but the right use of the Divine gifts. Characteristic for the Divine self-giving is that all the three persons, Father, Son and the Holy Spirit, are giving themselves

---

68 WA 26, 505, 38 - 506, 12 ≙ StA 4, 251, 22 - 252, 5: »Das sind die drey person / vnd ein Gott / der sich vns allen selbs gantz vnd gar gegeben hat / mit allen das er ist vnd hat. Der Vater gibt sich vns / mit hymel vnd erden sampt allen creaturen / das sie dienen vnd nütze sein müssen. Aber solche gabe ist durch Adams fal verfinstert / vnd vnnütze worden / Darumb hat darnach der son sich selbs auch vns gegeben / alle sein werck / leiden / weiseheit vnd grechtickeit geschenkt vnd vns dem Vater versunet / damit wir widder lebendig vnd gerecht / auch den Vater mit seinen gaben erkennen vnd haben möchten. Weil aber solche gnade niemand nütze were / wo sie so heymlich verborgen bliebe / vnd zu vns nicht komen kündte / So kompt der heilige geist vnd gibt sich auch vns gantz vnd gar / der leret vns solche wolthat Christi vns erzeigt / erkennen / hilfft sie empfahen vnf behalten / nützlich brauchen vnd austeilen / mehren vnd foddern / Vnd thut dasselbige beide innerlich vnd eusserlich / Ynnerlich durch den glauben vnd ander geistlich gaben. Eusserlich aber / durchs Euangelion / durch die tauffe vnd sacrament des altars / durch welche er als durch drey mittel odder weise / er zu vns kompt vnd das leiden Christi ynn vns vbet vnd zu nutz bringet der seligkeit.«

69 BSELK 661, 38 - 662, 1: »Per hujus doctrinae cognitionem amorem ac voluptatem Dei praeceptorum faciendorum consequimur videntes hic, quemadmodum Deus prorsus se nobis tradiderit cum omnibus, quae possidet, ut praesenti ope et auxilio in perficiendis praeceptis nos sublevet, pater cum omnibus suis creaturis, Christus vero omnibus suis operibus, porro autem spiritus sanctus omnibus suis dotibus.«

in and through created things. The Father gives himself with the heaven and the earth, and with all creatures, so that they serve human beings and are useful for them. However, because of the Fall of Adam this divine gift has become obscure and has lost its usefulness. It is important to note that both the correct regarding of the Father's giving nature and work and the right using of them have become impossible for the fallen human being. For this reason the Son has become man and given himself and his work, suffering, wisdom, and righteousness. In addition, he has reconciled us with the Father so that we, made alive and righteous again, could also know and have the Father with his gifts. However, such grace would be useless if it stayed secret and hidden, that is, if we could see in Christ only suffering, death and loss. So the Holy Spirit comes and gives himself fully, teaches us to know the good works of Christ, helps to receive, keep and to use them in a helpful manner and to deliver, increase and strengthen them.

3 Receiving Christ and His Good Works through the Word and Sacraments

The description of God's self-giving is closely connected with the thought that Christ is delivering the remission of sins in every article of the Christian faith. The self-giving of the Son with all his works is at the center of divine benefaction. Among other gifts Luther mentions the suffering of Christ which, again, contains the remission of sins. And giving the remission of sins contains the gift of Christ's righteousness. Luther sees Christ and all his deeds here clearly as gifts that are delivered or granted to human beings. In the third part of the summary he explains how these gifts can be received. They come to us through the Spirit, who teaches how to know, to receive, and to use them. The Spirit does this both outwardly and inwardly. Outwardly he brings Christ and his good works through the Gospel and the sacraments, baptism and the Lord's Supper. Inwardly he does this through faith and other spiritual gifts. Luther especially stresses that the Spirit comes to human beings through the three outward and created means, Gospel, Baptism, and the Lord's Supper, and practices the suffering of Christ in the believers for the good of their salvation. Only as a consequence of Christ's and the Spirit's self-giving and acting for the good of human beings does the self-giving of the Father with all his other gifts become known and useful again. As Luther writes in »That these words of Christ Still Stand Firm«, without the Word everything would be useful only in the bodily sense, but for the soul they are of no avail. But when the Word of God is added to the physical things, the heart uses the Word and enjoys spiritually what the body is using and enjoying outwardly and bodily.[70] Of course, the spiritual using of the physical things with the Word which is connected with them is possible only by faith. Consequently, Luther thinks that the correct understanding and using of the gifts of creation presuppose the delivering of Christ's suffering, death and the forgiveness of sins through the Word and sacraments and their reception and use by faith.

The delivering of Christ's merit through the Lord's Supper strengthens the new man. Luther calls this strengthening the fruit of the Sacrament. The idea is that the fruit is the food of the new, spiritual man.[71] Through Baptism Christians have already been born again and they have been set in a new being. But after the Baptism the old Adam has become furious. The new man encounters many dangers with which the flesh, the world and the devil are threatening him. In the struggle against these threats the new man gets tired and loses the power to continue. The Lord's Supper is given for the recovery of the new man. The heart that feels different temptations such as impatience, hate and envy should seek consolation from the Sacrament and eat and drink it in order to get more strength. This food and drink gives power and feeds the faith, chastity, patience, love and everything that belong to the new man. It feeds not only the soul but also the body which feels its influence and becomes cheered up.[72]

The Sacrament also strengthens the love of the new man. One may serve the neighbor either in the fleshly manner or spiritually. The fleshly service is of no avail. But if the service is done spiritually, so that one's heart does it out of faith in God's Word, it is life and beatitude. The spiri-

70 WA 23, 183, 23-28.
71 Luther's view of the Eucharist as nutrition of the new man is described thoroughly by Fredric CLEVE: Luthers nattvardslära mot bakgrunden av Gabriel Biels uppfattning av nattvard och sacrament (Luther's Eucharistic teaching in the light of Gabriel Biel's concept of the Eucharist and the sacraments). Åbo 1968, 351-371.
72 WA 30 I, 25, 1-23.

tual service is grounded in the Word of God, since the heart knows what the body is doing from the word ›love your neighbor«.[73] In the Confession Luther presents Christian love as a common order of God above all the other orders such as the Church, marriage, and worldly government. They who belong to this order of Christian love serve everyone who is in need and help others with all kinds of good works. They feed the hungry, give the thirsty to drink, forgive their enemies, pray for all human beings and suffer all kinds of evil. Luther accentuates that even though all the works of Christian love are holy, they do not form a way to salvation. The only way above all the divine orders is the faith in Jesus Christ.[74] As we see, by speaking of the value of service Luther does not mean that loving service of the neighbor earns eternal life and beatitude or leads to them as ends. Instead of that he says that the service itself is the holy life and beatitude. So, wherever faith and love are present, there also are the true divine life and salvation.

4 The Use of Christ's Merit in the Communion of Christians

At the end of the Confession Luther combines receiving the remission of sins with the communion of Christians or the spiritual body of Christ, which he also calls Christendom. According to him the Church is one. Physically it is dispersed everywhere in the world, but spiritually it is collected or united by one Gospel and one faith under the one head, Christ. By the »physical Church« Luther means the audible proclaiming of the Gospel and the visible delivering of the Sacraments. The remission of sins is there where this one Christendom is.[75] The communion of Christians and the forgiveness of sins are inseparable. They belong together, because where the Christendom is, there is also the kingdom of grace and true absolution.

And, as Luther stresses, where grace and forgiveness are, there is the Triune God himself. In the communion of Christians God Himself is also present delivering grace and forgiveness through the Gospel, the Baptism and the Lord's Supper. In the Confession Luther encourages Christians

---

73 WA 23, 189, 8-22.
74 WA 26, 505, 11-17 ≙ StA 4, 250, 18 - 251, 1.
75 WA 26, 506, 30-40 ≙ StA 4, 253, 1-12.

to receive the remission of sins as often as it is needed during this life.[76] Since the Lord's Supper delivers the merit of Christ that makes all the divine gifts useful again, receiving it is one of the necessary conditions of Christian spiritual living.

In the Large Confession Luther does not explicate the nature of the spiritual body of Christ. He concentrates there on the delivering and receiving of Christ's merit and emphasizes that the Christian community is there for that purpose. He continues and enlarges the discussion on this theme in some other texts of the same period. In the Large Catechism the connection between the Church and the forgiveness of sins is very clear. Although Christians have received grace through Christ and holiness through the work of the Holy Spirit in the unity of the Church, they need forgiveness constantly, because they are not yet without sin. In the Church forgiveness is granted through the sacraments and absolution as well as through the entire Gospel. So, according to Luther, everything in the Church is so ordered that Christians may daily obtain full forgiveness of sins and receive comfort for their conscience through the Word and the sacraments. The forgiveness given by God will then be used by Christians so that they forgive, bear with, and aid each other.[77] In the Christian communion the right use of God's mercy and of the remission of sins consists of a peaceful conscience before God and of mercifulness and forgiveness towards the neighbors. This mercifulness enables the Christians to mutual assistance and aid.

The idea of the Lord's Supper as the basis of the Christian communion is described even more fully in a Sermon on the Catechism which Luther delivered in the same year that the Confession was written. It is character-

---

76 WA 26, 507, 7-16 ≙ StA 4, 253, 18 - 254, 5: »Ynn dieser Christenheit vnd wo sie ist / da ist vergebung der sunden / das ist / ein kőnigreich der gnaden vnd des rechten ablas / Denn daselbst ist das Euangelion / die tauffe / das sacrament des altars / darynn vergebunge der sunden angeboten / geholet vnd empfangen wird / Vnd ist auch Christus vnd sein geist vnd Gott da selbst. [...]. Solche aber vergebung der sunden ist nicht auf ein mal / als ynn der tauffe gewarten / wie die Nouater leren / sondern so offt vnd viel mal / man der selbigen bedarff bis ynn den tod.«

77 The aspect of using God's forgiveness in the relations between the members of the Christian community is explicitly present in the Latin text of the Large Catechism: BSELK, 658, 10-52.

istic for Luther that he describes the nature of the Christian community directly for the congregation in his sermons. In this sermon he explains what he calls the signification of the Sacrament, namely Christian unity, love and community.[78] This signification is contained in the grains and grapes. Like the many grains are ground to meal and formed into one bread and like the many grapes which all have their own form are pressed into one common form, so the Christians should form one common and true spiritual body. In this body they have one head, Christ, and they are each other's members. They share the same faith and doctrine, and the same sacraments with another as well as the same weakness, foolishness, infirmity and poverty. If one is naked or hungry, the other shares his nakedness and hunger. This means that one member will not rest before the other is clothed or fed. Since the members of the communion have one spirit and one body, everything – both physical and spiritual goods and evils – is shared and no one lets another suffer any want.[79]

The communion will be realized when the Lord's Supper is received. The purpose of the eating of the Sacrament both physically by mouth and spiritually by faith is to strengthen the faith and after that to fulfill the meaning of the Sacrament, the communion.[80] When eating the Sacrament people enjoy Christ and unite themselves with him and he unites himself with them. The sinners come to Christ and give him all their sin and other evil, and from him they receive faith, righteousness, eternal life and willingness to live according to God's will. When the Christian is united with Christ he also allows the others to eat and drink him or her, so that the reciprocal eating and drinking fulfils the meaning of the verse »bear each other's burdens«. This reciprocal assistance is the law which Christians should follow because they are renewed by faith. Such goodness is to be exercised towards all whom they know. A Christian says to his neighbor: if you are poor, give your poverty to me; here you have bread and clothes.

---

78 WA 30 I, 26, 22-24: »Sicut baptismus aliquid significant / sic hoc quoque Sacramentum aliquid significant. Significatio eius est / quod in Christianitate sit unitas / lieb und gemeinschaft.«
79 WA 30 I, 26, 25 - 27, 4.
80 WA 30 I, 27, 16-18.
81 WA 30 I, 27, 6-16. 19-21.

Taking care of the neighbor's needs means for Luther both spiritual and material service; the neighbor may hear the Gospel, get consolation and receive what he or she needs for material living.[81] This example shows how the spiritual and material aspects merge together in the Christian community. A poor person can »change« her poverty to bread and clothes because her neighbor is able to receive the poverty as if it were his own and give what the poor person needs. In the Christian community people do this reciprocally for each other. There is no division between »the givers« and »the receivers« but all belong to both groups. Even though it is not mentioned explicitly in the sermon, it is clearly presupposed that the reciprocal assistance and aid originate in the mercifulness and forgiveness that are received through the Word and the Lord's Supper and then used in daily Christian living in the community.

VIII Conclusion

In his Confession from 1528 Luther states that in faith a Christian regards his or her fellow human and Christ in a new spiritual way. Regarding others in the spiritual manner means that one seeks what is best for them. And one, who knows Christ in the spiritual manner, understands that true life and glory are attained through suffering and death. In this context Luther does not explain concretely how one should seek the neighbor's good. He concentrates on the attaining of the true life. However, in certain sermons concerning the Lord's Supper he explains some aspects of the spiritual regarding of one's neighbor.

The true life is received in Christ's body and blood, that is, in his suffering and death, which are delivered to the believers in the Eucharist. Luther accentuates that in order to get the new, spiritual life one has to receive Christ's real body and blood because through them one participates in Christ's suffering and death, which hide his true glory and life. Luther explains how the Word of God makes this possible by producing the sacramental union between Christ's body and bread as well as between Christ's blood and wine. This happens when the Word out of the repletive ubiquity of Christ's body and blood produces their definitive presence in the concrete material elements of the Eucharist. In the sacramental union all the elements maintain their own essences but at the same time unite into new »things« which Luther calls »body-bread« and »blood-wine«. For Luther spirit is not contrary to body and blood. Christ's body as well as his blood are totally spiritual and thus able to make the believers' bodies completely spiritual also. So the resurrection of the bodies to the new life begins already through the receiving of Christ's body in the Lord's Supper.

By eating and drinking Christ's body and blood the believer receives the whole Christ and all His merits; suffering for others, mercy, forgiveness of sins, righteousness, salvation, and eternal life. She will also be united with Christ and all other believers so that they form a community where all members seek each other's best. The union with Christ is very concrete and real and it concerns both body and spirit. When Christ gives himself for the food of human beings, they receive him and his merits and Christ receives the believers and their sins. Through faith and sacrament Christ gives himself for the good of all human beings and those who believe this are using his suffering, death and other gifts for their salvation. They also become able to use Christ's merits for the good of their neighbors. So the Christians give themselves for the food and drink of their neighbors by serving them both spiritually and materially. In the Christian community, which is based on participation in Christ and his merits through the Word and sacrament, people share spiritual and material misery and evil as well as wealth and goodness. This sharing includes two aspects: Firstly, the Christians are united into one body so that each one's righteousness, strength and other spiritual gifts help the other's sinfulness, weakness and other spiritual distress. And secondly they serve each other and all human beings in their needs, poverty, hunger and thirst with their outward deeds. In practice these two aspects are always together in Christian life.

Der Mensch vor der Aufgabe ethischer Verantwortung

Anthropologie und Ethik in Luthers Genesisvorlesung

Von Pierre Bühler

Zum Einstieg: mein Vorhaben

Die Aufgabe, die mir anvertraut wurde, ist, über Luthers Anthropologie in seiner Genesisvorlesung zu sprechen. Diese sehr breit aufgefasste Aufgabe möchte ich mit folgenden Präzisierungen eingrenzen:

1. Es wird nicht möglich sein, die gesamte Genesisvorlesung zu berücksichtigen – sie macht bekanntlich in der Weimarer Ausgabe die drei Bände 42-44 aus! –.[1] Deshalb werde ich mich in ihr vor allem auf den Kommentar zum locus classicus theologischer Anthropologie, also dem Erzählzyklus von Schöpfung und Ursünde in Gn 1-3, konzentrieren.

2. Insgesamt ist dieser Kongress ja Luthers Ethik gewidmet – die Gesamtüberschrift lautet: »Luthers Ethik: christliches Leben in ecclesia, oeconomia und politia« –. Deshalb versuche ich, meine Aufgabe in Verbindung mit dieser Grundausrichtung zu bewältigen, das heißt: Luthers Anthropologie in Gn 1-3 unter dem besonderen Aspekt der ethischen Implikationen zu thematisieren. Das begründet meine Überschrift: Es soll um den Menschen »vor der Aufgabe ethischer Verantwortung« gehen. Die Verbindung von Anthropologie und Ethik wird also im Zentrum meiner Überlegungen stehen. Die etwas umständliche Formel »vor der Aufgabe« soll gleich das Forensische zum Ausdruck bringen, das darin liegt.[2]

---

1 Folgende Sekundärliteratur zur Auslegung von Luthers Genesisvorlesung steht im Hintergrund meiner Reflexion: Erich SEEBERG: Studien zu Luthers Genesisvorlesung: zugleich ein Beitrag zur Frage nach dem alten Luther. GÜ 1932; Peter MEINHOLD: Die Genesisvorlesung Luthers und ihre Herausgeber. S 1936; Hans-Ulrich DELIUS: Die Quellen von Martin Luthers Genesisvorlesung. M 1992; Ulrich ASENDORF: Lectura in Biblia: Luthers Genesisvorlesung (1535-1545). GÖ 1998; Johannes SCHWANKE: Creatio ex nihilo: Luthers Lehre von der Schöpfung aus dem Nichts in der Grossen Genesisvorlesung (1535-1545). B; NY 2004.

2 Gerhard Ebeling hat immer wieder auf die forensische Dimension in Luthers Anthro-

Antizipierend könnte die Grundfrage, um die es im Verhältnis zwischen Anthropologie und Ethik geht, folgendermaßen formuliert werden: Was macht für den Menschen die Schwierigkeit der ethischen Verantwortung aus, und woher könnte er ermächtigt werden, diese Verantwortung angemessener wahrzunehmen?

3. Obschon ich soeben das Thema eingegrenzt habe, möchte ich es nun trotzdem unter einem anderen Aspekt wieder etwas erweitern: Kurz nachdem Luther seine Genesisvorlesung im Juni 1535 angefangen hatte, wurde die Universität Wittenberg wegen Pestgefahr teilweise nach Jena verlegt und damit die Vorlesung unterbrochen. Sie brach bei Gn 3,14 ab. Man kann davon ausgehen, dass Luther im Januar 1536, bevor er seine Vorlesung bei Gn 3,15 weiterführte, als Zusammenfassung des Vorangegangenen die Thesen der »Disputatio de homine« für eine Übungsdisputation mit seinen Studenten verfasste, also das Erarbeitete auf Anthropologie hin synthetisierte. Damit wird die Thematik der Genesisvorlesung an einem entscheidenden Punkt fokussiert. Von meinem Thema her liegt es deshalb nahe, dass ich mich auch gelegentlich auf diese Disputation beziehe – freilich ohne den Anspruch zu erheben, mit Gerhard Ebelings (1912-2001) ausführlichem, dreibändigem Kommentar in Konkurrenz zu treten![3]

4. Obschon wir auf einem »Kongress für Lutherforschung« sind, verstehe ich meinen Beitrag nicht als rein historische Lutherforschung: Die Thematik der Ethik führt mich dazu, gemäß meiner Disziplin auch *systematisch* vorzugehen, also aus Luthers Texten Perspektiven zu gewinnen, die uns im Laufe des Kongresses für die Reflexionen zu heutiger ethischer Verantwortung weiterhelfen könnten. In diesem Sinne verstehe ich meine Reflexion als ein theoretisches Grundmodell, das auf Konkretisierungen aus ist.[4]

pologie hingewiesen und stets versucht, sie für seine eigene anthropologische Reflexion fruchtbar zu machen. Vgl. etwa Gerhard EBELING: Dogmatik des christlichen Glaubens. Bd. 1: Prolegomena. Erster Teil: Der Glaube an Gott, den Schöpfer der Welt. 3., durchges. Aufl. TÜ 1987, 334-355 (§ 14: Der Mensch coram Deo).

3 Gerhard EBELING: Lutherstudien. Bd. 2: Disputatio de homine. 3 Bde. TÜ 1977-1989. Für eine ausführlichere Darstellung des historischen Zusammenhangs der Disputation vgl. im ersten Band von Ebeling die Seiten 1-8.

4 Im Sinne von Max Webers (1864-1920) Verantwortungsethik geht es vornehmlich um die Wahrnehmung von Verantwortung in konkreten Situationen. Dazu leistet mein Beitrag sozusagen nur eine erste Vorarbeit.

Damit komme ich kurz zu meiner *Gliederung*: Ich steige zunächst bei einer Grundkategorie ein, nämlich der Kategorie des Zwischen-Seins, die ich von Ebelings Lutherinterpretation aufnehme. Diese Kategorie wird mich in einem zweiten Schritt dazu führen, ein systematisches Modell zu entwickeln, das es erlaubt, mit Luthers Hilfe die anthropologischen Spannungen wahrzunehmen, denen die ethische Verantwortung ausgesetzt ist. In theologischer Interpretation verbindet sich damit die Grunderfahrung der Sünde. In einem dritten Schritt soll dann, anhand desselben Verantwortungsschemas, gezeigt werden, wie Luthers Anthropologie versucht, diese Spannungen befreiend, ermächtigend anzugehen, sodass aus ihr für die Menschen, die sich auf vielfältige Weise in der Welt engagieren, ethische Perspektiven hervorgehen.

I Zwischen-Sein als Grundkategorie theologischer Anthropologie

Für die Darstellung von Luthers Anthropologie hat Ebeling in seinem Büchlein »Luther: Einführung in sein Denken« den Begriff des Zwischen-Seins entfaltet.

> »Die verschiedenen Weisen, wie die Existenz des Menschen als Zwischen-Sein in Erscheinung [tritt]: zwischen Geburt und Tod, zwischen Schöpfung und Auferstehung, zwischen Sünde und Gerechtigkeit, zwischen Gott und Nächstem und darum auch zwischen Gott und Welt, sind selbstverständlich nicht gleichzusetzen, wohl aber miteinander zusammenzudenken, wenn man das Zwischen-Sein des Menschen als die Urspannung, auf die alle Antithesen in Luthers Denken bezogen sind, in Wahrheit erfassen will.«[5]

Wenn dieses Zwischen-Sein vor allem beim jungen Luther betont wird – bereits ab der ersten Psalmenvorlesung –, so wird es doch ebenfalls in den späteren Disputationsthesen thematisiert. Das gilt ebenfalls von der Genesisvorlesung, und ganz besonders in Gn 1-3, sowohl in der Spannung zwischen dem geschöpflichen Urzustand und dem Zustand des gefallenen Sünders als auch in der Spannung zwischen dem Sündersein und der Verheißung des Gerechtfertigtwerdens, wird es zum allgegenwärtigen Thema. In der »Disputatio de homine« setzt sich Luther gleichfalls in-

---

5 Gerhard EBELING: Luther: Einführung in sein Denken. 4., durchges. Aufl. TÜ 1981, 182-186; Zitat 185f.

tensiv mit dem Zwischen-Sein zwischen Sündenwirklichkeit und Heils-
verheißung auseinander. Das hängt sicher mit der Stelle zusammen, an
der die Genesisvorlesung nach der Disputation weitergeführt werden soll:
nämlich bei der Verheißung eines Nachwuchses, welcher der ihn in die
Ferse stechenden Schlange den Kopf zertreten wird. In der traditionellen
Auslegungsgeschichte, auf die sich Luther öfters bezieht, wird mit dieser Stelle Gn 3,15 das sogenannte Protoevangelium verbunden: die erste
Verheißung des künftigen Christus, als Nachwuchs des Weibes, der die
Menschen von der Sünde erlösen soll. Die Betonung des Zwischen-Seins
hat also direkten Anhalt am biblischen Text, der hier den Bogen zwischen
Urgeschichte und Heilszukunft, zwischen Protologie und Eschatologie
spannt.

Dass dieses Zwischen-Sein auch in Hinsicht auf die Ethik zum Tragen
kommen kann, darauf wird bei Ebeling nur knapp, dennoch aber prägnant
hingewiesen:

> »Der Mensch ist nur dann am rechten Ort und das heißt: er ist nur dann
> wahrhaft Mensch, wenn er nicht wähnt, etwas für sich allein zu sein und auf sich
> selbst zu stehen, sondern im Zwischen-Sein zwischen Gott und dem Nächsten
> sein Zwischen-Sein zwischen Geburt und Tod, zwischen Sünde und Gerechtigkeit
> aushält.«[6]

An diesem Ort kommt es zu einer engen Verknüpfung von Anthropologie
und Ethik, und das wollen wir nun vertiefen.

II Die Grundspannungen ethischer Verantwortung und die Erfahrung der Sünde

1 Antwort und Verantwortung

Wie vorhin schon kurz erwähnt, muss, wenn von Verantwortung gesprochen wird, sogleich der forensische Charakter betont werden. Den
verknüpft Luther in seiner Vorlesung mit zwei wichtigen Aspekten von
Gn 1-3: Einerseits damit, dass Gott in Gn 1-2 mit dem als Ebenbild Gottes
erschaffenen Menschen spricht, wie bei keinem anderen Geschöpf, ihm
Anweisungen gibt, wie er mit der Schöpfung umgehen soll, was er im
Garten Eden darf und nicht darf, wie er den Garten bebauen und bewahren

---

6 Ebeling: Luther, 193.

soll, usw. Zentral ist hier also das Angeredetsein durch Gott. Das macht auch die Gottebenbildlichkeit des Menschen als fundamentale Relationalität aus. An dieser Stelle sieht Luther übrigens in seiner Genesisvorlesung auch die Begründung der ecclesia und der oeconomia: diese zwei Stände werden supralapsarisch eingesetzt. Die politia als dritter Stand hingegen wird seinem Urteil nach erst nach der Sünde nötig.[7]

Der zweite klare Hinweis auf das Forensische verbindet sich mit der Frage Gottes danach, wo der Mensch nach begangener Sünde sei: »Wo bist du?«[8] Dass hier die Frage als Ortsfrage gestellt wird, betont gerade die coram-Situation, die das darauf folgende Gespräch zwischen Gott und dem sündigen Menschenpaar auch prägt.

An beiden Stellen geht es also um Angesprochen-, Angeredetsein und Antworten. Die responsive Situation des Menschen ist also Grund für seine Verantwortung. Nicht von ungefähr haben im Lateinischen responsio und responsabilitas dieselbe etymologische Wurzel: Antwortend ist der Mensch auch *ver*antwortend, und seine Verantwortung geschieht deshalb immer vor einer bestimmten Instanz, die ihn zur Antwort und dadurch auch zur Verantwortung aufruft. Vor dieser Instanz verantwortet er nicht nur, was er tut und nicht tut, sondern auch wer er letztlich ist. Interessant ist hier, dass Luther bei Gn 3,10-13 mit großer Aufmerksamkeit notiert, wie unfähig die Menschen gerade sind, Verantwortung für das Geschehene wahrzunehmen, wie sie vielmehr die Verantwortung abschieben, ja schließlich Gott selbst zuschieben. Die Schwierigkeit ist eben, dass in der Wahrnehmung der Verantwortung der Mensch selbst auf dem Spiel steht, dass er zu sich selbst stehen müsste. Doch genau das gelingt dem Sünder nicht: Er versteckt sich, flieht, weicht aus. In diesem Sinne wird das Nichtwahrnehmen von Verantwortung, ihre Ablehnung die höchste Form der Sünde, die darin kulminiert, dass schließlich Gott zum »autor peccati« gemacht wird.[9]

---

7 WA 42, 79, 3-19; vor allem 79, 7-12: »Politia autem ante peccatum nulla fuit, neque enim ea opus fuit. Est enim Politia remedium necessarium naturae corruptae. [...]. Hoc enim unum et praecipuum agit Politia, ut peccatum arceat, [...].« Vgl. ebenfalls 87, 11 f: »Politia nulla opus fuit, cum natura esset integra et sine peccato.«

8 Gn 3,9.

9 Vgl. dazu vor allem WA 42, 132, 7 - 134, 10; insbesondere 134, 8 f: »Hic ultimus gradus peccati est Deum afficere contumelia et tribuere ei, quod sit autor peccati.«

2 Das Gewissen

Diese Grundstruktur der Verantwortung verbindet Luther anthropologisch mit der Kategorie des Gewissens, und es ist auffallend, wie stark diese Dimension auch in der Genesisvorlesung betont wird. Gewissen ist hier natürlich nicht vornehmlich als moralische Kategorie zu verstehen, im Sinne des guten oder schlechten Gewissens, sondern, wie das Ebeling in seiner Lutherinterpretation stets akzentuiert hat: als der Ort im Menschen, wo der Mensch selbst zur Entscheidung steht,[10] in Hinsicht auf alle Urteile, die von den unterschiedlichen Instanzen seiner Lebenswirklichkeit über ihn ausgesagt werden, wo der Mensch aufgerufen ist, auf diese Urteile antwortend sich selbst zu verantworten. Das heißt: Das Gewissen ist im Menschen der Ort der Verantwortung.

3 Die Spannungen der Verantwortung

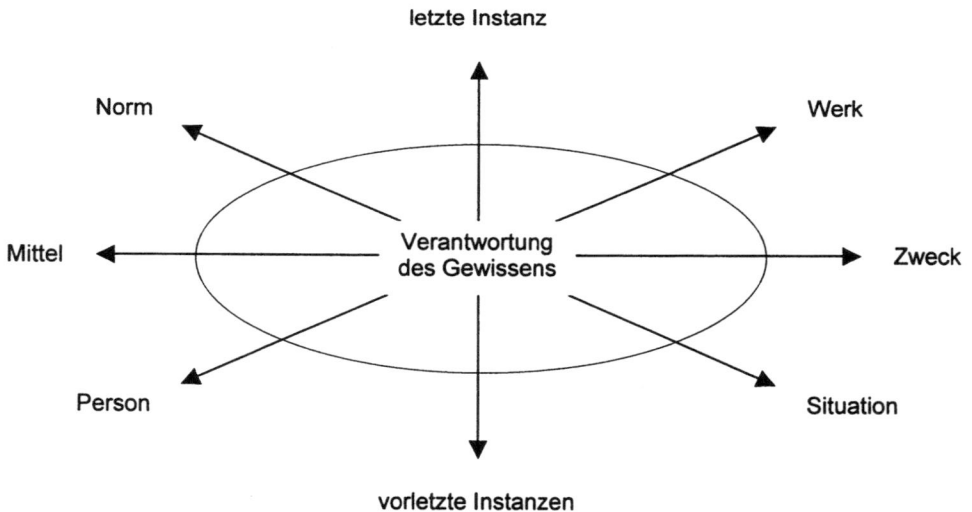

letzte Instanz

Norm   Werk

Mittel   Verantwortung   Zweck
              des Gewissens

Person   Situation

vorletzte Instanzen

---

10 Gerhard EBELING: Theologische Erwägungen zum Gewissen. In: Ders.: Wort und Glaube. 3. Aufl. TÜ 1967, 429-446; DERS.: Das Gewissen in Luthers Verständnis: Leitsätze. In: Ders.: Lutherstudien. Bd. 3: Begriffsuntersuchungen – Textinterpretationen – Wirkungsgeschichtliches. TÜ 1985, 108-125.

Aus dieser Grundperspektive des Gewissens lassen sich die Spannungen bestimmen, denen die ethische Verantwortung ausgesetzt ist. Sie sind im folgenden Schema dargestellt, wie eine Art Grundkoordinaten der Verantwortung.

Um unsere anthropologische Grundkategorie zu gebrauchen, können wir sagen: Diese Spannungen machen das Zwischen-Sein des Menschen vor der Aufgabe der ethischen Verantwortung aus. Sie seien hier kurz kommentiert.

1. Angesichts der forensischen Dimension der Verantwortung ist die grundlegende Spannung die der Instanzen: Immer wieder ist der Mensch als Gewissen der Frage danach ausgesetzt, was für ihn die letzte Instanz ist und was dieser gegenüber die vorletzten Instanzen sind, um die Spannung mit Dietrich Bonhoeffers (1906-1945) »Ethik« zum Ausdruck zu bringen.[11] In Luthers Terminologie könnte man sagen: Es steht zur Entscheidung, welche coram-Relation letztlich prägend ist.

2. Von dort her ist die zweite Spannung wahrzunehmen, nämlich die zwischen Person und Werk: In ethischer Perspektive muss ich mein Verhalten, mein Handeln verantworten. Zugleich aber bin ich auch immer als Person herausgefordert, und so stehe ich vor der schwierigen Aufgabe, die Fragen »Wer bin ich?« und »Was soll ich tun?« angemessen zu unterscheiden, das heißt: sie weder zu scheiden, noch zu vermischen.

3. Die dritte, damit verbundene Spannung ist die zwischen der Norm und der Situation. Situationen können Normen relativieren und Normen können Situationen ersticken. Wie es gelingen kann, beides miteinander aufzunehmen, so dass das eine nicht am anderen zu Grunde geht, sondern das eine dem anderen dient, gehört zu den schwierigen Herausforderungen der ethischen Verantwortung.

4. Schließlich verbindet sich damit die Spannung von Mittel und Zweck. Auch hier erweist sich das Zwischen-Sein als ein schwieriges: Verantwortung verfolgt gewisse Zwecke; zugleich gehört aber auch zu ihr, dass sie kritisch fragt, welche Mittel welchen Zwecken angepasst sind, ohne gleich der Tendenz zu verfallen, einseitig die Mittel durch die Zwecke zu heiligen.

---

11 Dietrich BONHOEFFER: Werke/ hrsg. von Eberhard Bethge ... Bd. 6: Ethik/ hrsg. von Ilse Tödt .... M 1992, 137-162: »Die letzten und die vorletzten Dinge«.

4 Die Störungen der Verantwortung und die Erfahrung der Sünde

Das Beieinander und Ineinander dieser Spannungen macht aus der Ausübung ethischer Verantwortung eine stets offene Aufgabe, im Sinne eines ständigen Zwischen-Seins. Es ist mir natürlich bewusst, dass es in Luthers Genesisauslegung keine solche Systematik gibt; das Schema ist mein eigener Systematisierungsversuch. Es beruht aber auf einer Reihe von anthropologischen Beobachtungen, die Luther bei seiner Kommentierung anstellt, indem er den biblischen Text im Sinne einer Aktualisierungshermeneutik mit kontextuellen Notationen seiner Zeit verbindet. In der Vielfalt von Störungen, die beim Austragen dieser Spannungen wahrzunehmen sind, sieht Luther die allgegenwärtige Sünde am Werk, unaufhörlich darüber klagend, wie stark diese das menschliche Leben zu einem mühsamen, schweren Leben macht. Dieses Motiv kommt vor allem in der Kommentierung der Folgen, die für die Menschen aus der Sünde hervorgehen,[12] zum Zuge.[13]

Zwar kann er auch hier immer wieder mit viel Humor den Text auslegen, so etwa, indem er den Schweiß des Adams nach den drei Ständen auslegt: Der sudor oeconomicus der Bauern beim Bebauen der Erde ist groß, aber der sudor politicus der Obrigkeit ist noch größer, denn sie muss sich mit allerlei schwierigen Problemen herumschlagen.[14] Am größten aber ist der sudor ecclesiasticus, wie sich etwa an Paulus zeigt: Die Bemühung, Kirchen zu begründen, zu leiten, zu bewahren, ist die allerschwierigste Aufgabe.[15] Freilich, so Luther, geht es dem Adam am schlechtesten, denn was wir unter uns aufgeteilt haben, muss er selber wahrnehmen, er ist zugleich Vater, König und Priester![16]

---

12 Gn 3, 16-19.

13 Vgl. WA 42, 148, 1 - 161, 42.

14 Zur Auslegung von Gn 3, 19: »In sudore vultus tui vesceris pane tuo«, vgl. WA 42, 157, 23 - 160, 27.

15 WA 42, 159, 17-19: »Distinguemus igitur sudorem secundum iustam proportionem. Oeconomicus sudor magnus, maior politicus, ecclesiasticus maximus. Nam Paulum vide et facile intelliges, quomodo ab eo desudatum sit.«

16 WA 42, 159, 30-36 ; insbesondere 31-35: »Nam ubi nos singuli in suo ordine sudamus, Adam unus sudorem oeconomicum, politicum et ecclesiasticum desudare coactus est. Nam solus haec officia apud posteritatem, dum vixit, omnia sustinuit: Aluit familiam, gubernavit eam, et instruxit eam ad pietatem, fuit Pater, Rex et Sacerdos.«

Dass die allgegenwärtige Sünde die Verantwortung dauernd stört, führt Luther in vielen Einzelaspekten aus, die sich ohne weiteres in unser Modell einfügen lassen. Wie vorhin schon betont, verhindert sie die Menschen zunächst daran, Verantwortung überhaupt wahrzunehmen: Sie schieben sie ab, schieben sie anderen zu, schließlich sogar Gott selbst. Doch auch dort, wo sie ein Stück weit wahrgenommen wird, gerät sie in Störungen hinein. Ausgehend von R 1 weiß Luther darum, dass die Gotteserkenntnis dadurch zerstört wurde, dass die Geschöpfe und der Schöpfer verwechselt wurden, dass die Geschöpfe an Stelle des Schöpfers verehrt wurden. In der Genesis kommt das im Versuch des Menschen zum Tragen, wie Gott sein zu wollen, gemäß der von der Schlange zugeflüsterten Versuchung. So kann Luther sagen: »Im Paradies wollten wir wie Gott werden, und unsere Sünde hat uns wie Satan gemacht.«[17] Der Mensch wird zum Ebenbild Satans entstellt, wie Luther sagen kann,[18] und zwar dadurch, dass er sich selbst zur letzten Instanz, zu Gott macht, und so vorletzte und letzte Instanz verwechselt. Durch diese forensische Verwirrung wird die Grundsituation der Verantwortung radikal tangiert.

Damit verbinden sich gleich weitere Störungen: Der vom Menschen verfolgte Zweck wird dann, wenn er sich zur letzten Instanz erklärt, die Verherrlichung seiner selbst, das Sich-selbst-Rühmen, das Sich-selbst-Rechtfertigen, und diesem Zweck müssen dann auch alle Mittel dienen. In vielfältigen Hinweisen notiert Luther diese Auswirkung der Sünde in der zeitgenössischen Frömmigkeit, vor allem der päpstlichen Kirche, aber auch bei den sogenannten Schwärmern und den Antinomisten. Ähnlich könnte man überlegen, ob solche Verkehrungen in den Verantwortungskoordinaten nicht auch negative Auswirkungen in heutiger Wirtschaft und Gesellschaft zeitigen, was die lateinamerikanische Befreiungstheologie als »strukturelle Sünde« thematisiert.

Dadurch kommt natürlich auch das Verhältnis von Person und Werk in ein schiefes Ungleichgewicht, wie das von Paulus bereits den Pharisäern vorgeworfen wird und es Luther – in Anlehnung an Paulus – ge-

---

17 WA 42, 208, 7-9: »Ecce hoc nostrum peccatum est. Nos in Paradiso voluimus fieri similes Deo, et sumus per peccatum Diabolo similes facti.«

18 Vgl. WA 24, 51, 12 f: »Der mensch mus ein bilde sein entwedder Gottes odder des Teuffels, Denn nach wilchem er sich richtet, dem ist er enhlich.«

gen die Werkgerechtigkeit seiner Zeit aufgreift: Die Sünde verleitet den Menschen, sich ganz auf seine Werke auszurichten, seine Person allein von dem her zu konstituieren, was er tut, und dabei ganz zu vergessen, dass – wie Luther es an anderer Stelle sagen kann – »fides […] facit personam«, der Glaube die Person letztlich ausmacht.[19]

So wird schließlich ebenfalls der Umgang mit den Normen, mit den Geboten, problematisiert, sei es in Form eines Legalismus, der mit der Werkgerechtigkeit einhergeht und das Gesetz so radikalisiert, dass es das Leben erstickt, oder in Form eines Antinomismus, der die Berechtigung des Normativen überhaupt in Frage stellt und sich darüber hinweg setzt. Mit beiden Positionen debattiert Luther in der Genesisvorlesung intensiv, ganz besonders bei der Kommentierung der Anweisungen Gottes an Adam in Gn 1 und 2. Ist der Umgang mit den Normen gestört, so wird der Mensch auch unfähig, angemessen auf die Situationen einzugehen.

Diese Schwierigkeiten in der Ausübung der Verantwortung werden durch Luthers Kommentar hindurch zum ständigen Erweis einer allgegenwärtigen, mächtigen Sünde. Es sei jedoch präzisiert: Nicht in einem moralischen Sinne, als Verfehlung, als schlechte Tat in weltlichen Bereichen. Luther achtet immer wieder auf diese Gefahr einer Moralisierung der Sünde. Sünde im Sinne von Ursünde gilt theologice, als Sünde vor Gott, und betrifft deshalb den Menschen in seinem Verhältnis zu sich selbst. Sie ist dieses selbstverschuldete Verhängnis, das den Menschen dauernd dazu führt, sich selbst zu verfehlen, sich selbst zur Falle zu werden, sich in sich selbst zu verfangen.

5 Ein kleines Zwischenspiel

Da wir in Lateinamerika sind und für Luthers Theologie der Bezug zur konkreten Situation nicht vernachlässigt werden darf, möchte ich, als eine Art Zwischenspiel am Übergang zum nächsten Teil, diese Erfahrung einer allgegenwärtigen Sünde mit Hilfe einer Zeichnung des argentinischen Zeichners Guillermo Mordillo illustrieren.

19 WA 39 I, 282, 16 - 283, 1: »Lex mandat et extorquet opera, fides autem facit personam, et hanc condit, parat ad opera bona. Sed lex et fides sunt inter se realiter distincta. Fides facit personam, lex erudit et monstrat opera.«

Diese Zeichnung[20] scheint mir dem lutherischen Sündenverständnis gut zu entsprechen: Selbstsicher, stolz, zieht der Mensch an der Fischrute, um seinen Fang, einen riesigen Tintenfisch, heraus zu holen. Er ahnt aber nicht, was wir als Betrachter wissen: Dass er auf dem Kopf seiner Beute steht und dass, in Anbetracht des bösen Blicks des Tintenfisches, er demnächst zur Beute werden könnte, und seine Beute zum Fänger …!

Doch gehen wir nun, nach diesem kleinen Zwischenspiel, zu unserem dritten Teil hinüber.

III Befreiende Ermächtigung des Menschen zur Verantwortung

1 Sünde und Protoevangelium

Bis hierher haben wir vor allem, in anthropologischer Perspektive, die Schwierigkeiten der Verantwortung thematisiert. Das entspricht dem Gewicht, das Luther in seiner Kommentierung von Gn 1-3 auf die Thematik der Sünde legt. Zugleich geht es ihm aber auch um das »ultimum et pulcherrimum opus Dei«, das letzte und schönste Werk Gottes, nämlich die vollendete Erschaffung des Menschen.[21] Das heißt: Es soll hier nun auch zum Zuge kommen, wie der Mensch zu neuer Wahrnehmung seiner Verantwortung ermächtigt werden kann, und das ist für Luther ebenfalls Thema seiner theologischen Anthropologie. Anders gesagt: Nur indem die Gottesbeziehung dieses Menschen erneuert wird, kann auch neue Verantwortung für die Welt daraus hervorgehen, aus geschenkter Freiheit. Pointiert kann man diese soteriologische Perspektive mit einer Überschrift aus Ebelings Kommentar zur »Disputatio de homine« zum Ausdruck bringen: »Das Sein des Menschen als Gottes Handeln an ihm«.[22] Das zeigt sich in den Thesen der Disputation daran, dass der ganze zweite Teil – im Kontrast zur philosophischen Definition des ersten Teils – einer theologischen Definition des Menschen gewidmet ist, die stark auf dieses Handeln Gottes am Menschen

---

20 [Guillermo] MORDILLO: Cartoons zum Verlieben (The Collected Cartoons of Mordillo ⟨dt.⟩)/ M 1971. Das Bild wurde beim Vortrag gezeigt, darf hier jedoch aus rechtlichen Gründen nicht reproduziert werden.

21 WA 42, 41, 34 f: »Sed accedamus iam ad ultimum et pulcherrimum opus Dei, ad hominis creationem.«

22 Ebeling: Disputatio de homine 3, 472.

ausgerichtet ist. In seiner Genesisvorlesung hängt für Luther diese neue Perspektive damit zusammen, dass – wie die Tradition sagte – inmitten der Geschichte der Ursünde das Protoevangelium, das »erste Evangelium« erklingt: »Und ich will Feindschaft setzen zwischen dir und dem Weibe, und zwischen deinem Nachkommen und ihrem Nachkommen: der soll dir den Kopf zertreten, und du wirst ihn in die Ferse stechen.«[23] Luther interpretiert diese Stelle sehr stark christologisch, teilweise in kritischer Auseinandersetzung mit der Auslegungsgeschichte, unter anderem dadurch, dass er eine mariologische Deutung sehr scharf ablehnt.[24] Aus dieser Verheißung Christi geht also bereits in Gn 3 Erlösung von der Sünde hervor!

2 Ermächtigung zur Verantwortung

In diese Richtung soll nun unser Versuch gehen, nämlich zeigen, wie aus der theologischen Anthropologie erneuerte ethische Verantwortung folgen kann. Dafür nehme ich nochmals dasselbe Verantwortungsschema auf, nun aber neu ausgerichtet mit Hilfe von Kategorien aus Luthers theologischer Anthropologie.

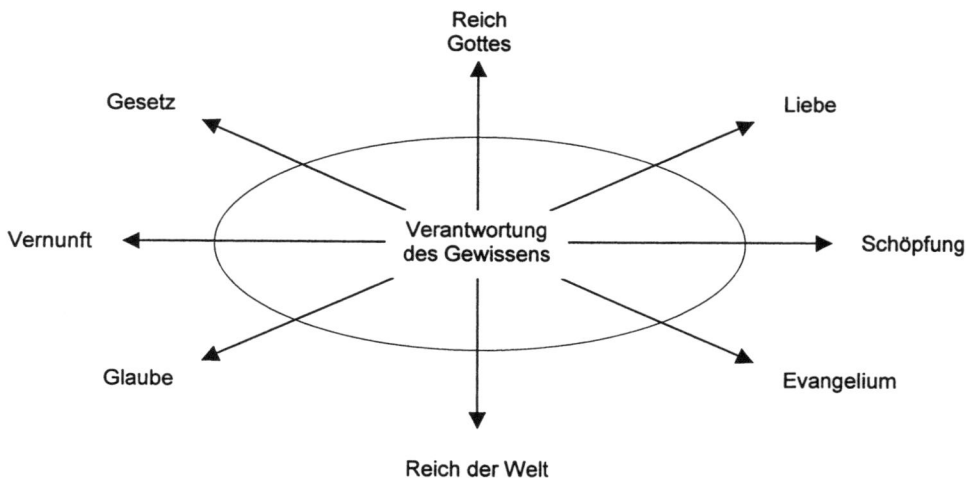

---

23 Gn 3, 15.

24 So z. B. WA 42, 138, 1-3: »Recentiorum autem notum flagicium est, qui [...] cum manifesto scelere detorserunt hunc locum ad beatam Virginem.« Vgl. auch WA 42, 143, 9-20.

1. Für die Kommentierung dieser theologischen Behandlung der Verantwortungskoordinaten möchte ich bei der Spannung von Norm und Situation einsteigen, denn hier ist wohl die entscheidende Wende angesiedelt. Wie wir gehört haben, erklingt im Protoevangelium bereits, aus dem Zorn heraus, den die Sünde auslöst, die verheißungsvolle Nachricht der göttlichen Gnade.[25] Von Grund auf verändert dieses Evangelium die Situation des Menschen vor Gott. Es schenkt diesem eine neue Beziehung zu sich selbst: Er wird sich selbst geschenkt, sodass er die Norm nicht mehr zu seiner Selbstrechtfertigung missbrauchen muss. Vom Evangelium her wird es möglich, die Norm, als Gottes Gesetz interpretiert, neu zu gebrauchen.[26] Das befreit den Menschen vom Legalismus, mit seiner zwanghaften Erfüllung des Gesetzes, wie die Auseinandersetzung des Paulus mit den frühchristlichen Judenchristen zeigt. Daraus darf jedoch nicht geschlossen werden, dass der Christenmensch nun durch seine Freiheit jenseits aller Normen steht. Der Antinomerstreit hinterlässt starke Spuren in Luthers Kommentierung von Gn 1-3: Die Befreiung vom Gesetz erlaubt nicht, das Gesetz hinter sich zu lassen, sondern befreit zu einem neuen Gebrauch des Gesetzes, in der Liebe, welche die Fähigkeit eröffnet, das Gesetz in jeder Situation neu, kreativ, befreiend auszulegen. In diesem Sinne darf die Spannung von Norm und Situation im Zeichen der ständigen Unterscheidung von Gesetz und Evangelium wahrgenommen und gelebt werden. In Anlehnung an das Protoevangelium ist diese Unterscheidung auf der Rechtfertigungsbotschaft begründet. Das zeigen die Thesen der »Disputatio de homine« an zentraler Stelle:

»32. Paulus faßt in Rm 3 [,28]: ›Wir erachten, daß der Mensch durch Glauben unter Absehen von den Werken gerechtfertigt wird‹ in Kürze die Definition des Menschen dahin zusammen, daß der Mensch durch Glauben gerechtfertigt werde.

33. Wer [vom Menschen] sagt, er müsse gerechtfertigt werden, der behauptet gewiß, daß er Sünder und Ungerechter sei und deshalb vor Gott schuldig, jedoch durch Gnade zu retten.«[27]

Damit verbindet sich ein wichtiges anthropologisches Motiv: Der Mensch wird nicht in einem unumstrittenen Status definiert, supralapsarisch, um

---

25 WA 42, 141, 36-38: »Hic enim incipit ex media ira, quam peccatum et inobedientia excitavit, elucere gratia et misericordia.«

26 Hier hat Luthers Lehre vom duplex usus legis ihre Wurzel; vgl. Ebeling: Luther, 137-156.

27 Ebeling: Disputatio de homine 1, 22 f.

nachher erst den Streitigkeiten ausgesetzt zu werden, sondern wird gerade am Ort seines Umstrittenseins definiert, also radikal infralapsarisch: als der durch Glauben zu rechtfertigende Sünder.

2. Wie wirkt sich das auf die Spannung zwischen Person und Werk aus? Wie wir bereits gesehen haben, geht Luther davon aus, dass der Glaube die Person macht. Das heißt: Nicht die Werke, die diese Person vollzieht oder nicht, machen ihren Wert vor Gott aus, sondern dass sie durch göttliche Gnade in all dem angenommen wird, was sie ist, und so, wie sie ist. Im Glauben an diesen gnädigen Gott, im Vertrauen auf ihn liegt der einzig wahre Grund des Menschen, und nicht in diesem Menschen selbst und was er zu produzieren vermag oder nicht. Dadurch wird die Person losgelöst von seinen Werken, was sie nicht davon entlastet, solche Werke zu vollziehen. Sie können aber nicht mehr der Grund ihrer Rechtfertigung sein, was zur Folge hat, dass sie erst recht zu guten Werken werden können, weil sie nicht mehr zur eigenen Rechtfertigung missbraucht, sondern zum Wohl der Welt und des Nächsten getan werden. Mit den befreiungstheologischen Begriffen von Luthers Freiheitsschrift zum Ausdruck gebracht: Der Glaube befreit den Menschen zur Liebe.

> »Aus dem allenn folget der beschluß, das eyn Christen mensch lebt nit ynn yhm selb, sondern ynn Christo und seynem nehstenn, ynn Christo durch den glauben, ym nehsten durch die liebe: durch den glauben feret er uber sich yn gott, auß gott feret er widder unter sich durch die liebe, und bleybt doch ymmer ynn gott und gottlicher liebe, [...].«[28]

3. Daraus folgt nun aber ebenfalls, dass der Konflikt der Instanzen aus einer neuen Perspektive angegangen werden kann: Ich habe hier die lutherische Zweiregimentenlehre ins Schema eingetragen. Diese wurde in Hinsicht auf die Ausübung der Verantwortung öfters kritisch betrachtet, denn sie kann in der Tat verantwortungshemmend wirken. Das ist vor allem dann der Fall, wenn sie im Sinne einer Trennung verstanden wird, die dazu führt, dass Gott und Welt, Glaube und Engagement, Kirche und Staat sich ganz voneinander lösen. Auch im umgekehrten Fall, wenn die zwei Reiche zu unmittelbar identifiziert, vermischt werden, wird freie Verantwortung schwierig. Deshalb muss man die Zweiregimentenlehre als Möglichkeit

---

28 WA 7, 38, 6-10; mit diesem Schluss werden die zwei Teile der Schrift in ihrer fundamentalen Zusammengehörigkeit unterstrichen.

betrachten, stets die letzte Instanz und die vorletzten Instanzen voneinander zu unterscheiden, ohne sie voneinander zu trennen noch miteinander zu vermischen. Der Welt in all ihrer herausfordernden Problematik kommt es nicht zu, letzte Instanz zu sein. Ich darf Gott Gott sein lassen, und der Welt das zukommen lassen, was ihr als vorletzter Instanz zukommt. Aus dieser Unterscheidung geht die befreiende Möglichkeit hervor, dem Reich der Welt in kritischer Loyalität zu dienen, das heißt: ihm Sorge zu tragen, es zu pflegen und zu bewahren, ihm aber auch die nötige Kritik zukommen zu lassen, gegen mögliche Missbräuche Widerstand zu leisten, wie das bei Luther auch stets der Fall war – darüber berichten weitere Referate des Kongresses. In diesem Sinne geht es hier nicht einfach um eine Aufteilung der Bereiche, sondern um eine Klärung der coram-Relationen des Gewissens, in Hinsicht darauf, wie es in christlicher Freiheit und Dienstbarkeit zugleich coram Deo und coram mundo leben kann. In diesem Sinne kann Luther in seiner Genesisvorlesung betonen, dass »das wahre Leben das Leben ist, das wir coram Deo leben dürfen«.[29] Erst von dort her lässt sich das Leben coram mundo befreiend gestalten.

4. Schließlich werden Zweck und Mittel, als vierte und letzte Spannung, neu bestimmt, und hier liegt wohl in ethischer Perspektive die wichtigste Umgestaltung. Ich habe sie – vielleicht etwas rätselhaft – mit dem Begriffspaar »Vernunft und Schöpfung« zum Ausdruck gebracht. Das sei hier etwas ausführlicher erörtert. Der Vernunft haftet, aus der Sicht der theologischen Anthropologie, eine starke Ambivalenz an. Das zeigt sich am eindrücklichsten in der »Disputatio de homine«: Im ersten Teil – Thesen 4-9 – wird die Vernunft gelobt, als »die Hauptsache von allem«, »das Beste im Vergleich mit den übrigen Dingen dieses Lebens«, ja als »[geradezu] etwas Göttliches«, »eine Sonne und eine Art göttlicher Macht«.[30] Zugleich wird aber dann im theologischen Teil der Thesen betont, dass »jene allerschönste und allerherrlichste Sache, welche die Vernunft nach dem Sündenfall geblieben ist«, sich dennoch »unter der Macht des Teufels« befindet.[31]

---

29 WA 42, 146, 27 f: »Per baptismum autem ad vitam spei, seu potius ad spem vitae restituimur. Nam haec demum vera vita est, qua coram Deo vivitur.«

30 Ebeling: Disputatio de homine 1, 16.

31 Ebeling: Disputatio de homine 1, 20 (These 24).

Wie wird nun aber dieser Ambivalenz der Vernunft begegnet? Als pervertierte, sündige Vernunft verfolgt sie leidenschaftlich den Zweck, sich durchzusetzen, Macht zu ergreifen, alles zu beherrschen, was sich auch in heutiger Zeit durch weltweite Ausbeutungsmechanismen zeigt. Deshalb muss hier der Zweck dem Zugriff der Vernunft entrissen werden. Das geschieht dadurch, dass er im Zeichen der Schöpfung verstanden, das heißt: ganz dem göttlichen Handeln anvertraut wird. Dabei sind zwei Dimensionen zu berücksichtigen, welche die Schöpfung sowohl nach hinten, als die bereits geschehene, als auch nach vorne, als die noch künftige Schöpfung betreffen.

In Hinsicht auf die erste, die bereits geschehene, betont Luther, dass die Vernunft von ihr her als Herrin eingesetzt wird. Das kommt sowohl bei der Kommentierung des Herrschaftsauftrags in Gn 1,28 als auch in These 7 der »Disputatio de homine« zum Ausdruck, wo das Gebot »Herrschet!« gerade als Auftrag zur Herrschaft interpretiert wird. Nicht die Vernunft greift autonom zur Herrschaft, sondern diese wird ihr vom Schöpfer gnadenhaft anvertraut. In Hinsicht auf die noch verheißene Schöpfung hingegen betont Luther, Protologie und Eschatologie verbindend, dass der Mensch hineingenommen wird in einen Verwandlungsprozess, der ihn auf die Wiederherstellung des verlorenen Ebenbildes Gottes in ihm ausrichtet:

> »35. So ist denn der Mensch dieses Lebens Gottes bloßer Stoff zu dem Leben seiner künftigen Gestalt.
> 36. Wie auch die Kreatur überhaupt, die jetzt der Nichtigkeit unterworfen ist, für Gott der Stoff zu ihrer herrlichen künftigen Gestalt ist.
> 37. Und wie sich Erde und Himmel im Anfang zu der nach sechs Tagen vollendeten Gestalt verhielt, nämlich als deren Stoff,
> 38. so verhält sich der Mensch in diesem Leben zu seiner zukünftigen Gestalt, bis dann das Ebenbild Gottes wiederhergestellt und vollendet sein wird.«[32]

Das Zwischen-Sein, das hier zur Sprache kommt, hat Luther öfters mit der Aussage gekennzeichnet, dass der Mensch in re Sünder und in spe Gerechter ist. Damit wird in der Anthropologie die eschatologische Dimension prägend, wie die soeben zitierten Schlussthesen aus der »Disputatio de homine« zeigen: Das Sein des Menschen wird als das Handeln Gottes

---

32 Ebeling: Disputatio de homine 1, 23.

an ihm verstanden, in der doppelten Bestimmung der protologischen und der eschatologischen Gestaltung des menschlichen Stoffes durch Gott. Mit dem Begriffspaar »materia – forma«, das hier in einem nicht-aristotelischen Sinn gebraucht wird, wird die Beziehung zwischen Gott und dem Menschen als protologisch-eschatologisches Gnadengeschehen charakterisiert. Für die Vernunft bedeutet das in ethischer Perspektive, dass ihr der Zugriff auf den Zweck aus den Händen genommen wird, sodass sie in aller Begrenztheit und Endlichkeit ihren eigentlichen Auftrag wahrnehmen kann, nämlich die Dinge in diesem irdischen Leben zu verwalten.[33] So wirkt sie – gemäß These 40 der »Disputatio de homine« – in den »Reichen der Vernunft«, im Zeichen der vergänglichen Gestalt der Welt.[34] Es geschieht hier also, im Zeichen der eschatologischen Schöpfungsverheißung, eine heilsame Bescheidung der Vernunft. Sie kann wieder zu sich selbst kommen, befreit von ihren Herrschaftsphantasien.

Wie sich diese Bescheidung in politischer Hinsicht im Einzelnen konkretisiert, hat Luther in seiner Schrift »Von weltlicher Oberkeit, wie weit man ihr Gehorsam schuldig sei« 1523 ausführlich erläutert.[35]

Damit vollzieht sich eine Stärkung des Gewissens, das inmitten dieser Verantwortungsaufgaben steht. Ihm kommt es zu, die Spannungen auszuhalten und so im Bewusstsein der Grenzen und Schwierigkeiten seine Entscheidungen zu treffen und seine Handlungen zu vollziehen. Deshalb soll es stets als grundlegende Perspektive anerkannt werden, wie es etwa Luther im Gegenüber zum Recht betonen kann:

> »Und man doch dasselbige recht, weil es gemein ist ynn der welt, nicht offentlich auff heben künde, so sol man doch fur Gott und heimlich ym gewissen mehr des gewissens denn des rechts achten, Und wenn ia eines weichen und reumen mus, so sol das recht weichen und reumen, auff das das gewissen los und frey werde. Denn das recht ist ein zeitlich ding, das zu letzt auffhören mus, Aber das gewis-

---

33 Ebeling: Disputatio de homine 1, 16 f (These 8): »... in diesem Leben dazu eingesetzt, [all] diese Dinge zu verwalten.«

34 1 K 7,31; Ebeling: Disputatio de homine 1, 24: »40. Deshalb hält Paulus diese Reiche der Vernunft nicht einmal für wert, sie ›Welt‹ zu nennen, sondern bezeichnet sie lieber als ›Schemen der Welt‹.«

35 WA 11, (229) 245-281. Zu Luthers Bestimmung der Vernunft vgl. auch Karl-Heinz ZUR MÜHLEN: Reformatorische Vernunftkritik und neuzeitliches Denken: dargestellt am Werk M. Luthers und Fr. Gogartens. TÜ 1980.

sen ist ein ewig ding, das nimer mehr stirbt, [...]. Das recht ist umb des gewissens willen, Und nicht das gewissen umbs rechts willen, Wo man nu beiden nicht zu gleich helffen kan, da helffe man dem gewissen und enthelffe dem Rechten.«[36]

3 »Simul iustus et peccator«

Mit dieser Erneuerung der Verantwortung sind nicht alle Probleme gelöst, sodass der Mensch diese Aufgabe der Verantwortung hinter sich lassen könnte, um sich anderem zu widmen. Es bleiben auch für den befreiten Menschen die Schwierigkeiten, wie sie im zweiten Teil skizziert wurden. Theologisch kommt damit zum Ausdruck, wie in der Genesisvorlesung öfters betont, dass der Mensch nicht ein für allemal gerechtgesprochen ist, sondern simul iustus et peccator, zugleich Gerechter und Sünder bleibt. In seinem Leben bleibt deshalb der Christenmensch im Zwischen-Sein, als einem Ort des Arbeitens, des Vorangehens, des Wanderns, des Wachsens. So hat es der junge Luther als Busse bestimmt:

> »immer in Sünde, in Rechtfertigung, in Gerechtigkeit, d. h. immer Sünder, immer in der Busse, immer Gerechter. Denn Busse ist die Bewegung vom Nichtgerechten zum Gerechten. Also ist Busse das Zwischen zwischen Ungerechtigkeit und Gerechtigkeit.«[37]

Auf ihre Weise betont das auch die »Disputatio de homine« in ihrer These 39 mit der Idee eines Interims, einer eschatologischen Zwischenzeit, die bestimmt wird als ein tagtäglicher Kampf des Sünders zwischen Rechtfertigung und Verunstaltung,[38] ausgerichtet jedoch auf die Verheißung der Wiederherstellung und Vollendung von Gottes Ebenbild in ihm.

Deshalb können die Menschen – wie es in der Genesisvorlesung heißt – frohen Gemüts, getrost und frei, die Strafe, die Gott ihnen zuweist, in Empfang nehmen; im Zeichen der Verheißung wird sie zu einer »glücklichen und lustigen Strafe« – »poena laeta et hilaris« –, weil in ihr zum Ausdruck kommt, dass Gott sie gerade nicht verwirft, sondern annimmt und liebt, ihnen seinen Segen nicht entzieht, sondern weiterhin – in neu-

36 WA 30 III, 246, 34-39; 247, 5-7; vgl. dazu den Beitrag von James M. Estes in diesem Jahrbuch.
37 WA 56, 442, 16-19 – zitiert in Ebelings Übersetzung; vgl. Ebeling: Luther, 182.
38 Ebeling: Disputatio de homine I, 24: »39. Bis dahin befindet sich der Mensch in Sünden und wird tagtäglich zunehmend gerechtfertigt oder verunstaltet.«

er Gestalt – zukommen lässt.[39] Angesichts der hoffnungsvollen Botschaft
darf die verzweifelte Wurzel wieder blühen.[40] Und deshalb bleibt Eva ge-
trosten Herzens und kann ihren Adam trösten.[41]

Zum Abschluss: Grundmodell und Konkretisierungen

Wie ich von Anfang an angekündigt hatte, bin ich anhand von Luthers Genesisvorlesung dem Verhältnis zwischen Anthropologie und Ethik nach-
gegangen. Grundvoraussetzung war dabei, dass sich dieses Verhältnis am
besten bei der Thematik der Verantwortung herauskristallisiert. In diesem
Sinne habe ich versucht, ein Verantwortungsmodell zu entwickeln, das
den anthropologischen Bezugsrahmen absteckt, innerhalb dessen sich das
Leben in den drei Ständen – in ecclesia, oeconomia und politia – vollzieht.
In einer ersten Etappe wurde die Verantwortung als allgemeinmensch-
liche Aufgabe entfaltet. Weil der Vollzug der Verantwortung durch die
Herrschaft der Sünde in Krise gerät, musste in einer zweiten Etappe reflektiert werden, wie der Mensch von dieser Sünde befreit und zu einem
neuen Umgang mit den Spannungen der Verantwortung ermächtigt werden kann. War die erste Etappe sozusagen schöpfungstheologisch, so war
die zweite eher soteriologisch angelegt.

Man könnte nun gleich fragen, wie sich dieses Modell auf konkrete
ethische Fragen auswirkt. Das war jedoch nicht meine Aufgabe, sondern
die der weiteren Referate des Kongresses. Mein Beitrag hat bewusst einleitenden Charakter. Ich hoffe aber, es sei mir gelungen, zu zeigen, wie bei
Luther ein theologisches Menschenbild für die ethische Verantwortung
zum Tragen kommen kann, indem es das Geflecht der Grundspannungen
der Verantwortung am Schnittpunkt zwischen Anthropologie und Ethik
reflektiert. Es darf für Luther jedoch nicht bei einem abstrakten Schema
bleiben, denn der Mensch, um den es hier geht, ist kein abstrakt kon-
zipiertes Gebilde, sondern ein immer schon in konkreten Situationen

---

39 WA 42, 148, 4: »Haec poena Mulieri est imposita, sed profecto laeta et hilaris.«
40 WA 42, 145, 36 f: »Sed tamen, quia Deus mentiri non potest, efflorescit radix illa sic des-
   perata.«
41 WA 42, 148, 35-37: »Itaque Heua sine dubio etiam in re tristissima, ut apparet, tamen
   gaudio plenum pectus habuit ac fortasse Adamum suum consolata est dicens: Peccavi.
   Sed vide, quam misericordem habemus Deum?«

lebendes Wesen. Theologischen Anthropologie ist deshalb grundsätzlich Lebensorientierung. Da muss sich die Verantwortung erproben lassen. Und wenn wir für diesen Kongress in Brasilien sind, dann sollte der Lebenskontext Brasiliens mit aufgenommen werden.[42] Deshalb bin ich gespannt auf mögliche Konkretisierungen der dargestellten Ansätze, in den Feldern der kirchlichen Gemeinschaften – ecclesia –, der wirtschaftlichen Strukturen – oeconomia – und der politischen Institutionen – politia –, in der Hoffnung, dass wir dabei nicht zu sehr ins Schwitzen kommen …!

---

42 Vgl. in diesem Jahrbuch den Beitrag von Gottfried BRAKEMEIER: Luthers Auftrag in Brasilien heute.

Luther's Attitude Toward the Legal Traditions of His Time

By James M. Estes

Questions of law confronted Luther at every turn. As an accused heretic, for example, he became the target of legal proceedings that were instituted either by Rome or the imperial government, and he defended himself with the advice of the Saxon government and its lawyers. More relevant to the theme of Luther's ethics in church and politics, however, is that throughout his entire career as a theologian and pastor he had to deal with problems posed by the codes of law that were in force in the church and state of his day. Unlike the Causa Lutheri, which has been much studied,[1] Luther attitude toward the law codes of his time has attracted surprisingly little attention from scholars. It is the topic to be addressed here.[2] The aim will be to explain Luther's view of the appropriate use of law in church and society without exploring in detail his views on any particular legal issue, such as usury or resistance to authority. In due course, however, it will become necessary to deal with certain aspects of Luther's view of marriage. As we shall see, the consistent element in all of Luther's utterances on the legal tradtions of his time was his preocupation with the relationship between law and conscience.

1 See especially Wilhelm Borth: Die Luthersache (Causa Lutheri) 1517-1524: die Anfänge der Reformation als Frage von Politik und Recht. Lübeck; HH 1970. See also Armin Kohnle: Reichstag und Reformation: kaiserliche und ständische Religionspolitik von den Anfängen der Causa Lutheri bis zum Nürnberger Religionsfrieden. GÜ 2001, chapters 1-3.

2 Much of the material dealt with in this paper has also been discussed by Gerald Strauss: Law, resistance, and the state: the opposition to Roman law in Reformation Germany. Princeton 1986, 191-224. Despite the rich array of primary and secondary sources cited, Strauss fails to make coherent sense of Luther's utterances on the subject of law. While I cannot here confront Strauss's argument directly, I shall implicitly take issue with his view that Luther was guilty of an »ambiguity« and »inconsistency« that »must have« undermined respect for the very law to which he demanded »unconditional obedience«. For a detailed analysis of the flaws in Srauss's argument, see Gottfried G. Krodel: Luther and the opposition to Roman law in Germany. LuJ 58 (1991), 13-42.

Of the codes of law that Luther had to deal with, the two most important were Roman law, the »Corpus Iuris Civilis«, and canon law, the »Corpus Iuris Canonici«. The two together constituted the »common law« (jus commune) of the Holy Roman Empire and were the basis of the teaching of law in German universities.[3] Important here is that canon law was not just the law of the church but rather a long-established, much revered, and highly useful complement to civil law in the adjudication of civil cases.[4] Then there were the various versions of Germanic law that were struggling to hold their own against the encroachments of the centralizing Roman law that was favoured by ambitious governments and their lawyers.[5] Finally, there was Mosaic law, which some individuals and groups argued should take precedence over all others in a Christian society. The criteria by which Luther judged these legal codes and the obedience owed them were, first, divine law as recorded in Scripture, and second, natural law (that sense of right and wrong which God has implanted in all human beings and is most succinctly summarized in the Decalogue). Although Luther had important things to say about all the legal traditions of his day, he had by far the most to say about canon law, which means that in the pages that follow it will receive more attention than the others. But before

3 »Common law« in the sense of the common system of law for the Empire, the provisions of which applied directly to all cases not governed by a local statute, custom, or privilege.

4 It was for this reason that, as we shall see in more detail below, evangelical jurists would stubbornly and successfully fight for the retention of much of canon law in the territories that adhered to the Reformation. It could not simply be thrown out without leaving huge gaps in law and legal procedure; see John WITTE, Jr.: Law and Protestantism: the legal teachings of the Lutheran Reformation. Cambridge 2002, 65-85; Rolf LIEBERWIRTH: Martin Luthers Kritik am Recht und an den Juristen. In: Martin Luther und seine Universität: Vorträge anläßlich des 450. Todestages des Reformators/ hrsg. von Heiner Lück. Köln; Weimar; W 1998, 53-72, here 65-67; Karl KÖHLER: Luther und die Juristen: zur Frage nach dem gegenseitigen Verhältniß des Rechtes und der Sittlichkeit. Gotha 1873, 34-36.

5 On the »reception« of Roman law and its integration into the German legal system alongside traditional Germanic law read in the light Roman law, see Strauss: Law, resistance, and the state, chapter 3; Isabelle DEFLERS: Lex und ordo: eine rechtshistorische Untersuchung der Rechtsauffassung Melanchthons. B 2005, 108-119.

discussing Luther's approach to any particular legal tradition, it is necessary to say something about his attitude toward law in general. That is at least as important as his attitude toward any particular law code.

II Luther's Attitude Toward Law in General

The earliest and most persistent element in Luther's attitude toward law was his belief that, in both church and state, laws should be enforced in conformity with the concept of »epieikeia« (aequitas, Billigkeit), which he had learned from Aristotle (384-322), the New Testament, and the works of the late-medieval conciliarists. The idea was that, since laws cannot be framed to cover all cases and problems, the severity of the law should be moderated, or indeed that the law should be set aside, if due consideration of the circumstances indicated that reason, justice, and humanity would best be served by so doing. We find Luther making the case for epieikeia as early as the »Dictata super Psalterium« of 1513-1515[6] and as late as February 1546, in one of the last of the entries in the »Tischreden«.[7] During the intervening years he was wont to take advantage of any opportunity to advocate this approach to the enforcement of law. There is, for example, a fine discussion of it in Part III of the treatise »Secular authority: to what extent it should be obeyed« (1523), even though in this particular case the word epieikeia (or its equivalents) is not used:

> »[...] no matter how good and equitable the laws are, they all make an exception in the case of necessity, in the face of which they cannot insist upon being strictly enforced. Therefore, a prince must have the law as firmly in hand as the sword, and determine in his own mind when and where the law is to be applied strictly or with moderation, so that law may prevail at all times and in all cases, and reason may be the highest law and the master of all administration of law. [...] [It is not] sufficiently praiseworthy merely to follow the written law or the opinions of jurists. There is more to it than that.«[8]

To be able to do this properly, the prince will have to pray for wisdom, heed God's word, be wary of the influence of »the high and mighty and of

6 WA 4, 323, 20-35 ≙ 55 II, 916, 734-750.
7 WA TR 6, 345 f (7031).
8 LW 4, 118 f ≙ WA 11, 272, 11-24.

flatterers«, place love and natural law above the content of law books, and thus be able to apply »untrammeled reason and unfettered judgment« to the just and equitable treatment of his subjects.[9]

While his intellectual formation as a theologian had thus taught Luther that good laws need to be enforced with wisdom and discretion, his conflict with ecclesiastical and civil authority from 1517 through 1521 taught him that bad laws might have to be resisted in the defence of truth and justice, and in the responsible exercise of a clergyman's pastoral duty. In his famous speech before Emperor Charles and the assembled estates at the Diet of Worms in April 1521, there is a brief passage that has attracted less notice than the much-cited »Here I stand« peroration at the end:

> »Another group of my books attacks the papacy and the affairs of the papists as those who [...] have laid waste the Christian world with evil that affects the spirit and the body. For no one can deny [...] *that through the decrees of the pope and the doctrines of men the consciences of the faithful have been most miserably entangled, tortured, and torn to pieces.* [...]. If, therefore, I should have retracted these writings, I should have done nothing other than to have added strength to this tyranny and I should have opened not only windows but doors to such great godlessness.«[10]

The immediate target of this outburst was the law of the church, canon law, a subject to be dealt with at length below. For the moment, however, the topic under investigation is still Luther's attitude toward law in general.

In the prolonged conflict with the defenders of the indulgence traffic and of papal absolutism, Luther had to do battle not only with scholastic theology but also with a body of ecclesiastical law which, in his view,

9 LW 45, 119-129 ≙ WA 11, 273-280; see also WA 6, 166, 32-37 (Confitendi ratio, 1520); WA 8, 662, 1 - 663, 2 (De votis monasticis M. Lutheri iudicium, 1521); 19, 632, 8-16 (Ob Kriegsleute auch in seligem Stande sein können); WA 25, 58, 28 - 60, 26 (Annotationes Lutheri in epistolam Pauli ad Titum, 1527); WA 51, 352, 20-26 (An die Pfarrherrn, wider den Wucher zu predigen, 1540). As an example of the need for such wise and pious jurisprudence Luther cited the judicial aftermath of the Peasants' War, in which those who had become involved in the rebellion against their will had been executed according to the strict letter of the law along with those who had been guilty of deliberate and intentional rebellion. This, he said, was a case in which the law ought to have yielded to justice; instead, a great injustice was done to many people and innocent blood was shed; WA 19, 630, 28 - 631, 7.
10 LW 32, 110 ≙ WA 7, 833, 8-13. 17-19 (Verhandlungen mit D. M. Luther auf dem Reichstage zu Worms, 1521); emphasis added.

required Christians to believe and to do things that God himself did not require Christians to believe or to do, or that God had in fact forbidden them to believe or to do. The residue of this experience was an abiding sense of the great propensity of human laws, ecclesiastical no less than secular, to be so at variance with divine law or natural justice as to inflict oppressive burdens and intolerable injuries on human consciences.[11]

The first product of this experience of the destructive potential of law was Luther's strategy for reform, which was marked by an acute anxiety that he not be guilty of erecting a new tyranny over consciences to replace the old one.[12] Hence his famous insistence, classically formulated in the Invocavit Sermons of 1522, that at the outset one should make no more reforms than were absolutely necessary and postpone more basic reforms until the instruction of the people from the word had prepared their con-

11 Few key words occur more often in Luther's writings, including those on law, than does »conscience« (conscientia, das Gewissen). It is a word that Luther does not trouble himself to define carefully, preferring to describe what conscience does rather than to offer precise definitions of what it is. Common to virtually all conceptions of conscience since classical antiquity, including Luther's, is the idea that it is the faculty of the soul (or mind) with which one observes one's self and renders moral judgements on one's own behaviour. According to St. Paul (R 2, 14f), even the heathen have this faculty by virtue of an innate, though vitiated, knowledge of natural law on the basis of which their consciences either accuse or excuse them. But Luther, less interested in consciences generally than in Christian consciences specifically, treats conscience as the forum in which the Christian hears, simultaneously, God's word in the form of the law, which condemns and terrifies, and the gospel, which liberates and consoles. »Das Gesetz bedrängt das Gewissen durch die Sünden, das Evangelium aber macht es frei und schenkt ihm Frieden durch den Glauben an Christus«; WA 56, 424, 16f. Because the action of conscience is both rational and emotional, Luther often equates »conscience« with »mind«, »spirit«, or »heart«. A conscience »captive to Word of God«, as Luther described his own conscience at Worms (WA 7, 835, 6-8), is one that is aware of the Christian's duty to obey God's law rather than human law. Luther knows nothing of the modern idea of conscience as an autonomous source of religious truth. Moreover, a free conscience is for Luther one freed from dependence on works and, consequently, free to live in a trusting relationship with God through faith. Although he acknowledges that erring consciences have rights that must (within limits) be respected, he knows nothing of »freedom of conscience« in the sense of an inalienable right to worship (or not) as one chooses; see Friedhelm KRÜGER: Gewissen. III: Mittelalter und Reformationszeit. 2: Reformation. TRE 13 (1984), 222-225.
12 This point is particularly well made by Scott HENDRIX: Luther and the papacy: stages in a Reformation conflict. Phil 1981, 138f.

sciences to accept changes without fear or compunction.[13] Hence also his insistent emphasis on Christian freedom in all externals not prescribed by divine law and his anxiety lest anyone think that the ceremonies and usages adopted in Wittenberg were in any way binding on Christians in other communities. External ceremonies, and the rules and regulations governing them, should, he said, be freely chosen and voluntarily submitted to by the communities affected.[14]

It was from this perspective that in 1523 Luther defended the right and duty of small communities to enact their own reforms in cases where the established authorities either could not or would not do so.[15] More important in the long run, however, was Luther's advice on how larger communities or territories should arrive at a common church order. The advice he gave is often taken as an example of Luther's shortcomings as an ecclesiastical organizer but is really an example of his preference for freedom over law. To the German-speaking community in Livonia, for example, he recommended in 1525 that their pastors should »get together in a friendly way and come to a common decision« about external ceremonies, thus establishing »one uniform practice«.[16] Once this was done, they would have to »instruct the people lest they [commit the old ›papist‹ error of regarding] such uniform practices as divinely appointed and absolutely binding laws«, the observance of which would contribute to their salvation, rather than viewing them simply as »useful and necessary [measures] for governing the people externally«. Even more instructive on this point is Luther's reaction to the effort of Landgrave Philip of Hessen (1504, 1518-1567) to impose an evangelical church order in his domains.

Landgrave Philip was the first Lutheran prince to act in response to the view of evangelical jurists that the recess of the Diet of Speyer in 1526 had established the right of the territorial princes to impose in

13 WA 10 III, 1-64 (Acht Sermone D. M. Luthers von ihm gepredigt zu Wittenberg in der Fasten [Invokavitpredigten vom 9.-16. März 1522]).
14 WA 12, 218, 33 - 219, 7; 19, 72, 1-24.
15 WA 11, 408-416 (Das eine christliche Versamlung ... Macht habe, alle Lehre ..., 1523).
16 LW 53, 45-50 ≙ WA 18, 417-421 (Eine christliche Vermahnung vom äußerlichen Gottesdienst und Eintracht an die in Livland); cf. the treatise »De instituendis ministris ecclesiae ad senatum Pragensem Bohemiae« (1523), where Luther gives the same advice to the clergy in Bohemia; WA 12, 193, 22 - 194, 20.

their territory an ecclesiastical order that would be valid at least until a general council.[17] The result was the »Reformatio ecclesiarum Hassiae«, which was adopted by the so-called synod of Homberg in October 1526 and quickly sent by the landgrave to Luther for his opinion.[18] In his reply to the landgrave, dated 7 January 1527,[19] Luther strongly advised that the »Reformatio« not be published »at this time«. In so doing he advanced no objection to the doctrines enumerated, eminently Lutheran all of them, or to the congregational-synodal polity prescribed, which was hardly objectionable even though it was not the wave of the future for German Lutheranism. Nor, indeed, did Luther object because the prince was taking the initiative in church reform. Instead, his complaint was that the »Reformatio« was »ein hauffen gesetze«, a great heap of laws whose enactment the Wittenberg theologians would not have dared to recommend in Saxony (where the Reformation was already much further advanced than it was in Hessen).

As Luther saw it, the »Reformatio« was an attempt prematurely to impose a uniform and highly detailed order on a territory in which there had still not been any communal reformation to speak of. He took the view that such enactments should be the culmination of a piecemeal process of law-making, not its beginning, and he pointed to the example of Moses, whose law code, he said, was for the most part a codification and harmonization of laws already long in force among the people of Israel. Experience has shown, he continued, that there is a great gulf between prescription and performance and that, if laws are made too early, in advance of practice and custom, they remain abstract thoughts about how things ought to be and do not really take root among the people and do not lend themselves readily to needed correction.

17 The recess declared that, with respect to the enforcement of the Edict of Worms (1521), the estates of the Empire would conduct themselves »wie ein jeder solches gegen Gott und kaiserliche Majestät hofft und vertraut zu verantworten«; Walch2 16, 210.
18 Text of the Reformatio in DIE EVANGELISCHEN KIRCHENORDNUNGEN DES SECHSZEHNTEN JAHRHUNDERTS/ hrsg. von Aemilius Ludwig Richter. Nachdruck der Ausgabe Weimar 1846. Nieuwkoop 1967, 56-59; see also Gerhard MÜLLER: Franz Lambert von Avignon und die Reformation in Hessen. Marburg 1958, 33-52.
19 WA Br 4, 157f (1071).

»For truly, making law is a big, risky, complicated business, and without the spirit of God no good will come of it. Therefore one must proceed with fear and humility before God, following these principles: brief and good, few and well made, gradually and always to the point.«[20]

This, said Luther, has been the experience of all lawgivers, including Moses, Christ, the Romans, and the popes. So the proper starting point in Hessen should be for the landgrave to see to it that local parishes and schools are provided with »good people«, who might be provided with brief and clear instructions about how to proceed. But it would be even better if »one, three, six, [or] nine« pastors were to make a start by agreeing to common practice on »three, five, [or] six matters« and continue in this fashion until all the pastors had agreed to adhere to a common order that could be written down in »a small booklet«.This procedure would lead to a result far more tailored to real needs and would thus be much easier to maintain in practice and to correct as needed. This, as Luther did not say directly, is what had happened in Saxony and should now happen in Hessen.

By the time Luther wrote this endorsement of law-making as the gradual process of introducing and harmonizing practices voluntarily agreed to, events in Saxony were already teaching him how difficult it was to achieve the desired voluntary agreement on a common church order. By the autumn of 1525 the Reformation had established itself in the vast majority of the leading communities in the elector's domains and, in the process, had produced a great deal of confusion and disorder in preaching, public worship, and church finances.

Seeing this, Luther decided that, for the sake of good order and effective ministry, a visitation of the parishes was needed to impose a common order in the territory. Since the evangelical church in Saxony had no bishop of its own to undertake such a visitation, Luther appealed to the elector »as Christian brother« to establish a commission that would

20 WA Br 4, 158, 33-36 (1071). Here, as in all other instances where the LW text is not cited, the translation is my own. The German of this passage is difficult, particularly in the second sentence: »Es ist fur war gesetz machen ein gros, ferlich, weitleufftig ding, vnd on Gotts geist wird nichts gutts draus. Darumb ist mit furcht vnd demut fur gott hie zu faren, Vnd diese mas zu halten: kurtz vnd gut, Wenig vnd wol, Sachte vnd ymer an.« The WA editors interpret »Sachte vnd ymer an« as »nicht zu hastig und stetig fort«.

undertake the episcopal office of visitation of the parishes. A year later, in the wake of the recess of the Diet of Speyer already mentioned, the elector agreed and the visitors began their work in the summer of 1527.

In his justification of this procedure – the introduction to the edition of the Saxon Visitation Articles published in 1528 – Luther, true to form, emphasized that neither he nor the other visitors had the authority to »issue any strict commands, as if [they] were publishing a new form of papal decrees«. At the same time, however, he emphasized that pastors who did not »willingly, without any compulsion« subject themselves to the visitation could expect the elector, as guardian of public peace and order, to »constrain them to preserve unity in teaching and faith«, just as the emperor Constantine had done in his day.[21] What this reveals is that, by the end of the 1520s, Luther's desire for Christian freedom in externals and his dislike of legalism were coming into conflict with the need for good laws and decent order that the rapid and unregulated spread of the Reformation had created.[22] In other words, Luther's emphasis on the defence of Christian freedom against the oppressive burden of papal law was giving way to an emphasis on the need to discipline evangelical freedom with good laws and wholesome order administered by ecclesiastical officials who were entitled to obedience. As a result, he would in the 1530s speak somewhat differently about law and government in church and state than he had up to that point. But before considering that development, it is necessary to go back to the beginning to consider, one by one, Luther's attitude toward the specific legal traditions of his time.

III Luther and Mosaic Law

Of the codes of law to which Luther had to address himself, the law of Moses can be dealt with most quickly and easily. In the early years of the Reformation there were, in Saxony and elsewhere, some who urged

21 LW 40, 269-273 ≙ WA 26, 195-201.
22 This tension is reflected in the Large Catechism (1529), where Luther explains at some length that the divine commandment to participate in the Sacrament of the Altar has to be observed without resorting to force or compulsion, »lest we institute a new slaughter of souls«; see THE BOOK OF CONCORD: the Confessions of the Lutheran Church/ ed. by Robert Kolb; Timothy J. Wengert. MP 2000, 471 f (§§ 40-52); German and Latin texts see BSLK, 716, 1 - 718, 35.

that »heathen law«, particularly Roman law, should give way to Mosaic law, or at least contain nothing contrary to it. Among these were Thomas Müntzer (ca. 1489-1525), the pamphleteer Eberlin von Günzburg (ca. 1470-1533), and possibly Andreas Bodenstein aus Karlstadt (1486-1541).[23] In 1524, when Duke John the Steadfast, soon to be Elector John (1468, 1525-1532), seriously proposed introducing such a radical measure into Saxony, Luther had to contribute private letters and memoranda to the (successful) effort to dissuade him from doing so.[24]

In August of the following year, Luther addressed the subject publicly in a sermon that was published under the title »How Christians should regard Moses«.[25] Luther's view was that, just as the fallen world could not be governed by the gospel, so the Germany of his day could not be governed by the »dead and gone« law of ancient Israel. The law of Moses, said Luther, was given to the Jews alone and not to the Gentiles, who were deliberately excluded. It is therefore not binding on Christians except in so far as it happens to agree with the New Testament or with natural law (as in the Decalogue), which has been given to the Gentiles as well as to the Jews. Mosaic law was, to be sure, God's word, but it was God's word for the Jews alone in ancient Israel and not for anyone else. Christians should obey the laws established by their own governments in the exercise of the authority over secular life that God has given them. One can, to be sure, find in Moses examples of good law-making and voluntarily imitate them. From time to time Luther himself sought guidance from Mosaic law, as,

---

23 Lieberwirth: Martin Luthers Kritik ..., 62 f. The charge that Karlstadt argued for the replacement of civil law (the Justinian code) by Mosaic law was made by Melanchthon in texts that date from after 1530. But no such argument can be found in Karlstadt's own writings, and there are good reasons to doubt that he ever argued the position attributed to him by Melanchthon; see Ulrich BUBENHEIMER: Consonantia Theologiae et Iurisprudentiae: Andreas Bodenstein von Karlstadt als Theologe und Jurist zwischen Scholastik und Reformation. TÜ 1977, 246-250.

24 WA Br 3, 254, 21-27 (720), Luther to Spalatin, 14 March 1524; 306, 4 - 307, 32 (753), Luther to Duke John Frederick, 18 June 1524.

25 Martin LUTHER: Eine Unterrichtung, wie sich die Christen in Mose sollen schicken; WA 16, 363-393; see also WA Br 3, 484, 1 - 485, 14 (861), Luther to the City Council in Danzig, 5 (7?) May 1525; and cf. WA 18, 67-84 (the section of the treatise »Wider die himmlischen Propheten, ...« entitled »Von den Bildsturmen«).

for example, in its rules governing marriage,[26] but he did not in the process attribute to it binding force for Christians. This remained Luther's position for the rest of his life.[27]

IV Luther and Secular Law in the 1520s

In the 1520s, the most significant expression of Luther's attitude toward secular law was his identification of a long list of clerical abuses as violations of it (because they constituted »robbery and theft«) and his insistence that popes, bishops, or any other clergymen found guilty of such violations were liable to appropriate punishment by the secular authorities. God, he said, has given secular government complete authority over such matters, which means that canon law's claims of clerical privilege are contrary to Scripture and reason and thus entirely bogus.[28] Apart from this, Luther's direct comments on secular law in these early years are not plentiful. When he does comment, it is to side, in rather general terms, with those who object to the wholesale reception of Roman law at the expense of local Germanic law. In the address »To the Christian nobility of the German nation concerning the reform of the Christian estates«, for example, he observes that »secular law [...] has become a [veritable] wilderness! Though it is much better, wiser, and more honest than the spiritual [i. e., canon] law [...] *there is far too much of it.*« Wise rulers aided by Holy Scripture ought to be law enough. It would be best, moreover, if »territorial laws and customs« were to take precedence over »general imperial laws«, for »brief laws« suitable to a people's »peculiar character« are better than »rambling and farfetched laws« that »burden the people« and are more of a hindrance than a help to the settlement of cases. That said, Luther defers to the judgement of those who have

26 As, for example, the treatise »Von Ehesachen«, 1530; WA 30 III, 214, 15 - 215, 14; 225, 10 - 227, 7; 232, 24-28; 241, 4-10.
27 The idea that Mosaic law should replace established law did not entirely die out. In 1542 Luther once again found it necessary to state his opposition to it and to insist on the Christian's duty to obey the established imperial and territorial laws. Lieberwirth: Martin Luthers Kritik ..., 64, citing WA TR 6, 127 f (6693).
28 See James M. Estes: Peace, order, and the glory of God: secular authority and the church in the thought of Luther and Melanchthon, 1518-1559. Leiden 2005, 10-14. 22 f.

given more attention to this problem than he has been able to do.[29] By 1530, however, Luther – having witnessed the Peasants' Revolt, with its denunciation of »new laws« and its demand for customary law – will have thought more about the matter and will have kinder things to say about Roman law as well as harsher things about Germanic law. Meanwhile, he had been devoting much attention to canon law.

V Luther on Canon Law

Strictly speaking, the category »canon law« includes any enactment of ecclesiastical authority that has acquired the force of law in the church. But when scholars speak or write of »canon law«, they are usually referring specifically to the codification of church law that we know as the »Corpus Iuris Canonici« (CIC). Since, however, that term was first officially used in 1582 and did not come into common use until the end of the seventeenth century, we do not find it in Luther's works. On the other hand, the five-part collection[30] now known as the CIC was already in existence by 1500, was already understood unofficially as a unity, and was already being printed in collected editions.[31] We know, moreover, that Luther himself understood as a unity the component parts of the CIC and that he did not confuse the contents of the collection with ecclesiastical laws and decrees that had not been included in it or that had come later.[32] Luther's vocabulary in referring

29 LW 44, 203 f ≙ WA 6, 459, 30 - 460, 5, emphasis added. On the subject of wise rulers aided by Scripture being »law enough«; WA 6, 554, 24-32: »Hoc scio, nullam rem publicam legibus foeliciter administrari. Si enim prudens fuerit Magistratus, ductu naturae omnia foelicius administrabit quam legibus: si prudens non fuerit, legibus nihil promovebit nisi malum, cum nesciat eis uti nec eas pro tempore moderare. ideo in rebus publicis magis curandum est, ut boni et prudentes viri praesint quam ut leges ferantur: ipsi enim erunt optimae leges, omnem varietatem casuum vivaci aequitate iudicaturi. Quod si assit eruditio divinae legis cum prudentia naturali, plane superfluum et noxium est scriptas leges habere. Super omnia autem, Charitas nullis prorsus legibus indiget.«

30 The Decretum Gratiani (circa 1140), the Liber Decretalium Gregorii IX (1234), the Liber Sextus of Boniface VIII (1298), the Clementina of Clement V (1314), and the Extravagantes of John XXII (1499-1502).

31 Sieghard MÜHLMANN: Luther und das Corpus Iuris Canonici bis zum Jahre 1530. Teil 1: Prolegomena. L 1972 – L, Univ., Theol. Fak., Diss., 1972 –, 103-107.

32 This is clearest in a letter of 10 December 1520 to Georg Spalatin, where he lists Decre-

to the CIC is not always free of ambiguity (Libri papae, des Papstes Gesetz, das geistliche Recht, decretum pontificum, and so on at great length), but his references to the collection are sufficiently abundant and sufficiently clear to establish that – most of the time, at least – the CIC was what he was talking about and that it was something that Luther dipped into frequently and carefully. He was certainly not »learned in the law« in the professional sense, but he knew enough about canon law to deal with it effectively where it impinged on in his work as a theologian and reformer.[33]

When one thinks of Luther and canon law, the image that immediately comes to mind is that of him throwing copies of it into a bonfire outside the Magpie Gate at Wittenberg on 10 December 1520. As is well known, that event, together with other evidence of seemingly indiscriminate hostility toward canon law,[34] cost Luther the support of many in the legal profession, including that of the most distinguished jurist of them all, Ulrich Zasius (1461-1536).[35] In the present context, however, it is important to emphasize that Luther's rejection of canon law was never as complete as the burning of it seemed to indicate and that he would, as we shall see, find positive uses for portions of it.

tum, Decretales, Sextus, Clementina, and Extravagantes; WA Br 2, 234, 4-7 (361). There are similar passages in WA 5, 259, 26; WA Br 1, 353, 28-32 (157); WA 10 III, 358, 29; 31 I, 241, 33-35. See also Mühlmann: Luther und das Corpus Iuris Canonici …, 109 f.

33 Mühlmann: Luther und das Corpus Iuris Canonici …, 299. In his confrontation with Cardinal Cajetan (1469-1534) at the Diet of Augsburg in 1518, for example, Luther proved more conversant with canon law than the cardinal expected. Cajetan appears to have assumed that Luther would be ignorant of the bull »Unigenitus« (1343), which was not included in the standard collections of canon law, and believed that when confronted with its definition of the treasury of the church as the merits of Christ, Luther would have to admit that his position on indulgences was in conflict with a valid papal decree. But Luther had in fact seen »Unigenitus« and had come to Augsburg prepared to reject its content as contrary to the plain sense of Scripture; see Hendrix: Luther and the papacy, 59.

34 As, for example, in the letter of 8 June 1521 to Justus Jonas that served as the preface to the »Rationis Latomianae pro incendiariis Lovaniensis scholae sophistis redditae, Lutheriana confutatio«, Luther advised Jonas, who at that moment was expected to lecture in canon law at the university, that he should devote his efforts to the refutation of its contents: »Ita, mi frater, facito, ut doceas dediscenda esse, quae doces, et sciant fugienda sicut mortifera, quaecunque Papa et Papistae statuunt ac sentiunt«; WA 8, 44, 39 - 45, 1.

35 Köhler: Luther und die Juristen, 34 f.

Luther's motive for burning canon law was that it was a treasury of everything in the doctrine and practice of the papal church that stood in contradiction to what he saw as the clear teaching of Scripture.[36] Above all, it was the embodiment in law of the theory of papal absolutism behind which the Roman hierarchy defended its catastrophic failure to nourish the people with the word of God.

> »For if you want to know in a few words what the canon law contains, then listen. It is, to put it briefly, the following: The pope is a god on earth over everything heavenly, earthly, spiritual, and secular, and all is his own. No one is permitted to say to him: ›What are you doing?‹«[37]

At the same time, however, Luther recognized in canon law a repository of much wholesome legislation that the papalists themselves chose to ignore or evade. From the beginning he was alert to any opportunity to point out that the those antagonists who demanded his obedience to some provision or other of canon law frequently excused themselves from heeding other and better provisions of it.[38] So it is no surprise that when, in the address »To the Christian nobility of the German nation ...« he declared that canon law should be blotted out »from the first letter to the last«, he made two important qualifications.[39] The first one was to add the words »especially the decretals«, i.e., especially the »Liber Decretalium Gregorii IX« which contained so much of the medieval legislation on which the claims of papal absolutism were based. By implication, this qualification granted a certain grudging recognition to the earlier »Decretum Gratiani«, which incorporated more of the legislation of the ancient church. Concerning it, Luther said – and this was his second qualification – that there was much in it that was good, even though the pope and his flatters assumed the right to ignore anything in it that they did not like.[40]

36 WA 7, (152) 161-182.
37 LW 31, 392 f ≙ WA 7, 177, 6-10 / 24-29.
38 For an abundance of examples, see Hendrix: Luther and the papacy, chapters 2-4 passim.
39 LW 44, 202 f ≙ WA 6, 459, 1-29.
40 This point is made more clearly in »Warum des Papstes und seiner Jünger Bücher von D. M. Luther verbrannt sind« (WA 7, 180, 11-18) than in »To the Christian nobility of the German nation ...«. Cf. Luther's statement 1530 at the end of the treatise »Von Ehesachen«: »[...] das geistliche recht [...] ist so unördig ynn einander gworffen und

Though his visceral antipathy toward canon law as a whole would never go away, and would indeed be reiterated with astonishing vehemence in the last years of his life, Luther would in the interim pay a good deal of attention to the »good things« in it. In this connection it is important that Luther was at the head of a movement, most of whose leaders had made their way to the Reformation via Erasmian humanism and were for that reason predisposed to view canon law, insofar as it incorporated the wholesome legislation of the ancient church, as a weapon in the battle for the reform of a church that they perceived as having departed from the apostolic purity of the ancients. No less a person than Erasmus of Rotterdam (1466/69-1536) had argued that canon law was not a compendium of eternal truths, all of them of equal value and force, but rather the accumulated residue of a historical development that was subject to critical examination and revision. To him it was clear that the legislation of the most ancient councils and synods was in closer harmony with Scripture and Christian virtue than that of later ages and that the authority that had made the laws could revise them in order to restore ancient purity. Luther himself *may* have been influenced by Erasmus in this respect via some of the latter's scriptural annotations.[41] Be that as it may, Luther was entirely in agreement with humanist scholars, including Philip Melanchthon, that canon law viewed historically was a useful tool in the hands of the reformers.

This historical-critical approach to canon law made it possible to see in it a repository of reliable information about the constitution of the ancient church that could be used selectively as a model for reforms in the present. So, for example, when in 1528 Luther needed to justify the Saxon visitation, he was able to refer to the example of the holy bishops who, »in the days of the ancient fathers«, diligently conducted visitations, »concerning which

offt widder einander, als das aus sendebrieffen des Bapsts, so auff mancherley zeit und sachen gegeben sind, zusamen gerafft«, that it is a difficult task to deal with it. »Est ist war, Es sind viel guter urteil und rechtsprüche drinnen, Etlich sind auch so hin [i. e., von mäßigem Wert]«; WA 30 III, 248, 1-8.
41 Wilhelm MAURER: Reste des kanonischen Rechtes im Frühprotestantismus. In: Ders.: Die Kirche und ihr Recht: gesammelte Aufsätze zum evangelischen Kirchenrecht/ hrsg. von Gerhard Müller; Gottfried Seebass. TÜ 1976, 145-207, here 154-169.

much is still to be found in the papal laws«.[42] More often, however, canon law was used polemically to refute the arguments of those who condemned the reformers as heretics. In 1527, for example, in a defence of communion sub utraque against a ban on it that had been published by Albert of Brandenburg, Cardinal-Archbishop-Elector of Mainz (1490, 1518-1545), Luther argued his case by citing from the »Decretum« papal decrees that were in accordance with his understanding of scriptural teaching on the proper distribution of the sacrament.[43] He did so, he said, not because he felt it necessary to confirm the clear teaching of Scripture with the authority of canon law but rather because he wanted to confront his adversaries with the content of their own law »and slay them with their own weapon«.[44]

It was in this same spirit that Luther expressed his pleasure with »Ein kurzer Auszug aus den päpstlichen Rechten der Dekrete und Dekretalien ...«, which Lazarus Spengler (1479-1534) published at Nürnberg in 1529.[45] This little volume of excerpts from the CIC, mostly the »Decretum« but with some from the »Decretales« as well, was intended to demonstrate that the ancient law of the church was essentially in harmony with Scripture as Luther and his followers understood it. Spengler found canonical justification for virtually every distinctly Lutheran doctrine and practice, including the precedence of Scripture over tradition, communion in both kinds, the priesthood of all believers, the marriage of priests, and the subjection of bishops to the authority of Scripture.[46] In the preface that

42 LW 40, 269 f ≙ WA 26, 196, 1-5.

43 WA 23, 416, 10 - 418, 26.

44 WA 2, 418, 27 - 419, 7. Luther then goes on to criticize Gratian for paying too little attention to Scripture and too much to »the pope and the Roman church« in the execution of his laudable aim of bringing order and coherence out of the »discordant« accumulation of ecclesiastical laws; WA 2, 419, 8-21. The same point is made 1539 in »Von den Konziliis und Kirchen«; 50, 543, 23-28.

45 The »Ein kurzer Auszug ...« is still not available in a modern critical edition. Thanks to the library of the Luther Seminary in Minneapolis, I was able to examine the microfiche of an edition of it printed at Strassburg in 1556 (HAB 420.3 Theol. 4º). But the summary of the contents of the » Ein kurzer Auszug ...« offered here is based on Maurer: Reste des kanonischen Rechtes ..., 188-204, where citations of the relevant portions of the CIC are given.

46 He also found in old canons (1) condemnation of the death penalty for heretics but at the same time the requirement that secular government should take action against false teachers and protect the church; (2) support for the emperor's role as the protector of

he wrote for the edition of the »Ein kurzer Auszug ...« that was printed at Wittenberg in 1530, Luther stated that he had often thought of producing such a volume himself in order to demonstrate that »the miserable people« who blindly reject the doctrine of the reformers are guilty not only of not obeying their own law but also of recklessly condemning it as heresy.[47]

In the wake of the publication of Spengler's »Ein kurzer Auszug ...« similar use of the CIC was made, with Luther's knowledge and approval,[48] in the »Confessio Augustana«, which was presented to the emperor at the Diet of Augsburg in the summer of 1530. Citations from the »Decretum« were used to support the argument that the doctrine and ceremonies of the emerging evangelical churches were closer to the biblical and apostolic purity of the ancient church than were those of the papal church. Cited, for example, were papal decrees that sanctioned the marriage of priests, that stipulated that communion must be distributed in both kinds, and that declared that rites and ceremonies do not need to be the same everywhere. More fundamentally, decrees were cited affirming that customs contrary to God's commands are not to be approved and that bishops have no authority to teach or command anything contrary to Scripture.[49] Moreover, the »Tischreden« of the early 1530s record several

Christendom who can demand even of a pope an accounting of his faith; and (3) justification for the German hope for a free Christian council.

47 WA 30 II, 219, 2-28.
48 Luther himself participated, along with Melanchthon, Bugenhagen, and Jonas, in the preparation of the so-called Torgau Articles, which contain several citations of the Decretum that Melanchthon incorporated, with still others, into the »Confessio Augustana«. The Torgau Articles, with notes identifying the citations of the Decretum are found in Sources and contexts of the Book of Concord/ ed. by Robert Kolb; James A. Nestingen. MP 2001, 94-104. For the original German of the passages used in the »Confessio Augustana«, see the critical apparatus of the pages of the BSLK cited in the following note. The complete German text of the Torgau Articles is in CR 26, 171-200.
49 See the conclusion to part one (following article 21) and articles 22-23, 25, 27-28 of the »Confessio Augustana« in BSLK 83d, 1-5; 85, 14-24; 86, 6-9; 87, 39 - 88, 5; 89, 29-33; 99, 11 - 100, 5; 111, 4f; 114, 13-15; 116, 5-13; 124, 22 - 125, 2; 126, 6-8 ≙ The Book of Concord, 59 (2). 62 (8). 63 (9). 64 (13). 66 (16). 74 (11). 84 (23). 86 (31f). 88 (10). 94 (27). 96 (31). Not surprisingly, canon law is put to similar use in the »Apologia Confessionis Augustanae« (1531), and the »Tractatus de potestate papae« (1537).

versions of Luther's remark that he would dearly like to see his papalist adversaries made to live by their own law: »I'd give my left hand to see the papists forced to observe their own canons; I think they would scream more loudly about that than about Luther.«[50] By the end of the 1530s, however, we find Luther once again decrying the hated papal law in language far more violent than any he had used in 1520 to justify consigning it to the flames. In the process, moreover, he had some breathtakingly rude things to say about the Wittenberg jurists. To see why this was so, it is necessary to return to 1530 and deal once more with Luther's attitude toward law in general.

VI Luther on Law in the 1530s

By 1530, as we have already seen, the rapid but disorderly development of the Reformation in Saxony had shifted Luther's attention from the task of freeing the territorial church from papal laws to that of providing it with good evangelical laws. Since 1527, the visitation commission that the elector had established at Luther's request had been engaged in the long and difficult task of imposing order and uniformity on the doctrine, ceremonies, and financial affairs of the Saxon church. Pleased with these developments and with the electors – John, and then from 1532, John Frederick (1503, 1532-1554) who presided over them, Luther, in his lectures and sermons of the early 1530s, was wont to take advantage of any biblical text – here particularly The Song of Solomon (1530/31) and Psalm 101 (1534/35) – that enabled him to sing the praises of a commonwealth in which church and state flourished under the rule of a godly prince. In the process, he elaborated a view of the cura religionis of Christian princes that was fundamentally identical to the one that Philip Melanchthon worked out and published in those same years.[51] More important in the present

50 Albert of Brandenburg, for example, would not be able to hold three bishoprics at once, including the imperial archbishopric of Mainz; WA TR 2, 72, 35-39; 73, 4-6 (1362); see also 489, 32 - 490, 1 (2496 b); 6, 239, 19 f (6862). The treatise »Von den Konziliis und Kirchen« contains a number of references to the damage to the pope's cause that would ensue if he actually kept certain of the decrees of the councils and the fathers that were incorporated into church law by Gratian; see for example WA 50, 531, 19 - 532, 5.
51 See Estes: Peace, order, and the glory of God, chapter 5.

context, however, is that Luther's concern for the welfare of church and state compelled him once more to address the question of the role of law in both. It will be evident that his observations were an elaboration of his view of the proper relationship between »the two kingdoms«.

In his lectures on the Song of Solomon, Luther offered the most detailed of all his discussions of the three hierarchies established by God for the good of mankind: family, government, church.[52] In the present context, it is the relationship between the latter two that is important. For Luther, the Song of Solomon was an »encomium of the political order«, a song in which Solomon thanks and praises God for »the divinely established and confirmed kingdom and government« in which Solomon had ruled over »the people of God« in peace and tranquillity. The mark of such a splendid politia is that in it both church and state are governed by the word of God. Whether one considers the population from its political or its ecclesiastical side, it is one and the same people of God living under two distinct but closely coordinated administrations. The politia, the secular regime, is God's left hand; the priesthood is his right hand. Significantly, Luther also uses the word »politia« with reference to the external church.[53] Just as the politia externa is governed by the magistratus politicus or corporalis, so the politia ecclesiastica is governed by the magistratus ecclesiasticus or spiritualis. Because the church on earth is a corpus mixtum that includes unbelievers and evildoers in its membership, it is no less in need of laws than is the politia externa. The crucial difference between the two is that ecclesiastical punishment consists only in the proclamation of God's judgement, something that affects only the conscience, while secular punishment imposes the physical penalties of human law.

Given this need of the church for laws, and given that such laws were by definition freely chosen human laws aimed at facilitating the church's divine mission,[54] it was both easy and natural to see positive value in

---

52 The text is in WA 31 II, 586-769. My summary of the relevant content is based entirely on Maurer: Reste des kanonischen Rechtes ..., 177-188.

53 Cf. Luther's commentary on Isaiah (1529), where the church is described as »novum genus vitae et Politiae«; WA 31 II, 507, 5-12.

54 On this point, see especially the treatise »Von den Konziliis und Kirchen« (1539); WA 50, 640, 7 - 650, 14.

many provisions of canon law. These included, for example, a long list of ceremonies and usages that were harmless adiaphora and could freely be observed in the interest of good order.[55] Also included, as we have already seen, were ancient canons on the office of bishop that could be cited to justify the Saxon visitation. For the evangelical jurists, moreover, the CIC was a gold mine of law upholding the rights and privileges of the clergy and the integrity of church property.[56] On the other hand, as we shall see presently, the jurists were attached to provisions of canon law that, in Luther's view, could not be enforced without great harm.

Meanwhile, Luther's lectures on the Song of Solomon were interrupted by the Diet of Augsburg in the summer of 1530. Unable as an imperial outlaw to attend the diet in person, Luther had to remain behind at the Koburg, the closest he could get to Augsburg on Saxon territory. One of the products of his forced idleness at the Koburg was the »Sermon on keeping children in school«,[57] portions of which are of direct interest to our topic. Alarmed that so few parents seemed willing to supply their children with education beyond basic instruction in German sufficient to the immediate needs of making a living, Luther admonished them to remember society's urgent need for learned men qualified to take on the vital task of governing church and state.

The church, he said, needs pastors, preachers, and schoolmasters who together make up the spiritual estate, which has been established by God and is therefore highly to be honoured.[58] Secular authority, too, is »a glorious ordinance and splendid gift of God, and it too needs learned men. Why? Because the government in our German lands is supposed to be guided by the imperial law of Rome«, which is its »wisdom and reason,

55 »Wir kunden auch on schaden alle Gebot halten, des Bapsts und seiner Concilien, so nicht stracks an jnen selbs wider Gottes Wort sind, wenn es nicht mehr betreffe denn eusserliche Ordnung und halten bestimpter zeiten, kleidung, speise etc. [...] solch eusserlich Mittelding, [...]«; WA 21, 499, 33-38.

56 Johannes HECKEL: Das Decretum Gratiani und das deutsche evangelische Kirchenrecht. Ders.: Das blinde, undeutliche Wort »Kirche«: gesammelte Aufsätze/ hrsg. von Siegfried Grundmann. Köln; Graz 1964, 1-48, here 33 f.

57 LW 46, 213-258 ≙ WA 30 II, (508) 517-588 (Eine Predigt, dass man Kinder zur Schule halten solle).

58 LW 46, 219-237 ≙ WA 30 II, 526-553.

given it by God«. In principle, a truly wise prince guided by Scripture is all that one needs for good rule. But since there are only one or two such »Wunderleute« in any generation, it is best to be guided by a code of written law. This law cannot be maintained by »fists and weapons; heads and books must do it. Men must learn and know the law and wisdom of our worldly government.« Secular government, in short, needs »jurists«, by which Luther means not only the doctors of law but the entire legal profession, including »clerks, judges, lawyers, notaries, and all who have to do with the legal side of government«. Their work is to be highly esteemed,

»for just as in the kingdom of Christ, a pious theologian and sincere preacher is called an angel of God, a saviour, prophet, priest, servant, and teacher [...], so a pious jurist and true scholar can be called, in the worldly kingdom of the emperor, a prophet, priest, angel, and saviour«.

Similarly, a false and faithless jurist is just as big a scoundrel, knave, and devil as is a heretical or false preacher. Indeed, it takes abler people to be jurists in secular administration than are required in the office of preaching. For

»in the preaching office, Christ does the whole thing, by his Spirit, but in the worldly kingdom men must act on the basis of reason [...], for God has subjected secular rule and all of physical life to reason. He has not sent the Holy Spirit from heaven for this purpose. This is why to govern temporally is harder, because conscience cannot rule; one must act, so to speak, in the dark.«[59]

There is a similar encomium of the secular realm and the role of reason in it in Luther's commentary on Psalm 101,[60] which is his portrait of godly rule in church and state as exemplified by King David. Because secular government is to have no jurisdiction over the welfare of souls but only over physical and temporal goods, God has made it subject to human authority and to reason. He has, moreover, lavished a high degree of

59 LW 46, 237-242 ≙ WA 30 II, 554-562, quotations 558, 27 - 559, 17; 562, 27-33. Although it is too complicated a matter to be dealt with here, it seems clear that in this new, positive view of Roman law as the epitome of God-given wisdom in the secular realm Luther had been decisively influenced by Melanchthon. For the development of Melanchthon's thought on the subject, see Guido KISCH: Melanchthons Rechts- und Soziallehre. B 1967, chapters 4 and 5.
60 LW 13, 198-200 ≙ WA 51, (197) 200-264, here 242, 1 - 243, 35.

reason, intelligence, wisdom, and learning upon the heathen, so much so that they make Christians look like »mere children, fools, and beggars by comparison«. Take, for example, the imperial law, according to which the Holy Roman Empire will continue to be ruled until the Last Judgement. It is nothing but heathen wisdom, established and written down before the Romans had ever heard of Christians or even about God himself. And yet it surpasses by far anything that all the jurists of today taken together could accomplish. The ancient lawmakers did their work wonderfully, but look »what a childish, silly, and bad thing the canon law is, even though the people who set it down were much holier and better« than the heathen authors of Roman law.[61] As the jurists themselves say, »A pure canonist is a jackass«, for they have got lost in their subject and taken little account of worldly wisdom. So, »whoever wants to learn and become wise in secular government, let him read the heathen books and writings« of Homer (fl. 8th century B.C.), Plato (ca. 429-347), Aristotle, Virgil (70-19), Demosthenes (384-322), Cicero (106-43), Livy (59 B.C.-A.D. 17), and »the fine old jurists«. They have portrayed secular government »quite beautifully and generously« and no one has yet equalled or surpassed them in this. Their works have been preserved so that »virtue, laws, and wisdom with respect to temporal goods, honor, and peace on earth« can be taught alongside Holy Scripture, which teaches about »faith and good works with respect to eternal life in the kingdom of heaven«.

While Luther's attitude toward Roman law had thus become far more positive than it had been in 1520, his attitude toward Germanic law was now far more critical. Specifically, he found the »Sachsenspiegel«, the most influential codification of German law, barbarous in its severity, and he expressed regret that it was far too deeply entrenched to be done away with in favour of uniform application of Roman law (ius caesareum), the common law of the Empire. What particularly stuck in his craw was that

---

61 Cf. WA TR 6, 239, 17-19 (6862): »Kaiser=Recht ist anders nichts, denn was menschliche Vernunft lehret; aber das geistlich Recht ist, was der Papst setzt, fartzet und träumet.« Cf. also 6, 328, 25-31 (7023): »Wenn man der Heiden Rechte im römischen Reich nicht hätte, so wären unsere Fürsten, Kaiser und Könige alle zu Narren worden. [...]. Der Heiden Rechte sind besser und ehrlicher, denn der vermeinten Christen. Aber des Papsts Rechte sind am Aergesten, und was Gutes drinnen ist, das ist aus den kaiserlichen Rechten genommen.«

the Saxon code was grossly unfair to married women. It stipulated that when a husband died, he was obliged to leave his widow only »a chair and a distaff« (einen Stuhl und Rocken), no matter how many years she had faithfully lived with him and cared for him. According to Luther, the jurists interpreted this »grammatice«, according to the strict letter, thus leaving widows with less than one might give to a servant or to a beggar at the door. Luther thought this provision of the law should be interpreted »allegorice«, with »Stuhl« taken to mean »Haus«, and »Rocken« taken to mean »Nahrung«. In other words, a just and equitable reading of the law would guarantee to a widow bed and board for the rest of her life.[62] In the present context, the most interesting feature of these comments, which he made 1537 and 1538, is not Luther's opinion of the »Sachsenspiegel« itself but rather his sharply critical attitude of the way in which jurists had interpreted one of its provisions. For the fact is that, in the period from 1530 through 1544, we find Luther nursing a growing animosity toward jurists, particularly the members of the faculty of law in Wittenberg.[63] He never retreats from his opinion of the importance and the dignity of the legal profession, but he is increasingly inclined to rail against what he regards as the abuse of it.

VII Luther and the Wittenberg Jurists, 1530-1544

This growing animosity toward jurists is most easily traced in the »Tischreden«, the earliest of which date from circa 1530 and continue from there to the end of Luther's life. They are liberally sprinkled with derogatory comments about jurists' disregard for truth, faith, and ideals, their preoccupation with what will work rather than with what is just, their greed for money and influence, their arrogance, and so on at length.[64] But it would

---

62 WA TR 3, 446f (3604 A-B), 1537; 4, 163f (4139), 1538.
63 Professors of law also functioned as members of the Hofgericht and (from 1539) the Wittenberg consistory, the membership of which included two jurists and two theologians; Heiner Lück: Die Spruchtätigkeit der Wittenberger Juristenfakultät. Köln; Weimar; W 1998, 67-87, here esp. 83-85. For more on the consistory, see below, 21-28.
64 Two examples from among many will suffice. Luther described the Saxon chancellor, Gregor Brück (1485-1557), as the only true Christian he knew among jurists, and then added that »die Anderen gemeiniglich allzumal gottlos [sind und] suchen nur ihren

take something far more serious than these perceived ethical shortcomings of the legal profession as a whole to provoke Luther to attack the Wittenberg jurists from the pulpit.[65]

At first, all seemed well. At the famous conference of Saxon jurists and theologians at Torgau in the autumn of 1530, Luther and the other theologians yielded courteously, if not exactly gracefully, to the opinion of the jurists that the evangelical princes did indeed have the right in law to offer armed resistance should the emperor make war on them because of their support for the true faith.[66] Luther did not complain (or even mention) that the jurists had supported their argument with extensive citations from canon law as well as from civil law.[67] In the aftermath, he was concerned only to make clear that he as a theologian had not counselled resistance but had simply taken the position that it was for jurists rather than theologians to know what the law said and to bear responsibility for their reading of it.[68] By 1532, however,

Genieß und Nutz, ziehen das Recht, und drehen es nach ihrem Vorthel, machen aus Recht, Unrecht, und aus Unrecht, Recht, mit irer Deuteley und Sophisterey, allein umbs Geldes willen«; WA TR 3, 619, 7-9 (3793). The same point could be made more succinctly: »Juristen sind oft Christi Feinde, wie man sagt: ein rechter Jurist, ein böser Christ«; WA TR 1, 143, 10f (349). Such sentiments were scarcely new in the 1530s, nor were they unique to Luther in particular or to theologians in general. They were, rather, widely shared in society at large. See Lieberwirth: Martin Luthers Kritik ..., passim.

65 Unfortunately, much less is known than one would like concerning the things that the Wittenberg jurists said and did to provoke Luther's wrath. This is because »die Geschichte der Wittenberger Juristenfakultät und deren Wirksamkeit in der europäischen und deutschen Rechtswissenschaft keinesfalls aufgearbeitet ist«; Heiner LÜCK: Die Wittenberg Juristenfakultät im Sterbejahr Martin Luthers. In: Martin Luther und seine Universität, 73-93, here 74.

66 WIDERSTANDSRECHT ALS PROBLEM DER DEUTSCHEN PROTESTANTEN, 1523-1546/ hrsg. von Heinz Scheible. GÜ 1969, 67 f.

67 See Widerstandsrecht als Problem ..., 63-66, for footnote references to the relevant sections of the CIC. The jurists' argument was based largely on principles of legal procedure, an area in which, as Luther conceded, canon law offered much that was good and useful for the practice of civil law: »Was er [Papst] aber Guts hat in seinen Rechtsbüchern, das zu Gerichtshändeln und Policey gehört, und weltlichen kaiserlichen Rechtes ist, da ist er gar ein Kaiser«; WA TR 2, 490, 33f (2496 b), 22 January - 28 March 1532.

68 WA TR 1, 40f (109), 9.-30. November 1531; 6, 322f (7007) ≙ WA Br 6, 16, 9 - 17, 24 (1772), Luther to Wenzeslaus Linck 15 January 1531.

Luther was already complaining that the jurists were entirely too fond of canon law and consequently tempted to interfere in matters of conscience, which were the proper concern of the theologians.[69] By 1537 these general grumblings had turned into specific complaints about the jurists's advocacy of certain provisions of canon law on marriage that Luther judged to be contrary to Scripture and reason.[70] He thought it preposterous, for example, that the jurists wanted to enforce the canonical rule that a widowed clergyman who took another wife was guilty of »digamy« and could no longer hold a spiritual office.[71] If Solomon could have several hundred wives all at once, why could not a poor pastor have two or three wives in succession? What would the enforcement of this canon achieve apart from either preventing or dishonouring a legitimate marriage and depriving the church of good pastors?[72] Similarly, Luther

69 WA TR 2, 489-491 (2496 a-b), 624 f (2738 a), both of 1532.
70 The leader of the jurists in Wittenberg was Hieronymus Schurff, aka Schürpf (1481-1554). An early convert to Luther's cause who had been his legal adviser at the Diet of Worms in 1521, Schurff participated actively in the Saxon visitation that commenced in 1527. On the other hand, he embodied the attachment to »received law«, particularly with respect to marriage, that would produce serious estrangement between Luther and the Wittenberg jurists; see Theodor MUTHER: D. Hieronymus Schürpf. In: Ders.: Aus dem Universitäts- und Gelehrtenleben im Zeitalber der Reformation. Nachdruck der Ausgabe Erlangen 1866. Amsterdam 1966, 178-229; Hermann DÖRRIES: »Der Juristen Schwitzbad«: das beirrte Gewissen als Grenze des Rechts. In: Festschrift für Erich Ruppel: zum 65. Geburtstag am 25. Jan. 1968/ hrsg. von Heinz Brunotte ... Hannover; B; HH 1968, 63-88, here 73 f, with footnote 45; Deflers: Lex und ordo, 133-139. For information on other members of the faculty of law involved, including Melchior Kling (1504-1571), the student of Schurff who, following the reorganization of the faculty of law in 1536, was appointed professor of church law, see Otto MEJER: Anfänge des Wittenberger Consistoriums. In: Ders.: Zum Kirchenrechte des Reformationsjahrhunderts: drei Abhandlungen. Hannover 1891, 3-83; Lück: Die Spruchtätigkeit der Wittenberger Juristenfakultät, 80-85; Ralf FRASSEK: Eherecht und Ehegerichtsbarkeit in der Reformationszeit: der Aufbau neuer Rechtsstrukturen im sächsischen Raum unter besonderer Berücksichtigung des Wittenberger Konsistoriums. TÜ 2005, 102-111.
71 In contrast to bigamy, which consisted of having two wives simultaneously, digamy consisted of having two or more wives in succession. On the history of digamy as a cononical impediment to holy orders, see James A. BRUNDAGE: Law, sex, and Christian society in medieval Europe. Chicago 1987, 97 f. 142. 196. 207. 252 f. 318 f. 405-407. 479. 540.
72 WA TR 3, 452 f (3609 A-B), 18 June - 28 July 1537 / 16 April 1539.

vehemently disapproved of the desire of the jurists to restore the canonical rule, long since banished from the church in Saxony,[73] that a couple who secretly became engaged, without parental knowledge or approval, had thereby entered into a marriage that could not be dissolved by the subsequent decision of either party to marry someone else.[74] He sided with Roman law in his insistence that public engagements entered into with parental consent were the best way to prevent hot-blooded young people from rushing into ill-considered unions, with unhappy consequences for everyone involved. To dismiss parental approval as irrelevant was, in Luther's view, to deny parents the authority over their children given them by God in the Fourth Commandment.[75]

On two separate occasions, in 1539 and again in 1544, Luther angrily and abusively attacked the Wittenberg jurists from the pulpit. On the first occasion, the charge was that they were poisoning the minds of their students by teaching canon law, and Luther made his point with specific reference to the matter of digamy.[76] On the second occasion, digamy was not forgotten,

73 Luther reports that Elector John Frederick had, at the request of the theologians, issued an order to this effect but that the jurists continued to insist that it was their duty to point out what established law prescribed; WA TR 6, 330, 18-28 (7024); WA 49, 300, 28 - 301, 10.

74 Canonists actually disliked clandestine marriages and sought to discourage them. But, given their view that marriage had its origin in mutual consent that could be given privately and without witnesses, they were adamant in their insistence that secret marriages were valid and binding; see Brundage: Law, sex, and Christian society ..., 239. 276 f. 289. 335 f. 361-364. 440-443.

75 Luther's position on this question, already evident in the 1520s, had been clearly set out in 1530 in his treatise »Von Ehesachen« (WA 30 III, 207-217 ≙ LW 46, 268-281), where he observed (WA 30 III, 208, 1 f ≙ LW 46, 268) that »the ancient canons and [...] the best points of canon law [...] forbid such secret engagements«. Only the LW editors supply the canon law reference, which is to the Decretales, lib. iv, tit. III. For the reiteration of Luther's views in the period 1539-1544, see WA TR 4, 242-247 (4345), February 1539, which records his detailed response to an inquiry from Basilius Monner (ca. 1501-1566), a jurist and member of the consistory. See also WA Br 10, 500 f (3958), Luther to Elector John Frederick, 22 January 1544.

76 WA 47, 670, 16 - 671, 4 (sermon of 23 February 1539); 676, 3 - 678, 15 (sermon of 2 March 1539). See also WA TR 4, 280-284 (4382 a-b: three versions of the sermon of 23 February); 462-464 (4743: further accounts of the sermon of 23 February, where 462, 15 - 463, 25 could actually refer to the sermon of 2 March); 465 (4745: brief account of sermon of 2 March). In WA 47, 676, 27, the text speaks of »bigamia« rather than »digamia«.

but Luther's principal complaint was that the Wittenberg consistory[77] had erred outrageously in decreeing that Kaspar Beyer (documented 1537-1545), a law student whom Luther had befriended, was obliged marry the young woman to whom he had become secretly engaged in 1541 rather than the one to whom he had become publicly engaged in 1542.[78] Of the two issues, that of clandestine engagements was by far the more important to Luther because it involved a much more direct challenge to the authority of theologians and pastors in the church, and it was only that issue that provoked him into a decisive confrontation with the Wittenberg jurists.[79] The attempt here will be to summarized Luther's general argument as it was most fully developed in 1544, taking full account of things said in 1539 as well, but without becoming involved in the details of the dispute over digamy or those of the case of Kaspar Beyer.[80]

77 Established in 1539, the consistory functioned primarily as a marriage court with two jurists and two theologians as sitting members (see above note 64). On the history of the establishment and early development of the consistory (to 1545), see Mejer: Anfänge des Wittenberger Consistoriums, and Frassek: Eherecht und Ehegerichtsbarkeit ...

78 WA 49, 297, 14 - 307, 12 (sermon of 6 January 1544); 316, 1 - 317, 30 (sermon of 13 January 1544); 318-324 (sermon of 20 January 1544); and 340, 16 - 343, 9 (sermon of 3 February 1544). See also WA TR 6, 329-335 (7024: from the sermon of 6 January). 335-337 (7025: from the sermon of 20 January). 337f (7026: again from the sermon of 6 January). 340-343 (7028: from the sermon of 3 February). See further Luther's letter of 22 January 1544, written to the elector in support of Kaspar Beyer's appeal to the elector against the decision of the consistory – WA Br 10, 500-504 (3958) –, as well as the letter of 21 June 1544 to Gregor Brück, thanking him for his role in the settlement of the case; WA Br 10, 598-600 (4006).

79 At the time of the Beyer case, the jurists on the consistory were Benedikt Pauli (1490-1552) and Konrad Mauser († 1548), but the Wittenberg jurists stood together as a group in support of the views of Schurff and Kling (neither of whom ever served on the consistory) against Luther's objections. See Mejer: Anfänge des Wittenberger Consistoriums, 73; Frassek: Eherecht und Ehegerichtsbarkeit ..., 114f.

80 The complicated but not very well documented history of the Beyer case is ably summarized in WA Br 10, 498-500 (3958). 598f (4006); Mejer: Anfänge des Wittenberger Consistoriums, 64-80; Dörries: »Der Juristen Schwitzbad«, 65f; and in Frassek: Eherecht und Ehegerichtsbarkeit ..., 111-114. As is clear from those accounts, however, many aspects of the confrontation between Luther and the jurists over this issue remain unclear (cf. above note 66). The WA editors assert that Luther's denunciation of the consistory's decision was unfair, but Dörries, 75, note 54, finds Luther's judgement of it to be fair and accurate. Be that as it may, I have, for the purposes of this article, accepted Luther's

As Luther saw it, the basic problem was that the jurists were not content to stick to their proper sphere of responsibility, which was secular matters, but were, rather, determined to intervene in spiritual matters and rule over consciences, which are in Christ's kingdom and are the divinely appointed responsibility of the theologians. For four hundred years, he said (i. e., during the period that he regarded as the life-span of the medieval papacy), jurists ruled the church and despised the theologians. Now that their power has been taken from them and they are not permitted to govern the church, they are upset and want to recover the ground lost to the theologians,[81] whom they deride as »jackasses and dunces« (Esel und Bachanten) who do not understand the law.[82] To Luther it seemed that the jurists had seized upon the establishment of the Wittenberg consistory as an opportunity to reassert their lost authority.[83]

Not content simply to intervene in spiritual matters that do not concern them, the jurists, said Luther, want to do the devil's work of bringing back into force in the church that heap of stinking papal filth,[84]

version of events at face value. In the absence of more information to work with, it is difficult to do anything else.

81 WA TR 6, 344, 10-19. 25-27 (7029), undated but with clear references to the consistory's verdict in the case of Kaspar Beyer: »Die [Juristen] haben nun vier hundert Jahre regieret, und je die Theologos verachtet, und sind ihnen gram gewesen. [...]. Nu, weil man ihnen das Regiment nimmt, und ihr Ding umstößt, [...], und man will sie nicht lassen die Kirchen regieren und Pfarr bestellen, das thut ihnen faul. [...]; sie wollen in der Kirchen seyn, und die Conscientias mit regieren; das wollen wir [Theologen] nicht leiden.« Denn wir »haben ja fein distinguiret, wie weit die Juristen mit ihrem Regiment gehen sollen; aber sie wollens nicht thun, sie wollen alleine über Alles herrschen«.

82 WA 47, 670, 23; 676, 8f.

83 See Luther's letter of 18 January 1545 to Elector John Frederick; WA Br 11, 23, 27-32 (4070). What is not clear from this letter or from the other sources is *how* the jurists managed their little *coup* in the Beyer case. Of the two theologians on the consistory at the time, one was Georg Major (1502-1574), a friend and student of both Luther and Melanchthon, who had joined the faculty of theology in 1536. In the case of the other, however, not even his name appears in the records. It is quite possible that he, like his immediate predecessor, Magister Ambrosius Berndt († 1541), was not even a member of the theological faculty. See Frassek: Eherecht und Ehegerichtsbarkeit ..., 108. 109f. What, if anything, the theologians said or did in defence of Luther's position on clandestine vows is not known. What is known is that Luther's wrath came down exclusively on the heads of the jurists.

84 Luther's language here (i. e., in the texts cited in the following note) is graphically scato-

the canon law that was long ago burned and banished from the church and denounced in the »Confessio Augustana«.[85] At the most elementary level, as in branding widowed priests who remarried as digamists unfit for clerical office, or as in trying to force a young man into an unsuitable marriage, this constituted the kind of unwarranted severity that violated of the principle of epieikeia.[86] More seriously, it constituted a wanton disturbance of the established order of the church in Wittenberg and Saxony, which the lawyers should treat with respect and not oppose.[87] Most seri-

logical. Canon law is »des Papsts Unflat«, »des papsts esels dreck vnd furtze«, »päpstlicher, stinkender Dreck«, and so on, with frequent repetition. The same language is found passim in the texts of 1544. As for those »große Eselsköpfe«, the jurists, Luther observed in 1544 that »[es] ist des Papsts Recht, daran sie hangen, wie dem Teufel im Hintern«; WA TR 6, 329, 26 (7024); cf. 338, 41 f (7026). It should be remembered that when Luther resorted to scatological language, it was not because he routinely spoke that way or that he had lost control of his temper but rather that he perceived himself to be locked in a vitally important battle with the devil, against whom scatological language was taken to be an appropriate and effective weapon; see Heiko A. Oberman: Luther: man between God and the Devil (Luther: Mensch zwischen Gott und Teufel ⟨engl.⟩)/ transl. by Eileen Walliser-Schwarzbart. New Haven; LO 1989, 106-109.

85 WA TR 4, 280-283 (4382), 2 March 1539; WA 47, 670, 16-18; 671, 6 f (2 March 1539). The reference to the »Confessio Augustana« is doubtless to Art. 28, which stipulates that bishops have no authority to teach or prescribe anything contrary to Scripture. In 1544 Luther accused the jurists of being »gut mainzisch« as well as »gut päpstlich«, i. e., of acting in the interests of Archbishop Albert of Mainz and taking money from him; WA 49, 298, 10-12; 305, 14 f; 341, 14-17. 29-34; WA TR 6, 332, 24 f; 333, 6 f; 334, 39 f (7024). I have no idea what was behind this accusation. Muther: D. Hieronymus Schürpf, 211; 226, note 94, asserts, without explaining why, that the accusation was probably aimed at Melchior Kling, the professor of church law.

86 Luther does not cite this principle by name, but he does refer to the need to »weichen von der scherffe des rechten, wo man kan«; WA 49, 316, 34. To highlight the consequences of indiscriminate enforcement of the law, Luther pointed out that if canon and imperial law were to be enforced *in toto* and with full rigour, the elector would not only have dismiss him from the ministry and send him back to the monastery but also, because he had married a nun, order his decapitation and declare his children unfit to be his heirs; WA 49, 341, 23-27; WA Br 11, 23, 59 - 24, 65 (4070).

87 WA 47, 670, 18-23. 25 (23 February 1539): »Ideo freundlich bit [to you jurists], ut non agatis contra Ecclesiam nostram. [...]. Non volumus nec possumus leiden, das ir meam Ecclesiam solt zerreissen. Nolumus papae Ecclesiam. [...], nolumus des Bapsts furtzen etc.« WA TR 4, 280, 14-21 (4382 a), 2 March 1539: »Ist derhalben meyn freuntlich bitte vnd beger an euch [Juristen], das yrs mit vns haldet, wie mans offentlich in der kirchen

ously of all, it amounted to doing the devil's work of restoring »popery« in the sense of laws that »perplex consciences« (die Gewissen verwirren) by imposing restrictions or burdens that are not required by God's word or sound reason. Luther repeatedly identified this »inexpressible perplexity of poor consciences« as the chief source of his anger at »the filthy jurists«[88] and insisted that this was a matter in which human law of every sort must yield to God's law: »Oportet Deo magis quam hominibus obedire.«[89] So determined was he to place the welfare of stricken consciences above the letter of the law that he was even prepared to set aside the Second Table of the Decalogue if that were necessary to prevent the loss of a soul.[90]

Luther cannot here be accused of having invented a new argument to bolster his case in a jurisdictional dispute with the Wittenberg jurists. Quite the contrary, he was defending a position that he had already stated clearly in 1530 in the treatise »On marriage matters«. In that work, which is replete with examples, drawn from his own experience as pastor and theologian,[91] of how consciences can be entangled and tormented by

helt in d[ies]em furstenthum, landgrauenthum vnd [andere lender vnd stende], wie sie in der confession vnterschrieben sind. [...] wir [Theologen] wollens nicht leiden, das ir sollet vnser kirchen zu reissen; wollet yrs aber thun, so thuts anderswu. Wir wollen des baptsts esels dreck vnd furtze nich haben; frest irs selber!«

88 WA 49, 316, 27-32: »Ich kans nit leiden, das sie [Juristen] die gewissen verwirren, das ist die ursache meins zorns, [...]. Es heist Perplexitas, ist nit new, Ich habs nit erst erdacht, Im Bapstumb haben sie viel gehabt, Non est toleranda perplexitas in via Dei [...]« WA TR 6, 332, 14f (7024): »Drüm will ichs nicht leiden, daß sie [die garstigen Juristen] in meiner Kirche eine Perplexität anrichten, und die Gewissen verwirren wollen mit ihrem beschmissenen Rechte.«

89 WA 49, 317, 4f / 19f (cf. Act 5, 29). Luther recognized that judges themselves could be subjected to »preplexity of conscience« by the teaching of the jurists that a judge who knows absolutely that a defendant is innocent must nonetheless find him guilty (or else resign from office and let someone else do it) if the formal requirement of imperial law is met that guilt is established by the testimony of two or three witnesses. Luther insists that the judge should declare the man innocent even if there were 10,000 witnesses against him. Is that contrary to imperial law? »Ich schiß ins keysers recht, das dem armen Man unrecht thut. [...]. Jurist hat kein Conscientz, drumb fragen sie auch nicht nachm periculo conscientiae«; WA 49, 303, 19 - 304, 38, esp. 304, 29-38.

90 »Ehe ich ein seel verlieren sol, ehe die 7 praecepta hin werffen«; WA 49, 317, 3f.

91 Besides dealing with marital matters as a pastor, Luther was also heavily burdened with

the enforcement of »crazy, unreasonable, unnatural, and godless laws«, Luther advises pastors and clergy to treat marriage as a worldly matter covered by secular laws and to abstain from involvement in marriage matters as much as they can. Only where matters of conscience are involved, as, for example, when jurists enforce the law in such a way as to »entangle and confuse consciences«, should clergymen intervene. In cases where either

> »conscience or the law has to yield and give way, then [says Luther] it is the law which is to yield and give way, so that the conscience may be clear and free. The law is a temporal thing that must ultimately perish, but the conscience is an eternal thing that never dies. [...]. The law exists for the sake of the conscience, not the conscience for the sake of the law. If one cannot help both at the same time, then help the conscience and oppose the law.«[92]

Given that Luther's entire career can be viewed as a campaign to establish the free and orderly exercise of a Christian ministry that liberates Christian consciences from the tormenting burden of man-made laws, and given that he had risked everything by defying pope and emperor in order to launch and sustain that campaign, it is perhaps not surprising that at the end of his life he should have mounted so ferocious a defence of this ministry against the latest attempt of Satan to undermine it.[93] Not content simply to assert in general that clergymen exercise God-given authority in the spiritual realm of conscience[94] and are entitled to

requests from the authorities for his opinion in difficult marital cases. By 1530, he had already written forty such Ratschläge: Lieberwirth: Martin Luthers Kritik, 67.

92 LW 46, 317-319 ≙ WA 30 III, 246, 23 - 247, 23. It is worth noting in passing that in 1539 this view of the relationship between law and conscience figured significantly in the decision of the Wittenbergers to grant Philip of Hessen a dispensation to take a second wife; see Martin BRECHT: Martin Luther. Bd. 3: Die Erhaltung der Kirche, 1532-1546. S 1987, 206.

93 Cf. the apt observation of Dörries: »Der Juristen Schwitzbad«, 68, concerning the importance of Luther's experiences as a father-confessor in his career as a reformer: »Wie sein Angriff auf den Ablaß durch seine Erfahrung als Beichtvater ausgelöst war, so auch der gegen die heimlichen Verlöbnisse. Dort weckte er die Gewissen, die sich in trügerischer Sicherheit wiegten, hier will er bedrängte Gewissen aus gesetzlicher Verstrickung befreien. Von Anfang an sind es diese Beichterfahrungen, die ihn zum Handeln treiben.«

94 See, for example, WA TR 6, 339, 32-34 (7027): »Ihr [Juristen] sollt uns Theologen nicht

obedience,[95] Luther asserted specifically his own personal prerogatives as preacher in Wittenberg. »They are meddling with *me* in *my* jurisdiction.«[96] The Wittenberg church, he insisted, was *his* and *he* would have to give answer for it in the Day of Judgement. He exercised authority in that church, »not as Doctor Martinus but rather as a servant of Christ, acting on his orders«, and for that reason he should be obeyed. He would tolerate no clandestine engagements in his church; indeed, he would abandon his pulpit rather than tolerate any such thing.[97] »I was not put here so that jurists might teach me what it means to govern and to console consciences.«[98] If the jurists do not mend their ways, »we will drive them out of the church to the devil, and they shall know that the consistory is not to be subject to their law but rather to the authority of the pastor«.[99]

regieren, noch uber uns herrschen. Die Herrschaft und das Regiment (in der Kirchen) gebührt uns, [...].« 344, 29-35: »Unsere Juristen sprechen mir im Consistorio ein Urthel, quod pertinet ad conscientiam regendam; das gehöret hieher in die Kirche für mich Doctor Martinum und andere Theologen. Extra conscientiam sollen sie [die Juristen] sprechen, nicht intra conscientiam; sie sollen haben iura corporum et famae, da fragen wir Theologen nichts nach. Aber daß sie wollen fallen in die Spiritualia, und die conscientias regieren, das können wir nicht leiden.« See also WA TR 4, 280-284 (4382 a-b).

95 According to the Epistle to the Hebrews (H 13, 17, as Luther translates it): »Gehorchet ewren Lerern, vnd folget jnen, denn sie wachen vber ewre Seelen, als die da rechenschafft dafur geben sollen, [...]«; WA DB 7, 381-383. See WA TR 6, 341, 34-40 (7028).

96 WA 49, 307, 15-17: »Ich bin zornig und wils auch sein, Denn sie greiffen mir in mein Regiment. Das wil Ich nicht haben, das Bapst und Meintz Wittenberg solt regiren, [...].«

97 WA 49, 318, 4 -319, 3: »[...] verum est Ecclesiam Witenbergensem esse meam. Ja ich mus dafür antworten am jüngsten gericht, [...]. Cum ergo sim is, qui hic in Ecclesia das hochste ampt füret und sols verantworten etc. so wil ich sagen, was ich tragen et non tragen kan. [...] In mea Ecclesia sol man kein heimlich verlubnis einreissen noch gelten lassen, es geschehe, wie es wölle. Ich wils nit halten, wils nicht leiden nec verantworten. [...]. Kan ich solchs nicht erhalten so wil ich mich des predigstuels enthalten [...].« WA TR 6, 340, 24-33 (7028): »Ich, als ein Prediger, muß strafen, und sagen, was unrecht ist, bey Verlust meiner Seelen Seligkeit, wie Gott im Propheten Ezechiel [3, 17f] ernstlich gebeut, daß ich für dich soll Rechenschaft geben. [...]. Weil ichs [...] thue [nicht als D. Martinus, sondern] als ein Diener Christi, und sage dirs aus Befehl Gottes , [...], der michs geheißen hat, daß ich dirs sagen und verkündigen, und dich warnen soll, sollt du mir billig gehorchen.« See also WA Br 10, 501, 41 - 502, 56 (3958).

98 WA TR 6, 338, 16 f (7026).

99 WA TR 6, 333, 13-16 (7024). In Wittenberg, »the pastor« was Johann Bugenhagen, whom Luther as preacher acknowledged as his ecclesiastical superior.

Not surprisingly, the jurists were indignant at what they took to be an assault on their professional honour, and they were not inclined to bow the knee to the theologians. Indeed, at some point in the proceedings they denounced Luther to the elector.[100] It took the intervention of the elector and the skilful mediation of chancellor Gregor Brück to produce an agreement in which the judgement against Kaspar Beyer was overturned and Luther's rejection of clandestine engagements was made the law of the land.[101]

VIII Conclusion

What shall we conclude from all this? From Luther's standpoint, the Beyer case was not just a contest over jurisdiction between jurists and theologians. Nor was it simply an attempt to keep tidy the boundary between spiritual authority and secular authority. It was of course, both of those things, but it was more besides. The emotion that Luther invested in this particular case – including the clear threat to abandon his ministry and excommunicate the jurists if he did not get his way – makes sense only if one takes seriously his claim that he was faced with a diabolical attempt to undo the liberation of Christian consciences from the tyranny of human law as enshrined in canon law. This being so, one is entitled to conclude that Luther's career as a reformer ended exactly where it had begun. The Luther who mounted the pulpit 1544 to denounce the jurists and their papal canons because they were causing grave »perplexity of conscience« in parishioners for whose spiritual welfare he was responsible, was the same Luther who in 1521 had stood before the emperor and refused to retract his books attacking the papal decrees by which »the consciences of the faithful [had] been most miserably entangled, tortured, and torn to pieces«. Freeing consciences from the oppression of »crazy, unreasonable,

---

100 Mejer: Anfänge des Wittenberger Consistoriums, 73f. Their complaint appears to have predated somewhat Luther's attack on them from the pulpit and to have focused on the Luther's alleged intention to write against them.

101 Dörries: »Der Juristen Schwitzbad«, 76-79; Mejer: Anfänge des Wittenberger Consistoriums, 76-80. Luther's own account of the final agreement with the jurists is in a letter of 18 January 1545 to Elector John Frederick; WA Br 11, 22-25 (4070).

unnatural, and godless laws« was, to a large degree, what Luther's reformation was all about. Through it all he maintained that the writ of human
law stops at the boundary of the human conscience and that the ministers
of God's church have the solemn duty to defend that boundary. Of all the
things he had to say about the legal traditions of his time, that was to him
the most important.

Günther Wartenberg in memoriam

Gedenken an Professor Dr. Günther Wartenberg vor dem Elften Internationalen Kongress für Lutherforschung an der Universidade Luterana do Brasil in Canoas, RS, Brasilien, Dienstag, 24. Juli, 9.00 Uhr

Von Michael Beyer

Meine Damen, meine Herren, liebe Freunde,
ich bin dankbar dafür, dass wir jetzt miteinander ein Gedächtnis halten für den verstorbenen Vorsitzenden des Fortsetzungsausschusses, Günther Wartenberg, der dem Internationalen Kongress für Lutherforschung seit 1997 durch zwei Kongressperioden hindurch gedient hat. Lassen Sie mich beginnen mit einer leicht veränderten Zeile aus einem Gedicht von Matthias Claudius: »Ach, wir haben / einen guten Mann begraben / und er war uns mehr.« In das »uns« möchte ich einschließen die Familie des Verstorbenen, seine Kolleginnen und Kollegen von nah und fern, diesen Kongress und nicht zuletzt den Kreis der Mitarbeiterinnen und Mitarbeiter des Leipziger Instituts für Kirchengeschichte. Wer Günther Wartenberg näher kannte, erinnert sich zuerst an sein freundliches, verbindliches Wesen, das Konflikte aushielt und auf Ausgleich bedacht war, ohne jedoch die sachlichen Ziele in seinen vielen Ämtern aus den Augen zu verlieren. Im engeren Leipziger Umfeld, eben im Institut, das er von Helmar Junghans übernommen hatte und nach dem frühen Tod seines Kollegen Kurt Nowak über längere Zeit allein leitete, förderte er die lange Tradition fröhlicher Gemeinschaft und des guten Miteinanders bei der Vielzahl der persönlichen und gemeinsamen Projekte. Neben seiner Familie war ihm das Institut ein Stück Heimat, und bis wenige Tage vor seinem Tod am 9. Juli hat er sich trotz zusehends schwindender Kräfte regelmäßig eingefunden und das Haus zu bestellen versucht. Ich hoffe, dass wir unserem »guten Mann« in seiner schweren Zeit ein Weniges von dem »mehr«, das er uns war, haben zurückgeben können.
Am Dienstag voriger Woche, dem 17. Juli 2007, 11.00 Uhr, haben die Universität Leipzig und ihre Theologische Fakultät Günther Wartenberg in einem akademischen Trauergottesdienst unter großer Beteiligung von

Freunden und Kollegen aus ganz Deutschland die letzte Ehre erwiesen. Und ich weiß, dass uns viele Freunde aus der Ferne im Gebet verbunden waren. Sein Sarg war aufgestellt unter der Kanzel der Stadtkirche St. Nikolai, die er als Mitglied des Konvents der Universitätsprediger selbst oft bestiegen hatte. Im Universitätsgottesdienst und in anderen Gottesdiensten das Evangelium zu verkündigen, war Günther Wartenberg ebenso wichtig wie die akademische Forschung und Lehre. Noch wenige Wochen vor seinem Tod hat er einen Studenten getraut und dessen Frau und Kind getauft. Im Trauergottesdienst hat der Erste Universitätsprediger Martin Petzold gepredigt über Is 43,1: »Fürchte dich nicht, denn ich habe dich erlöst; ich habe dich bei deinem Namen gerufen, du bist mein.« Der Prediger hat mit diesem Wort die Not aufgenommen, die dem Verstorbenen mit der spät erkannten und nicht mehr aufzuhaltenden Krankheit bereitet war. Und er hat die Familie und uns alle, die wir erschrocken und tief traurig und voller Angst den schnellen Verfall des so tatkräftigen Mannes angesehen hatten, hinein genommen in das Evangelium von der Erlösung aus Angst und Furcht: Du bist – ihr seid – mein.

Der Dekan der Theologischen Fakultät, Rüdiger Lux, hat Günther Wartenbergs wissenschaftlichen Werdegang nachgezeichnet, der Rektor der Universität, Franz Häuser, hat die großen Verdienste des Verstorbenen gewürdigt, die er sich als langjähriger Prorektor in der Zeit nach der Friedlichen Revolution 1989 erworben hatte. Seiner Alma Mater Lipsiensis hat er bis zuletzt als Vorsitzender der Historischen Kommission für das 600-jährige Universitätsjubiläum 2009 gedient.

Der Sohn einer Pfarrerfamilie aus Nordhausen am Harz, der am 17. Mai 1943 geboren wurde, wollte eigentlich Geschichte studieren. Aufgrund der politischen Verhältnisse, in die er sich nicht hinein verbiegen lassen wollte, wurde es dann doch die Theologie, was, wie sich zeigen sollte, keine schlechte Wahl gewesen ist. Wie viele seiner Generation wurde er in Leipzig durch den Reformationshistoriker und Lutherforscher Franz Lau geprägt, studierte neben der Theologie noch Altphilologie und erwarb in diesem Fach seinen ersten Doktorgrad. Noch am 22. Juni hat Günther Wartenberg im Rahmen eines wissenschaftlichen Ehrenkolloquiums für Franz Lau zum 100. Geburtstag seinem Lehrer Dank abgestattet und über Lau als Professor an der Theologischen Fakultät Leipzig gesprochen: sein

Schwanengesang. Günther Wartenberg gebührt zurecht ein Platz in der über 100-jährigen Leipziger Kirchengeschichtstradition, in der sich allgemeine Reformationsgeschichte immer eng mit der Lutherforschung und der sächsischen Territorialkirchengeschichte verbunden hat.

Hervorheben möchte ich seine jahrzehntelange, federführende Mitarbeit an der »Politischen Korrespondenz des Herzogs und Kurfürsten Moritz von Sachsen«, die 2006 nach einer schwierigen, mehr als 100-jährigen Editionsgeschichte vollendet werden konnte. Sie bot Günther Wartenberg die Quellengrundlage für seine Neubewertung des umstrittenen Kurfürsten und seiner Kirchenpolitik, war auch Ausgangspunkt seiner Forschungen, die u. a. Martin Luther im Spannungsfeld von Glaube und Macht zum Gegenstand hatten und nicht zuletzt auch die Melanchthonforschung beeinflussten. Ich meine, dass sich die Beschäftigung mit dem begabten Politiker Moritz von Sachsen durchaus auch auf Günther Wartenbergs eigenes diplomatisches Gespür ausgewirkt hat. Wenn man ihm das halb im Ernst und halb im Scherz sagte, dann hat er das zwar abgewehrt, aber dabei gelächelt.

Günther Wartenberg hat mehrer Bände der Martin-Luther-Studienausgabe redaktionell mitbetreut und war einer der Herausgeber der Lateinisch-deutschen Luther-Studienausgabe, an deren noch ausstehendem dritten Band er bis in die letzten Wochen seines Lebens mitarbeitete. Vor Jahren schon hatte er einen eigenen Band mit Lutherbriefen herausgegeben.

Viele Jahre lang hat Günther Wartenberg dem Leiterkreis des Theologischen Arbeitskreises für Reformationsgeschichtliche Forschung angehört und ihn geleitet. Dessen traditionelle Bindung an das Lutherhaus in Wittenberg im Zusammenspiel von Kirche und wissenschaftlicher Theologie lag ihm besonders am Herzen. Viele der heute hier Anwesenden haben mit ihm an gemeinsamen Forschungs- und Tagungsprojekten gearbeitet. Diese Projekte können hier nicht alle im Einzelnen Erwähnung finden. Erwähnen möchte ich aber sein Engagement für die Kirchen in der Diaspora in Theorie und Praxis, das seinen Ausdruck fand durch die Mitgründung und Leitung des Leipziger Instituts für Diasporawissenschaft. Lange hat er der Arbeitsgemeinschaft für Sächsische Kirchengeschichte als Geschäftsführer, stellvertretender Vorsitzender und schließlich als Vorsitzender gedient und das territorialkirchengeschichtliche Jahrbuch »Herbergen der Christenheit« herausgegeben.

Die weit gespannten Interessen und Tätigkeitsfelder des Verstorbenen, die bis in die deutsche Hochschulpolitik hineinreichten, haben einander oft glücklich ergänzt. Nicht zuletzt der Internationale Kongress für Lutherforschung verdankt ihm viel. Ich erinnere mich an das Abschlussdinner des Kopenhagener Kongresses im August 2002 mit einem fröhlichen und gelösten Chairman Wartenberg, der sich geradezu tatendurstig gemeinsam mit Nestor Beck auf den Weg zu diesem Kongress hier in Canoas machte. Er hat diesen Weg nicht mehr bis zum Ende gehen können.

Ach, wir haben / einen guten Mann begraben – heute vor einer Woche, am späten Mittag auf dem Leipziger Südfriedhof – und er war uns mehr.

Lasst uns nun einen Moment gemeinsamen stillen Gedenkens an unseren Freund Günther Wartenberg haben, und hört dann noch einen Liedvers, der von unserer Hoffnung gegen allen Augenschein kündet, und in dessen Trost ich mich fürbittend für den sterbenden Freund geflüchtet habe:

>>Ach Herr, lass dein lieb Engelein
an meinem End die Seele mein
in Abrahams Schoß tragen
Der Leib in seim Schlafkämmerlein
gar sanft ohn alle Qual und Pein
ruh bis zum Jüngsten Tage
Alsdann vom Tod erwecke mich
dass meine Augen sehen dich
in aller Freud, o Gottes Sohn
mein Heiland und mein Gnadenthron
Herr Jesus Christ, erhöre mich, erhöre mich
ich will dich preisen ewiglich.<< Amen.

Als Nekrologe sind inzwischen erschienen: Michael BEYER: In memoriam Günther Wartenberg. LuJ 74 (2007), 7-10; Markus HEIN: In memoriam Günther Wartenberg (1943-2007). HCh 31 (2007), 9-12: Portr.; Helmar JUNGHANS: In memoriam Günther Wartenberg. In: Die sächsischen Kurfürsten während des Religionsfriedens von 1555 bis 1618/ hrsg. von Helmar Junghans. L; S 2007, 7-9; Rüdiger Lux: Zum Gedenken: Günther Wartenberg. ThLZ 132 (2007), 1162 f.

Luther als Berater im politischen Bereich – Zwölf Thesen[1]

Von Armin Kohnle

1. Luthers Stellungnahmen zu politischen Fragen erfolgen durchweg von transpolitischen, nämlich theologischen Voraussetzungen her. Der Politiker Luther ist immer ein »Derivat des Theologen«[2].
2. Für Luther hat jedes politische Problem zugleich eine religiöse Dimension, insofern es gilt, Gottes Willen in einer bestimmten Situation zu erkennen. Dies legitimiert die Stellungnahme des Theologen.
3. Luthers Bewertungen politischer Sachverhalte und Vorgänge seiner Zeit basieren auf direkter Parallelisierung von biblischen, historischen und aktuellen Situationen. Die biblische und weniger prominent die außerbiblische Geschichte dienen ihm als Argumentationsbasis und Orientierungshilfe auch für politische Fragen der Gegenwart. Weil er die Weltgeschichte als Geschichte Gottes mit dem Menschen versteht, ist an jedem Punkt der Geschichte Gottes Handeln mit dem Menschen abzulesen, wenn auch nicht vorherzusagen.
4. Gott wirkt in der Geschichte zwar mit dem Menschen zusammen (Cooperatio-Gedanke), und der Mensch ist Werkzeug Gottes in der Geschichte, doch bleiben ihm Gottes Zwecke und Absichten verborgen, wo Gott seinen Willen nicht offenbart. Dies setzt jedem rein politischen Kalkül eine unüberwindliche Grenze. Politische Rationalität steht für Luther in der Gefahr, das Gottvertrauen zu verlieren.

---

1 Die am Dienstag, dem 24. Juli 2007, in Canoas vorgetragenen Thesen, mit denen kurzfristig die durch den Tod Günther Wartenbergs im Vortragsprogramm entstandene Lücke geschlossen werden sollte, werden hier in nur geringfügig überarbeiteter Form wiedergegeben. Belegt werden wörtliche Zitate und wenige ausgewählte Sachverhalte.
2 Eike WOLGAST: Die Wittenberger Theologie und die Politik der evangelischen Stände: Studien zu Luthers Gutachten in politischen Fragen. GÜ 1977, 13.

5. Indem Luther vor allem auf das Alte Testament als »Spiegel des Lebens«[3] zurückgreift, erschließt sich ihm ein Reservoir an Exempeln von Gott wohlgefälligen beziehungsweise mißfälligen Handlungen, das er benutzt, um der eigenen Zeit Handlungsanweisungen zu geben.

6. Diese Übertragung des Schriftprinzips auf die Tagespolitik hat zur Folge, daß Kategorien, die üblicherweise zur Beurteilung politischer Sachverhalte dienen wie Erfahrung, Vernunft, Opportunität, Recht oder Macht, bei Luther, wenn überhaupt, dann nur subsidiär eine Rolle spielen. Wenn Luthers politische Ratschläge gelegentlich als weltfremd erscheinen, dann deshalb, weil er die Gesetze der Politik nicht als letztverbindlich akzeptierte und weil er an politische Handlungen andere Maßstäbe anlegte als die Politiker.

7. Da die Zukunft in der Gewalt Gottes und nicht des Menschen liegt, zählt für Luther der Augenblick. Langfristige politische Strategien spielen für ihn keine Rolle. Der Mensch ist allerdings verpflichtet, die von Gott im Augenblick bereitgestellten Mittel anzunehmen und den Kairos zu nutzen.

8. Zum Verständnis von Luthers politischen Ratschlägen ist die Unterscheidung der beiden Regimente grundlegend, denn der Raum der Politik ist das weltliche Regiment. Die Verderbtheit der Welt und des einzelnen Menschen begründet das Schwertamt der Obrigkeit, die folglich an ihrer Aufgabe, dem Bösen zu wehren, gemessen werden muß. Dem Theologen kommt hier ein Wächteramt zu, er hat die christliche Obrigkeit an ihre Verantwortung vor Gott zu gemahnen, nämlich den Frieden und die Ordnung zu bewahren.

9. Luther erteilt politische Ratschläge als Seelsorger mit dem Ziel, die Gewissen zu unterrichten. Mit seinen Ratschlägen will er zugleich ein schriftgemäßes Verhalten bei den Beratenen evozieren. Luther ist demzufolge kein Politikberater, sondern ein Seelenberater. Die Gefahr, dass auf diese Weise eine neue geistliche Autorität errichtet werden könnte, analog zu der, die im Papsttum gerade überwunden wurde, hat er erkannt.

3 Heinrich Bornkamm: Luther und das Alte Testament. TÜ 1948, 9.

10. Für die Fürsten und andere politische Entscheidungsträger, die Luther um Rat angehen, steht das Motiv der Gewissensentlastung im Vordergrund. Der Bedarf an Gewissensentlastung war bei den Landesherrn Luthers aber unterschiedlich ausgeprägt. Entsprechend schwankt der Einfluß der Theologen auf die kursächsische Politik.

11. Friedrich der Weise entscheidet relativ unabhängig von den Theologen; sein Nachfolger Kurfürst Johann will als bewusst evangelischer Fürst die Theologen zu vielen politischen Fragen hören. In seiner Regierungszeit (1525-1532) ist ihr Einfluß am größten. Unter Kurfürst Johann Friedrich (1532-1554) werden sie zur Gewissensentlastung gelegentlich hinzugezogen, ohne daß man ihren Ratschlägen in jedem Fall folgt[4].

12. Luther spielt als Gutachter in politischen Fragen bis etwa 1530 die entscheidende Rolle, hält sich nach der »Torgauer Wende« aber stärker zurück. Fortan gewinnen die Kollektivgutachten der Wittenberger Theologen an Bedeutung. Immerhin ein Drittel aller gutachterlichen Stellungnahmen der Wittenberger betreffen (religions)politische Fragen im weiteren Sinne.[5] Neben der Beratung des Landesherrn gewinnt die Beratung auswärtiger Instanzen an Gewicht. Die Wittenberger Autorität beruht aber weiterhin auf der Beteiligung Luthers und Philipp Melanchthons.

---

4 Vgl. Armin KOHNLE: Luther und das Reich. In: Luther Handbuch/ hrsg. von Albrecht Beutel, TÜ 2005, 196-205.
5 Vgl. Armin KOHNLE: Wittenberger Autorität: die Gemeinschaftsgutachten der Wittenberger Theologen als Typus. In: Die Theologische Fakultät Wittenberg 1502 bis 1602: Beiträge zur 500. Wiederkehr des Gründungsjahres der Leucorea/ hrsg. von Irene Dingel; Günther Wartenberg. Redaktion: Michael Beyer. L 2002, 189-200.

Prof. Dr. Dr. Dr. h. c. Günther Wartenberg (1943-2007)
Chairman des Fortsetzungsausschusses für den Zehnten und den Elften
Internationalen Kongress für Lutherforschung

Aus den Lutherstätten

Neue Dauerausstellungen und archäologische Funde

Von Stefan Rhein

Vorbemerkung

Der Bericht über die Lutherstätten im »Mutterland der Reformation« fand eine erfreuliche Resonanz auf dem Elften Internationalen Kongress für Lutherforschung, sodass er auch in schriftlicher Form wiedergegeben werden soll. Er konzentriert sich auf die Aktivitäten der vier Gedenkstätten, die 1997 in der Stiftung Luthergedenkstätten in Sachsen-Anhalt institutionell zusammengefasst wurden: Lutherhaus und Melanchthonhaus in Wittenberg sowie Luthers Geburtshaus und Sterbehaus in Eisleben. Er greift aber auch darüber hinaus, wenn er die archäologischen Grabungsergebnisse in Mansfeld-Lutherstadt vorstellt.[1]

I Neue Dauerausstellung im Lutherhaus Wittenberg

Seit dem 6. März 2003 präsentiert das Wittenberger Lutherhaus eine neue Dauerausstellung, die in vielfältiger Hinsicht eine neue Etappe in der seit 1883 andauernden Museumsgeschichte von Luthers ehemaligem Wohngebäude darstellt. Sie löste die zum 500. Geburtstag Luthers 1983 eingerichtete Dauerausstellung »Martin Luther 1483-1546« ab. In ihr waren in dichter Exponatenfolge Themen abgehandelt worden, die von »Eine Gesellschaft

---

1 Über die Wittenberger Lutherstätten hat zuletzt Martin Treu berichtet; vgl. Martin TREU: Die Lutherhalle Wittenberg zwischen 1980 und 1991: ein Bericht. LuJ 60 (1993), 118-138. Für die Jahre 1945 bis 1989 vgl. Stefan RHEIN: Deponieren und Exponieren: Einblicke in das Lutherhaus. In: Wissensspuren: Bildung und Wissenschaft in Wittenberg nach 1945/ hrsg. von Jens Hüttmann und Peer Pasternack. Wittenberg 2004, 57-70, und Edeltraud WIESSNER: Zur Geschichte des Melanchthonhauses nach 1945. In: Wissensspuren, 110-116. Vgl. auch Stefan RHEIN: Die Stiftung Luthergedenkstätten in Sachsen-Anhalt: Anspruch und Aufgaben. Mitteldeutsches Jahrbuch für Kultur und Geschichte 6 (1999), 246-248.

im Umbruch – Wende 15./16. Jahrhundert« bis hin zu »Bleibende Spuren« reichen. Trotz einiger kritischer Stimmen – hier ist vor allem Hartmut Boockmanns (1934-1998) Polemik gegen das im 19. Jahrhundert verwurzelte DDR-Geschichtsbild zu nennen[2] – konnte die Ausstellung von 1983 den politischen Umbruch von 1989 unbeschadet überstehen, da die damalige Direktorin Elfriede Starke sich für ein ideologieresistentes hermeneutisches Verfahren entschieden hatte: Statt aktueller Beschreibungsformeln wie »frühbürgerliche Revolution« wurden zeitgenössische, v. a. wörtliche Zitate Luthers genommen, sodass die verschiedenen Themen in der Kommentierung durch den Reformator selbst zur Sprache kamen. Die nach 20 Jahren notwendig gewordene Neukonzeption der Dauerausstellung war also weniger der Kritik an den Inhalten geschuldet, sondern musste auf veränderte Seh- und Informationsgewohnheiten und v. a. auf die technische und konservatorische »Abnutzung« der Präsentation reagieren. Mehr als 1 200 000 Besucher hatten die Ausstellung bis zu ihrer Schließung im Dezember 2000 gesehen, allerdings mit sinkenden Jahresquoten.

Bauliche Voraussetzung für die neue Dauerausstellung war die Instandsetzung des Lutherhauses und der Neubau eines Eingangsgebäudes mit den Funktionen Shop, Kasse, Toiletten, Garderobe. Die Sanierungsarbeiten wurden von einer intensiven Bauforschung vorbereitet und begleitet, welche die archivalische Überlieferung sowie die restauratorischen Befunde auswertete. Erstmals wurde die »Biografie des Gebäudes« ernst genommen. Spektakuläre Funde förderten z. B. den authentische Ziegelfußboden im Erdgeschoss in dem Raum hinter dem Katharinenportal und eine hausinterne Abfallgrube zutage. Komplexe Forschungen zum ursprünglichen Verlauf der Treppen, zu Feuerstellen oder zu den Decken der »Lutherwohnung« vermehrten eindrucksvoll unser Wissen von Luthers Haus.[3]

Um das seit 1996 als UNESCO-Weltkulturerbe ausgezeichnete Lutherhaus vor weiterer Vernutzung zu schützen, wurden die Büros und die Werkstätten ausgelagert. So entstand eine Ausstellungsfläche, die

2 Hartmut BOOCKMANN: Die Lutherhalle in Wittenberg heute: Probleme einer historischen Ausstellung. ARG 85 (1994), 287-302.

3 Insa Christiane HENNEN: Das Lutherhaus Wittenberg: ein bauhistorischer Rundgang. 2. Aufl. Wittenberg 2007; Anne-Marie NESER: Luthers Wohnhaus in Wittenberg: Denkmalpolitik im Spiegel der Quellen. L 2005.

Lutherstadt Wittenberg, Lutherhaus, Lutherstube

mit 1800 m² das bisherige Flächenangebot von 700 m² weit überragt und nunmehr vom Keller über das Erdgeschoss und 1. Obergeschoss bis in das 2. Obergeschoss das gesamte Haus umfasst. Entsprechend den zwei Typen von Lutherhaus-Besuchern – einmal den touristischen Gruppen mit ca. 1 Stunde Aufenthaltszeit, zum anderen den z. T. umfassend interessierten Einzelbesuchern – wurde eine abgestufte Ausstellungsstruktur gewählt: Der »Biografische Rundgang« bietet die wichtigsten Räume – Refektorium, Großer Hörsaal, Lutherstube – und die wertvollsten Exponate wie Lutherkanzel, Kutte, 10-Gebote-Tafel Cranachs, Luther-Porträts Cranachs und Gemeiner Kasten. Er ordnet die Objekte in lockerer Folge, gibt kurze Erklärungstexte und kann in etwa 50-60 Minuten erlebt werden. Hinzu treten vertiefende Zusatzausstellungen wie »Zu Haus bei Katharina«, »Die Reformation als Medienrevolution«, »Luthers Bild und Lutherbilder«

und eine Schatzkammer mit Zimelien aus neun Jahrhunderten, die mit verdichteten Exponatenfolgen und Texten den Gesamtanspruch, eine Ausstellung zu »Martin Luther – Leben, Werk, Wirkung« zu präsentieren, einlösen.[4] Die Engführung auf »Luther in seinem Haus« schlägt sich auch in der Umbenennung des Hauses nieder, nämlich »Lutherhaus« statt der 1883 eingeführten und häufig irreführenden Bezeichnung »Lutherhalle«.[5]

Die neue Dauerausstellung geht neue Wege in der Gestaltung des Lutherhauses: Die Beschriftung ist durchgängig zweisprachig (deutsch/englisch). Neue Themen sind aufgenommen: Alltags-, Medien- und Rezeptionsgeschichte. Neue Präsentationsmedien sind eingebracht: v. a. Multimediastationen und digitale Faksimiles. Das Ziel der Ausstellung ist Besucherorientierung durch Anschaulichkeit: Modelle von Alltagsszenen, zahlreiche Objekte statt der früher dominierenden »Flachware« von Grafik, Handschrift, Buch. Während im »Biografischen Rundgang« die bekannten Exponat-Highlights – wie Kanzel, Kutte, 10-Gebote-Tafel etc. – präsentiert werden, mussten für die neuen thematischen Ergänzungsausstellungen neue Vermittlungsansätze gesucht werden. Die gerade für das Haus der Familie Luther passende Darstellung der Alltagsgeschichte kann kaum mit Originalgegenständen aufwarten, da nicht zuletzt die Nutzung des Hauses durch die Universität nach Luthers Tod alle Nachlassenschaften mit Ausnahme der Ausstattung der Lutherstube vergessen und verloren machte. Der alltäglichen Geschichte der Familie war nicht die Dignität der Musealisierung zugesprochen worden, sodass erst die Ausstellung von 2003 ihr Proprium, im Haus Luthers und seiner Familie zu sein, ernst nimmt. Eine

4 Die Ausstellungsteile werden ausführlich vorgestellt in drei Rundgängen: Martin TREU: Martin Luther in Wittenberg: ein biographischer Rundgang. 2. Aufl. Wittenberg 2006; DERS.: Martin Luther in Wittenberg: a biographical tour (Martin Luther in Wittenberg: ein biographischer Rundgang ⟨engl.⟩) / übers. durch Tradukas: Gesellschaft freier Übersetzer und Übersetzerinnen von [Will Firth]. Wittenberg 2004; Antje HELING: Zu Haus bei Martin Luther: ein alltagsgeschichtlicher Rundgang. Wittenberg 2003; Volkmar JOESTEL; Jutta STREHLE: Luthers Bild und Lutherbilder: ein Rundgang durch die Wirkungsgeschichte. Wittenberg 2003. Die herausragenden Exponate erfahren in einer neuen Publikation eine Würdigung in Text und Bild:. LUTHERS SCHATZKAMMER: Kostbarkeiten im Lutherhaus Wittenberg/ hrsg. von Volkmar Joestel. Dößel 2008.

5 Vgl. Karl-Heinz FIX: Lutherhaus – Reformationshalle – Lutherhalle: zur Namensgeschichte des Wittenberger reformationsgeschichtlichen Museums. In: Reformationserinnerung und Lutherinszenierung/ hrsg. von Stefan Laube; Karl-Heinz Fix. L 2002, 241-263.

erste Hinwendung zum familiären Alltag hatte bereits das Katharina-von-Bora-Jahr 1999 eröffnet, das durch Ausstellung und Publikationen zu einem besonderen Publikumserfolg des Wittenberger Lutherhauses wurde.[6] Die Not der Objektarmut und des konservatorisch unzuträglichen Kellerklimas wendet die neue Dauerausstellung in eine Tugend, indem sie wichtige Alltagsszenen in liebevoll geschnitzten Holzmodellen zur Anschauung bringt. Auf der Grundlage breiter Recherchen v. a. in Luthers Briefen und Tischreden sind Familienszenen wie das Bierbrauen, das Abfischen der Teiche oder die Viehhaltung szenisch ausformuliert worden. Die Gartenarbeit gehört zu diesen Szenen, zumal es wohl keinen besseren Ort gibt als Luthers Haus samt Umgebung, um die Erfahrung des Reformators – »wenn ich am Leben bleibe, will ich Gärtner werden«[7] – von der erholsamen Arbeit in Gottes Schöpfung nahe zu bringen.

Die Sammlung des Lutherhauses – herausragend durch ihre Lutherdrucke am authentischen Ort – ist indessen vor allem dadurch charakterisiert, das Nachleben Luthers in Grafik, Medaillen, Schrifttum bis hin zu Souvenirs vielfältig illustrieren zu können. Diese Sammlungsstärke kam in den früheren Dauerausstellungen durch deren Fokussierung auf Luthers Leben und Werk kaum zum Tragen. Deshalb kann der rezeptionsgeschichtliche Ausstellungsteil »Luthers Bild und Lutherbilder« aus dem Vollen schöpfen, zumal er sich vorrangig auf die visuelle Wirkungsgeschichte konzentriert. Von 1546 bis 1983 wird ein weiter Bogen gespannt, der von einem monumentalen, elfteiligen ganzfigurigen Luther-Holzschnitt der Cranach-Werkstatt bis hin zur Vielfalt der künstlerischen Auseinandersetzung mit Luther aus Anlass des 500. Geburtstags des Reformators reicht. Für die populäre Lutherverehrung werden aussagekräftige Objekte gezeigt, darunter z. B. Becher und Kelche, die aus dem Holz der Lutherbuche bei Altenstein in Thüringen – die am 4. Mai 1521 »Zeuge« von Luthers vermeintlicher Gefangennahme war und am 18. Juli 1841 einem Orkan zum Opfer fiel – hergestellt wurden, außerdem zahlreiche Alltagsgegenstände des 19. Jahrhunderts, d. h.

---

6 Vgl. Martin Treu: »Lieber Herr Käthe« – Katharina von Bora: die Lutherin; Rundgang durch die Ausstellung. Wittenberg 1999, und Katharina von Bora, die Lutherin: Aufsätze anläßlich ihres 500. Geburtstages/ hrsg. von Martin Treu. Wittenberg 1999.

7 WA Br 4, 310, 13 (1189), Luther an Wenzeslaus Linck am 29. Dezember 1527 aus [Wittenberg]; zu Luthers Gartentätigkeit vgl. Heling: Zu Haus bei Martin Luther, 33-44.

Johann Gottfried Schadow (1764-1850): Lutherbüste, Gips, patiniert, 62 cm hoch, 1807
Modell für das 1821 auf dem Wittenberger Marktplatz eingeweihte Lutherdenkmal

Tassen, Teller, Pfeifenköpfe, Dosen, Spieluhren mit Luther-Darstellungen,
oder auch Luthersouvenirs aus dem 20. Jahrhundert. Rund neun Spielfilme
haben sich seit der Stummfilmzeit bis zur Gegenwart mit Person und
Werk Martin Luthers beschäftigt; einzelne Szenen – z. B. Thesenanschlag,
Wormser Reichstag 1521, Bauernkrieg, Eheschließung – werden in einer

Collage unterschiedlicher Filmsequenzen mit einer erstaunlichen Interpretationsbreite visualisiert: »Hier stehe ich, ich kann nicht anders« etwa triumphalisch-aggressiv bis hin zu verhalten-demütig.[8]

Seit der Eröffnung der neu gestalteten Ausstellung konnte der Anteil der ausländischen Besucher – ca. 40 % – und der Familien gesteigert werden. 2007 betrug die Gesamtbesucherzahl im Lutherhaus 79.300. Dazu trägt überdies bei, dass die Stiftung Luthergedenkstätten im Lutherhaus seit einigen Jahren ihr Veranstaltungsprogramm und ihre museumspädagogische Angebote ausgebaut hat.[9]

II Neue Dauerausstellung in Luthers Geburtshaus Eisleben

Das 1693 nach der Zerstörung des ursprünglichen Gebäudes infolge eines verheerenden Stadtbrands neu errichtete Geburtshaus diente seit seiner Entstehung als Memorialgebäude und vereinigte unter einem Dach ein eindrucksvolles Miteinander unterschiedlicher Funktionen: Untergebracht war eine Armenfreischule mit Klassenzimmern und Lehrerwohnung. Im sogen. »Schönen Saal« fanden die Feierlichkeiten zu den einschlägigen Jahrestagen Luthers und der Reformation statt. Und jeden Sonntag wurden in diesem Saal den Bedürftigen der Stadt Almosen ausgeteilt. Das Gedenken an den Reformator war also nicht nur durch die Exposition von Büchern, Handschriften und Grafiken gegeben – erst ab Beginn des 19. Jahrhunderts konnten entsprechende Sammlungen aufgebaut werden –, sondern war eng mit Schule und Diakonie verbunden und erhielt daraus seine Aktualität und Vitalität. Da die Schülerzahl immer größer wurde, musste ein zusätzliches Gebäude in unmittelbarer Nachbarschaft errichtet werden, das nach maßgeblicher Finanzierung durch den preußischen König Friedrich Wilhelm III. 1819 eingeweiht und bis 1953 für schulische Zwecke genutzt wurde.

8 Vgl. die aus diesem Filmpräsentationsprojekt entstandene Untersuchung von Ester P. Wipf-ler: Vom deutschnationalen Titan zum Herzensbrecher: zur Geschichte des Luther-Bildes in Kinematographie und Fernsehen. Lu 75 (2004), 25-41, auch zum neuesten Lutherfilm mit Joseph Fiennes in der Hauptrolle (2003), der für die Dauerausstellung im Lutherhaus noch nicht berücksichtigt werden konnte.
9 Vgl. die Stiftungswebsite www.martinluther.de mit aktuellem Veranstaltungskalender und Beschreibung der museumspädagogischen Aktionen und Führungen nicht nur im Lutherhaus Wittenberg, sondern auch im Geburtshaus Eisleben.

Lutherstadt Eisleben, »Luthers Geburtshaus«, Hofseite

Um die bislang sehr begrenzte Ausstellungsfläche von circa 150 m²
zu erweitern, wurde 2006/07 ein neues Ausstellungsgebäude in moderner
Architekturformensprache errichtet, das die beiden historischen Häuser –
Geburtshaus und Lutherarmenschule – verbindet und ein zusammenhän-
gendes Ensemble schafft, in dem sich eine neue Ausstellungsfläche von
über 700 m² ausbreitet. Über das bloße Faktum der Geburt hinaus konnte
deshalb der inhaltliche Rahmen der neuen Dauerausstellung weiter gesteckt
werden. Prägender Lebenskontext der Familie Luder war der Bergbau, in
dem Vater Luder schon in seiner thüringischen Heimat bei Möhra tätig war
und der ihn um 1483 wegen der weitaus besseren Verdienstmöglichkeiten
in das boomende Kupferabbaugebiet Mansfeld führte. Dort – vor allem
nach dem Umzug in die Stadt Mansfeld – wurde Hans Luder rasch ein er-
folgreicher Hütten- und Bergwerksbesitzer. Seine archivalisch belegbaren
Bergwerke und Schmelzöfen werden in der Ausstellung erstmals auf einer

Karte verzeichnet. Luder erwarb außer einem Anwesen in der Stadt, das er ausbaute, Äcker und Wiesen rund um Mansfeld. Schließlich konnte er sein Einkommen sogar durch Geldverleih erhöhen.

Die archivalischen Recherchen im Vorfeld der neuen Dauerausstellung, die das Bild vom Unternehmer Hans Luder mit neuen Fakten bereicherten,[10] flossen in die Konzeption der Ausstellung ein: In zwei Räumen widmet sie sich dem jahrhundertelang – von 1200 bis 1990 – Landschaft, Wirtschaft und Kultur prägenden Bergbau. Entgegen den heutigen ökonomischen Schwierigkeiten in dieser Region können die Texte und Exponate der Ausstellung samt einem Modell der Stadt Eisleben zur Lutherzeit eine völlig andere Situation beschreiben: Das 15. und 16. Jahrhundert erscheint als Zeit wirtschaftlichen Aufschwungs in der Grafschaft Mansfeld.

Zentrales Ereignis war für Luther seine Taufe in der dem Geburtshaus benachbarten Kirche St. Peter und Paul. Die Ausstellung illustriert dies mit einem Taufstein aus der Taufkirche, der dort seit 1518 stand und seit dem 19. Jahrhundert in einem Garten lange Jahrzehnte als Blumenkübel »missbraucht« wurde. Eine eindrucksvolle Galerie bieten die Epitaphien aus dem Kronenfriedhof, der auf Ratschlag Luthers 1533 außerhalb der Stadtmauern angelegt wurde. Die Epitaphgemälde, die ab 1558 überliefert sind und deren Qualität an die Cranach-Schule erinnern, nehmen immer wieder auf Luther Bezug, zeigen die ältesten erhaltenen Ansichten der offensichtlich bereits damals als »Lutherstadt« imaginierten Stadt Eisleben und werden erstmals als Ensemble in der neuen Dauerausstellung der Öffentlichkeit nach eingehender Restaurierung präsentiert.

Aus der Familie Luder – die Ausstellung differenziert prononciert den herkömmlichen Familiennamen von der späteren Selbstbezeichnung des Reformators Martin Luther[11] – hat der Vater vor allem in psychohis-

10 Hier sind v. a. die aufschlussreichen Forschungen von Michael Fessner zu nennen; Michael FESSNER: Die Familie Luder und das Bergwerks- und Hüttenwesen in der Grafschaft Mansfeld und im Herzogtum Braunschweig-Wolfenbüttel. In: Martin Luther und Eisleben/ hrsg. von Rosemarie Knape. L 2007, 11-31; fortgeführt und erweitert – z. B. zur Kupfergewinnung in und um Möhra – von DEMS.: Die Familie Luder und das Berg- und Hüttenwesen. In: Luthers Lebenswelten/ hrsg. von Harald Meller; Stefan Rhein; Hans-Georg Stephan. Halle (Saale) 2008, 235-243.

11 Vgl. Bernd MOELLER; Karl STACKMANN: Luder – Luther – Eleutherius: Erwägungen zu Luthers Namen. GÖ 1981.

Lutherstadt Eisleben, »Luthers Geburtshaus«, Taufraum
mit Taufstein, Sandstein, 1518, aus Luthers Taufkirche St. Petri und Paul

torischer Perspektive[12] weitaus mehr Beachtung gefunden als etwa die
Mutter. Von ihr hat der Sohn 1535 eine Liedzeile überliefert: »Mir und dir
ist niemand hold, das ist unser beider Schuld.«[13] Die Suche nach einer
musikalischen Notierung führte letztendlich zu einer volksliedhaften
Fassung aus dem Jahr 1544, die jetzt in der Ausstellung erstmals zu Ge-
hör gebracht wird; damit wird eine der wenigen Erinnerungen Luthers an
seine Mutter wieder lebendig

12 Erik Erikson: Der junge Mann Luther: eine psychoanalytische und historische Studie
(Young man Luther: a study in psychoanalysis and history ⟨dt.⟩)/ übers. von Johanna
Schiche. M 1958.
13 WA 38, 338, 5-7; vgl. auch WA TR 4, 414, 6 f (4640), 5. Juni 1539. Die erste Zeile findet sich
mit Noten in einem Quodlibet von Wolfgang Schmeltzel (um 1500 - nach 1560); Das
deutsche Lied des XV. und XVL. Jahrhunderts in Wort, Melodie und mehrstim-
migem Tonsatz/ hrsg. von Robert Eitner. Bd. 1. B 1876, 81.

Zum Erfolg anschaulicher Vermittlung tragen zum einen die zeitgenössischen Skulpturen aus den Kirchen Eislebens bei, die für das religiöse Umfeld der Lutherkindheit stehen, zum anderen die Inszenierung im Erdgeschoss des Geburtshauses, mit der die Einrichtung der Wohn- und Schlafstube von 1483 nach historischen Vorlagen nachempfunden wird. Das Obergeschoss nimmt die barocke Entstehungszeit des Geburtshauses ernst und lässt im Schönen Saal die Musik und die überlieferten Reden der Einweihungszeremonie vom 31. Oktober 1693 an Hörbeispielen nacherleben.[14]

III Archäologische Funde in Mansfeld

Das Luther-Gedenken findet in der kleinen, heute von ca. 3000 Menschen bewohnten Stadt Mansfeld-Lutherstadt an verschiedenen Orten seinen Platz: Elternhaus, Kirche St. Georg, Luthers Schule – deren historische Bausubstanz durch einen Umbau 1999/2000 fast vollständig abgerissen wurde –, der Lutherbrunnen von 1913 mit Szenen aus Luthers Leben und das über der Stadt thronende Schloss Mansfeld mit der Lutherkanzel in der Kapelle. Im Rahmen der Stadtsanierung wurden 2003 umfangreiche Grabungen auf dem Areal des Elternhauses durchgeführt, die einen Fundkomplex von Keramik, Tierknochen, vielfältigen Gebrauchsgegenständen und Kleidungszubehör zu Tage brachten. Sie erweitern die Kenntnisse über Luthers Familie über die Textquellen hinaus durch Zeugnisse der materiellen Kultur.

Luthers Vater, Hans Luder, erwarb das Gebäude vermutlich 1491, das auch nach seinem Tod am 29. Mai 1530 von der Familie Luder bewohnt wurde.[15] Martin Luther verbrachte in der Stadt Mansfeld seine Kindheit von 1484

14 Die neue Dauerausstellung wird mit ihren Themen und Exponaten vorgestellt in Martin Treu: »Von daher bin ich«: Martin Luther und Eisleben: ein Rundgang durch die Ausstellung im Geburtshaus. Wittenberg 2007. Die verschiedenen Aspekte der Dauerausstellung – von Luthers Taufe bis zu seiner Familie, vom Bergbau bis zur wirtschaftlichen Situation Eislebens um 1500 – werden ausführlich behandelt in dem Band Martin Luther und Eisleben/ hrsg. von Rosemarie Knape. L 2007.

15 Das heutige »Elternhaus« war nach aktuellen Recherchen nur der kleinere Teil einer größeren Liegenschaft im Eigentum der Luders (Lutherstraße 24, 25, 26), vgl. Andreas Stahl: Historische Bauforschung an Luthers Elternhaus: archivalische Voruntersuchungen und erste Baubeobachtungen. In: Luther in Mansfeld: Forschungen am Elternhaus des Reformators/ hrsg. von Harald Meller. Halle (Saale) 2007, 113-137.

bis 1497 und wohnte wahrscheinlich in dem sogen. »Elternhaus« von 1491 bis 1497. Die in der Grube gefundenen 160 Münzen, insbesondere Eisleber Pfennige der Grafen von Mansfeld, datieren die Abfallgrube auf die Zeit um 1500.[16] Der Gesamtfund hat unter der Überschrift »Luthers Murmeln«[17] ein großes Presseecho hervorgerufen, da zwei Schellen, zwei Murmeln und zwei aus Gänseknochen gefertigte Pfeifen als Kinderspielzeug gedeutet wurden. Unter den Küchenabfällen nehmen die Tierknochen einen breiten Raum ein – »mehrere Tausend Fundstücke« –, so z. B. von jungen Schweinen, Schafen/Ziegen und Rindern, viele Geflügelknochen (v. a. Gänse und Hühner, aber auch Enten, Tauben, Rebhühner), außerdem Reste kleiner Singvögel, die zur Ernährung gefangen wurden (v. a. Singdrossel, Dorngrasmücke, Rotkehlchen, Buchfink, Goldammer), sowie Reste von Süßwasserfischen (Karpfen, Hecht, Brassen, Plötze, Rapfen, Zander, Flussbarsch, Aale) und Meeresfischen (Hering, Dorsch, Scholle), die in ihrer Vielfalt den Haushalt einer wohlhabenden Familie zeigen.[18] Damit finden die archivalischen Quellen, die Luder bereits 1491 als »Vierherr«, also als einen aus der Mitte der städtischen Oberschicht bestimmten Vertreter der Bürgerschaft, notieren, ihre gleichsam materielle Bestätigung. Die Funde veranschaulichen den sozialen Aufstieg von Luthers Vater, der nach Aussage seines Sohnes in seiner Jugend als »armer Heuer« seine Tätigkeit im Bergbau aufnahm.[19]

Das Jahr »1491« ist erschlossen: Hans Luder ist 1491 als Vierherr nachgewiesen, ein Amt, das Hausbesitz in der Stadt voraussetzte. Zudem ist für 1506 belegt, dass Luder bereits längere Zeit das Anwesen abbezahlte. Gleichwohl bleibt festzuhalten: Es ist nicht auszuschließen, dass Martin Luther niemals in dem sogen. »Elternhaus« lebte.

16 Ulf DRÄGER: Die Münzen – Eine verlorene Haushaltskasse? In: Luther in Mansfeld, 159-168, worin folgender Schluss gezogen wird: »Der Fundkomplex steht aber sicherlich nicht in einem ursächlichen Zusammenhang mit dem Vermögen und den Geschäften des wohlhabenden Hans Luder, sondern weist eher auf die Barschaft einer Magd oder eines Bediensteten hin«; ebd, 159.

17 Unter dieser Überschrift ist er auch in der Mansfelder Bevölkerung präsent; vgl. etwa Mitteldeutsche Zeitung (29. Okt. 2003): »Mansfelder hoffen, dass Luthers Murmeln mehr Geld in Kassen bringt« oder (21. Jan. 2004): »Luthers Murmeln gehen auf Reisen«.

18 Vgl. Hans-Jürgen DÖHLE: Schwein, Geflügel und Fisch – bei Luthers zu Tisch. In: Luther in Mansfeld, 169-186; MANSFELD. In: Fundsache Luther: Archäologen auf den Spuren des Reformators/ hrsg. von Harald Meller. [S 2008], 165-217.

19 WA TR 3, 51, 8 f (2888 a), 2.-26. Juni 1533. Dieter STIEVERMANN: Sozialer Aufstieg um 1500: Hüttenmeister Hans Luther und sein Sohn Dr. Martin Luther. In: Martin Luther und der

IV »Lutherturm« in Wittenberg – auf der Suche nach dem Ort des Turmerlebnisses

Der Gedenkort für Luther in seinem Wittenberger Haus war lange Zeit hindurch ausschließlich die Lutherstube, die nach Luthers Tod nicht wesentlich verändert und bereits 1655 »Museum Lutheri« genannt wurde.[20] Dass das gesamte Haus als denkmalwürdig aufgefasst wurde, war eine Folge preußischer Denkmalpolitik, die durch den Berliner Architekten Friedrich August Stüler (1800-1865) allen Stockwerken und Räumen eine umfassende Sanierung angedeihen ließ – weniger im Sinne des Erhalts vorhandener Bausubstanz als vor allem der historisierenden Imagination. Die bereits oben skizzierte Öffnung des gesamten Lutherhauses für die Öffentlichkeit im Rahmen der neuen Dauerausstellung seit 2003 vollendet letztendlich den Ansatz des 19. Jahrhunderts, das Lutherhaus als komplett begehbares

Bergbau im Mansfelder Land/ hrsg. von Rosemarie Knape. Lutherstadt Eisleben 2000, 45, interpretiert allerdings diese Aussage als »Tief-Stapeln« im stolzen »Bewußtsein um den ganz persönlichen sozialen Aufstieg«. Dagegen Helmar JUNGHANS: Neue Erkenntnisses und neue Fragen an Martin Luthers Leben und Umwelt. In: Fundsache Luthers, 142-149, bes. 146.

Materielle Kultur und Textüberlieferung treten übrigens auch in Eisleben in einen fruchtbaren Dialog: Das dortige Kloster St. Annen gehört wegen seiner vom Marktplatz aus gesehen etwas entfernten Lage nicht zu den häufig aufgesuchten Lutherstätten in der Geburtsstadt des Reformators – im Gegensatz zum Geburtshaus, der Taufkirche St. Petri und Paul, der St. Andreaskirche mit Lutherkanzel und dem »Sterbehaus«. In das heute fast ausschließlich privat genutzte Klostergebäude kam ich nur in Begleitung von Pfarrer Hauke Meinhold und war fasziniert, was im Dachgeschoss sich bis heute verbirgt: original erhaltene Klosterzellen! Dendrochronologische Untersuchungen des Landesamtes für Denkmalpflege und Archäologie Sachsen-Anhalt erbrachten die Bauzeit Winter/Frühjahr 1515/16, sodass die Darlegungen von Wilhelm Ernst Winterhager über den Distriktvikar Luther, der am Fronleichnamstag 1516, dem 22. Mai, das Kloster einweihte, ihre sinnfällige Bestätigung finden; Wilhelm Ernst WINTERHAGER: Martin Luther und das Amt des Provinzialvikars in der Reformkongregation der deutschen Augustiner-Eremiten. In: Vita Religiosa im Mittelalter: Festschrift für Kaspar Elm zum 70. Geburtstag/ hrsg. von Franz J. Felten; Nikolaus Jaspert. B 1999, 707-738. Zum Eisleber Kloster St. Annen als Lutherort vgl. künftig die Beiträge von Christian Philipsen und Reinhard Schmitt in DER MÖNCH MARTIN LUTHER IN SEINER LEBENSWELT/ hrsg. von Johannes Schilling. L 2010 (im Druck).

20 Vgl. Stefan LAUBE: Das Lutherhaus Wittenberg: eine Museumsgeschichte. L 2003, 93-99.

Lutherstadt Wittenberg, Lutherhaus, Anbau an der Südwand des
Augustinereremitenklosters, der 2004 freigelegt wurde

Denkmal zur Ehre seines berühmtesten Bewohners zu begreifen. Zu den
Baumaßnahmen der 1840er Jahre gehörte auch die freistellende Monumentalisierung des Lutherhauses, indem ein Anbau an der Südfassade abgerissen und eingeebnet wurde. Eben dort entstand der »Luthergarten«, der
bis Sommer 2004 als vermeintlich idyllischer Aufenthaltsort der Familie
Luther die Besucher erfreute. Der Anbau aber war vielmehr im Stadtgraben
errichtet worden. In alten Plänen des 18. und 19. Jahrhunderts tituliert der
Anbau als »Küchengebäude« oder »Waschhaus«, doch zeigt die erhaltene
ursprüngliche Fußbodenheizung des Erdgeschosses, dass es sich dabei
um spätere Funktionen handelte. Der als Erweiterung zum Südflügel des
Klosters wohl um 1515 errichtete Anbau – die Datierung wird durch Bau-

rechnungen nahe gelegt – diente offensichtlich als Wohnung eines heraus-
gehobenen Mitglieds des Konvents. Diese Nutzung ergibt sich durch die
im Untergeschoss erhaltene Toilette und die erwähnte Fußbodenheizung,
aber auch durch die Sandsteingewände der Türen und Fenster und die ge-
gliederte Fassade aus gelben Backsteinen. Zugänglich war der Anbau nur
vom Haupthaus und zwar im Erdgeschoss und im 1. Obergeschoss, wie
restauratorische Untersuchungen feststellten. Über drei Stockwerke – Untergeschoss, Erdgeschoss, Obergeschoss – erstreckte sich also dieser Anbau,
der offensichtlich, so jedenfalls auf frühen Stadtdarstellungen, von einem
Giebeldach bedeckt war.[21]

1983 wurde im 1. Obergeschoss des Lutherhauses ein Durchgang zu
einem Stadtmauerturm gefunden und als Zugang zu Luthers Studierstube
verstanden.[22] Bei der Baumaßnahme 2000/03 wurden die Grundmauern
dieses Südwestturms gefunden, die hinter den starken Quadersteinen
einen nutzbaren inneren Raum von lediglich 4 m² freigeben – unter der
Voraussetzung, dass die dicken Quadersteine des Fundaments die Mauer-
stärke des gesamten Turmes bestimmen. Hier wurde seit langem Luthers
ursprüngliches Arbeitszimmer lokalisiert,[23] während der neue Anbau zunächst als repräsentatives Priorat und nach Aufhebung des Klosters und
Wegzug des Priors Konrad Helt († 1548) 1522 als neues, nunmehr größeres
Arbeitszimmer Luthers identifiziert wurde.[24] Luthers Position war indes im

21 Der Anbau an der Südfassade des Lutherhauses wurde 2004 ausgegraben. Der Fundkomplex umfasst rund 50 000 Objekte, die größtenteils auf 1500-1560/70 zu datieren und
   vor allem glasierter Irdenware, Tierknochen, unglasierter Keramik und Kachelkeramik
   zuzurechnen sind. Zu den einzelnen Objekttypen vgl. im Sammelband »Luthers Lebenswelten« die Beiträge von Hans-Georg Stephen (insbesondere Keramik), Sonja König
   (Wandbrunnen), Ulf Dräger (Münzen), Verena Schwartz (Ofenkacheln), Hans-Jürgen
   Döhle (Tierreste) und Monika Hellmund (Pflanzenreste). Zahlreiche Fundstücke sind
   mit kompetenten Erklärungstexten vorgestellt in: Fundsache Luther, 233-303.
22 Vgl. die Abbildung in MARTIN LUTHER 1483-1546: Katalog der Hauptausstellung in der
   Lutherhalle Wittenberg/ bearb. von Volkmar Joestel. B 1993, 184.
23 Ernst KROKER: Luthers Arbeitsstube. ARG 17 (1920), 301-315; Heinrich Gisbert VOIGT: Die
   entscheidende Stunde in Luthers religiöser Entwicklung: ihre Örtlichkeit, Zeit und Bedeutung. Zeitschrift des Vereins für Kirchengeschichte der Provinz Sachsen und des Freistaates
   Anhalt 24 (1928), 32-70; DERS.: Luthers Wittenberger Turm. Ebd 26 (1930), 166-175.
24 So Martin TREU: Waschhaus – Küche – Priorat: die neuen archäologischen Funde am
   Wittenberger Lutherhaus. Lu 76 (2005), 132-140.

Augustinerkloster bereits seit 1515 herausgehoben, seitdem er als Distrikt-vikar von zunächst zehn, dann nach Einweihung des Eisleber Klosters 1516 von elf Klöstern fungierte und als solcher Priores ernennen und entlassen konnte. Dass im Mai 1519 nicht Prior Helt, sondern Luther sich in Baufra-gen des Wittenberger Klosters an Kurfürst Friedrich den Weisen wandte, belegt diese besondere Stellung Luthers.[25] Im engen Stadtmauerturm ist bei den Ausgrabungen keine Latrine gefunden worden – im Gegensatz zum Anbau, dessen Grundmaße von 9 x 9 m über drei Stockwerke gezogen einen turmähnlichen Eindruck vermitteln konnten. So verweist Luthers bekannte Verknüpfung der reformatorischen Erkenntnis mit der »Cloaca« naheliegend auf den Anbau und situiert diesen als Ort des »Turmerleb-nisses«.[26] Als der Anbau samt Arbeitszimmer durch Befestigungsarbeiten 1532/33 in die Gefahr, abgerissen zu werden, geriet, beschwerte sich Luther beim Rat der Stadt und kämpfte selbstbewusst für »das Stüblein, woraus ich das Papsttum gestürmt habe, weswegen es ewigen Gedächtnisses würdig ist«.[27] Dieses »Stüblein« lag also ohne Zweifel im Anbau. Nach 1533 wurde ein Wall aufgeschüttet und eine hohe Mauer errichtet, die eben diesen und nur diesen Anbau schützte, was nicht nur den Einfluss Luthers in Wittenberg, sondern auch die tiefe Anhänglichkeit Luthers an sein »Stüblein« im Turm und sein Wissen um die Geschichtsmächtigkeit dieses »Stübleins« eindrucksvoll unterstreicht.[28]

25 WA Br 1, 386 (173).
26 Zur »Cloaca« vgl. WA TR 2, 177, 8 f (1681): »Dise kunst [Erkenntnis] hatt mir der Spiritus Sanctus auf diss Cloaca eingeben.« Offenkundig hat Luther 1532 in seinem Arbeitszimmer in »deiktischer« Nähe zur »Cloaca« gesprochen. Die theologiegeschichtliche Debatte um Prozess oder Durchbruch der reformatorischen Erkenntnis kann hier unerörtert bleiben; vgl. Reinhard SCHWARZ: Luther. 2., überarb. Aufl. GÖ 1998, 40-44, und zuletzt Volker LEPPIN: Einleitung: Die Erforschung von Luthers reformatorischer Entwicklung auf dem Weg von »Wende-Konstrukt« zur Kontextualisierung. In: Luther und das monastische Erbe/ hrsg. von Christoph Burger; Volker Leppin; Andreas Lindner. TÜ 2007, 1-7, zumal beide – Prozess oder Durchbruch – ihre Lokalisierung in Luthers »Stüblein« besitzen.
27 »Lebe ich noch ein jar, so mus mein armes stublin hinweg, daraus ich doch das bapstumb gesturmet habe, propter quam causam dignum est perpetua memoria«; WA TR 2, 509, 10-12 (2540 a).
28 Damit ist m. E. die Frage von Martin Treu – »Ungeklärt ist dabei bis heute, warum der Wall etwa in der Mitte des Lutherhauses nach Norden zurückschwenkt, so dass der östliche Teil des Gebäudes aus der Befestigung ungeschützt hervorragt« – beantwortet; vgl. Treu:

Luthers Arbeitszimmer befand sich in diesem turmähnlichen Anbau an der südlichen Außenwand des Schwarzen Klosters. Luther war sich des epochalen Umbruchs in Folge der Geschehnisse des 31. Oktober 1517 sehr wohl bewusst, sodass die emphatische Beschreibung dieses seines Arbeitszimmers als Ausgangsort des antipäpstlichen Sturms die Erschütterungen des »Turmerlebnisses« wie auch des »Thesenanschlags« widerzuspiegeln scheint.[29] Luthers Arbeitszimmer im Anbau ist gewiss Realität 1532, höchstwahrscheinlich auch bereits nach 1522, nach dem Wegzug des Priors, m. E. aber schon bereits ab ca. 1515.[30]

V »Luther 2017 – 500 Jahre Reformation«

Das große Reformationsjubiläum 2017 wirft schon heute seine Schatten, die am zentralen Gedenk- und Festort Wittenberg, aber auch in den anderen mitteldeutschen Lutherorten wie Eisenach, Erfurt, Eisleben und Torgau bereits heute sicht- und spürbar sind. Die Diskussion um die Authentizität des

Waschhaus – …, 139, und Stefan RHEIN: »Mythos Luther«: oder wie sich das Nachleben vom Leben löst. In: Mythos: Dokumentation einer Veranstaltung der UNESCO-Stätten im Raum Dessau-Wittenberg/ Red. Marie Neumüllers; Stefan Rhein. Calbe 2008, 30-37.

29 Vgl. zum »erinnerungswürdigen« biografischen Einschnitt des Ablassstreites Luthers Briefdatierung 1. November 1527: »Wittembergae die Omnium Sanctorum, anno decimo Indulgentiarum conculcatarum, quarum memoria hac hora bibimus utrinque consolati, 1527«; WA Br 4, 275, 25-27 (1164). Luther selbst datierte 1531 den Beginn seines »schreibenden« Kampfes gegen den Papst auf 1516; vgl. WA TR 1, 441, 38 (884); 2, 376, 9 (2250).

30 Oder war Luther sogar bereits seit 1513 Bewohner des im Unterschied zum Südwestturm mit einer Fußbodenheizung ausgestatteten Anbaus – dessen Errichtung müsste dann vorverlegt werden –, da er sein Doktorat (Okt. 1512) und vielleicht auch den Beginn seiner universitären Lehrtätigkeit 1513 mit einem beheizbaren Arbeitszimmer verknüpfte: »Doctor creatus mihi ipsi fui calefactor«; WA 1, 99, 24f (5375); vgl. Treu: Waschhaus – …, 138; Kroker: Luthers Arbeitsstube, 301-315? Zu einem anderen Ergebnis kommt Helmar Junghans in seinem Beitrag »Zeitpunkt und Ort von Luthers Turmerlebnis angesichts neuer Ausgrabungen« für den geplanten Sammelband »Der Mönch Martin Luther in seiner Lebenswelt«. Er erläutert eingehend die Textquellen zum Turmerlebnis und zu Luthers Arbeitszimmer und kommt zu dem Ergebnis, dass Luthers reformatorische Anfänge nicht im Südanbau, sondern im Südwestturm des Lutherhauses zu lokalisieren sind. Dieser in den Klosterbau einbezogene Südwestturm des Lutherhauses war Teil der mittelalterlichen Stadtbefestigung. Sein Feldsteinfundament wurde 2000 freigelegt und ist heute im neuen Eingangsbereich des Lutherhauses zu besichtigen.

Thesenanschlags scheint durch die Neubewertung einer handschriftlichen Notiz Georg Rörers – »Anno Domini 1517 in profesto omnium Sanctorum p[...] Witembergae in valvis templorum propositae sunt pro[positiones] de Indulgentiis a Doctore Martino Luthero« –, die in der Thüringer Universitäts- und Landesbibliothek Jena aufbewahrt ist, passgenau zehn Jahre vor dem Ereignis neu aufgeflammt zu sein und hat auch in der deutschen Öffentlichkeit die Aufmerksamkeit auf die Geschehnisse des 31. Oktobers 1517 gelenkt.[31]

Die unter dem institutionellen Dach der Stiftung Luthergedenkstätten in Sachsen-Anhalt arbeitende Geschäftsstelle »Luther 2017« hat die Aufgabe, mit allen kirchlichen, wissenschaftlichen und kulturellen Partnern – in enger Abstimmung mit der Geschäftsstelle der EKD in Wittenberg – die Vorbereitungsphase – »Lutherdekade« – und das Jubiläumsjahr zu konzipieren und zu gestalten. Tagungen, Disputationen, Seminare, aber auch touristische Angebote, Bauinvestitionen und öffentlichkeitswirksame Events wie Theater, Musikfestivals etc. werden in den nächsten Jahren stattfinden, um dieses Jubiläum mit weltweiter Ausstrahlung angemessen zu kommunizieren.[32]

Der Internationale Lutherforschungskongress ist herzlich eingeladen, 2017 in der Lutherstadt Wittenberg zu tagen – und mitzufeiern.

31 Neben den Leserbriefspalten der »Frankfurter Allgemeinen Zeitung« im März 2007 vgl. Martin TREU: Der Thesenanschlag fand wirklich statt: ein neuer Beleg aus der Universitätsbibliothek Jena. Lu 78 (2007), 140-144, und zweifelnd Volker LEPPIN: Geburtswehen und Geburt einer Legende: zu Rörers Notiz vom Thesenanschlag. Ebd, 145-150. Vgl. LUTHERS THESENANSCHLAG – FAKTUM ODER FIKTION/ hrsg. von Joachim Ott; Martin Treu. L 2008, hier neben den Darlegungen von Martin Treu und Volker Leppin zusätzliche Argumente für die Faktizität des Thesenanschlages durch Bernd Moeller, Helmar Junghans und Timothy J. Wengert, außerdem Beiträge zur Wirkungsgeschichte des Thesenanschlages und der Iserloh-Debatte von Konrad Repgen, Vinzenz Pfnür, Reinhard Brandt, Henrike Holsing und Esther P. Wipfler.
32 Die verschiedenen Gremien und Akteure sowie die geplanten Veranstaltungen werden laufend aktualisiert vorgestellt auf www.luther2017.de

Luthers Antworten auf wirtschaftliche und soziale Herausforderungen seiner Zeit

Von Ricardo W. Rieth

Wenn Luther soziale und ökonomische Probleme seiner Umwelt reflektierte, verfuhr er in der Regel nach einer bestimmten Methode.

Sowohl in den sogenannten »Wucherschriften«, in der Adelsschrift und in den Schulschriften als auch in Auslegungen von Bergpredigt und Dekalog, in Abhandlungen, Vorlesungen und Predigten begann sein Nachdenken normalerweise mit der Feststellung und der Beschreibung der zu analysierenden Probleme. In diesem Zusammenhang sollten die ständige Berufung auf die geschichtliche Erfahrung und das intensive Beobachten und Auseinandersetzen mit der alltäglichen Wirklichkeit beachtet werden, wie es exemplarisch aus zahlreichen Predigten und Tischgesprächen spricht.

Seiner Betrachtung des Problems stellte er dann die für ihn in der Heiligen Schrift betreffenden Aussagen gegenüber.

Nach diesen zwei ersten fundamentalen Schritten gab er dann sein eigenes Urteil ab, wobei er die Argumente für ein unrechtes Verhalten bzw. für eine ungerechte Struktur im Sozialgefüge durch die Konfrontation mit den grundlegenden biblischen Geboten kritisierte. Je nachdem, wen Luther ansprach, ob die Obrigkeit, die ihre Verantwortung im weltlichen Regiment wahrzunehmen hätte, oder den Glaubenden in seinem Stand und in seinem Beruf, wies er auf die nach seiner Überzeugung gegebenen Möglichkeiten des Handelns hin.[1]

Im Folgenden wird dargestellt, wie Luther sich im Rahmen seiner Gesellschaftsauffassung aufgrund dieser Verfahrenweise (1) generell mit Wirtschaftsfragen beschäftigte und wie er spezifisch Probleme mit Bezug auf (2) Handel sowie (3) Geldwirtschaft (Wucher) erörterte.

---

1 Vgl. Gerta SCHARFFENORTH: Den Glauben ins Leben ziehen ...: Studien zu Luthers Theologie. M 1982, 320-335; Helmar JUNGHANS: Sozialethisches Denken und Handeln bei Martin Luther. Standpunkt 17 (1989), 67f.

Das Wort »Stand«, das für die Bezeichnung der verschiedenen Gruppen im Sozialgefüge des Spätmittelalters verwendet wird, kann inhaltlich nur mit großer Schwierigkeit beschrieben werden. Es wurde im 16. Jahrhundert keineswegs einheitlich gebraucht. Jeder Einzelne bzw. jede Gruppe mit eigenem Verständnis von »Stand« wollte nicht nur die soziale Wirklichkeit darstellen, sondern sie auch in ihrer Gestaltung bestimmen, je nach der Intention des beschreibenden Subjektes.[2] Eine weitere Tatsache ist, dass die spätmittelalterliche »Ständegesellschaft« keine absolute und statische soziale Formation darstellte, in der jedes ihrer Mitglieder von Geburt an bis zum Tod zu einer bestimmten Schicht gehörte, die das Verhältnis des Einzelnen z. B. zum Besitz von Land oder zu den Ausbildungsmöglichkeiten endgültig festlegte, obwohl für einen großen Teil der Bevölkerung außerhalb des städtischen Raumes die Überwindung einer niedrigeren ständischen Barriere immer noch ausblieb.

Luther wurde in seinem Verständnis über die Stände stark von der in drei Teile gegliederten aristotelischen Moralphilosophie – Individualethik, politische Ethik und Wirtschaftsethik – beeinflusst, die im Spätmittelalter in Erfurt gelehrt wurde. Er sprach von drei durch Gott eingesetzte Ordnungen bzw. Hierarchien bzw. Ständen – ecclesia (Priesteramt), oeconomia (Ehestand) und politia (politische Obrigkeit) – im Gegensatz zu der für ihn falschen Vorstellung einer Aufteilung in nur dem Dekalog verpflichteter Laien einerseits und in Mitglieder monastischer Orden andererseits, die zusätzlich den evangelischen Räten und der Bergpredigt Jesu verpflichtet waren. Das zeigt bereits, dass Luther mit »Stand« eigentlich keine Beschreibung des ihn umgebenden Sozialgefüges anbieten wollte. Deswegen blieb er auch terminologisch nicht an ein Wort gebunden, sondern verwandte »Stand« auch, um »Amt«, »Regiment« und »Beruf« auszudrücken.

Auf diese Weise könnte »Stand« bei Luther als der Bereich bezeichnet werden, wo jeder – und vor allem die Christen in ihrer Verantwortung vor Gott – seine Aufgabe in der Welt erfüllt. Ein »Stand« beinhaltete für ihn

---

2 Vgl. Otto Gerhard OEXLE: Stand, Klasse II: »Stand« in der Antike und im Mittelalter. In: Geschichtliche Grundbegriffe: historisches Lexikon zur politisch-sozialen Sprache in Deutschland/ hrsg. von Otto Brunner … Bd. 6: St-Vert. S 1990, 159.

ebenfalls viele weitere Stände und dieselbe Person konnte in verschiedenen Bereichen tätig sein.[3] Luther übernahm mit »Stand« einen zentralen Begriff seiner Zeit, den er schöpferisch in seine Theologie einbaute.

Luther arbeitete niemals systematisch an einer allgemeinen Analyse der wirtschaftlichen Wirklichkeit seiner Zeit. Seine Reflexionen waren vielmehr praktische Anweisungen und Richtlinien zu verschiedenen Aspekten des Ökonomischen – vor allem zu Fragen der Geldwirtschaft, der Preis- und Lohnpolitik sowie der Güterversorgung – durch einen Bibelausleger und Seelsorger, der großen Wert auf die Beobachtung der ihn umgebenden Realität legte und unermüdlich die Wahrnehmung der christlichen Verantwortung für die Verbesserung dieser Realität forderte. Trotz des Fehlens einer derartigen allgemeinen Analyse der Wirtschaft soll versucht werden, aufgrund der oben erwähnten praktischen Anweisungen und Richtlinien, einige Grundzüge von Luthers allgemeinem Urteil über das Ökonomische darzulegen.

Schon zu seinen Lebzeiten wurde die Autorität Luthers von manchen der durch seine Kritik betroffenen Leute in Frage gestellt, wenn er zu den Fragen der Wirtschaft Stellung nahm. In der Schrift »Vermahnung zum Gebet wider den Türken« verteidigte sich der Wittenberger 1541 aufgrund des für ihn selbstverständlichen Zusammenhangs von rechter Durchführung des Predigtamtes und Wirtschaftskritik:

> »Und da ich wider jn [den Wucher] schreib, Lacheten mein die heiligen Wůcherer und sprachen: Der Luther weis nicht, was Wůcher ist, Er mag seinen Mattheum und Psalter lesen. Nu wolan, bin ich denn ein prediger Christi, und mein wort Gottes Wort ist, als ich keinen zweivel hab, so sol dich verfluchter Wucher entweder der Tůrcke oder sonst ein ander zorn Gotts leren, das der Luther wol verstanden und gewust habe, was Wucher sey, das gelte einen guten gůlden.«[4]

Die Aktivitäten eines Christen im wirtschaftlichen Bereich spielten sich für Luther keineswegs unabhängig von seinem Leben im Glauben ab. Alles, was der Christ unternehme und erreiche, befinde sich im Rahmen

3 Vgl. Reinhard SCHWARZ: Luthers Lehre von den drei Ständen und die drei Dimensionen der Ethik. LuJ 45 (1978), 15-19. 28-34; Michael BEYER: Martin Luther und das Kirchengut: ekklesiologische und sozialethische Aspekte der Reformation. L 1984, 148-158. (MS) – L, Univ., Theol. Fak., Diss., 1984; Junghans: Sozialethisches Denken …, 67-71.

4 WA 51, 589, 29 - 590,20. Luther bezog sich auf seine 1524 erschienene Schrift »Von Kaufshandlung und Wucher«; WA 15 (279), 293-322; sowie »[Großer] Sermon von dem Wucher«; 6, (33-), 36-60.

des von ihm ausgeübten Gottesdienstes und die daraus stammenden Güter sollten als Gottes Segen betrachtet und nach dem Gesetz der Liebe verbraucht werden: »Also sehen wyr, das haushallten soll und mus ym glauben geschehen, so ist gnug da, das man erkenne, Es lige nicht an unserm thun, sondem an Gottes segen und beystand.«[5]

Die Realität zeige jedoch, dass die meisten aus einer anderen Überzeugung und nicht in christlicher Verantwortung handeln. In der Römerbriefvorlesung setzte sich Luther mit einer Auslegung von Faber Stapulensis (um 1455-1536) zu R 13, 1 auseinander, wo dieser von einer doppelten – der geordneten und der ungeordneten – Gewalt sprach. Solche Auslegung gefiel Luther nicht, weil keine Gewalt im Gemeinwesen ungeordnet sei. Eigentlich würde diese Gewalt lediglich in unordentlicher Weise durch den Menschen betrachtet und verwaltet. Güter verlören ihre Güte nicht infolge eines falschen Gebrauchs, anderenfalls müsste sich z. B. Geld durch Diebstahl verschlechtern. Mit diesem Beispiel stellte Luther das Ökonomische im Rahmen der »potestas« auf eine Ebene mit dem Politischen. Im ungeordneten Trachten nach der von Gott geordneten Gewalt und in ihrer ungeordneten Verwaltung liege der Spielraum der Habsucht im Umgang der Menschen mit den Gütern.[6]

Im Rahmen seiner Bibelauslegung war das siebente Gebot ein wichtiger Text, mit dem Luther grundsätzlich die Wirtschaft seiner Zeit erörterte. Eine wichtige Quelle dafür sind – außer seinen katechetischen Schriften – zahlreiche Predigten. Im Jahre 1518 sprach er von vier Werken gegen dieses Gebot: Diebstahl, gewaltsame Beschlagnahme des Besitzes des Nächsten, Wucher und Betrug im Handel.[7] Für die Beurteilung dieser Vorkommnisse in der Wirtschaft hatte die theologische Reflexion nach Luthers Ansicht ihr Proprium. Die Juristen, wenn sie von fünf verschiedenen Formen des Diebstahls – von furtum simplex, sacrilegium, peculatus, abigeatus und plagiatus – redeten, verstünden das siebente Gebot lediglich aufgrund der dagegen begangenen äußeren Werke. Theologisch gesehen irre sich jedoch derjenige, der sich auf das Verständnis der Juristen beschränke. Schon das Begehren der Güter anderer Menschen sei eine Übertretung dieses Gebotes

5 WA 15, 366, 12-14.
6 WA 56, 124, 21-23.
7 WA 1, 500, 28 - 502, 26.

gegenüber Gott. Wenn es allerdings kein »Dein-und-mein« mehr gebe, löse sich automatisch das Recht auf und die Juristen müssten ihr Brot mit irgendeiner anderen Tätigkeit verdienen.[8]

Im Verlauf der Genesisvorlesung äußerte sich Luther oft grundsätzlich über das Ökonomische, sogar oft und z. T. ausführlicher als in anderen Quellen dieser Gattung. Aufgrund von Gn 1, 28 sagte er, dass die Menschen mit ihrer verdorbenen Natur keine Vorstellung vom Umgang mit den anderen Geschöpfen in einem vollkommenen Zustand hätten, wie es vor dem Sündenfall einmal gewesen sei. Adam habe die Kreaturen anders gebraucht, als es zur Zeit Luthers üblich sei. So habe er sich z. B. nicht vom Fleisch der Tiere ernährt. Gerade als der Mensch die Herrschaft über alle Dinge besaß, habe er weder Kleidung noch Geld gehabt. Ohne den Sündenfall bestimmte nicht die Habsucht den Umgang der Nachkommenschaft Adams mit den anderen Geschöpfen, und die Kreaturen dienten lediglich dem heiligen Vergnügen und zur Bewunderung Gottes. Das ganze Gemeinwesen sei durch die Habsucht geschädigt.[9]

Bei Gn 47, 3f erörterte Luther die Strafe Gottes gegen Ägypten, das dieser in eine Wüste verwandelte,[10] nachdem Joseph – »vere politicus et theologus« genannt – alles mit großer Einsicht und Glaube verwaltet hätte. Ähnliches passierte mit Italien und Thüringen. Thüringen vor allem hätte früher den fruchtbarsten Boden im Vergleich mit anderen deutschen Ländern besessen. Jedoch müssten die Thüringer Bauern jetzt sieben Jahre lang arbeiten, um dieselbe Quantität zu produzieren, für die sie ehemals lediglich drei Jahre zu ernten brauchten. Wenn Gott ein Land bestrafe, litten damit nicht allein die Ansässigen, sondern er nehme auch den Saft der Erde. Die Ursache für eine solche ökologische Katastrophe sei die menschliche Bosheit, vor allem in Form des Wuchers, durch den die Menschen alles wagten, um diese Regionen bis ins Elend auszuschöpfen und zu berauben.[11]

Luther war sich auch der Auseinandersetzungen und Widersprüche auf wirtschaftlicher Ebene zwischen Menschen bzw. Interessengruppen aus verschiedenen Ständen bzw. aus dem gleichen Stand bewusst. Schon in

8 WA 1, 500, 21-37.
9 WA 42, 54, 18-30.
10 Ps 107, 33f.
11 WA 44, 658, 13. 29-38.

der Römerbriefvorlesung machte er auf den Kampf zwischen dem Bischof Wilhelm III. von Honstein (um 1470, 1506-1541) und der Stadt Straßburg in Sachen des Kanonikus Hepp von Kirchberg aufmerksam.[12] In derselben Vorlesung erwähnte er den damaligen Streit zwischen Vertretern des höheren Adels und der Bauern, weil erstere Ländereien in Besitz nahmen, die eigentlich dem Gemeinwesen gehörten.[13] Luther beschäftigte sich auch mit ökonomischen Auseinandersetzungen zwischen Angehörigen des Bürgertums. In einem Brief wandte er sich 1525 an Bürgermeister und Rat von Nürnberg wegen des Diebstahls von Teilen seiner Bibelübersetzung aus Wittenberger Druckereien durch in jener Stadt angesiedelte Drucker. Damit verhinderten diese Drucker die Verbreitung des Evangeliums.[14]

Der Wittenberger hatte klar vor Augen, dass die Spielregeln unter den bestehenden wirtschaftlichen Verhältnissen zunehmend durch außerlokale und sogar außerterritoriale Faktoren bestimmt waren. Gerade da, wo der Interdependenz und Internationalisierung der Wirtschaft die Benachteiligung und Ausbeutung einzelner Gruppen und Gemeinschaften im sozialen Gefüge entsprachen, stellte er die Beteiligung vom unrechten Handeln fest. Gerade deshalb machte er über die großen Handelsgesellschaften und -monopole sehr kritische Bemerkungen. Als Folge des Wuchers beobachtete er: Hatte jemand früher das ganze Jahr hindurch mit hundert Gulden seinen Unterhalt bestreiten können, so brauchte er um 1540 für dieselbe Zeitspanne dagegen mindestens doppel soviel. Obwohl sich die Wucherer in Leipzig, Augsburg und Frankfurt am Main befänden, wirke sich ihr Wucher spürbar auf den Wittenberger Markt oder die eigene Küche aus.[15]

Da das eigennützige wirtschaftliche Handeln immer eine ungerechte Güterverteilung im Gemeinwesen mit sich bringe, sei es zu verstehen, dass es auch im Fall von Überfluss Teuerung und Hunger gebe. So war das Jahr 1531 nach Luthers Meinung durch Gott im Überfluss mit Gütern gesegnet, aber die Leute hätten es verdorben.[16] Aus demselben Grund kam er 1540 zu der düsteren Auffassung, der Wucher hätte am Ende seines Lebens

12 WA 56, 479, Anm. 11.
13 WA 56, 190, 15-30.
14 WA Br 3, 577, 15 - 578, 21 (924).
15 WA 51, 417, 24-31.
16 WA 31 I, 432, 24-30.

die deutschen Länder zugrunde gerichtet. Die Meinung Senecas (um 4 v. Chr. - 65 n. Chr.), dass dort kein Raum für Rettung bleibt, wo allgemeine Sitte geworden ist, was vorher als Laster galt, treffe insbesondere auf die deutschen Territorien zu.[17]

II Handel

Öfters äußerte sich Luther über den Handel im Rahmen der Auslegung des siebenten Gebotes. Im Jahre 1518 nannte er den Betrug im Handel als das vierte Werk gegen dieses Gebot.[18] In der Schrift »Von den guten Werken« verstärkte er 1520 die Stellung der wirtschaftlichen Verbrechen unter den Sünden gegen dieses Gebot und bot eine Liste von einzelnen Machenschaften an:

> »Auch dieses Gebot fordert ein Werk, das sehr viele gute Werke umfaßt und vielen Lastern entgegenwirkt. Es heißt auf deutsch Freigebigkeit [Mildickeit]. Es bestehe darin, daß jedermann bereit ist, mit seinem Besitz zu helfen und zu dienen. Es streitet nicht allein gegen Diebstahl und Raub, sondern gegen alle Einbuße an zeitlichem Besitz, wie sie einer dem andern zufügen kann, z. B. durch Geiz, Wucher, Übersteuern, Übervorteilen und den Gebrauch von falscher Ware, falschem Maß und falschen Gewichten. Wer könnte all die raffinierten Erfindungen aufzählen, die sich täglich in allen Gewerben mehren, wodurch jedermann seinen Vorteil sucht zum Nachteil des anderen und das Gesetz vergißt, welches lautet: ›Was du willst, daß dir andere tun, das tu ihnen auch‹ (Matth. 7, 12).«[19]

In der 1524 erschienenen Schrift über Handel und Wucher beschrieb Luther dann sehr ausführlich jeden dieser Verstöße gegen den Willen Gottes und das Gesetz der Liebe. Theodor Strohm fasste sie folgenderweise zusammen:

»1. Jeder gibt das Seine, so teuer er kann, und orientiert sich nicht an einem aus Arbeitsaufwand und Beschaffungsrisiko genau ausgewiesenen Preis.

17 WA 51, 331, 21-25 ; Lucius Annaeus SENECA: Ac Lucilium epistolae morales 4, 10 (39), 6; DERS.: Ad Lucilium epistolae morales I-LXIX = An Lucilius: Briefe über Ethik 1-69/ übers., eingel. und mit Anm. vers. von Manfred Rosenbach. DA 1999, 310 / 311.

18 WA 1, 502, 20-26.

19 WA 6, 270, 27-36; zitiert aus Martin LUTHER: Evangelium und Leben/ bearb. von Horst Beintker. B 1983, 124. (Martin Luther Taschenausgabe; 4)

2. Es werden persönliche Bürgschaften geleistet, die geradezu zur Leib-eigenschaft führen müssen und in Gottes providentielles Herrschaftsrecht spekulativ eingreifen.

3. Wo man Geld oder Ware oder Gerät leiht und dafür mehr oder Bes-seres fordert, handelt es sich um Wucher, und der ist ›in allen Rechten verdammt‹. Alle, die fünf, sechs oder mehr aufs Hundert vom geliehenen Geld nehmen, sind Wucherer.

Aus diesen drei Quellen entspringen viele weitere Übel. Einige seien erwähnt:

1. Anstelle von Bargeschäften wird auf Zins verkauft, um größere Ge-winne zu erzielen. […].

2. Der Preis wird durch Zurückhalten der Ware (Austrocknen des Marktes) in die Höhe getrieben, um dadurch aus dem Mangel des Nächsten Kapital zu schlagen. […].

3. Die Ware wird aufgekauft, um den Preis willkürlich diktieren zu können (Monopolwirtschaft). […].

4. Man treibt Dumping-Preispolitik, um den Markt zu beherrschen. […].

5. Man verkauft Ware, über die man noch gar nicht verfügt, […], teurer als man sie schließlich erwirbt.

6. »gorgel stecher odder kelstecher« sind solche, die über angeworbene Zwischenkäufer in Zahlungsnot geratene Kaufleute um ihre Waren prellen, indem sie diese für bares Geld unter dem üblichen Preis aufkaufen.

7. Preisabsprachen und Kartellbildungen: […].

8. Einem in Not Geratenen wird die Ware auf Zins (also zu überdurch-schnittlichem Preis) verkauft, um sie ihm alsdann über einen angeworbenen Zwischenkäufer für bares Geld, dafür unter dem Normalpreis, wieder abzuhandeln. […].

9. Risikofreie Zinseinlagen.

10. Warenmanipulation (das Hübscheste zuoberst legen).«[20]

Die Stelle Dt 25,13 beziehe sich auf das Thema der Veränderung von Verträgen im Geschäftsverkehr, wie Luther in »Deuteronomion Mosi cum annotationibus« schrieb. Der Verkäufer sollte mit richtiger und äquivalenter

20 Theodor STROHM: Luthers Wirtschafts- und Sozialethik. In: Leben und Werk Martin Luthers von 1526 bis 1546/ im Auftrag des Theologischen Arbeitskreises für Reformati-onsgeschichtliche Forschung hrsg. von Helmar Junghans. 2. Aufl. Bd. 1. B 1985, 216.

Ware dem Geld des Käufers gegenüberstehen. Das sei von großer Bedeutung, denn hier finden unglaubliche Leichtfertigkeit und Betrug in Form von Verfälschung, Veränderung und Vermischung der Waren statt.[21] Andererseits identifizierte er bei Am 8, 46 die dort erwähnten Unterdrücker der Armen mit den Kaufleuten seiner Zeit. Mit diesem Wort strafe der Prophet den Hass gegen die religiösen Feiertage – weil man an ihnen nicht Handel treiben dürfe –, das Zurückhalten von Getreide, das Verringen des Maßes, das Steigern der Preise, das Verfälschen der Waage und das Verkaufen von Spreu für Korn.[22]

Luther verurteilte die unbegrenzte Macht, welche die Kaufleute durch ihre Aktivitäten im ökonomischen Bereich auf das gesamte Gemeinwesen ausübten. Sie betrachteten ihr Geld als Voraussetzung ihrer Macht und benutzten es, um sie zu erweitern. So stellte er 1541 fest:

> »Aber die Geitzwenste erwuchern, ergeitzen, rauben und stelen jre Göttliche ehre und herrschafft über die armen und dürftigen, Haben freude und lust dran, das sie von gelde reich, und andere arm, das sie mit gelde Herrschen, andere sie anbeten mussen.«[23]

Die Steigerung der Preise mittels bewusst herbeigeführter Verknappung von Nahrungsmitteln war für Luther Grund genug, die Urheber solcher Umstände als Räuber und Mörder zu bezeichnen.[24]

Nach Luthers Meinung, wie bereits erwähnt, bestünde die Hauptregel der Kaufleute darin, dass jeder seine Waren so teuer verkaufe, wie es nur möglich sei. Das Prinzip des Dienstes am Nächsten bliebe damit beiseite, und die Preise würden schon vom Ansatz her zum Nachteil, ja Schaden des Mitmenschen festgelegt.[25] Weder die vom Kaufmann geleistete Arbeit, noch die Qualität der Waren, noch die Risiken bei Ankauf und Transport spielten bei der Preisbildung eine Rolle, sondern nur die eigennützige Ausbeutung des anderen in seiner Not.[26] Nach Luthers Meinung sollte sich freilich der von einem Christen unternommene Handel auf die Not

---

21 WA 14, 719, 11-16.
22 WA 13, 151, 24 - 152, 6; vgl. auch 198, 1-16.
23 WA 51, 395, 19-30.
24 WA 51, 421, 29 - 422, 30.
25 WA 15, 294, 25-30.
26 WA 15, 295, 4-13.

und auf die Bedürfnisse des Nächsten ausrichten. Der Unterschied zu der oben genannten Praxis der Kaufleute seiner Zeit bestehe darin, dass sie sich durch Vorteil und Profit aus der vom Mitmenschen erlebten Situation der materiellen Abhängigkeit bereichern wollten und durch den Handel nicht das Ziel verfolgten, den Bedürftigen bei der Überwindung dieser Situation zu helfen.[27]

Nach Luthers Überzeugung übernimmt das Geld für viele Kaufleute eine ganz andere Bedeutung als die eines einfachen Zahlungs- und Tauschmittels. Vor allem zeigten die Bergpredigt Jesu[28] und die tägliche Erfahrung, inwiefern man das Geld nicht als Mittel dafür suche, um das Notwendige für die Bedürfnisse zu erwerben. Das Geld werde als Gegenstand mit Wert an sich gesucht. Das ständige und wachsende Anhäufen werde lebensnotwendig.[29] Hinter dieser Praxis stünde der Gedanke, der Kaufmann selber habe geschaffen, was er besitze. Deshalb halte er es für gerechtfertigt, die Preise seiner Waren zu steigern und den Markt nach seinen Gunsten zu manipulieren.[30]

Luther räumte zwar ein, dass die Kalkulation eines gerechten Preises nicht einfach sei. Das liege in der Natur des Handels. Ganz besonders für den Kaufmann bedeute das berufliche Leben ein ständiges Ringen mit dem eigenen Gewissen.[31] So lautet der Tenor eines am 12. Februar 1544 an Georg Spalatin (1484-1545) geschriebenen Briefes. Spalatin hatte Luther wegen der Preisfestlegung für Getreide durch christliche Kaufleute angefragt. Für Luther ließ sich diese Frage nicht mit einer exakten Definition lösen, weil es große Unterschiede in Bezug auf die Arten, die Zeiten, die Personen, die Orte, die Situationen oder die einzelnen Fälle gebe. Das Problem sollte daher dem Gewissen des einzelnen Kaufmannes überlassen werden, damit er sich unter Berücksichtigung des natürlichen Gesetzes – der Goldenen

27 WA 19, 657, 13-32. Siehe dazu Andreas Pawlas: Die lutherische Berufs- und Wirtschaftsethik: eine Einführung. NK 2000, 141-150; Hans-Jürgen Prien: Luthers Wirtschaftsethik. GÖ 1992, 110-118.

28 Mt 6, 20 f.

29 Vgl. WA 32, 441, 36 - 442, 3; 51, 375, 23-27.

30 Vgl. WA 31 I, 443, 27-31.

31 WA 15, 297, 21 f: »Denn zu solchen feyl [Fehlkalkulation des Preises] dringt dich die not vnd art des wercks / nicht der muttwille vnd geytz.« Über den Kaufmann und sein Gewissen vgl. auch WA 15, 296, 26-28.

Regel[32] – entscheide. Jemand mit gutem Gewissen sollte auch die Bi-
beltexte von Prv 11, 26 und Am 8, 5 wahrnehmen. Da Spalatin etwas über
Preisfestlegung im Zusammenhang mit dem Verhalten gerechter Leute – de
bonis – wissen möchte, beträfen beide Stellen eigentlich nicht seine Frage.
Zuletzt sollte ein jeder für sich in seinem Handeln die richtige Antwort bei
so unsicheren und nicht gesetzlich geregelten Dingen geben.[33]

Die Frage des Sündigens bei der Festlegung von Preisen bliebe ebenfalls
ungelöst, wenn die Kaufleute das zu Unrecht Erworbene für Arbeit der
Kirche stifteten. Es stimme nicht mit der Nächstenliebe überein, dass die
Kaufleute ihre Waren mit falschem Gewicht verkauften bzw. andere For-
men von Unrecht betrieben und Handwerker ihre Produkte immer mehr
verteuerten, damit sie »dar nach ein groschen odder drey umb Gottes wil-
len geben«. Nach Luthers Meinung behält immer noch Is 61, 8 Gültigkeit:
»Ich der Herr hab das recht lieb und bin feynd dem opffer das aus dem
raub ist.« Daher sollten betroffene Kaufleute und Handwerker, ehe sie ihre
»Opfer« vor den Altar brächten, sich der Lehre Christi gemäß[34] mit dem
Nächsten durch Worte und Tat versöhnen und das durch sie verursachte
Übel wiedergutmachen.[35]

Die meisten Kaufleute ignorieren Luther zufolge bei ihren Unterneh-
mungen die Bestimmungen des Evangeliums – vor allem die Nächstenliebe –, sodass er selber sich niemals große Hoffnungen machte, durch
seine Vorschläge und seine Kritik die ungerechten Verhältnisse im ökonomischen und sozialen Gefüge wesentlich zu verbessern.[36] Das war jedoch
für ihn kein Grund, seine prophetische Aufgabe der Anklage der Habsucht
aufzugeben. Luther fühlte sich verpflichtet, die verschiedenen Formen des
Betrugs im Handel zu enttarnen, insbesondere wenn Kaufleute christliche
und biblische Motive zum Verdecken verbrecherischer Machenschaften
ausnutzten. Das Opfern für die Kirche aus ungerechtem Gewinn und die
damit verbundene Entschuldigung wurden bereits erwähnt. Die Kaufleute
könnten ihren »kauffgeytz« auch nicht mit dem biblischen Vorbild Jose-

32 Mt 7, 12.
33 WA Br 10, 532, 7-17 (3970).
34 Mt 5, 23.
35 WA 19, 324, 27 - 325, 9. 15-22.
36 WA 15, 293, 16-28; 51, 331, 21-25.

phs[37] rechtfertigen. Denn mit dem Anhäufen von Nahrungsmitteln habe Joseph auf das Überleben der Menschen gezielt und die weitere Existenz Ägyptens gesichert. Die Kaufleute seiner Zeit dagegen suchten seiner Ansicht nach den eigenen Vorteil, ohne darauf zu achten, ob das zum materiellen Verderben der Bevölkerung beitrüge oder nicht.[38]

Die Handelsgesellschaften müssten als »eyttel rechte Monopolia« beurteilt werden.[39] Für Luther gab es zum einen Teuerungen, die natürliche Ursachen hatten, und zum anderen Teuerungen, die mit Absicht durch solche Personen und Gruppen verursacht würden, die auf diese Weise größere Gewinne erzielten. Er beschäftigte sich am intensivsten mit der letzteren Art von Teuerung. So erwähnte er z. B. in einem am 9. April 1539 datierten Brief an Kurfürst Johann Friedrich (1503, 1532-1547, 1554), sowohl die Teuerung des vergangenen als auch die des laufenden Jahres, die sich nicht so sehr aus Mangel, sondern mehr durch den Einfluss der reichen »Junker« abgespielt hätten. Luther nahm die Anschuldigung auf, dass die Adligen das gesamte Getreide aufgekauft hätten, um mit den Preisen spekulieren zu können.[40] Eine natürliche Ursache für eine Teuerung war für den Wittenberger das extreme Bevölkerungswachstum. Wenn die Bevölkerung zu stark anwachse, entstünden Teuerung und zuletzt Hunger. Die Teuerung bringe »Buben« mit sich, die »geizig werden«. In dieser Hinsicht wäre ihm die Pest lieber als Teuerung, denn unter weniger Leuten käme es nicht zu so großer Verknappung bei der Versorgung mit Nahrung.[41] Theologisch gesehen spielte Teuerung für Luther eine große Rolle als Teil der Strafe Gottes. Wenn die Gemeinschaft nichts mehr für Schulen und Kirchen geben wolle, weil »geytz« und »sorge der narung« die Leute regierten, verdienten sie Katastrophen wie eine Teuerung.[42] In solchen Fällen konnten Luthers Äußerungen zu Themen der Wirtschaft sehr häufig eschatologische Züge übernehmen.

37 Gn 41, 36.
38 WA 15, 306, 19-23.
39 WA 15, 312, 1-4.
40 WA Br 8, 404, 9-11 (3319). Das war Luthers Meinung auch in der 1540 erschienenen Wucherschrift, vgl. WA 51, 395, 19-26.
41 WA Br 8, 612, 5-13 (3416), Luther an Sixt Ölhafen am 26. November 1539 aus [Wittenberg].
42 WA 15, 361, 15-18.

III Geldwirtschaft und Wucher

Luther besaß ein umfangreiches Verständnis für die Bedeutung des Wortes »Wucher«. Wucher im breiteren Sinne bedeutete für ihn sowohl die Zinsforderung als Gegenleistung für ein Gelddarlehen – nach der philosophisch-theologischen Tradition »Wucher« im engeren Sinne – als auch jede Preissteigerung und das Ausnutzen einer Notlage durch Zurückhalten oder Aufkauf von Waren. So nannte Luther z. B. 1540 in seiner Wucherschrift an die Pfarrherren alle diejenigen »Wůcherer«, die fünf Prozent oder mehr in der Form von Zinsen auf das geliehene Geld forderten. Sie seien »des Geitzs oder Mammon abgottissche Diener« und gingen der Seligkeit verlustig, wenn sie nicht Buße täten. Der Wucher bestehe aber auch darin, den Preis für ein zu verkaufendes Produkt über seinen realen Wert hinaus festzulegen.[43] An vielen Stellen in Luthers Schrifttum ist es jedoch für den Leser eindeutig, dass er vom Wucher im engeren Sinne sprach.

Beim Zinsnehmen handelte es sich damals um eine brisante Frage. Denn noch immer galt das kanonische Zinsverbot, obgleich die wirtschaftliche Entwicklung – vor allem im Fernhandel – zu einer schnellen Ausbreitung und Intensivierung von Bank- und Geldgeschäften führte. Für Theologen war das Nachdenken über Kreditgeschäfte – und über Wirtschaftsthemen überhaupt – gerade in einer Epoche selbstverständlich, in der die Naturalwirtschaft zunehmend durch die Geldwirtschaft abgelöst wurde.[44]

Großes Ansehen gewannen am Anfang des 16. Jahrhunderts die Bemühungen Johann Ecks (1486-1543), dieser Frage mehr Aufmerksamkeit zu schenken.[45] Schon Konrad Summenhart (um 1450-1502), Ecks Lehrer in Tübingen, und vor ihm Gabriel Biel (1410-1495), hatten versucht, den Begriff »Wucher«, wie er in der Tradition der Kirche verstanden wurde, in Bezug auf die Kreditgeschäfte einzugrenzen und neu zu definieren. Vor allem

---

43 WA 51, 332, 34 - 333, 21.

44 Vgl. vgl. Hans-Günther ASSEL: Das kanonische Zinsverbot und der »Geist« des Frühkapitalismus in der Wirtschaftsethik bei Eck und Luther. Erlangen [1948], Teil 1. – Erlangen, Univ., Phil. Fak., Diss., 1948.

45 Vgl. Assel: Das kanonische Zinsverbot …, Teil 3; Heiko Augustinus OBERMAN: Werden und Wertung der Reformation: vom Wegestreit zum Glaubenskampf. TÜ 1977, 161-200.

Summenhart legte großen Wert auf die Intention des Kapitalgebers beim Geldleihen, die vor der Öffentlichkeit unbekannt bleibe. Dem äußeren Anschein nach sei eine risikolose Partnerschaft zwischen Geldgeber und Schuldner nicht von der Sünde des Wuchers zu unterscheiden, obwohl sie in der Tat als partnerschaftlicher Kapitalvertrag grundsätzlich legitim sei, denn beide Vertragspartner seien am Kapital beteiligt. Um das Gewissen des Nächsten nicht zu verwirren, der in seiner Unkenntnis diese Form von Geschäften für Wucher hielt, sollten sie jedoch vermieden werden. Damit zeigte Summenhart seine seelsorgerliche Intention, das Gewissen der an Kreditgeschäften Beteiligten zu entlasten, ohne diese jedoch im Rahmen des öffentlichen Lebens zu billigen.[46]

Eck führte die Konzeption seines Meisters fort, jedoch mit dem Unterschied, dass er das Argument des Anstoßes für die Außenstehenden zurückwies. Beim Zinsnehmen sollte nach seiner Meinung immer die gute Intention der am Geschäft Beteiligten und nicht der verwerfliche Vorsatz zum Wuchertreiben vorausgesetzt werden. Schon 1514 schlug er einen Drei-Stufen-Vertrag vor, in dem kein Wucher vorhanden sein sollte. Zuerst müsse von beiden Parteien ein erstes Abkommen zur Gründung der Partnerschaft geschlossen werden; danach sei ein zweites Abkommen zu vereinbaren, wodurch die ursprüngliche Beteiligung – fünfprozentiger Zinssatz – zur Investition werde, ohne jedoch die Unsicherheit und das Risiko auszuschließen. Zuletzt müsse eine dritte Vereinbarung getroffen werden, die das Anrecht auf einen möglichen, aber nur erhofften, festen und sicheren Gewinn – größer als fünf Prozent – einräume.[47]

Am 15. Juli 1515 veranstaltete Eck in Bologna eine Disputation über das Zinsnehmen, wo er seine Thesen – nach eigener Auskunft – mit großem Erfolg vertrat. Kritik gegen ihn übten Mitglieder der humanistischen Bewegung, insbesondere Angehörige des Nürnberger Kreises. Die Nichtübereinstimmung mit dem Gedankengut der Antike und der Kirchenväter

---

46 Oberman: Werden und Wertung ..., 171-174; Hugo Ott: Zur Wirtschaftsethik des Konrad Summenhart. Vierteljahresschrift für Sozial- und Wirtschaftsgeschichte 53 (1966), 1-27.

47 Oberman: Werden und Wertung ..., 174 f; vgl. besonders zu Ecks Auffassungen über das Zinsnehmen Assel: Das kanonische Zinsverbot ..., Teil 3; J[oseph] Schneid: Dr. Johann Eck und das kirchliche Zinsverbot. Historisch-politische Blätter für das katholische Deutschland 108 (1891), 241-259. 321-335. 473-496. 570-589. 659-681. 789-810.

in dieser Frage, aber vor allem das immer wieder von Humanisten betonte enge Verhältnis zwischen Eck und dem Haus der Fugger, bildeten den Ausgangspunkt dieser kritischen Infragestellung des seelsorgerlichen Bemühens von Eck. Der Ingolstädter Professor – trotz des Fehlens von Belegen gab es die Vermutung, Eck habe diese Stelle mit Hilfe von Jakob Fugger (1459-1525) bekommen – hatte Kontakte zu dem Augsburger Bankhaus über Konrad Peutinger (1465-1547). Eine erste Gelegenheit über die Zinsfrage zu disputieren hatte er in dem mit den Fuggern verbundenen Karmeliterkonvent zu Augsburg genutzt. Zur direkten Konfrontation zwischen Humanisten und Eck kam es im Oktober 1514, als er sich eine Disputation über dasselbe Thema in Ingolstadt wünschte, die aber durch den von Christoph Scheurl (1481-1542) beratenen Gabriel von Eyb (1455, 1496-1535), Bischof von Eichstatt und Kanzler der dortigen Universität, untersagt wurde. Die Reise Ecks samt einer Delegation 1515 nach Bologna wurde durch Fugger finanziert.

Luther kannte die oben erwähnten Auseinandersetzungen um die Kreditgeschäfte.[48] Er selbst aber äußerte sich in seiner Polemik gegen Eck anscheinend niemals explizit zu den Inhalten von dessen Lehre. Luther verurteilte mehrfach die wirtschaftliche Übermacht der Fugger und ihren Gewinn bei Machenschaften mit kirchlichem Besitz, erwähnte aber Eck nicht in diesem Kontext. Dennoch lässt sich aufgrund von Luthers starker Betonung der bestimmenden Rolle vom Selbstinteresse in Handel und Kreditwesen schlussfolgern, dass er keineswegs die grundsätzliche Voraussetzung einer guten Intention seitens der Geschäftspartner – wie Eck es wollte – als theologisch sachgemäß anerkannt hätte.

Von großem Gewicht für Luthers Erfahrung in der Frage des Zinsnehmens war die Auseinandersetzung zwischen Wittenberger Theologen – Luther und Melanchthon – und dem aus Basel stammenden ehemaligen Dominikaner und damaligen Eisenacher Hofprediger Jakob Strauß (um 1480 – vor 1530) von 1523/24.[49]

Im Gegensatz zu Eck, der die Frage von dem Standpunkt des Kreditgebers her erörterte, dachte der durch die bedrückende Situation vieler Leute in Eisenach beeindruckte Strauß – ähnlich wie Luther – von der Perspektive

---

48 Vgl. Ulrich von Hutten: Schriften/ hrsg. von Eduard Böcking. Bd. 1. L 1859, 200. 787.
49 Vgl. Hermann Barge: Luther und der Frühkapitalismus. GÜ, 1951, 19 f; Joachim Rogge: Der Beitrag des Predigers Jakob Strauß zur frühen Reformationsgeschichte. B 1957, 71-86.

der Verschuldeten aus. In 51 Thesen legte er 1523 seine Ansicht dar und stellte grundsätzlich fest, dass die Meinung von Päpsten und Konzilien niemals die von Gott gegebenen Gebote überwinden könnte. Als biblische Grundlage seiner Auffassung über das von Christen zu fordernde Verhalten gegenüber dem Zinsnehmen dienten Dt 15, 2 und L 6, 35. »Zins« und »Wucher« hielt Strauß für identische Begriffe. Der Wucher stünde seiner Natur nach gegen die Nächstenliebe und das göttliche Gebot und sei gerade deshalb eine schwerwiegende und offenbare Todsünde. Die These, die am stärksten die Polemik anregte und später auch von Luther angegriffen wurde, war die 17.: »Vnselig und des glaubens gar entsetzet ist der, der yn seyner armuet wuecher zu raichen bewylliget.«[50]

Die Ansichten von Strauß verbreiteten sich schnell und wurden von vielen aufgenommen und in die Praxis umgesetzt. Unter den damit benachteiligten Kreditgebern verurteilten die Vertreter geistlicher Einrichtungen, die ihre Existenz dem regelmäßigen Zinsempfang verdankten, die von seinen Auffassungen ausgelösten Umstände am heftigsten. Die Mehrheit des Eisenacher Rates und Herzog Johann von Sachsen (1468-1532) schienen auf seiner Seite zu stehen. Auf Anfrage des Kanzlers Gregor Brück (1485-1557), der angeblich durch den Kurprinzen Johann Friedrich dazu bewegt worden war – beide vertraten eine andere Auffassung als Strauß –, äußerte sich Luther im Oktober 1523 zu den Thesen. Obwohl auch er für die Abschaffung des Zinskaufs war, fand er das Handeln von Strauß als übereilt. Besonders die Auffassung, Zahlung von Zinsen sei Sünde, könne man nicht verteidigen. Der Zinskauf sei eine sehr komplizierte Materie. Er habe keinen Vorschlag dazu, aber damit so umzugehen, wie Strauß es fordere, sei nicht ratsam.[51]

Anfang Juni 1524 milderte Strauß seine Stellung in einer weiteren Schrift. Die Schuldner sollten nicht von sich aus zum Unrecht des Zinskaufs beitragen, indem sie die Zinszahlung unterließen. Darüber hinaus aktualisierte er die mosaischen Bestimmungen über das Sabbatjahr und das Halljahr in deutlicher Anlehnung an Luthers 1520 erschienenen »[Großen] Sermon von dem Wucher«.[52] Strauß lehnte den Vorschlag Johann Fried-

50 Vgl. FLUGSCHRIFTEN DER FRÜHEN REFORMATIONSBEWEGUNG: (1518-1525)/ hrsg. von Adolf Laube; Sigrid Looß. Bd. 2. B 1983, 1073-1077, bes. 1074, 6 f.
51 WA Br 3, 176-179 (673), Luther an Georg Brück am 18. Oktober 1523 aus Wittenberg.
52 Jakob STRAUSS: Daß Wucher zu nehmen und zu geben unserem christlichen Glauben

richs ab, sich mit Luther und Melanchthon in Wittenberg über diese Frage auseinanderzusetzen. Ihm wäre ein öffentliches Gespräch lieber. Auf eine Anfrage von Johann Friedrich – ebenfalls im Rahmen der Gutachten um die Äußerungen von Strauß –, ob ein Fürst den Zinskauf zulassen dürfe, sprach sich Luther für dessen Neuregelung aus. Da es sich aber beim Zinskauf um eine allgemeine Konvention handele, sollte der Schuldner seiner Zahlungspflicht nachkommen, die Verweigerung der Zinszahlung keineswegs von der Obrigkeit angenommen und geschützt werden. Der Zinssatz sollte auf keinen Fall höher als fünf Prozent liegen.[53] Auch nach der Milderung seiner Auffassung über das Zinsnehmen in der zweiten Schrift stand Strauß nach Luthers Ansicht unter dem Verdacht, das Volk zum Aufruhr zu bewegen. Ohne Zweifel hatte aber der Eisenacher Wucherstreit entscheidenden Anteil an der Herausgabe von Luthers Schrift »Von Kaufshandlung und Wucher« im Jahr 1524.

Luther selbst verurteilte – mit wenigen Ausnahmen – alle Formen von Kreditgeschäften. In der Wucherschrift des Jahres 1540 charakterisierte er sie mit den Worten »mut williger, Geitziger, unnotiger Wucher«, weil sie nur mit der Sünde zu tun hätten und mitnichten zum Guten der Gemeinde beitrügen.[54] In derselben Schrift kritisierte er die Ausrede mancher Leute, dass die fünf, sechs oder zehn Prozent Zinsen, die der Gläubiger für ein Darlehen von hundert Gulden bekomme, lediglich ein Geschenk des Schuldners, ein Zeichen seiner Dankbarkeit sei. Für Luther offenbarte gerade dies den Versuch vonseiten des »Geitzwanst«, seinen Gewinn und Wucher in Form eines Geschenkes zu tarnen. Gewinn und Wucher waren aber aus dem Opfer des »dürfftigen in seiner nott« entstanden.[55]

Die von Luther am meisten kritisierte Modalität des Kreditgeschäftes war der Zinskauf, eine Form, das kanonische Zinsverbot zu umgehen. Dieses Kreditgeschäft war als Kaufgeschäft getarnt. Der Kreditgeber erwarb für das bei ihm vom Eigentümer eines Grundstückes entliehene Geld einen

entgegen sei. In: Flugschriften der Bauernkriegszeit/ hrsg. von Adolf Laube; Hans Werner Seiffert. 2. Ausgabe. Berlin 1978, 178-189; WA 15, 322, 10-18.

53 WA Br 3, 307, 33-59 (753), Luther an Herzog Johann Friedrich von Sachsen am 18. Juni 1524 aus Wittenberg; 310, 23-43 (754), Herzog Johann Friedrich an Luther am 24. Juni 1524 aus Weimar.

54 WA 51, 373, 31-33.

55 WA 51, 341, 27 - 342, 18.

Anteil an jenem Ertrag, den der Kreditempfänger durch seine Arbeit auf diesem Grundstück erwirtschaften musste, den sogenannten Zins. In der Form des »Zinskaufs auf Wiederkauf« verpflichtete sich der Schuldner, außer dem geliehenen Geld auch bestimmte Zinsen zu zahlen, die der Kreditgeber »kaufte«.

Bereits in seiner 1518 veröffentlichten Reihe von Predigten über den Dekalog erläuterte Luther die päpstliche Intention, mit der der Zinskauf – contractus reemptionis – erlaubt worden wäre. Sie bestünde darin, 1. alten Leuten, Kindern und Kranken eine Überlebensmöglichkeit zu schaffen; 2. den Dienern des Wortes – Geistlichen, Prälaten, und Priestern – gleichwie 3. den Dienern des Gemeinwesens – Fürsten, Räten, Bürgermeistern eine Unterhaltungsform anzubieten, damit sie über die notwendige Zeit zur Erfüllung ihrer Amtspflichten verfügten. Tatsächlich aber wird nach Luthers Ansicht durch den Zinskauf viel mehr dem Eigennutz gedient. Mit den Zinsen wollten die meisten ihren Gewinn erhöhen und darüber hinaus ohne Arbeit und Risiko Sicherheit in Bezug auf die Güter erlangen.[56]

Die Vorsteher des Gemeindekastens in Leisnig sollten genau überprüfen, ob die aus ehemaligen geistlichen Einrichtungen zum allgemeinen Nutzen gesammelten Güter und Gelder ihren Ursprung im »zinßkauff auff widderkauff« gehabt hätten. Wenn ja, sei das Grund genug, sie zu verwerfen.[57]

Luther schloss aus theologischer Überzeugung das Gelddarlehen auf Zinsen als wirtschaftliche Tätigkeit von den durch den Glauben gebilligten Möglichkeiten aus. Für ihn war dies lediglich eine Modalität für solche Menschen – z. B. Witwen oder Kranke –, die ihren Unterhalt sich nicht durch Arbeit erwerben konnten. Bei allen übrigen Gelddarlehen auf Zinsen gehe es immer um die Habsucht: »Sonst wo es ein mut williger, Geitziger, unnotiger Wucher were, der auff eitel handel und gewinst gericht were, da wolt ich nicht mit stimmen (Denn Leihen sol und kan kein handel, gewerbe odder gewinst sein) noch raten, […].«[58]

Die gewaltige Ausbreitung der Praxis des Zinskaufes demonstrierte Luther zufolge, wie sehr man die evangelische Lehre in Bezug auf den Umgang mit Hab und Gut vernachlässigte. Wenn das Gebot Christi – die

56 WA 1, 505, 15-31.
57 WA 12, 14, 25-35.
58 WA 51, 373, 31-33.

Güter »fahren lassen«, geben und leihen[59] – mit größerer Rücksicht befolgt würde, könnte der Zinskauf nicht so allgemein und intensiv im Gebrauch sein. Luther beobachtete, dass sogar für sehr geringe Geldsummen eine Zinsleistung gefordert wurde, die über den gesamten ausgeliehenen Betrag hinausging:

»Er [der Kreditgeber] reyst aber eyn yn die groschen und pfennig, [...], und will doch nit geytz genent seyn.«[60] Für Luther war der Zinskauf ein neuerfundenes Geschäft, bei dem das praktizierte Unrecht im Umgang mit Geld und Gütern verborgen blieb. Der Zinskauf spiele sich deshalb sehr oft auf als ein »frumen vnd getrewen schutz herrn des verdampten geytzs vnd wucher«.[61]

Neben der Kritik des Zinskaufes als Tarnung vom Wucher setzte sich der Wittenberger auch mit der vom Geldgeber im Zinskauf gesuchten Sicherheit auseinander. Luther meinte, dass sich Zinskauf und Wucher sehr ähnlich seien. Für ihn sei der Zinskauf gegen Gott, die Liebe und das Naturrecht, denn damit suche der Geldgeber seinen Vorteil beim Mitmenschen in seiner Not. Auf diese Weise zeige sich das Unrecht, in dem der Kreditgeber im Zinskauf allein auf die Sicherheit seiner Zinsen und Güter achte und nicht auf dem Wohlstand seines Nächsten.[62]

Luther protestierte auch gegen andere Erscheinungen im damaligen Umgang mit finanzieller Verschuldung. In einem am 2. Januar 1540 an Gregor Brück datierten Brief forderte er konsequente Maßnahmen seitens der Obrigkeit gegen die Praxis des »Einreitens«. Beim »Einreiten«[63] sollte ein Schuldner, der seinen Verbindlichkeiten gegenüber dem Gläubiger nicht genügte, dessen Gäste empfangen und bewirten. Normalerweise bedeutete dies den totalen Ruin des Schuldners, der weder die früheren Schulden abzahlen noch sich den Aufwand der Verpflegung des Gläubigers leisten konnte. Die Fürsten seien nach Luthers Meinung verpflichtet, das »Einreiten« zu verhindern, sonst machten sie sich selber zu Teilnehmern dieser

59 Mt 5, 40-42.
60 WA 6, 6, 32-38.
61 WA 15, 294, 29 - 295, 2; 6, 51, 12-19.
62 WA 6, 8, 14-21.
63 Auf Lateinisch: »obstagium«, auf Deutsch: »Einlager«, »Geiselschaft« oder »Leistung«; WA Br 9, 3f, Anm. 3.

ungerechten Praxis und sollten die Verantwortung aus dem damit entstandenen Schaden tragen. Der Wittenberger bedauerte, dass die Menschen sich auf diese Weise untereinander fraßen, aufrieben und verdarben.[64]

Der Lebensunterhalt der Mönche im Augustinerkloster von Wittenberg war teilweise – wie es in der Regel bei anderen Klöstern ebenfalls geschah – durch die Einnahme von Zinsen für vom Kloster verliehene Geldsummen garantiert. Infolge des reformatorischen Umbruches fühlten sich die Schuldner auch dort berechtigt, ihren Verpflichtungen nicht mehr nachzukommen.

Schon im Mai 1522 zahlten die Schuldner des Klosters keine Zinsen mehr. Um Malz zum Bierbrauen kaufen zu können, machte der Prior Eberhard Brisger († 1545) Schulden, für die sich Luther verbürgte. Das Kloster musste seinerseits jährlich 20 Gulden an Christoph Blanck († 1541), einen Kanoniker des Wittenberger Allerheiligenstifts, zahlen, war aber dazu nicht in der Lage, weil die eigenen Zinseinnahmen ausblieben. Im November 1523 bat Luther den Kurfürsten, einen Zahlungsbefehl an Christoph von Bressen auf Motterwitz ergehen zu lassen, der dem Kloster Zinszahlungen im Wert von 90 Gulden schuldete. Er sei der letzte Insasse des Klosters. Der ebenfalls noch verbliebene Brisger, stünde im Begriff zu heiraten. Da das Kloster später auf jeden Fall unter die Macht des Kurfürsten käme, erbitte er aus diesen Einkünften seinen Lebensunterhalt bis zu seinem Tode. Luthers Forderung in eigener Sache stimmt mit seinen Empfehlungen zur Versorgung von Insassen aus in Auflösung befindlichen Klöstern in der Vorrede zur »Ordnung eines gemeinen Kasten« überein.[65]

Später nahm Luther Stellung zu seiner persönlichen Beziehung zum Kreditwesen. In einem Brief vom 1. Februar 1527 antwortete er Brisger, der ihn um ein Darlehen von 8 Gulden gebeten hatte. Der Wittenberger beschrieb sehr ausführlich seine finanzielle Lage. Er sei auch wegen des teuren Haushaltes sehr verschuldet und überrascht vom Ausmaß der Schulden Brisgers. Es sei richtig, dass Brisger diesen falschen Schritt der Verschuldung bereue und ihn als göttliche Versuchung akzeptiere, denn auf diese Weise werde er nicht von Gott in einer solchen Lage allein gelassen. Infolge der eigenen Unvorsichtigkeit sei Luther selbst an mehreren Stellen

---

64 WA Br 9, 3, 6-30 (3428).
65 WA Br 3, 173, 4-11 (670); 185, 28 - 186, 37 (681); WA 12, 12, 29 - 13, 7.

mit insgesamt beinahe 100 Gulden verschuldet. Dies sei seine Strafe, aber er hoffe, vom Herrn wieder befreit zu werden. Lukas Cranach (1472-1553) und Christian Döring (1490-1533) hätten ihm sogar untersagt, weiter die Funktion eines Bürgen beim gemeinen Kasten zu übernehmen. Zwar könnte er, um an Brisger die gewünschte Summe auszuleihen, Wertgegenstände als Unterpfand hingeben, wie er es schon mit drei Pokalen für 50 Gulden und einem vierten für 12 Gulden getan habe. Doch wäre das nichts weiter, als Almosen von fremdem Gut zu geben. Er sei bereit, mit anderen Leuten darüber zu reden, welche die Bitte von Brisger vielleicht erfüllen könnten. Nach dem Standpunkt Luthers kann seine Entscheidung in Bezug auf den Wunsch seines Freundes nicht als Knauserei – parcitas – verurteilt werden, denn sogar mit dem von anderen ausgeliehenen Geld ginge er verschwenderisch um.[66]

Die Diskussion, ob Luther sich entweder als mittelalterlicher oder als neuzeitlicher Denker mit Themen beschäftigte, die heute der Wirtschaft zugerechnet werden, stand sehr oft im Vordergrund sowohl der wirtschafts- und sozialgeschichtlichen als auch der theologiegeschichtlichen Forschung.[67] Eine Frage, die möglicherweise durch den Fortschrittsglauben bestimmt wurde, der die Wissenschaft für eine lange Zeit prägte. Der Stellenwert dieser Diskussion sollte relativiert werden. Die Entfaltung von wirtschaftstheoretischen Auffassungen in der Zeit vor und nach der ersten Hälfte des 16. Jahrhunderts erlaubt nicht die Fixierung einer angeblichen Zäsur zwischen Mittelalter und Neuzeit, weil ihre Grundlinien – trotz der einzelnen Nuancen und Differenzen bei den verschiedenen Denkern – vielmehr durch Kontinuität bestimmt werden.

Luther setzte sich als Ausleger der Heiligen Schrift mit den Problemen seiner Zeit auseinander, um das Unrecht anzuklagen und zu bekämpfen. Er wollte damit konkrete »Besserung« erzielen und fragte sich keineswegs, ob er mit seinem Handeln bestimmte Entwicklungen hemme oder ob seine theoretische Begründung für dieses Handeln rückständig sei. Seine

66 WA Br 4, 164 f (1078).

67 Vgl. Ricardo RIETH: »Habsucht« bei Martin Luther: ökonomisches und theologisches Denken, Tradition und soziale Wirklichkeit im Zeitalter der Reformation. Weimar 1996, 15-40.

realistische und nicht skeptische bzw. negative Überzeugung, dass die Welt anderenfalls zugrunde gehe, lässt sich ebenfalls nicht unbedingt als »mittelalterlich« bezeichnen.

Insbesondere heute gewinnt Luthers Überzeugung viel an Aktualität: Zunehmend fühlt sich die Menschheit herausgefordert, das Vorhaben der Schaffung einer »moderneren« und durch »Wohlstand« geprägten Welt für ihre Nachkommenschaft preiszugeben und an seine Stelle das Vorhaben zu setzen, ihrer Nachkommenschaft überhaupt etwas von der Welt übrigzulassen.

Luther's New View on Marriage, Sexuality and the Family

By Jane Strohl

»[…] for God has created man and woman so that they are to come together with pleasure, willingly and gladly with all their hearts. And bridal love or the will to marry is a natural thing, implanted and inspired by God. This is the reason bridal love is so highly praised in the Scriptures and is often cited as an example of Christ and his church.«[1] »To be sure, when I consider marriage, only the flesh seems to be there. Yet my father must have slept with my mother and made love to her, and they were nevertheless godly people. All the patriarchs and prophets did likewise. The longing of a man for a woman is God's creation – that is to say, when nature's sound, not when it's corrupted as it is among Italians and Turks.«[2]

Luther's early reflections on marriage concentrate on its importance as a defense against lust and as a safe channel for the expression of human sexuality.[3] His anti-monastic polemic is constant.[4] He distinguishes sharply between

---

1 LW 46, 304 ≙ WA 30 III, 236, 9-14.

2 LW 54, 161 ≙ WA TR 2, 167, 3-7 (1659).

3 »The concupiscence or fleshly self-centeredness of man forces him into all kinds of im-morality and unchastity. Even though ›concupiscence‹ is described by Luther basically in terms of egoism rather than sexual lust, he is still impressed by the frightening ease with which man's sinful personality can unleash such uncontrollable passions«; William H. LAZARETH: Luther on the Christian home: an application of the social ethics of the Reformation. Phil 1960, 7. It is important to note that rapacious sexual desire is only one manifestation of the incurvatus in se nature of the fallen human being. One must not minimize the danger such desire presents, but one must see it as one among many ways in which concupiscence manifests itself at the expense of the neighbor. Luther himself puts lust into perspective: »Youth feels its own evils; then manhood does. For the flesh is plagued by lust, the heart by greed, wrath, hatred, and similar emotions, which trouble the mind in various ways. But these conflicts involve the Second Table *and gradually subside.* Therefore when the struggle seems to be over, this new and sharper battle involving the First Table confronts us, the fight against presumption, vainglory, and the confidence we have in ourselves because of our gifts«; LW 3, 6 (emphasis added) ≙ WA 42, 552, 23-29.

4 Roman Catholic teaching with regard to the social and spiritual good of marriage and

the true charism of chastity and what he denounces as the sham, brutally imposed celibacy of the monastic life. If God favors a person with the former, there is reason for rejoicing, not because it exempts one from the whole difficult business of sexual relationship but because, as Paul points out, it frees one from the entanglements of marriage for uninterrupted service and worship of God.[5] Luther insists, however, that one cannot by one's own efforts generate such a calling; it comes only as a divine gift and quite rarely at that. Those who take upon themselves vows of celibacy that they prove unable to keep had far better marry, thereby honoring their created nature and corralling their sinful need. Christians remain male and female like other people and have the same innate desire to reproduce their kind. Despite the sin that infects the longing of male and female for one another, it remains in God's eyes a good part of the creation.

The view of marriage as the antidote to sin predominates in the early years.[6] Over time, however, Luther also speaks of marriage as a divine calling. It is no longer chiefly about what marriage prevents; it is about what it allows to happen in terms of obedience to God and service to the neighbor. Despite Luther's praise of the celibate state – in contrast to the monastic – one ultimately comes away with the impression that the entanglements and challenges of married life generate the discipleship that is most pleasing to God. Luther emphasizes the holiness of the married estate,[7] but he insists that it is a civil ordinance established as part of

the sanctity of procreation mirrored Protestant positions in many respects. What is offensive to Luther is the hypocrisy of honoring marriage while relegating it to a status far inferior to that of monastic celibacy.

5 LW 44, 264 ≙ WA 8, 585, 12-17.

6 »Although the remedial and defensive coloration of this initial view was to be complemented after 1523 by a more positive emphasis, it is important to note that it enjoyed virtually exclusive stress for some six years after the posting of the *Theses*, and even thereafter continued to remain prominent in Luther's view for the rest of his life«; Lazareth: Luther on the Christian home, 208 f.

7 »[…] Luther allows all human occupations and institutions a *relative* autonomy in the realm of creation, and yet maintains that ›in, with, and under‹ them the living Word of God is at work transforming them into divine vocations for all who have the faith to ›see‹. In this manner, the realms of redemption and creation are neither separated nor equated, but permitted to remain in fruitful tension until the Day of Judgment«; Lazareth: Luther on the Christian home, 161.

God's rule of creation.[8] Marriage and attendant concerns – betrothals, divorce – should be handled exclusively by the temporal authorities. Luther rejects the church's teaching that marriage is a sacrament and denounces as illegitimate and abusive its involvement in the regulation of marital matters. The only proper engagement on the church's part is with issues of conscience, and then pastors can only advise troubled souls embroiled in marital conflicts, not legislate.

For Luther the vocation of husband or wife is inseparable from that of parent, and ultimately he holds the latter to be the more important. He speaks often of the word of God that is joined to marriage and is the one thing that distinguishes it from fornication, for the two look the same in their externals.[9] He appeals to several different biblical passages: »It is not good that the man should be alone; I will make him a helper fit for him«;[10] »Therefore a man leaves his father and his mother and cleaves to his wife, and they become one flesh«;[11] »What therefore God has joined together, let no one put asunder«;[12] but most often he makes reference to God's command to the man and woman at creation, »Be fruitful and multiply«.[13] There is for Luther no greater blessing than the birth of children into a family and no weightier responsibility for husband and wife than becoming effective parents. He even links their eternal salvation to their diligence in this vocation.[14] The parent-

---

8 In contrast to monasticism: »For though [marriage] is a worldly estate, yet does it have God's word in its favor and was not invented or instituted by men, as was the estate of the monks and nuns. Therefore, it should be accounted a hundred times more spiritual than the monastic estate, which in truth should be considered the most worldly and fleshly of all, because it was invented and instituted by flesh and blood, out of worldly reasons and considerations«; LW 53, 112 ≙ WA 30 III, 75, 15-21.

9 WA 34 I, 53, 19-30.

10 Gn 2, 18. All citations are from the »New Oxford annotated Bible. Rev. standard version«.

11 Gn 2, 24.

12 Mt 19, 6.

13 Gn 1, 28

14 »Think what deadly harm you do when you are negligent and fail to bring up your children to be useful and godly. You bring upon yourself sin and wrath, thus earning hell by the way you have reared your own children, no matter how holy and upright you may be otherwise. Because this commandment is neglected, God also terribly punishes the world; [...]«; THE BOOK OF CONCORD: the confessions of the Evangelical Lutheran Church/ ed. by Robert Kolb; Timothy J. Wengert. MP 2000, 410, 176 f ≙ WA 30 I, 157, 2-7.

child relationship is also one of love. Yet this is a stern affection that must instill fear and exact obedience to be appropriately loving, for its purpose is to produce responsible citizens and faithful disciples.

This paper will discuss Luther's primary writings on marital matters in chronological order. It will then look at divorce and some aspects of the parent-child relationship and conclude with an exploration of Luther's portrayal of the patriarchs and matriarchs as married couples.

I The Early Writings

In his »A sermon on the estate of marriage, 1519« Luther begins by emphasizing the unique nature of marriage which God grants only to human beings and not to any of the other animals. The importance to God of this relationship is evident in the care God takes in creating Eve for Adam and giving her to him. Luther then distinguishes among three kinds of love: false love, natural love, and married love. False love is self-serving and uses the desired object to satisfy its own appetites, things such as money, sex or prestige. In reality false love is greed and covetousness posing as love. Natural love is that which binds us to parents, siblings, friends and family members. The third form, married love, is or should be the greatest and purest of all loves, writes Luther. It trumps the claims of natural love, since husband and wife leave father and mother to be joined to one another and create a new family.

> »But over and above all these is married love, that is, a bride's love, which glows like a fire and desires nothing but the husband. She says, ›It is you I want, not what is yours; I want neither your silver nor your gold; I want neither. I want only you. I want you in your entirety, or not at all.‹ All other kinds of love seek something other than the loved one: this kind wants only to have the beloved's own self completely.«[15]

Luther then qualifies this paean to nuptial rapture with the observation that since the fall such love is no longer pure. It has been corrupted by the presence of false love, that is, the drive to use the other as the means to satisfying one's own desires. Such love is about the self, not the beloved. Luther then concludes that marriage now can be little more than a pro-phylactic measure against lust.[16]

15 LW 44, 9 ≙ WA 2, 167, 29-34.
16 »Therefore, the married state is now no longer pure and free from sin. The temptation

At this point he still considers marriage to be a sacrament. Because it signifies the sacred reality of Christ's union with the church, a married man should perform his conjugal duty, the act of making one, without fear of the wicked lust of the flesh that inevitably afflicts him in this most intimate of acts. The taint of lust is also counteracted by the covenant of fidelity that constitutes marriage.[17] Because the couple stays within the limits of their committed relationship, God defends them from the sin of illicit desire. Moreover, within these confines husband and wife are allowed to give relatively free rein to their sexual lives.

> »In this way God sees to it that the flesh is subdued so as not to rage wherever and however it pleases, and, within this plighted troth, permits even more occasion than is necessary for the begetting of children. But, of course, a man has to control himself and not make a filthy sow's sty of his marriage.«[18]

The third way in which marriage undermines the damning power of lust is by producing children. However, Luther insists, birth within the bonds of matrimony is only the beginning. Even heathens produce offspring, Christians must raise their children to a life of godliness. Maintaining the covenant of marriage becomes almost a secondary concern.

The following year, 1520, in »The Babylonian captivity of the church«, Luther rejects the sacramental status of marriage. He argues that marriage does not impart saving grace and has no divinely instituted sign, although it is a divine institution. Since marriage has existed from the beginning of the world and is found among all peoples, not just Christians, there is no reason to regard it as a sacrament of the Gospel under the governance of the church. Luther then catalogues at great length what he judges to be the church's abusive policies in the regulation of

of the flesh has become so strong and consuming that marriage may be likened to a hospital for incurables which prevents inmates from falling into graver sin«; LW 44, 9 ≙ WA 2, 168, 1-4.

17 »Second, [the doctors say] that marriage is a covenant of fidelity. The whole basis and essence of marriage is that each gives himself or herself to the other, and they promise to remain faithful to each other and not give themselves to any other. By binding themselves to each other, and surrendering themselves to each other, the way is barred to the body of anyone else, and they content themselves in the marriage bed with their one companion«; LW 44, 10f ≙ WA 2, 168, 38 - 169, 3.

18 LW 44, 11 ≙ WA 2, 169, 3-7.

marriage.[19] The treatise concludes with a discussion of specific marital situations – for example, what should an impotent man's wife do, if she wants children? – and of divorce.[20] In the years following Luther devoted increasing amounts of attention to such cases of marital difficulty.

II Rejection of Monasticism

Luther's ›The judgment on monastic vows, 1521« is an unconditional denunciation of the monastic practice of his day and in particular of the required vow of celibacy. He argues that there is no biblical warrant for the imposition of this discipline. Jesus only discusses it with reference to eunuchs; he neither invites nor calls his hearers to take it up. The same, writes Luther, is true of Paul.[21]

He insists once again that true celibacy is a divine gift, not a human accomplishment. To demand it is a form of works righteousness and a violation of Christian freedom.[22] Most monastics have tormented con-

---

19 »Among endless other monstrosities, which are supposed to instruct the confessors, whereas they most mischievously confuse them, there are enumerated in this book eighteen impediments to marriage. If you will examine these with the just and unprejudiced eye of faith, you will see that they belong to those things which the Apostle foretold: ›There shall be those that give heed to the spirits of demons, speaking lies in hypocrisy, forbidding to marry‹ (I Tim. 4:1-3). What is ›forbidding to marry‹ if it is not this - to invent all those hindrances and set those snares, in order to prevent people from marrying, or, if they are married, to annul their marriage?«; LW 36, 96 f ≙ WA 6, 553, 29 - 554, 4.

20 »[...] the content of Luther's early marital counsel, whatever the motivation and the circumstances, is naïve at best and illegal at worst«; Lazareth: Luther on the Christian home, 189.

21 »›But virginity and celibacy is a counsel‹, [they say]. Clearly Christ did not counsel it, but rather discouraged it. It was only when eunuchs had been mentioned that he referred to it and praised it by saying, ›He who is able to receive this precept, let him receive it‹ [Mt 19, 12]. And again, ›Not all can receive this precept‹ [Mt 19, 11]. Are these not the words of someone who prefers to advise against virginity and celibacy and discourage their application? He neither invites anyone to take up celibacy, nor calls men to it. He simply refers to it. Paul, however, says ›I give this counsel [...]‹ [1 K 7, 25], but he does not invite anyone to take up celibacy either; rather, he discourages them and deters them when he says, ›But each has his own special gift from God‹ [1 K 7, 7]. Paul neither persuades nor dissuades; he leaves the matter open«; LW 44, 261-62 ≙ WA 8, 583, 30-37.

22 »The virgin would then think like this, ›Although I could marry, I am content to remain unmarried, not because it is commanded, not because it is advised, not because it is

164

sciences because they have vowed to do that which they cannot. They are denied the proper outlet for their sexual nature in marriage, and so, argues Luther, they inevitably fall into rampant lust and hypocrisy. Moreover, their celibacy serves no one but themselves; it has nothing to do with the worship of the Lord or the love of the neighbor. Indeed, it excuses them from the very works of mercy Christ has enjoined upon all believers.

Luther concludes »The Judgment ...« with some comments on marriage. He acknowledges that the married person, because of care for the family and involvement in worldly matters, has less time to tend to the Word of God than does the true celibate. Commenting on Isaiah 56, 4f. [23] Luther acknowledges that virginity and chastity are greater works and greater gifts than marriage. We know too, he writes, that in our Father's house are many mansions and that one star differs from another in brightness. »But in relation to the true God and the eunuchs there is no name other than the one we all enjoy, and that name is Christ.« [24] Marriage does not come across here as a way of life with the potential for joy. It is not for the faint of heart, but its hardships are far preferable to the tormented conscience of the person unable to keep a vow of chastity. Besides, connubial endurance has biblical precedent.

> »We do not advocate marriage as an easy way out, nor do we hold out any promises that it will be such. We want it to be permitted, to be a matter of option, so that the man who is able may be continent for as long as he wants. We want the conscience to be free from offense, not from marriage. How much happier a state of affairs it is to tolerate a marriage irksome twice over than to be tortured by the constant pangs of conscience! This kind of trouble has been laid on us by God, and all the holy patriarchs have borne it.« [25]

greater and more sacrificial than all other virtues, but because this seems to me to be the right way to live, just as marriage or farming may seem right to somebody else. I do not want the responsibilities of married life, I want to be free of responsibilities and have time for God.««; LW 44, 307 ≙ WA 8, 611, 37 - 612, 2.

23 For thus says the Lord: »To the eunuchs who keep my Sabbaths, who choose the things that please me and hold fast my covenant, I will give in my house and within my walls a monument and a name better than sons and daughters; I will give them an everlasting name which shall not be cut off.« .

24 LW 44, 375 ≙ WA 8, 653, 16f.

25 LW 44, 395 ≙ WA 8, 665, 27-32.

In this treatise Luther does not celebrate married life. It is marked by the cross of Christ, but the light of its grace is less radiant than that of the truly celibate, the eunuchs for the kingdom of heaven. Over time, however, Luther comes more and more to see in the life of the family within the community of neighbors not an arena of potential distraction from the Word of God but the primary setting for experiencing and enacting the Gospel.

In »An exhortation to the knights of the Teutonic Order that they lay aside false chastity and assume the true chastity of wedlock, 1523« Luther appeals to the knights to abandon their vows without delay and get married. He makes his case using Gn 2,18: »God says, ›It is my will that you have a helper and not be alone; this seems good to me.‹ Man replies, ›Not so; you are mistaken; I vow to you to do so without a helper; to be alone seems good to me.‹«[26] Vows of celibacy fly in the face of this divine word and so cannot be binding. Here the issue is not »marry rather than violate your conscience with a vow of chastity you can't keep«, but »you have no right to make such a vow in the first place when it is God's intent for you to marry«.[27] Luther emphasizes once again the hardship that married life entails: »For in the sight of God it is a precious and noble good work to bring up children and train them, to rule your wife and servants in a godly manner, to support yourself by the sweat of your face, and to endure much misfortune and unhappiness at the hands of your wife, children, servants, and others.«[28] Married life is the real spiritual discipline, whereas the monastic life, by avoiding such challenges, is pretending to greater suffering while in reality taking a far easier route.

26 LW 45, 145 ≙ WA 12, 234, 22-25.

27 »For this reason God has done marriage the honor of putting it into the Fourth Commandment, immediately after the honor due to himself, where he commands, ›Honor your father and your mother‹ [Ex 20,12]. Just look! Show me an honor in heaven or on earth, apart from the honor of God, that can equal this honor! Neither the temporal nor the spiritual estate has been so highly honored. And if God had told us nothing more about married life than this Fourth Commandment, we should still have learned sufficiently from it alone that in the sight of God there is no higher office, estate, condition, or work (next to the gospel, which concerns God himself) than the estate of marriage«; LW 45, 154 ≙ WA 12, 241, 10-17.

28 LW 45, 153 f ≙ WA 12, 241, 3-6.

III »The Estate of Marriage« 1522

The 1522 treatise »The estate of marriage« opens with a statement of reluctance on Luther's part to get further involved with the subject of marriage. He fears that there will be no end to the work of straightening out the confusion and damage caused by papal law and by the failure of the secular authority to fulfill its responsibilities. Luther objects that arbitrary restrictions imposed by the church that make it difficult for couples to marry are illegitimate and abusive.[29] Moreover, following the letter of even sound civil law in marital matters may be inadequate for the accomplishment of God's will and the spiritual health of the believer. In such cases of emergency Luther feels compelled to speak out on behalf of troubled consciences caught in conflict. It is here that the created order of marriage spills over into the realm of law and Gospel, where the peace of the conscience before God is of paramount concern.[30]

29 Luther discusses at length eighteen impediments which were recognized as grounds for preventing or dissolving a marriage. These include issues of consanguinity, relationship through marriage, impotence, prior betrothal, coercion, etc. Of the eighteen Luther recognizes only the fourteenth, »unfitness for marriage« – impotence – as a valid ground for ending a marriage. Otherwise these restrictions represent for him an illegitimate interference with the freedom of a Christian. He concludes: »It is a dirty rotten business that a bishop should forbid me a wife or specify the times when I may marry, or that a blind and dumb person should not be allowed to enter into wedlock. So much then for this foolishness [...]«; LW 45, 30 ≙ WA 10 II, 287, 8-11.

30 Luther's advice concerning impotence given in »The Babylonian captivity ...« is reiterated here: »What I said was this: if a woman who is fit for marriage has a husband who is not, and she is unable openly to take unto herself another – and unwilling, too, to do anything dishonorable – since the pope in such a case demands without cause abundant testimony and evidence, she should say to her husband, ›Look, my dear husband, you are unable to fulfill your conjugal duty toward me; you have cheated me out of my maidenhood and even imperiled my honor and *my soul's salvation*; in the sight of God there is no real marriage between us. Grant me the privilege of contracting a secret marriage with your brother or closest relative, and you retain the title of husband so that your property will not fall to strangers. Consent to being betrayed voluntarily by me, as you have betrayed me without my consent.‹

I stated further that the husband is obligated to consent to such an arrangement and thus to provide for her the conjugal duty and children, and that if he refuses to do so she should flee from him to some other country and there contract a marriage. I gave

While upholding the principle of Christian freedom, that a person may marry or not, depending on his or her abilities and inclinations, Luther does insist on a certain natural necessity that drives the human being to mate. »Be fruitful and multiply«, he writes, is more than a command; it is a divine ordinance which it is not our prerogative to hinder or ignore. He compares it to such natural instinctual acts as sleeping and waking, eating and drinking, and the emptying of bladder and bowels. God does not command people to be man or woman but creates them as one or the other. Neither does God command human beings to multiply but creates them so that they are driven to do so. Vows of celibacy are a vain attempt to reverse the tide and a dishonoring of God's created order. »And wherever men try to resist this, it remains irresistible nonetheless and goes its way through fornication, adultery, and secret sins, for this is a matter of nature and not of choice.«[31] You either honor the nature God has given you or you degrade it by trying to become what you were not meant to be. There is for Luther nothing admirable or meritorious in such a vain struggle.

In the second part of »The estate of marriage« Luther discusses divorce, which will be taken up below. The final section of the treatise is devoted to the topic of how to live a Christian and godly life in marriage.

Luther is a realist. He points out that to recognize marriage as a holy estate is something quite different from merely being married. Family life is inevitably fraught with conflict and full of drudgery and hardship. Without the eyes of vocation that is all one will see. The person who knows herself called to this spouse and this home, however, will be strengthened by the assurance that all that she does and all that she suffers is pleasing to God. Moreover, she will find in her marriage delight, love and joy without end. The devil has a vested interest in defaming marriage, and so men and women must be on their guard lest they be lured into deni-

this advice at a time when I was still timid. However, I should like now to give sounder advice in the matter, and take a firmer grip on the wool of a man who thus makes a fool of his wife. The same principle would apply if the circumstances were reversed, although this happens less frequently in the case of wives than of husbands [...]. It will not do to lead one's fellow-man around by the nose so wantonly in matters of such great import involving his body, goods, honor, and salvation«; LW 45, 20f (emphasis added) ≙ WA 10 II, 278, 10 - 279, 5.
31 LW 45, 18 ≙ WA 10 II, 276, 29-31.

grating one another and rejecting the call to the marital estate.[32] Luther gives particular emphasis to the generation of children which results from the relationship of husband and wife, comparing it to the sterility, both physical and spiritual, that he finds in monastic life. He also acknowledges the rich satisfactions that come out of the relation of husband and wife, in addition to the fulfillment of shared child-rearing.

>>Observe that thus far I have told you nothing of the estate of marriage except that which the world and reason in their blindness shrink from and sneer at as a mean, unhappy, troublesome mode of life. We have seen how all these shortcomings in fact comprise noble virtues and true delight if one but looks at God's word and will, and thereby recognizes its true nature. I will not mention the other advantages and delights implicit in a marriage that goes well – that husband and wife cherish one another, become one, serve one another, and other attendant blessings […].<<[33]

Luther makes clear that even within marriage copulation is not without sin. Yet, he writes, >>God excuses it by his grace because the estate of marriage is his work, and he preserves in and through the sin all that good which he has implanted and blessed in marriage.<<[34] The very same act outside of wedlock has no such coverage and, even when it leads to reproduction, is corrupting and wholly shameful. Fornication, he writes,

---

32 >>What we would speak most of is the fact that the estate of marriage has universally fallen into such awful disrepute. There are many pagan books which treat of nothing but the depravity of womankind and the unhappiness of the estate of marriage, such that some have thought that even if Wisdom itself were a woman one should not marry […]. I imagine that if women were to write books they would say exactly the same thing about men. What they have failed to set down in writing, however, they express with their grumbling and complaining whenever they get together<<; LW 45, 36 ≙ WA 10 II, 292, 22-26; 293, 10-13.

>>In order that we may not proceed as blindly, but rather conduct ourselves in a Christian manner, hold fast first of all to this, that man and woman are the work of God. Keep a tight rein on your heart and your lips; do not criticize his work, or call that evil which he himself has called good. He knows better than you yourself what is good and to your benefit, as he says in Genesis 1 [2;18], ›It is not good that the man should be alone; I will make him a helper fit for him.‹ There you see that he calls the woman good, a helper. If you deem it otherwise, it is certainly your own fault, you neither understand nor believe God's word and work. See, with this statement of God one stops the mouths of all those who criticize and censure marriage<<; LW 45, 37 ≙ WA 10 II, 293, 26 - 294, 7.

33 LW 45, 42 f ≙ WA 10 II, 299, 1-8.

34 LW 45, 49 ≙ WA 10 II, 304, 9-12.

destroys not only the soul but also the body, property, honor and family.[35] The union of man and woman outside of marriage is no more a legitimate response to the divine imperative »Be fruitful and multiply« than the monastic withdrawal from the world of sexual relationship. Both represent a sinful self-assertion over against the will of God.

IV »I Corinthians 7« on Sexual Relations 1523

Sex outside of marriage is for Luther irredeemably sinful, but sex within marriage is obligatory. It is the obedient response to God's command and a good work on behalf of one's closest neighbor, one's spouse. As we shall see, the inability or unwillingness to fulfill one's conjugal duty is grounds for divorce. In his commentary on I Corinthians 7 (1523) Luther discusses the sexual commitment of married couples with reference to verses 1-7:

> »Now concerning the matters about which you wrote. It is well for a man not to touch a woman. But because of the temptation to immorality, each man should have his own wife and each woman her own husband. The husband should give to his wife her conjugal rights, and likewise the wife to her husband. For the wife does not rule over her own body, but the husband does; likewise the husband does not rule over his own body, but the wife does. Do not refuse one another except perhaps by agreement for a season, that you may devote yourselves to prayer; but then come together again, lest Satan tempt you through lack of self-control. I say this by way of concession, not of command. I wish that all were as I myself am. But each has his own special gift from God, one of one kind and one of another.«[36]

Marriage is embraced by the law of love, which requires a person to put the neighbor's need before his/her own desire. Consequently, the partners surrender their bodies to each other. When lust assaults one partner, the other is to minister to him/her, and the commitment to

35 »For we see how a licentious and wicked life not only brings great disgrace but is also a spendthrift life, more costly than wedlock, and that illicit partners necessarily occasion greater suffering for one another than do married folk. Beyond that it consumes the body, corrupts flesh and blood, nature, and physical constitution. Through such a variety of evil consequences God takes a rigid position, as though he would actually drive people away from fornication and into marriage. However, few are thereby convinced or converted«; LW 45, 43 f ≙ WA 10 II, 299, 21-27.
36 From Luther quoted LW 28, 9-15 ≙ WA 12, 95, 6-19, Das 7. Kapitel zu den Korinthern.

offer oneself to one's spouse is indissoluble. The boundaries are clearly drawn; you cannot give yourself to another, your body is no longer yours to give.[37] »For the wife does not rule over her own body, but the husband does; likewise the husband does not rule over his own body, but the wife does.«[38]

Luther is of the opinion that Christians should discipline themselves and conduct their sexual lives with moderation. However, he is adamant that no rules should be imposed on sexual activity, limiting the times and conditions in which intercourse is permissible. Citing the saying »Whoever is too passionate in love-making commits adultery against his own wife«,[39] Luther rejects the idea as impossible.[40] Sex within marriage, as St. Paul writes, is given as a defense against lust and unchastity. Under no circumstances should it be restricted, and the couple thereby left vulnerable to temptation. Moreover, such interference is a violation of God's will. How, asks Luther, can anyone forbid me access to the body which God has decreed should be given to me? St. Paul stipulates that only by common agreement may the partners in a marriage abstain from sexual relations in order to devote themselves to prayer. Luther notes that their sexual relationship takes priority. Both parties must agree, and prayer and fasting must yield to conjugal demand rather than either spouse withholding himself/herself from the other's need. Luther concludes, »Now prayer is a most precious good work, but it must give way to what seems a base thing. The law of love, by which they are bound, brings this about.«[41]

37 From this we see how adultery is the greatest robbery and theft on earth. For it gives away a living body, which belongs to another, and also takes a living body, that is not free for the taking«; WA 12, 101, 21-24 ≙ LW 28, 13.
38 LW 28, 13 ≙ WA 12, 95, 11-13.
39 »Wer zu hitzig ist ynn der liebe, der ist an seynem eygen weybe eyn ehebrecher‹ Aber eyn heyde hatts geredt, darumb acht ich seyn nicht, und sage, es sey nicht war«; WA 12, 101, 30 - 102, 1 ≙ LW 28, 13.
40 Luther adds an interesting exception to this: »Es kann freylich niemant an seynem weybe eyn ehebrecher werden, er wolt sie denn nicht fur seyn weyb hallten, oder nicht als seyn weyb berüren«; WA 12, 102, 1-3 ≙ LW 28, 13. It would appear that if the husband mistreats his wife sexually, then he has committed a sin on the order of adultery, using her body rather than receiving it within the covenant of their mutual self-giving.
41 LW 28, 14 ≙ WA 12, 103, 6-9.

»The order of marriage for common pastors«, dating from 1529, says nothing of the potential joys of the marital relationship but concentrates instead on its difficulties and dangers.

> »For whoever desires prayer and blessing from the pastor or bishop indicates thereby – even if he does not express it in so many words – into what peril and need he enters and how greatly he stands in need of the blessing of God and common prayer for the estate which he enters. For every day we see marriages broken by the devil through adultery, unfaithfulness, discord, and all manner of ill.«[42]

Luther gives Gn 2, 18. 21-24 as the first reading after the couple enters the church; this is the word that establishes marriage as a divine ordinance. Then follows a reading from Ephesians setting forth the duties of husband and wife.[43] The third reading speaks of the cross which God has laid upon marriage.[44] The last reading offers comfort to the couple, reiterating the first reading in the affirmation of God's blessing on their union.[45] The closing prayer, however, comes back to the issue of marriage's vulnerability to the machinations of the devil and the assaults of human sinfulness.

> »O God, who hast created man and woman and hast ordained them for the married estate, has blessed them also with fruits of the womb, and hast typified therein the sacramental union of thy dear Son, the Lord Jesus Christ, and the church, his bride: We beseech thy groundless goodness and mercy that thou wouldst not permit this thy creation, ordinance, and blessing to be disturbed or destroyed, but graciously preserve the same; through Jesus Christ our Lord. Amen.«[46]

The service is marked by a somber tone which, rather than celebrating the present love of the couple, focuses on the daunting challenges of married life between sinful individuals in a fallen world. The couple's exchange of

42 LW 53, 113 ≙ WA 30 III, 76, 9-15.
43 E 5, 22-29.
44 Gn 3, 16-19.
45 »So God created man in his own image, in the image of God he created him; male and female he created them. And God blessed them, and God said to them, ›Be fruitful and multiply, and fill the earth and subdue it; and have dominion over the fish of the sea and over the birds of the air and over every living thing that moves upon the earth.‹ [...]. And God saw everything that he had made, and behold, it was very good«; Gn 1, 27f.31. »He who finds a wife finds a good thing, and obtains favor from the Lord«; Prv 18, 22.
46 LW 53, 115 ≙ WA 30 III, 80, 8-13.

Hans Sebald Beham (1500-1550): Das Liebespaar, Holzschnitt
(Lutherstadt Wittenberg, Lutherhaus)

vows constitutes the marriage. The liturgy makes it clear, however, that the couple is to look to the promise of God rather than their own affections and expectations to sustain their commitment.

In the Large Catechism, also dating from 1529, Luther has much to say about marriage in his explication of the sixth commandment, »You are not to commit adultery«. Indeed, Luther has more to say about marriage than about adultery *per se*. He emphasizes once again its status as divinely ordained and God-pleasing and insists on its pre-eminence among social institutions and vocations.

> »[God] has established [marriage] before all others as the first of all institutions, and he created man and woman differently (as is evident) not for indecency but to be true to each other, to be fruitful, to beget children, and to nurture and bring them up to the glory of God. God has therefore blessed this walk of life most richly, above all others, and, in addition, has supplied and endowed it with everything in the world in order that this walk of life might be richly provided for.«[47]

Once again Luther emphasizes the naturalness of the sexual urge as a physical drive implanted by God. Flesh and blood remain flesh and blood, writes Luther, and natural inclinations and stimulations function without fail. Marriage is the proper conduit into which these should flow; otherwise they will lead to licentiousness, for flow they must.

The issue of sexual fidelity is embedded for Luther in a deeper understanding of the relationship between marital partners. Chastity has its roots first and foremost in the affectional life of the spouses. Where husband and wife live together in love and harmony, chastity follows spontaneously, argues Luther. When one receives one's spouse as a gift from God, as the particular husband or wife given *for me*, then the boundaries are plainly drawn. It is clear now both where one is called to love and where one is forbidden to act on one's natural instincts.

VI »The Sermon on the Mount« 1532

Luther discusses the issue of licit and illicit desire at greater length in his study of Mt 5, 27-30. The temptation of lust is impossible to avoid. Men and women will be thrown together in society. Moreover, it is pleasing to

47 The Book of Concord, 414, 207 f ≙ WA 30 I, 161, 28-34.

God that men look at women, talk, laugh and have a good time with them. People are supposed to fall in love. Indeed, they need to be swept off their feet in order to risk getting married. After that, safeguarding love and desire is crucial to sustaining a marriage.

> »Without it there is trouble: from the flesh, because a person soon gets tired of marriage and refuses to bear the daily discomfort that comes with it; and from the devil, who cannot stand the sight of a married couple treating each other with genuine love and who will not rest until he has given them an occasion for impatience, conflict, hate, and bitterness. Therefore it is an art both necessary and difficult, and one peculiarly Christian, this art of loving one's husband or wife properly, of bearing the other's faults and all the accidents and troubles. At first everything goes all right, so that, as the saying goes, they are ready to eat each other up for love. But when their curiosity has been satisfied, then the devil comes along to create boredom in you, to rob you of your desire in this direction, and to excite it unduly in another direction.«[48]

Luther takes the reality of lust and the temptation to adultery quite seriously, but he is no alarmist. A man may look at another woman, but he must not look at her the way he should look only at his wife. It does not take a rocket scientist to tell the difference. Such temptation will inevitably befall us. It comes with the territory of being social creatures, gifted with the capacity for passion and affection and blinded by the love of self. Luther is refreshingly matter of fact about it.

> »Yet we should not make the bowstring too taut here, as if anyone who is tempted and whose lust and desire for another woman are aroused would be damned for it. I have often said that it is impossible to be alive and to have flesh and blood without any sinful and evil inclination, whether in this or in all the other commandments.«[49]

It is impossible for us to keep sinful thoughts from occurring; just don't let them take root, cautions Luther. Of course, the lustful thought is sin, but no one lives in the flesh without a great many sins, and »everyone must have his devil«[50] The best protection against adultery is, as Luther says in the Large Catechism, to remind oneself that one's wife is God's special gift, and that she alone has the surpassing beauty of God's Word to adorn her. With that the allure of any other woman cannot compare.

---

48 LW 21, 89 ≙ WA 32, 374, 1-11.
49 LW 21, 88 ≙ WA 32, 373, 6-10.
50 LW 21, 89 ≙ WA 32, 373, 28 f.

The biblical passage with which Luther is working here deals specifically with the sin of adultery. He sees unfaithfulness at work among married couples in other ways as well. There will be dissension and distrust; angry words get spoken; feelings cut deep. The one you share bed and board with will sometimes seem like your worst enemy.

> »Husband and wife can become alienated from no one else as readily as from each other. All it takes is one little word, spoken in passing or jokingly, which pierces the heart and cannot be forgotten. And thereafter they both brew pure poison and bitterness in their souls.«[51]

Your eyes may not be turning toward a new sexual partner, but when your heart is closed to the one you have married, then you are breaking the sixth commandment.[52] You need once again to pay heed to the Word of grace shining through your marriage.[53]

VII Divorce

Luther recognizes the need for divorce in a sinful society and regards its regulation as a matter for the civil authority. At the same time he wants Christians to do their best to exceed secular expectations and hold their marriages to a higher spiritual standard. In »The estate of marriage, 1522« Luther identifies three legitimate grounds for marital dissolution: inability to fulfill one's conjugal duty (impotence or frigidity) so that one's spouse is deprived of children, adultery, and refusal to fulfill one's conjugal duty or to live with one's spouse. The resistance of the partner in the last case may well become the cause of the other's fall. Luther suggests that he/she be called to public accountability,[54] and if that doesn't shame the errant spouse into cooperation, divorce is appropriate. The issue here is one of fraud.

51 WA 34 I, 61, 25-29.
52 »Let it be said in conclusion that this commandment requires all people not only to live chastely in deed, word, and thought in their particular situation (that is, especially in marriage as a walk of life), but also to love and cherish the spouse whom God has given them«; The Book of Concord, 415, 219 ≙ WA 30 I, 163, 14-17.
53 WA 34 I, 56, 32-36.
54 »Only first the husband should admonish and warn his wife two or three times, and let the situation be known to others so that her stubbornness becomes a matter of common knowledge and is rebuked before the congregation«; LW 45, 33 f ≙ WA 10 II, 290, 10-12.

»When one resists the other and refuses the conjugal duty she is robbing the other of the body she had bestowed upon him. This is really contrary to marriage, and dissolves the marriage. For this reason the civil government must compel the wife, or put her to death.[55] If the government fails to act, the husband must reason that his wife has been stolen away and slain by robbers.«[56]

Luther makes it clear, however, that this does not apply to a couple where one partner is unable to meet his or her conjugal responsibilities because of infirmity. Indeed, caring for an invalid spouse is an extraordinary spiritual discipline. He assures the reader that God is far too faithful to deprive a person of his spouse through illness without simultaneously subduing his carnal desire.

Luther discusses one additional situation that does not fit under the three major headings with which he began. This is the case of what today we would call »irreconcilable differences«: where husband and wife cannot get along together for some reason other than the matter of the conjugal duty. Luther points out that even the Scriptures make reference to such women »more bitter than death«,[57] and he acknowledges that there are also rude, brutal, and unbearable husbands. In such cases, which would include domestic abuse, Luther allows dissolution of the marriage as long as neither party remarries. He concludes this section with the observation that it would be a fine instance of Christian witness if one or the other of

---

55 In this early treatise Luther also suggests that the civil authorities impose the death penalty on adulterers: »You may ask: What is to become of the other [the guilty party] if he too is perhaps unable to lead a chaste life? Answer: It was for this reason that God commanded in the law [Deut. 22:22-24] that adulterers be stoned, that they might not have to face this question. The temporal sword and government should therefore still put adulterers to death, for whoever commits adultery has in fact himself already departed and is considered as one dead. Therefore, the other [the innocent party] may remarry just as though his spouse had died, if it is his intention to insist on his rights and not show mercy to the guilty party. Where the government is negligent and lax, however, and fails to inflict the death penalty, the adulterer may betake himself to a far country and there remarry if he is unable to remain continent. But it would be better to put him to death, lest a bad example be set«; LW 45, 32 ≙ WA 10 II, 289, 8-17.

56 LW 45, 34 ≙ WA 10 II, 290, 20 - 291, 1.

57 »And I found more bitter than death the woman whose heart is snares and nets, and whose hands are fetters; he who pleases God escapes her, but the sinner is taken by her«; Eccl 7, 26.

the spouses in such a dysfunctional relationship could endure the misery. This is not terrified submission but a conscious sacrifice by the wronged party for whom the marriage is the devil's battleground.

>Now if one of the parties were endowed with Christian fortitude and could endure the other's ill behavior, that would doubtless be a wonderfully blessed cross and a right way to heaven. For an evil spouse, in a manner of speaking, fulfils the devil's function and sweeps clean him who is able to recognize and bear it. If he cannot, however, let him divorce her before he does anything worse, and remain unmarried for the rest of his days.«[58]

It is the Christian's obligation to bear the cross, and in Luther's view the path of suffering in a miserable relationship can have unique spiritual benefits. If you refuse that opportunity, you don't get the chance to work out your salvation with fear and trembling in a second marriage.[59]

In his commentary on Mt 5,31f in »The sermon on the mount« Luther again stipulates that divorce is a secular, external matter that is rightly regulated by the law in its first use. When Christ speaks to the issue, it is not as a lawyer or ruler but as a preacher. He is not prescribing policy but instructing Christian consciences in the godly use of divorce law. Luther sees himself functioning in a similar vein. His conclusion from Jesus' teaching in »The sermon on the mount« is that those who want to be Christians should not be divorced, »but every man should keep his own spouse, sustaining and bearing good and ill with her, even though she may have her oddities, peculiarities, and faults. If he does get a divorce, he should remain unmarried.«[60]

Luther offers a good dose of commonsense realism in his reflections on the matter. Writing on Mt 19,8, Luther states that it was better to allow the sin of divorce to the people of Israel than to court greater evil. He goes on to

---

58 LW 45, 34f ≙ WA 10 II, 291, 15-20.

59 In »On marriage matters, 1530« Luther, again referring to 1 Corinthians 7, 10f, comments: »But if sometimes one party runs away from the other out of anger or rage, it is quite a different matter [...]. Here we can see what to do from St. Paul, 1 Cor. 7 [:11], namely, they are to be reconciled or, if the reconciliation does not succeed, remain single. There may well be a case where they are better off separated than together, otherwise St. Paul would not have permitted them to remain single if they did not wish to be reconciled. And who can enumerate all the cases like these or make laws to deal with them? Sensible people must be the judges here«; LW 46, 314 ≙ WA 30 III, 243, 31 - 244, 2.

60 LW 21, 94 ≙ WA 32, 378, 5-7.

say that a similar accommodation to contemporary social reality might be advisable, if lamentable: »[...] certain queer, stubborn, and obstinate people, who have no capacity for toleration and are not suited for married life at all, should be permitted to get a divorce. [...]. Frequently something must be tolerated, even though it is not a good thing to do, to prevent something worse from happening.«[61]

Luther knows that people can be dangerously deluded. There is no getting around the tedium of daily life, the predictable burdens of family and the aggravations imposed by the outside world. One just has to deal with them. Still many think they can escape the disappointments, most readily by transferring their affections to a new spouse. But if you can't see the hand of God at work in your life in the first place, then it will just go on as the »same old, same old« no matter how you try to spice up the domestic scene.[62] Luther's response to such people is unsparing: get real, grow up, work at your marriage – vocations require effort after all – remember what the forgiveness of sins is all about, and pray.

Having dealt with the whiners, Luther then turns to more serious problems. Adultery is legitimate grounds for divorce, for the adulterer has in truth already dissolved the marriage by his actions. Luther hopes that the other partner, although set completely free, will nonetheless choose to reconcile.[63] He recognizes, however, that there may be no hope for

---

61 LW 21, 94 ≙ WA 32, 377, 37 - 378, 3.

62 »The only source of trouble here is the fact that marriage is not thought of on the basis of the Word of God, as His work and ordinance, and that His will is ignored. He has given every man his spouse, to keep her and for His sake to put up with the difficulties involved in married life. To them it seems to be nothing more than a purely human and secular state, with which God has nothing to do. Therefore they tire of it so quickly; and if it does not go the way they would like, they immediately want a divorce and a change. Then God so arranges things that they are not better off as a consequence. A person who wants to change and improve everything and who refuses to put up with any inadequacies, but insists on having everything clean and comfortable, will usually get in exchange something twice as uncomfortable or ten times as uncomfortable. [...]. A change is a fast and easy thing, but an improvement is a rare and doubtful thing«; LW 21, 94f ≙ WA 32, 378, 10-22. 32f.

63 »To those who really want to be Christians, we should give this advice. The two partners should be admonished and urged to stay together. If the guilty party is humbled and reformed, the innocent party should let himself be reconciled to him and forgive him in Christian love«; LW 21, 96 ≙ WA 32, 379, 27-31.

improvement and a renewal of spousal fidelity, and then the partners must go their separate ways, with only the innocent party free to marry again. The other issue Luther raises here is that of abandonment. He is outraged by the »dead beat dad«, the man who takes off from his family, leaving them to fend for themselves and expecting them to take him back whenever he chooses to return. Luther judges such a person to be worse than an unbeliever and less tolerable than an adulterer. He recommends that the authorities issue a summons, and if the offender does not respond within the stated time, that the wife be set completely free. Luther's indignation is evident; the person who would default not just on his commitment to his spouse but on his obligations to his children is beneath contempt.

VIII Parents and Children

As has already been noted Luther extols the vocation of marriage chiefly because it produces family life.

> »But the greatest good in married life, that which makes all suffering and labor worth while, is that God grants offspring and commands that they be brought up to worship and serve him. In all the world this is the noblest and most precious work, because to God there can be nothing dearer than the salvation of souls. Now since we are all duty bound to suffer death, if need be, that we might bring a single soul to God, you can see how rich the estate of marriage is in good works. God has entrusted to its bosom souls begotten of its own body, on whom it can lavish all manner of Christian works. Most certainly father and mother are apostles, bishops, and priests to their children, for it is they who make them acquainted with the gospel. In short, there is no greater or nobler authority on earth than that of parents over their children, for this authority is both spiritual and temporal.«[64]

Parental responsibility to serve one's children as »their apostle and bishop« consists of four crucial duties: to provide the sacrament of baptism for infants, to form children in the true faith as they mature, to attend to their education for vocation, and to provide them with a suitable spouse in a timely fashion, that is, before the force of their natural sexual instincts puts them at risk of sin. For the purposes of this paper, we will focus on the last of the four.

64 LW 45, 46 ≙ WA 10 II, 301, 16-27.

In 1524 Luther wrote a brief piece entitled »That parents should neither compel nor hinder the marriage of their children, and that children should not become engaged without their parents' consent«. Luther reminds the reader that God has established parental authority to build up, not destroy. Indeed there are strict limits set on it; it cannot go so far as to inflict damage on the child, especially not on his or her conscience. Thus a father violates his sacred trust and acts against God when he forces his child into a marriage without love.[65] He does the same when he prevents his child from marrying. Luther allows that interference with a relationship to a particular person can be justified, but it is a gross sin to prevent the child from marrying altogether and force him or her into a life of celibacy. No parent can demand of their children that they go against their created nature.[66] God has made human beings to eat, drink, procreate, sleep and

65 Luther addresses the same issue with great passion in »On marriage matters, 1530«: »Yes, my dear fellow, if you want to accept the gospel when it gives you power over your child and demands filial obedience to you, then you should also accept it when it commands you to treat your child in a paternal way and forbids you to use your power shamefully and criminally in this matter, since the salvation of your child is in danger, for you cannot give your child the desire and love for his spouse that he should have according to the commandment of God, who desires that husband and wife shall love one another. If you now can make a big thing out of the sin of filial disobedience on the basis of the gospel, then one can also make a big thing out of your unnatural crime on the same basis, and if filial disobedience is a sin, then your unnatural criminal power is two sins«; LW 46, 306 ≙ WA 30 III, 237, 27-36.

66 Luther speaks sharply about the same subject in »On marriage matters, 1530«, chiding fathers who refuse to let their daughters marry because the women are more useful to them at home: »Before I would tolerate such peasant caprice with paternal power on the part of these rude louts, I would rather advise their children and tell them to get engaged without the consent of such fathers. For paternal power is not given to the fathers by God for their caprice or to do harm to their children, but to further and help them. And anyone who uses paternal power in any other way or to the disadvantage of his children forfeits it thereby and is not to be considered a father, but an enemy and destroyer of his own children«; LW 46, 308 ≙ WA 30 III, 239, 15-22.

Luther advises that in such cases the authorities act *in loco parentis* and take custody of the child, as they do with abandoned children and orphans, and insure that the father cannot hinder an honorable and advantageous marriage. In addition, the authorities should punish the father as a public enemy of his child, God, and the entire community. If the authorities default, then the pastor should help as he can and »give to the child, as one deserted by her father and prevented by him, the free right before God

respond to other physical needs, writes Luther. Not even the father in his vast God-given authority can alter that. Finally, if he fails to help his child make a suitable match, he again defaults on his parental responsibility. In such a case, if the child has sought the father's assistance in vain, the child may proceed as if the father or guardian were dead and make his or her own marital arrangements.

Luther considers one hypothetical case that calls for some artful pastoral counsel on his part. What should a young person do when his father intends to force him into an unwanted marriage? Strictly speaking, responds Luther, he should do as his father demands and take up his cross in obedience to Christ.

> »For Christ has the ready answer: Let that be my concern; why do you have no faith in me? Obey my command, and I can so govern events that none of the misfortunes you foresee will occur, and all will be good fortune and happiness. Would you transgress my certain and blessed commandment on account of an uncertain future misfortune? Or would you do evil, that good might result? Paul condemns this in Romans 3[:8]. And even though misfortune were certain for the future, indeed already at hand, should you on that account disregard my commandment, when you are in duty bound to hazard body and soul temporally and eternally for my sake?«[67]

It is not clear how enduring a loveless and potentially destructive marriage qualifies as faithful Christian discipleship. What appears to be at stake for Luther is obedience to the fourth commandment, even when

> to become engaged in good conscience, and confirm this marriage for the reason that paternal power is not created by God to be free wantonness but is an obligation first of all to serve the children with advice and help for their benefit and honor and with all diligence to further and seek the improvement and increase of the community. And the pastors are publicly to point out most emphatically the malice of these crude people as most shameful, so that they will have some conscience about it. And even if they do not fear God., they must still be ashamed before men and obey the authorities«; LW 46, 309 ≙ WA 30 III, 239, 35 - 240, 5.
>
> Luther is very clear that marriage is a community affair; the community depends upon it for the increase of its citizenry. Thus it has a vested interest in acting against parents who would prevent their children from taking up their marital and childbearing responsibilities. It is also worth noting how the fourth commandment comes into play here: authority of the spiritual father, the pastor, trumps that of the biological father of the girl in this case.

67 LW 45, 389 ≙ WA 15, 166, 13-20.

paternal authority is exercised tyrannically and cruelly. But Luther offers escape routes for »weak Christians« – and are there any other kind in his theology? If you can't bear the yoke of Christ in a forced marriage, then turn to the civil authorities for aid, »[...] that they may put a stop to such outrageous injustice, deprive the father of his devilish power, rescue the child from him, and restrict him to the proper use of his parental authority.«[68] Now the burden of honoring the fourth commandment falls on the father. The Christian is called to endure injustice, but the temporal authority is responsible for preventing it and punishing perpetrators. Luther concludes that if the government fails to do its duty, the child might flee and settle somewhere else, out of the reach of both parent and ruler.[69] There is precedent for this, he writes, citing certain »weak Christians« in the Old Testament who fled tyrants.

Luther is equally concerned about the conduct of children in the process of betrothal and marriage. He is adamant that no union should be based on a secret engagement. Clearly the easiest way around parental objections or interference was to join oneself to another without their knowledge. Protestant and Roman teaching held the free mutual consent of the parties in an exchange of vows to constitute a marriage. However, Luther did

---

68 LW 45, 389 ≙ WA 15, 166, 21-25.

69 Luther addresses a similar case in »On Marriage Matters, 1530«. Here he is more sanguine about the efficacy of intervention on the part of the authorities, including the pastor, and does not suggest flight as a potential last resort. On the other hand, he is callous about the lack of power that would contribute to a young person's being railroaded into a disagreeable marriage by coercive parents. »What if a child has already been forced into marriage? Shall this be and remain a marriage? Answer: Yes, it is a marriage and shall remain one, for although she was forced into it, she still consented to this coercion by her action, accepted it, and followed it, so that her husband has publicly acquired conjugal rights over her, which no one can now take from him. When she feels that she is being coerced, she should do something about it in time, resist, and not accept it, call upon some good friends, and if that were of no avail she should appeal to the authorities or complain to the pastor or give public, verbal testimony that she did not want to do it, and thus cry out openly against the compulsion. For these four means, namely, calling upon good friends, appealing to the authorities, complaining to the pastor, and protesting openly, should be powerful enough to prevent a forced marriage. Indeed, the authorities with the law or the pastor with good counsel can probably do it alone«; LW 46, 307 ≙ WA 30 III, 238, 4-16.

183

not acknowledge the validity of freely exchanged promises between two parties of legally marriageable age if they were made without public witnesses or parental consent, whereas Roman canon law did recognize such unions. Luther objected on four grounds: 1) that such commitments led too easily to conflicts of conscience;[70] 2) that marriage is critical to the life and health of the community and therefore should be contracted publicly before one's neighbors and with the recognition of the secular authorities; 3) that a betrothal contracted without the approval of one's parents violates the fourth commandment; and 4) that no word of God is proclaimed over the couple's action and consequently God has not joined them together. The bride, says Luther, has only the fine words and promise of her seducer to go by and on these she dare not rely.

Luther also condemns children who, presuming on the fact that they should not be forced into a marriage, resist a union that is honorable and desirable. It is their duty to abandon what Luther calls their »foolish young love« and honor their family's judgment. Parents, however, can only go so far in leading a child to wisdom. Once they offer their counsel, their consciences are clear. If children reject their considered opinion and persist in

---

70 »Here I want to show what impelled me, even before I had considered these causes, to advise and act against secret engagements. It often happened that a married couple came to me (not counting those who came to others all over the world), one or both of whom had previously become secretly engaged to others, and now there was misery and distress. Then we confessors or theologians were supposed to counsel these captive consciences. But how could we do this? There was the law and custom of the officials which decreed that the first secret betrothal was a true marriage in God's sight, and that the second one was an open act of adultery. So they went ahead and tore up the second marriage and ordered them to keep the first secret betrothal, even if they had ten children together in the second marriage and had joined their inheritance and property into one [...]. Further, if this engagement was so secret that it could not be attested by a single witness, and the second one was openly confirmed in the church, then they were forced to comply with both: first, they must consider the secret betrothal as the true marriage in their consciences before God, and on the other hand the woman was forced on pain of excommunication and by obedience to share the table and bed of the second man as her true husband, because this marriage was publicly attested, while the former secret engagement no one dared to acknowledge except she herself, and that in her conscience before God. What should a poor conscience do in a case like this?«; LW 46, 270 f ≙ WA 30 III, 209, 10-21. 24-32.

their intention to make a match to which their parents object, the parents are free to leave them to their own devices, commit the matter to God, and consider their parental obligation met.

IX The Patriarchs and Matriarchs as Married Couples

Luther makes creative use of biblical narratives to support his arguments concerning the holy status of marriage and family life. Husbands and wives do not figure significantly as actors in the New Testament, but the stories of the Old Testament patriarchs and matriarchs provide him with rich material. Indeed, Luther expands with relish on what he finds there, decking these figures out with a full range of emotions and domestic virtues. Given the promise made to Abraham that God would make of him a great nation, these couples are deeply concerned with child-bearing. Luther comments that it is hard for us to imagine the anguish and shame caused by barrenness in the days of the matriarchs and patriarchs. Indeed, the worst stresses fall on these marriages when infertility becomes an issue.[71] Consequently,

71 Infertility afflicts Sarah, Rebekah, and Rachel, although they all ultimately become mothers. Eve is the exception; she has a lot of stressors on her marriage, but an inability to conceive is not one of them. Tamar is not barren, but she is deprived of her rights to bear children due to the death of her first husband (slain by God for his wickedness) and the sexual malpractice of her second.

Of the latter Luther writes: »Onan must have been a malicious and incorrigible scoundrel. This is a most disgraceful sin. It is far more atrocious than incest and adultery. We call it unchastity, yes, a Sodomitic sin. For Onan goes in to her; that is, he lies with her and copulates, and when it comes to the point of insemination, spills the semen, lest the woman conceive. Surely at such a time the order of nature established by God in procreation should be followed. Accordingly, it was a most disgraceful crime to produce semen and excite the woman, and to frustrate her at that very moment. He was inflamed with the basest spite and hatred«; LW 7, 20f ≙ WA 44, 316, 39 - 317, 6.

Luther's concern for Tamar's experience in this sexual encounter is noteworthy. Judah, the father of these two men, promises Tamar the third son in marriage but fails to follow through. Tamar then disguises herself as a prostitute and seduces Judah, is impregnated by him and thus secures her right to childbearing of which his family had defrauded her. Although Luther charges Tamar with incest, he sees her case as complicated. She transgresses boundaries in a rightful cause: »To be sure, she sins gravely, but it is the unwillingness to bear reproach which provides the occasion for this sin. She grieves because the highest honor of women is being taken from her, namely, to be a wife, especially of

the greatest manifestation of God's goodness is the opening of the womb, so that the childless woman is able to take her place in the line of those carrying God's promises to future generations.

When commenting on the creation story in his »Lectures on Genesis«, Luther notes that with the work of the fifth day God not only »saw that it was good», God also »blessed them«. Only with the fifth day does God bring living things into being,[72] and the blessing given to them and not to the inanimate part of the creation has to do with their distinctive method of reproduction: »But here there is procreation from a living body into a living body. This, therefore, is a new work, that a living body grows and multiplies out of its own body.«[73] This capacity to bear live young is the effect of the Word making fruitful the common act of reproduction.[74]

When discussing Adam and Eve, Luther understands Gn 2, 18 – »Then the Lord God said, ›It is not good that the man should be alone [...].‹« – to be concerned with what he calls the common good of the species rather

this son of Judah, and because she is being deprived of all the adornments of a lady of the house. Her wrath was justified and almost excusable«; LW 7, 34f ≙ WA 44, 326, 36-40.

Moreover, her conduct plays a key role in the plan of salvation, since Christ is descended from her and Judah's son Perez. Thus Jesus can trace his ancestry back to some very bold sinners. However, later in his commentary on Genesis [38] Luther counts Tamar among the excellent saintly matrons who administer the household and care for the stock. Once the time of crisis is over, she settles back into modesty and domesticity.

72 Gn 1, 20-22: »And God said, ›Let the waters bring forth swarms of living creatures, and let birds fly above the earth across the firmament of the heavens.‹ So God created the great sea monsters and every living creature that moves, with which the waters swarm, according to their kinds, and every winged bird according to its kind. And God saw that it was good. And God blessed them, saying, »Be fruitful and multiply and fill the waters in the seas, and let birds multiply on the earth.‹«

73 LW 1, 53 ≙ WA 42, 39, 37-39.

74 »What, then, is the reason for this remarkable procreation? The hen lays an egg; this she keeps warm while a living body comes into being in the egg, which the mother later on hatches. The philosophers advance the reason that these events take place through the working of the sun and her belly. I grant this. But the theologians say, far more reliably, that these events take place through the working of the Word, because it is said here: He blessed them and said: ›Increase and multiply.‹ This Word is present in the very body of the hen and in all living creatures; the heat with which the hen keeps her eggs warm is the result of the divine Word, because if it were without the Word, the heat would be useless and without effect«; LW 1, 53 ≙ WA 42, 40, 5-12.

than the personal good of Adam. The other created living beings had companions with whom they could mate, but »so far Adam was alone; he still had no partner for that magnificent work of begetting and preserving his kind«.[75] He required Eve so that he could fulfill his duty to be fruitful and multiply. It is only after the fall that he has need of her to ward off the sin of illicit desire.[76] The animals, Luther notes, do not have to contend with lust, but neither do they have the kind of spiritual, affective relationship that comes with human marriage. Luther laments the damage done to the intimacy between husband and wife by the loss of innocence. Delight gives way to shame and resentment.

God tells the woman, »I will greatly multiply your pain in childbearing; in pain you shall bring forth children, yet your desire shall be for your husband, and he shall rule over you.«[77] In this Luther hears as much good news as bad. Yes, the flesh will suffer, but God does not repudiate Eve. Nor is she deprived of the blessing of procreation or separated from her husband to live in solitude. Most of all, in keeping what Luther calls the glory of motherhood, she also has the assurance that the Seed who will crush the head of her betrayer will come from her. The discomfort of pregnancy and the danger of childbirth pale in comparison, concludes Luther. Then he writes:

> »Without a doubt, therefore, Eve had a heart full of joy even in an apparently sad situation. Perhaps she gave comfort to Adam by saying: ›I have sinned. But see what a merciful God we have. How many privileges, both temporal and spiritual, He is leaving for us sinners! Therefore we women should bear the hardship and wretchedness of conceiving, of giving birth, and of obeying you husbands. His is a fatherly anger, because this stands: that the head of our enemy will be crushed, and that after the death of our flesh we shall be raised to a new and eternal life through our Redeemer. These abundant good things and endless kindnesses far surpass

75 LW 1, 116 ≙ WA 42, 87, 36-38.
76 Luther speaks from the male perspective: woman is man's defense against lust. The following is typical: »In Paradise woman would have been a help for a duty only. But now she is also, and for the greater part at that, an antidote and a medicine; we can hardly speak of her without a feeling of shame, and surely we cannot make use of her without shame«; LW 1, 118 ≙ WA 42, 89, 34-37. Considering the universal nature of the fall, it is a given that women too are plagued with selfish, raging desire that threatens to use rather than honor the partner in every aspect of a relationship. Eve also needs Adam to be able to subject lust to love.
77 Gn 3, 16.

whatever curse and punishments our Father has inflicted on us.‹ These and similar conversations Adam and Eve undoubtedly carried on often in order to mitigate their temporal adversities.«[78]

Adam and Eve, caught in sin and facing the trauma of life in the post-fall world, represent marriage at its best. The couple accepts the arduous work that lies before them as God's charge, and they stand together as companions, sharing words of comfort and faith. Clearly there is more going on in the relationship of husband wife than the containment of lust and the raising of children.[79]

Abraham and Sarah serve Luther as a model for the discipleship of Christian couples first and foremost because of their faith. Both of the elderly people give up the home they know to answer God's call to go forth to a strange land. When promised the birth of a child at their advanced ages, they are shocked but confident of God's truthfulness. Luther also praises their daily discipleship because of the commonplace duties and normal domestic tedium it entails. He contrasts this in most pejorative terms to the idle, inflated »spiritual« life of the monastics and assures his readers that the menial tasks that occupy Sarah and Abraham, done as they are in faith, are more precious than any trumped up work of holiness and celibacy.

> »Therefore shut out from your heart and eyes the outward appearance, and see what God has commanded; do this, and you will not go wrong, even if in outward appearance it is small, ordinary, and insignificant. Antony withdraws into the desert, and Jerome makes a pilgrimage to sacred places and advocates devotion to chastity. These works the world regards as great. But the fact that Sarah stands at the hearth and busily prepares food for the guests – this not only has no outward appearance of a good work but seems to stand in the way of good works. Yet to one who has regard for the Word it will be evident that Sarah did a holier work than all the hermits did.«[80]

78 LW 1, 199 ≙ WA 42, 148, 35 - 149, 5.
79 In relation to Gn 2,22 Luther writes: »Let us, therefore, obey the Word of God and recognize our wives as a building of God. Not only is the house built through them by procreation and other services that are necessary in a household; but the husbands themselves are built through them, because wives are, as it were, a nest and a dwelling place where husbands can go to spend their time and dwell with joy«; LW 1, 134 ≙ WA 42, 100, 17-21.
80 LW 3, 216-17 ≙ WA 43, 30, 5-12.

When, Luther says, you are confident of doing full justice to your calling and of having no need to pray »forgive us our trespasses« because of negligence, dissatisfaction, or impatience, then feel free to go into the desert and busy yourself with showy works of holiness.

Luther finds in Sarah a treasury of housewifely virtues. He makes much of the fact that when the three guests inquire as to Sarah's whereabouts, Abraham answers, »She is in the tent.«[81] Women, writes Luther, are given to a certain levity and indecent curiosity. They either run around or hang out conspicuously at their doors to pick up the latest gossip. Such women on the loose are susceptible to moral laxity. Sarah, however, is right where she belongs, within their home, leaving her husband and his guests in peace while she prepares the meal and manages the household responsibly.

Yet one should note that Sarah is not always so amiable and modest. Luther maintains that in the matter of Hagar and Ishmael Abraham is lax in protecting the promise made to him and Sarah concerning their descendants. He loves the slave woman and their son with a natural affection and does not see their impudence. Sarah is the one who obliges him to expel them, lest Ishmael presume on his primogeniture at Isaac's expense. Although Luther is at some pains to protect Sarah's wifely modesty, stating that she humbly implores but does not command Abraham, he recognizes the reality of dissension and anger in their marriage and by extension in every marriage. The endurance of such arguments by husband and wife is a spiritual discipline, a formation in holiness, far excelling anything concocted by the monks.

> »Therefore they call the life of married people a »secular« life, but it surely has a place among the highest levels of spiritual life. For the loftiest sentiments of married people toward God and man are being cultivated.
>
> In this passage Abraham is an instance. He is compelled by a two-fold right, the natural and the divine, to defend his lawful wife and son. Because of this feeling he is unable to see the promise clearly. On this account a violent outburst of anger occurs, and there is a very sharp quarrel – to give us an example and to comfort us, in order that when slight offenses arise, we may be mindful of the life and the lot that are common to all men.«[82]

81 The story is told in Gn 18, 1-16.
82 LW 4, 22 $\hat{=}$ WA 43, 151, 28-36.

In this instance Sarah, in fulfilling her »secular« responsibilities as wife and mother, acts as the unlikely but indispensable champion of the Word. Through bearing Isaac and protecting his position as heir to the promise, she becomes the mother of the faithful.[83]

Luther's commentary on the courtship of Jacob and Rachel offers some interesting observations on the realities of physical attraction. Reflecting on Jacob's infatuation with Rachel and indifference to Leah, Luther offers the opinion that ugly women are usually the most fertile. By rights men should love women simply for the sake of procreation; strictly speaking they should not be swayed by appearance. However, God indulges the male's preference for beautiful women to help sweeten the conjugal pot.

> »Because of so many great troubles and difficulties of marriage it is not wicked if one chooses a beautiful woman with her bodily strength unimpaired in order that he may be able to endure this bond of marriage with all its troubles longer and more easily.«[84]

Because of original sin man's sexual urges are unpredictable and urgent. He needs to marry, and if it takes feminine beauty to get the deed done, so be it.

Luther speaks of Jacob the suitor with fond amusement. According to his calculations the patriarch is 84 years old when he first meets Rachel. He is already an old man, but in the presence of this beautiful girl he is rejuvenated.[85] He single-handedly rolls away the stone from the mouth of

---

83 One finds a similar dilemma in the narrative of Isaac and Rebekah, when the wife transgresses the bounds of propriety and obedience to her husband in order to preserve the divine promise. In this case Rebekah disguises Jacob as Esau so that he might secure the paternal blessing due the first born, despite the aged Isaac's stated intent of bestowing it on Esau.

84 LW 5, 290 ≙ WA 43, 628, 33-36.

85 »Then, when in his exile he found Rachel, his blood relation, he took courage and gained great hope that at last he would obtain what he had in mind and what his father had commanded him with respect to taking a wife. Therefore he is immediately inflamed with love at first sight, and natural desire toward his kinswoman comes to the fore, so that the two-fold impulse of faith and love made his body and heart more animated. For he wanted to show himself as a man of strength and agility – in order that he might capture the maiden's heart and entice her to fall in love with him«; LW 5, 281 ≙ WA 43, 622, 33 - 623, 2.

the well so that she might water her sheep. Luther praises Jacob's extraordinary chastity; he has remained continent from his youth, some 68 years, until now, which is at it should be. But continence is destined to end in marriage. As Luther describes it, this is not a surrender to carnal necessity but a venture into love from the very start, when the patriarch kisses Rachel at the well before they have even been introduced. Old Jacob makes a bit of a fool of himself. And it is surpassingly pleasing to God.

> »Other histories about very great events – about the burning of Sodom, about the sacrifice of Isaac – [the Holy Spirit] has described with very few words and has summed up in barely five or six verses. But when He comes to these sordid, carnal, and foolish matters, He is wordy beyond measure, in order that we may know that the Lord takes pleasure in those who fear Him (Ps. 147:11). For if we believe and are sure of the freely offered mercy of God, we should not doubt that everything we do pleases God very much and that He has numbered even the hairs of our head (cf. Matt. 10:30), yes, that the kisses and embraces are pleasing to Him, likewise the removal of that stone. All these things are recounted in this passage as very great and extraordinary works in the eyes of God and the angels. God could not forget them but wanted them recorded for our instruction and consolation.«[86]

Luther does not dismiss the ardor and delight of new love as frivolous. They will not sustain a couple through the challenges of years of married life, but such enchantment is a real fine place to start.

X Conclusion

Human beings are fallen creatures. For Luther our sexual nature is no more and no less vitiated by sin than our other qualities and abilities. Sexuality still unfolds in the wondrous way God intended it to: men and women are drawn to one another; they fall in love and discover for themselves that it is not good for the man to be alone; they long for children. God has created marriage to make these things possible. God has formed us to want what God wants: that we leave our parents and cleave to our spouse; that we be fruitful and multiply. In the fallen world marriage grants additional blessing, although Luther does not regard it as a sacramental means of saving grace. God does not call a person to marriage in general; God calls you to be married to a particular person. The word of God's command and favor

---

86 LW 5, 283 ≙ WA 43, 624, 12-22.

is spoken over *this* union. It is absolutely clear that this is the spouse you are to have and no other. The certain boundary will frustrate couples at times, but its clarity is also a kindness. Husband and wife can persevere in the demanding work of marriage, confident that their efforts are pleasing to God, their failures forgiven, and their commitment to one another enduringly blessed.

The same is true in the realm of the family. Its routine activities are hardly glorious in human eyes, but for God they are acts of praise. In tending to the needs of those who populate our daily lives we carry out our calling to be little Christs one to another. Regarding the responsibility of parents for their children in particular, Luther speaks sternly. One's child, like one's marriage, is a sacred trust. A parent who violates a child by abuse, betrayal or neglect falls under the wrath of God. Luther recognizes that it does indeed take a village to raise the young, and in such cases he expects the wider community – collateral relatives, friends of the family, the civil authorities, the pastor – to intervene.

Luther holds marriage in the highest regard as the created norm for the life of Christian and non-Christian alike. He is clear, however, that no one is saved by matrimony – or the absence thereof. Marital status is an adiaphoron. One can wed or not as one pleases; in terms of salvation it is of no importance to God. However, in terms of sexuality marriage is the deal-breaker. Fulfilling conjugal obligations is the only legitimate form of sexual activity. God beholds sex within marriage and declares that it is still good, covering its lustful deficits with grace.[87] But outside of marriage sexual activity plunges a person into a morass of sin and condemnation. It is hardly surprising that Luther did not take a new view on this matter. Unfortunately, it makes it difficult for many of his contemporary heirs, who do not share that judgment, to appreciate what Luther does have to say to those who choose to marry and to the communities obliged to support their family life. On these matters he gives us much worth taking to heart.

---

87 In his sermon on H 13,4 from January 1531 Luther speaks beautifully of the coverlet – Decke – which God spreads over the bed shared by the married couple, »damit es geschmückt wird und ein schön, rein, unbefleckt bette heisst, [...]«; WA 34 I, 74, 10 f.

Models of the Christian Life in Luther's Genesis Sermons and Lectures

By Robert Kolb

In his »Recultivating the vineyard« Scott Hendrix concludes that Martin Luther set out »to provide a religious environment in which believers would develop as fully as possible into the model Christians described by him in *Freedom of a Christian*: free through faith to serve others in love. The creation of these ›real Christians‹ (to use his term) took precedence over other agendas that interpreters have occasionally tried to impose on Luther [...].«[1] Hendrix quotes Luther's treatise »On both kinds of the sacrament«: if his readers would abandon »unfaithfulness, hatred, envy, wrath, and unbelief«, then »we would at last become again a group of Christians«, in contrast to being »almost completely pagan and only Christian in name.«[2] Luther's concept of a »real« Christian incorporated two elements, Hendrix concludes. The first is »righteousness,« which signified for Luther that someone faithfully is and expresses what he or she is supposed to be. The second is »piety«, which Luther himself transformed from a word for general upright and honorable living to a designation for living a life of faith in God which produces love and service to others.[3] As he communicated his call to his parishioners and students in Wittenberg to live the godly life in sermons and lectures, Luther cultivated a biblical sense of righteousness and piety through many means and rhetorical de-

---

1 Scott HENDRIX: Recultivating the vineyard: the Reformation agendas of Christianization. Louisville, KY; LO 2004, 37. The addition of »real« before Christians is not in the German but conveys the sense of Luther's comment.
2 Hendrix: Recultivating the vineyard, 40; Martin LUTHER: Von beider Gestalt des Sakraments zu nehmen; WA 10 II, 39, 10f ≙ LW 36, 264.
3 Hendrix: Recultivating the Vineyard, 59f; cf. Walter SPARN: »Wahrlich, dieser ist ein frommer Mensch gewesen!«: Überlegungen zu einem evangelischen Begriff von Frömmigkeit. In: Post-Theism: reframing the Judeo-christian tradition/ ed. by Henri Andriën Krop; Arie Leendert Molendijk; Hendrik Johan Adriaanse de Vries. Louvain 2000, 447-465.

vices. Among them was the story, above all the biblical stories, which he retold and elaborated with suitable explanation and application to model the Christian life for his people.

I The Whole Life of a Christian Is a Life of Repentance

Luther's recultivation of the Christian life rested on several axioms. First, his own experience, as well as his reading of Scripture, had impressed upon him that the mystery of the continuation of sin and evil in the lives of the baptized defied explanation, but the unshakable actuality of this mystery caused him nonetheless to define the Christian life as a continuing struggle. For the remnants of sinners' defiance of God and disdain for the welfare of other creatures disrupt the peace which God designed to frame human living.

For, he knew from his own experience, this mystery of continuing sin and evil in Christians' daily living made it necessary to wage a never-ending struggle against wickedness and impiety day in and day out. God and believers waged this struggle through the use of the law, which strikes sinners dead, and the gospel, which gives new life through Christ's death and resurrection. Although medieval antecedents framed what Luther meant when in 1517 he wrote, »the whole life of a Christian is a life of repentance«,[4] it is clear that by 1529 his concept of repentance had come to focus upon the repetition of God's baptismal action of killing sinners and making them into children of God: »[…] the old creature in us with all sins and evil desires is to be drowned and die through daily contrition and repentance, and on the other hand, a new person is to come forth and rise up to live before God in righteousness and purity forever«, as he wrote in the Small Catechism.[5] This action of God's condemning law and his life-

4 See Volker Leppin: »Omnem vitam fidelium penitentiam esse voluit«. ARG 93 (2003), 7-25, who demonstrates that in 1517 Luther was echoing the conviction of the fourteenth-century devotional writer and preacher Heinrich Tauler (circa 1300-1361) regarding the continuing necessity of humbling oneself before God. See also the critique of this position in Martin Brecht: Luthers neues Verständnis der Buße und die reformatorische Entdeckung. ZThK 101 (2004), 281-291.

5 The Book of Concord: the confessions of the Evangelical Lutheran Church/ ed. by Robert Kolb; Timothy J. Wengert. MP 2000, 360 (12-14) ≙ BSLK 516, 29 - 517, 7.

restoring gospel permeated Luther's interpretation of both New and Old Testaments, according to Heinrich Bornkamm (1901-1977).[6] In his lecture on Abraham's pleading for the people of Sodom,[7] Luther repeated an earlier allegorical treatment of God's command not to take the lower and upper millstone from the needy at the same time,[8] an interpretation that he had made more than a decade earlier in lecturing on Deuteronomy. Then he had not sketched the distinction of law and gospel with his later clarity:

> »The lower and upper millstone are properly said to denote hope and fear, or law and gospel. The law is the word of wrath, the upper millstone; it preserves fear and humbles people through the recognition of sin. The gospel, the word of grace, preserves the conscience by faith, so that it does not tremble. The preaching of both is necessary.«

But then he counseled not to overdo either, neither punishing sin too strictly and terrifying too greatly nor treating the sinner too gently and consoling too strongly.[9] In 1538 he stated,

> »The upper millstone is the fear and judgment of God. This the lower millstone supports; it signifies the hope and feeling of mercy. Thus, the ministry of the Word should connect law and gospel, repentance and the forgiveness of sins.«[10]

Luther presumed that this struggle to leave godlessness behind and to practice true humanity, that is, to return to being a righteous or pious human being, took place in the two dimensions of human life that formed the heart of his anthropology. He understood that God had constructed humanness to be lived out in two relationships quite distinct from each other, though inextricably and inseparably linked with each other. He first set forth this anthropology at length in his treatises on three kinds and two kinds of »righteousness« in 1518/19,[11] and claimed that this distinction characterized »our theology« in 1531.[12] Sometimes

---

6 Heinrich Bornkamm: Luther and the Old Testament/ trans. by Eric W. and Ruth C. Gritsch. Phil 1969, 262f.

7 Gn 18, 29-33.

8 Dt 24, 6.

9 WA 14, 717, 3-10 ≙ LW 9, 244.

10 WA 43, 45, 2-5 ≙ LW 3, 237.

11 WA 2, (39) 43-47; (143) 145-152 ≙ LW 31, 297-306.

12 WA 40 I, 45, 24-27 ≙ LW 26, 7.

more explicitly, sometimes less explicitly, this anthropological foundation for his thinking accompanied his proclamation of the gospel throughout his career.[13]

For Luther, Christian living did not simply involve doing good works although he did define human activity as an essential element of piety. His more comprehensive definition of the faithful Christian life can be found in his »Warning to his dear German people« of 1531. There he reflected on the »success« of his efforts over the past decade, commenting, »It has, praise God, come to this, that men and women, young and old, know the catechism and how to believe, live, pray, suffer, and die«.[14] This suggests that Luther gauged the success of his Reformation in terms of five elements that constituted for him the Christian life:

1) Trust in God, Creator, Redeemer, and Sanctifier replaces trust in false gods of human invention. Luther's use of examples from biblical figures served to nurture dependence on God and confidence in his merciful disposition toward his baptized children.[15]

2) Suffering of all kinds haunts much of life on earth. Luther turned to the likes of Abraham and Joseph, for example, to demonstrate how hearers and readers could flee to the refuge and haven of their providential Creator and Savior for support and comfort in times of affliction. Luther also regarded the God-pleasing conduct of daily life as a significant element of piety. That daily life embraced two aspects of righteous or pious activity for a preacher with as strong convictions about sin as Luther had.

3) »Mortifying the flesh«, that is, defeating temptations to stray from trusting in God and loving the neighbor is necessary as preparation for

4) the practice of humanity as God had designed it, in love toward other, performing God-commanded virtues within the context of callings or vocations.

13 See Robert KOLB: Die Zweidimensionalität des Mensch-Seins: die zweierlei Gerechtigkeit in Luthers De votis monasticis judicium. In: Luther und das monastische Erbe/ hrsg. von Christoph Bultmann; Volker Leppin; Andreas Lindner. TÜ 2007, 207-220; and Robert KOLB: God and his human creatures in Luther's Sermons on Genesis: the reformer's early use of his distinction of two kinds of righteousness. CJ 33 (2007), 164-184.

14 »Aber nu ists, Gott lob, dahin komen, das man und weib, jung vnd alt, den Catechismum weis, Und wie man gleuben, leben, beten, leiden und sterben sol, [...]«; WA 30 III, 317, 32-34 ≙ LW 47, 52.

15 Bornkamm: Luther and the Old Testament, 23 f.

5) Exemplary living prepares for exemplary dying. To be sure, Luther treated these aspects of pious living on the basis of a variety of biblical genre, but important among them were those models for such living sprang from biblical narratives on which Luther preached and lectured.

II Luther as Narrative Theologian

»Narrative« became a major topic in biblical studies, homiletics, and systematic theology a quarter century ago. »Narrative« can refer in these settings to the style of preaching that relies on stories of real or imagined people and events from Scripture, history, or contemporary experience to foster the hearers' absorption of the preacher's message. It also refers to the biblical accounts of God's and human actions and reactions to each other. From that focus on the biblical text narrative theology also reached out to embrace discussions of the »metanarrative« that stands behind individual stories and/or the entire biblical report of God's interaction with this human creatures. Biblical narrative serves a number of purposes, among them specifically the cultivation of human righteousness and the pious life.[16]

According to the analysis of Yale systematic theologian Hans Wilhelm Frei (1922-1988), whose work has guided much recent thinking on »narrative«, »Western Christian reading of the Bible in the days before the rise of historical criticism [...] was usually strongly realistic, i. e. at once literal and historical, and not only doctrinal or edifying«,[17] though for Luther it certainly was that, too. Like a stream of previous biblical preachers, above all Augustine (354-430), the Wittenberg reformer »envisioned the real world as formed by the sequence told by the biblical stories [...] from creation to the final consummation to come«.[18] The reformer was convinced that neither the God who designed human life nor the course of human living had changed substantially between Abraham's time and his own. Luther's

16 Gordon J. WENHAM: Story as Torah: reading Old Testament narrative ethically. Grand Rapids, MI 2004.
17 Hans W. Frei: The eclipse of Biblical narrative: a study in eighteenth and nineteenth century hermeneutics. New Haven, CT 1974, 1.
18 Ibid.

practice in using Scripture also reflected Frei's observation about his time that »since the world truly rendered by combining biblical narratives into one was indeed the one and only real world, it must in principle embrace the experience of any present age and reader.«[19]

Frei acknowledged his debt to the literary theory of German-Jewish émigré scholar Erich Auerbach (1892-1957),[20] who used the contrast between Greek epic ways of telling tales of human life and the biblical record as the basis for his observations about the representation of reality in Western literature. Auerbach classified biblical narratives as intrinsically historical in intent – even though he did not necessarily regard them as historically true in point of fact –, contrasting them with those of Homer, and he found a deep cleft separating the two literary traditions. Readers gain full benefit from the story of Odysseus, Penelope, and Euryclea, Auerbach argued, without being compelled to believe they existed, »but the Biblical narrator [...] had to believe in the objective truth of the story of Abraham's sacrifice« of Isaac, and »had to believe in it passionately«. Auerbach labeled this not an orientation toward »realism« but toward truth that simply subjects readers to itself.[21] And yet the biblical text's hegemony over its readers is not exercised so simply as this might make it seem. Biblical narratives depict human life through stories full of »gaps«, Auerbach emphasized. The episodic nature of the Old Testament »requires an interpreter even though the message does emerge clearly from the texts«.[22] The interpreter must retell its stories for new hearers in new times and places, filling in the gaps on the basis of the claim of the text to provide a new application of the story to real experiences and thus to authentic human life. Luther slipped easily into this role. He accepted the challenge which one of Auerbach's disciples, the Jewish exegete Meir Sternberg later saw in this style of narrative: the »ubiquity of gaps about character and plot exposes to us our own ignorance: history unrolls as a continuum of discontinuities, a sequence of non sequiturs, which challenge us to repair the omissions by our native

19 Frei: The eclipse of Biblical narrative, 3.
20 Frei: The eclipse of Biblical narrative, vii.
21 Erich AUERBACH: Mimesis: the representation of reality in western literature/ trans. by Willard R. Trask. Princeton, NJ 1953, 14-16.
22 Auerbach: Mimesis, 17.

wit.«²³ Luther employed the gaps in the biblical narrative to explain how God works in behalf of his human creatures and what he requires from them, while at the same time illuminating the mysterious nature of the continuation of sin and evil in the lives of the baptized through these gaps. The hearer has no illusion of being able to take control of knowledge or direction in such situations: the children of God can only listen and hearken to the Word of the Lord.

Two other observations from Auerbach illumine Luther's use of Scripture. First, the biblical narrative engages the reader in the midst of daily life. This engagement with reality takes place because »a part of the genius of these stories is that they depict neither simple heroes nor, consistently, upper class life, as Homer did. The Old Testament figures […] can fall much lower in dignity.«²⁴ Biblical people »are bearers of the divine will, and yet they are fallible, subject to misfortune and humiliation […].«²⁵

Second, »if the text of the Biblical narrative, then, is so greatly in need of interpretation on the basis of its own content, its claim to absolute authority forces is still further in the same direction«.²⁶ Sternberg attributed the biblical text's authority and hold on its readers to two factors:

1) the omniscience of the biblical narrator produces a view of his stories that is derived from the omniscience of God, whose servant and voice the narrator is; thus, the text claims irrevocably to be true.²⁷

23 Meir STERNBERG: The poetics of biblical narrative: ideological literature and the drama of reading. Bloomington, IN, 1985, 47.
24 Auerbach: Mimesis, 22.
25 Auerbach: Mimesis, 18.
26 Auerbach: Mimesis, 15.
27 Sternberg: The poetics …, 12 f. Sternberg describes the connection between the biblical presentation of the person of God and the authors' art in depicting him and his actions: »The building of supernatural premises into the action, the preference of the dramatic method over commentary, the foreshadowing-fulfillment structure of repetition, the manifold patterning of redundancy, speech as creative act, the manipulation of sequence in units ranging from the entire Bible to a verse, similarly variable play of perspectives, forms of serialization, shifts between overt and covert providence, spatiotemporal bounding, and so on: the strategy coordinating such an array bespeaks an ideological crux of the first magnitude. Anchored in this composition, moreover, the effect and the narrative stance of intermediacy from which it is generated afford an equally powerful explanation for a set of other measures, great and small. Above all, their ideological

2) the Old Testament narratives are, therefore, first and foremost the stories of God, his actions and his address of his human creatures. This »history unfolds a theology in action – one distinctively grounded in God's control and providence [...] history-writing doubles as a sacred contract, uniquely explaining the processes of time by reference to a covenantal relation with divinity«.[28] Luther treated biblical narration in this way, taking for granted that readers of Scripture were engaging and engaged by the person of the Almighty Father and real human creatures who had interacted with him.[29] He trusted the biblical reports regarding God's power and reliability as well as their reflection of the course of real human living.

Sternberg observes that in its narratives the Old Testament seldom tells the reader of the moral or theological significance of the reported events.[30] While this is true, those narratives are set in the context of such interpretations of God and human life. Luther's application of the narratives did not simply retell the story and presume that sixteenth century hearers would understand. His use of the narratives involved extensive interpretive comment at several levels. This can be clearly in his several treatments of Genesis, which form the basis of this essay, from earlier sermons (1519-1521, 1523 [published 1527] and later lectures (1535-1545).[31] The

imperative accounts for the narrator's drastic self-effacement in the handling of a plot that foregrounds God's omnipotence«; Sternberg: The poetics ..., 118.

28 Sternberg: The poetics ..., 44f.

29 Bornkamm makes this point; Bornkamm: Luther and the Old Testament, 6f. 261.

30 Sternberg: The poetics ..., 38.

31 See the commentary of the editor Ernst Thiele (1856-1922) in WA 9, 320-323 on the sermons and Glossa of 1519-1523. On the sermons preached in 1523/24, published 1527, see the introduction to the printed edition in WA 24, xiii-xlvii, and to the notes taken on the sermons as they were delivered; WA 14, 92-96. The text of notes from Georg Rörer (1492-1557) and Stephan Roth (1492-1546) are found in WA 14, 97-488. See J[ohannes] P. BOENDERMAKER: Heet eerste word blijft gelden: Luthers preken over de vijf boeken van Mozes 1523-1525, inleiding en enkele teksten. In: Luther na 500 jaar: teksten, vertaald en besproken/ ed. by Jan T. Bakker; Johannes P. Boendermaker. Kempen 1983, 99-123. The lectures are found in WA 42-44. I have dated individual parts of these lectures according to the analysis of Gustav Koffmane (1852-1915) in the introduction of WA 42, vii-viii. Despite some lingering doubts about the validity of the text of the Genesis lectures of 1535-1545, the more convincing argument is made by critics of the view advanced by Erich SEEBERG: Studien zu Luthers Genesisvorlesung: zugleich ein Beitrag zur Frage nach

comparison of these stages of Luther's interpretation of the book could form an interesting essay in itself, but because the fundamental elements of Luther's understanding of the Christian life are present in the early 1520s in his preaching and remained, with certain developments in detail and emphasis, to be sure, in his lectures in 1535-1545, we will not in this study pursue these comparisons.

Indeed, Luther employed other literary forms in cultivating the life of repentance, and he treated biblical stories as more than only recitals of how daily life works. He used »figural« interpretations of the people who inhabited biblical narratives, such as Leah and Rachel, in his treatment of Christ and his church.[32] But he cultivated piety by retelling, refashioning, the stories of daily life and its encounters with God, sin, and neighbor. Already in 1521, as Luther dictated Scholia on Genesis, he noted that »all the books of the entire Scripture are either »historiae« or »historice narrationes, [scilicet] Exempla tum legum, tum operum divinorum, vel docent fidem.«[33] God's law taught human beings what they should do, and the recital of God's work taught them the gospel and faith. The story of Samuel's mother had initiated his fascination with Scripture as a youth, Luther recalled at table.[34] David Steinmetz compares Luther's handling of Old Testament narratives to the techniques of modern authors who combine fictional elaboration with biographical or historical description, such as André Maurois and Gamaliel Bradford. Luther's »narrative imagination« – »his intuitive response to the Bible as a work of art« – »grasps his readers not only at the level of their discursive reason but also at the level of their imaginative participation in their common humanity.«[35]

dem alten Luther. GÜ 1932, and Peter MEINHOLD: Die Genesisvorlesung Luthers und ihre Herausgeber. S 1936, critics such as Bernhard KLAUS: Die Lutherüberlieferung Veit Dietrichs und ihre Problematik. ZBKG 53 (1988), 33-47, and Ulrich ASENDORF: Lectura in Biblia: Luthers Genesisvorlesung (1535-1545). GÖ 1998, 33-42.

32 Sabine HIEBSCH: Figura ecclesiae: Lea und Rachel in Martin Luthers Genesispredigten. MS 2002; see also David C. STEINMETZ: Luther and the blessing of Judah. LuJ 71 (2004), 159-178, on Luther's figural treatment of Old Testament passages.

33 WA 9, 353, 8-10.

34 WA TR 1, 44, 16-20 (116); Bornkamm: Luther and the Old Testament, 8 f.

35 David C. STEINMETZ: Luther and the drunkenness of Noah. In: David C. Steimetz: Luther in context. Bloomington, IN 1986, 110 f.

Luther's education had made him sensitive to the literary constructions of the biblical stories.[36] As a re-teller of biblical stories Luther presumed that only an osmotic membrane separated Jerusalem from Wittenberg, ancient Israel from contemporary Saxony. To be sure, Luther retold the narratives with some historical sensitivity in spite of his belief that human life was largely the same in Abraham's time and his own. The manner in which Joseph ran the civil government of Egypt[37] defied the professor's imagination, and he was quite sure it would not have worked in his day and place.[38] Nonetheless, Mickey Mattox's judgment in regard to Luther's »charitable« reading of Hagar accurately describes the underlying relationship of biblical text, history, and application: »While Luther's is a decidedly anachronistic interpretation in the sense that he lacks a modern sense of historical change, moreover, it possesses at least the advantage that it yields characters whose struggles parallel those of the contemporary Christian.«[39] Therefore, as Mattox has noted, Luther accepted the invitation of the biblical text to enter into its world of thought »enthusiastically, never hesitating to imagine the biblical characters into his world or himself into theirs«.[40] He presumed that he was fundamentally like all other readers of Scripture who read the text under the Holy Spirit's guidance, and he assumed the role of the teacher of other readers, whether present parishioners or future preachers.

36 Eberhard WINKLER: Luther als Seelsorger und Prediger. In: Leben und Werk Martin Luthers von 1526 bis 1546: Festgabe zu seinem 500. Geburtstag/ im Auftrag des Theologischen Arbeitskreises für Reformationsgeschichtliche Forschung hrsg. von Helmar Junghans. Bd. 1. B, 1983, 236. According to Ulrich NEMBACH: Predigt des Evangeliums: Luther als Prediger, Pädagoge, und Rhetor. NK 1972, 131-174, Luther's preaching followed the form of Quintilian's (um 30-96) genre of advice for the people, but Gerhard Krause (in a review of Nembach in: ThLZ 99 [1974], 274f) and Helmar Junghans (LuJ 41 [1974], 149f, and DERS.: Rhetorische Bemerkungen Luthers in seinen Dictata super Psalterium. Theol. Versuche 8 [1977], 97-128) placed his rhetoric in a broader stream of tradition. Bornkamm: Luther and the Old Testament, 35-42, details some of Luther's literary treatment of Old Testament texts.

37 Gn 47, 13f.

38 WA 44, 666, 5-13 ≙ LW 8, 119.

39 Mickey Leland MATTOX: Defender of the most holy matriarchs: Martin Luther's interpretation of the women of Genesis in the Enarrationes in Genesin, 1535-45. Leiden; Boston 2003, 165.

40 Mattox: Defender ..., 1.

In that way he replicated what Sternberg sees as the role of the biblical narrator at the same time he was in the process of examining the text literarily and theologically. Sternberg conjectured that for the biblical narrator »the intervention of the Holy Spirit levels all the barriers that normally divide the far from the near, the private from the public, the interior from the exterior«,[41] and Luther seems to have presumed something similar. American homileticist John McClure holds that preachers should »*both* ›textualize experience‹, thereby inviting their hearers to see their lives on the terms of the biblical narrative, *and* ›experientialize the text‹, thereby allowing current experience to illustrate the meaning and ongoing significance of the text.«[42] Luther did both.

Bornkamm contended that Luther could do so because he experienced in Old Testament texts a »mirror of life« in sixteenth century Germany. Therefore, Luther explained biblical texts out of contemporary German life, as in the case of Lot's incest in a drunken state.[43] Luther regarded Lot's incest as an inadvertent rather than a purposeful sin, similar to a young boy's imprudently setting a fire and being spared by the law because he clearly was not an arsonist, or similar to »a brawl, in which angry people engage in a fight«, but are excused by civil authorities as having committed an imprudent sin due to circumstances. The biblical reports record not »impossible things« but rather things that are »natural and in harmony with experience«.[44] Likewise, Luther evaluated or explained contemporary German life on the basis of biblical texts.

Luther often commented on the usefulness of examples for teaching various elements of Christian living although he did not formulate a pedagogical-psychological theory as to how examples actually teach or motivate. He presumed that hearers would make the necessary associations, trusting in God's promise to them, obeying his commands for their lives. He did not presume this so completely, however, that he dispensed

41 Sternberg: The poetics ..., 76.
42 In a review of Charles L. CAMPBELL: Preaching Jesus: new directions for homiletics in Hans Frei's postliberal theology. Grand Rapids, MI 1997. In: Journal for preachers 21 (1998) number 2, 36, as quoted by David J. LOSE: Confessing Jesus Christ: preaching in a postmodern world. Grand Rapids, MI 2003, 123.
43 Gn 19, 31-33.
44 WA 43, 96, 36 - 97, 6 ≙ LW 3, 309 f.

with his own commentary; it was designed to teach in very specific terms precisely what the hearers were to gain from the story. The stories hover in the background of discourses often pages long in print as the preacher or professor drew careful applications.

Luther marveled at the fact that God engages his human creatures in conversation and urged his readers and hearers to pay close attention to the stories in which God's personal dialog directed the lives of ancient believers.

> »Those who read the bible stories perfunctorily regard them as though Claus Schmid were talking with Hans Mist, one person to another. But if you look at these stories correctly, it is a great and wonderful thing that the divine majesty talks with people as with a child. There is no more precious sign of God's grace and favor than when he lets himself be heard, and no greater plague than when he is silent.«

Therefore, the Wittenberg parishioners were to recognize the magnificence of God in these stories of his engagement with human beings and take them to heart as strengthening for their faith and encouragement to good works.[45] As Ulrich Asendorf noted, Luther found in the books of Moses »examples of faith, love, and the cross« in the patriarchs, who teach believers to trust and love God.[46]

However, Luther also distinguished between good examples and extraordinary – he sometimes called them »miraculous« – interventions by God in the patriarchs' lives. The latter should not serve as models for breaking out of the framework God's plan for usual, normal human life had set. Thomas Müntzer (circa 1489-1525) had used the examples of Abraham's freeing Lot by the sword[47] and David's fighting the Syrians precisely in this manner,[48] and Luther admonished, »one should note that the examples of the saints and of the children of God must not be understood as something to imitate and as rules for all except when they follow the rule laid down in the Word«.[49]

---

45 WA 24, 294, 17 - 295, 26; cf. WA 14, 245, 9 / 30 - 246, 4 / 15. Cf. the similar comments on Genesis 26 and God's address of Isaac; WA 14, 334, 5 / 14 / 24 - 337, 1 / 11/ 32; 24,447, 19 - 450, 25.
46 Ulrich ASENDORF: Die Theologie Martin Luthers nach seinen Predigten. GÖ 1988, 342, with reference to WA 24, 11, 26-12; 4, 15, 2-5.
47 Gn 14.
48 WA 42, 531, 7-13 ≙ LW 2, 374; WA 42, 570, 24-30 ≙ LW 3, 30 f; WA 43, 61, 33 - 63, 5 ≙ LW 3, 260-262; WA 43, 640, 32 - 641, 18 ≙ LW 5, 307 f; WA 43, 653, 12-34 ≙ LW 5, 325-326.
49 WA 43, 322, 39-41 ≙ LW 4, 261.

Luther often reminded parishioners and students that the biblical narratives reported on real, live, flesh and blood people because the Holy Spirit »delights in playing and trifling when describing things that are insignificant, childish, and worthless; and he hands this down to be taught in the church for its most significant edification«.[50] Luther's doctrine of the created order and its worth expressed itself in his reveling in the details of the common and ordinary. He assured the Wittenberg congregation that as long as sin is not in control, »no natural emotion is evil, as we see in Christ, who had feelings and affections according to his nature as any other human being«, as he talked of Jacob's love for his children and his »natural fatherly heart«, comparing his love to that of Mary for Jesus.[51] To his students Luther commented on Abraham's emotions, frequently with a comment denying that the patriarch was a block of wood or stone.[52] In the reformer's view Abraham and Jacob shared his own feelings and perceptions of human life.

In amplifying the humanity of the real people who crossed the biblical stage, Luther could not leave God out of the stories because he was unable to think of human creatures apart from their relationship to their Creator, just as he warned against trying to think about God apart from his revelation of himself to those human creatures, hidden beyond human grasp. Luther insisted on understanding what made God God in a different way than had his scholastic instructors. God's treatment of Abimelech after he had taken Sarah to himself[53] reveals that

> »God's righteousness is not, as they have taught in the schools, the severity, sternness, or violent anger with which God condemns. It is the righteousness through which he has mercy on the humble as he protects them against unjust violence and punishes the guilty.«[54]

50 WA 43, 671, 32-37 ≙ LW 5, 352..
51 WA 14, 467, 12-23 / 28-34; 24, 15-27.
52 WA 43, 92, 12-14 ≙ LW 3, 303; WA 43, 162, 12-16 ≙ LW 4, 37; WA 43, 277, 10-24 ≙ LW 4, 196 f;
   WA 43, 285, 25-30 ≙ LW 4, 208; WA 44, 525, 38 - 526, 3 ≙ LW 7, 305. Cf. WA 43, 96, 15-22 ≙ LW
   3, 309; WA 43, 149, 27 - 150, 11 ≙ LW 4, 19 f; WA 44, 187, 39 - 188, 13 ≙ LW 6, 253; WA 44, 395,
   29-34 ≙ LW 7, 131; WA 44, 588, 36 - 589, 12 ≙ LW 8, 13; WA 44, 591, 4-7 ≙ LW 8, 16; WA 44, 593,
   42 - 595, 14 ≙ LW 8, 20-22.
53 Gn 20, 1-5.
54 WA 43, 113, 6-9 ≙ LW 3, 331; cf. WA 44, 485, 25 - 486, 38 ≙ LW 7, 251-253.

When this God identified himself to Abram in Gn 17, 1, Luther again noted that God spoke not to stones, wood, or beasts of burden, but to real human beings, for »the word ›God‹ indicates a relationship. It refers to him whom the descendants of Abraham believe to be God and who, in turn, reveals himself to them as God and their eternal benefactor«.[55] For Luther the human story is a vital part of God's story, and God's story is the centerpiece of the human story, a key element in his definition of human righteousness.

III Fearing, Loving, and Trusting in God above All Things

Piety begins and ends with trust in God in which combat against Satan and love for the neighbor are enveloped. Luther presupposed that God had fashioned people with a two dimensional set of relationships that determined, first of all, their identity as his faithful children, and, second, their performance of his expectations for his children in his world.[56] Throughout both the sermons of the 1520s and the lectures of 1535-1545 Luther found examples in Genesis of the two dimensional nature of human life, or as he called it in describing Jacob, »two kinds of holiness«.[57] In introducing his sermons on Genesis in 1527 he reminded readers that God had given many examples and sayings in which he made it clear that faith alone lies at the basis of human living.[58] The first dimension of human righteousness focused on the First Table of the law and what God does for his human creatures, the second on the Second Table and what human creatures are made to do for God, as becomes clear at many points in the unfolding of Abraham's story.[59]

The story of Cain and Abel revealed how human righteousness in God's sight depends simply and alone on God's favorable disposition toward his people.[60] In 1535 the professor told his students,

55 WA 42, 609, 33-35 ≙ LW 3, 86.
56 WA 2, 43-47. 145-152.
57 »Duplex sanctitas«, that which the Word establishes in relationship to God and that which human creatures perform; WA 43, 575, 22 - 576, 35 ≙ LW 5, 213 f; cf. WA 43, 588, 37 - 589, 37 ≙ LW 5, 232 f.
58 WA 24, 17, 14-19. Luther repeated this theme throughout the sermons, among many examples; cf. WA 24, 296, 19-37; 318, 30 - 321, 34.
59 WA 43, 484, 6-17 ≙ LW 5, 79 f.
60 WA 9, 338, 24-30.

»This is the chief point [summa] of our teaching [...] that a person rather than his work is acceptable to God and that a person does not become righteous as a result of a righteous work, but that a work becomes righteous and good as a result of a person's being righteous and good. [...] Abel, rather than his work, was righteous and that work was pleasing because of the person, not the person because of his work.«[61]

Abraham served as Luther's prime instance of a life that clearly differentiated and united the two dimensions of what it means to be human. On the basis of Abraham's story

»we do not deny that works must be performed [...] faith and works indeed fit together well and are inseparably joined, but it is faith alone that obtains salvation. [...] faith alone justifies [...]. Works do not save; they do not have this glory. No, they are the fruits of the person who has been saved. Our righteousness comes through faith.«[62]

Abraham is the classic paradigm for the way the Creator who brought the world out of nothing in Gn 1 re-creates sinners. Commenting on the call of Abraham in Gn 12, Luther told his students, »God chooses as patriarch an idolater, who is estranged from God and a prisoner of Satan«.

»Abraham is merely the material that the Divine Majesty seizes through the Word and forms into a new human being, into a patriarch. And so this rule is universally true, that of himself the human creature is nothing, is capable of nothing, and has nothing but sin, death, and condemnation, but through his mercy Almighty God brings it about that he is something and is freed from sin, death, and condemnation through Christ, the blessed seed.«[63]

Again and again, Abraham's story revealed for Luther that the relationship between all believers and their Lord was created alone by God through his Word.[64]

The stories of this relationship between Creator and creature take place within a framework which Luther found in his reading of Scripture, one that attributed to God the almighty power and total responsibility for his world of which his Ockhamist instructors had spoken.[65] At the same

61 WA 42, 190, 37 - 191, 5 ≙ LW 1, 257; cf. WA 42, 191, 5 - 192, 13 ≙ LW 1, 257-259.
62 WA 43, 256, 36-42 ≙ LW 4, 166.
63 WA 42, 437, 42 - 438, 2; 437, 31-36 ≙ LW 2, 247.
64 WA 42, 439, 9-13 ≙ LW 2, 249.
65 Heiko Augustinus OBERMAN: The harvest of medieval theology, Gabriel Biel and late medieval nominalism. 3. ed. Durham, NC 1983, 30-56.

time Luther believed that God demands performance that expresses that unconditionally and freely given identity as his children. For he had given them responsibility for the working of his world. Sternberg posed the biblical problem:

> »Does the Almighty control the human heart? If no, where is his omnipotence? If yes, where is man's free will, hardly less novel in terms of ideology and equally underscored at the beginning of Genesis? Biblical narrative gives no straightforward answer, because the question is unanswerable, and no consistent treatment, except for the consistency of maneuvering between the two extremes.«[66]

Luther's sense of the mystery of what it means to be human plotted another solution to the tension between narratives which focus on God's power and responsibility and those which focus on human responsibility and calling to obedience in God's world. He kept these two responsibilities in tension and refused to homogenize and harmonize them by assigning partial responsibility to God, partial responsibility to human creatures.

Occasionally, he reviewed this tension in presenting biblical stories to students and parishioners. He did not presume to unravel the mystery of how God and human creature can both be responsible within the functioning of God's creation, but he did believe that God is at work when it appears as though human agents are in charge. In the sermon on Gn 6 Luther spoke of Noah's exercising his own responsibility for rescuing his family in the midst of the Flood. If you say, »God will sustain me«, and get lazy and not work, it will not happen.

> »It is true that he gives all things; he sustains and preserves everyone. But if you do not want to use what you are able to put to use, that is tempting God. It is his will that you put to use what you have at hand, that he has given you and placed at your disposal, not that you close your mouth and let his creation go. He has given it to you. He will not perform a miracle for you when it is not necessary.«[67]

At least twice in his lectures the reformer summarized Augustine's observation that »God governs the things he has created so that he nevertheless allows them to function with their distinctive impulses [...] God makes use of definite means and tempers his exercise of his miraculous powers so

66 Sternberg: The poetics ..., 110.
67 WA 24, 181, 6-9 / 19-26.

208

that he makes use of the service of nature and of natural means.«[68] Luther warned his students in lecture against saying »I am the pastor of a church about which I know that God is concerned. Therefore I shall do nothing and shall not be concerned about my ministry.«[69] God's total responsibility lies alongside total human responsibility, and Luther refused to harmonize and homogenize the two, preaching both as he distinguished God's gospel from the law that describes proper human actions.

God not only forgives sin and bestows new life and salvation in Christ. He also exercises his providential control over his universe. Although Luther's reading of Genesis often treated Christ in a variety of prophetic connections, his retelling of narratives of daily life often focused on God's providential care, a great comfort to Luther. That God sustained Jacob as he went to meet Esau[70] reminded Luther that the whole course of nature and human life reveals more good than evil, demonstrates that »a very small part of life is subjected to the devil's power«.[71] This results alone from God's goodness and mercy. Even when the ungodly forget God and their obligations to him, he is leading and governing them as well as the godly in all their actions.[72] Believers persist in trust, as Noah had, even when evil seems to triumph.[73] This trust clings to God on good days and bad days, not only for death but also for life.

IV Suffering as Child of God and Enemy of Satan

In the mystery of evil's invasion of the Creator's world, both suffering and sin shaped Luther's agenda. In daily life Christians continually flee to God, sometimes as victims of evils visited by others, sometimes as rebels who must be turned from defiance of God and changed to living in the consciousness of being his child.

---

68 WA 42, 316, 21-25 ≙ LW 2, 76; WA 42, 512, 19 f ≙ LW 2, 350. Cf. Augustinus: De trinitate 3, 4; Aurelius Augustinus: De trinitate libri XV: (libri I-XII). Turnholt 1968, 135-137. (Corpus christianorum: series latina; 50)
69 WA 44, 461, 37 - 462, 5; 463, 22-32 ≙ LW 7, 219. 221 f.
70 Gn 32.
71 WA 44, 67, 9 f ≙ LW 6, 90.
72 WA 44, 168, 1-27 ≙ LW 6, 92.
73 WA 24, 168, 31 - 169, 23.

One of the foremost characteristics of the pious or righteous believer was the presence of suffering in one of several forms. Luther taught how to deal with this variety of suffering on the basis of faith by calling attention to how the ancient patriarchs had done so. Abraham offered a number of good examples of the fact that »the godly who are burdened with a cross and in various ways are hard pressed and groan under this weight have need of God's promises in order to be buoyed up by them«.[74] Both confrontations with their enemies and the continuing childlessness of Abraham and Sarah tested the faith of the couple, Luther explained to the congregation.[75] In retelling Isaac's encounter with Abimelech Luther observed,

> »you see how kind the Lord is to his saints. To be sure, he tests them, sends them into exile, lets them be exposed to danger to reputation and life, and permits them to be afflicted with famine and misfortunes of every kind; yet he provides excellent, quiet, and safe hospitality and grants peace in the midst of their enemies.«

This confirmed what he had shown on the basis of several of Abraham's experiences.[76]

The worst of these sufferings come from God's afflicting his saints or seeming to be absent in the midst of afflictions, as Abraham experienced when he deceived Abimelech to protect himself.[77] Luther explained to the Wittenberg parishioners that God's delaying his promises to Abram laid a cross and suffering upon the patriarch, alongside the difficulties caused by being a stranger in Egypt. But God still was governing the course of Abram's and Sarai's life and gave them consolation in the midst of their trials.[78]

74 WA 43, 33, 19f ≙ LW 3, 221.
75 WA 14, 221, 20 / 36 - 222, 24 / 30; WA 24, 248, 29 - 249, 23.
76 WA 43, 465, 3-7 ≙ LW 5, 53; cf. WA 43, 436, 37 - 437, 8 ≙ LW 5, 12. On Abraham WA 14, 291, 3 / 23 - 292, 23 / 25; 24, 361, 29 - 363, 30; 42, 526, 32-37 ≙ LW 2, 369; WA 42, 533, 32-36 ≙ LW 2, 378f and above all, at the call to sacrifice Isaac WA 43, 200, 30 - 268, 10 ≙ LW 4, 91-183. Similar incidents provided for good narrative and similar observations in Hagar's life; WA 42, 599, 29-36 ≙ LW 3, 71f; in Jacob's life WA 43, 526, 32 - 529, 17 ≙ LW 5, 142f; WA 44, 174, 30 - 175, 8 ≙ LW 6, 235f; in Joseph's life WA 44, 390, 14 - 394, 35 ≙ LW 7, 123-129; WA 44, 419, 37 - 420, 32 ≙ LW 7, 161-164
77 Gn 20; WA 43, 111, 28-36 ≙ LW 3, 329.
78 WA 14, 224, 13-23 / 32-40. On Luther's use of his concept of the »hidden God« in depicting Abraham; see Juhani FORSBERG: Das Abrahambild in der Theologie Luthers: pater fidei sanctissimus. S 1984, 31-38.

As he introduced Joseph to the congregation in Wittenberg, he labeled the stories of this patriarch »the true ›golden legends‹«, in which God »teaches how he boils and fries his saints, how he plays with them, as if everything he had promised was a lie«.[79] God remained hidden for Joseph, but he continued to trust that God was with him even as Potiphar's wife tempted him and had him thrown into prison, the German version of his 1523 sermons explained to readers.[80] Luther spoke of God's playing with the saints in a similar way to his students.[81] Nonetheless, Luther took seriously the terror and confusion of the saints when God is at work in their lives »under the appearance of the opposite« of his true disposition toward them. Luther's appeal to God's reliability and steadfast lovingkindness in these situations remained the closest he got to a theodical address of the problem. He refused to find explanations for questions regarding the origen of evil or its ultimate cause in human reasoning. Instead he looked to the person of his creator, whose demonstration of love for his rebellious human creatures in Christ's death on the cross provided all the justification God needed.

Satan and his minions are responsible for many of the attacks and afflictions of both a temporal and a spiritual nature from which Christians suffer, both from inside themselves and from others. The very presence of the faithful people of God provokes the devil to visit catastrophe upon them and their surroundings. The death of Abel at the hands of his brother Cain gave the preacher the opportunity to instruct the Wittenberg congregation regarding the persecution of God's people by evildoers.[82] In commenting on the famine at Isaac's time, Luther pointed out to the Wittenberg congregation that the devil attempts to disrupt lives of those who serve God through hardship and persecution as well as temptation.[83] The whole life of the righteous is engaged in eschatological conflict.

---

79 WA 14, 467; 24, 613, 31-33.

80 WA 24, 632, 21 - 635, 26.

81 WA 42, 529, 37 f ≙ LW 2, 373; WA 43, 218, 3-5 ≙ LW 4, 115; WA 43, 229, 36 - 230, 3 ≙ LW 4, 131; WA 43, 371, 24-39 ≙ LW 4, 326; WA 44, 97, 10-24 ≙ LW 6, 130; WA 44, 466, 22-26 ≙ LW 7, 225; WA 44, 536, 8-20 ≙ LW 7, 319; see Forsberg: Das Abrahambild ..., 39-41.

82 WA 24, 136, 28 - 136, 23.

83 WA 14, 342, 2 / 16 / 21 - 344, 7 / 13 / 38; 24, 454, 29 - 458, 18.

Abraham's lie to Abimelech[84] reminded Luther that »not only passive evils are inflicted upon us, bringing good upon us, but also the active ones, that is, the evils which we ourselves do«, for they produce the blessing of repentance.[85] Evil does not only invade the righteous and pious life from outside believers. It also comes from within, and therefore those who are sinful as well as righteous simultaneously are constantly engaged in the mortification of the flesh, the destruction of their own sinful desires and habits. Therefore, as Eberhard Winkler observes, the devil's inflicting suffering in the battle between Satan and God sometimes atually works against the Tempter's intentions. When this happens, »comfort is often closely associated with admonition«.[86]

Scholars have noted that Luther's treatment of the sins of the patriarchs differs from other commentators in the medieval tradition and among his contemporaries, but this approach to those who were at the same time the saintliest saints and the most sinful of sinners conforms to Luther's understanding of the Christian life as a life in constant confrontation with the mystery of the continuation of sin and evil in the lives of the baptized.[87] His treatment of Judah's intercourse with Tamar gave his students insight into the larger context of the phrase »simul justus et peccator«.

> »The very saintly fathers and sons of such great patriarchs, Judah and others, are described as men full of the weakness and the very great blemishes to which this wretched nature is subject. God guided them in a wonderful manner by his Holy Spirit, yet in such a way that he permitted them to bare their own inclinations, that is, the sin and fruit of the original evil.«

As these events teach and console God's people, they also call them to put their evil desires and deeds to death. Abraham and Isaac »were lights [...] of the whole world and of the church of God.]...]. They were perfect in faith, hope, and love, but at the same time abysmal and horrible sin-

84 Gn 20, 1-17.
85 WA 43, 115, 7f ≙ LW 3, 334.
86 Winkler: Luther als Seelsorger ..., 228.
87 See Bornkamm: Luther and the Old Testament, 20-27.

ners.« Their examples serve »the preaching of repentance and faith or of the forgiveness of sins, lest anyone be presumptuous because of his own righteousness and lest those who have fallen despair«.[88] The struggles of the Old Testament paragons of faith served both to warn believers against falling into sin and to make clear their inherent weakness and inclination toward wrongdoing.

These warnings undergirded one of the most important constitutive elements of Luther's understanding of Christian piety in a sinful world. To attain the practice of active righteousness and to abolish the false gods that continually lure believers, they must actively strive to kill their own desires to live life on their own terms; mortification of the flesh is the negative side of the fulfilling of God's commands in the context of God's callings. Luther often repeated his principle that killing off the sinful identity of his people and bestowing or renewing their identity as his children is God's natural way of doing things in a sinful world. He used this description of God's activities among sinner-saints both in reference to their core identities in relationship to him and their practice of their callings in his world. In his portrayal of the relationship of Abraham with Sarah and Hagar, Luther found the patriarch mortified in regard to both the first and the second table of the law.[89] God's command to Abraham to sacrifice Isaac constituted true mortification, »sitting in sackcloth and ashes«.[90] In retelling the story of God's covenant with Abram in Gn 15, Luther noted,

> »It is also the purpose of this passage to teach us what God's nature is. He is indeed the deliverer and liberator from death. But before he delivers, he destroys; before he makes alive, he plunges into death. He is accustomed to act in this way, ›so that out of nothing he may make everything.‹«[91]

He takes no pleasure in afflicting us but uses powerful and bitter remedies to make the deformity and foulness of the depraved sinful nature clear to his people and to cleanse them, as the story of Joseph's leading his

---

88 On Rebecca WA 44, 309, 29 - 310, 8 ≙ LW 7, 10 f; cf. on Isaac WA 43, 446, 37 - 447, 41 ≙ LW 5, 27; WA 14, 371, 1 / 10 - 373, 5 / 28; 24, 483, 19-34.

89 WA 43, 167, 22-34 ≙ LW 4, 44f.

90 WA 43, 213, 29-31 ≙ LW4, 109.

91 WA 42, 572, 21-23 ≙ LW 3, 33. Cf. the treatment of this concept in Luther's treatment of Joseph's mortification WA 44, 454, 36 - 456, 12 ≙ LW 7, 210 f.

brothers to repentance shows.[92] Therefore, the believer's struggle against sin must be conscious and active, seeking to diminish or eradicate sin at every turn, as Reuben did by diverting his brothers from murdering Joseph.[93] His is not a perfect example of avoiding sin, but Luther moved beyond the text to make application for his students even though the story did not fit his point perfectly.[94] The mortification of the flesh constituted a critical element in the life of repentance.

VI Carrying out God's Commands in the Context of His Callings

Luther regarded the life of repentance in the believer's obedience to God's commands within the context of one's calling as the positive counterpart to the mortification of the flesh. The life of repentance is lived out of a faith that God has given; it does not change in so far as it is the trust that holds fast to God's gift of his love and the new identity of the child of God. But the fruits of faith can be renewed and expanded, trained and cultivated, as believers grow in their faithful expression of God's love. Luther pointed out to the Wittenberg congregation that the stories of Abram displayed the patriarch's love for the neighbor.

> »Faith and love for God govern love for the neighbor, so that we do not love other human beings more than God. When love for God takes proper form, love for the neighbor will also. Love for the neighbor governs alls external works, so that people perform what love demands. All commands are directed by love.«

Luther believed that this meant, first of all, converting others, both Jews and pagans, and bringing them to faith and then demonstrating every other kind of love that truly benefits the neighbor and does no harm to faith, even beyond specific commands of the law.[95] This concern remained a constant theme, also in Luther's later lectures. Faith produces a life of love that »advances daily, when we gradually learn more and more to hope, trust, and be patient. It is one and the same faith that begins, makes progress, and reaches perfec-

92 WA 44, 468, 22 - 469, 42 ≙ LW 7, 228-230; cf. WA 44, 569, 7-12 ≙ LW 7, 362; and WA 44, 582, 37 - 585, 38 ≙ LW 8, 5-8.
93 Gn 37, 21-22.
94 WA 44, 282, 16-19 ≙ LW 6, 377.
95 WA 24, 275, 19-32; cf. WA 24, 407, 17 - 410, 9.

tion,« Luther reflected as he placed the young Joseph before his students.[96] His desire to promote sound Christian living accompanied his desire to give assurance of God's love in Christ to his people throughout his life.

That growth takes place not in a religious environment set apart from this world but in the midst of daily life, Luther repeated with frequent polemical references to monasticism and other medieval religious observances.[97] God has liberated his people for the faithful performance of divinely ordained virtues within the believer's vocations. Luther presumed that the examples of the patriarchs, their families, and their contemporaries provided guidance for the conduct of daily life in the sixteenth century. Of Genesis 24 Luther could say in 1521, »there are several topics in this chapter that pertain to moral actions, for forming human life and training the spirit«.[98] His sermon on the chapter two years later elaborated on the lessons to be learned as sixteenth century Germans followed the example of their ancient fellow believers. These lessons included children's valuing their parents' planning of their marriages and all Christians' recognizing how God cares for his people, also in governing marriage and married life.[99] Even though many have only contempt for the common and ordinary details of family found in the stories of Abraham and Sarah, Luther was convinced that the Holy Spirit had intended to instruct all readers of Scripture in the proper way of conducting human life.[100] The reformer put to use a host of examples in his treatments of Genesis, which, rather than relating tales of extravagant

96 WA 44, 401, 30 - 402, 7 ≙ LW 7, 139. Luther clearly distinguishes between the justification by which God gives the person he calls to be his child identity as that child and the expectations which this newborn child of God meets through new obedience. Thus, Forsberg's assertion that in depicting Abraham's justification Luther taught that »incarnate faith« brings to the justifying of the sinner »secondly also the works, that is the love. ›In concreto‹ the human being is saved only through this incarnate faith«; Forsberg: Das Abrahambild ..., 83. In effect, Forsberg returns with this false interpretation of Luther to the medieval understanding of salvation by faith formed through love, »fides a charitate formata«, a view that Luther specifically and repeatedly rejected.

97 WA 43, 30, 20-34 ≙ LW 3, 217; WA 43, 108, 18 - 109, 11 ≙ LW 3, 325. See also Luther's long critique of monastic vows on the basis of the example of Jacob's vow to God in Gn 28, 20-22; WA 14, 387, 4 / 14 - 399, 2 / 11 / 34; 24, 499, 29 - 510, 21.

98 WA 9, 369, 17f.

99 WA 14, 317, 14 / 34 - 320, 13 /29; WA 24, 419, 31 - 423, 19.

100 WA 42, 474, 1-5 ≙ LW 2, 296. On Luther's treatment of Sarah see Mattox: Defender ..., 117-128.

religious performances – as was the case in the medieval »Legenda aurea«, tell how »the fathers live in their households with their children, wives, servants, and cattle. Here there is no outward show of religion, but there is only one coarse sack of household life.«[101] God's gift of a relationship with himself freed Abraham to serve in the world. Because God is

> »gracious, ready to forgive, and kind, I go out and turn my face from God to human beings, that is, I tend to my calling. If I am a king, I govern the state. If I am the head of a household, I direct the servants; if I am a schoolmaster, I teach pupils, mold their habits and views toward godliness. [...]. In all of our works we serve God, who wanted us to do such things and, so to speak, stationed us here.«[102]

Luther's sketch of Christian living placed God's commands into the context of the callings God gives; he used the stories of Genesis to depict and describe the virtues to practice and the vices to avoid within the setting of vocation. The reformer's contrast of the lifestyles of the inhabitants of Sodom and of Lot's family[103] led him to assert that God has provided a specific structure for human living even though he has given human creatures a good deal of freedom in deciding the details of how to carry out his will as well.

> »A human creature does not have such freedom that if God has commanded something, he can do it or not do it. So far as the commands of God are concerned, people are not free but must obey the voice of God or endure the sentence of death. Freedom is operative in regard to those things about which God has given no command [...].«[104]

Jacob and Esau offered one contrast between the latter's smug pride and contempt for his brother and the former's modesty, humility, agreeable, and guileless.[105]

The narrative of Genesis placed a large number of instances of the practice of godly commands or virtues at Luther's disposals, and he often made the most of them. He admonished hearers to live in peace with each other, to serve one another, and to be content and satisfied in fulfilling

101 WA 43, 432, 38-40 ≙ LW 5, 6.
102 WA 42, 632, 1-7 ≙ LW 3, 117.
103 Gn 13.
104 WA 42, 512, 21-24 ≙ LW 2, 350. Cf. similar statements in WA 43, 29, 34-39 ≙ LW 3, 216; and WA 43, 477, 29 - 478, 21 ≙ LW 5, 70-72.
105 WA 43, 408, 28 - 409, 11 ≙ LW 4, 379.

their callings to help others and care for their needs. In the practice of the virtues which God commands, Abraham's intervention in behalf of Sodom and Gomorrah presented a »magnificent example« of love for the neighbor.[106] Joseph's practice of a range of virtues also provided a model for Luther's contemporaries.[107]

Luther often taught obedience to God's commands and the practice of the virtues he ordained by contrasting them with vices. Because the reformer laid so much worth on contentment with what God gives, he warned against grumbling as he lectured on the relationships within Jacob's family.[108] His sharp words of criticism rang out as he noted that Joseph's humility and acceptance of his lot in life stood in stark contrast to the pride and the impatience which it nurtures so common in his own day, a »diabolical poison« that interferes with devotion to God and service to others.[109]

Luther did not trap himself in legalistic definitions of virtues and vices, however. Instead, he presumed a general standard for human behavior that he found in Aristotle's concept of epieikeia. Although he harshly criticized the influence of Aristotle's »Ethics« for its constructing a definition of what it means to be human apart from life's Creator,[110] in assessing Joseph's life he turned to the balance and wisdom expressed in Aristotle's term. The reformer presumed that human beings are righteous in two ways, in two dimensions of life; they continue to be addressed both by God's promise and his commands. Therefore, »the law must not be cast aside because of the promise of grace but must be taught in order that discipline and the teaching concerning good works may be retained and we may be taught to know and humble ourselves after we have sinned«, so that people may »govern and direct their conduct in a godly and prudent manner according to the norm of the law«.[111] Beyond what Aristotle could prescribe stood the faith that exercised itself in study of God's Word and prayer as the pre-

---

106 WA 14, 276, 10 / 22 / 34 - 278, 4 / 19 / 32; 24, 337, 15-28.
107 WA 44, 591, 26-39 ≙ LW 8, 17.
108 WA 44, 238, 32 - 239, 31 ≙ LW 6, 320-321.
109 WA 44, 432, 3 - 433, 32 ≙ LW 7, 179-181.
110 Theo DIETER: Der junge Luther und Aristoteles: eine historisch-systematische Untersuchung zum Verhältnis von Theologie und Philosophie. B; NY 2001.
111 WA 44, 703, 30-40 ≙ LW 8, 170 f.

supposition for all performance of vocation and virtue in the horizontal relationships of human life. Repeatedly Luther emphasized the dependence of the Christian life on listening to God. Even though God had spoken directly to the patriarchs, for Luther's contemporaries, that meant hearing or reading God's Word from Scripture. When God speaks, his children not only listen but reply. Abraham's struggling in prayer to God on behalf of Sodom presented a model of prudent but resolute and unrelenting prayer, a pattern for bold beseeching that seemed to Luther to portray a prayer aimed at compelling God to forgive.[112] The practices of daily life began in conversation with God and proceeded to living out God's callings according to his commands.

VII Dying Well

Such a life lived within God's callings in accord with God's commands prepared the baptized to die well. Early in his career Luther adapted the medieval genre of the ars moriendi to his own message,[113] and he continued to prepare his hearers for dying through good counsel on how to live in faith and love throughout his life from the pulpit and in his lectures. Noah lived in dependence on God, Luther reminded readers of his Genesis sermons, confident that his life was pleasing to God because of God's merciful regard for him. So must all live that they may be prepared to die.[114]

Baptismal death and resurrection shaped the words Luther used to describe God's blessing of departure from this life to the better life with him, for instance, in describing God's promise to Jacob as he was about to depart for Egypt.[115] When death comes to God's faithful people they will have the peace that God gave Abraham, as Luther interpreted Gn 25, 8. Luther described death as a most pleasant sleep which holds no dread for those who know that Christ takes them from this life. Luther also knew

---

112 WA 14, 282, 1 / 12 /27 - 283, 3 /21; 24, 342, 29 - 343, 29; 43, 41, 30 - 44, 9 ≙ LW 3, 232-236.
113 WA 2, 685-697 ≙ LW 42, 99-115. See also Robert Kolb: »Ein kindt des todts« und »Gottes Gast«: das Sterben in Luthers Predigten. LThK 31 (2007), 3-22, and Neil Leroux: Martin Luther as comforter, writings on death. Leiden 2007, 45-80.
114 WA 24, 3-16.
115 WA 44, 637, 37 - 640, 26 ≙ LW 8, 79-83.

the questions Christians ask, and so he posed for his students the query, »Where did Abraham go?« What does it mean to be gathered to his people? These words Luther found to be »evidence of the resurrection and the future life, […] a comfort for all who trust in God«.

> »We have a clear and extensive knowledge about death and life since we are certain that our Savior Christ Jesus is sitting at the right hand of God the Father and is waiting for us when we depart this life. Therefore, when we depart from the living, we go forth to the Guardian of our souls, who receives us into his hands.«[116]

The example of the patriarchs could also be put to use in instructing parishioners in the proper reaction to the death of a loved one. Abraham provided such a model in his care for the burial of Sarah, a good work that the preacher commended to the Wittenberg congregation. He explained that Abraham's sorrow and tears had been recorded not as a bad example but because such sorrow and suffering is a result of the love for others that faith produces.[117] Not fear of death but rather confidence in the promised resurrection in Christ typified Luther's attitude toward death.[118] In living and dying trust in God that leads to love for God and neighbor governed Christian existence.

VIII Conclusion

Luther's desire to recultivate the garden of Christendom fit effectively together with his way of reading and conveying the biblical text as the record of God's addressing real, flesh-and-blood people in the midst of daily lives. God's message centered on his own love for his people that had led him to create them and, once fallen, to re-create them through the work of Jesus Christ. Therefore, God's commands reflected his original expectations of what would result from their recognizing him as God and themselves as his

---

116 WA 43, 357, 23 - 358, 14 ≙ LW 4, 309 f. Luther continues with consolation for the dying and the grieving on the basis of Abraham's death, and with an extensive treatment of questions related to death; WA 44, 358, 15 - 364, 5 ≙ LW 4, 310-318.

117 WA 14, 311, 20 / 35 - 313, 20 / 35; 24, 408, 29 - 411, 35.

118 Robert KOLB: »Life is king and lord over death«: Martin Luther's view of death and dying. In: Tod und Jenseits in der Schriftkultur der Frühen Neuzeit/ hrsg. von Marion Kobelt Groch; Cornelia Niekus-Moore. Wiesbaden 2008, 23-45.

beloved human creatures; those commands do not set forth his expectations that had to be met to restore a relationship with him. For restoring that relationship, like creating it in the first place, lies beyond the capabilities of human creatures to create, whether sinners or not.

To carry out the task of recultivating the lives of God's people, to conduct the conversation between a life-restoring God and those dead in trespasses and sin, Luther turned to a number of communicative devices. One of them was the story of the faithful, for instance, as depicted in Genesis. Against the background of these stories, which he presumed matched and illuminated the experiences of his contemporaries, Luther cultivated the life of repentance that is based upon trust in God as he has revealed himself in Christ, a trust that sustains in suffering and puts to death the desires that lead to false gods and false living, so that believers may live out their callings according to God's command, and die as they have lived, relying on God.

Gottesdienst als Quelle des christlichen Lebens bei Martin Luther

Von Carl Axel Aurelius

I »... mit unaussprechlichem Seufzen«

Das Bild des christlichen Lebens kommt für Luther am deutlichsten in den Psalmen zum Ausdruck. Die Mischung von Freude und Leid, Klage und Lobgesang, die in den Psalmen zu finden ist, kennzeichnet das christliche Leben. Die Psalmen entsprechen den verschiedenen Gemütszuständen oder Affekten eines Christenmenschen. In seiner zweiten großen Auslegung des Psalters – den »Operationes in psalmos«, 1519-1521 – sagt Luther:

> »Denn die Angefochtenen müssen dann und wann getröstet werden, damit sie aushalten können. Deshalb werden fröhliche Psalmen und Klagepsalmen in mancherlei Ordnung unter einander vermengt, sodass diese Mischung verschiedener Psalmen und diese verworrene Ordnung, wie man meint, ein Exempel und Bild des christlichen Lebens sein sollte, das unter mancherlei Trübsalen der Welt und Tröstungen Gottes geübt wird.«[1]

Einige von den Psalmen lassen uns tief in die schwersten Anfechtungen hineinblicken. Wir bekommen ein Bild von den Gefühlsregungen dieser Situation, zum Beispiel in Ps 6 oder Ps 13. Sie sind beide seltsame Psalmen, und zwar in doppelter Hinsicht. Zum einen ist es ja merkwürdig, dass sie überhaupt da sind. Der Angefochtene befindet sich offensichtlich in einer Lage, wo er sich fragen muss: Lohnt es sich wirklich zu beten? Aber das tut er trotz allem. Warum?

Zum anderen sind diese beide Psalmen seltsam wegen der plötzlichen Veränderung der Tonart. Mitten im Psalm geht die Tonart von Moll nach Dur über. Klage verwandelt sich in Lobgesang. Was passiert eigentlich? Luthers Auslegung beantwortet beide Fragen.

1 WA 5, 287, 16-20.

Wie gesagt, zeigen uns die beiden Psalmen die schwerste Anfechtung. Es handelt sich nicht länger um die Trübsale der Welt. Der Angefochtene kämpft nicht mehr mit Menschen, sondern mit Gott. Er sinkt tiefer und tiefer in die Verzweiflung hinunter. Äußerlich leidet er oder sie an etwas, das uns nicht bekannt ist. Innerlich aber, wie dieser Mensch sein Leid aufnimmt, das wissen wir genau. Er denkt: In seinem Zorn hat Gott mich auf ewig verworfen. Dies ist die Spitze der Anfechtung. Der Angefochtene befindet sich in einem chaotischen Dunkel. Luther weist auf zwei Bibelworte hin: Gn 1,2 und R 8,26. Hier geht es offensichtlich um folgenden Gedankengang: Das Dunkel, das den Betroffenen umgibt, steht in Analogie zu dem chaotischen Dunkel, das vor der Schöpfung »über der Tiefe war«. Der Geist, der damals »über den Wassern schwebte«, ist der Geist, der jetzt im Angefochtenen wirksam wird und ihn »vertritt mit unaussprechlichem Seufzen«.

Luther versteht also die Klage der Angefochtenen nicht als einer letzten Kraftanstrengung, sondern als Ausdruck dafür, dass der Heilige Geist in ihm wohnt und in ihm betet. Der Geist hilft ihm die Anfechtung zu überstehen, hilft ihm auszuhalten. Es ist also das Werk des Geistes, dass überhaupt gebetet wird und dass diese Gebete in den Psalmen gesammelt sind.

Außerdem ist der Heilige Geist wirksam in den Fürbitten der Heiligen für den Betroffenen. Der Heilige Geist ist für Luther vor allem interpellator et consolator, genau so wie es in R 8,26 gesagt ist. Regin Prenter (1907–1990) nennt gerade dieses Bibelwort »das Zentrum des Verstehens, von dem aus Luthers Gedanken über den Geist orientiert sind«. Er fügt hinzu: »Keine *gratia infusa* kann den Menschen mit unaussprechlichem Seufzen vertreten. Das kann nur Gottes eigene lebendige Person.«[2]

Die Wende der beiden Psalmen kommt durch ein Wort von außen zustande, das Wort von Gottes Anwesenheit und Barmherzigkeit, das Wort Christus: »[...], non tamen nisi per verbum dei et Ihesum Christum«[3] Und so fängt der Lobgesang an. Nach außen hin hat sich die Situation des Betroffenen gegenüber früher vielleicht wenig geändert. Er wird immer noch angegriffen. Aber durch das Wort der Barmherzigkeit Gottes ist seine *Deutung* der Situation eine ganz andere geworden. Das Wort macht der

2 Regin PRENTER: Spiritus creator: studier i Luthers teologi. 2. Aufl. København 1946, 39.
3 WA 5, 216, 2.

Angst und seiner Herrschaft ein Ende. Es ruft die Hoffnung hervor. Luther kann sagen, Gott habe sich für den Beter verändert. Jetzt tritt Gott hervor als der barmherzige Vater, von dem man alles Gute erwartet:

> »Nun aber, da du mein Herr und mein Gott geworden bist, so kehre dich nun zu mir, nicht allein um mich zu hören, sondern auch um mich zu *er*hören, und nicht anders zu tun als mich zu retten und zu erhalten, damit ich statt eines zornigen Richters einen barmherzigen Gott habe.«[4]

Die Überwindung der Anfechtung ist für Luther ein Schöpfungsakt, der wie jener erste in einem chaotischen Dunkel – aus dem Nichts (ex nihilo) und durch das Wort – geschieht. Die Doppelbelichtung der Schöpfung und Erlösung, die in der Bibel häufig ist, wird ganz deutlich hervorgehoben. Gottes Erlösung heißt, von Anfang an zu beginnen. Erlösung ist neue Schöpfung.

Die Überwindung der Anfechtung ist außerdem auch ein trinitarisches Geschehen. An der Stelle des zornigen Gottes tritt der barmherzige Vater, der durch das unaussprechliche Seufzen seines Geistes und die verlorene Liebe seines Sohnes den angefochtenen Menschen umarmt.

Ein katechetischer Text aus derselben Zeit des Psalterkommentars erzählt, wie der Geist den Weg öffnet zum Vater »durch Christum und in Christo«. Der Wortlaut erinnert im hohen Maß an die Erklärung des dritten Artikels im Kleinen Katechismus:

> »Ich glaub nit allein, das der heylig geyst eyn warhafftiger gott ist mit dem vatter und sun, ßondern auch ynn und tzu dem vatter durch Christum und seyn leben, leyden, sterben und alles was von yhm gesagt ist, niemant kummen noch ettwas desselben erlangen mag on des heyligen geysts werck, mit wilchem der vatter und der sun mich und alle die seynen ruret, wecket, ruffet, tzeucht, durch und ynn Christo lebendig, heylig und geystlich macht, und alßo zum vatter bringt, dan er ist das, da mit der vatter durch Christum und ynn Christo alles wirckt und lebendig macht.«[5]

Luther benennt die Anfechtung und die Überwindung der Anfechtung ein »Spiel Gottes«. Erst nachher ist es möglich, das Geschehen so anzusehen und zu erleben, wie Jakob an der Furt des Jabbok in Gn 32. In Luthers Auslegung, sowohl in den frühen Predigten aus den zwanziger Jahren als

4 WA 5, 388, 19-21.
5 WA 7, 218, 25-32.

auch in seinem großen Genesiskommentar, handelt es sich um die allerschwerste Anfechtung, genau so wie in Ps 6 und Ps 13. Seine Auslegung dieser Geschichte von Gebet und Kampf Jakobs kann vielleicht unser Verständnis der Überwindung der Anfechtung und der Wende von Klage in Lobgesang, der wir schon in den Psalmen begegnet sind, noch vertiefen. Luther versteht Jakobs Kampf als Erzählung einer Erhörung. Jakob rief zu Gott, dass er ihn errette vor der Hand Esaus, seines Bruders. In seinem Gebet erinnerte Jakob Gott an seine Verheißung in Bethel. Doch Gottes Erhörung sieht, zumindest am Anfang, gerade wie das Umgekehrte aus: Gott will uns umbringen. Darum ist Gottes Handeln für die Vernunft unmöglich zu verstehen – aber für den Glauben nicht.

Jakob kommt aus dem Regen in die Traufe. Sein hoher Wunsch ist es, die Begegnung mit seinem Bruder Esau zu vermeiden. Das ist seine Bitte. Aber statt Esau begegnet er Gott. Der Gegner Jakobs ist für Luther nicht ein Engel, sondern Gott selbst. Während des Kampfes hielt Jakob an Gottes Verheißung – promissio – fest. Darin liegt seine Stärke, die ihm zu einem Sieg verhilft.

Wie kann Jakob Gott, der doch allmächtig ist, überwinden? Mit Gott kämpfen und siegen heißt für Luther, den zornigen Gott zu überwinden, den Gott der mich ewiglich verstossen und verlassen hat. Genauso wie in den genannten Psalmen geht es um Folgendes: Wie versteht ein Mensch, der sich in der tiefsten Anfechtung befindet, sein Leiden? Wie sieht er Gott und das ganze Dasein an? Es ist nicht eine Frage von Gott »an sich«, sondern eine Frage von Gott »in mir«:

> »So heisset nu das Gott uberwinden: nicht seine gewalt uberwinden, sondern das jhenige, das er ynn unserm gewissen ist und gefület wird, uberwinden, Wie die schrifft redet, das sich Gott verwandlet, wenn wir verwandlet werden, Er ist on wandel an yhm selbs, [...].[6]

Gott ist immer derselbe. Aber Gott wird für mich anders, wenn die Anfechtung überwunden ist.

Für diese Veränderung ist das Hören und Festhalten an Gottes Wort und Verheißung von entscheidender Bedeutung, auch wenn gerade dieses Wort im Dunkel der Anfechtung in Zweifel gezogen ist:

6 WA 24, 578, 28-31.

»Wenn ich yhn also ynn mir uberwinde, so habe ich Gott uberwunden, dadurch, dass ich das wort von seiner güte ergreiffe und halte und schlage das hynweg, das yhn zornig wil machen, Also uberwindet man nicht seine Majestet, sondern sein werck, das er an uns thut.«[7]

Luther redet hier vom fremden Werk Gottes, sein opus alienum. Gott tötet, um lebendig zu machen, er vernichtet, um aufs neue zu schaffen aus dem Nichts. So bewahrt Gott den Mensch im Glauben und in der Demut. »So thut nu Gott, wenn er will die seinen vollig starck machen, [...].«[8]

Die trinitarische Bewegung, die schon in der Auslegung der Psalmen zu spüren war, findet sich auch hier wieder. Jakobs Gegner ist »Gott selber, oder Gottes Sohn, der ins Fleisch zu kommen war«[9] Christus ist der Gegner! Luther vergleicht den Kampf Jakobs mit dem Kampf, den die kananäische Frau zu kämpfen hatte in Matt 15. Christus lehnte sie mit schroffen Worte ab, aber sie gab nicht auf. Sie fuhr fort, ihn um Hilfe zu bitten. Und schließlich legte Christus seine Maske ab. Er fing an, tröstend und herzerquickend mit ihr zu reden: »O Weib, dein Glaube ist groß!«[10]

In so einem Kampf ist es unmöglich, ohne die Anwesenheit des Heiligen Geistes in unserer Schwachheit auszuhalten. Er vertritt uns aufs Beste mit unaussprechlichem Seufzen. Wie sonst weist Luther auf die Worte vom Geist in R 8,26 hin. Die Überwindung der Anfechtung ist beinahe mit denselben Worten wie in den Psalmen beschrieben. Gott, der in den Augen der Betroffenen ein zorniger Richter war, tritt jetzt als der liebevolle Vater hervor.[11] Die trinitarische Bewegung ist dieselbe: *Mit* dem Geist – *durch* den Sohn – *zu* dem Vater.

II Der Gottesdienst als Ort der Rechtfertigung

Das Werk des Geistes besteht darin, Menschen in und durch Christus zum Vater zu führen. Der Geist vermittelt die reale Gegenwart Christi. Wo geschieht dies? Die Reformatoren meinten zwar, das Gott es wann und wo

7 WA 24, 579, 7-11.
8 WA 24, 578, 22.
9 WA 44, 96, 40: »[...], Deus ipse, sive filius Dei incarnandus, [...].«
10 Mt 15, 28: »O mulier, magna est fides tua.«
11 WA 44, 105, 20.

er will geschehen lassen kann. Aber sie waren auch überzeugt davon, dass Gott Zeit und Ort angibt. Mit Prenter möchte ich deshalb vom Gottesdienst als dem Ort der Rechtfertigung reden, in reformatorischer Perspektive:

> »Der Ort [...], wo Jesus Christus, Gott und Mensch, mit seiner stellvertretenden Genugtuung dem Glauben als die einzige Gerechtigkeit des Sünders geschenkt wird, ist der Gottesdienst mit seinem Wort und Sakrament.
>
> Wenn wir nämlich allein durch die stellvertretende Genugtuung Jesu Christi vor Gott gerecht werden, muss diese Genugtuung uns von Gott selbst ausgeteilt werden. Dies geschieht eben in der Messe, durch die Predigt des Evangeliums und die Darreichung des Abendmahles. Die Messe ist sozusagen die Rechtfertigung durch den Glauben in Funktion.«[12]

Wenn dem nun so ist, wie Prenter sagt, dass der Gottesdienst der Ort der Rechtfertigung ist, dann hat die Rechtfertigung ihre künstlerische Darstellung in St. Marien in Wittenberg bekommen. Ich denke dabei an das Altarbild von Lukas Cranach d. Ä. (1472-1553). Dieses besteht eigentlich aus vier Bildern.

Im Zentrum steht ein Bild von der Einsetzung des Abendmahls. Einer der Teilnehmer ist Martin Luther, der Mann mit Bart, der den Kelch empfängt. So sah Luther aus, als er – unerreichbar für seine Widersacher – als Junker Jörg auf der Wartburg lebte. Es ist kein Zufall, dass gerade er den Kelch empfängt. Luther hatte ja – genau wie 100 Jahre zuvor Jan Hus (um 1370-1415) – dem Volk nicht nur das Brot, sondern auch den Kelch gegeben. Zur Linken sehen wir, wie Philipp Melanchthon ein Kind tauft, mit Cranach selbst als dem Taufpaten. Bemerkenswert ist, dass Melanchthon tauft, obwohl er nicht ordiniert war. Zur Rechten macht der Gemeindepfarrer, Johannes Bugenhagen (1485-1558), von den Schlüsseln des Himmelreichs Gebrauch. Er wird flankiert von einem bußfertigen Mann, der niederkniet, und einem unbußfertigen, der sich im Zorn – von ihm – abwendet. Darunter, in der sogenannten Predella, sehen wir Luther einer Gemeinde predigen, zu der u. a. Luthers Ehefrau Katharina, die Tochter Magdalena und der Sohn Hans gehören. Inhalt der Predigt ist der gekreuzigte Christus.

Bildinterpretation ist eine heikle Aufgabe, die eigentlich in zwei Phasen erfolgen sollte: Zuerst die intuitive Begegnung mit dem Bild, die der Kontemplation Raum lässt, danach die methodische Ausdeutung. In der

---

12 Regin PRENTER: Das Augsburgische Bekenntnis und die römische Meßopferlehre. Kerygma und Dogma 1 (1955), 45.

zweiten Phase kann man vier Aspekte unterscheiden: den materiellen, den verbalen, den plastischen und den ikonografischen. Der letztgenannte interessiert uns dabei am meisten, aber auch zur verbalen und zur plastischen Bedeutung muss etwas gesagt werden.

Von *verbaler Bedeutung* spricht man, wenn ein Bild schriftliche Botschaften oder Zeichen enthält. Dies gilt nicht für die eigentlichen Bilder, wohl aber für den Rahmen. Ganz oben finden wir ein Bibelwort und darunter zwei Jahreszahlen. Das Bibelwort, das den Altar krönt, steht in 1 K 3, 11: »Einen anderen Grund kann niemand legen als den, der gelegt ist, welcher ist Jesus Christus.« Möglicherweise ist der Bibelvers erst später eingefügt worden, aber er passt ohne Zweifel sehr schön zum Bild des Gekreuzigten auf der Predella. Das T-Kreuz vermittelt den Eindruck, dass alles von den ausgestreckten Armen des Gekreuzigten getragen wird.

Die Jahreszahl 1547 ist bemerkenswert, wenn man bedenkt, dass das Altarbild das Zentrale der Reformation wiedergeben will. Gerade in diesem Jahr schien doch alles zu Ende zu gehen. Luther war im Jahr zuvor gestorben. Der Kurfürst Johann Friedrich von Sachsen (1503, 1532-1547, 1554) wurde nach der Niederlage auf der Lochauer Heide bei Mühlberg in die Gefangenschaft geführt. Cranach selbst musste sein Amt als Bürgermeister von Wittenberg niederlegen und folgte seinem Kurfürsten in die Gefangenschaft. Melanchthon hatte die Stadt verlassen. Der evangelische Herzog Moritz von Sachsen (1521, 1541-1553) machte mit den Kaiserlichen gemeinsame Sache und erhielt als Belohnung die Kurfürstenwürde. Die Stadt wurde von den Truppen des Kaisers belagert und kapitulierte am 19. Mai 1547. Der Kaiser selbst stand an Luthers Grab in der Schlosskirche. Bugenhagen blieb zwar in der Stadt, aber seine Stellung wurde geschwächt. Seine Dankbarkeit für die Verschonung von Stadt und Universität und seine Teilnahme am Abschluss der verschiedenen Interimsentwürfe wurden als Nachgiebigkeit und mangelnde Treue zur reformatorischen Sache gedeutet. Das Altarbild steht da als ein Stück Theologie in Notzeiten, auf das einzig Notwendige konzentriert in einer Zeit, als die Grundfesten bebten.

Die *plastische Bedeutung* handelt von der Perspektive und dem Spiel der Formen und Farben. Hier können wir konstatieren, dass das Altarbild als Ganzes von sehr einheitlicher Prägung ist. Alles spielt sich im selben Raum ab. Das Gewölbe und das Fenster im rechten Flügel finden sich seitenverkehrt im linken. Das mittlere Bild ist quadratisch und umfasst die kreisrunde Abendmahlstafel. Quadrat und Kreis sind die vollkommensten geometrischen Figuren. Die Kreisform findet sich auch ganz oder teilweise im Taufstein, in der Kanzel und tatsächlich auch in der Seelsorge-Szene. Es kann eine gerade Linie gezogen werden vom Bindeschlüssel über den Löseschlüssel, hinab über den pelzverbrämten Kragen des bußfertigen, knienden Mannes und hinauf über das Schwert des unbußfertigen. Das Bild macht einen einheitlichen Eindruck, und doch keinen verschlossenen. Der Abendmahlssaal ist offen, hin zur Welt. Wir ahnen eine Weltlandschaft, die von der Kunstgeschichte als typisch für die Malerei der Renaissance bezeichnet wird. Das Feld, der Fluss, das Dorf und die Burg geben dem Bild Tiefe. Als Theologen möchten wir vielleicht hinzufügen, dass das Leben dort draußen, in Familie und Gesellschaft, dass die Weltlandschaft der Verstehenshorizont des Evangeliums ist. Damit sind wir bei der *ikonografischen Bedeutung* angelangt.

Das Altarbild bildet nicht nur von dem plastischen, sondern auch von dem ikonografischen Blickwinkel her gesehen eine Einheit. Alle vier Gemälde bringen ein und dasselbe zum Ausdruck: Die Austeilung des Evangeliums an das Volk. Die Worte aus den »Schmalkaldischen Artikeln« liegen nahe:

> »Wir wollen nu wieder zum Evangelio kommen, welchs gibt nicht einerleiweise Rat und Hulf wider die Sunde; denn Gott ist reich in seiner Gnade: erstlich durchs mundlich Wort, darin gepredigt wird Vergebung der Sunde in alle Welt, welchs ist das eigentliche Ampt des Evangelii, zum andern durch die Taufe, zum dritten durchs heilig Sakrament des Altars, zum vierden durch die Kraft der Schlussel und auch per mutuum colloquium et consolationem fratrum, Matth. 18.: ›Ubi duo fuerint congregati‹ etc.«[13]

Der Gottesdienst ist der »Ort der Rechtfertigung«, genau wie Prenter es sagt. Alles geschieht im Rahmen des Gottesdienstes, in der Begegnung der Menschen mit dem lebendigen Gott, wo Gott seinen Mantel der Rechtfertigung um den in seiner Sünde frierenden Menschen legt. Luthers Unterscheidung zwischen dem Faktum des Leidens Christi, factum passionis, und dessen Brauch, usus passionis, gibt das Verhältnis zwischen Vergangenem und Gegenwärtigem an:

---

13 BSLK, 449, 6-14.

»Von der vergebunge der sůnden handeln wyr auff zwo weyse. Eyn mal, wie sie erlangt und erworben ist, Das ander mal, wie sie ausgeteylt und uns geschenckt wird. Erworben hat sie Christus am creutze, das ist war, Aber er hat sie nicht ausgeteylt odder gegeben am creutze, Im abentmal odder Sacrament hat er sie nicht erworben, Er hat sie aber daselbst durchs wort ausgeteylet und gegeben, wie auch ym Euangelio, wo es predigt wird, Die erwerbunge ist eyn mal geschehen am creutze, Aber die austeylunge ist offt geschehen vorhyn und hernach von der wellt anfang bis ans ende, [...].«[14]

Die Austeilung, die nun geschieht, liegt für Luther ganz auf einer Linie mit der Entäußerung, die schon die Inkarnation kennzeichnet, wo die Ehre unter der Entehrung/Kränkung und die Macht unter der Ohnmacht verborgen ist. Luther spricht von der »Mühe des Abendmahls«:

»Unsers Gotts ehre aber ist die, so er sich umb unser willen auffs aller tieffest erunter gibt, yns fleisch yns brod, ynn unsern mund, hertz und schos, Und dazu umb unsern willen leidet, das er unehrlich [unverehrt, achtungslos] gehandelt wird beyde auff dem creutz und altar, [...].«[15]

In einer Beschreibung des Altarbildes, die ich in Wittenberg erstanden habe, kann man lesen, dass »die vier Bildfelder den siebten Artikel der von Melanchthon verfassten Confessio Augustana widerspiegeln«.[16] Doch das Altarbild ist kaum die Illustration eines dogmatischen Gedankenganges. Viel eher verhält es sich so, dass Melanchthon dogmatisch formuliert, was Cranach gleicherweise künstlerisch gestaltet, nämlich den Gebrauch des Evangeliums und die Gemeinschaft am Tisch des Herrn – usus evangelii et communio mensae Domini –.

Die Artikel des Bekenntnisses erklären den Gebrauch – usus – des Evangeliums und verteidigen ihn gegen jeden Missbrauch – abusus –. Nathan Söderblom (1866-1931), Erzbischof vor 100 Jahren, ermunterte zum Studium der Bekenntnisschriften mit folgender Begründung: »Die großartige geistliche Arbeit, die darin enthalten ist, hat ganz wesentlich zum Ziel, zu verhindern, dass die Freude getrübt würde, die Gott in Christus verleiht.«[17]

14 WA 18, 203, 28-35.

15 WA 23, 157, 30-33.

16 Albrecht STEINWACHS; Jürgen M. PIETSCH: Der Reformations-Altar von Lucas Cranach d. Ä. in der Stadtkirche St. Marien Lutherstadt Wittenberg. L 1998, 5.

17 Nathan SÖDERBLOM: Herdabref till prästerskapet och församlingarna i Uppsala (Hirtenbrief an die Geistlichkeit und die Versammlungen in Uppsala). Uppsala 1914, 26.

Der Gottesdienst, mit Wort und Sakrament, ist unsere Freude – der Ort wo Jesus Christus, Gott und Mensch, mit seiner stellvertretenden Genugtuung dem Glauben als die einzige Gerechtigkeit des Sünders geschenkt wird. Die Bekenntnisschriften erklären und verteidigen diese Freude.

III Am Anfang war der Gottesdienst

Eine kurze Beschreibung der grundlegenden Struktur in jedem Gottesdienst findet sich in 2 K 4, 15: »Denn es geschieht alles um euretwillen, damit die überschwängliche Gnade durch die Danksagung vieler noch reicher werde zur Ehre Gottes.«

Das griechische Wort für Gnade ist »charis«, das für Dankbarkeit und Danksagung ist »eucharistia«. Somit sind die zwei Bewegungen des Gottesdienstes angegeben: Gott ruft, und die Menschen antworten, die Austeilung der Gnade unter den Menschen und deren Dank zu Gottes Ehre. Dieses Grundmuster des Gottesdienstes hebt Luther zuallererst in seiner Predigt zur Einweihung der Schlosskirche in Torgau hervor, am 5. Oktober 1544. Dort heißt es einleitend:

> »MEin lieben Freunde, Wir sollen itzt dis newe Haus einsegnen und weihen unserm HERrn Jhesu CHRisto, Welches mir nicht allein gebůrt und zustehet, Sondern jr solt auch zu gleich an den Sprengel und Reuchfass greiffen, auff das dis newe haus dahin gericht werde, das nichts anders darin geschehe, denn das unser lieber Herr selbs mit uns rede durch sein heiliges Wort, und wir widerumb mit jm reden durch Gebet und Lobgesang, […].«[18]

Mit der Austeilung der Gnade meint Luther nicht nur die Gaben, die Gott schenkt. Er spricht auch vom dreifaltigen Sich-Geben Gottes, im »Vom Abendmahl Christi. Bekenntnis« von 1528. Gott schenkt sich uns selbst, voll und ganz, als Vater, Sohn und Heiliger Geist: »Das sind die drey person und ein Gott, der sich uns allen selbs gantz und gar gegeben hat mit allem, das er ist und hat.«[19]

Der Vater schenkt sich uns mit Himmel und Erde und allen Geschöpfen. Aber durch Adams Fall ist diese Gabe verdunkelt worden, und damit von geringerem Nutzen für uns. Der Sohn hat sich uns gegeben mit seinem

18 WA 49, 588, 12-18.
19 WA 26, 505, 38 f.

Leiden und seiner Gerechtigkeit. Er hat uns mit dem Vater versöhnt, damit wir den Vater wieder kennenlernen und uns an seinen Gaben freuen können. Eine solche Gnade aber wäre von keinerlei Nutzen, wenn sie verborgen bliebe. Deshalb kommt der Heilige Geist und gibt sich uns selbst, voll und ganz. Der Geist lehrt uns und hilft uns, die Wohltat Christi anzunehmen, zu bewahren und weiterzugeben. Dies geschieht innerlich durch den Glauben, und äußerlich durch die Gnade, das heißt durch die Predigt des Evangeliums, durch Taufe und Abendmahl. So wirkt das Leiden Christi in uns zur Seligkeit.[20]

Im Folgenden wollen wir uns auf die zweite Bewegung im Gottesdienst konzentrieren, nämlich unser Empfangen der Gnade und unsere Danksagung. Wir gehen von denselben Texten aus wie im ersten Teil, hauptsächlich dem späten Kommentar zur Genesis.

In der Lutherbibel von 1534 findet sich ein Holzschnitt, der Gott Vater als den Schöpfer von Himmel und Erde zeigt. Darunter sind der Erdkreis mit dem von Wasser umgebenen Paradies, Adam und Eva, Bäume und Flüsse, und der Himmel mit Vögeln, Sonne, Mond und Sternen zu sehen. Alles war vollendet. Gott ruhte am siebten Tag.[21] Und Gott segnete und heiligte diesen Tag.[22] Damit bestimmte Gott schon von Anfang an den siebten Tag für den Gottesdienst: »Igitur Sabbatum ab initio mundi destinatum est ad cultum Dei.«[23]

Wenn die Menschheit im Zustand der Unschuld verblieben wäre, hätte sie also trotzdem den siebten Tag heilig gehalten. Und die Ordnung für den Gottesdienst wäre an Kinder und Kindeskinder weitergegeben worden. Wir sind also geschaffen, um Gott zu loben und anzuerkennen. Gerade dies bedeutet der Sabbat: Gott spricht mit uns durch sein Wort, und wir sprechen unsererseits mit Gott im Gebet und im Glauben.[24] Der Mensch ist nicht nur für das physische Leben geschaffen, sondern auch für das ewige Leben, die Ruhe in Gott, in welche Adam übergegangen wäre, ohne zu sterben.

20 Vgl. WA 26, 505, 39 - 506, 12.
21 Hans VOLZ: Martin Luthers deutsche Bibel: Entstehung und Geschichte der Lutherbibel/ eingel. von Friedrich Wilhelm Kantzenbach; hrsg. von Henning Wendland. HH 1978, 161 (247).
22 Gn 2, 3.
23 WA 42, 60, 18 f
24 WA 42, 61, 14 f: »Hoc significat Sabbatum seu quies Dei, in quo Deus nobiscum loquitur per verbum suum et nos vicissim cum eo per invocationem et fidem.«

Den Gottesdienst, der mit dem Sabbat verbunden ist, nennt Luther einen »inneren und geistlichen« Gottesdienst, der aus Glaube und Liebe besteht. Aber Gott will auch, dass der Mensch seinen Gottesdienst »äußerlich und körperlich« ausübt.[25] Deshalb verordnete Gott nicht nur eine Zeit, sondern auch einen Platz, an dem Gottesdienst gehalten werden soll. So sah Luther die Bedeutung des einen der beiden Bäume, die mitten im Paradies standen: des Baumes der Erkenntnis des Guten und Bösen, von dessen Früchten die Menschen nicht essen durften.[26] Dieser Baum war »Adams Kirche, Kanzel und Altar«.[27]

Hier wird die Kirche gegründet. »Ecclesia« kommt also vor »oeconomia« und «politia«. Die Reihenfolge bezeugt nach Luther, dass der Mensch zu einem anderen Zweck und Ziel als die anderen Geschöpfe geschaffen ist, nämlich zum unsterblichen, ewigen Leben. Hier sollten Adam und sein Geschlecht Gott den angemessenen Gehorsam leisten, Gottes Wort und Willen kennenlernen, Gott für alle Gaben danken und ihn um Hilfe gegen die Versuchung anrufen. Dort sollten sie sich versammeln, nachdem sie von den Früchten vom Baum des Lebens gegessen hatten, um dem Herrn zu danken und ihn zu loben. Beispiele für die Gestaltung solcher Dank- und Lobgesänge findet Luther u. a. in den Psalmen 148 und 149, wo alles Erschaffene, Sonne, Mond, Blitz und Hagel, Höhen und Berge, Bäume und Tiere etc. zum Lobpreis gerufen wird.

Dies ist Gottesdienst in seiner »nacktesten, reinsten und einfachsten« Form.[28] Nichts anderes ist vorgeschrieben, nur dies eine, dass man Gott lobt und dankt, sich im Herrn freut und ihm Gehorsam leistet, indem man nicht vom verbotenen Baum isst. Zu einem Teil hat Christus diesen Gottesdienst für uns wieder aufgerichtet, aber vollständig hergestellt wird er erst im Himmel.

---

25 WA 42, 72, 10-12 »Sic necessarium fuit, ut animalis homo etiam cultum animalem seu externum haberet, quo secundum corpus exerceretur in obedientia erga Deum.«

26 Gn 2, 9.16 f.

27 WA 42, 72, 20-23: »Sed templum, altare et suggestum Adae fuit arbor haec scientiae boni et mali, in qua praestaret Deo debitam obedientiam, in qua agnosceret verbum et voluntatem Dei, ac Deo ageret gratias, imo etiam, ad quam invocaret Deum contra tentationem.«

28 WA 42, 80, 41 - 81, 1: »Utile autem est, ut hoc quoque consideremus: Deum Adae verbum, cultum et religionem dedisse nudissimam, purissimam et simplicissimam, in qua nihil laboriosum, nihil sumptuosum fuit.«

Wenn man den reinen Gottesdienst so beschreibt, ist es interessant zu sehen, wie Luther die Frage des Opfers behandelt. Zum ersten Mal werden Opfer in Gn 4 erwähnt, wo von den Opfern Kains und Abels die Rede ist.

Luther betont, dass die Opfer ein Ausdruck des Glaubens und des Dankes an Gott sind. Der Gedanke wird trinitarisch entwickelt. Adam und Eva sind nicht nur Eltern, sondern haben auch priesterliche Aufgaben. Deshalb können sie, erfüllt vom Heiligen Geist und im Wissen um den kommenden Christus, bei ihren Kindern die Hoffnung auf eine kommende Befreiung wecken, wie auch die Dankbarkeit für Gottes große Barmherzigkeit.[29]

Das Opfer soll außerdem als das äußere Zeichen verstanden werden, das Gott immer zu seinem Wort hinzufügt, um die Menschen an seine Barmherzigkeit zu erinnern und um ihren Glauben zu erleichtern. So war es auch mit anderen sichtbaren Zeichen des alten Bundes, wie z. B. dem Regenbogen oder der Beschneidung. Sie alle waren Zeichen der Gnade Gottes, genau wie Taufe und Abendmahl uns Zeichen des neuen Bundes sind. Was für uns die Sakramente sind, das war das Opfer nach der Zusage an Adam. Sowohl die alten als auch die neuen Zeichen zeugen von Gottes unablässiger Sorge um die Menschen, auch nach dem Sündenfall.[30]

Diese sichtbaren Zeichen der Gnade Gottes sind die Antwort auf die Frage nach der Kirche, wo sie sei. Sie sind Kennzeichen: »[…], ubi est Eucharistia, Baptismus, Verbum, ibi sit Christus, remissio peccatorum et vita aeterna.«[31] Die Worte erinnern an den Gedankengang Luthers zu den Kennzeichen der Kirche – notae ecclesiae – in der Schrift »Von den Konziliis und Kirchen« von 1539. Dort geht es gerade darum, wie ein armer, verlorener Mensch ein heiliges christliches Volk finden soll. Was die Kirche konstituiert, sind auch die sichersten Kennzeichen.[32]

Es gibt noch weitere Verse in den einleitenden Kapiteln der Genesis, die Luther vom Gottesdienst reden lassen. So z. B. die abschließende kurze Anmerkung zu Gn 4, 26, dass man zu dieser Zeit anfing, den Namen des Herrn anzurufen. Luther nennt diese Passage die »allerschönste Beschreibung

---

29 WA 42, 183, 39 f: »Nullum enim alium finem traditorum sacrificiorum fuisse statuendum est.«
30 Vgl. WA 42, 184, 13-28.
31 WA 42, 185, 6 f.
32 Vgl. WA 50, 632, 35 - 633, 11.

dessen, was es heißt, einen rechten Gottesdienst zu feiern«, nämlich den Namen des Herrn anzurufen. Der »Name des Herrn« weist auf Christus, den verheißenen Samen, der den Kopf der Schlange zertreten wird.[33]

Luther kann einen solchen Gottesdienst auch einen rechten Gottesdienst gemäß den Geboten der ersten Tafel nennen.[34] Auch diesen Sprachgebrauch erkennen wir wieder in »Von den Konziliis und Kirchen«, wo Luther von den Zeichen nach der ersten und der zweiten Tafel spricht.[35] Den Namen des Herrn anzurufen meint nämlich, das Wort zu predigen, mit dem Herzen zu glauben und mit dem Mund zu bekennen. Dies alles gehört zusammen und folgt aufeinander, genau wie Paulus es in R 10, 13 f sagt. Den Namen des Herrn anzurufen kommt aus dem Glauben des Herzens, der wiederum von der Predigt dessen kommt, der zur Verkündigung gesandt ist. Alles entspricht dem, was Gott in der ersten Tafel gebietet. Das erste Gebot fordert, zu glauben, dass Gott zu unserer Rettung eilt. Das zweite Gebot fordert Bekenntnis und Gebet, dass wir den Namen Gottes in der Stunde der Gefahr anrufen und dass wir Gott danken. Das dritte Gebot fordert, dass wir die Wahrheit predigen, sowie die rechte Lehre bewahren und verteidigen.[36]

Auch die zweite Tafel gehört mit dem Gottesdienst zusammen, jedoch nicht so unmittelbar, weil das dort Gesagte vom Verhältnis der Menschen untereinander handelt. Wenn aber erfüllt ist, was die erste Tafel fordert, dann folgen spontan auch alle anderen Werke der zweiten Tafel. Diese sind als gottesdienstliche Handlungen nach der zweiten Tafel zu betrachten, entsprungen aus der Erfüllung der Gebote der ersten Tafel.[37] Sie sind also sekundär. Das bedeutet, dass die Werke der zweiten Tafel als Kennzeichen weniger sicher sind, aber es gibt sie, weil ein guter Baum immer gute Früchte bringt. So betrachtet Luther das ganze christliche Leben, das Leben nach der ersten und nach der zweiten Tafel, als Gottesdienst. Es ist ein Leben im Glauben an Gott und in Liebe zum Nächsten.

33 Vgl. WA 42, 241, 6-23.
34 WA 42, 241, 6-8.
35 WA 50, 643, 27-37.
36 WA 42, 241, 8-10; 242, 5-13.
37 WA 42, 242, 14-18: »Primam tabulam requirit, ut audias, mediteris, doceas verbum, ut ores, ut Deum timeas. Hoc cum fit, sequentur quasi sua sponte etiam secundae tabulae cultus seu opera. Est enim impossibile, ut, qui primae tabuale cultus praestat, non etiam praestet secundam tabulam« (Hervorhebung von mir).

Sexuality and Marriage in Luther's Theology

Seminar Leader: Sammeli Juntunen
Reporter: Christopher Boyd Brown

Sammeli Juntunen: »Luther on Sex« — Luther's views must be set in context of late medieval valuation of celibacy over marriage, ideas of courtly love, and practices of marriage such as clandestine engagements. Luther's central concern is to help overcome troubles of conscience about sex. His counsel is founded in his theology of creation, established by God's will but distorted by sin, and an essentialist anthropology of humans as male and female, founded in the Bible, but also corresponding to natural law and reason as Luther understood them. Sexual responsibility is exercised within the natural orders created by God and governed by the Law; neither celibacy nor marriage is a way of salvation, but marriage is regulated by God through the worldly regiment.

Luther criticizes the medieval theology of celibacy as contrary to nature and a manifestation of self-righteousness. For all but a very few, marriage is a necessary remedy against unchastity. Within marriage, sex is not only licit but commanded. Nevertheless, Luther continues to assert the Augustinian-Stoic criticism of sex even within marriage as irrational exstasis. On the other hand, Luther's rejection of the ordo caritatis as fundamental theological principle might lead to a more positive appreciation of sex.

Children are central to Luther's theology of marriage, not only as the goal of sexuality but also as the central good work of married life. Luther, drawing on mysticism, speaks highly of married love – Braut-Liebe –, which is commanded within the estate of marriage. Although Luther gave more flexible pastoral advice in exceptional cases his normative teaching on sexuality was grounded in his sense of natural law and of marriage as part of the created order.

Robert Guy Erwin: »Neither sacrament nor covenant: Martin Luther, marriage, and the modern world« — Medieval Christian teaching and regulation on marriage developed rather late, in the canonical synthesis of a tangled matrix of Biblical texts, Roman laws, and patristic reflections. The definition of marriage as sacrament took place alongside the exaltation of celibacy as spiritually superior. Divergence from rules requiring clerical celibacy was practically institutionalized in much of Europe.

Luther's early rejection of ecclesiastical regulation of marriage was bound up with his broader rejection of canon law. Marriage belonged to the created order, not the order of salvation – though the sharp systematization of a theology of orders belongs to the 19th century, not to Luther –. As a condition of human life, marriage is natural and universal, and belongs to the civil order to regulate, though practically Luther had to help fill the gap left by the rejection of canon law on marriage. Luther thus desacralizes marriage while seeing it as part of the social order existing after the Fall for the restraint of sin.

Luther's views are to be contrasted with Reformed and Anglican descriptions of marriage as a divine covenant as well as with Enlightenment descriptions of marriage as a contract. Luther can inform a critique of contemporary attempts to resacralize marriage as well as proposals to yield discussion of marriage entirely to the state; at the same time Luther's own presuppositions must be called into question in a secular and pluralistic world.

Harold Ashley Hall: »Some Notes on Marriage and Sexuality in the Early Church and in the Works of Philipp Melanchthon« — The theology of marriage and sexuality in the early church developed under the presupposition of fundamental agreement between Christian morality and the best pagan moral teaching. In that context, homosexuality was tolerated, though criticized, so long as it did not interfere with the social obligation to marry. The central importance of marriage was that of procreation to support the state. The praise of religious celibacy among Christians also drew on classical models of praise for celibate philosophical life. Celibacy spread from monasticism to become the model for bishops as well.

Augustine defends conjugal intercourse and the goodness of marriage while criticizing disordered sexual desire. Despite Pelagian criticism, Augustine maintained a close connection between lust and the transmission of original sin. His ideas had long influence in the Western theological tradition.

Philipp Melanchthon stands firmly within this tradition at many points. He is firmly anti-Pelagian and accepts the description of lust as primary example of the disorder of original sin. He declines to lecture on classical texts – the »Symposium« – that reflect »unnatural« sexual practices. He goes beyond Augustine in elevating marriage over celibacy, a distinctive Protestant voice within the Christian tradition. Tradition does serve Melanchthon as a source for the defense of clerical marriage.

In his writing on marriage, Melanchthon is particularly, though not exclusively, concerned with practical matters. An extended discussion was incorporated into the »Loci theologici« from 1543 on.

James Arne Nestingen: »Luther on Marriage, Vocation, and the Cross« — Luther's doctrine of vocation, standing together with justification as the »twin centers« of his theology, guides his frequent return to the subject of marriage in his writing, lecturing, and preaching: marriage is the primary context for creaturely calling as well as the place in which the cross is applied to believers.

Luther's theology of marriage is shaped by his redefinition of spirit and flesh in terms of faith and unbelief, in light of which »marriage is the most religious state of all«. It is also informed by his theology of creation: Luther counts the household among the three orders in which God's creative work continues, though provisionally in relation to God's kingdom which stands beyond. The household is more primary than civil government, but also regulated by law, summarized in the Commandments and the »Haustafel«. »In the Spirit«, however, the demands of the law upon the household become a Christian vocation of service, one so important that Luther uses otherwise problematic language of cooperation with God to describe its work, a gracious partnership beyond law.

The family is also a place particularly characterized by the cross amid the troubled but shared relationships of household life, a place therefore also where the Spirit brings repentance out of despair and resurrection comes out of the deep freedom of the forgiveness of sins. Luther's marriage with Katherine von Bora was both matrix and exemplar for these insights.

Pernilla Parenmalm: »The calling to parenthood and parenting: reflections on Luther's view of men, women, and Vocation« — Luther's ideas must be seen in the context of late medieval society and religion, including changing opportunities for women's work in rural and urban environments both in common with a husband or alone, witchcraft, and prostitution. Religiously, virginity – especially for women of the upper classes – was considered superior to married life.

Luther set his description of marriage in polemical opposition to monastic life, as a superior context for good works, located within the temporal regiment and the status oeconomicus. He recognized sexuality as an important and healthy element in human life.

Especially important is Luther's understanding of married life and parenthood as a vocation, an antidote to human egocentricity. It is a gift of God, though it has been corrupted by sin. He gives special attention to the work of raising children as part of the vocation of marriage. Parents are to show love for their children by teaching and disciplining them. If the parents fail in their primary responsibility, however, the civil authorities should intervene. Luther's sense of marriage as vocation was expressed in his testament which appointed Katharina as guardian.

Luther's emphasis on honor and obedience within hierarchical relationships within the family raises questions in contemporary perspective. Limits on obedience are not always clearly developed. However, Luther's understanding of reciprocity in relationships is helpful and challenging for contemporary ethics.

Christopher Boyd Brown: »The Reformation of Marriage among Luther's Students« — The wedding sermons of Luther's students – here, especially Johann Mathesius (1504-1565), Cyriacus Spangenberg, (1528-1604) and Hieronymus Mencel (1517-1590) – were a key means by which Luther's theology of marriage was – selectively and creatively – transmitted to a large public. Though Luther preached a few such sermons, his students were largely responsible for developing the genre using material from Luther's Genesis lectures, Table Talk, and treatises as well as medieval precedents.

Lutheran preaching, however, abandons the medieval subordination of praise of marriage to the praise of celibacy. A very wide range of Biblical texts, especially Old Testament narratives, serve as the basis for sermons – the New Testament epistles have a surprisingly small role –. Wedding sermons gave clergy opportunity for presenting themselves as »Hausväter« as well as pastors and for both critique and defense of popular customs.

Lutheran preachers give little attention to moral critique of sexual activities within marriage. The crucial boundary is between marriage and everything that takes place outside. Sin attending married sexuality is relativized by the understanding that all human activity is inevitably attended by sin. They also use language of »delight« and »play« to describe marital relations and praise passionate love between husband and wife.

Lutheran preaching about the »Ehecreutz« is a key application of the theologia crucis to daily life and a contrast to medieval preaching in which such misfortunes as the birth of handicapped children were understood as divine punishment for particular sexual sins.

In describing relations between husbands and wives, patriarchal authority is presupposed, though the sermons labor to emphasize reciprocal obligations, such as the husband's duty to heed the advice of a godly wife. They regard the household as a place of emotional solace and relative informality in contrast to the strict roles assumed in the public sphere.

Jeannine Olson: »John Calvin's views of marriage and divorce as evidenced in the marital laws of Geneva« — About a year after Calvin arrived in Geneva in 1536 he and the other pastors proposed to the city council, which ruled the city, that the council appoint a committee to deal with marital matters and discipline, given the absence of the canon law of the Church of Rome. The council did not accept this proposal. However, when Calvin returned to Geneva in 1541

after his years in Strasbourg (1538-1541), he could press the issue again. In the mid-1540s he proposed laws that gradually took effect. They were formally accepted in 1561. Young people could marry without parental consent at the ages of eighteen for women and twenty for men. The impediments to engagement and marriage were those of close relationship. First cousins could not marry, for instance. Also infectious disease could be an impediment as could the discovery that the bride was not a virgin. Engagements were enforced. Within six weeks of the engagement, couples were expected to marry, which they did at a regular worship service before the sermon. Once married, divorces were granted for adultery or for extended absence, assuming the spouse was dead or had abandoned the marriage. They were difficult to obtain, and more men successfully obtained them than women. Brutality was not a reason for divorce although it was discourgaged. The ultimate penalty for repeated adultery was death, although this was exceptional.

Darci Drehmer also participated in the seminar.

Seminar über Luthers Briefe

Seminarleiterin: Ute Mennecke
Berichterstatter: Johannes Schilling

Luthers Briefe lohnen immer und immer wieder die Lektüre, als Quellen für sein Leben und Werk, als Zeugnisse ihrer Zeit und ihrer Epoche, als literarische Texte.

Ute Mennecke, Professorin für Kirchengeschichte an der Evangelisch-Theologischen Fakultät der Universität Bonn und selbst Autorin eines ausgezeichneten Buchs über

»Luthers Trostbriefe« (GÜ 1988), hatte das Seminar als ein Laboratorium gemeinsamer Lektüre geplant und vorbereitet.

Als hervorragende Kennerin der Quellentexte gab sie zu Beginn eine Einführung in Überlieferung, Textbestand und Forschungssituation. Einzelne Referate wurden nicht vorgetragen; vielmehr galt die ungeteilte Aufmerksamkeit aller Seminarteilnehmer den von der Seminarleiterin ausgewählten Texten. Diese wurden einer genauen Lektüre unterzogen. Dabei erwies es sich als erhellend, dass die deutsch- bzw. englischsprachigen Teilnehmer bei der Übersetzung der lateinischen Briefe in die jeweilige Zielsprache – oder auch bei der Übersetzung deutscher Texte ins Englische bzw. Amerikanische – ihr jeweiliges Verständnis in die Diskussion einbrachten. Im Einzelnen ging es vor allem um die Stellung von Luthers Briefen im Kontext der humanistischen Korrespondenzen, ihren rhetorischen Charakter sowie seelsorgerliche Konstellationen und Situationen, in denen Luther brieflich agierte.

Die gemeinsame Arbeit ließ allen Teilnehmern deutlich werden, welch großen Gewinn eine genaue, ruhige Lektüre darstellt; gerade im Prozess des Übersetzens stellten sich zahlreiche neue Erkenntnisse ein. Vor allem bei einem Teil der amerikanischen Teilnehmer, die sich zuvor nur ansatzweise mit Luthers Briefen befasst hatten, dürfte das Seminar nachhaltige Wirkung erzielt und eigene Forschungen angeregt haben.

Vita christiana nach Luthers Freiheitsschrift (1520)

Seminarleiter: Steffen Kjeldgaard-Pedersen
Berichterstatter: Steffen Kjeldgaard-Pedersen

Das Seminar zielte auf historisch fundierte Beiträge zur theologischen Interpretation des lateinischen Freiheitstraktats – WA 7, 49-73 –, wobei Fragen nach Aktualität und Applikation nicht von vornherein ausgeschlossen sein sollten.

In der ersten Sitzung hat zunächst *Steffen Kjeldgaard-Pedersen* als Hypothese erwogen und zur Diskussion gestellt, ob sich der lateinische, auf humanistisch gebildete Leser deutlich ausgerichtete Freiheitstraktat vielleicht auch stillschweigend gegen Erasmus (1466/69-1536) wendet. Dafür könnte sprechen, dass Luther an mehreren Stellen anscheinend auf Formulierungen des Erasmus in dessen »Enchiridion militis christiani« adversativ anspielt. Außerdem wurde eine Reihe von Beobachtungen zur trinitarischen Struktur der Gedankenfolge in den beiden Hälften des nach der Distinktion »innerer Mensch – äußerer Mensch« gegliederten Textes näher besprochen.

Dass Luther in »De libertate christiana« sozusagen mit dem dritten Glaubensartikel und dem Heiligen Geist anfängt, entspricht seinen Ausführungen zum sachlich richtigen Verständnis der Heiligen Schrift in den »Operationes in psalmos«, mit denen der

Freiheitstraktat ja in enger Beziehung steht; vgl. Wilhelm Maurer: Von der Freiheit eines Christenmenschen: zwei Untersuchungen zu Luthers Reformationsschriften 1520/21. GÖ 1949.

Dies wurde in der zweiten Sitzung deutlich gemacht durch *Lars Christian Vangslevs* Analyse der Auslegung Luthers in den »Operationes in psalmos« von Ps 1,3 und Ps 14,1 vor dem Hintergrund der hermeneutischen und theologischen Grundeinsichten der gesamten zweiten Psalmenvorlesung, inklusive der beiden Vorreden Luthers, und – unter Hervorhebung der wichtigsten, zum Teil fast wortwörtlichen Übereinstimmungen zwischen Vorlesung und Traktat – im Hinblick auf ein präzises Verständnis der entsprechenden Abschnitte in »De libertate christiana«. Der These Maurers beipflichtend, dass Universitätstheologie und »Erbauungsschriftstellerei« bei Luther eng zusammenhängen, hat Vangslev im letzten Teil seines Beitrages eine Aktualisierung von Luthers Anliegen versucht und davor gewarnt, das Christentum als Religion der Freiheit und den Islam als Religion des Gesetzes auf einen Nenner zu bringen.

In der dritten Sitzung konzentrierte *Knut Alfsvåg* die Diskussion des Seminars auf die prima fidei virtus – WA 7, 53, 34 –, die am Anfang von Luthers Darstellung der Freiheit und Gerechtigkeit des inneren Menschen – WA 7, 50-59 – erörtert wird. Unterstrichen wurden dabei der christologische Ausgangspunkt Luthers, seine Aufnahme von Gedankengut der griechischen Väter und seine Nähe zur Rhetorik der Renaissance. Indem das Euangelium Christi als die einzig mögliche Verwirklichung wahrer Menschlichkeit gesehen wird, verknüpft Luther durch seine Betonung der Vereinigung des Glaubenden mit Christus forensische und

effektive Aspekte der Rechtfertigung, und die prima fidei virtus wird dann gleichbedeutend mit der christlichen Freiheit, die durch die Verbindung der Seele mit dem alle göttlichen Güter schenkenden Wort zustande kommt. Luthers Sicht der Vergöttlichung des Menschen muss in dieser Perspektive verstanden werden.

Anschließend hat *Joachim Fischer* in einem kurzen Bericht über die Rezeption von Luthers Freiheitstraktat in Brasilien die Doppelheit von Herrsein und Dienstbarkeit des Christen, das christliche Leben in Glauben und Liebe und den Christen als Christus für seinen Nächsten als die drei immer wieder – auch in der sogenannten Befreiungstheologie – zitierten Hauptsachen der Schrift hervorgehoben.

Ein Referat über »The inner man: justification in Luther's ›Freedom of a Christian‹« von *Diane Bowers* lag den Verhandlungen der vierten und letzten Sitzung zugrunde. Anstöße von Bengt R. Hoffmann und der neuen finnischen Lutherforschung positiv aufnehmend und die Unterscheidung zwischen innerem und äußerem Menschen in den Vordergrund stellend, hat Bowers dafür argumentiert, dass Rechtfertigung nach dem Freiheitstraktat ein sowohl forensisches als effektives Ereignis sei, das im inneren Menschen stattfinde und von Luther als »altera fidei virtus« – WA 7, 53, 34 – und »tertia fidei gratia« – WA 7, 54, 31 – weiter differenziert werde, und zwar parallel zur Distinktion zwischen gratia und donum in der Schrift gegen Latomus (1475-1544). Der fortlaufende Prozess der Heiligung sei demgegenüber als Einwirkung der Gabe der göttlichen Gnade auf den äußeren Menschen zu verstehen. Bowers hat u. a. das radikal forensische Verständnis der Rechtfertigungslehre Luthers bei Gerhard O. Forde (1927-2005) zum

Vergleich herangezogen, um schließlich auf eine durch Luthers doppeltes Verständnis der Rechtfertigung ermöglichte Verbesserung des ökumenischen Gesprächs, der – lutherischen – Theologie und des christlichen Gemeinschaftslebens hinzuweisen.

Doctrine and Life in Luther and Melanchthon

Seminar Leader: Bo Kristian Holm
Reporters: Bo Kristian Holm and Lubomir Batka

The seminar focused on the relationship and interaction between doctrine and life, with special attention to the relationship between theology and piety, doctrinal content and Christian conduct, doctrinal clarity and pastoral certainty, theology and pedagogy, with the aim of establishing a foundation for comparisons between Luther and Melanchthon, and with the intention of elucidating how doctrine is used and how doctrinal differences shape practical approaches and vice versa.

With the paper »You shall sanctify the holy day: Luther's view on worship in some of his catechetical writings« *Paulo W. Buss* began the discussion by grounding the function of doctrine in the midst of worship. He states a shift from an emphasis on the sabbatical rest of the soul in the earlier writings, towards a growing emphasis on the hearing of the Word in the sanctification of the holy day. Luther's strong pedagogical understanding of the function of worship, focusing on the right understanding of the word of God, is counterbalanced by an emphasis on the congregation's activity in praising, singing and praying. It is God who is acting, giving his justice to sinful man. And justified sinners are nothing but receivers, but that especially in sanctifying God's holy day. In this response there is, according to Buss, an analogy between worship and the act of creation.

Lubomir Batka, in his paper »Original sin: a comparison of Luther and Melanchthon«, led the discussion into interrelatedness of clarity and certainty. Comparing Luther's Introduction to the Epistle to the Romans (1522) and Melanchthon's »Loci communes rerum theologicarum seu Hypotyposes theologiae« (1521), he focuses on the fundamental shift in the understanding of original sin in reformation theology. While Luther is very clear in his identification of sin with disbelief, Melanchthon is more concerned with sin as lack of justice. Luther accepts the Pauline teaching about the foreknowledge of God as a doctrinal consequence of the fact that sinful man cannot save himself and that salvation for this very reason totally depends on God, but is not developed any further, leaving it as a concept of consolation. Contrary, Melanchthon begins with the foreknowledge of God and the merits of Christ in order to understand the proclamation of salvation. If for Luther the word of God opens the doctrinal system, then for

Melanchthon the doctrinal system opens the word of God. Comfort, however, is not lacking in Melanchthon's theology. Quoting the Apology, Batka states that Christian teaching for Melanchthon is exactly what brings the abundant consolation that devoted consciences need.

The seminar was led a step further into the understanding of the interrelatedness of doctrine and preaching in Luther's work in *Paul R. Hinlicky's* »›The deity has withdrawn‹: Luther's doctrinal preaching of Christ forsaken by God according to Psalm 8«. As his source he used both the original and the version edited by Poach in 1572. In discussion with Joachim Mörlin (1514-1571), Andreas Poach (1515-1585) emphasises that Christ is not a perfect man who wins a prize and shares it with his friends, but the incarnate Son of God who wins those dead in their sins back to life. The final part of Luther's sermon, therefore, gives Poach trouble. Here Luther speaks about the withdrawal of the deity from Christ, which seems to lead to a notion of Christ as an autonomous man fulfilling the legal demand for faith in God in extremis, and in this way actually to support Major's doctrine: bona opera sunt necessaria ad salutatem. Poach tries to solve the problem by distinguishing between the immanent Trinity and the economic Trinity and by the anti-Nestorian doctrine of communicatio idiomatum; doctrines that are in accord with Luther's theology but have scant basis in the actual sermon. For Hinlicky, the study of the texts shows the interface between doctrine and life in three different ways: First of all, it illustrates how theology has to be understood as pathos not poiesis, neither as construction nor as a strong distinction between first-order kerygma and second-order doctrine. Second, the text

points at a potential misleading formulation made by Luther. Poach's solution is therefore theologically sound as he uses Luther to correct himself, seeing Luther's Christology close to the theopaschite Neo-Chalcedonism of the Fifth Council and Maximus Confessor (580-662). Finally, Anfechtungen understood as the »Gethsemane of the soul« points at the ultimate, martyrological surrender to the will of God, as the doctrine of Christ forms the believer's life.

Jussi Koivisto ended the »Luther section« by investigating »The tension between doctrine and life in Luther's later Commentary on Galatians (1531/1535)«. Koivisto begins his paper by noting the alterations in the world view separating us from Luther's time. Passions are no longer understood as either God-sent or Devil-sent. Virtues have lost their function of controlling the passions. To understand the relation between doctrine and life in Luther, we therefore need to take Luther's doctrine on virtues into consideration. By identifying doctrine with heaven and life with earth, Luther gives doctrine the highest value possible, and, through the doctrinal virtue of faith, the Christian takes part in the immutable God. This identification and partaking is a clear separation of doctrine from life. At the same time, the theological virtues connect two separate realms: as faith is the power in love, the heavenly and immutable doctrine is the power in life. Although Luther never rejects the value of Aristotelian philosophy for living in the world, he totally rejects its value in spiritual matters. Instead his understanding of doctrine and theological virtues, according to Koivisto, brings him closer to both Paul and Plato, who shared the opinion that virtues have divine origin.

242

Chris Croghan contributed with the paper »Examen eorum: a case study in Melanchthon's pedagogical method and the assimilation of Aristotle«. Melanchthon's emphasis on rhetoric and dialectics becomes a necessary background for understanding »Examen eorum qui audiuntur ante ritum publicae ordinationis qua commendatur eis ministerium euangelii« in the first part of the paper. The second part draws attention to Melanchhon's use of the Aristotelian method of inventio, the correct use of demonstrative questions. The third part deals more specifically with Melanchthon's assimilation of Aristotle, and the fourth part with the application of Aristotle in »Examen eorum …«. A comparison between Melanchthon's use of the topic »poenitentia« as an example of the process of dialectical inventio in »Elementorum rhetorices libres II« and the same topic in »Examen eorum …« shows striking similarities, which, according to Croghan, contributes to the understanding of the context and concepts that shaped the teaching, preaching and polemics in later Lutheranism.

The development in the theology of the later Melanchthon was the subject of *Bo Kr. Holm's* paper »Doctrine and life in Melanchthon's German and late Latin Loci«, which focused on the seldom read, but now reedited, Heubtartikel Christlicher Lere. Caused by Melanchthon's response to Osiander's accusation, and due to the more cathetical function of the German Loci, the presence of Christ plays a much more central role than previously in Melanchthon's theology. This could give the impression that Luther's Christological qualification of divine presence is more suitable for catechetical purposes than is the traditional pneumatological qualification normally found

in Melanchthon, and that the actual context of communication thus shapes doctrinal formulations. In both cases, more studies are needed. However, it clearly shows how Melanchthon himself, despite his aftermath, ends in a position even closer to Luther than generally presumed, especially when this »fourth Loci« is taken into consideration.

In the final paper »Promise, liberty, and persecution: exploring Philipp Melanchthon's contextual theology«, *David Lumpp* presents the »Unterricht der Visitatoren an die Pfarrherrn im Kurfürstentum Sachsen« (1528) and the »Leipzig articels« (1548) as sources for understanding Melanchthon's role as both teacher and reformer, aware of his public responsibilities. In »Unterricht der Visitatoren …«, the discussion of tribulation gives Melanchthon an opportunity to integrate doctrine and life, sketching the knowledge that tribulations are to be met with. The differences in these works show how actual circumstances, pastoral and catechetical consideration and »damage control« shape the formulations. In Melanchthon's Unterricht, the promise is articulated by using language of atonement and satisfaction, while the »Leipzig articles« explicitly uses the language of justification. In 1518, liberty is defined more explicitly and Melanchthon asserts the necessity of good works. In 1548, he works harder to define the boundaries of liberty rather than the concept itself. Lumpp ends by arguing in defence of the intent of the »Leipzig articles« and, at the same time, a theological clarification and correction of its language, especially concerning the necessity of virtues etc. for salvation.

The result of the seminar discussion can be summarised in the following main points:

1.1 For the reformers, doctrine is an assertion of truth against the lie, dealing with immutable divine things. At the same time, there is a constant interplay between faith and doctrine. Doctrine is the result of faith. At the same time, faith is determined by the historical consensus of the church, as expressed in doctrine. Doctrine surrounds the practical life as heaven surrounds the earth.

1.2 Based on the consensus of the church, some doctrines are more fundamental than others: the Canon, Trinity, Christology, the teaching on Grace. All these lead to the doctrine of Justification as the central expression of Reformation theology.

2 The primary function of doctrine is related to the practical life of a Christian. Doctrine gives what it explains. Therefore doctrine is intertwined with a process of communication. True doctrine is determined by its consolatory value as a powerful weapon against the assaults of the Devil. There is a need to make a decent explanation of the content of faith to the listener. For Luther and Melanchthon, true doctrine communicates God's salvation to sinful man. Not as mere information, but doctrine is always at the same time a matter of divine self-giving, although the emphasis on the identity of the divine gift with the divine giver is stronger in Luther.

3 Emphasising the consolatory effect of doctrine, it is necessary to distinguish between the Gospel with its consolatory ef-fect and the stated consolatory effect of the formulated doctrine. This distinction establishes a critical interplay.

3.1 Consolation needs a firm basis to be certain. The right doctrine – and not the wrong doctrine – is what helps to console the conscience. The clear articulation of faith in doctrine, at least according to Melanchthon, thus makes the way for the Gospel. The observation was made that Melanchthon's early understanding of faith as fiducia was later altered to include the comprehension of faith as notitia. Consolation comes through understanding the Gospel by clear teaching.

3.2 Luther puts the emphasis on the aspect of preaching as the proper place for communicating Gospel with its consolatory aspect. Consolation comes through clear formulations that increase faith. In this way it is right to say that true doctrine is dependent on its ability to function as Gospel.

3.3 A concept of doctrine oriented towards its actual communication needs a secure basis. This secure basis, however, is again a matter of actual communication, since the only guide is the actual use of the Bible. It contains the divine title of immutability – not the inspiration of letter, but of the Spirit. In dealing with the Bible, Luther emphasises the narrative character of the message of Jesus Christ, while Melanchthon emphasises the right theological method as a clear deductive science.

Luther's Ethics in the Realms of Church, Household, and Politics

Seminarleader: Risto Saarinen
Reporter: Jonathan Mumme

How can a seminar on »Luther's ethics in the realms of church, household, and politics«, function as a subsection of a congress on »Luther's ethics in the realms of church, household, and politics«? *Risto Saarinen*, having set the theme for his seminar before the congress had set its own, decided not to answer that question. Instead, wishing to further pursue his own findings on divine ordinance and the three orders, he offered one seminar group the opportunity to engage the theme of the congress directly.

Michael Beyer opened the forum by way of a guided tour through the seventeenth to nineteenth sections of Luther's »Ein Sermon von dem heiligen hochwürdigen Sakrament der Taufe« (1519) – WA 2, 734, 14 - 737, 13 –. Beyer's analysis explained baptism as the justified identity of the Christian in a fallen world and the three orders or hierarchies as the places in which Christians variously live out this one baptism. Living out baptism within these orders means nothing other than work and labor, suffering and dying. Baptism's work is to kill sin and the flesh, and it adopts these orders as its theater to that destructive end. Within the three orders baptism continually labors to break any tranquil satisfaction with earthly life, preparing the Christian in his or her given »Stand« for death.

Written as edifying literature for the pious reader, this early sermon stood in sharp contrast to the piety of its day. The reader is not encouraged to reach above and beyond his or her »Stand« in order to merit a given standing with God. Rather, as baptized and justified the reader is to find his or her given work in the given »Stand«. The mathematical gradations of a late medieval merit-based system fall apart before baptism's common quantity – »gemein Maß« –. These gradations having falling by the wayside, the baptized Christian finds a unique life in his or her given »Stand«, in which action amounts to the praise of God and the service of neighbor.

The fact that this sermon deals with these orders under the headings of »Estate of Marriage« – »ehelicher Stand« –, »Spiritual Estate« – »geistlicher Stand«, here pertaining to monasticism – and »Governing Estate« – »regierender Stand«, here pertaining to bishops and parsons –, which estates are themselves arranged into a graduated hierarchy, led to a lively discussion of Luther's understanding of the three orders – »Dreiständelehre« – over against his understanding of the two fields of ruling or operating – »Zwei Regimente« – and his and/or Augustine's (354-430) understanding of the two kingdoms – »Zwei Reiche« –.

Continuing his presentation under the heading »Luthers Drei-Stände-Welt als Ort christlicher Existenz: das Miteinander der befreiten Knechte« Beyer sought to present Luther's understanding of the three orders as an essential element of early-modern life.

In this regard the churchliness of all three orders was stressed as well as their tendency to overlap and intertwine.

»The three orders or life-forms and the three motifs«, the paper presented by *Bernhard Erling*, wrestled with difficulties and ambiguities associated first with reconciling and then with applying Luther's understanding of the two kingdoms and of the three orders in the modern context.

Erling approached the topic on the basis Anders Nygren's (1890-1978) work in »Agape and eros« (Phil 1953). Here Nygren identifies three motifs, that is, three factors or virtues that give particular thought systems and outlooks their character. These motifs he calls »agape«, »eros«, and »nomos«. These motifs underlie the answers given by various systems of thought and world-outlooks to fundamental questions of belief and behavior, of faith and ethics. After articulating Nygren's thesis that »agape« – essentially Christian and »eros« – essentially Greek – were synthesized by Origen (circa 185/86 - circa 253/54) and especially by Augustine into »charitas«, a synthesis subsequently shattered by Luther, Erling went on to show how these three motifs harmonize with Luther's tri-fold distinction of ecclesia, oeconomia, and politia. Adding in the parallel distinctions of Lehrstand, Nährstand, and Wehrstand, the categories for the rest of the paper and the group's discussion were ordered as follows: ecclesia / agape / Lehrstand, oeconomia / eros / Nährstand, politia / nomos / Wehrstand.

Posing numerous concrete, contemporary questions, Erling kept his eye to fundamental differences between the modern and Reformation contexts. In Luther's articulation of the three orders at least two things may be observed. First, there is an overlap, a sort of giving and receiving, between the three orders. Second, Luther assumed and foresaw a system in which the ecclesia had an intentional and definitive teaching function in the oeconomia and the politia; see Luther's 1530 »A sermon on keeping children in school«; WA 30 II, 517-588 ≙ LW 46, 207-258. This teaching function – Lehrstand – was embodied in the person of »the teaching pastor«. Clearly, one is presented with a different situation today. Whether viewed from the perspective of the American context, where one finds a strict division of church and state, or from the Finnish or German contexts where the politia regulates religious and moral education, the ecclesia as Lehrstand does not hold the place it did in Luther's day. Yet the »separation of church and state« alleged in the United States – or in the Americas, as *Daniel Beros* affirmed of Argentina –, dare not obstruct the permanent fact, that religious and moral education is inherent in all educational systems – a fact at least recognized in the lands of Erling's European interlocutors –.

Erling's paper provided much grist for the milling conversation, touching not only on education, but also on political and socioeconomic systems. His central thesis is that Luther's understanding of the three orders can best be approached and applied in the modern context from the standpoint of the three motifs. Identifying Luther and his understanding of Christian love, and thereby his ethic, with the agape motif, Erling suggests that a society could approach moral and religious education under the categories of agape, eros, and nomos. The given educational system would present and teach about all faiths active in the given land, but under this threefold heading. One would expect that the agape motif, characterized by self-giving love and thankful response to this love, would come to predominate the other two motifs, making room for the voice of the ecclesia in its Lehrstand function, to educate not only the family – one half of the oeconomia – but also the socio-economic workings – the other half of the oeconomia – and the government – politia – of the given society.

Risto Saarinen's paper, presented midweek as a short presentation, could well have served as an introduction to the whole of this seminar's discussions. Herein *Saarinen* deals with his own particular interest in this seminar's theme, namely a consideration of the three orders as divine ordinances.

Considering Luther in relation to the ethical systems of his day, Saarinen deals especially with Aristotelian (384-322) ethics as received in the medieval tradition. With Luther he finds both an appropriation and adaptation of Aristotelian ethics in the latter middle ages. Here Luther's tri-fold ordering of ecclesia, politia, and oeconomia reflects the divisions of Aristotle's ethics as received in the middle ages: ethica monastica – from Nichomachean Ethics –, ethica politica – from Politics – and ethica oeconomica – from Oeconomics –. »Luther replaced ethica monastica with the ecclesial order«, argues Saarinen. It is this »ecclesial order«, somewhat resembling though not identical to Aristotle's understanding of prudence – phronesis –, which his paper then labors to define.

Through following the research of other Luther scholars Saarinen identifies a deficiency in the failure to observe the medieval notion of ordinatio Dei as an essential element of Luther's articulation of the three orders. The language of divine ordinance was most common in late medieval discus-

sions of grace and justification under the term »potentia ordinata«, and, in addition, it played a role in this period's consideration of covenant, testament and donation/gift. The late medieval consideration of divine ordinance was enriched by analysis from the perspective of Aristotle's four causes, to which late medieval theology added the category of instrumental cause, divided into the subcategories of primary and secondary instrumental causes. Saarinen sees Luther appropriating these distinctions as he articulates a positive place for Christian action in »the earthly kingdom«, in the oeconomia and politia, understanding Christians as secondary instrumental causes. Luther's ethics in regard to the ecclesia, however, remain more nuanced. He claims a reticence by Luther to speak of human beings as instrumental causes in the ecclesia, »the spiritual kingdom«, since this would amount to Pelagianism.

Illustrating his observations in part by way of Luther's exposition of Psalm 127 – 1532; WA 40 III, 268, 1 - 269, 4 –, Saarinen arrives at a »twofold view of human agency«; in the oeconomia and politia human action may be understood as a secondary instrumental cause, but in the ecclesia human action may only be considered »ecclesial« if it proceeds from faith and love. Late-medieval considerations of covenant and testament suffice to articulate a sort of two-party action in »the earthly kingdom«, but fall short of being able to define a theological causality of faith and love. Thus the three orders come to »represent a graduated moral hierarchy«.

Saarinen cautions against extracting any discussion of ethics from the whole of Luther's theology, the danger in this case being that one may slip into Pelagianism. He concludes that theological »doing« and philosophical/ethical »doing« are fundamentally different. In the latter the doing flows from reason and a rightly disposed will, in the former the doing flows solely from faith.

Saarinen continued his contribution to the forum with his paper on »Renaissance ethics and the European Reformation«. In his section on the Lutheran Reformation Saarinen identifies a young Luther well acquainted with Aristotle's Nichomachean Ethics. Although Luther theologically rejected Aristotle's understanding of virtue along with medieval understandings of merit that sprung from the same, Melanchthon skillfully adapted Aristotle's ethics in 1546 for his »Philosophiae moralis epitomes libri duo emendati & aucti«, and preserves its place in the Protestant university.

Melanchthon's attention to Luther's distinction of Law and Gospel and his understanding of the two regiments allows for the articulation of ethics and the law within the state, falling entirely into the »worldly kingdom«, and in the household, which »remains between worldly and ecclesiastical orders«.

Opening this seminar's first session, Saarinen remarked that his interest in Luther's understanding of the three orders had been sparked by previous seminars of the Luther Congress led by Oswald Bayer. The 2007 seminar may well not be the last that the Luther Congress is to see on this topic. Especially in regard to the ecclesia, this group's discussions evidenced that there is still work to be done before clarity is reached.

Luther on Work and Vocation

Seminar leader: Roger Jensen
Berichterstatter: Roger Jensen

This seminar titled »Work an Vocation« explored Luther's notion of the ethical person, with special reference to the reformer's understanding of everyday work and vocation. We focused our attention on both Luther's writings and the tradition of scholarly interpretation. Although we missed the contributions of several seminar members who, at the last minute had to cancel, our work led to a consensus that the theology of Luther – particularly his understanding of vocation – represents a vital resource for modern ethical reflection.

Initially *Roger Jensen* gave a short presentation of how the term »calling« has been interpreted differently in the history of Luther research. Jensen argued that older – i. e., pre-Holl – investigators emphasized Luther's supposed division between church and society into separate spheres. Therefore, argued Jensen, the work of early Luther researchers such as Christian Ernst Luthardt (1823-1902), Karl Eger (1864-1945), and Ernst Troeltsch (1865-1923) – as well as that of P. H. Schifferdeckers (* 1902), Wilhelm Stapel (1882-1954) and Arno Deutelmoser (1907-1983) – could not adequately account for either the proper relationship of faith to »calling«, or »calling« to faith.

Jensen maintained that Karl Holl's (1866-1926) work marked a new era in the history of Luther research on this issue. Holl's »Der Neubau der Sittlichkeit« – In: Ders.: Gesammelte Aufsätzer zur Kirchengeschichte. Bd. 1: Luther. TÜ 1921, 155-287 –, underlined that Christians are to form society according to faith – which is the particular task of the Christian –. For Holl, love is the crucial factor behind Christian action. The form of the act of love, however, differs according to the situation. Holl writes, »Beim wirklichen Christen werden ›Freiheit und Form‹ für ihn eins, so daß die Form nicht die Freiheit ertötet und die Freiheit nie zur Formlosigkeit ausartet.« In Holl's way of understanding Luther's ethics, the ratio – which is to give the act a concrete form – is »die christlich bestimmte Vernunft«, das »christliche Liebesgebot«.

In analyzing Holl's article »Die Geschichte des Worts Beruf. (1923)« – In: Karl Holl: Gesammelte Aufsätze zur Kirchengeschichte. Bd. 3: Der Westen. TÜ 1928, 189-219 – *Andreas Pawlas* argued that Luther's ethics are best understood in relation to his understanding of calling / vocatio / Beruf. In Holl's rediscovery of Luther's understanding of the calling, the calling becomes the place upon which personal ethics are founded. Pawlas in particular points to the famous place in the Kirchenpostille (1522) where Luther for the first time equals Beruf to Stand, Amt, Befehl. Pawlas underlined that, although this text is central to the understanding of Luther, it is hardly a »Neuschöpfung« of the Reformation. Further, Pawlas contended that Luther's understanding of the calling is not to be understood in a purely secular

way, i. e. that Luther's way of understanding the calling represented a secularization of the calling – cf. Martin Honecker –, as it is God that is the subject of the calling, is the Caller.

John Pless focused his attention on Gustav Wingren's (1910-2000) doctoral dissertation »Luther lära om kallelsen« (Lund 1942) / »Luthers Lehre vom Beruf« (M 1952) and found that he agreed with Pawlas on the question of secularization. Pless argued that – citing Wingren – »Luther does not use Beruf or vocatio in reference to the work of a non-Christian.« Still, Pless underlined, this does not imply a distinction between the Christian and the non-Christian as to how one serves one's neighbor. This does imply, however, a difference regarding knowing the source of the calling, because Christians know the Caller. Although recognizing the importance of Wingren's work, Pless criticized the Swede's tendency to separate, rather than distinguish between, the two realms in Luther's ethics.

In comparing Wingren and Holl, *Jensen* pointed to Holl's argument that »Vernunft« in Luther is to be understood as a »christlich bestimmte Vernunft«, and that morality in Luther is »einer streng auf das Religiöse gebauten Sittlichkeit«. Wingren, on the other hand, argued that there is neither Christian reason nor Christian ethics/morals. However, said Jensen, there is a central similarity between Holl and Wingren – that ethical practice in Holl is to be based on »Freiheit und Form« whereas in Wingren it is, similarly, to be based on »fasthet och bevegelighet«.

Furthermore, in analyzing Wingren's later work on vocation, the article »Beruf II: Historische und ethische Aspekte« in the »Theologische Realenzyklopädie. Bd. 5. B 1980,

657-671, Jensen showed the shift that took place in Wingren's later writings with regard to his understanding of the relevance of Luther today. In his TRE-article, Wingren showed an awareness of the historical distance between the time of the Reformation and the present, from a pre-industrial/pre-modern society to a industrialized/modern. Also, Wingren pointed to the significance of salvation with regard to the understanding of the body, a fact that he finds underdeveloped in Luther. Further, Wingren maintained that Luther too starkly divided the two realms. Although upholding his historical work on Luther and vocation, the later Wingren becomes more critical with regard to the relevance of Luther on vocation for the present.

William Russell argued that the later Wingren in his article from 1980 anticipated some of the critiques, which scholars have directed at the earlier Wingren – or at least his interpreters –. Russell pointed to the work of both Kenneth Hagen – with respect to the historical sources – and Miroslav Volf – with respect to current applicability–.

Naomichi Masaki, challenging both the traditional way of locating the vocational ethics of Luther in the first article and the present popular way of locating theological ethics in the third article, argued that the vocational ethics of Luther in the Large Confession (1528) are based on the second article. In the following discussion Masaki emphasized that he did not intend a Barthian ethics.

Jin-Seop Eom gave a description of Korean culture in relation to the Christian evangelization that has been going on in Korea for some time. *Jin-Seop* argued that a one-sided – pietistic – evangelical focus has led to a deficit with regard to the understanding of creation and the first article. This has led to a lack of »life« and »practice« among some Christians.

Recognizing that the term »vocatio/Beruf« has religious connotations in Luther – cf. Pawlas and Pless –, *Jensen* raised the question of what implication the vocational ethics of Luther, understood as based on the first article, could have for thinking about ethics today. If based on the first article, can the structure of thinking about ethics, be expressed in a way that is understandable outside of faith? The question can partially be answered by pointing to the Danish theologian Knud E. Løgstrup (1905-1981), said Jensen, and his phenomenological approach to ethical reflection, which was inspired by Luther. The later Wingren often pointed to Løgstrup as a model for thinking about ethics in the present – while maintaining that Løgstrup did not give sufficient attention to the centrality of the distinctively theological aspects of Luther's ethics –.

Jensen argued that there in Luther is an unused source in thinking about ethics today. In pointing to »Von den guten Werken« (1520), »Von der Freihet eines Christenmenschen« (1520) and Kirchenpostille (1522), Jensen argued that Luther represents a pragmatic approach to thinking about ethics based on a relational anthropology. Jensen gave special attention to the interpersonal aspect of vocational ethics, the significance of ethical knowledge, and the moral good.

The papers of our seminar are available at ⟨http://web.mac.com/roger2.jensen2/iWeb/Brasilseminar07/Welcome.html⟩

Christentum als Herrschertugend – Lutherische Ethik in Fürstenspiegeln der frühen Neuzeit

Seminarleiter: Armin Kohnle; Susan Richter
Berichterstatter: Armin Kohnle

Das Seminar fügte sich in den thematischen Rahmen des Kongresses insofern, als es die Frage eines nach lutherischer Auffassung verantwortbaren Verhaltens politischer Entscheidungsträger in den Mittelpunkt stellte, mithin also ein Thema der politischen Ethik des frühneuzeitlichen Luthertums behandelte.

Das Seminarthema betrat wissenschaftliches Neuland in mehrerlei Hinsicht. Die Befragung frühneuzeitlicher Fürstenspiegel auf eine konfessionsspezifische Fürstenethik hin bedeutete einen originellen Zugang zu einer Textgattung, deren Quellenwert bislang notorisch unterschätzt wird. Einige der behandelten Texte wurden in der historischen und kirchenhistorischen Forschung bislang kaum beachtet und für die Frage einer lutherischen Fürstenethik nie herangezogen. Den Seminarleitern ging es aber nicht primär darum, diese Texte und ihre Autoren bekannt zu machen, sondern im Mittelpunkt stand die Frage, ob und in welcher Weise sich Luthers Vorstellungen vom Amt des Fürsten und vom Charakter der christlichen Obrigkeit bei konfessionell lutherisch geprägten Autoren der folgenden Jahrhunderte niederschlugen. Das Augenmerk lag nicht ausschließlich auf dem 16. Jahrhundert, sondern Ziel war es, in einer Längsschnittbetrachtung die Entwicklungen von der Frühzeit der Reformation bis in das 18. Jahrhundert nachzuzeichnen. Auf die Einbeziehung humanistischer Texte, vor allem

Erasmus von Rotterdam (1466/69-1536), wurde aus Zeitgründen verzichtet, in den Diskussionen auf das Fortleben erasmianischer Vorstellungen aber immer wieder hingewiesen.

Da lediglich eine strenge Auswahl an Texten behandelt und diese wegen ihres gelegentlich beträchtlichen Umfangs nur in Auszügen gelesen werden konnten, musste das Seminar gründlich vorbereitet und die vorgesehenen Texte auf ihre Brauchbarkeit im Sinne der Fragestellung hin geprüft werden. Im Sommersemester 2007 diskutierten die Seminarleiter deshalb mit einer Gruppe von Studierenden im Rahmen einer Übung am Heidelberger Historischen Seminar eine Vorauswahl an Texten und sammelten auf diese Weise Erfahrungen, die in das Seminar in Canoas eingebracht werden konnten. Da für die Übung die überwiegend nicht leicht zu beschaffenden, weil nur in den Originaldrucken greifbaren Texte bereits vorliegen mussten, war die Zusammenstellung eines Textreaders im Verlauf des Sommersemesters im wesentlichen abgeschlossen. Wegen der Unsicherheit des Postwegs wurden sämtliche Texte digitalisiert und elektronisch an die Seminarteilnehmer verschickt. Kenntnis der zu behandelnden Texte konnte in Canoas also vorausgesetzt werden.

Wie es auf dem Internationalen Kongress für Lutherforschung üblich ist, fand das Seminar an vier Nachmittagen in Einheiten von jeweils dreieinhalb Zeitstunden statt. Die erste Arbeitssitzung diente der Einführung in die Problematik des Seminars. Lutherische Ethik wurde von *Armin Kohnle* im Einführungsvortrag nicht nur als Frage der privaten Lebensführung definiert, sondern im politischen Kontext – im Sinne einer Fürstenethik – auch als Regelwerk für die Leitung eines Gemeinwesens charakterisiert. Als zu erreichendes Ziel des Seminars wurde nicht in erster Linie die Beantwortung der Frage vorgegeben, wie die Fürsten der frühen Neuzeit tatsächlich waren, sondern wie sie gemäß lutherisch-konfessioneller Auffassung sein sollten. Als weitere Leitfragen für die kommenden Sitzungen wurden besonders die Problematik der Herrschaftsbegründung, der Herrschertugenden sowie der Herrscherpflichten ausgegeben; im Mittelpunkt sollten außerdem die Bedeutung der Fürstenerziehung, das Verhältnis der Fürsten zu den Regierten, zu Gott sowie die Rechte und Pflichten der Untertanen stehen. Ein weiteres Augenmerk sollte auf die Fürstenspiegel als Dokumente der Zeitkritik gelegt werden.

In einem zweiten Schritt der Einführung in das Thema stellte *Susan Richter* die frühneuzeitlichen Fürstenspiegel als Textgattung vor, wobei sie auf Vorarbeiten im Zuge ihrer Dissertation zurückgreifen konnte. Unterschiedliche Definitionen von Fürstenspiegeln wurden präsentiert und voneinander abgegrenzt. Als Arbeitsdefinition für das Seminar wurde unter Fürstenspiegeln eine lehrhafte Literaturform verstanden, in der aus der Perspektive eines Untertanen und gelegentlich durchaus interessegeleitet ein Panorama von Herrschertugenden entwickelt und dem Fürsten als Spiegel vorgehalten wurde. Nicht die Herrscherethik eines bestimmten Fürsten läßt sich in diesen Texten demzufolge auffinden, sondern in ihnen schlugen sich kollektive Wertvorstellungen nieder, in der konfessionelle Überzeugungen nicht der einzige, aber doch ein wichtiger Faktor waren. Ein Blick auf die Gesamtzahl der frühneuzeitlichen europäischen Fürstenspiegel – ca. 300 – und ihre Verfasser machte außerdem deutlich, dass Fürstenspiegel zu überwiegenden Teilen lutherischen oder reformierten Ursprungs waren und nur in wenigen Exemplaren auf römisch-katholische Verfasser zurückgingen.

Der zweite Seminarblock behandelte lutherische Fürstenspiegel des 16. Jahrhunderts beginnend mit Martin Luther selbst, dessen Obrigkeitslehre und politische Ethik von *Armin Kohnle* vorgestellt wurden. Luther äußerte sich mehrfach zur Frage des christlichen Fürsten, zwei Schriften aus seiner Feder weisen Charakterzüge eines Fürstenspiegels auf: die Obrigkeitsschrift von 1523 und die Auslegung des 101. Psalms von 1534/35. Die sogenannte Zweiregimentenlehre und ihre Folgen für Luthers Verständnis christlicher Herrschaft wurden rekapituliert, die Haltung von 1523 mit den modifizierten Positionen aus der Mitte der 1530er Jahre verglichen, um eine gesicherte Basis für die Frage einer lutherischen Fürstenethik zu gewinnen. Luthers ethische Anforderungen an einen christlichen Fürsten waren hoch. Er musste sich nicht nur an Gottesfurcht und Demut als den zentralen Fürstentugenden messen, sondern sich von Gottes Wort leiten lassen und Recht und Vernunft in der richtigen Weise gebrauchen. König David diente Luther als exemplarischer Fürst, das Bild des Hausvaters, der in Güte, Liebe und Gerechtigkeit, notfalls aber auch mit Strenge über die ihm Anvertrauten wacht, war eine von Luther selbst und von lutherischen Autoren gerne gebrauchte Umschreibung dieses Ideals. Nicht ausschließlich Luthers theologische Aussagen wie die Herleitung der Obrigkeit aus göttlicher Einsetzung oder die Zweiregimentenlehre wirkten in das frühneuzeitliche Luthertum hinein, sondern vor allem auch seine Methode, eine Fürstenethik unmittelbar aus der Bibel, vor allem aus dem Alten Testament, zu entwickeln. Die Bibel diente Luther und den lutherischen Autoren nicht als historischer Text, sondern als aktuelle Beispielsammlung.

Als erster Vertreter des Luthertums des 16. Jahrhunderts wurde Urbanus Rhegius (1489-1541) und sein »Enchiridion oder Handtbüchlein eines Christlichen Fürstens« herangezogen, in dem zwar viel ausführlicher als bei Luther selbst, aber in den theologischen Grundentscheidungen und in der Methodik der Bibelexegese analog zu diesem das Bild eines christlichen Fürsten entworfen wird. Nach Rhegius zählt es zu den Aufgaben des Fürsten, den Irrglauben abzustellen. War Luther in der Frage des Einsatzes der weltlichen Gewalt zur Durchsetzung der evangelischen Wahrheit noch sehr vorsichtig gewesen, dominierte bei Rhegius bereits das Interesse am inneren Ausbau lutherischer Landeskirchen mit der Folge, dass der Obrigkeit weitgehende kirchenordnende Funktionen und Kompetenzen zuerkannt wurden.

Bei einem weiteren lutherischen Autor des 16. Jahrhunderts, dem Juristen und Mansfelder Kanzler Georg von Lauterbeck (um 1510-1578), dessen Regentenbuch von 1556 ein wahrer Verkaufsschlager war, wurde diese Tendenz deutlich fortgesetzt. Auch er zählte die Förderung der wahren – das heißt evangelischen – Religion zu den Amtspflichten des Fürsten und die Ausrottung falscher Lehre zu seinen wesentlichen Aufgaben. Bei von Lauterbeck findet sich auch die für das Luthertum typische Argumentation, dass zwischen rechter Lehre und politischem Erfolg ein unmittelbarer Zusammenhang

bestehe, dass Abgötterei und falscher Gottesdienst zum Untergang von Reichen führen müssen. Deutliche Kritik äußerte von Lauterbeck an den Fürsten seiner Zeit, deren vermittelnden Standpunkt in religiösen Dingen er verurteilte und denen er allzu große Lust an der Kriegführung vorwarf. Zwar kannte von Lauterbeck ein ganzes Tableau von Kriegsgründen, doch nicht der kriegerische, sondern der friedliebende Fürst, wie Friedrich der Weise von Sachsen ihn verkörperte, war sein Ideal.

Die lutherische Fürstenethik um und nach 1600 – Seminarblock 3 – wurde mit einem Referat von *Louis Reith* über die Fürstenerziehung in Württemberg in der Zeit Herzog Christophs (1515, 1550-1568) eingeleitet, das den Erziehungsaspekt als einen Grundpfeiler der lutherischen Fürstenethik nachdrücklich in Erinnerung rief. In den württembergischen Kontext des konfessionellen Zeitalters gehört auch der Hofprediger Michael Schäfer (1573-1608), dessen 7. Predigt vom Amt der Obrigkeit Gegenstand der Seminarlektüre war. Deutlicher als bei anderen Autoren explizierte Schäfer das Idealbild des Fürsten als Hausvater mit umfassender Fürsorgpflicht für die ihm Anvertrauten, vor allem für die schwächsten unter ihnen, für Witwen und Waisen. Die Rechenschaftspflicht des Fürsten im Jüngsten Gericht war für alle lutherischen Autoren eine Selbstverständlichkeit, bei Schäfer allerdings findet sich eine bemerkenswerte alttestamentarische Vorstellung von göttlicher Gerechtigkeit, die ganz im Taliationsrecht aufgeht: Gott zahlt mit gleicher Münze heraus und straft nicht nur die fürstlichen Übertreter selbst, sondern auch ihre Frauen und Kinder. Dem Hausvaterideal auf fürstlicher Seite entsprach bei Schäfer das Ideal des Untertanen als eines frommen und gehorsamen Kindes. Ein Recht auf Fürsorge der christlichen Obrigkeit hat nur, wer sie ergeben und auf Gottes Hilfe vertrauend erwartet.

In Seminarblock 4 wurde die Linie in das 17. und 18. Jahrhundert ausgezogen. Als Textbeispiel eines Autors des 17. Jahrhunderts diente Caspar von Liliens (1632-1687) Schrift »Christ-Fürstliche Jesus-Nachfolge« von 1677, wo der selbst regierende, selbst richtende und selbst strafende Herrscher als Ideal gezeichnet und ähnlich wie bei Schäfer eine alttestamentliche Gerechtigkeitsvorstellung vorgetragen wird. Der gute Fürst ist der gerechte Fürst. Gerecht ist aber nur, wenn die Strafe dem Vergehen entspricht – Auge um Auge –. Ein Fürst, der nicht nach diesem Maßstab bestraft, wird selbst von Gott bestraft werden. Das 18. Jahrhundert war vertreten durch den Juristen Johann Daniel Aßmuth (ca. 1724-1776), einen Hofrat aus Waldeck-Pyrmont, dessen »Abhandlung von den Pflichten der Regenten« zwischen 1751 und 1753 erschien. Von den Texten der Reformationszeit und des konfessionellen Zeitalters unterscheidet sich Aßmuths Arbeit nicht nur durch eine rationalere und säkularisiertere Sprache, sondern auch durch eine Aufnahme aufklärerischer Kategorien wie dem Nützlichkeitsdenken bei gleichzeitiger Abwehr aufklärerischer Religionskritik. Aßmuth verteidigte die Pflicht des Fürsten, die Religion zu schützen, er verteidigte aber auch das landesherrliche Kirchenregiment, schrieb der Religion aber primär eine nützliche Rolle bei der Beförderung der irdischen Wohlfahrt zu. Auf der anderen Seite stemmte er sich gegen eine allzu tolerante Haltung gegenüber religiösen Abweichlern, indem er am Ideal des territorialen Monokonfessionalismus grundsätzlich festhielt und die Duldung anderer Konfessionen der Klugheit des Fürsten empfahl. Spötter und Atheisten mussten nicht geduldet werden, Juden schon, die zugleich aber bekehrt werden sollten.

Das Seminar kam insgesamt zu neuen Einsichten in die Vielgestaltigkeit und Wandelbarkeit der lutherischen Fürstenethik in der frühen Neuzeit. Es wurde deutlich, dass die notwendige Beschränkung auf wenige ausgewählte Autoren die vermutlich vorhandene Bandbreite an Vorstellungen und Argumentationen zwar erahnen, aber nicht wirklich ausmessen ließ. Das Thema enthält das Potential für ein größeres Projekt, das den gesamten vorhandenen Quellenbestand auswerten müsste. Auch eine andere Beschränkung des Seminars fiel ins Gewicht. Die konfessionell-lutherische Fürstenethik müsste in einem zweiten Schritt verglichen werden mit Texten aus dem reformierten und römisch-katholischen Bereich, um Gemeinsamkeiten und konfessionelle Spezifika besser erkennen zu können. Dass es eine konfessionell-lutherische Fürstenethik gegeben hat, ja dass die Abfassung von Fürstenspiegeln ein überwiegend lutherisches Phänomen war, hat das Seminar aber deutlich gezeigt. Warum dies so war, bedürfte der weiteren Diskussion. Im Blick auf die Gegenwart, in der »good governance« und ethisch verantwortbares Verhalten von Politikern angesichts einer verbreiteten Korruptionspraxis in vielen Ländern der Welt intensiv diskutiert werden, eröffnete die Thematik viele Möglichkeiten der Aktualisierung und Adaptierung auf die Situation eines in der abendländisch-christlichen Tradition stehenden Schwellenlandes wie Brasilien. Diese aktuellen Bezüge gaben dem Seminar eine besondere Note.

Außer den Genannten nahmen James S. Estes, Valter Kuchenbecker, Tine Reeh und Ricardo Willy Rieth an dem Seminatr teil.

Armen- und Krankenfürsorge in den Ordnungen der Reformation

Seminarleiter: Kaarlo Arffman
Berichterstatter: Kaarlo Arffman

In dem Seminar wurden Texte Martin Luthers und lutherische Ordnungen unter dem Aspekt der Kranken- und Armenfürsorge – der Diakonie – betrachtet. Im Seminar gab es sechs Teilnehmer. *Theodor Strohm*, der die Leitung des Seminars übernehmen sollte, musste seine Teilnahme leider absagen. Doch hatte er den Teilnehmern Artikel und Quellentexte zugesandt, die in dem von ihm zusammen mit *Michael Klein* herausgegebenen Sammelband »Die Entstehung einer sozialen Ordnung Europas: historische Studien und exemplarische Beiträge zur Sozialreform im 16. Jahrhundert« (2 Bde. HD 2004) enthalten sind. Dies erleichterte die Vorbereitung und die Arbeit des Seminars, gab gleichzeitig auch seinen Teilnehmern ein Gesamtbild der neuesten Forschung zum Themenkreis. Zwei Vorträge waren für das Seminar geschrieben worden.

Zuerst wurden »Vierzehn Thesen über die Beziehung der Rechtfertigung und Armenfürsorge in der lutherischen Reformation« von *Kaarlo Arffman* vorgetragen und erläutert. Darin wurde gezeigt, dass die Rechtfertigung und die Armenfürsorge in der bisherigen Forschung zu wenig als eine Einheit betrachtet wurden. Die lutherische Lehre von der Rechtfertigung wurde bisher beinahe nur von Vertretern der systematischen Theologie analysiert. Dagegen haben sich für die Armenfürsorge der lutherischen Reformation zunächst Kirchengeschichtler, Soziologen mit geschichtlichem Interesse und Forscher der Geschichte der Diakonie interessiert. In Finnland jedoch brachten die Systematiker die Forschung beider Themenkreise in einen Zusammenhang.

Nach Arffman hatte Luther um 1520 festgestellt, dass es genügend sei, wenn die Menschen an Christus glauben würden. Die »guten Werke«, die Nächstenhilfe würden ohne Weiteres dem Glauben folgen. Die Lutheraner ordneten ihre neuartige Armenfürsorge nach diesem Grundsatz. Sie wurde im Rahmen der Kassen der Kirchengemeinden organisiert. Das Luthertum hat die Armenfürsorge nach dem Vorbild der in der Apostelgeschichte geschilderten Jerusalemer Urgemeinde als Aufgabe der Kirchgemeinden gesehen. Anfangs sah es so aus, als ob die neue Armenfürsorge sich gut bewähren würde, was zugleich die Verbreitung des Luthertums förderte. Jedoch schon bald nach dem Bauernkrieg nahm die Lust zum Helfen ab. Die guten Werke folgten dem rechten Glauben nicht von selbst, automatisch. Die Reformatoren – einschließlich Luther und ihre Nachfolger – waren enttäuscht, und manche begannen zu überlegen, wie es möglich wäre, die Ermahnung zum Helfen und die Bezugnahme auf den menschlichen Willen mit der Lehre von der Rechtfertigung allein aus der Gnade zu verbinden, was auch zu den lang andauernden innerlutherischen Streitigkeiten über die Rechtfertigung beigetragen hat. Auch diese Streitigkeiten haben bald nach dem Baurnkrieg begonnen.

Im Gespräch wurde besonders die vorgetragene These, dass die lutherischen Reformatoren die Armenfürsorge als eine Aufgabe der christlichen Gemeinde gesehen hätten, kritisiert. Manche Teilnehmer erklärten, dass die Reformatoren nicht von der Kirche und Gesellschaft, sondern von geistlichem und weltlichem Regiment ausgingen. Weil alle Menschen, um die es ging – die wenigen Juden ausgenommen –, Christen waren, schien eine Grenzziehung gerade im Hinblick auf Fürsorge zwischen den Regimenten unwichtig. Darüber sollte man verhandeln und den Konsens erreichen. Geistliche und weltliche Obrigkeit müssen zusammenwirken, jede auf ihrem Gebiet – die geistliche Obrigkeit für Predigt und Sakramente, die weltliche für die Sicherheit der Menschen und für das täglich Nötige zum Leben. Deshalb sei die Kranken- und Armenfürsorge nach den lutherischen Reformatoren auch eine Aufgabe der weltlichen Obrigkeit. Die Stadt- und Kirchenordnungen der Reformationszeit enthielten sowohl dem geistlichen als auch dem weltlichen Regiment zuzurechnende Aufgaben.

Weiter wurde auch die Spontaneität der vom Glauben hervorgebrachten guten Werke erörtert. Was meinte Luther, als er um 1520 schrieb, dass die guten Werke dem Glauben automatisch, »von sich selbst« folgen würden? Wie sind solche Äußerungen mit Luthers Betonung des »simul iustus et peccator« zu verbinden?

Auch *Ulrich Bubenheimer* – ein angekündigter Teilnehmer des Seminars – konnte an dem Kongress nicht teilnehmen. Doch hatte er seinen Vortrag »Die Wittenberger Stadtordnung vom Januar 1522 und Karlstadts Beitrag zu einer Sozialreform« gesandt. Darin analysiert Bubenheimer kurz die Entstehung und Überlieferung der Stadtordnung, die in der Stadtordnung enthaltene Gottesdienst- und Sozialreform sowie die theologischen und sozialethischen Motive Karlstadts.

Zu Beginn der Erörterung wurde festgehalten, dass Bubenheimer, der die Wittenberger Bewegung im Winter 1521/22 schon früher behandelt hatte, in seinem Vortrag die von Arffman gestellte Frage nach der Grenzziehung zwischen dem geistlichen und weltlichen Regiment wieder aufgriff. Kann man sagen, dass das für Wittenberg geplante Hilfesystem mit einem gemeinen Kasten, mit dem die ganze Wirtschaft der Kirchgemeinde geführt werden sollte, ein »städtisches/weltliches« Fürsorgewesen gewesen sei? Die meisten Teilnehmer antworteten auf diese Frage bejahend. Sie gehört eng zu der Frage nach der Art der Zahlung, welche die Wittenberger nach dem jeweiligen Bedarf dem gemeinen Kasten leisten sollten: War diese Zahlung eine Armensteuer oder eine vom Glauben hervorgebrachte freiwillige Gabe? Darüber hinaus kreiste die Diskussion der Seminarteilnehmer um die Frage nach angemessenem Zinssatz und die Rolle der Kleriker als Kreditgeber.

Nach der Behandlung der Vorträge wurden einige zentrale Kranken- und Armenfürsorge betreffende Texte analysiert. Die »Beutelordnung« (1521/22) und die »Kastenordnung« (1522) der Stadt Wittenberg waren mit dem Vortrag Bubenheimers verbunden. In der Analyse wurde die verschiedene Behandlung der Zünfte und der Bruderschaften in der Kastenordnung problematisiert. Die Zünfte konnten nicht abgeschafft werden, weil nur ihre Mitglieder das Recht auf die Handwerke hatten. Darum sollten sie nur ihre Zinsen in den gemeinen Kasten bezahlen. Dagegen sollten das Vermögen und die Einnahmen der Bruderschaften ihm ganz einverleibt werden. Auch die Art des Diakonenamtes und die Entlohnung des Pfarrers und der Diakone wurden thematisiert, da die Texte auf diese Fragen keine Antwort geben.

Anschließend wurden zwei Texte Luthers – »Ein Sermon von dem hochwürdigen Sakrament des heiligen wahren Leichnams Christi und von den Bruderschaften« (1519) und »An den christlichen Adel deutscher Nation von des christlichen Standes Besserung« (1520) – näher betrachtet. Im Gespräch wurde festgestellt, dass die Bruderschaften für Luther Beispiele solcher Gemeinschaften gewesen sind, die nur ihren eigenen Nutzen gesucht haben und die sich nun auf den gemeinsamen Nutzen richten sollten. Auch wenn festgehalten werden musste, dass die Bruderschaften auch anderswo als in Wittenberg Unzufriedenheit weckten, sind doch Luthers Texte keine objektive Schilderungen, sondern vor allem ein Blick auf die negative Seiten der Bruderschaften, gerade im Hinblick auf das reformatorische Geschehen und Wollen.

Schließlich wurde noch ein »Der ehrbaren Stadt Hamburg Christliche Ordnung« (1529) zur Diskussionsgrundlage gemacht. Dabei wurde deutlich, dass hier die Finanzierung der geplanten Kassen eine Rolle spielt. Für Hamburg hatte man zweierlei Kassen geplant, die ersten für die Armenfürsorge, die zweiten für sonstige kirchliche Tätigkeit. Auch die kirchliche Wirtschaft hat sich nun nicht mehr ganz auf freiwillige Gaben aufgebaut, sondern die Einwohner sollten dafür eine Steuer zahlen.

Zusammenfassend kann man sagen, dass die Teilnehmer im Wesentlichen ihre Ansichten zu den diskutierten Fragen teilten. In einigen Stellen wurden aber auch unterschiedliche Meinungen sichtbar. Als besonders befruchtend wurde die Teilnahme von Frau *Ruthild Brakemeier*, einer in Brasilien tätigen Diakonisse, empfunden, die gerade die Diakonie als ein eminent auch theologisch-geistliches Anliegen immer wieder anmahnte und in der Diskussion deutlich machen konnte, dass die Praxis des sozialen Engagements und der Armenfürsorge nicht zu trennen ist vom Evangelium.

Insgesamt zeigte sich, dass die Armen- und die Krankenfürsorge der lutherischen Reformation noch einer Forschung bedürfen, gerade, wenn es um die Verbindung der theologischen Ideen mit ihrer praktischen Umsetzung geht.

Außer den Genannten nahmen noch Albert Collver, Markus Hein, Jeffrey Jaynes und Antti Raunio am Seminar teil.

Luthers Wochenpredigten über Matthäus 5-7[*]

Seminarleiter: Silfredo Bernardo Dalferth
Berichterstatter: Silfredo Bernardo Dalferth

I Einführung

Die Teilnehmer hatten sich mit verschiedenen Fragestellungen vorbereitet, die im Wesentlichen im Seminar bearbeitet wurden. Alle Teilnehmer haben dazu beigetragen, dass es ein interessantes Seminar geworden ist. Viele Informationen wurden in kurzen Vorträgen eingebracht. Dazu hat *Igor Kiss* die Interpretation der Bergpredigt auf dem Hintergrund des Mittelalters dargestellt.[1]

II Einleitung: Predigt und Theologie in der Reformation

Besonders wichtig sind die Einzigartigkeit und der Ursprung der reformatorischen Theologie. Die Originalität in der Bewegung der Reformation besteht in der »Theologie des Wortes« – der Interpretation des biblischen Textes – in einem unauflöslichen Zusammenhang mit der Verkündigung des Wortes, der Predigt. Für Luther ist Theologie Auslegung der Heiligen Schrift für das Leben der

Kirche.[2] Es ist interessant zu beobachten, dass ungefähr ein Drittel der in der Weimarer Ausgabe edierten Texte Predigten sind.

III Analysis des Textes vorgetragen von Scott H. Hendrix

Nach Paul Pietsch (1849-1927) hat Georg Rörer (1492-1557) die Nachschrift von den Predigten Luthers über die Bergpredigt als Grundlage für den Herausgeber und Redakteur geliefert.[3] Obwohl es kein Konsens über die Identität des Herausgebers und Redaktors der ersten Veröffentlichung gibt, denkt Pietsch eher an Caspar Cruciger (1504-1548) oder auch an Veit Dietrich (1506-1549), denn »in der Sprache erinnert manches an ihn«.[4] Es ist bekannt, dass Luther die kompetente Art Crucigers für den Text seiner Predigten zur Veröffentlichung sehr schätzte.[5]

Der in WA 32 aufgenommene Text erlebte schon in den ersten Jahren drei Veröffentlichungen: 1532 bei Joseph Klug († 1552) in Wit-

[*] Martin LUTHER: Das fünfte, sechste und siebente Kapitel Matthaei gepredigt und ausgelegt, 1532; WA 32, 299-544.

[1] Siehe dazu insbesondere Karin BORNKAMM: Umstrittener »spiegel eines Christlichen lebens« – Luthers Auslegung der Bergpredigt in seinen Wochenpredigten von 1530 bis 1532. ZThK 85 (1988), 409-454.

[2] Cf. Ulrich ASENDORF: Martin Luther als Prediger: Anmerkungen zur Bedeutung seiner Predigten im Rahmen seiner gesamten Theologie. In: Kirche in der Schule Martin Luthers = Festschrift für D. Joachim Heubach/ hrsg. von Bengt Hägglund; Gerhard Müller. Erlangen 1995, 11-22, bes. 14.

[3] WA 32, lxxvi.

[4] WA 32, lxxvi.

[5] WATR 3, 42, 27-32 (2869b) 1532; WA 22, xvi.

tenberg, 1533 bei Franciscus Rhodus († 1559) in Marburg und 1538 bei Johannis Weiss († 1544?) in Wittenberg.[6] Für den Text in WA 32 wurden fünf Exemplare – die sich infolge von Korrekturen voneinander unterscheiden – des Druckes von 1532 (A) und die auf ihm basierenden letzten Veröffentlichungen (B & C) untersucht und verglichen.

Während der Bearbeitung des Textes für die Veröffentlichung verlor der Text seine originale Predigtnatur.[7] So sind z. B. alle Einführungen in die einzelnen Predigten, die es bei Rörer gegeben haben muss, entfallen. Glücklicherweise sind zwei von diesen Nachschriften erhalten geblieben, die Luthers Sonntagspredigten über Mt 7,15 und 7,16-20 am 30. Juli 1531 enthalten.[8] Der einfache Vergleich der Nachschriften mit dem Text von WA 32 bietet ein Beispiel für die Unterschiede der Texte und auch der ausgelassenen Einführungen.[9]

Beachtenswert ist die Information, dass Johannes Bugenhagen (1485-1558) von Ende Oktober 1530 bis Ende April 1532 von Wittenberg 77 Wochen abwesend war. Während dieser Zeit hat er in Lübeck geholfen, die Reformation einzuführen. In dieser Zeit hat Luther 45 Mal über das Evangelium nach Johannes am Sonntag gepredigt und wahrscheinlich dieselbe Anzahl Predigten über die Bergpredigt am Mittwoch gehalten. Die längste Zeit, in der Luther nicht innerhalb der Woche predigte, war zwischen 9. Dezember 1531 und 10. Februar 1532. Zu dieser Zeit

litt er unter Heiserkeit und war außerdem überarbeitet.[10] Er hatte bereits am 24. November 1531 Bugenhagen gebeten, nach Wittenberg zurückzukehren.

Da das Schlusswort – »Beschluß« – vom gesamten Text eigentlich ein wenig aus der Art schlägt, entsteht der Verdacht, dass er als »Nachgedanken« angefügt, vielleicht sogar vom Herausgeber verfasst worden ist. Es scheint so, dass der Herausgeber aus Sorge die Absicht hatte, die Laien – die Leser – vor Missverständnissen zu bewahren. Diese Unsicherheiten bezüglich einer Bearbeitung eines Textes für die Veröffentlichung sind nicht nur bei dieser Predigtreihe zu finden. In diesem Zusammenhang ist die Frage zu stellen was Luther tatsächlich selbst predigte und lehrte. Es ist ein Anzeichen dafür, dass die Theologie Luthers eigentlich vor allem auch ein Prozess unter Mitwirkung vieler Menschen ist – ein Teamprojekt –, sodass es besser ist, sie »Wittenberger Theologie« zu nennen und auf diesem Wege den Kollegen Luthers die verdiente Anerkennung zu geben.

IV Diskussion über die Bergpredigt nach Matthäus

Danach haben wir uns mit dem biblischen Text der Bergpredigt befasst. Matthäus bemüht sich um eine Einheit von Zuspruch des Trostes und Anspruch des Gesetzes. Dabei geht es nicht nur um ein »Ihr sollt«, sondern auch um eine »indikative Identität«, nämlich um das »Ihr seid«, denn im Unterschied zur Welt sind die Christen Licht und Salz. Sie leben in der Situation der Ver-

6 Josef BENZING: Lutherbibliographie. Baden-Baden 1966, 352 f. 6 (3011-3014. 20).

7 Vgl. den Revisionsnachtrag WA 32 RN, 14 zu LXXVI.

8 WA 34 II 594 f (70 f); 31-42. 43-53.

9 Vgl. den Revisionsnachtrag WA 32 RN, 14 zu LXXVI.

10 Martin BRECHT: Martin Luther. Bd. 2: Ordnung und Abgrenzung der Reformation; 1521-1532. S 1986, 416.

folgung. Die Radikalität des Gesetzes am Beispiel der Feindesliebe ist nicht Moralität, sondern die äußerste Betonung von der Einheit von Gnade und Tun. Im Duktus des »Ihr seid« wird nicht die Gesetzesfrage »wer kann das schon?« hervorgehoben, sondern eine Situation des Leidens und eine authentische christliche Existenz.

V Die Bergpredigt als Ausgangspunkt der Theologie Luthers vorgetragen von Silfredo B. Dalferth[11]

Die Bergpredigt bei Luther ist in dem Sinne nicht nur eine Sammlung von Predigten, sondern bildet eine Grundkoordinate der Theologie des Reformators überhaupt. Für Luther gilt die Bergpredigt Jesu uneingeschränkt für die gesamte Christenheit und ihre Schärfe kann nicht in der Unterscheidung von christlichen Ständen minimiert werden. Die Zweireiche- und Zweiregimentenlehre ist daher eine Konsequenz dieser wortwörtlichen Interpretation der Bergpredigt. Die Zweireiche- und Zweiregimentenlehre ist die Vornahme einer gesellschaftlich-relationalen Differenzierung: Da nicht alle freiwillig dem Evangelium folgen und die Menschen im eigenen Interesse handeln, gibt es das Gesetz in seinem usus theologicus und seinem usus civilis, damit die Gesellschaft von den Konsequenzen des Bösen geschützt werden kann. Das ist das theologische Argument für die Notwendigkeit des Rechts im Interesse der Allgemeinheit.

11 Siehe dazu Silfredo B. DALFERTH: Prédicas semanais sobre Mateus 5-7: introdução. In: Martinho Lutero: Obras selecionadas. Bd. 9: Interpretação do Nuovo Testamento/ hrsg. von Darci Drehmer ... São Leopoldo 2005, 17-21.

In diesem Grundgedanken geht es um eine Alternative gegen den kirchlichen »Dualismus« der Römisch-Katholischen Kirche und gegen den Monismus der Schwärmer, wo das Evangelium als gesellschaftliches Gesetz gehandhabt wird, resultierend in eine eigenartige gesellschaftliche Dynamik, die der Bergpredigt widerspricht. Daher ist nach reformatorischer Theologie die Grundfrage eines Christenmenschen, ob ethisches Handeln in Relation zu einer öffentlich-rechtlichen Angelegenheit steht. Diesbezüglich bedeutet die biblische Unterscheidung zwischen dem »inneren« und dem »äußeren« Menschen eine anthropologische Kontinuität in einem relational differenzierten Ethos, ohne Dualismus.[12] In dieser Interpretation ist die Bergpredigt in ihrer Wortwörtlichkeit eine bleibende Provokation.

Die Theologie Luthers ist eine Theologie der Herrschaft Gottes auf verschiedene Weisen: durch die Predigt des Wortes – Gesetz und Evangelium – und Politik – Obrigkeit und Recht – sowie als deus absconditus regiert er mit dem, was menschlicher Verstand nicht erkennen kann, auch durch das Böse.

Exkurs: In diesem Rahmen wurde von *Pierre Bühler* auf die Theologie Karl Barths (1886-1968) hingewiesen: Barth denkt in Analogien. Die Welt ist zwar kein Gleichnis für das Himmelreich, aber dennoch gibt es im Denken Barths in den Differenzen weiterhin analogische Strukturen im Handeln Gottes und dem Handeln des Menschen. Im eschatologischen Handeln Gottes – die Referenz der Analogie – ist Analogie zwischen der Gerechtigkeit der Bürgergemeinde und der Christengemeinde möglich.[13]

12 Siehe dazu Brecht: Martin Luther 2, 354.
13 Siehe dazu Eberhard JÜNGEL: Barth-Studien. GÜ 1982, 323.

VI Zum Inhalt der Predigten Luthers

1 Gnade und Verdienst

Nach Luther redet Christus selbst nirgendwo davon, dass es so etwas wie ein Prozess zum Glauben gibt. Der Glaube ist kein Ankunftspunkt, sondern ein Ausgangspunkt. Es gibt keine Belohnung für Menschen, die Christen sein »werden« in einem Prozess, sondern für die Glaubenden ein Trost für das Leiden: »Was sagstu aber dazu, das soviel sprüche sind von dem lohn und verdienst? Dazu sagen wir jtzt also fur die einfeltigen, Das es eitel trostung sind fur die Christen.«[14]

Die ganze Logik der Belohnung entfällt. Luther hat diesen Zusammenhang in einer Predigtreihe vom Jahre 1522 mit dem Wort »volge« an Stelle von »belonung« beschrieben. Der Trost ist »ein lockung und reytzung«, dass er den Glaubenden »lustig mach zur frumkait, got zu dienen und loben«, nicht als Belohnung, sondern »gleich wie der geschmack dem wein volgen muß«.[15]

Im Schlusswort der Wochenpredigten bleibt im Grunde dieser Gedanke, aber die Terminologie ist eine andere: anstatt »Folge« ist das Schlüsselwort »vergeltung des leidens«.[16] Der Sinn ist auch hier der Logik der Belohnung der Werkgerechtigkeit zu entkommen. Auch der Begriff »Vergeltung« wird von dem Trost Gottes her gedeutet, im Zusammenhang mit der Gnade als Geschenk.[17] Aus dieser Basis beruht die Gleichheit von allen Glaubenden in der Gemeinde, dass es keinen Unterschied mehr gibt und wahre Gemeinde möglich wird.[18]

2 Bergpredigt und Dekalog

Bei Luther gibt es zwar ein Wachsen an Klarheit vom Dekalog des Sinai zur Bergpredigt, aber er lässt auch diese Relation als Ganzheit stehen, sodass es letztlich eine theologische Kontinuität zwischen Dekalog und Bergpredigt gibt, wo sich »die zehen gebot in die acht seligkait schliessen« lassen.[19] In diesem Duktus bezieht er die erste Seligpreisung der Bergpredigt und das erste Gebot des Dekalogs aufeinander[20] und dadurch interpretiert Luther die Bedeutung von »geistlich arm« von dem Glauben her.[21]

Die Begriffe »geistlich arm« und »arm« werden komplementär interpretiert. Der Reformator bringt das »Weh« gegen die Reichen von L 6 gegen eine Theologie des Segens ein, nämlich, gegen die Einstellung, wenn es »einem menschen wol gienge hie auff erden, der were selig und wol dran«, und aus dieser Einstellung, dass wenn Menschen »frumm« wären und »Gott dieneten, das jn Gott gnug solt geben auff erden und nichts gebrechen lassen«.[22]

Luther bemüht sich, jede Grundlage für eine Legitimation von Armut und Reichtum zu entziehen.[23] Das Reichtum und das Wohlergehen sind keinerlei »zeichen« für Gottes Gnade oder Verdammung. Denn gerade dagegen wurde »das buch Hiob gemacht«, gegen die Meinung »er müsse etwas grosses widder Gott verschuldet haben, und auff jn wissen, das er so gestrafft werde«.[24] Diese Logik, in der äußerliches Wohlergehen mit Gottes Gnade verbunden wird, geht es nicht

---

14 WA 32, 540, 21-23.
15 WA 10 III, 401, 14-26.
16 WA 32, 543, 1-9.
17 WA 32, 543, 19 f.
18 Siehe dazu WA 32, 536, 24-27.

19 Siehe dazu WA 10 III, 401, 33 - 402, 7.
20 WA 10 III, 402, 8-18.
21 WA 32, 318, 30-35.
22 Siehe WA 32, 305, 33 - 306, 2.
23 Siehe WA 32, 306, 7-12.
24 Siehe dazu WA 32, 306, 12-21.

um den rechten Glauben, sondern um »den rechten abgott Mammon«. Die Konsequenz ist der materielle Ansporn: »Jst der selig, dem es wolgehet und guts gnug hat, so mus ich zusehen, das ich auch nicht am wenigsten habe.«[25]

Luther sieht in dieser Verbindung von äußerlichem Wohlergehen und Gottes Gnade eine Art »religio«. Er nennt diese Form der Wahrnehmung ein »aller wellt glaube« oder »religio auff erden«. Da geht es gar nicht mehr um eine spezifische Religion, sondern um eine Art geistliche Anthropologie, also die Religion der Menschen, »darauff alle menschen nach fleisch und blut bleiben« und »konnen auch kein anders fur seligkeit achten«.[26]

Luther entzieht der Theologie jeder Form von sozialgeschichtlicher Begründung, so ungewöhnlich dies auch klingen mag. Die Armut gilt nicht als Leistung für den Erwerb

des Himmelreichs. Sonst kämen die Reichen und die Armen ins Geschäft, wo die ersten das Himmelreich den Armen abkaufen könnten: »Es heisst [...] selbs arm sein [...].«[27] Zugleich entzieht »das wortlin ›Geistlich arm‹« die Legitimation der Armut.[28] Es wäre sinnvoll an dieser Stelle ein Vergleich mit Max Webers (1864-1920) Wahrnehmung des Protestantismus vorzunehmen.

Zu vermerken ist, dass bei Luther die Begriffe in einer gewissen dialektischen Relation treten, sodass der eine Begriff vor einer falschen Deutung des anderen Begriffes schützt. Diese feststellbare dialektische Relation zwischen biblischen Begriffen wie »geistlich arm« und »arm«, wo in dieser Relation die Legitimationsgrundlage gerade eines sozialgeschichtlichen Missbrauchs verhindert wird.

Außer den Genannten nahmen Annika Laats und Albrecht Heim am Seminar teil.

25 Siehe dazu WA 32, 306, 22-29.
26 Siehe dazu WA 32, 306, 30-38.

27 Siehe dazu WA 32, 307, 8-10.
28 Siehe dazu WA 32, 307, 11-15.

Kreuz und Metapher – Luthers Auslegung von Psalm 22

Seminarleiter: Jens Wolff
Berichterstatter: Jens Wolff

Das kleinste unter den Seminaren des Lutherkongresses beschäftigte sich mit der Sprachgstalt von Luthers Christusverkündigung. Die »Operationes in psalmos«, kürzlich als frische Quelle reformatorischer Christologie wiederentdeckt, dienten als Orientierungspunkt gemeinsamer Seminararbeit. Ne-

ben Ps 22, der im Fokus der Aufmerksamkeit stand, kamen weitere Referenztexte hinzu, darunter »De servo arbitrio« und die Schrift gegen den Löwener Theologen Latomus. Die gemeinsame Interpretationsarbeit zeigte, dass sich die Aufmerksamkeit innerhalb der jüngeren Forschung dergestalt verschiebt, dass

dass nun nicht mehr die eine idealisierte Quelle der Heidelberger Disputation zum Ausgangspunkt einer Rekonstruktion von Luthers Kreuzestheologie gewählt wurd, wie dies z. B. in dem lange bestimmenden Werk von Walther von Loewenich (1903-1992) der Fall war. Luther ist Kreuzestheologe vielfach auch da, wo er nicht den Ausdruck »theologia crucis« benutzt. Deshalb ist es nicht sinnvoll, sich sehr literal am Begriff »theologia crucis« zu orientieren. Vielmehr ist es weiterführend, Symbolisches und Imaginäres einzubeziehen und den Gekreuzigten auf diese hermeneutisch neue Weise zu thematisieren. Wegweisend für den ein enges begriffszentriertes Konzept verlassenden Ansatz ist Luthers »Antilatomus«, der in zeitlicher und sachlicher Nähe zu der Auslegung von Ps 22 in den »Operationes in psalmos« entstand.

Joar Haga eröffnete das Seminar mit einem systematischen Referat über »Humanity and divinity in Luther`s interpretation of Psalm 22«: Luther betont ähnlich wie Kyrillos von Alexandrien († 444) stärker die Einheit der Naturen und weist die nestorianische Trennungschristologie zurück. Von den altkirchlichen Autoren unterscheidet er sich durch stärkere Betonung der Soteriologie. Christi Erfahrung der Verlassenheit am Kreuz besteht in einem heftigen Affekt. Er besetzt Christi Gewissen und führt zur Verzweiflung. Das Denken von Gottes Gegenwart am Kreuz bleibt aber trotz dieses Affekts möglich: Gott selbst wird in der Auslegung von Ps 22 als Allergegenwärtigster dargestellt. Hier finden sich Spuren der Ubiquitätslehre. Gleichwohl ist Christus verlassen. Er verinnerlicht diesen Schmerz. Er leidet. Sein Herz zerschmilzt wie Wachs – vgl. Ps 22,15f –. Diese konkrete Erfahrung, die metaphorisch kodiert ist, sprengt den Rahmen einer metaphysisch-philosophischen Vermögenspsychologie und vereint Gottverlassenheit mit Gottes Gegenwart.

Der kirchenhistorische Beitrag von *Anna Vind* »Christus factus est peccatum metaphorice«, in dem sie sich mit der theologischen Verwendung rhetorischer Figuren im »Antilatomus« (1521) unter Einbeziehung des Quintilianus (um 30-96) befasste, bot den metapherntheoretischen Rahmen für das Seminarthema. Luther zieht im »Antilatomus« in einer figuralen Bibelauslegung 2 K 5,21 zur Begründung der Remetaphorisierung des Christusereignisses heran. Der modus loquendi scripturae wird mit sprachwissenschaftlichen Mitteln als metaphorisch ausgewiesen. Vind zeigt durch sorgfältige Interpretation einschlägiger Quellen, dass es nicht eine Entdeckung von Metapherntheoretikern des 20. Jahrhunderts ist, metaphorische als eigentliche Rede zu verstehen. Diese These vertritt bereits Luthers Lieblingsrhetor Quintilianus. Sehr plausibel führte Vind aus, dass die Rede von »Metapher« für Luthers umfassendes Sprachschaffen zu eng ist. Vielmehr vollzieht sich die Erneuerung theologischer Rede von Christus in einem umfassenden medialen Sprachprozess – Stefan Streiff –, der mit der neuen Sprache von Metaphern Gemeinsamkeiten aufweist. Vind führte diese These auch im Hinblick auf Luthers Abendmahlsschrift von 1528 durch.

Marius Mjaaland näherte sich dem Thema aus systematischer Perspektive zwischen Dekonstruktion und Hermeneutik unter dem Titel »Duplex obscuritas: writing and difference in De servo arbitrio (1525) illuminated by some obscure passages from Luther`s Commentary on Ps 22 (1521)«. Mit seinem Titel griff er einen meist überlesenen Doppelbegriff aus der Schrift vom unfreien Willen auf. Er fällt in jener berühmten Passage, die zwischen claritas externa und claritas interna unterscheidet. Die Betonung der »Externität« sei jedoch antihermeneutisch im Vergleich mit neuerer Hermeneutik, da der Wittenberger die verstehende Subjektivität reduziere. Luthers Schrifttheorie, die sich in eine generelle Theorie der Textinterpretation für jegliche Art von Schrift(en) transformieren lasse, respektiere deutlicher als Erasmus (1466/69-1536) die Andersheit von Texten – vgl. Jacques Derrida (1930-2004) –. Gleichwohl müsse Luthers Theorie der inneren Klarheit ausgeweitet werden, wozu sich die Illuminationslehre anbiete, da sie die Differenz zwischen Leser und Text offenhalte. Dieses an Søren Kierkegaard (1813-1855) angelehnte Leser-Text-Modell betont den Vorrang der Schrift. Luther unterscheide beim Verstehen der Schrift topisch zwischen Dunkelheit und Licht. Für diese Hell-Dunkel-Topik lässt sich die Operatio zu Ps 22 anführen. Mjaaland betont, dass Luthers claritas externa den Verzicht auf metaphorische oder tropologische Interpretation bedeute, da es nur auf die schlichte grammatikalische Bedeutung der Texte ankomme.

»Das Skandalon des Kreuzes in Luthers Auslegung von Ps 22,7-11 im Verhältnis zur mittelalterlichen Tradition« war *Jens Wolffs* kirchenhistorisches Thema. Er ist der Ansicht, dass christologische Niedrigkeitsausssagen bereits zu Ps 22 metaphorisch verdichtet erscheinen, d. h. zeitlich vor dem »Antilatomus«: »Ich bin ein Wurm und kein Mensch« – Ps 22,7 –. Hieronymus (347/348-420), Augustinus (354-430) und Cassiodorus (um 485 - nach 580) sowie mittelalterliche Exegeten – vgl. die »Glossa ordinaria« – vertreten hier abschwächende Deutungen. Nach Luthers Auslegung bezieht sich »Wurm« auf eine verachtete Person, die sich im Dreck suhlt. Die Passion stinkt wie Fäulnis. Die

in diesem Metaphorisierungsprozess dargestellte Passion meint wegen ihrer Zugehörigkeit zu Christus alle Christen. Luthers Ethik ist aus der Perspektive der Kreuzestheologie Nachfolge im Leiden. Christi Passion zielt jedoch auf ein befreiendes Wort ab. Wie das Wort vom Leiden, so ist die fröhliche Botschaft des Evangeliums metaphorisch kodiert: Christus, der das Wasser der Taufe heiligt, heiligt alle starken Flüsse, d. h. die Leiden der Christen. Christenmenschen tragen Christi Kreuz im Herzen. Christi Passion ist singulär, nicht seine Würde wie bei Cassiodorus. Ps 22,10 f »Du hast mich aus dem Mutterleibe gezogen« redet nicht von der Jungfrauengeburt, sondern ist affektzündende Geborgenheitsmetaphorik. Christus spricht mit diesen lieblichen Umschreibungen Gott an. Er war von Kindheit an sein curator und tutor. Die »Jungfrauengeburt« wird metaphorisch transformiert: Der in der Krippe liegende Christus zeigt, dass Gott zu Kindereien aufgelegt ist.

Die gemeinsame Seminararbeit machte deutlich, dass es gewinnbringend ist, Quellen auszuschöpfen, die zunächst am Rande der Aufmerksamkeit liegen. Das Gespräch diente der Schärfung des Problembewußtseins, dass Luther Kreuz und Metapher bereits in der Operatio zu Ps 22 zu Redefiguren verbindet, die mit dem üblichen begriffsgeschichtlichen Instrumentarium nicht angemessen beschrieben werden können. Zu 2 K 5,21 – im »Antilatomus« der zentrale Bezugspunkt – hebt Luther bereits in der Operatio zu Ps 22 metaphorisch den »Glanz« der Aussage hervor, dass Christus am Kreuz für uns zur Sünde gemacht wurde.

Die Pluralität der Interpretationen, die während der Seminararbeit sichtbar wurde, spiegelt die hohe metaphorisch-begriffliche Vielfalt von Luthers Text- und Lebenswelt

wider. Das Abebben der begriffsgeschicht-
liche Bewegung in Nachbardisziplinen wie
Geschichte und Literaturwissenschaft vermag die vielgestaltige Lutherforschung nicht
nur im Bereich der Kreuzestheologie auf
neue Wege zu führen. Es wurde deutlich,
dass mit der Wahl der Operatio zu Ps 22
weder eine normative Metaphorologie inten-
diert ist noch ein neuer Kanonisierungspro-
zess dieses Textes in Gang gesetzt werden
soll. Vielmehr zeigte die Arbeit des international besetzten Seminars zu »Kreuz und
Metapher«, dass zur Analyse dieses Themas
eine problembewusste Kombination histori-

scher und systematischer Methoden notwendig ist. Es war für das interdisziplinäre
Gespräch deshalb besonders fruchtbar, dass
der Kreis paritätisch besetzt war und die
Teilnehmenden dieses kleinsten Seminars
vor einem systematischen und kirchenhistorischen Horizont argumentierten. Inwiefern das zu »Kreuz und Metapher« Herausgearbeitete weitere Bereiche von Luthers
theologischer Text- und Lebenswelt erhellen
mag, konnte in Brasilien wegen der Kürze
der Zeit nicht geklärt werden. Hier bleibt
eine Aufgabe für die Zukunft deren Lösung
Zeit erfordern wird..

Catechisms and Catechetics

Seminar leader: Mary Jane Haemig
Reporter: Mary Jane Haemig

This seminar considered a variety of topics related to the history and theology of
Luther's catechisms.

Ninna Jørgensen presented on the »History and theology of the Decalog in Catechisms«, focusing on the use of the commandments in the century before Luther.
She first considered their use as a layperson's
guide to heaven as demonstrated in vernacular devotional literature and then discussed
their use in pulpit and confessional as reflected in model sermons, episcopal statutes,
and confessors' manuals.

Jeffrey Silcock presented on »The conclusion to the Ten Commandments in the
Large Catechism«. He addressed the issue of whether Luther allowed the law to

overshadow the gospel in that conclusion.
He argued that the key to correctly understanding the Ten Commandments and the
place of the gospel lies in the structure of
the three main parts of the catechism. Further, he argued that Luther's reference to
reward and punishment does not obscure
the gospel or compromise the doctrine of
justification.

Gordon Jensen discussed »The theology
of the cross in Luther's Catechisms«, arguing that the emphases of the theology of
the cross, as expressed in the Heidelberg
disputation, were carried on through and
developed in Luther's early sermons on catechetical pieces, the Betbüchlein, and Small
and Large Catechisms.

Clovis Prunzel noted that much research on Luther's theology of the Lord's Supper stresses polemical aspects related to disputes with Rome and the Enthusiasts. His paper, »Lord's supper in the Large Catechism: a pastoral approach«, focused on pastoral aspects in Luther's instructions, exhortations, and counseling concerning the Lord's Supper.

Several presentations looked at catechesis and the use of Luther's catechisms in particular locations.

Simo Heininen in his presentation »The first Finnish Catechism« compared the Finnish Reformer Michael Agricola's (1509-1557) ABC book (1539) with Luther's Small Catechism (1529) as well as catechisms by Philip Melanchthon (1536) and by Andreas Osiander (1498-1552) (1539). Agricola, like Melanchthon, included an introductory rhyme. Like Luther, Agricola included table, morning, and evening prayers. Unlike the other three, Agricola included the alphabet and letters as well as the Ave Maria and prayers to be said when bells were rung.

Ninna Jørgensen examined the reception of Luther's Small Catechism in Denmark in the 18th through 20th centuries, considering editions of the catechism as well as the use of the catechism in hymnals.

Klaas Zwanepol in »The reception of Luther's Small Catechism in the Netherlands« reviewed editions of Luther's Small Catechism in the Netherlands from the 16th century to the present day. He also examined the use of the Small Catechism during these centuries. A special section considered the reception of the text on the office of the keys and confession in Dutch editions of Luther's Small Catechism and corresponding developments concerning confession and absolution in the Netherlands.

Mary Jane Haemig examined catechesis and the use of Luther's Small Catechism by an important early Lutheran leader in North America in her presentation »Early Lutheran catechetical efforts in Colonial America: the correspondence of Henry Melchior Mühlenberg, 1742-1752«.

Die Rezeption und Unterscheidung von vita contemplativa und vita activa bei Luther

Seminarleiter: Volker Leppin
Berichterstatter: Matthias Mikoteit

Im Seminar wurden mit Hilfe einer Reihe von mittelalterlichen, wirkungsgeschichtlich hochgradig bedeutsamen Texten Deutungsmodelle der Unterscheidung von vita contemplativa und vita activa rekonstruiert. Diese Rekonstruktion ermöglichte es, eine Reihe von Texten Luthers so zu interpretieren, dass dessen Modell des christlichen Lebens in seinem Verhältnis zu den mittelalterlichen Traditionsströmen erfasst werden konnte. Wie sich herausstellte, sind für das Verhältnis zur Tradition bei Luther die Begriffe »Anknüpfung« und »Abgrenzung« charakteristisch, wenn es um das Verständnis der vita christiana geht.

Die Texte, die dem Seminar zugrunde lagen, enthalten die Unterscheidung von vita contemplativa und vita activa nicht alle explizit. Sie gehen aber alle entweder auf die Frage nach den Sozialformen des christlichen Lebens, nach der Frömmigkeitskultur oder nach der Begründung der Ethik ein.

Es folgen die Textinterpretationen in Kurzfassung:

Nach der »Glossa ordinaria« – erstes Drittel des 12. Jahrhunderts; Patrologiae cursus completus/ besorgt von Jacques-Paul Migne. Series latina. Bd. 113-114. P 1852, einem maßgeblichen mittelalterlichen Lehrbuch aus der Schule des Anselm von Laon (um 1050-1117), das bis in das 16. Jahrhundert hinein auf die Bibellektüre gewirkt hat –, repräsentiert das Schwesternpaar Martha und Maria – L 10, 38-42; dazu 114, 287 – die vita activa bzw. die vita contemplativa als zwei gleichberechtigt nebeneinander stehende »vitae spirituales« bzw. »vitae innocentes«:

Die vita activa der »Martha« beinhaltet die karitative Tätigkeit, aber auch die Predigtmission und die Seelsorge; die vita contemplativa der »Maria« umfasst die Liebe zu Gott und dem Nächsten, wobei allerdings das äußere Tun ruht und die Schau Gottes das sehnsüchtig angestrebte Ziel ist. Das Konzept der vita contemplativa schließt somit die Nächstenliebe ein, wenn es auch deren Auswirkungen ausschließt. Den mystischen raptus freilich schließt es explizit nicht mit ein.

Vita activa und vita contemplativa stehen als gleichberechtigte vitae spirituales bzw. innocentes nach der »Glossa ordinaria« der »vita iniqua« gegenüber. Der Übergang von der nicht geistlichen in eine der geistlichen

Lebensweisen geschieht laut »Glossa ordinaria« in dem Moment, in dem »Martha« und »Maria« ihr Leben in direktem und evidentem Bezug zu Christus, der »fons vitae«, zu leben beginnen. Angesprochen ist offenbar der Übergang vom Leben in der oeconomia und politia zum Leben in der ecclesia, wobei vorausgesetzt ist, dass das Leben sich nicht zugleich in ecclesia, oeconomia und politia vollziehen kann.

Vita activa und vita contemplativa meinen in der »Glossa ordinaria« mithin exklusiv das Leben in der ecclesia.

In der populärsten mittelalterlichen Legendensammlung, die von dem Dominikaner Jacobus de Voragine (1228/30-1298) stammt, der »Legenda aurea« – um 1263/1273; kritisch hrsg. von Giovanni Paolo Maggioni. Firenze 1998 –, wird Maria, die Schwester von Martha, mit Maria Magdalena identifiziert (Kap. XCII). Aufschlussreich ist hier die Deutung des Namens »Maria« im Dreischritt als »amarum mare«, »illuminatrix« und »illuminata« – Vers 1-8 –. In Anlehnung an das traditionelle Dreierschema zur Beschreibung des mystischen Aufstiegs – purgatio, illuminatio, perfectio; vgl. Pseudo-Dionysius Areopagita – wird amarum mare auf die geistliche Stufe der »poenitentia«, illuminatrix auf die der »contemplatio interna« und illuminata auf die der »coelestis gloria« bezogen.

Die Seelsorgetätigkeit, die in der »Glossa ordinaria« der Lebensweise der Martha zugeordnet wurde, wird hier der Maria zugeschrieben: Als illuminatrix nämlich widmet sie sich nach der contemplatio interna ihren Mitmenschen in Südfrankreich als Predigerin, die »ausgießt«, was sie »geschöpft« hat. Vita contemplativa und vita activa bilden somit auf dieser Stufe bei ihr eine Einheit. Als illuminata befindet sich Maria dann freilich auf einer Stufe, auf der die vita activa aufhört und die vita contemplativa sich vollendet. Während Maria als illuminatrix nur mit einem unvollkommenen Licht ausgestattet ist, besitzt sie als illuminata das »perfekteste Licht der Erkenntnis«. Als illuminata gelangt sie sogar zur Verklärung ihres Körpers.

Die sich anschließende biografische Schilderung in der »Legenda aurea« illustriert dieses differenzierte Schema des geistlichen Lebens. In ihr wird u. a. die »Süße der Beredtsamkeit« – Vers 38 – der Maria hervorgehoben und von einer äußerlich sichtbaren körperlichen Erhebung – vgl. Vers 135 – berichtet, wie sie – der Überlieferung nach – in Beginengemeinschaften vorkam.

Kaum ein mittelalterlicher Autor geht so ausführlich auf die Begründung des geistlichen Lebens ein wie der Dominikaner Thomas von Aquino (um 1225-1274). Er liefert eine theologisch-ethische Begründung von dessen Sozialform. In der Schrift »De perfectione vitae spiritualis« (um 1269/70) – Thomas von Aquino: Opera omnia/ hrsg. im Auftrag von Leo XIII. Bd. 41. Romae 1970, B 69-111 –, mit der er die Bettelorden in Paris mit ihrer strikten Armutsforderung verteidigt, betont er, dass die Vollkommenheit des geistlichen Lebens hauptsächlich in der Vollkommenheit der Liebe besteht (Kap. II), wobei »Liebe« zuerst und hauptsächlich die Gottesliebe, an zweiter Stelle dann auch die Nächstenliebe meint. Der Einfluss der aristotelischen Soziallehre auf Thomas wird sichtbar, wenn er andeutet, dass die Nächstenliebe sich auf dem Boden des ius sociale ereignet (Kap. III). Die dem Menschen mögliche Gottesliebe realisiert sich nach Thomas vollkommen erst auf dem Weg der Befreiung, der durch die Befolgung der »Räte« »Armut«, »Keuschheit« und »Gehorsam« beschritten wird (Kap. VII-

XIII). Thomas arbeitet heraus, dass es auf die innere Befolgung der »Räte« ankommt, und konzediert, dass die Befolgung derselben deshalb außerhalb des Standes der Religiosen möglich ist. Er macht gleichwohl unmissverständlich klar, dass die »Räte« eigentlich diesen Stand erfordern.

Meister Eckhart (um 1260-1328) setzt sich als dominikanischer »Lebemeister« konkret mit problematischen Entwicklungen im geistlichen Leben bestimmter Beginengemeinschaften auseinander. Zu diesem Zweck knüpft er in seiner Predigt über »Maria und Martha« – um 1313/1326; Meister Eckhart: Die deutschen Werke/ hrsg. und übers. von Josef Quint. Bd. 3: Predigten. S 1973-1976, 481-492, im Folgenden zitiert nach der neuhochdeutschen Übersetzung ebd, 592-599 – an die einschlägigen Texte in der »Glossa ordinaria« und in der »Legenda aurea« an. Auch seiner Meinung nach sind die beiden vitae spirituales der Maria und der Martha gleichwertig – vgl. 596, 14-31 –. Allerdings macht er deutlich, dass das noch nicht zu der Zeit gilt, als Maria zu Jesu Füßen sitzt, wo sie nämlich »im Wohlgefühl und in süßer Empfindung« – 598, 20 – verharrt. Meister Eckhart liegt alles daran, zu zeigen, dass die sinnlich gefärbte vita contemplativa, die Maria anfangs repräsentiert, gegenüber der von Martha repräsentierten vernunfterhellten vita activa defizitär ist.

Nun kann Meister Eckhart freilich aufgrund der hagiografischen Überlieferung der »Legenda aurea« bei Maria eine Entwicklung konstatieren, die durch die Angleichung an Martha zustande kam. Äußerst prägnant beschreibt er diese Entwicklung folgendermaßen: »Maria ist erst [eine solche] Martha gewesen, ehe sie [die reife] Maria werden sollte« – 598, 17f –.

An dieser Stelle interpretiert er die in der »Legenda aurea« dargestellten Phasen im Leben der Maria als einen dialektischen Prozess: Maria gelangte auf dem Weg der vernunfterhellten vita activa zu sich selbst, weil sie auf ihm den Weg der vita contemplativa, von dem sie hergekommen war, neu – nämlich als rein geistigen Weg – entdeckte.

Das Ideal des geistlichen Lebens, an dem sich die Beginen orientieren sollen, ist folglich nach Meister Eckhart die vita activa in ihrer Einheit mit der vernunftgemäß transformierten vita contemplativa.

Der Dominikaner Johannes Tauler (um 1300-1361) hat aus Eckharts Schriften bestimmte Grundgedanken übernommen. So verwundert es nicht, dass auch bei ihm vita activa und vita contemplativa nachweislich – Dietmar Mieth – eine Einheit bilden. In seiner Weihnachtspredigt – Die Predigten Taulers/ hrsg. von Ferdinand Vetter. B 1910, 7-12 –, mit der er ursprünglich Dominikanerinnen, darüber hinaus auch sog. Gottesfreunde und Beginen adressiert, beschreibt er die vita contemplativa in zeitlos gültiger Form. Ihr Ziel ist nach seiner Darstellung die Geburt Gottes bzw. des Sohnes Gottes bzw. des ewigen Wortes Gottes in der Seele.

In ihrer strengen Bezogenheit auf die Gottesgeburt enthält die vita contemplativa eine aktive und eine passive Komponente. Die aktive besteht darin, dass die Seele sich wie die Jungfrau Maria in sich selbst einschließt und sich von allem abkehrt, nicht nur »von zitlichen uzlöffungen, die ettewaz gebrestlich schinent«, sondern auch »von sinnelicher übunge der tugende« – 11, 25 f –. Die aktive Komponente geht in dem Moment in die passive über, in dem durch die genannte Aktivität ein völliges »swigen« – 11, 31 u. ö. – entsteht und dieses seine Funktion als »mittel« des »unmittelichen inganges diser ewiger geburt« – 12, 4 – erfüllt – vgl. 11, 34 f –.

Für Tauler ist die aktiv angestrebte Passivität aufseiten des Menschen die notwendige Bedingung für die Gottesgeburt in der Seele bzw. für die Vereinigung von Gott und Seele entsprechend der von ihm rezipierten allgemeinen Regel: »Wan wenne zwei súllent eins werden, so mús sich daz eine halten lidende und daz ander wúrckende; [...]« – 9, 34-36 –.

Jean Gerson (1363-1429) wendet die Unterscheidung von vita contemplativa und vita activa konkret an, um den Seelsorgeklerus aufzuwerten, wie es *Christoph Burger* in einem Referat darstellte:

Als Hochschullehrer der Theologie und Kanzler der Pariser Universität sieht sich der Weltgeistliche Gerson, der »Kirchenvater des 15. Jahrhunderts« – Bernd Moeller –, mit dem Anspruch von Kollegen aus den Bettelorden konfrontiert, ihr »schauendes Leben« stehe höher als das »tätige Leben« der Säkularkleriker. In »De consiliis evangelicis et statu perfectionis« – um 1400; Jean Gerson: Œuvres complètes/ hrsg. von Palémon Glorieux. Bd. 3. P 1962, 10-26 – rückt Gerson Weltgeistliche nahe an Bischöfe heran: vermittelten doch die Angehörigen beider Stände Vollkommenheit, während Mönche sie erst anstrebten. Die »Evangelischen Räte« seien lediglich Werkzeuge dazu, geistlich vollkommener zu werden. Auf die Nachfolge Christi komme es an.

In »De comparatione vitae contemplativae ad activam« – um 1401; ebd, 3, 63-77 – schreibt Gerson, weil der Sündenfall viele Nöte im menschlichen Leben verursacht habe, sei eine Lebensweise zu empfehlen, in der ein Christ sich nicht ausschließlich der an und für sich vorzüglicheren Gottesschau hingebe, sondern auch für seinen Nächsten wirke. Prälaten und »andere Heilige« vereinbarten Gottesschau und tätiges Leben miteinander – vita mixta –.

In beiden Schriften relativiert der Pariser Theologe den Anspruch der Bettelordenstheologen, ihre Lebensweise sei vollkommener.

In seinen Randbemerkungen zu Taulers Predigten – um 1516; WA 9, 97-104 – zeigt Luther, dass er die traditionelle typologische Deutung des Schwesternpaares Martha und Maria als die Verbindung von vita activa und vita contemplativa übernimmt. Er kommentiert mit diesem Schema die genannte Weihnachtspredigt, die es voraussetzt, aber expressis verbis nicht enthält – vgl. 98, 14-34 –:

Luther bezieht die beiden Lebensweisen aufeinander, ohne einer von beiden den Vorrang zu geben. Gott wird nämlich einerseits – damit fasst er die Ausführungen Taulers zusammen – »in nobis secundum statum vitae contemplativae« geboren, andererseits – und damit ergänzt er dessen Ausführungen – »moraliter [...] in operatione virtutum secundum statum vitae activae«.

Luther betont dabei, dass die vita contemplativa nur dann ihr Ziel erreichen kann, wenn sie strikt von der vita activa abgegrenzt wird, weil »in contemplatione et operatio virtutum impedit nativitatem dei in anima«, und wenn die vita activa ihr vorgeordnet wird; denn wer zur Ruhe der »contemplatio« eilt, muss nach Luther gemäß Is 1, 16 zuvor Leidenschaften, Laster und böse Werke zur Ruhe bringen.

Den Abschluss bzw. Höhepunkt seiner Argumentation bildet eine Überlegung zum Theologiebegriff: Die Theologie, welche die geistliche Geburt des inkarnierten Wortes zu ihrem Gegenstand hat, erwächst aus der Erfahrung dieser Geburt und ist deswegen als eine »sapientia experimentalis« zu bezeichnen.

Das Interesse, das Luther bei der Anwendung des Schemas um 1516 leitet, ist somit höchstwahrscheinlich ein wissenschaftstheoretisches, nämlich die Überwindung des aristotelischen Wissenschaftsbegriffs durch die positive Aufnahme der Kategorie der Erfahrung in den Theologiebegriff.

In den »Operationes in psalmos« – 1518-1521; WA 5 ≙ AWA 2 als Neuedition von Ps 1-10 – spricht Luther von der vita passiva, die man als Synthese von vita contemplativa und vita activa verstehen kann. Diese These erläuterte *Ilmari Karimies* in seinem Referat:

Wenn Luther Ps 2, 6 kommentiert, scheint er die Unterscheidung zwischen aktivem und kontemplativem Leben zu akzeptieren. Später kritisiert er in dem umfangreichen Exkurs »De spe et passionibus« – AWA 2, 284, 1 - 321, 5 – jedoch an beiden Lebensweisen, dass sie auf dem Tun des Menschen gründen.

Unter Zuhilfenahme mystischer Begrifflichkeit beschreibt er in diesem Exkurs die Wirkung der eingegossenen göttlichen Tugenden Glaube, Hoffnung und Liebe – vgl. AWA 2, 302, 9 - 304, 6; 305, 14 - 306, 7; 307, 3 - 308, 17; 317, 7 - 319, 3 –: Sie verbinden die Seele mit dem unsichtbaren Wort Gottes und machen die menschlichen Verdienste zunichte, sodass für sie als »Tugenden« kein anderer Grund übrig bleibt als Gott. Das verursacht für das Fleisch Leiden, weil es unfähig ist, das Unsichtbare zu begreifen. Nach Luther ist das rechte christliche Leben deshalb ein Leben des Leidens, das er an besagtem Ort »vita passiva« – 302, 15; vgl. 303, 5 – nennt: leidendes, passives, rezeptives Leben.

Zu beachten ist nun, dass er zwischen dem Innen- und dem Außenaspekt der göttlichen Tugenden unterscheidet – vgl. AWA 2, 320, 15 - 321, 5 –. Während diese sich in Bezug auf das Wort Gottes im Inneren rein rezeptiv vollziehen, vollziehen sie sich nach außen hin, in Bezug auf den Nächsten, allerdings aktiv: Sie nehmen in Taten der Nächstenliebe Gestalt an. In solchem äußeren Tun fungiert das menschliche Wollen wie ein Werkzeug, das die Bewegung, in der es sich befindet, nicht selbst begonnen hat, aber das Ergebnis seiner Bewegung sehr wohl mit bewirkt.

Luthers Idee von der vita passiva in den »Operationes in psalmos« nimmt demnach Elemente der beiden mittelalterlichen Lebensweisen in sich auf: das Element der Erfahrung der unsichtbaren Realität und das der praktizierten Nächstenliebe.

Die Neubegründung des christlichen Lebens im Glauben führt Luther zur Neubewertung der ihm begegnenden Sozialformen des christlichen Lebens. In der Schrift »De votis monasticis iudicium« – 1521 auf der Wartburg entstanden; WA 8, (564) 573-669 – weist er nach, dass die Aufteilung des Evangeliums in »Räte« und »Gebote« unhaltbar ist, weil sie erstens aus dem Evangelium ein Gesetz mache und weil sie zweitens verkenne, dass die sog. »consilia« in Wirklichkeit »necessaria mandata« seien – 581, 31 –. Er folgert daraus, dass es nur den einen, allgemeinen Weg der Christen in der Nachfolge Christi gibt – vgl. 583, 25 f –. Trotz einiger Spitzensätze, die Anderes vermuten lassen – vgl. z. B. 583, 20-28; 596, 1-4 –, bedeutet dies für Luther nicht, dass die Sozialform des Mönchtums nicht bestehen bleiben könnte. Akzeptabel bleibt es für ihn, wenn sein Sinn ausschließlich in der leiblichen Askese, der karitativen Tätigkeit und der Schriftmeditation gesehen und es somit nicht prinzipiell von den weltlichen Berufen unterschieden wird – vgl. 604, 18-23 –.

Mit dem Sermon »Von den guten Werken« – bereits im Jahr 1520 entstanden, in seiner Bedeutung vergleichbar mit den sog.

reformatorischen Hauptschriften; WA 6, (196) 202-276 – legt Luther den Entwurf einer für jeden Christen verbindlichen »Ethik aus dem Glauben« – Martin Brecht – vor. Er fordert in diesem Zusammenhang nicht nur, dass bei der weltlichen Arbeit »geistlich betenn« – 234, 36 –, d. h. ein inneres Reden mit Gott, geschieht, sondern dass bei der weltlichen Arbeit und überhaupt bei jeder Form menschlicher Aktivität »ein ruge und auffhoren gescheh aller unser werck, wort, gedancken unnd lebenn« – 244, 15 f –, so »das wir allein got in uns wircken lassen« – 244, 5 –.

Luther bestimmt hier die Alltagswelt der Christen neu, indem er sie als den Ort begreift, an dem sich vita activa und vita contemplativa stets aktuell miteinander verbinden, und macht zugleich deutlich, dass sich durch das Ineinander derselben in der Welt für jeden Christen die Möglichkeit und auch die Notwendigkeit ergibt, Taulers mystisches Konzept einer auf Gott konzentrierten Passivität in transformierter Weise, nämlich in der Zuwendung zur Welt, fortwährend zu realisieren.

Luthers neues Konzept der Verbindung von vita activa und vita contemplativa als von Gott regierte weltzugewandte vita passiva liegt auch seinem Kommentar zum Magnifikat – L 1,46b-55; WA 7, (538) 544-604 – aus den Jahren 1520/21 zugrunde. Wie *Christoph Burger* in einem weiteren Referat ausführte, zeigt gerade dieser Kommentar, dass dieses Konzept Gedanken mittelalterlicher Mystiker aufnimmt und umbildet:

Zum zentralen Thema der Schrift macht Luther Gottes gnädiges An-Sehen Marias. Zu L 1,46b schreibt er, Marias ganzes Gemüt, ihr Leben und alle ihre Sinne seien hingerissen. Gott selbst erhebe sie zu seinem Lobe – vgl. WA 7, 550, 2-18; 554, 19-29 –. Diese Ausdrucksweise ist vertraut aus dem

Sprechen von Mystikern über das Hingerissensein – raptus –. Freilich vermeidet Luther jede Aussage, die so missverstanden werden könnte, als vereinige sich Marias Geist mit dem Geist Gottes. Da er zu diesem Zeitpunkt noch keine negativen Erfahrungen mit Spiritualisten gemacht hat, kann er ungeschützt sagen, Gottes Wort verstehe nur recht, wer es unmittelbar vom Heiligen Geist habe – vgl. 546, 24-29 –. Mystisch klingt auch sein Reden von Gelassenheit – vgl. 555, 21-35; 581, 24-31; 582, 27-29 –. Rechtes Regieren eines Herrschers – vita activa – habe seine Grundlage darin, dass er sich von Gott leiten lasse – vita passiva; vgl. 544, 21-29 –, was durch das eigene Beten ermöglicht werde – vita contemplativa; vgl. 602, 30 - 603, 6 –. In der Lebensform, in der ein Christ sich von Gott leiten lässt – vita passiva –, kommen vita activa und vita contemplativa für Luther zusammen.

Dass Luthers reformatorisches Konzept der vita passiva worttheologisch fundiert ist, erkennt man dort, wo er sich in seiner dritten Psalmenvorlesung – 1532-1535; WA 40 II, (185) 193-312. (313) 315-470. (471) 472-610; 40 III, (1) 9-475. (476) 484-594 – positiv zur Erfahrung der »unio cum deo« äußert. Diese Stelle – WA 40 III, 199, 5-13 – analysierte *Matthias Mikoteit:*

Luther grenzt sich hier von der brautmystischen Intention ab und empfiehlt die »unio cum deo« im Sinne einer »unio« mit dem Wort Gottes als tägliche Übung. Damit betont er jedoch nur scheinbar die menschliche Aktivität. Das wird deutlich, wenn man einige Abschnitte der gegen Ende der dritten Psalmenvorlesung im Jahr 1535 verfassten Gebetsanleitung für Peter Beskendorf – WA 38, (351) 358-375 – zur Interpretation seiner Empfehlung heranzieht – vgl. 363, 9-16; 366, 10-15; 372, 31 - 373, 7 –.

Luther unterscheidet dort nämlich zwei Phasen des Umgangs mit dem biblischen Text: In der ersten Phase betätigt der Beter den Text mit einem kalten Herzen wie einen Feuerstein. In der zweiten Phase bewirkt der Heilige Geist, dass durch den Text ein Feuer im Herzen entsteht, welches das Herz erwärmt. Während der Beter in der ersten Phase in Erwartung der Aktivität des Geistes aktiv sein soll, soll er in der zweiten Phase im Erleben der Aktivität des Geistes passiv sein.

Die Übung der »unio« mit dem Wort Gottes gipfelt für Luther im idealen Fall, den er selbst nach eigenem Bekunden »offt« – WA 38, 363, 9 – erlebt hat, in der Aktivität des Heiligen Geistes. Sie besteht darin, dass dieser als Bibelausleger spontan selber »predigt« – 363, 13 –, wodurch er die Passivität des Menschen gegenüber dem Wort Gottes überhaupt erst ermöglicht – dass nämlich der Mensch »mit stille« zuhört; wie Luther es an dieser Stelle ausdrückt.

Streit um das theologische Erbe Martin Luthers

Seminarleiterin: Irene Dingel
Berichterstatterin: Irene Dingel

Die Reformationsgeschichtsforschung hat lange Jahre hindurch ihren Schwerpunkt in den Entwicklungen der ersten Hälfte des 16. Jahrhunderts gesehen und sich mit der Etablierung der Reformation und den frühen Schriften Martin Luthers beschäftigt. Untersucht wurden Korrespondenzen, die beginnende reformatorische Predigt und das Lied, Flugschriften und die großen reformatorischen Programmschriften. Seltener kam die zweite Hälfte des 16. Jahrhunderts und die Konsolidierung der Reformation in den Blick. Auch die entscheidende Rolle der mündlich und später vor allem schriftlich ausgetragenen Kontroversen mit ihrer lehrmäßig konsolidierenden Kraft wurde eher vernachlässigt, wenn nicht sogar als unnützes Theologengezänk abgewertet. Im Zusammenhang heutiger Forschung und neuer Perspektiven auf das beginnende Zeitalter der Konfessionen scheint es angemessener von einer »Streitkultur« zu sprechen. Problemlösung und Wahrheitssuche über den Weg des Gesprächs, d. h. über die Konfrontation von Rede und Gegenrede, war schon zu Beginn der Reformation nichts Neues, sondern ein gängiges Mittel der Verständigung. Die Wurzeln dafür liegen im Disputationswesen der mittelalterlichen Universitäten. Sie wurden angewandt und weiterentwickelt in den Religionsgesprächen, aber auch in den in der zweiten Hälfte des 16. Jahrhunderts aufbrechenden Kontroversen um das theologische Erbe Martin Luthers. Diese Auseinandersetzungen innerhalb des Protestantismus, die schließlich auf das lutherische Konkordienwerk hinführten, sind aber nicht nur von ihren theologischen Inhalten her zu begreifen. Vielmehr sind die zeitliche Ausdehnung der Konflikte, oft über 10 bis 15 Jahre, sowie die inhaltlichen Schwerpunktsetzungen, welche auch nach der Erstellung der Konkordienformel weiter diskutiert wurden, sowie die Intensität, mit der die Debatten geführt wurden, nur einsichtig, wenn man sich die komplexen Entstehungsbedingungen und Begründungszusammenhänge vor Augen führt. Hier sind in erster Linie drei Faktoren zu nennen: a) die historisch-politischen Rahmenbedingungen; b) die Infragestellung und der Verlust der reformatorischen Autoritäten; c) Territoriale Rivalitäten und theologische Identitätsfindung. Die in diesem Kontext im Anschluss an das Interim aufbrechenden Kontroversen drehten sich im Grunde alle um die Frage, in welcher inhaltlichen Ausprägung man die reformatorische Wittenberger Theologie an die kommenden Generationen vermitteln wollte: entweder in bewusster und ausschließlicher Konzentration auf die Lehre Martin Luthers oder in einer die Theologie Luthers und Melanchthons integrierenden Form oder aber in Betonung der von Melanchthon ausgegangenen Impulse für Lehre und Leben der Kirche. Insofern stellen die Streitigkeiten den Versuch dar, zu einer theologischen Klärung zu gelangen. Sie sind ein ausschlaggebender Prozess im Streben nach konfessioneller Identitätsbildung.

Diese Prozesse nachzuvollziehen, hatte sich das Seminar zum Ziel gesetzt und dazu eine Arbeitsform gewählt, welche die

Präsentation von Referaten mit Quellenlektüre und Diskussion verband. In einer aus sechs Personen bestehenden internationalen Gruppe konnten ein intensiver wissenschaftlicher Austausch gepflegt und vielfältige Impulse aufgenommen werden, auch wenn – aufgrund unvorhersehbarer, kurzfristig eingetretener Ereignisse – sich die ursprüngliche Teilnehmerzahl reduzierte und von den eigentlich vorgesehenen sieben Referaten schließlich nur vier gehalten wurden.

Die *Seminarleiterin* steckte zunächst durch eine problembezogene Einleitung das Untersuchungsfeld ab, das – orientiert an dem Hauptthema des Kongresses – seinen ersten Schwerpunkt auf dem »Interim und seinen Wirkungen auf ecclesia, oeconomia und politia« hatte. Als ein ausgewähltes Beispiel dafür diente die nach dem Erlass dieses kaiserlichen Religionsgesetzes (1548) im Zusammenhang mit Fragen von Lehre und Bekenntnis einsetzende »Kultivierung des Exulantentums im Luthertum«, das sie am Beispiel des Nikolaus von Amsdorf (1483-1565) in dem ersten Referat des Seminars entfaltete. Dabei konnte sie zeigen, dass eine ganze Gruppe von entschiedenen Lutheranhängern – meist hochgebildeten Theologen – die Selbstbezeichnung des »Exul« oder »Exul Christi« gezielt zur Legitimierung und wirksamen Propagierung ihrer in Luthers Theologie gründenden Lehre einsetzten. Wer sich als »Exul«, »Exul Christi« oder sogar als »Exul et Servus Jesu Christi« auswies, nahm für sich in Anspruch, Glied der wahren, auf dem Boden des Evangeliums stehenden Kirche in der Nachfolge Martin Luthers zu sein. Die auf diese Weise in Erinnerung gebrachte Verfolgung um ihres Bekenntnisses willen galt als Beleg für die Rechtmäßigkeit des eigenen evangelischen Glaubens. Auch von Amsdorf nahm das

Exil als identifikatorisches und legitimatorisches Kennzeichen in Dienst, konstruierte dabei allerdings auch einen nicht unbedingt den historischen Tatsachen entsprechenden Blick auf die eigene Biografie und trug mit bei zur Herausbildung einer »Theologie der kleinen Herde« sowie eines regelrechten Exulanten-»Standes«.

Mit dem anschließenden Referat eröffnete *Timothy Wengert* den zweiten Schwerpunkt des Seminars, nämlich die Frage nach den Wirkungen der Theologie Luthers und lutherischer Bekenntnisbildung in ecclesia, oeconomia und politia. Wengerts Ausführungen über »Luther als Freund und Feind im Osiandrischen Streit, 1550-1553« zeigten, dass das platonische Denken als Grundlage für die Hermeneutik Andreas Osianders d. Ä. (1498-1552) und sein Lutherverständnis, wie es im Verlauf des Streits Gestalt gewann und angepasst wurde, als ausschlaggebende Komponenten in Anschlag zu bringen sind. Zugleich führte er vor Augen, dass die damalige Auseinandersetzung um die Rechtfertigungslehre sich im Grunde an Fragen von Definitionen und Autoritäten entzündete. Die differenzierte Rekonstruktion des Streitablaufs und die Analyse der jeweils zugrunde liegenden Hermeneutik machten sowohl die Berechtigung des Anspruchs Osianders als auch den seiner Gegner auf das Erbe Luthers deutlich.

Theodor Dieter erweiterte die eröffneten Perspektiven durch die seinem Beitrag vorangestellte Frage »Was macht ein Werk zu einem guten Werk?: Beobachtungen bei Martin Chemnitz«. Dazu fragte er zunächst nach den typischen Merkmalen der Theologie Luthers, um diese in den Schriften des Chemnitz auf ihre kontextbezogenen Veränderungen hin zu überprüfen. In diesem Zusammenhang trat dessen Melanchthonschülerschaft klar hervor, zumal er sich eindeutig an dem von Melanchthon formulierten Gesetzesverständnis orientierte und so die unklare begriffliche Fassung des »guten Werks« bei Luther wenigstens zum Teil überwinden konnte. Die von Luther vertretene Radikalität des Sündenverständnisses musste – so Dieter – die Gefahr heraufbeschwören, dass nicht mehr differenziert ausgesagt werden konnte, was die gute Frucht des guten Baumes – des Glaubenden – ist, wenn doch der Glaubende zugleich Sünder bleibt, sodass im Laufe der Geschichte als Reaktion darauf eine Fülle von Heiligungsbewegungen entstanden. Seine Analyse mündete in das Fazit, dass in Luthers Ethik Differenzierungen zwischen verschiedenen Ebenen der Gutheit des menschlichen Wollens und Handelns, etwa zwischen Legalität und Moralität, nur unzureichend entwickelt werden, obwohl solche Differenzen den Menschen trotz ihres Sünderseins zugutekommen und deshalb auch theologisch bedacht werden müssen. Dieters systematisch-theologische Perspektive ließ nicht zuletzt die Gegenwartsrelevanz solcher Überlegungen aufscheinen und nach Kontrastmustern in der scholastischen Theologie des Mittelalters fragen.

Mit *Amy Burnetts* Referat traten die konfessionellen Entwicklungen in Basel in den Blickpunkt, die ebenfalls als Auseinandersetzung mit dem Erbe Luthers zu beschreiben sind: »Luther's theological legacy in Switzerland: the evolution of Simon Sulzer's eucharistic theology«. In kritischer Stellungnahme zu überkommenen Forschungsmeinungen stellte sie heraus, dass Simon Sulzers (1508-1585) intensive Korrespondenz mit Johannes Marbach (1521-1581) ihn längst nicht zu einem Lutheraner im eigentlichen Sinne mache. Weder in der Abendmahlsleh-

re, die er im Sinne der Wittenberger Konkordie auslegte, noch in der Christologie, die weit von der des Johannes Brenz (1499-1570) entfernt war, konnte er eigentlich dem lutherischen Lager zugerechnet werden. Sie plädierte deshalb für eine weitaus differenziertere Sicht der Entwicklungen in Basel als dies bisher in der Forschung der Fall ist. Denn selbst als sich in den sechziger Jahren des 16. Jahrhunderts der gnesiolutherische Einfluss verstärkte, versuchte Sulzer, seinen konfessionell offenen Kurs zu halten. Diese theologische Option fand nicht zuletzt Rückhalt in seiner Einbindung in die Netzwerke der führenden Basler Familien.

Die an alle Referate anschließende gemeinsame Quellenlektüre und Interpretation sowie die ausführlichen Diskussionen vertieften die gesetzten Schwerpunkte und führten immer wieder vor Augen, wie wenig die Quellen des in diesem Seminar behandelten Zeitalters und Problemfelds bisher Beachtung gefunden haben, obgleich gerade hier die Weichen für die weitere Entwicklung einer sich sodann in Konfessionen aufgliedernden Theologie gestellt wurden. Betont wurde von allen Beteiligten, und nicht zuletzt durch die weiterführenden Diskussionsbeiträge *Simo Peuras* und *Günther Franks*, wie sehr auf die Eigenständigkeit der theologischen Positionen auch der Protagonisten der zweiten und dritten Reformatorengeneration zu achten ist. Dies implizierte die Forderung nach einem differenzierteren Blick auf die theologischen Entwicklungen in der durch Politik und Gesellschaft des 16. Jahrhunderts jeweils unterschiedlich vorgegebenen Gemengelage, denen der übliche konfessionelle Schematismus nicht gerecht werde. An den hier diskutierten Beispielen, welche die Entwicklungen der Rechtfertigungstheologie, die

Modifikationen in der Lehre von den guten Werken, Fragen des Abendmahlsverständnisses, aber auch die Legitimation solcher Lehren durch gesellschaftlich-politische Erfahrungen, wie der des Exulantentums, zur Sprache brachten, wurde deutlich, wie notwendig auch die Entwicklung einer neuen Terminologie ist, die der Vielfalt lehr- und bekenntnismäßiger Positionen Rechnung zu tragen und sie wiederzugeben vermag.

Lutherrezeption in Kontexten der sog. Dritten Welt

Seminarleiter: Claus Schwambach
Berichterstatter: Claus Schwambach

Welche Bedeutung kommt der Theologie Luthers innerhalb der weltweiten Kirchen der Reformation heute zu? Unter welchen Gesichtspunkten kann oder muss sie heute, besonders in Kontexten der sog. Zweidrittelwelt, rezipiert werden? Kann die heutige Theologie – eben in diesen Kontexten – diese »alten« Aussagen noch festhalten? Müssen sie kontextuell umgeformt oder gar ganz preisgegeben werden? Diese Fragen, die im Verlauf der breiten Wirkungs- und Rezeptionsgeschichte Luthers immer wieder gestellt wurden,[1] sind in diesem Seminar von Teilnehmern aus verschiedenen Kontinenten – Europa, Asien, Australien, Afrika, Nord- und Südamerika – behandelt worden. In ihren Beiträgen wurde rasch deutlich, wie stark das letzten Endes allen Kontinenten mehr oder weniger gemeinsame geistesgeschichtliche Phänomen der Neuzeit sich als eine überaus wichtige Instanz herauskristallisierte, die diese Wirkungsgeschichte der Theologie Luthers nachhaltig bestimmt hat. Die Veränderungen, welche die Neuzeit zeitigte, führten im Blick auf das allgemeine Bewusstsein zu einer Herauslösung aus dem traditionellen Weltbild, das mit mehr oder weniger Intensität in allen Ecken der Welt gespürt wird. Die Diskussion, wie weit der neuere Umgang mit der abendländischen christlichen Tradition – einschließlich der Theologie Luthers – eher als eine »Umformung des christlichen Denkens« – Emanuel Hirsch (1888-1972)[2] – im

1 Vgl. Heinrich Bornkamm: Luther im Spiegel der deutschen Geistesgeschichte: mit ausgewählten Texten von Lessing bis zur Gegenwart. 2., neu bearb. und erw. Aufl. GÖ 1970; ferner Gerhard Ebeling: Der kontroverse Grund der Feiheit: zum Gegensatz von Luther-Enthusiasmus und Luther-Fremdheit in der Neuzeit. In: Luther in der Neuzeit: wissenschaftliches Symposion des Vereins für Reformationsgeschichte/ hrsg. von Bernd Moeller. GÜ 1983, 9-33.

2 Emanuel Hirsch: Die Umformung des christlichen Denkens in der Neuzeit: ein Lesebuch. Fotomech. Nachdruck der Ausgabe TÜ 1938/ mit Nachwort

Sinne einer Säkularisierung als »Auflösung der Eigenständigkeit der Religion und die Verwaltung ihres Nachlasses allein in den Formen des Tuns und des Wissens bzw. die Übernahme ihrer Funktionen durch diese Formen«,[3] oder als Umformung eine durch allen Wandel sich haltende Identität zu verstehen ist, entbrannte rasch unter den Teilnehmern. Muss der Historismus der Neuzeit als »Schicksal«,[4] als eine die Theologie konstituierende irreversible und eherne, unvermeidliche und nicht wieder preiszugebende schicksalhafte Logik angesehen werden? Kommt der Neuzeit also eine alles andere bestimmende geschichtsaxiomatische Bedeutung zu? Die theologische Bewertung der Neuzeit spielt also nach wie vor eine wichtige Rolle für die Lutherrezeption. Ist dieser Prozess zu bejahen?[5] Oder ist von ei-

ner Grundlagenkrise[6] der Theologie[7] – auch im Rahmen der Lutherforschung – zu reden?

Beide Meinungen wurden in verschiedenen Nuancierungen im Seminar vertreten und ließen die Frage nach den *Kriterien* der Lutherrezeption stärker hervortreten: Geht es bei der Rezeption von Luthertexten eher um das Kriterium der Verständlichkeit vor

und bibliograf. Anhang hrsg. von Hans Martin Mueller. TÜ 1985; vgl. DERS.: Geschichte der neueren evangelischen Theologie. Bd. 5. GÜ 1954, 621-626.

3 Oswald BAYER: Theologie. GÜ 1994, 455; vgl. ferner die Ausführungen ebd, 456-487.

4 Hirsch: Die Umformung …, V (Vorrede): »Das Tor zur christlichen Vergangenheit ist uns allen zugeschlagen, seitdem dies Schicksal über uns gekommen ist: nur in den Formen der Sehnsucht und des Selbstbetrugs ist für den, an dem die Reflexion der letzten Jahrhunderte ihr Werk getan hat, noch ein Verhältnis zur alten Gestalt christlichen Glaubens und Denkens möglich«; ders.: Geschichte … 5, 621-626.

5 Einige exemplarische Beispiele: Wolfgang TRILLHAAS: Dogmatik. B 1962, 80: Der Historismus »ist zunächst einfach der Vollzug eines unvermeidlichen

Schicksals in der Wissenschaft«; Hans GRASS: Der theologische Pluralismus und die Wahrheitsfrage. (1965). In: Ders.: Theologie und Kritik: gesammelte Aufsätze und Vorträge. GÖ 1969, 91: »Der theologische Pluralismus ist in der evangelischen Theologie nicht nur als Schicksal hinzunehmen, […], sondern er ist durchaus zu bejahen.« Friedrich MILDENBERGER: Theorie der Theologie: Enzyklopädie als Methodenlehre. S 1972, 57, spricht von einer »Unausweichlichkeit der historisch-kritischen Reflexion«, zu der die »Unausweichlichkeit der empirischen Kritik« hinzukommt.

6 Zu den theologischen Sachproblemen um die Ablehnung des reformatorischen Schriftprinzips innerhalb der deutschen Systematischen Theologie der Gegenwart vgl. die Studie von Armin WENZ: Das Wort Gottes – Gericht und Rettung: Untersuchungen zur Autorität der Heiligen Schrift in Bekenntnis und Lehre der Kirche. GÖ 1996, 126-306. Zur Autorität der Schrift in den evangelisch-lutherischen Bekenntnisschriften und im Kirchenkampf vgl. ebd, 15-87. 88-125.

7 Reinhard SLENCZKA: Kirchliche Entscheidung in theologischer Verantwortung: Grundlagen – Kriterien – Grenzen. GÖ 1991, 94.

dem Forum der menschlichen Vernunft, der theoretischen bzw. praktischen Relevanz oder auch der gesellschaftlichen Akzeptanz im neuzeitlichen, modernen bzw. postmodernen Kontext, oder geht es um das Kriterium deren Schriftgemäßheit?[8] Wie man auch immer diese Frage beantworten mag, so besteht doch Konsens: Nicht Luther als Denker vergangener Zeiten, der er für uns nun einmal auch ist, sondern als Zeuge des lebendigen Wortes Jesu Christi kann der heutigen weltweiten Theologie von orientierender Bedeutung sein. Was dabei heute und zu allen Zeiten auf dem Spiel steht, ist nichts anderes als die Einheit des christlichen Bekenntnisses selbst. Diese hermeneutische Grundentscheidung schließt das kritische Eingehen der Theologie vom Standpunkt der Schrift bzw. der Reformation Luthers her auf das Denken der Neuzeit bzw. der Moderne und Postmoderne keineswegs aus, sondern notwendig ein.

Es kann heute nicht um eine Repristination von Luthers Theologie im Sinne einer Wiederherstellung eines früheren geistesgeschichtlichen Zustandes gehen, welcher nicht mehr gegeben ist. Vielmehr geht es darum, sich dem Wahrheitsanspruch von Luthers Lehre zu stellen, der nicht durch distanzierende Historisierung erledigt werden kann, sondern aufgrund des Charakters des Zeugnisses und des Bekenntnisses zeitübergreifend ist. Dies lässt sich anhand prägnanter Sätze *Hans Joachim Iwands* (1888-1960) verdeutlichen:

»Luther ist nicht der Begründer einer christlichen Richtung oder Partei, sondern er ist der Reformator der Kirche. Darum sind seine Lehren kein konfessionelles Sondergut, sondern Gemeingut der Kirche. Es ist sogar so weit gekommen, daß Luther in wesentlichen Lehrstücken heute dem modernen Protestantismus ebenso entgegensteht wie damals dem scholastisch-katholischen Lehrsystem.«»Das meinen wir, wenn wir von Luthers Lehre reden: es ist seine Lehre nicht! Es ist falsch, seine Lehre mit den Besonderheiten seiner Zeit, mit der Entwicklung seiner Person zu erklären, wie es leider immer wieder in unserem psychologistischen Zeitalter geschieht; denn damit wird die Verbindlichkeit seiner Lehre aufgehoben. Es geht um die schlichte Frage von wahr und falsch, um die Frage, ob man mit dieser Lehre selig wird oder verloren geht.«[9]

Die Zweite Größe neben der Neuzeit, die viele, besonders in der Zweidrittelwelt, als für die Rezeption Luthers für entscheidend empfinden, ist die Größe »Kontext«. Dieser Kontext wurde lange Zeit vor allem, aber nicht nur von sog. Befreiungstheologen als Kontext von wirtschaftspolitisch verursachter Verarmung, Auslandsschulden, frühzeitigem Tod, sozialer Ungerechtigkeit, gesellschaftspolitischer Unterdrückung und vielfachen Aktionen und Befreiungsbemühungen vor allem im gesellschaftspolitischen Bereich gekennzeichnet. Wie stark der Kontext eine entscheidende Rolle bei der Frage nach der Lutherrezeption spielt, zeigten im Verlauf des Seminars Berichte aus den verschiedenen Erdteilen. Es war besonders beeindruckend, einiges über Lutherrezeption in Australien unter Menschengruppen wie die Aborigenes zu hören, oder auch über Lutherrezeption in Afrika, Asien und Brasilien.

8 Zur Schriftgemäßheit vgl. Reinhard SLENCZKA: Was heißt und ist schriftgemäß? KD 34 (1988), 304-320; ders.: Kirchliche Entscheidung …, 94-118, bes. 112-115.

9 Hans Joachim IWAND: Glaubensgerechtigkeit nach Luthers Lehre. M 1941, 4. 7 (Vorwort).

Dort tauchen sich durchaus erheblich von denen in Deutschland, Skandinavien oder Nordamerika unterscheidende Fragekomplexe auf. Wenn man auch eine andersartige Fragestellung in diesen Ländern feststellt, so lässt sich doch eine – wenn auch recht bescheidene – Lutherrezeption in den meisten dieser Länder wahrnehmen. Man findet nur eine geringe Zahl von Publikationen »einheimischer« Autoren. Es gibt auch lediglich eine kleine Zahl von Forschungen oder Arbeiten, die publiziert wurden. Von einer intensiven Rezeptionsgeschichte kann in den meisten dieser Länder nicht die Rede sein. Man findet aber immerhin Ansätze dazu.

Ein paradigmatisches Beispiel eines bestimmten Ansatzes der Lutherrezeption in Kontexten der Zweidrittelwelt lässt sich bei der Konferenz lutherischer theologischer Lehrer der Dritten Welt, die 1988 in São Leopoldo, Brasilien, stattfand, wie auch im Rahmen der VIII. Vollversammlung des Lutherischen Weltbundes 1990 in Curitiba, Brasilien, feststellen. In diesen zwei Begegnungen wurde Luthers biblisch-reformatorische Theologie danach befragt, welche Impulse sie für die Bewältigung der lateinamerikanischen Probleme, die als primär sozialpolitisch gelten, geben kann, wobei der Kontext selbst – gemäß dem methodischen Dreischritt »*Sehen – Urteilen – Handeln*« – den Ausgangspunkt bildet, von dem her an die Theologie Luthers herangegangen wird.[10] Es ging um die kontextuelle Relevanz Luthers im Blick auf die konkreten täglichen Kämpfe lateinamerikanischer Menschen ums Überleben.

In diese Richtung plädierte die Mehrheit der Referenten und Teilnehmer der Conferência de Educadores Teológicos Luteranos do Terceiro Mundo, die vom 5. bis 11. September 1988 in der Escola Superior de Teologia in São Leopoldo, RS, versammelt war. Ziel und Thema war die Erarbeitung von Richtlinien für eine »Relektüre der Theologie Luthers in Kontexten aus der Dritten Welt«. Die Teilnehmer, theologische Lehrer aus der Dritten Welt, kamen aus 18 Ländern aus vier Kontinenten. Die Beiträge sind von der Spannung zwischen dem Rückgriff auf die lutherische Theologie und dem für unausweichlich gehaltenen Bezug auf den lateinamerikanischen Kontext gekennzeichnet. Die alle Beiträge durchziehende Grundsorge, von der her allein eine Lutherrezeption heute noch für sinnvoll gehalten wird, ist die nach der Notwendigkeit des Erweises der ökumenischen, sozialen und kulturellen Relevanz Luthers in diesem Kontext.

Gottfried Brakemeier betonte in seinem Grußwort: »Somente se tivermos algo a contribuir em nosso contexto ecumênico, social e cultural, será significativo o esforço por manter uma Igreja minoritária, como o é a Igreja Evangélica de Confissão Luterana no Brasil. Estamos comprometidos a demonstrar, sempre de novo, a relevância da confissão luterana.« Der lutherische Beitrag in diesem Kontext besteht aber nicht so sehr »em tópicos dogmáticos«, sondern in der Betonung von Luthers Denkweise, die bekannt »kritisch« ist, und »feststehende Autoritäten« zu hinterfragen vermag.[11]

10 Vgl. die Ergebnisse der Konferenz theologischer Lehrer der Dritten Welt: Luthers Theologie muss in der Dritten Welt vom Standpunkt der Verpflichtung für die Sache der Armen neu gelesen werden; Releitura da teologia de Lutero em contextos do Terceiro Mundo/ hrsg. von Nelson Kirst. São Leopoldo 1990, 103.

11 Releitura da teologia de Lutero …, 11 f (Saudação).

Unter Heranziehung einer Fülle von Lutherstellen betonte *Albérico Baeske*, dass es weder darum gehe, Luther zu kopieren, noch darum, spezifische Inhalte oder zeitgebundene Handlungsmodelle zu übernehmen, sondern um »confissão – com coração, boca e mãos – atual, concreta, sem igual«. Baeske betont die Notwendigkeit, heute von Luthers Freiheitsverständnis auszugehen, um sich in der Freiheit des Glaubens an Christus für die Probleme des Kontextes zu engagieren.[12]

Naozumi Eto sieht es als eine Aufgabe an, die Zweiregimentenlehre Luthers nicht im Sinne einer Weltflucht oder einer konservativen Haltung zu verstehen. Er insistiert auf einem Ganzheitsverständnis von Heil. Es sei notwendig, die Gnade in Christus mit der sozialen Ethik zu verbinden, wobei der westlich-abendländische Individualismus überwunden werden müsse, um der Dimension der Gemeinschaft, die der Denkweise in der Dritten Welt eher entspricht, mehr Bedeutung einzuräumen.[13]

Aufgrund einer Analyse von Luthers Freiheitstraktat und unter Hervorhebung des von Luther dort zugrunde gelegten *totus–homo–Aspektes* hebt *Ricardo Pietrantonio* Luthers Unterscheidung von Glaube und Liebe hervor und versucht zu zeigen, dass sich der christliche Liebesdienst im lateinamerikanischen Kontext vor allem durch Engagement für die sozialpolitische Befreiung der lateinamerikanischen Völker auszeichne.[14]

Auch *Davasahayam W. Jesudoss*, Direktor des Gurukul Lutheran Theological College & Research Institute in Madras, Indien, der sich mit dem Thema »Rechtfertigung aus Glauben und Mission in einem multikulturellen und multireligiösen Kontext« beschäftigt, betont die Notwendigkeit der Kontextualisierung der Rechtfertigungsbotschaft, die z. B. in Indien meistens auf großes Unverständnis aufseiten der Bevölkerung stößt. Angesichts der Tatsache, dass die Botschaft von der Rechtfertigung in heutiger Zeit zunehmend missverstanden wird – und zwar aufgrund des veränderten Kontextes – plädiert er dafür, dass heute die Heiligung in der Liebe zum zentralen Thema der Theologie erhoben werde: »Assim meu apelo seria este: vamos fazer da *santificação no amor o tema central da teologia*. Afinal, justificação e santificação não se opõe totalmente, mas constituem os dois lados da mesma moeda.« Er plädiert außerdem dafür, dass die Ausbildung nicht elitär gestaltet, sondern den Problemem der mehrheitlich ärmeren Volksschichten zugewandt sein sollte.[15]

Naaman Laiser will zwar von der Botschaft der Rechtfertigung nicht abrücken, wohl aber hebt er unter Berufung auf die IV. Vollversammlung des Lutherischen Weltbundes in Helsinki die Notwendigkeit hervor, sie im Blick auf die heutigen Fragen in die verschiedenen kulturellen und religiösen Kontexte zu übersetzen und in anderer Form zu präsentieren.[16]

Philip Moila, der über das Thema »Reich Gottes und politische Verpflichtung« referierte, hält es für angebracht, in der Drit-

---

12 Releitura da teologia de Lutero ..., 15. 17. 19.

13 Releitura da teologia de Lutero ..., 36-38 (Reação à Baeske).

14 Releitura da teologia de Lutero ..., 41-63 (Libertação).

15 Releitura da teologia de Lutero ..., 75-77 (Justificação) – Hervorhebung von mir.

16 Releitura da teologia de Lutero ..., 81f (Reação à Jesudoss).

ten Welt von einer Auffassung der »Beschaffenheit des Menschen« auszugehen, die diese nicht als Unglaube – Karl Barth (1886-1968), Helmut Thielicke (1908-1986) – Hoffnungslosigkeit und Verlust des historischen Glaubens – Wolfhart Pannenberg (* 1928) –, Rebellion bzw. Entfremdung – Paul Tillich (1886-1965) – oder Chaos, ökologische Unordnung – Charles W. Cobb (1892-1976), Paul F. Knitter (* 1939), sondern als »Unterdrückung, soziale Ungleichheit [und] Gefangenschaft« – Jon Sobrino (* 1938), Johann Baptist Metz (* 1928) – versteht. Aufgrund der condition humaine in der Dritten Welt, die von gesellschaftspolitischer Gefangenschaft und wirtschaftspolitischer Unterdrückung gekennzeichnet ist, müsse die Botschaft vom Reiche Gottes als etwas verkündigt werden, das wesentlich mit der »Befreiung« zu tun hat. Er fordert, dass die Kirche Christi in Lateinamerika eine Option für die Armen treffen solle: »[…] a igreja como serva do reinado de Deus está sob a obrigação de comprometer-se em favor da luta contra a pobreza, em continuidade plena com o testemunho bíblico acerca do empenho em favor dos pobres.« Moila, der Luthers Verständnis vom Reich Gottes in starker Parallelität zur römisch-katholischen Auffassung Leo Boffs (* 1938) deutet, insistiert darauf, dass das Reich als Inbegriff des eschatologischen Heils »implicações de profundo alcance para as estruturas sociais« haben müsse, sodass heute der Orthopraxis der Vorrang vor der Orthodoxie zukomme. Die Kirche ist ein »agente do reinado de Deus« und hat – insofern sie auch eine säkulare Instituition ist – die Aufgabe, im Rahmen des weltlichen Regimentes gegen das Böse zu kämpfen. Das Ziel des Reiches Gottes in der Dritten Welt ist nach Moila die Hinterfragung und die Vernichtung von po-

litischen und ökonomischen Strukturen, die unterdrückerisch sind – »desafiar e destruir as estruturas políticas e econômicas opressivas existentes« –. Persönliches Heil müsse in der Dritten Welt die »participação ativa no reino de Deus« zur Folge haben, mit dem Ziel der »transformação de estruturas sociais malignas«.[17]

Walter Altmann stimmt Moila im Wesentlichen zu, hebt aber hervor, dass die Erhebung des lateinamerikanischen Kontextes, in den Luthers Theologie hineinzuwirken habe, viel intensiver vom Konnex zwischen westlichem Neokolonialismus und lateinamerikanischer Abhängigkeit definiert werden müsse. Luthers Theologie müsse vom Standpunkt eines engagierten Einsatzes für die Befreiung aus gelesen werden, wobei seine Zweiregimentenlehre von Dualismen befreit werden müsse. Luthers dynamische Theologie dürfe nicht in eine statische Theologie verwandelt werden. Altmann hält es heute für eine wesentliche Aufgabe, die weitverbreitete Meinung, Luthers Theologie sei mit der Befreiungstheologie inkompatibel, aus dem Weg zu räumen. Die Vielfältigkeit von Luthers Unterscheidungen im Rahmen seiner Zweiregimentenlehre seien daher von zentraler Bedeutung für die theologische Bestimmung der Aufgabe von Kirche und Christen im Blick auf Veränderungen in der Gesellschaft.[18]

Für eine solche Weise der Lutherrezeption in dem lateinamerikanischen Kontext plädierte vor allem Walter Altmann, einer der wichtigsten Vertreter dessen, was man eine evangelisch-lutherische Befreiungs-

17 Releitura da teologia de Lutero …, 83. 84-86. 85. 87 f. 90. 92 (Reinado).
18 Releitura da teologia de Lutero …, 98-102 (Reação à Moila).

theologie nennen kann. Altmann legte die auf lateinamerikanischem Boden sicherlich umfangreichste Studie über die gesamte Theologie Luthers vor.[19] Altmann bemüht sich um eine kritische Vermittlung zwischen der Theologie Luthers und der Befreiungstheologie. Er erörtert die verschiedenen Themen im Grunde in einem methodischen Dreierschema: Wirklichkeitsanalyse – Darstellung der Theologie Luthers – Herausstellung der Relevanz von Luthers Theologie für die zunächst erhobene kontextuelle Wirklichkeit. Im Anschluss an die IV. Vollversammlung des Lutherischen Weltbundes 1963 in Helsinki kritisiert Altmann eine repristinatorische Rezeption Luthers.[20] Kritisch steht Altmann vor allem jeder ethischen Passivität,[21] einem individualisierenden und spiritualisierenden Rechtfertigungsverständnis[22] und Dualismen im Rahmen der Deutung von Luthers Zweiregimentenlehre gegenüber.[23] Er betont immer wieder die Notwendigkeit des Aktivwerdens von Christen vom Evangelium Christi her.[24] Altmann setzt sich also insgesamt dafür ein, dass Luthers Theolo-

gie heute von der kontextuellen Perspektive der Befreiungstheologie aus rezipiert wird.[25] Er möchte die Rechtfertigung aus Glauben grundsätzlich im Sinne von umfassender Befreiung verstehen.[26]

Dies waren also Beispiele, wie die Ansätze zur Lutherrezeption in jüngerer Zeit in Kontexten der sog. Zweidrittelwelt, v. a. in Lateinamerika, ausgesehen hat.

Die Sorgen, welche die meisten Teilnehmer dieses Seminars im Blick auf die heutige Lutherrezeption bewegten, kreisten um die Herausforderungen, die mit dem multimedialen postmodernen Denken gegeben sind. Einerseits wird überall die Relevanzkrise lutherischer Theologie festgestellt. Andererseits besteht ein durchgehender Konsens darüber, dass es um ein reiches Erbe geht und dass es sich lohnt, sich den neuen Herausforderungen auszusetzen und darauf kritisch einzugehen. Die Frage – über die auch kein Konsens besteht – ist die, welches Kriterium bei der Lutherrezeption vorzuziehen ist: das Kriterium der Schriftgemäßheit dem der Kontextgemäßheit bzw. der Kontextrelevanz oder umgekehrt.

Ein letzter Aspekt ergab sich bei Berichten von Lutherforschern aus Afrika, Asien und Südamerika. Es fiel besonders auf, dass das, was für Europäer, Nordamerikaner und Skandinavier geradezu selbstverständlich ist, für sie ein Problem darstellt: der Zugang zu Luther in den jeweiligen Muttersprachen. Obwohl es bereits seit mehr als 180 Jahren eine Evangelisch-lutherische Kirche in Brasilien gibt, begann man erst seit Ende der 80er Jahren des 20. Jahrhunderts mit der Vorbereitung, eine umfangreichere Luther-

19 Walter ALTMANN: Lutero e libertação: releitura de Lutero em perspectiva latino-americana. São Paulo 1994.
20 Altmann: Lutero e libertação, 32. 40. 256. 283 f.
21 Altmann: Lutero e libertação, 69 f. 87 f. 112. 150. 233; zur Berufung auf Helsinki vgl. z. B. 283.
22 Altmann: Lutero e libertação, 87 f.
23 Altmann: Lutero e libertação, 160 f..
24 Vgl. z. B. Altmann: Lutero e libertação, 180: »Em última análise, as pessoas cristãs e as igrejas não vivem do resultado de sua ação, mas do evangelho gratuito de Jesus Cristo. Isso lhes dá (ou poderia dar) uma particular liberdade para a ação.«

25 Vgl. dazu v. a. die Überlegungen Altmann: Lutero e libertação, 281 f.
26 Altmann: Lutero e libertação, 289.

ausgabe in Portuguiesisch herauszubringen. Bis dahin beschränkte sich die Produktion auf das Übersetzen einiger wenige zentrale Texte – z. B. des Großen und Kleinen Katechismus und der Freiheitsschrift. Das Nichtvorhandensein von Luthers Werken in der jeweiligen »einheimischen« Sprache wird noch akuter in Afrika und Asien und bedeutet faktisch, dass nur eine sehr geringe Zahl von Personen wirklich Zugang zu Luther hat. Normalerweise beschränkt sich dies auf diejenigen – immer weniger werdende –, die noch Deutsch können oder auf diejenigen, welche die Möglichkeit haben, in Deutschland, Skandinavien oder Nordamerika zu studieren. Wenn daher die Lutherrezeption weltweit auch in Zukunft gefördert werden soll, müssen nach wie vor die Überseztungen seiner Werke in den jeweiligen einheimischen Sprachen intensiviert werden. Ohne einem umfassendern Zugang zu Luther – nicht nur in den Ausgaben in den ursprünglichen Sprachen Deutsch und Latein!, die selbstverständlich in den Bibliotheken weltweit vorhanden sein sollten –, sondern auch in den einheimischen Sprachen, bleibt eine »weltweite Lutherrezeption« auf ein Minimum beschränkt und den neuen Generationen von Theologen, Theologiestudenten und Pfarrern letzten Endes unzugänglich. Diese Tatsache erweist sich gerade als sehr schwierig bei der Bildung einer starken und soliden lutherischen Identität in den Kirchen der Diaspora. Inclusive erkärt sich daraus, dass auch in den Ländern, in denen die Säkularisierung noch nicht so intensiv in ihren sozial-gesellschaftlichen Folgen zu sein scheint, wie in Europa, von einer intensiven Auflösung des lutherischen Erbes zu reden ist. Besser, in manchen Fällen kam es bis heute überhaupt noch nicht zur Bildung eines richtigen lutherischen Denkens. Es fand demensprechend schlichtweg kaum eine Lutherrezeption statt. Wo hingegen Luthers Werke in den Sprachen der (Diaspora)länder – wenn auch spät – herausgegeben werden, wie z. B. in Brasilien, stellt sich – freilich auch erst langsam – ein erneutes, vertieftes und intensiveres Interesse an Luther auch vonseiten der jüngeren Generation ein. Die Existenz von Luthers Werken in Portuguiesisch wurde z. B. feierlich begrüßt im Rahmen der Foschung und auch vonseiten von Pfarrern und Theologiestudenten. Nach 180 Jahren Lutherischer Kirche in Brasilien begann Luther ganz neu entdeckt zu werden. In den theologischen Fakultäten entstehen nun langsam Untersuchungen und Forschungen über bestimmte Themen lutherischer Theologie. Auch und gerade die elementaren Sachverhalte werden oft mit Begeisterung entdeckt. Und dies gibt Hoffnung im Blick auf die weltweite zukünftige Lutherrezeption.

Canoas/RS, Universidade Luterana do Brasil, University chapel (Foto: Arnim Kohnle)

Die Teilnehmenden des Elften Internationalen Kongresses für Lutherforschung in Canoas/RS 2007

Soweit es in Erfahrung gebracht werden konnte, sind Anstellungen, Titel, Post- und E-Mail-Adressen aktualisiert worden.

Pastor Michael J. ALBRECHT, Saint James Lutheran Church, 453 W. Annapolis Street, St Paul, MN 55118 USA; malbrecht@saintjameslutheran.com

Associate professor Dr. Knut ALFSVÅG, School of Mission and Theology – Department of Historical and Systematic Theology, Misjonsveien 34, N-4024 Stavanger, Norway; knut.alfsvaag@mhs.no

Professor Dr. Kaarlo ARFFMAN, University of Helsinki – Faculty of Theology – Department of Church History, Aleksanterinkatu 7, P. O. Box 33, FIN-00014 Helsinki, Finland; kaarlo.arffman@helsinki.fi

Bischof Dr. Carl Axel AURELIUS, Diocese of Gothenburg – Church of Sweden, Postbox 11937, SE-404 39 Göteborg, Sweden; carlaxel.aurelius@svenskakyrkan.se

Professor Dr. Hans-Martin BARTH, Philipps-Universität Marburg – Fachbereich Evangelische Theologie, Auf dem Schaumrück 31, D-35041 Marburg, Germany; barthh-m@staff.uni-marburg.de

Professor Dr. Lubomir BATKA, Comenius University – Evangelical Theological Faculty – Department of Systematic Theology, Bartokova 8, SK-81102 Bratislava, Slovakia; batka@fevth.uniba.sk

Professor Dr. Nestor Luiz João BECK, Universidade Luterana do Brasil (ULBRA), Avenida Farroupilha 8001 – Bairro São José, BR-92425-900 Canoas/RS, Brasil; beck@ulbra.br

Pastor Rui Leopoldo BERNHARD, Igreja Evangélica de Confissão Luterana do Brasil (IECLB), Rua Zamenhof 117 – ap. 201, BR-90550-090 Porto Alegre/RS, Brasil; rbernhard@uol.com.br

Dr. Daniel BEROS, Evangelische Kirche am La Plata (IERP), Culpina 159, 3 D – Ciudad de Buenos Aires, 1406, Argentina; dani-caro@web.de

Akademischer Mitarbeiter Dr. Michael BEYER, Universität Leipzig – Theologische Fakultät – Institut für Kirchengeschichte, Schönbach, Kirchweg 14, D-04668 Großbothen, Germany; michaelbeyer@t-online.de

Reverend Diane BOWERS, Graduate Theological Union, 2908 Florence Street, Berkeley, CA 94705-2004 USA; dvbphd@sbcglobal.net

Professor Dr. Gottfried BRAKEMEIER, Rua José Neumann Filho 120, Caixa Postal 110, BR-95150-000 Nova Petrópolis/RS, Brasil; gbrakemeier@gmx.net

Assistant Professor Dr. Christopher Boyd BROWN, Boston University – School of Theology, 745 Commonwealth Avenue, Boston, MA 02215 USA; cbbrown@bu.edu

Professor Dr. Pierre Bühler, Universität Zürich – Institut für Hermeneutik und Religions-philosophie, Kirchgasse 9, CH-8001 Zürich; Pierre.Buehler@access.uzh.ch

Professor Dr. Christoph Burger, Vrije Universiteit – Faculteit der Godgeelerdheid, De Boele-laan 1105, 14 A 36, NL-1081 HV Amsterdam, The Netherlands; CPM.Burger@th.vu.nl

Dr. Amy Nelson Burnett, University of Nebraska – Department of History, 626 Oldfather Hall, P. O.. Box 880327, Lincoln, NE 68588-0327 USA; aburnett1@unl.edu

Dr. Albert Collver, The Lutheran Church – Missouri Synod (LCMS) – World Relief and Human Care, 1333 South Kirkwood Road, St. Louis, MO 63122-7295 USA; albert.collver@lcms.org

Pfarrer Dr. Silfredo Dalferth, Igreja Evangélica de Confissão Luterana do Brasil (IECLB) / Evangelische Landeskirche in Württemberg – Referent bei Dienst für Mission, Ökumene und Entwicklung (DIMOE), Römerstraße 19, D-72805 Lichtenstein, Germany; shdalferth@t-online.de

Dr. Theodor Dieter, Institute for Ecumenical Research, 8 rue Gustave Klotz, F-67000 Stras-bourg, France; t.dieter@ecumenical-institute.org

Professor Dr. Irene Dingel, Institut für Europäische Geschichte, Alte Universitätstraße 19, D-55116 Mainz, Germany; dingel@ieg-mainz.de

Dr. Timothy Dost, Concordia Seminary, 801 Seminary Place, St Louis, MO 63105 USA; tpdost@msn.com

Pastor Darci Drehmer, Igreja Evangélica de Confissão Luterana do Brasil (IECLB) – Escola Superior de Teologia, Caixa Postal 14, BR-93001-970 São Leopoldo/RS, Brasil; darcid@sinos.net

Professor Dr. Jin-Seop Eom, Luther University/Seminary, Sanggal-dong 17, Gihengu-gu, Youngin-si, Kyunggi-do 446-700, Republic of Korea; js_eom@hotmail.com

Professor Emeritus Svante Bernhard Erling, 1412 S Washington avenue, St. Peter, MN 56082-1527 USA; erling@gac.edu

Professor Dr. Robert Guy Erwin, California Lutheran University – Department of Religion, 60 W Olsen Road 3900, Thousand Oaks, CA 91360 USA; erwin@clunet.edu

Professor Emeritus Dr. James Estes, University of Toronto, Victoria College, 73 Queen's Park Crescent, Toronto, Ontario M5S 1K7, Canada; james.estes@utoronto.ca

Dr. Joachim Fischer, Igreja Evangélica de Confissão Luterana do Brasil (IECLB), Rua São Paulo, 605/202, São Leopoldo/RS, Brasil († 5. Juli 2008)

Assesoria Mag. Douglas Moacir Flor, Universidade Luterana do Brasil (ULBRA) – Comuni-cação Social, Avenida Farroupilha 8001, BR-92425-900 Canoas/RS, Brasil; comunicacao@ulbra.br

Professor Dr. Günter Frank, Melanchthonhaus Bretten, Melanchthonstraße 1, D-75015 Bretten, Germany; info@melanchthon.com

Professor Dr. Robert Carl Fr. von Friedeburg, Erasmus Universiteit Rotterdam – Faculteit der Historische en Kunstwetenschappen, Burg. Oudlaan 50, L-Gebouw, Postbus 1738, NL-3000 DR Rotterdam, The Netherlands; vonfriedeburg@fhk.eur.nl

Dr. h. c. Johannes Hermann GEDRAT, Universidade Luterana do Brasil (ULBRA), Avenida Farroupilha, 8001 – Bairro São José – Canoas/RS, Brasil; gedrat@ulbra.br

Professor Dr. Hans-Peter GROSSHANS, Universität Münster – Evangelisch-Theologische Fakultät – Seminar für Systematische Theologie, Österbergstraße 4, D-72074 Tübingen, Germany; grosshans@uni-muenster.de

Associate Professor Dr. Mary Jane HAEMIG, Luther Seminary, 2481 Como Avenue, St. Paul, MN 55108 USA; mhaemig@luthersem.edu

Mr. Joar HAGA, Menighetsfakultet Norwegian School of Theology, P. O. Box 5144 Majorstuen, N-0302 Oslo, Norway; joar.haga@mf.no

Harold Ashely HALL, Fordham University – Department of Theology, The Bronx, NY 10458, USA, haroldashleyhall@gmail.com

Pfarrer Albrecht HEIM, Alleenstraße 10, D-72622 Nürtingen; Albrecht.Heim@gmx.net

Professor Dr. Leopoldo HEIMANN, Universidade Luterana do Brasil (ULBRA), Avenida Farroupilha 8001, Predio 11, sala 24 , BR-92420-280 Canoas/RS, Brasil; dirteologia@ulbra.br

Dr. Markus HEIN, Universität Leipzig – Theologische Fakultät – Institut für Kirchengeschichte, Körnerstraße 10, D-04107 Leipzig, Germany; hein@uni-leipzig.de

Professor Simo HEININEN, University of Helsinki – Faculty of Theology – Department of Church History, Aleksanterinkatu 7, PO Box 33, FIN-00014 Helsinki, Finland; simo.heininen@helsinki.fi

Professor Emeritus Scott H. HENDRIX, Princeton Theological Seminary, 1196 Fearrington Post, Pittsboro, NC 27312 USA; scott.hendrix@ptsem.edu

Professor Dr. Paul R. HINLICKY, Roanoke College, 221 College Lane, Salem, VA 24153 USA, hinlicky@roanoke.edu

Privatdozent Dr. Vesa HIRVONEN, University of Helsinki – Faculty of Theology – Department of Systematic Theology, P.O. Box 33, FIN-00014 Helsinki, Finland; vehirvon@mappi.helsinki.fi

Associate Professor PhD Bo Kristian HOLM, University of Aarhus – Faculty of Theology – Department of Systematic Theology, Taasingegade 3, DK-8000 Aarhus C, Denmark; bh@teo.au.dk

Professor Dr. Jeffrey JAYNES, Methodist Theological School in Ohio – Warner Chair of Church History, 3081 Columbus Pike, P. O.. Box 1204, Dellaware, OH 43015 USA; jjaynes@mtso.edu

Professor Dr. Gordon JENSEN, Lutheran Theological Seminary Saskatoon, 114 Seminary Crescent, Saskatoon, SK S7N 0X3, Canada; gordon.jensen@usask.ca

Professor Dr. Oddvar Johan JENSEN, Norsk Lærerakademi, Krokåsvegen 24, N-5300 Kleppestø, Norway; ojj@nla.no

Senior Research Fellow Dr. Roger JENSEN, University of Oslo – Faculty of Theology – Department of Systematic Theology, Postboks 1023 Blindernvn 9, N-0315 Oslo, Norway; roger.jensen@teologi.uio.no

Associate Professor Dr. Ken JONES, Grand View University – Department of Philosophy &

Department of Religion, 1200 Grand View Avenue, Des Moines, IA 50316 USA, kjones@grandview.edu

Research Associate Professor Dr. Ninna Jørgensen, University of Copenhagen – Faculty of Theology – Department of Church History, Købmagergade 44-46, DK-1150 København K, Denmark; nj@teol.ku.dk

Dr. Sammeli Juntunen, University of Helsinki – Faculty of Theology – Department of Systematic Theology, Aleksanterinkatu 7, P. O. Box 33, FIN-00014 Helsinki, Finland; sammeli.juntunen@helsinki.fi

Pastor Postgraduate Student Ilmari Karimies, Diocese of Helsinki, Leskirouva Freytagin Kuja 15 B 15, FIN-00790 Helsinki, Finland; ilmari.karimies@helsinki.fi

Professor Dr. Igor Kišš, Palisády 46, CSFR-811 06 Bratislava, Slovakia; prof.kiss@abela.sk

Professor Dr. Steffen Kjeldgaard-Pedersen, University of Copenhagen – Faculty of Theology – Department of Church History, Købmagergade 44-46, DK-1150 København K, Denmark; skp@teol.ku.dk

Professor Dr. Armin Kohnle, Universität Leipzig – Theologische Fakultät – Institut für Kirchengeschichte, Otto-Schill-Straße 2, D-04109 Leipzig, Germany; kohnle@rz.uni-leipzig.de

Researcher Jussi Koivisto, University of Helsinki – Faculty of Theology – Department of Systematic Theology, Aleksanterinkatu 7, P. O. Box 33, FIN-00014 Helsinki, Finland; jussi.koivisto@helsinki.fi

Vice-Reitor Dr. Valter Kuchenbecker, Universidade Luterana do Brasil (ULBRA), Avenida Farroupilha 8001, BR-92425-900 Canoas/RS, Brasil; valterk@ulbra.br

Doctoral student Annika Laats, University of Helsinki – Faculty of Theology – Department of Systematic Theology, Männiku tee 85 A-1, EST-11213 Tallinn, Estonia; annika.laats@eelk.ee

Professor Dr. Volker Leppin, Universität Jena –Theologische Fakultät – Kirchengeschichte, Fürstengraben 6, D-07743 Jena, Germany; volker.leppin@uni-jena.de

Diretor Mag. Gerson Linden, Seminário Concórdia – Igreja Evangélica Luterana do Brasil (IELB), Avenida Getúlio Vargas 4388, BR-93025-000 São Leopoldo/RS, Brasil; linden@ulbranet.com.br

Professor Dr. David Lumpp, Concordia University St. Paul – Religion & Theology, 275 North Syndicate, St. Paul, MN 55104 USA; lumpp@csp.edu

Rony Ricardo Marquardt, Igreja Evangélica Luterana do Brasil (IELB), Avenida Cel. Lucas de Oliveira 894 – Bairro Mont´Serrat, BR-90440-010 Porto Alegre/RS, Brasil; rony@ielb.org.br

Assistent Professor Dr. Naomichi Masaki, Concordia Theological Seminary – Systematic Theology, 6600 North Clinton, Fort Wayne, IN 46825 USA; masakin@ctsfw.edu

Professor Mark Mattes, Grand View University – Department of Philosophy, 1200 Grandview Avenue, Des Moines, IA 50316-1599 USA; mmattes@grandview.edu

Professor Dr. Ute MENNECKE, Universität Bonn – Evangelisch-Theologisches Fakultät – Abteilung für Kirchengeschichte – Kirchengeschichte der Reformation und der Neuzeit, An der Schlosskirche 2-4, D-53113 Bonn, Germany; ute.mennecke@freenet.de

Pfarrer Dr. Matthias MIKOTEIT, Evangelische Kirche von Westfalen, Blaufärberweg 10, D-46325 Borken, Germany; Matthias.Mikoteit@t-online.de

Dr. Marius MJAALAND, University of Oslo, Postboks 1023 Blindern, N-0315 Oslo, Norway; m.g.t.mjaaland@teologi.uio.no

Professor Dr. Viggo MORTENSEN, University of Aarhus – Faculty of Theology – Department of Systematic Theology, Taasingegade 3, DK-8000 Århus C, Denmark; vm@teo.au.dk

Jonathan MUMME, Schildhornstraße 68, D-12163 Berlin; jonathanmumme@hotmail.com

Professor Emeritus Dr. James A. NESTINGEN, Luther Seminary, 2481 Como Ave W, St. Paul, MN 55108 USA; jnesting@luthersem.edu

Reverend Dr. Theol. Kjell Ove NILSSON, Bredgatan 9 E, SE-22221 Lund, Sweden; kjellovenilsson@hotmail.com

Professor Dr. Jeannine OLSON, Rhode Island College – Faculty of Arts and Sciences – History Department, 88 Arbor Drive, Providence, RI 02908 USA; jolson@ric.edu

Ph. D. student & VDM Pernilla PARENMALM, Uppsala University – Faculty of Theology – Studies in Faith and Ideologies – Ethics, Odensgatan 13, SE-75114 Uppsala, Sweden; Pernilla.Parenmalm@teol.uu.se

Pastor Professor Dr. Andreas PAWLAS, Nordelbische Evangelisch-Lutherische Kirche – Kirchengemeinde Barmstedt, Chemnitzstraße 28, D-25355 Barmstedt, Germany; andreas.pawlas@web.de

Bishop Dr. Simo PEURA, University of Helsinki – Faculty of Theology – Department of Systematic Theology, Piispank. 2 A 2, FIN-62100 Lapua, Finland, simo.peura@evl.fi

Assistant Professor John T. PLESS, M. Div., Concordia Theological Seminary, 6600 N. Clinton Street, Fort Wayne, IN 46825 USA; plessjt@ctsfw.edu

Professor Mag. Clóvis Jair PRUNZEL, Seminário Concórdia – Igreja Evangelica Luterana do Brasil (IELB), Avenida Getúlio Vargas 4388, BR-93025-000 São Leopoldo/RS, Brasil; prunzel@ulbranet.com.br

Professor Dr. Antti RAUNIO, University of Helsinki – Faculty of Theology – Department of Systematic Theology, Alesanterinkatu 7, P. O. Box 33, FIN-00014 Helsinki, Finland; araunio@mappi.helsinki.fi

Ph. D. student Tine RAVNSTED-LARSEN REEH, University of Copenhagen – Faculty of Theology – Department of Church History, Købmagergade 44-46, DK-1150 København K, Denmark; trr@teol.ku.dk

Professor Dr. Austra REINIS, Missouri State University – Department of Religious Studies, BR-901 South National Avenue, Springfield, MO 65897 USA; austra.reinis@missouri-state.edu

Rare Book Cataloger Dr. Louis J. REITH, Georgetown University Library, P. O. Box 571174, Washington, DC 20057-1174 USA; reithl@georgetown.edu

Direktor Dr. Stefan RHEIN, Stiftung Luthergedenkstätten in Sachsen-Anhalt, D-06886 Lutherstadt Wittenberg, Germany; ilona.kunze@martinluther.de

Dr. Susan RICHTER, Universität Heidelberg – Historisches Seminar, Grabengasse 3-5, D-69117 Heidelberg, Germany; susan.richter@zegk.uni-heidelberg.de

Professor Dr. Ricardo Willy RIETH, Igreja Evangélica de Confissão Luterana do Brasil (IECLB) – Escola Superior de Teologia / Universidade Luterana do Brasil (ULBRA), Amadeo Rossi 476, BR-93001-970 São Leopoldo/RS, Brasil; ricardo.rieth@ulbra.br

Rev. Dr. William RUSSELL, Strayer University, 3355 Northeast Expressway, Suite 100, Atlanta, GA 30341 USA; russellwllm@aol.com

Professor Dr. Risto SAARINEN, University of Helsinki – Faculty of Theology – Department of Systematic Theology, P. O. Boks 33, FIN-00014 Helsinki, Finland; risto.saarinen@helsinki.fi

Pastor Basil SCHILD, Finke River Mission –Lutheran Church of Australia, 29 Mallam Crescent, Alice Springs 0870, Australia; basil.schild@lca.org.au

Professor Dr. Dr. Johannes SCHILLING, Universität Kiel – Theologische Fakultät – Institut für Kirchengeschichte, Leibnizstraße 4, D-24118 Kiel, Germany, jschilling@kg.uni-kiel.de

Professor Dr. Claus SCHWAMBACH, Faculdade Luterana de Teologia (FLT), Rua Walli Malschitzky 164 – Mato Preto, 89290-000 São Bento do Sul/SC, Brasil; diretoria@flt.edu.br

Assistent Professor Paulo SEIFERT, MPhil, Universidade Luterana do Brasil (ULBRA) – Pro-Reitoria de Graduação, Avenida Farroupilha 8001, Prédio 11, sala 229, BR-92450-900 Canoas/RS, Brasil; logos@ulbra.br

Bishop Dr. Tomas SHIVUTE, Evangelical Lutheran Church in Namibia, Onipa, PvT Bag 2018 – Ondangwa, Namíbia; westdio@mweb.com.na / gen.sec@elcin.org.na

Rev. Dr. Jeffrey SILCOCK, Australian Lutheran College, 104 Jeffcott Street, SA-5006 North Adelaide, Australia; silcock.jeffrey@alc.edu.au

Professor Dr. Jane STROHL, Pacific Lutheran Theological Seminary – Reformation History and Theology, 2770 Marin Avenue, Berkeley, CA 94708 USA; amycher@comcast.net / jstrohl@plts.edu

Pastor Eric J. SWENSSON, Holy Trinity, Evangelical Lutheran Church of America (ELCA), 30 Lockwood Avenue, New Rochelle, NY 10801 USA; ericswe@regent.edu; ejswensson@gmail.com

Ph. D. student Lars Christian VANGSLEV, University of Copenhagen – Faculty of Theology – Department of Church History, Købmagergade 44-46, DK-1150 København K, Denmark; lva@teol.ku.dk

Assistant Professor Ph. D. Anna VIND, University of Copenhagen – Faculty of Theology – Department of Church History, Købmagergade 44-46, DK-1150 København K, Denmark, av@teol.ku.dk

Prof. Dr. Wilhelm Wachholz, Igreja Evangélica de Confissão Luterana do Brasil (IECLB) – Escola Superior de Teologia, Martin Lutero 274, BR-93030-120 São Leopoldo/RS, Brasil; wwachholz@est.com.br

Dozent STM Paulo Proske Weirich, Seminário Concórdia – Praktische Theologie, Avenida Getúlio Vargas 4388, BR-93025-000 São Leopoldo/RS, Brasil; weirich@ulbranet.com.br

Professor Dr. Timothy Wengert, Lutheran Theological Seminary at Philadelphia – History of Christianity, 7301 Germantown Avenue, Philadelphia, PA 19119-1794 USA; Twengert@ltsp.edu

Pfarrer Dr. theol. Jens Wolff, Martin-Luther-Universität Halle-Wittenberg – Fachbereich Sprach- und Literaturwissenschaften – Germanistisches Institut, D-06099 Halle/Saale, Germany; jenswolff@aol.com; jenswolff@germanistik.uni-halle.de

Professor Dr. Klaas Zwanepol, University of Utrecht (ELS), Leeuwerikstraat 78, NL-3853 AE Ermelo, The Netherlands; kzwanepol@hetnet.nl

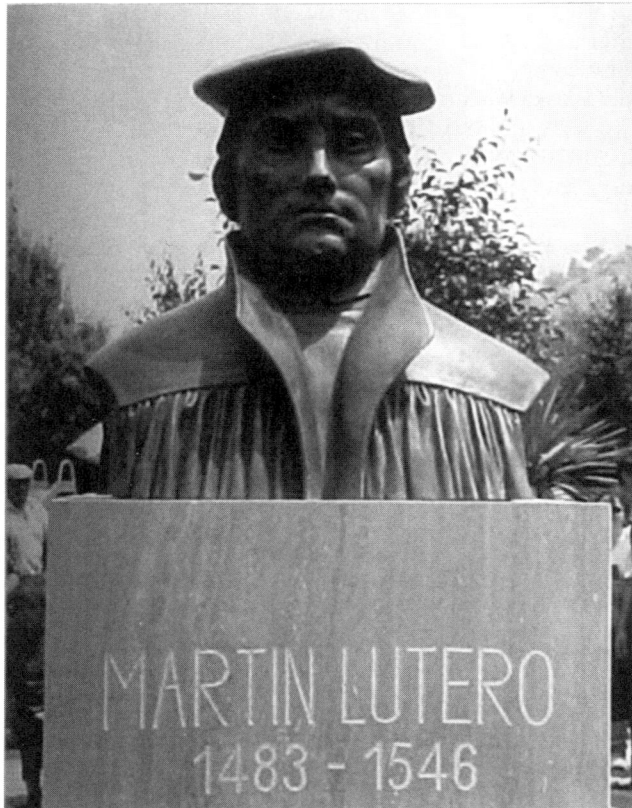

Serena Piacentini: Lutherbüste, Bronze, circa 95 cm auf Marmorsockel circa 155 cm hoch
Inschrift: Martin Luthero / 1483-1546 / sola gratia y sola fide – solus christus – sola scriptura
Santiago de Chile, eingeweiht am 31. Oktober 2002
Das von Pfingstlern und beiden lutherischen Kirchen in Chile errichtete erste
Lutherdenkmal in Lateinamerika wurde unter großer Beteiligung der Öffentlichkeit
eingeweiht. Es steht im Stadtteil Huechuraba, der zu den ärmsten gehört und in dem
relativ viele Evangelische wohnen, auf der umbenannten »Plaza de la Reforma«.
Die Einweihungsfeier war nicht nur ein ökumenisches – neben Pfingstlern und Lutheranern
beteiligten sich die Antiochenisch-orthodoxe und die Römisch-katholische Kirche sowie
die Heilsarmee –, sondern auch ein gesellschaftliches Ereignis, auf dem sowohl die
Bürgermeisterin als auch ein Minister das Wort ergriffen. Sie deuteten das Denkmal
als Zeichen für friedliches Zusammenleben, für Gleichheit und Freiheit in Chile.
(Lutherstadt Wittenberg, Lutherhaus – Martin-Luther-Bund)

Buchbesprechungen

AUSTRA REINIS: Reforming the art of dying: the ars moriendi in the German Reformation (1519-1528). Aldershot, Hampshire; Berlington, VT: Ashgate, 2007. VI, 290 S. (St. Andrews studies in Reformation history)

Diese Veröffentlichung enthält die überarbeitete Dissertation, die 2003 am Princeton Theological Seminary angenommen wurde und für welche die Autorin 2000/01 in Wittenberg als Martin-Luther-Stipendiatin ihre Forschung betrieben hat. Infolge sorgfältiger Textanalysen eines überschaubaren Quellenmaterials bietet sie detaillierte Ergebnisse.

Anhand spätmittelalterlicher Schriften der ars moriendi arbeitet die Vfn. heraus, dass deren Vorbereitung auf den Tod vor allem Gottes Gericht vor Augen hatte. Der Sterbende wurde ermahnt, seine Todsünden vollständig zu bekennen und das zu leisten, wozu er in der Lage ist, um ein barmherziges Urteil zu erlangen. Allerdings gab es zwischen den einzelnen Schriften Unterschiede. Während manche Autoren, welche die weniger Frommen im Auge hatten, darauf drängten, sich mit allen Mitteln auf die Vergebung durch das Sakrament vorzubereiten, dachten andere an diejenigen, die angesichts von Gottes Gericht ängstlich und verzweifelt waren, und versuchten, ihre Skrupel, nicht genügend zum Empfang des Sakramentes getan zu haben, zu mindern. Trotz dieser Unterschiede hatten die spätmittelalterlichen Schriften eins gemeinsam: Sie bezeugten keine Heilsgewissheit, sondern waren darauf aus, den Sterbenden zu guten Werken zu aktivieren.

Als Quellen für die Darstellung der reformatorischen Vorbereitung auf das Sterben dienen 16 Schriften, die zwischen 1519 und 1528 entstanden sind. Luthers »Ein Sermon von der Bereitung zum Sterben« steht als erste reformatorische Schrift der ars moriendi am Anfang. Da mit dem Erscheinen von Luthers Katechismen 1529 ein neuer Abschnitt in der Sterbeliteratur begann, wurde die Entwicklung begründet nur bis 1528 untersucht.

Die Vfn. verfolgt den großen Einfluss von Luthers Sterbebüchlein auf andere Autoren, die darüber hinaus Ausführungen Luthers auch aus dessen späteren Schriften übernahmen, so den Hinweis des Sterbenden auf seine Taufe. Neben Luther wurden auch andere Reformatoren berücksichtigt. So griff Johannes Oekolampad (1482-1531) besonders auf Ulrich Zwingli (1484-1531) zurück. Die Vfn. stellt heraus, dass die Sterbebücher für die Verbreitung der reformatorischen Botschaft von der Rechtfertigung durch den Glauben und von der Heilsgewissheit weit über den akademischen Raum hinaus eine große Bedeutung hatten. Sie benennt die jeweiligen Adressaten der Sterbebücher. Es waren hervorragende Persönlichkeiten, in einem Fall die Kleriker, vor allem aber Laien, die Hilfe zur Sterbebegleitung erhalten sollten. Zwei Sterbebücher enthalten vorausgegangene Predigten. Der

Inhalt der Sterbebücher zielte also nicht nur auf eine Begleitung in den Letzten Stunden, sondern auch auf eine allgemeine Vorbereitung auf das Lebensende überhaupt. Das große Interesse an dieser Literatur lässt sich daran erkennen, dass Luthers Sterbebüchlein von 1519 bis 1528 in 25 Auflagen erschien. Außerdem fand es als Bestandteil von Luthers Betbüchlein weite Verbreitung.

Bei der Analyse der Schriften achtet die Vfn. auf deren rhetorischen Aufbau und die Verwendung rhetorischer Ausdrucksmittel. Sie benennt aber nicht nur die rhetorische Form, sondern beschreibt vor allem die Absicht, welche die Autoren mit deren Verwendung verfolgten. Dadurch wird herausgestellt, woran die Autoren ein besonderes Interesse hatten, was sie dem Leser einprägen wollten. Aber nicht nur das. Es wird dadurch auch deutlich, wo sie belehren und wo sie »bewegen«, Emotionen bewirken wollten.

Die Vfn. achtet auch darauf, welche Elemente aus der spätmittelalterlichen Sterbeliteratur aufgenommen, ausgeschieden oder umgewandelt wurden. Vor allem aber weist sie auf den Bruch zwischen dem Spätmittelalter, in dem der Wille des Sterbenden angesprochen wurde und Heilsungewissheit blieb, und der Reformation hin, die den Sterbenden auf das Heilswerk Christi verwies, der Tod, Sünde und Hölle besiegt hat, und eine darauf gegründete Heilsgewissheit vermittelte. Es kam nicht mehr darauf an, sich auf die Sakramente – 1519 zählt Luther noch Beichte, Letzte Ölung und Abendmahl auf – richtig vorbereiten zu wollen, um Vergebung zu erlangen, sondern darauf, sie als Zeichen dafür zu verstehen, dass Christus Tod, Sünde und Hölle besiegt hat. Die tröstende Seelsorge am Totenbett gründete nun auf den Glauben an die Verheißungen der Sakramente und brachte damit eine grundlegend Veränderung.

Die große Bedeutung der reformatorischen Sterbekunst verdeutlicht die Vfn., indem sie den spätmittelalterlichen und den evangelischen Totenkult gegenüberstellt. Sie hebt den grundlegenden Unterschied zwischen beiden hervor: Nachdem die Christen durch ihren Glauben gerechtfertigt wurden und ihres Heils gewiss waren, bedurfte es keiner Handlungen mehr, um Seelen von einem zornigen Gott zu erlösen. Messen zugunsten Verstorbener hörten auf. Führte das zu einer Trennung der Lebenden von den Toten, wie behauptet wurde? Die Vfn. unterscheidet in ihrer Antwort zwischen religiösen und sozialen Pflichten. Die religiösen Verpflichtungen für Verstorbene hörten auf, die Trauerfeier richtete sich vor allem auf die Hinterbliebenen aus. Es entstand aber eine soziale Verpflichtung zur Totenehrung. Luther und Melanchthon sorgten 1525 für eine feierliche Ausgestaltung der Bestattung Friedrich des Weisen. Die zunehmende Totenehrung fand ihren Ausdruck in Leichenpredigten, die neben der Verkündigung des Evangeliums auch einen Lebenslauf des Verstorbenen enthielten und zum Teil gedruckt wurden, sowie in Grabmalen. Die Beziehung zwischen den Lebenden und den Verstorbenen besteht nun in der Bewahrung der Erinnerung.

Helmar Junghans   Leipzig

HEIMO REINITZER: Gesetz und Evangelium: über ein reformatorisches Bildthema, seine Tradition, Funktion und Wirkungsgeschichte. 2 Bde. HH: Christians, 2006. 535 S.: Ill.; 415 S.: Ill.

Dieses Werk untersucht die Darstellungen des Themas »Gesetz und Evangelium« auf Gemälden, Retabeln, Kanzeln, Wänden, Epitaphien, Grafiken, Bucheinbänden, Titelblättern sowie in Büchern, auf Glasfenstern, Kabinettscheiben, Tellern, Krügen, Wandteppichen, Truhen, Ofenplatten und an Kaminen von Anbeginn bis in das 18. Jahrhundert und führt noch Nachwirkungen bis 1905 an. Sie werden auch mit »Gesetz und Gnade« oder »Sündenfall und Erlösung« oder »Die Rechtfertigung des Sünders allein aus dem Glauben« bezeichnet. Der Cranachforscher Dieter Koepplin hat die schwerfällige Bezeichnung »Die Rechtfertigung des Sünders vor dem Gesetz durch die Gnade Gottes und den Glauben« eingeführt, der Vf. die prägnante »Gesetz und Evangelium« vorgezogen und bei den jeweiligen Darstellungen die überlieferten Benennungen beibehalten.

Das Werk hat drei Teile: Die ikonografische *Einleitung* verfolgt Entstehung und Entwicklung der Darstellung »Gesetz und Evangelium« im 16. Jahrhundert (I, 11-137). Der *Katalog* erfasst alphabetisch nach Fundorten geordnet 860 Objekte, von manchen unter einer Nummer mehrere Auflagen (I, 143-491). Band 2 enthält über 285 *Abbildungen*.

In einem Kapitel wendet sich der Vf. dem Entstehen des Bildthemas »Gesetz und Gnade« zu, das er als Lehrbild bezeichnet. Er geht davon aus, dass im nichtdeutschen Sprachbereich ein besonderer Bedarf bestand, Luthers Rechtfertigungslehre anschaulich zu machen. Daher sei es einsichtig, dass die erste Darstellung mit französischen Inschriften entstand, ob in Paris oder der französischen Gemeinde in Antwerpen ist offen. Als Entstehungszeit des Holzschnittes komme 1522/23 in Betracht. Die ausführliche Beschreibung geht zwar auf spätmittelalterliche Beispiele einzelner Elemente ein, hebt aber hervor, dass diese in neue Beziehungen gesetzt wurden und eine andere Funktion erhielten. Vf. benennt die biblischen Grundlagen und hebt

hervor, dass dabei alttestamentliche Szenen nach neutestamentlichen Zitaten dargestellt wurden, also die Gegenüberstellung von Gesetz und Gnade in bestimmten Szenen schon vorgebildet war. Vf. weist durchgehend die Übereinstimmung der Darstellungen mit Bibelstellen, vor allem aber mit Aussagen Luthers nach. Er betont entschieden, dass das Thema »Gesetz und Gnade« zuvor keine bildliche Darstellung gefunden hatte und die Rechtfertigungslehre Luthers zum Inhalt hat. Gleichzeitig widerspricht er der Anschauung, dass die bildliche Darstellung der Rechtfertigungslehre in Wittenberg entstanden und von Lucas Cranach d. Ä. (1472-1553) entworfen worden sei. Als baldige neu gestaltete Kopien führt er den »Erlanger Holzschnitt«, eine Flugschrift des Urbanus Rhegius (1489-1541) von 1525 – in der nur die Gnadenseite aufgenommen wurde – und ein Gemälde des Hans Holbei d. J. (1497-1543) an, das um 1600 noch zweimal kopiert wurde.

Ein eigenes Kapitel ist Cranach d. Ä. gewidmet, der laut Vf. für ein mit 1525 datiertes Gemälde – das heute in Prag erhalten ist – sowohl den französischen als auch den Erlanger Holzschnitt verarbeitet hat. Bedeutender erscheint das Gothaer Tafelgemälde von 1529, auf dem Cranach nun das Thema »Gesetz und Evangelium« darstellte und eine evangelische Bildpredigt gestaltete, die mit Luthers Theologie übereinstimmte. Es steht nun nicht mehr ein Mensch unter Gesetz und Evangelium, sondern in jeder Bildhälfte ist ein Mensch in zwei unterschiedlichen Situationen dargestellt. Vf. sieht hier ein Ringen um »Visualisierung von Theologie«, das bildliche Darstellung und die darunter geschriebenen Bibelzitate zu einer evangelischen Bildpredigt vereinigt, die schreckt und tröstet, die nicht nur belehrt, sondern verkündigt und selbst Evangelium ist (50 f).

Bei einem undatierten Holzschnitt, welcher der Cranachwerkstatt zugewiesen wird, führt der Vf. die Übereinstimmungen mit dem Gothaer Tafelgemälde an, bemerkt aber zugleich, dass Maria und Johannes der Täufer als Fürbittende neben dem Weltenrichter theologisch einen Rückschritt bedeuteten und im Widerspruch zu Luther standen. So spreche der theologische Inhalt für eine Frühdatierung bis um 1525, die Entwicklung der Bildelemente aber eher für die Zeit um 1529. Hier ist wohl die Frage aufzuwerfen, wie groß die Selbständigkeit von Cranachs Mitarbeitern war.

Den Schneeberger Altar von 1539 stellt der Vf. unter die Überschrift »Das Ende des Predigtbildes«. Da ein Wandelaltar zu gestalten war, kam die Darstellung von »Gesetz und Evangelium« auf einer Predella zu stehen, die das Abendmahl darbot. Auf der Rückseite wurde das Weltgericht mit Sintflut und Vernichtung von Sodom und Gomorra gezeigt. Die reformatorische Rechtfertigungslehre wurde – den Eindruck störend – auf vier Flügel verteilt, auf denen die Bibelzitate zurücktraten, der Charakter des Predigtbildes ging verloren, es blieb nur die Illustration eines Teiles einer umfangreicheren Konzeption.

Die Fülle der behandelten Kunstwerke und deren Deutung kann hier nicht einmal skizziert werden. Vf. verfolgt die weitere Entwicklung des wandlungsfähigen Bildes »Gesetz und Evangelium« und unterscheidet zwischen Lehrbild, Andachtsbild, Epitaphbild und Bekenntnisbild. Dabei versucht er, den jeweiligen geschichtlichen Kontext aufzuspüren und daraus resultierende Akzentsetzungen – z.B. antinomistische, unionistische, polemische – zu benennen. Er fragt stetig nach den jeweiligen Vorlagen, was zu dem Ergebnis führt, dass eine breitgefächerte Entfaltung sichtbar wird, die keinesfalls im-

mer in der von Cranach geprägten Tradition stand, auch nicht immer mit Luthers Theologie übereinstimmte, dennoch aber immer genuin evangelisch war. Dass dies auch die Zeitgenossen so empfanden, lässt sich daraus erkennen, dass die Gegenreformation diese Bildwerke beseitigte. In dem Kapitel »Evangelisch – katholisch« führt Vf. Bildwerke an, welche protestantische Bildmotive übernahmen oder auch stark von reformkatholischer Haltung geprägt wurden.

Der *Katalog* verzeichnet »Bilddenkmäler möglichst ›vollständig‹, wenn sie das vom dürren/grünen Baum, vom Kreuz oder vom Weltgericht im Zentrum beherrschte Thema von ›Gesetz und Gnade‹ beeinhalten, …« (I, 141). Systematisch konnte allerdings nur in Deutschland, Österreich und dem ehemaligen Schlesien recherchiert werden. Außerdem wurden – ohne Anspruch auf Vollständigkeit – damit zusammenhängende Darstellungen aufgenommen. Die Beschreibungen der Objekte sind – abhängig von Quellen und Literatur – teils sehr ausführlich, teils sehr knapp. Sie sind unabhängig von der Einleitung abgefasst, sodass sie ohne diese benutzbar sind. Es wäre aber hilfreich gewesen, in den gegebenen Fällen auf die jeweilige Stelle in der Einleitung zu verweisen.

Die ausführlichen Beschreibungen schildern die Einzelheiten des Bildes und zitieren die vorhandenen oder auch nur überlieferten Über-, In- und Unterschriften des Bildwerkes. Besonders nützlich ist dies dann, wenn in Bd. 2 keine dazugehörende Abbildung vorhanden oder die Schrift auf ihnen nur sehr schwer lesbar ist. Das trifft z.B. auf die Federzeichnung zu, die um 1550 enstand und durch »Altes Testament : Neues Testament mit Gegenwartbezug« charakterisiert ist. Auf ihr ist zwischen einer Reihe mit alttestamentlichen und einer Reihe neutestamentlichen Szenen eine Reihe mit Szenen aus dem Schmalkaldischen Krieg eingefügt und zu den jeweils darüber und darunter biblischen Szenen in Beziehung gesetzt. Jeder Szene ist ein gereimter Text zugeordnet (1, 206-213 [177]; 2, 346 f [250]).

Zu dem *Katalog* gehören ein Quellen- und ein Literaturverzeichnis, ein Register der Autoren, Auftraggeber, Drucker, Künstler, Sammler, Stifter, Verleger und Widmungsempfänger sowie der auf Epitaphien und auf Gedächtnisbildern genannten Personen. Auf das Register der Druckorte folgt das der Themen, das erlaubt, die Verwendung bestimmter Elemente – z.B. Abraham, Auferstehung Christi oder Eherne Schlange in den 860 Bildwerken zu verfolgen. Besonders bemerkenswert ist das Register der Bibelzitate, das die biblische Grundlage der Bildwerke erschließt. Dem Register der Gattungen folgt eine Zeittafel, in welcher die 860 Objekte den Jahren von 1020/25 bis 1905 zugeordnet sind. Den Schluss bildet das Register der »Typen zu Gesetz und Gnade/Evangelium«. Der Vf. unterscheidet anhand der Stellung einzelner Elemente vier Typen der Bilddenkmäler, die dann weiter spezifiziert sind (1, 141 f). Soweit ein Bildwerk einer dieser Typen zugeordnet werden kann, ist dies hinter seinem Titel in runder Klammer angegeben. Das Register erlaubt es nun, Objekte desselben Typs zu vergleichen. Der Katalog ist also bemerkenswert gut erschlossen.

Die *Abbildungen* in Bd. 2 folgen in ihrer Anordnung weder der Einleitung noch dem Katalog, sondern in sieben Kapiteln sachlichen Gesichtspunkten: 1. Vorreformatorische Darstellungen mit Elementen, die später in reformatorische mit dem Thema »Gesetz und Evangelium« aufgenommen wurden. 2. Solche Darstellungen, »auf denen der sündige, erlösungsbedürftige Mensch

sich zugleich unter Gesetz und Evangelium gestellt sieht«. 3. Die Chranachdarstellungen mit jeweils zwei Menschen, »einen, der in die Hölle getrieben, den anderen, der auf das Kreuz Christi verwiesen wird«, und ihre Rezeptionen. 4. Bildwerke, die den Gekreuzigten ins Zentrum stellen. 5. Darstellungen mit Gott Vater oder Christus als Weltenrichter. 6. »Ohne Bezug auf einen bestimmten Bildtypus wird Gesetz und Evangelium dargestellt in der Gegenüberstellung von dürren und grünen Bäumen oder Zweigen; ...« 7. Wie es bei sachlichen Anordnungen der Fall zu sein pflegt, bleiben auch hier Varia übrig. Unter »Andere Entwürfe« sind auch Bilder, die nur Elemente aus der Ikonographie von »Gesetz und Evangelium« aufnehmen. Die Abbildungen sind im Rahmen einer großzügigen Gestaltung in guter Qualität reproduziert. Sie haben eine knappe Bildunterschrift mit Verweis auf den Katalog, der sich im 1. Bd. befindet und somit mühelos mit seinen detaillierten Ausführungen dazu herangezogen werden kann.

Vf. hat ein grundlegendes Werk zu einer »Bild-Text-Komposition« geschaffen, welcher nach seiner Überzeugung »ein besonderer Ort in der Kunst-, Geistes- und Kulturgeschichte« zukommt, weil keine zweite »so gekonnt einen grundlegenden theologischen Lehrsatz ins Bild setzt« und weil nicht viele komplexe Bildkompositionen genannt werden können, »die in sich so vielfältig und sinntragend variiert und die so vielen unterschiedlichen Überlieferungsträgern anvertraut wurden« (1, 136). Vf. bemerkt selbst, dass sein Werk nicht erschöpfend ist, weil er nicht alle dazugehörenden Bildwerke erfassen konnte. Er weiß aber auch, dass die erfassten unterschiedlich gründlich erforscht sind. Das wird an dem unterschiedlichen Umfang der Beschreibungen im Katalog sehr deutlich. Er bedauert, dass er zu den auf Epitaphien genannten Personen nicht mehr – gegebenenfalls unter Einbeziehung von Leichenpredigten – erheben konnte. Das Werk enthält aber so viele Informationen und Gesichtspunkte, dass es für die weitere Forschung und für den an der Deutung eines entsprechenden Bildwerkes Interessierten als Handbuch dienen kann.

Leipzig   Helmar Junghans

PHILIPP MELANCHTHON: Ethicae doctrinae elementa et enarratio Libri quinti Ethicorum/ hrsg. und eingel. von Günter Frank unter Mitarb. von Michael Beyer. S-Bad Cannstatt: Frommann-Holzboog, 2008. XLII, 271 S. (Editionen zur Frühen Neuzeit; 1)

Dieser Edition einer der ethischen Schriften Melanchthons liegt ein Wittenberger Druck aus dem Jahr 1550 zugrunde. Melanchthon hatte sich seit etwa 1526 erneut Aristoteles zugewendet, nachdem er sich vorher mit Luther von diesem abgewendet hatte. Konkret ging es dabei allerdings mehr um eine Kritik an der scholastischen Aristotelesrezeption, die im reformatorischen Verständnis zu einer totalen Missdeutung biblischer Aussagen geführt hatte. Im Kontext einer reformatorischen und zugleich humanistischen Universitätsreform gewannen nun auch antike Autoren wieder an Bedeutung.

In der instruktiven Einleitung skizziert der Hrsg. die humanistische Aristotelesrezeption, die im 15. Jahrhundert einsetzte und durch die vor den Türken nach Italien geflohenen griechischen Gelehrten einen starken Auftrieb erhielt. Damit wird einerseits die Betrachtungsweise korrigiert, die ihren Blick einseitig nur auf die durchaus wirkungsvolle Platonrezeption der Humanisten richtet, und

andererseits deutlich, dass die neue Wittenberger Aristotelesrezeption nichts mit einer Rückkehr zur Scholastik zu tun hat. Denn die humanistische Aristotelesrezeption war äußerst kritisch gegenüber der scholastischen Aristotelesrezeption.

Der Herausgeber macht aber nicht nur deutlich, dass Melanchthon in die humanistische Aristotelesrezeption gehörte, sondern zugleich noch vielmehr eine reformatorische Aristotelesrezeption gestaltete. Er informiert darüber, wie Melanchthon seine Kommentierung der Nikomachischen Ethik des Aristoteles 1529 mit einem »In Ethica Aristotelis commentarius« eröffnete, um schließlich 1550 den nun edierten Text herauszubringen. Anhand von Melanchthons eignen Worten kann er bewusst machen, wie sehr Melanchthon zwischen einer theologischen und einer philosophischen Ethik unterschied, Aristoteles auf die philosophische Ethik beschränkte und diese als – durch Theologie – ergänzungsbedürftige charakterisierte. Hrsg. beschreibt dieses Vorgehen Melanchthons: »Die für Luthers Theologie bestimmende Gesetz-Evangelium-Dialektik wird als theologisches Strukturprinzip auf das aristotelische Konzept einer praktischen Philosophie appliziert« (XXXIX). Obgleich damit auf eine von Melanchthon selbst vorgenommene Unterscheidung zurückgegriffen wird (8/9-10/11), lässt sich Melanchthons Ethik auch gut im Rahmen der reformatorischen Vorstellungen interpretieren, die wir heute unter dem Begriff »Zweiregimentenlehre« zusammenfassen.

Der Hrsg. hält nicht nur fest, dass Melanchthon sich im Rahmen von Luthers Theologie bewegte, sondern vermerkt auch ausdrücklich, wie sehr es verwundern muss, dass von Luther trotz seiner entschiedenen Kritik an Aristoteles »keine Kritik an Melanchthons Studien und Lehrbüchern zur aristotelischen Ethik überliefert ist« (XXIII). Er erklärt das damit, dass Melanchthon »in der konkreten Ausführung der Schriften zur aristotelischen Ethik und Politik ... dem theologischen Interesse Luthers Rechnung trug« (XXIV). Er kommt zu dem Ergebnis, »dass es sich um den Entwurf einer reformatorischen Ethik« handelt (XXXIX).

Bei dem edierten Text handelt sich also nicht um einen historischen Kommentar zur Nikomachischen Ethik des Aristoteles, sondern um eine evangelische Ethik, die Probleme und Definitionen von Aristoteles aufnimmt und unter dem Titel »Grundbegriffe der Ethik und Auslegung des fünften Buches der Nikomachischen Ethik« erschien. Sie ist in zwei Bücher eingeteilt, wobei das erste Buch Probleme der Ethik und einzelne Tugenden erörtert, das zweite aber – wie das fünfte Buch in der Nikomachischen Ethik – sich der Gerechtigkeit widmet.

Der Hrsg. geht am Ende seiner Einleitung noch auf eine Aporie der aristotelischen Ethik ein. Aristoteles wollte »einer größtmöglichen Glückseligkeit aller Bürger im besten Staat« dienen. Er sah sie in der vita contemplativa, die aber nur dem philosophierenden, keineswegs allen Menschen erreichbar ist. Melanchthon fand den Streit, ob die vita activa oder die vita contemplativa vorzuziehen sei, lächerlich und erklärte, beide bedingten sich gegenseitig. Er löste die Aporie auf und lehrte eine Ethik für alle »Menschen unter den Bedingungen der gefallenen Menschennatur« (XL-XLII).

Der vorliegende Band eröffnet die Reihe »Editionen zur Frühen Neuzeit: lateinisch-deutsche Quelleneditionen«. Sie will »bislang unveröffentlichte, kulturhistorisch bedeutende Quellen des Zeitalters der Reformation« zugänglich machen. Das geschieht nicht

zuletzt durch die deutsche Übersetzung im Paralleldruck, die darauf gerichtet ist, in einer klaren Sprache der Gegenwart den Inhalt des lateinischen Textes zu vergegenwärtigen.

Die Angaben zur Textgestaltung sind knapp geraten, sodass nicht deutlich wird, dass der Text des »Corpus reformatorum« kollationiert wurde und Michael Beyer den lateinischen Text und die Übersetzung abschließend redigiert hat.

Die für die neue Reihe ausgewählte Melanchthonschrift ist ein wichtiger, für an der Wittenberger Reformation Interessierte sehr nützlicher Text. Er dokumentiert die Gemeinsamkeit von Luther und Melanchthon, die Breite der reformatorischen Bildung, konkretisiert die reformatorische Aristotelesrezeption und vermittelt last not least Einsichten über grundlegende Begriffe und Vorstellungen, deren Kenntnis für das Verständnis reformatorischer Texte äußerst hilfreich ist.

Leipzig   Helmar Junghans

Andreas Waschbüsch: Alter Melanchthon: Muster theologischer Autoritätsstiftung bei Matthias Flacius Illyricus. GÖ: V&R, 2008. XII, 208 S. (Forschungen zur Kirchen- und Dogmengeschichte; 96)

Nach Luthers Tod erlebten seine Weggefährten in Wittenberg durch die politischen Wirren der Jahre 1547 bis 1549 eine schwere Krise. Trotzdem behielt Wittenberg seine Stellung als Zentrum der reformatorischen Bewegung. Stadt und Universität waren unauslöschlich mit dem Namen Luthers verbunden. Melanchthon bemühte sich unermüdlich um den Erhalt der Universität und die Weiterführung der theologischen Tradition Wittenbergs. Jedoch wurde ihm seit

1548 der Vorwurf gemacht, er habe das Erbe
Luthers verraten. An der Etablierung dieses
Vorurteils war maßgeblich Matthias Flacius
Illyricus (1520-1575) beteiligt. Um diese Sicht
auf seinen Lehrer durchsetzen zu können,
bediente sich Flacius des Mediums der Flugschriften, die er von Magdeburg, das so den
Namen »Herrgottskanzlei« erhielt, zwischen
1548 und 1556 zu Hunderten ausgehen ließ.

Wie kam es zum Zerwürfnis zwischen
Lehrer und Schüler? Wo lag die Bruchlinie
im Verhältnis zwischen beiden? Dieser span-
nenden Frage geht Vf. in seiner 2005 in Göttingen eingereichten und nun veröffentlichten
Dissertation nach. Die Stärke der Arbeit liegt
eindeutig auf der präzisen philologischen
Erschließung der Quellen im zweiten Teil des
Buches (47-160), der mit »Lesestücke« betitelt
ist. Zu Beginn der Arbeit steht ein Kapitel
»Historien« (1-46), in dem »Gegenstand und
Problemstellung« der Studie geklärt, »Die
Karriere [des Flacius] bis 1546« und »Die Lage
im Reich« erläutert werden. Dieser Teil bietet
bekanntes Material zum Lebensweg des Flacius, stellt es aber unter die besondere Frage nach
»der autoritätsstiftenden Publizistik des Flacius« (10), indem insbesondere seine rhetorische
Ausbildung Beachtung findet. Rhetorische
Traditionen der Antike, die Flacius sowohl
in Venedig wie auch ab 1541 bei Melanchthon
in Wittenberg kennen und vorzüglich beherrschen lernte, dienen Vf. zur Analyse der
Flugschriften der Jahre 1548 und 1549.

Nachdem Flacius im Juli 1548 Melanchthons nicht für die Öffentlichkeit bestimmte »Iudicium IV« zum »Augsburger Interim«
als »Bedenken der Wittenberger Theologen«
herausgegeben hatte, konnte Melanchthon
nicht mehr so agieren, wie er es gern getan
hätte. Das Interim galt fortan in Kursachsen
als mangelhaft und der Kaiser war über die
Angriffe auf seine Religionspolitik verärgert

(38f). Flacius löste so eine Diskussion über
den Text aus, die von Melanchthon und auch
Kurfürst Moritz von Sachsen (1521, 1547-1553)
nicht beabsichtigt war. Zugleich zog diese
Herausgabe eine verschärfte Zensurverord-
nung nach sich. Melanchthon musste fortan
den Kompromiss suchen.

Den weiteren Verlauf der Verhandlungen
verfolgte und kommentierte Flacius mit Flugschriften, die jeweils unter verschiedenen
sprechenden Pseudonymen – z.B. Johannes
Waremundus oder Christianus Lauterwar –
erschienen (54). Vf. arbeitet deutlich heraus,
dass Flacius lange an seinem Lehrer festhielt,
diesen nicht direkt angriff, sondern dessen
Position ohne Namensnennung als gefähr-
lich beschrieb. Dabei bildeten sich von einer
Flugschrift zur nächsten Argumente heraus,
die immer pointierter wurden. Flacius demonstrierte seine meisterhafte Beherrschung der
rhetorischer Figuren und Topoi von Cicero
oder Aristoteles.

Für jedes Titelblatt seiner Flugschriften
wählte Flacius mindestens ein Zitat aus der
Heiligen Schrift aus, das die aktuelle Situation kommentieren sollte. Inwieweit das
typisch für die Zeit oder etwas Besonderes für
Flacius war und ihn somit von anderen Autoren unterschied, wird von Vf. leider nicht
thematisiert. Interessant ist allerdings das
Ergebnis, dass Flacius seine Autorität durch
die Autorität der Schrift untermauert sah.
Somit schützte ihn das Bibelwort nicht nur,
sondern legitimierte zugleich seine Position
als Gotteswort. Flacius war gewissermaßen
nur das Sprachrohr Gottes.

Nach Weihnachten 1548 verschärfte Flacius seine Angriffe auf das »Augsburger Interim«, indem er gegen den Messkanon, die
Opfervorstellung der Messe sowie Johann
Agricola (1492/94-1566) polemisierte, der an
der Abfassung entscheidender Textpassagen

beteiligt war. In zunehmendem Maße geriet er so in Opposition zu seinen Wittenberger Kollegen, die er wiederum nicht nannte, deren Positionen er aber als Verrat am Evangelium angriff. Ende März 1549 musste er schließlich Wittenberg verlassen.

In allen behandelten Flugschriften erweist sich Flacius als brillanter Melanchthonschüler, der seinen Lehrer mit seinen eigenen Waffen schlug, indem er rhetorische und hermeneutische Figuren und Argumentationsmuster sicher verwendete, um die Leser von seiner das »Augsburger Interim« ablehnenden Position zu überzeugen. Schließlich kommt Vf. auf die Apologie des Flacius zu sprechen, an der er das zuvor in den Flugschriften herausgearbeitete Ergebnis erneut zeigen und vertiefen kann (129-151).

1557 reflektierte Flacius in seiner Jenaer Antrittsvorlesung über die historischen und religionspolitischen Ereignisse, die zu seinem Weggang aus Wittenberg führten (151-160). Während in seinen vorangegangenen Texten Luther keine Rolle spielte, rückte er ihn hier verstärkt in den Blick. Allerdings nur im Deuteschema Melanchthons, der bereits 1548 die besondere Rolle des Reformators in der aktuellen Periode der Kirchengeschichte herausstellte. Verdienstvoll ist die Edition der Jenaer Antrittsvorlesung vom 17. Mai 1557 am Ende des Bandes (171-189), die so der Forschung leichter zugänglich gemacht wird.

Vf. vertieft in dieser Arbeit die Forschungen zu Flugschriften, die vornehmlich von der »Herrgottskanzlei« zu Magdeburg ausgingen. Bei der Lektüre ist allerdings die Kenntnis der bisherigen Arbeiten zu diesem Thema insbesondere von Thomas Kaufmann – »Das Ende der Reformation« – unerlässlich. Im Gegensatz zur Biografie Oliver Olsons – »Matthias Flacius and the survival of Luther's reform« – hebt Vf. den Graben zwischen Luther und Melanchthon gar nicht erst aus, sondern konzentriert sich in seiner Untersuchung auf Argumentationsmuster. Flacius wird dabei als »Alter Melanchthon« nicht zu einem besseren Melanchthon, indem er zum Retter des Luthertums stilisiert würde, vielmehr kann der Autor zeigen, dass gerade die innerlutherische Binnendifferenzierung nach Luthers Tod notwendig war, um in ein neues »Apostolisches Zeitalter« (167) eintreten zu können.

Das Lesevergnügen wäre größer gewesen, wenn der Band weniger Fehler, insbesondere Satzfehler enthielte.

Stefan Michel   Jena

Matthias A. Deuschle: Brenz als Kontroverstheologe: die Apologie der Confessio Virtembergica und die Auseinandersetzung zwischen Johannes Brenz und Pedro de Soto. TÜ: Mohr Siebeck 2006. XVI, 343 S. (Beiträge zur historischen Theologie; 138).

Die Berliner Dissertation stellt mit der zwischen 1555 und 1559 entstandenen Apologie der »Confessio Virtembergica« eine – mit Ausnahme des Abendmahlskapitels – bisher wenig beachtete kontroverstheologische Spätschrift des Johannes Brenz in den Mittelpunkt. Sein Gegner, der spanische Dominikaner, Beichtvater Karls V. und Professor in Dillingen Pedro de Soto (um 1495-1563), eröffnete die Auseinandersetzung 1555 mit einem Angriff auf die dem Konzil von Trient vorgelegene »Confessio Virtembergica«. Brenz, angeregt durch Herzog Christoph von Württemberg (1515, 1550-1568), räumte der Aufgabe der Widerlegung de Sotos höchste Priorität ein, wobei er aber anders als der Herzog die Chancen einer Religionsvergleichung von Anfang an skeptisch beurteilte und auch nicht primär die auf dem Wormser Kolloquium 1557 zu Tage getretene Uneinigkeit der Evangelischen überwinden, sondern deren Trennung von der römischen Kirche begründen wollte. Auch die in der Apologie entwickelte Ubiquitätslehre diente in erster Linie der Abgrenzung von römischen Auffassungen und zielte nur indirekt auf die Streitigkeiten im eigenen Lager (51).

Nach einer Analyse der gegen Brenz gerichteten Theologie de Sotos, der mit dem Anspruch auftrat, nicht nur seine eigene, sondern die römisch-katholische Lehre schlechthin zu vertreten (vgl. 85), sowie nach einem Blick auf die Weiterungen der Kontroverse, die europäische Dimensionen erreichte, ist der Hauptteil der Untersuchung der Apologie selbst gewidmet (Teil 3, 147-289). Brenz eröffnete sie mit Prolegomena und präformierte damit die Unterscheidung von Prolegomena und materialer Dogmatik, wie sie im Zeitalter der Orthodoxie üblich wurde (vgl. 136 f). Seine Auseinandersetzung mit de Soto gestaltete sich als Kampf um die drei Prinzipien Schrift (statt Tradition), Christus als Haupt der Kirche (statt Papst) und Glaubensgewissheit (statt Zweifel). Wegen dieses grundsätzlichen Charakters der Auseinandersetzung kann die Apologie als Ausdruck der reifen Form der Theologie des Johannes Brenz überhaupt verstanden werden.

Breiten Raum nimmt die Verteidigung der Schriftlehre gegen de Sotos Angriffe ein. Brenz bestimmte das Wesen der Schrift von ihrer Funktion her: Sie ist Gottes Wort und dient dazu, dass durch sie das zum Heil Notwendige erkannt und das Heil gewirkt wird. Suffizient ist sie insofern, als in ihr alles Heilsnotwendige enthalten ist (154), klar ist sie, wenn sie ihrem Sinn entsprechend richtig ausgelegt wird (165). Die von de Soto angeführte Autorität der Tradition als Wort Gottes weist Brenz mit dem Grundsatz zurück, dass alle Tradition an der Schrift zu messen sei. Angesichts der Klarheit und Suffizienz der Schrift scheidet die Kirche als hermeneutische Instanz aus. Ob Schriftworte für die eigene Gegenwart Geltung haben, muss durch sorgfältige Auslegung ermittelt werden. Auf keinen Fall aber können gegenwärtige Verhältnisse zum Maßstab für die Gültigkeit biblischer Weisungen gemacht werden (175). Die Schrift ist zuerst durch die Schrift selbst auszulegen, wobei dem Literalsinn besondere Bedeutung zukommt. Eine Verschiebung der hermeneutischen Position gegenüber früheren Schriften ergibt sich aber insofern, als Brenz in der Apologie zwischen Gesagtem und Gemeintem stärker unterscheidet und einen »systematisch verantworteten Wortsinn« (207) vertrat und damit den Boden Melanchthonischer Hermeneutik verließ.

Auf ekklesiologischem Feld ging es Brenz vor allem darum, »das Herrsein Christi in der Kirche zur Geltung zu bringen« (208). Das Prädikat »katholisch« beanspruchte Brenz gegen de Soto für die eigene Kirche. Erkennungszeichen der wahren katholischen Kirche sind die reine Predigt des Evangeliums und der richtige Gebrauch der Sakramente, beides in steter Bindung an die Schrift. Von dieser wahren äußeren, sichtbaren Kirche unterscheidet er die wahre innere, verborgene Kirche der Glaubenden, die nur Gott alleine kennt. Beides grenzt er von der falschen äußeren Kirche seines Gegners ab. Gegen de Soto entwickelt Brenz – vom geistlichen Priestertum aller Gläubigen ausgehend – auch sein Verständnis des kirchlichen Amts, das als Dienst für die Kirche verstanden wird. Die Kirche bedarf zwar des Amtes, die Amtsträger sind aber nicht die Kirche. Die Notwendigkeit einer kirchlichen Urteilsinstanz in der Lehre lehnte Brenz entschieden ab. Vielmehr hat jeder Christ eine Urteilskompetenz und kann selbst mit Hilfe des Heiligen Geistes Gewissheit aus der Schrift schöpfen. Die von de Soto bestrittene Kompetenz des Fürsten, in kirchliche Belange einzugreifen, verteidigte Brenz mit dem Argument der Fürsorgepflicht des Fürsten für die Religion. Wie jeder Christ ist aber auch der Fürst bei der Beurteilung der rechten Lehre an die Schrift gebunden, und seine Kompetenz endet bei der Formulierung und Verkündigung der Lehre, die Aufgaben der Theologen bleiben. Eine Besonderheit der Brenzschen Konzeption sieht der Vf. gerade »in der Verbindung von allgemeinem Priestertum und landesherrlichem, vom Herzog und seiner Behörde verantworteten Kirchenregiment« (239).

Gegen de Sotos Behauptung, ein spezieller Glaube an die gewisse Vergebung der Sünden allein um Christi willen sei nicht nötig, formulierte Brenz schließlich sein Verständnis des Glaubens, der nichts anderes ist »als die Gewißheit, dass Gott uns um Christi willen gnädig ist« (242). Zweifel am eigenen Glauben sind in diesem Leben zwar nicht völlig auszuräumen, der vergebenden Güte Gottes dürfen und müssen wir aber gewiss sein. Zum Glauben gehört individuelle Gewissheit, ein Vertrauensakt des einzelnen. In der Rechtfertigungslehre bescheinigt der Vf. Brenz zwar ähnliche Anliegen, wie sie Andreas Osiander d. Ä. (1498-1552) vertrat, dennoch war Brenz »kein Osiandrist« (276).

Die Studie stellt insgesamt nicht nur einen wichtigen Beitrag zur Theologie des späten Brenz dar, sondern sie lenkt darüber hinaus den Blick auf die über den Religionsfrieden hinaus weiterbestehende theologische Frontstellung zwischen Luthertum und Katholizismus im Reich. Die Brenzforschung wird nicht zuletzt durch die Erkenntnis bereichert, dass die kontroverstheologische Frontstellung – und hier waren die Differenzen mit der römischen Seite für Brenz wichtiger als die innerevangelischen Kontroversen – sein theologisches Denken bis zuletzt bestimmte: »Zeit seines Lebens war Brenz Kontroverstheologe« (291).

Leipzig   Armin Kohnle

FRÜHNEUHOCHDEUTSCHES WÖRTERBUCH/ hrsg. von Ulrich Goebel; Anja Lobenstein-Reichmann; Oskar Reichmann; begr. von Robert R. Anderson; Ulrich Goebel; Oskar Reichmann. Bd. 6. Lfg. 4: gesicht-gewonheit/ bearb. von Oskar Reichmann. B; NY: de Gruyter, 2009, Sp. 1505-2016.

Diese Lieferung ist weiterhin Wörtern mit der Vorsilbe »ge« gewidmet, die bereits seit Sp. 195 erläutert werden und von denen mit »gewonheit« auf der letzten Spalte noch nicht alle erfasst sind, sodass der Bd. 6 noch einer weiteren Lieferung bedarf. Diese große Anzahl von Wörtern mit der Vorsilbe »ge« erklärt sich daraus, dass sie im Frühneuhochdeutschen häufiger verwendet wurden als im heutigen Hochdeutschen. Dabei lässt sich eine vielfältige Entwicklung beobachten.

Manche Wörter sind noch heute mit der Vorsilbe »ge« im Gebrauch, aber mit weniger Bedeutungen, manchmal sogar nur mit einer im Frühneuhochdeutschen noch unbekannten. So ist für »gesuch« die Bedeutung »einen Antrag stellen« nicht belegt. Im Frühneuhochdeutschen kann es einfach »suchen« bedeuten, aber auch »Weide, Weidefläche« und als Metonymie – ein Tropus, in dem eine reale Beziehung zur eigentliche Sache besteht – »Recht auf Nutzung der Weide«, ja überhaupt »Recht auf Nutzung einer Sache«, sogar ganz allgemein »menschliches Tun und Lassen, Lebenswandel, feindseliges Handeln«. Das Frühneuhochdeutsche Wörterbuch belegt auch hier ausführlich die Verwendung des Wortes in religiösen Texten im Sinne von »auf eigenen Vorteil, Nutzen orientiertes Handeln des Menschen«. Es stellt in der Erläuterung heraus, dass die Mystik damit ein dem Menschen naturgegebenes, ichbezogenes Vorteilsstreben kritisierte, das selbst in den religiösen Bemühen ein »ichbezogenes Schielen nach dem Himmelreich« einschloss. In den reformatorischen Texten hingegen stehe »gesuch« im »Gegensatz zum selbslosen, in christlicher Freiheit gründenden Handeln«, womit auch der Wucher kritisiert wurde. Neben der negativen Konnotation standen aber auch eine wertneutrale Verwendung oder gar positive Bedeutungen wie Zinsen, Abgaben, Forderungen oder Gewinn und Nutzen einschließlich der Erlösung und der Seligkeit des Menschen (6, 1674-1680).

Bei einige Wörter haben sich Formen ohne die Vorsilbe »ge« mit derselben Bedeutung wie im Frühneuhochdeutschen durchgesetzt, wie z. B. »gesingen« oder »getöten«.

Bei andere Wörtern sind Formen ohne die Vorsilbe »ge« und zum Teil mit anderen Vorsilben im Gebrauch geblieben, so z. B. »gewarten« in den Verben »warten, erwarten, abwarten« (6, 1867-1871). Für »geweigern« ist heute »sich weigern, etwas verweigern« üblich (6. 1882).

Der relativ umfangreiche Artikel »gewalt«– die übrigens im Frühneuhochdeutschen überwiegend maskulin verwendet wurde – unterscheidet elf Bedeutungsvarianten (6, 1784-1803). Er verdeutlicht besonders gut, wie sehr semantische Erläuterungen in die von der Sprache beschriebenen Sachverhalte

eindringen. Die Einleitung zu diesem Artikel folgert: »*gewalt* bedeutet […] das auf religiösem, sozialem, rechtlichem, politischem, physischem, natürlichem, persönlichem Ungleichgewicht beruhende Gefälle zwischen den Handlungs- und Verfügungsmöglichkeiten sowie -befugnissen beider umschriebener Bezugsgrößen [die über Gewalt verfügende und die von Gewalt betroffene], auch zwischen ihren als religiös, natürlich oder sozial vorausgesetzten bzw. anerkannten Seinsweisen.« Dementsprechend beginnt der Artikel mit Aussagen über Gottes Gewalt, gefolgt von solchen zur Naturgewalt und den einzelnen Bereichen bis zu der allgemeinen Bedeutung »Nachdruck, Entschiedenheit, Ernst» in der Wendung »*mit gewalt*«.

Die angeführte Bedeutung »Recht, Verfügungsrecht und -gewalt« kann für das Verständnis von Luthers Aussage in seiner Schrift »Von dem Papsttum zu Rom wider den hochberühmten Romanisten zu Leipzig« – die 6, 1795 zum Teil zitiert ist – Hilfreich sein. Luther warf die Frage auf: »Ja warumb vorpeut der Bapst der gantzen priesterschafft den ehelichen standt nit allein wider die figur [Vorbild], sondern auch widder got, widder recht, wider vernunft und natur, des er keinen fug, gewalt noch recht hat, […].« Mancher Leser könnte versucht sein, die Differenz zwischen den letzten drei Begriffen herauszufinden. Mit dem Frühneuhochdeutschen Wörterbuch kann er erkennen, dass es zwischen diesen drei Begriffen keinen sachlichen Unterschied gibt, sondern dass Luther hier vielmehr eine doppelte repetitio mit drei synonymen Begriffen einsetzte, um affektvoll zum Ausdruck zu bringen, dass der Papst für das Eheverbot für Geistliche nicht das allergeringste Recht hat.

Leipzig   Helmar Junghans

Lutherbibliographie 2009

Mit Professor Dr. Matthieu Arnold, Strasbourg (Frankreich); Professor Dr. Zoltán Csepregi Budapest (Ungarn); Professor Dr. Jin-Seop Eom, Kyunggi-do (Südkorea); Studierektor Dr. Roger Jensen, Oslo (Norwegen); ; Universitätsassistent Dr. Rudolf Leeb, Wien (Österreich); Professor Dr. Pilgrim Lo, Hong Kong (China); Informatiker Dr. Leo Näreaho, Helsinki (Finnland); Bischof Sen. D. Janusz Narzyński, Warszawa (Polen); Professor Dr. Paolo Ricca, Roma (Italien); Professor Dr. Ricardo W. Rieth, São Leopoldo (Brasilien); Professor Dr. Maurice E. Schild, Adelaide (Australien); Dr. Rune Söderlund, Lund (Schweden); Bibliographer Assistant Rose Trapiano, Milwaukee, WI (USA); cand. theol. Lars Vangslev, København (Dänemark); Professor Dr. Jos E. Vercruysse, Antwerpen (Belgien); Dr. Martin Wernisch, Praha (Tschechien) und Professor Dr. Klaas Zwanepol, Utrecht (Niederlande) bearb. von Professor em. Dr. Helmar Junghans; Akadem. Mitarbeiter Dr. Michael Beyer sowie Dr. Stefan Reichelt,, Leipzig (Deutschland).

Der Leiterin und den Mitarbeiterinnen der Außenstelle Theologie der Universitätsbibliothek Leipzig und den Mitarbeiter(inne)n von Die Deutsche Bibliothek – Deutsche Bücherei Leipzig, danke ich für ihre Unterstützung herzlich, besonders aber der Wilhelm-Julius-Bobbert-Stiftung für ihre finanzielle Förderung.

ABKÜRZUNGSVERZEICHNIS

1   Verlage und Verlagsorte

ADVA	Akademische Druck- und Verlagsanstalt	HD	Heidelberg
AnA	Ann Arbor, MI	HH	Hamburg
B	Berlin	L	Leipzig
BL	Basel	LO	London
BP	Budapest	LVH	Lutherisches Verlagshaus
BR	Bratislava	M	München
CV	Calwer Verlag	MEES	A Magyarországi Evangélikus Egyház
DA	Darmstadt		Sajtóosztálya
dtv	Deutscher Taschenbuch Verlag	MP	Minneapolis, MN
EPV	Evangelischer Presseverband	MRES	A Magyarországi Református Egyház
EVA	Evangelische Verlagsanstalt		Zsinati Irodájának Sajtóosztálya
EVW	Evangelisches Verlagswerk	MS	Münster
F	Frankfurt, Main	MZ	Mainz
FR	Freiburg im Breisgau	NK	Neukirchen-Vluyn
GÖ	Göttingen	NV	Neukirchener Verlag
GÜ	Gütersloh	NY	New York, NY
GVH	Gütersloher Verlagshaus	P	Paris

PB	Paderborn	SH	Stockholm
Phil	Philadelphia, PA	StL	Saint Louis, MO
PO	Portland, OR	TÜ	Tübingen
PR	Praha	UMI	University Microfilm International
PUF	Presses Universitaires de France	V&R	Vandenhoeck & Ruprecht
PWN	Pánstwowe Wydawníctwo Naukowe	W	Wien
Q&M	Quelle & Meyer	WB	Wissenschaftliche Buchgesellschaft
S	Stuttgart	WZ	Warszawa
SAV	Slovenská Akadémia Vied	ZH	Zürich

2 Zeitschriften, Jahrbücher

AEKHN	Amtsblatt der Evang. Kirche in Hessen und Nassau (Darmstadt)	EP	Evanjelický Posol spod Tatier (Liptovsky Mikuláš)
AG	Amt und Gemeinde (Wien)	EThR	Etudes théologiques et religieuses (Montpellier)
AGB	Archiv für Geschichte des Buchwesens (Frankfurt, Main)	EvD	Die Evangelische Diaspora (Leipzig)
AKultG	Archiv für Kulturgeschichte (Münster; Köln)	EvEG	Evangelium – ›euaggelion‹ – Gospel (Bremen)
ALW	Archiv für Liturgiewissenschaft (Regensburg)	EvTh	Evangelische Theologie (München)
ARG	Archiv für Reformationsgeschichte (Gütersloh)	GTB	Gütersloher Taschenbücher (Siebenstern)
		GuJ	Gutenberg-Jahrbuch (Mainz)
ARGBL	ARG: Beiheft Literaturbericht (Gütersloh)	GWU	Geschichte in Wissenschaft und Unterricht (Offenburg)
BEDS	Beiträge zur Erforschung der deutschen Sprache (Leipzig)	HCh	Herbergen der Christenheit (Leipzig)
BGDS	Beiträge zur Geschichte der deutschen Sprache und Literatur (Tübingen)	He	Helikon (Budapest)
		HThR	The Harvard theological review (Cambridge, MA)
BlPfKG	Blätter für pfälzische Kirchengeschichte und religiöse Volkskunde (Otterbach)	HZ	Historische Zeitschrift (Müchen)
		IL	Igreja Luterana (Porto Alegre)
BlWKG	Blätter für württembergische Kirchengeschichte (Stuttgart)	ITK	Irodalomtörténeti Közlemények (Budapest)
BPF	Bulletin de la Société de l'Histoire du Protestantisme Fançais (Paris)	JBrKG	Jahrbuch für Berlin-Brandenburgische Kirchengeschichte (Berlin)
BW	Die Bibel in der Welt (Stuttgart)	JEH	Journal of ecclesiastical history (London)
CAZW	Confessio Augustana mit Zeitwende (Neuendettelsau)	JHKV	Jahrbuch der Hessischen Kirchengeschicht-lichen Vereinigung (Darmstadt)
ChH	Church history (Chicago, IL)	JLH	Jahrbuch für Liturgik und Hymnologie (Kassel)
CJ	Concordia journal (St. Louis, MO)		
CL	Cirkevné listy (Bratislava)	JNKG	Jahrbuch der Gesellschaft für Niedersäch-sische Kirchengeschichte (Blomberg/Lippe)
Cath	Catholica (Münster)	
CThQ	Concordia theological quarterly (Fort Wayne, IN)	JGPrÖ	Jahrbuch für Geschichte des Protestantis-mus in Österreich (Wien)
CTM	Currents in theology and mission (Chicago, IL)	JRG	Jahrbuch für Regionalgeschichte und Landeskunde (Weimar)
DLZ	Deutsche Literaturzeitung (Berlin)	JWKG	Jahrbuch für Westfälische Kirchen geschichte (Lengerich/Westf.)
DPfBl	Deutsches Pfarrerblatt (Essen)	KÅ	Kyrkohistorisk årsskrift (Uppsala)
DTT	Dansk teologisk tidsskrift (København)	KD	Kerygma und Dogma (Göttingen)
EÉ	Evangélikus Élet (Budapest)	KR	Křestanská revue (Praha)
EHSch	Europäische Hochschulschriften: Reihe …	LF	Listy filologické (Praha)
EN	Evangélikus Naptár az … èvre (Budapest)	LK	Lutbersk kirketidende (Oslo)
		LP	Lelkipásztor (Budapest)
		LQ	Lutheran quarterly N. S. (Milwaukee, WI)

LR	Lutherische Rundschau (Stuttgart)	STK	Svensk theologisk kvartalskrift (Lund)
LThJ	Lutheran theological journal (Adelaide, South Australia)	StZ	Stimmen der Zeit (Freiburg im Breisgau)
LThK	Lutherische Theologie und Kirche (Oberursel)	TA	Teologinen aikakauskirja / Teologisk tidskrisft (Helsinki)
Lu	Luther: Zeitschrift der Luther-Gesellschaft (Göttingen)	TE	Teológia (Budapest)
LuB	Lutherbibliographie	ThLZ	Theologische Literaturzeitung (Leipzig)
LuBu	Luther-Bulletin (Kampen)	ThPh	Theologie und Philosophie (Freiburg im Breisgau)
LuD	Luther digest (Shorewood, MI)		
LuJ	Lutherjahrbuch (Göttingen)	ThR	Theologische Rundschau (Tübingen)
MD	Materialdienst des Konfessionskundlichen Institutes (Bensheim)	ThRe	Theologische Revue (Münster)
		ThSz	Theológiai Szemle (Budapest)
MEKGR	Monatshefte für evangelische Kirchengeschichte des Rheinlandes (Köln)	ThZ	Theologische Zeitschrift (Basel)
		TRE	Theologische Realenzyklopädie (Berlin; New York, NY)
MKSz	Magyar Könyvszemle (Budapest)		
NAKG	Nederlands archief voor kerkgeschiedenis (Leiden)	TTK	Tidsskrift for teologi og kirke (Oslo)
		US	Una sancata (München)
NELKB	Nachrichten der Evangelisch-Lutherischen Kirche in Bayern (München)	UTB	Uni-Taschenbücher
		Vi	Világosság (Budapest)
NTT	Norsk teologisk tidsskrift (Oslo)	VIEG	Veröffentlichungen des Instituts für Europäische Geschichte Mainz
NZSTh	Neue Zeitschrift für systematische Theologie und Religionsphilosophie (Berlin)		
		ZBKG	Zeitschrift für bayerische Kirchengeschichte (Nürnberg)
ODR	Ortodoxia: Revista Patriarhiei Romine (București)		
		ZEvE	Zeitschrift für evangelische Ethik (Gütersloh)
ORP	Odrodzenie reformacja w Polsce (Warszawa)	ZEvKR	Zeitschrift für evangelisches Kirchenrecht (Tübingen)
PBl	Pastoralblätter (Stuttgart)		
PL	Positions luthériennes (Paris)	ZHF	Zeitschrift für historische Forschung (Berlin)
Pro	Protestantesimo (Roma)		
PTh	Pastoraltheologie (Göttingen)	ZKG	Zeitschrift für Kirchengeschichte (Stuttgart)
RE	Református Egyház (Budapest)		
RHE	Revue d'histoire ecclésiastique (Louvain)	ZKTh	Zeitschrift für katholische Theologie (Wien)
RHPhR	Revue d'histoire et de philosophie religieuses (Paris)	ZRGG	Zeitschrift für Religions- und Geistesgeschichte (Köln)
RL	Reformátusok Lapja (Budapest)	ZSRG	Zeitschrift der Savigny-Stiftung für Rechtsgeschichte: Kanonistische Abteilung (Wien; Köln)
RoJKG	Rottenburger Jahrbuch für Kirchengeschichte (Sigmaringen)		
RSz	Református Szemle (Kolozsvár, RO)	ZThK	Zeitschrift für Theologie und Kirche (Tübingen)
RuYu	Ru-tu yun-ku (Syngal bei Seoul)		
RW	Rondom het woord (Hilversum)	Zw	Zwingliana (Zürich)
SCJ	The sixteenth century journal (Kirksville, MO)	ZZ	Zeitzeichen (Berlin)

3   Umfang der Ausführungen über Luther

L"   Luther wird wiederholt gestreift.
L 2-7   Luther wird auf diesen Seiten ausführlich behandelt.
L 2-7+" Luther wird auf diesen Seiten ausführlich behandelt und sonst wiederholt gestreift.
L•   Die Arbeit konnte nicht eingesehen werden.

01 **Angeklagt und anerkannt:** Luthers Rechtfertigungslehre in gegenwärtiger Verantwortung/ hrsg.
von Hans Christian Knuth. Erlangen: Martin-
Luther-Verlag, 2009. 154 S. (Veröffentlichungen
der Luther-Akademie Sondershausen-Ratzeburg
e. V.; 6) – Siehe Nr. 292 f. 313. 327. 330.

02 **Bauernkrieg zwischen Harz und Thüringer Wald**/
hrsg. von Günter Vogler. S: Steiner, 2008. 522 S.
(Historische Mitteilungen: Beiheft; 69) – Siehe
Nr. 636-641. 643-645. 647-649. 651.

03 **La Bible lue au temps des Réformes (XVIᵉ siècle)**/ hrsg. von Guy Bedouelle; Annie Noblesse-
Rocher. P: Cerf, 2008. 96 S. (Cahiers évangile:
supplément; 146) – Siehe Nr. 368 f.

04 **Buchwesen in Spätmittelalter und Früher Neuzeit**
= Festschrift für Helmut Claus zum 75. Geburts-
tag/ hrsg. von Ulman Weiß. Epfendorf/Neckar:
Bibliotheca academica, 2008. 484 S.: Ill., Faks.,
Frontispiz. – Siehe Nr. 9. 12. 441. 452. 605. 664.
778 f. 964. 969.

05 **Calvin Handbuch**/ hrsg. von Herman J. Selderhuis. TÜ: Mohr Siebeck, 2008. IX, 569 S. – Siehe
Nr. 677. 680. 688. 694. 696. 700. 703.

06 **Calvijn:** handboek (Calvin Handbuch (niederl.))/
hrsg. von Herman J. Selderhuis; übers.: W. G.
Hurksman; M. J. Boon. Kampen: Kok, 2008.
653 S.: Ill. – Siehe Nr. 678. 681. 689. 695. 697. 701.
704.

07 **Christlicher Glaube und weltliche Herrschaft:**
zum Gedenken an Günther Wartenberg/ hrsg.
von Michael Beyer; Jonas Flöter; Markus Hein.
L: EVA, 2008. 392 S. (Arbeiten zur Kirchen- und
Theologiegeschichte; 24) – Siehe Nr. 245. 347. 350.
460. 620. 615. 617. 635. 724. 761.

08 **De la guerre juste à la paix juste:** aspects con-
fessionels de la construction de la paix dans
l'espace franco-allemand (XVIᵉ-XXᵉ siècle)/ hrsg.
von Jean-Paul Cahn. Villeneuve d'Ascg: Presses
Univ. du Septentrion, 2008. 313 S. – Siehe Nr. 344.
358. 851.

09 **Deutsche Geschichte:** vollständige Ausgabe/
hrsg. von Joachim Leuschner. Lizenzausgabe auf
CD-ROM. 10 Bde. B: Directmedia, 2006. 5160
Bildschirm-S. (Digitale Bibliothek; 151) – Siehe
Nr. 727. 795.

010 **Dictionnaire du monde germanique**/ hrsg. von
Elisabeth Décultot; Michel Espagne; Jacques Le
Rider. P: Bayard, 2007. 1308 S. L". – Siehe Nr. 148.
572.

011 **Ecriture, protestantisme et oecuménisme:** hom-

mage ... Albert Greiner pour ses 90 ans/ hrsg.
von Matthieu Arnold. P: Positions Luthériennes,
2008. 184 S. (PL; 56 (2008) Heft 1) – Siehe Nr. 210.
530. 886. 940.

012 **125 Jahre Verein für Reformationsgeschichte**/
hrsg. von Luise Schorn-Schütte. [GÜ]: GVH;
HD: Verein für Reformationsgeschichte, 2008.
443 S. (Schriften des Vereins für Reformationsgeschichte; 200) – Siehe Nr. 835. 839. 849. 855. 859.
948. 955. 959. 966.

013 **Eröffnung der Lutherdekade:** Reformationsjubiläum 2017. EPD-Dokumentation (2008) Nr. 42.
18 S. – Siehe Nr. 883. 893-895. 909. 913.

014 **Europa in der Frühen Neuzeit:** Festschrift für
Günther Mühlpfordt zum 75. Geburtstag/ hrsg.
von Erich Donnert. Bd. 6: **Mittel-, Nord- und
Osteuropa.** Köln; Weimar; W: Böhlau, 2002. IX,
819 S.: Ill., Frontispiz. – Siehe LuB 2004, Nr. 848;
LuB 2009, Nr. 718.

015 **Europa in der Frühen Neuzeit:** Festschrift für
Günther Mühlpfordt zum 85. Geburtstag/ hrsg.
von Erich Donnert. Bd. 7: **Unbekannte Quellen.
Aufsätze zu Entwicklung, Vorstufen, Grenzen
und Fortwirken der Frühneuzeit in und um
Europa. Inhaltsverzeichnisse der Bände 1-6. Per-
sonenregister der Bände 1-7.** Köln; Weimar; W:
Böhlau, 2008. XXV, 1242 S.: Ill. – Siehe Nr. 377.
731. 829.

016 **Fragmentarisches Wörterbuch:** Beiträge zur biblischen Exegese und christlichen Theologie; Horst
Balz zum 70. Geburtstag/ hrsg. von Kerstin
Schiffner; Klaus Wengst; Werner Zager. S: Kohlhammer, 2007. 470 S.: Frontispiz. – Siehe Nr. 256.
324. 362. 408. 413. 428. 434. 853.

017 **Frühneuzeitliche Konfessionskulturen:** Wittenberg 30.9. - 2.10.2004/ hrsg. von Thomas Kaufmann ... GÜ: GVH, 2008. 384 S.: Ill. (Schriften
des Vereins für Reformationsgeschichte; 207)
(Nachwuchstagung des VRG; 1 (2004)) – Siehe
Nr. 359. 386. 563. 633. 733. 773.

018 **Fundsache Luther:** Archäologen auf den Spuren
des Reformators; [Begleitband zur Landesausstel-
lung »Fundsache Luther – Archäologen auf den
Spuren des Reformators« im Landesmuseum für
Vorgeschichte Halle (Saale) vom 31. Oktober 2008
bis 26. April 2009] / hrsg. von Harald Meller. S:
Theiss; Halle: Landesamt für Denkmalpflege
und Archäologie Sachsen-Anhalt, 2008. 343 S.:
Ill. – Siehe Nr. 62. 76. 84. 92. 98. 108. 115. 137.
139.

019 **Gebundene Freiheit?:** Bekenntnisbildung und theologische Lehre im Luthertum/ hrsg. von Peter Gemeinhardt; Bernd Oberdorfer. GÜ: GVH, 2008. 289 S. (Die luth. Kirche: Geschichte und Gestalten; 25) – Siehe Nr. 173. 235. 237. 240 f. 271. 397. 577. 827.

020 **Une germanistique sans rivages:** mélanges en l'honneur de Frédéric Hartweg/ hrsg. von Emmanuel Béhague; Denis Goeldel. Strasbourg: Presses Universitaires de Strasbourg, 2009. 496 S,: Ill., Kt. – Siehe Nr. 398. 650. 714. 770. 881. 941.

021 **Gewalt erkennen – Gewalt überwinden:** Beiträge zu einem Symposium der Kirchlichen Hochschule Wuppertal und der Vereinten Evangelischen Mission/ hrsg. von Michael Klessmann; Jochen Motte. Wuppertal: Foedus, 2002. 127 S. – Siehe Nr. 652. 873.

022 **Glaube und Geschlecht:** fromme Frauen – spirituelle Erfahrungen – religiöse Tradition/ hrsg. von Ruth Albrecht; Annette Bühler-Dietrich; Florentine Strzelczyk. Köln; Weimar: Böhlau, 2008. 284 S.: Ill. (Literatur-Kultur-Geschlecht: Große Reihe; 43) – Siehe Nr. 492. 841.

023 **Grund und Gegenstand des Glaubens nach römisch-katholischer und evangelisch-lutherischer Lehre:** theologische Studien/ hrsg. von Eilert Herms und Lubomir Žak. TÜ: Mohr Siebeck; [Citta del Vaticano]: Lateran University, 2008. XVI, 610 S. – Siehe Nr. 186. 208. 229. 251. 309. 311. 325. 329. 335.

024 Hamm, Berndt; Welker, Michael: **Die Reformation:** Potentiale der Freiheit. TÜ: Mohr Siebeck, 2008. 133 S. – Siehe Nr. 121. 547. 921.

025 **Hochadelige Herrschaft im mitteldeutschen Raum (1200 bis 1600):** Formen – Legitimation – Repräsentation/ hrsg. von Jörg Rogge; Uwe Schirmer. L: Sächsische Akademie der Wissenschaften zu Leipzig; S: Steiner, 2003. 506 S. (Quellen und Forschungen zur sächsischen Geschichte; 23) – Siehe Nr. 78. 732.

026 **Introduction à la théologie systématique/** hrsg. von André Birmelé ... Genève: Labor et Fides, 2008. 622 S. – Siehe Nr. 25. 177. 179. 181. 212. 236. 294 f. 372. 475. 875-877. 888.

027 **Iustus ordo e ordine della natura:** sacra doctrina e saperi politici fra XVI e XVIII secolo; convegno di studi, Milano, 5-6 marzo 2004 (Iustus ordo und Naturordnung: heilige Lehre und politische Weisheit vom 16. bis 18. Jh.)/ hrsg. von Fausto Arici. Padova: Cedam, 2007. XIV, 328 S. (Biblioteca di lex naturalis; 5) – Siehe Nr. 351. 813.

028 **Der Jakobuskult in Sachsen/** hrsg. von Klaus Herbers und Enno Bünz. TÜ: Narr, 2007. 340 S. – Siehe Nr. 2. 535. 900.

029 **»Justice et grâce« dans les commentaires sur l'épître aux Romains/** hrsg. von Annie Noblesse-Rocher unter Mitarb. von Christian Krieger. Strasbourg: Faculté de Théologie Protestante, 2008. 263 S. – Siehe Nr. 290. 323. 561. 578.

030 Kettmann, Gerhard: **Wittenberg – Sprache und Kultur in der Reformationszeit:** kleine Schriften/ hrsg. von Rudolf Große. F; B; Bern; Bruxelles; NY; Oxford; W: Lang, 2008. 213 S. (Leipziger Arbeiten zur Sprach- und Kommunikationsgeschichte; 16) – Siehe Nr. 387-393.

031 Korsch, Dietrich; Leppin, Volker: **Luther im Gespräch/** red. Vorbemerkung: Hellmut Zschoch. Lu 79 (2008), 45-55. – Siehe Nr. 110-112.

032 **Krisztusra tekintve hittel és reménységgel:** ünnepi kötet Reuss András 70. születésnapjára (Mit Glaube und Hoffnung auf Christus schauen: Festschrift für András Reuss zum 70. Geburtstag)/ hrsg. von Tamás Béres; Eszter Kodácsy-Simon; Gabor Viktor Orosz. BP: Luther 2008. 381 S. (Eszmecsere; 4) – Siehe Nr. 221. 282. 374. 394. 668. 885. 890. 945. 949.

033 **Landeskirchengeschichte:** Konzepte und Konkretionen; Tagung des Arbeitskreises Deutsche Landeskirchengeschichte im Kloster Amelungsborn vom 29. bis 31. März 2006/ hrsg. von Hans Otte; Michael Beyer; Christian Winter. L: EVA, 2008. 176 S. (HCh: Sonderbd.; 14) – Siehe Nr. 74. 766. 939. 943.

034 **Lay bibles in Europe 1450-1800/** hrsg. von M[athijs] Lamberigts ... Leuven: University: Peters, 2006. XI, 360, 4 S.: Ill. (Biblioteca Ephemeridum theologicarum Lovanensium; 198) – Siehe Nr. 613. 713.

035 **Life in all fullness:** Latin American Protestant churches facing neoliberal globalization/ hrsg. von René Krüger. Buenos Aires: Instituto Universitario ISEDET, 2007. 434 S. – Siehe Nr. 338. 867.

036 **Luther in Mansfeld:** Forschungen am Elternhaus des Reformators/ mit Beiträgen von Björn Schlenker ... hrsg. von Harald Meller. Halle (Saale): Landesmuseum für Vorgeschichte, 2007. 209 S. Ill. (Archäologie in Sachsen-Anhalt: Sonderbd.; 6) – Siehe Nr. 60. 63 f. 81 f. 90. 95. 135. 734.

037 **Lutherjahrbuch:** Organ der internationalen Lutherforschung/ im Auftrag der Luther-Gesellschaft hrsg. von Helmar Junghans. Bd. 74: Jahrgang 2007. GÖ: V&R, 2008. 276 S.: Ill. – Siehe Nr. 8. 230. 371. 435. 440. 449 f. 618. 871. 951. 956.

038 **Lutherjahrbuch:** Organ der internationalen Lutherforschung/ im Auftrag der Luther-Gesellschaft hrsg. von Helmar Junghans. Bd. 75: Jahr-

gang 2008. GÖ: V&R, 2008. 288 S.: Ill. – Siehe Nr. 165. 207. 289. 300. 448. 455. 540. 590. 910. 944. 952. 957.

039 **Luthers Lebenswelten**/ hrsg. von Harald Meller; Stefan Rhein; Hans-Georg Stephan. Halle (Saale): Landesamt für Denkmalpflege und Archäologie Sachsen-Anhalt, Landesmuseum für Vorgeschichte, 2008. 387 S.: Ill. (Tagungen des Landesmuseums für Vorgeschichte Halle; 1) – Siehe Nr. 7. 48. 59. 65. 67. 77. 85. 87. 91. 96. 136. 138. 140-142. 144-146. 333. 494. 735.

040 **Luthers Thesenanschlag – Faktum oder Fiktion**/ hrsg. von Joachim Ott; Martin Treu. L: EVA, 2008. 207 S.: Ill. (Schriften der Stiftung Luthergedenkstätten in Sachsen-Anhalt; 9) – Siehe Nr. 14. 20. 66. 124. 127. 608. 769. 861 f. 872. 920. 935.

041 **Maria von Ungarn (1505-1558)**: eine Renaissancefürstin/ hrsg. von Martina Fuchs; Orsolya Réthelyi; Mitarb.: Katrin Sippel. MS: Aschendorff, 2007. 416 S. (Geschichte in der Epoche Karls V.; 8) – Siehe Nr. 744. 747.

042 **Masculinity in the Reformation era**/ hrsg. von Scott H. Hendrix; Susan C. Karant-Nunn. Kirksville, MO: Truman State University, 2008. XIX, 228 S.: Ill. (Sixteenth century essays & studies; 83) – Siehe Nr. 486 f. 491. 502.

043 **Medizin und Sozialwesen in Mitteldeutschland zur Reformationszeit**/ hrsg. von Stefan Oehmig. [Wolfgang Böhmer zum 70. Geburtstag]. L: EVA, 2007. 369 S.: Ill., Taf. (Schriften der Stiftung Luthergedenkstätten in Sachsen-Anhalt; 6) – Siehe Nr. 339. 346. 353. 357. 361. 584. 588. 659. 719.

044 **Melanchthons Wirkung in der europäischen Bildungsgeschichte**/ hrsg. von Günter Frank; Sebastian Lalla. HD; Ubstadt-Weiher; Weil a. Rhein; BL: Regionalkultur, 2007. 267 S. L''. (Fragmenta Melanchthoniana; 3) – Siehe Nr. 427. 574 f. 585. 591 f. 607. 626. 789.

045 **Nikolaus von Amsdorf (1483-1565)**: zwischen Reformation und Politik/ hrsg. von Irene Dingel. Redaktion: Johannes Hund; Henning P. Jürgens. L: EVA, 2008. 379 S. (Leucorea-Studien zur Geschichte der Reformation und der Luth. Orthodoxie; 9) – Siehe Nr. 6. 11. 72. 586. 589. 593. 601. 776. 780. 787. 790. 794. 797. 805 f. 809. 823.

046 **Orthodoxies and heterodoxies in early modern German culture**: order and creativity 1500-1750/ hrsg. von Randolph C. Head; Daniel Christensen. Leiden: Brill, 2007. XII, 284 S.: Ill. (Studies in central European histories; 42) – Siehe Nr. 546. 548. 801. 816.

047 **Paul Gerhardt – Dichtung, Theologie, Musik**: wissenschaftliche Beiträge zum 400. Geburtstag/ hrsg. von Dorothea Wendebourg. TÜ: Mohr Siebeck, 2008. VIII, 374 S. – Bespr.: Junghans, Reinhard: LuJ (2008), 228-231. – Siehe Nr. 793. 819.

048 **Perspektiven der Reformationsforschung in Sachsen**: Ehrenkolloquium zum 80. Geburtstag von Karlheinz Blaschke/ hrsg. von Winfried Müller. Dresden: Thelem, 2008. 184 S.: Ill. auf Taf. (Bausteine aus dem Institut für Sächsische Geschichte und Volkskunde: kleine Schriften zur sächsischen Geschichte und Volkskunde; 12) – Siehe Nr. 17. 611.

049 **A péteri szolgálat a harmadik évezred küszöbén** (Der Petrusdienst an der Schwelle des dritten Jahrtausends). BP: Vigilia, 2008. 234 S. (Sapientia füzetek; 12) – Siehe Nr. 279. 287.

050 **Piety and family in early modern Europe**: essays in honour of Steven Ozment/ hrsg. von Marc R. Foster; Benjamin J. Kaplan. Aldershot, Hampshire; Burlington, VT: Ashgate, 2005. X, 242 S. (St. Andrews studies in Reformation history) – Siehe Nr. 274. 479. 528. 911.

051 **Politik und Religion**: Eigenlogik oder Verzahnung?; Europa im 16. Jahrhundert/ hrsg. von Robert von Friedeburg; Luise Schorn-Schütte. M: Oldenbourg, 2007. VI, 165 S. (HZ: Beihefte: N. F.; 45) – Siehe Nr. 545. 565.

052 **Reform and expansion, 1500-1660**/ hrsg. von R[onny] Po-chia Hsia. Cambridge, UK; NY: Cambridge University, 2007. XXI, 749 S.: Ill. (The Cambridge history of Christianity; 6) – Siehe Nr. 106. 541. 656. 720. 792. 811.

053 **Reformation und Mönchtum**: Aspekte eines Verhältnisses über Luther hinaus/ hrsg. von Athina Lexutt; Volker Mantey; Volkmar Ortmann. TÜ: Mohr Siebeck, 2008. VI, 276 S. (Spätmittelalter, Humanismus, Reformation; 43) – Siehe Nr. 122. 515. 520. 523. 527. 818. 828. 842. 961. 967.

054 **Religion past and present**: encyclopedia of theology and religion (Religion in Geschichte und Gegenwart. 4., adaptierte Aufl. ⟨engl.⟩)/ hrsg. von Hans Dieter Betz ... Bd. 1: **A-Bhu**/ übers. von Jennifer H. Adams-Maßmann ... Leiden: Brill, 2007. CIII, 719 S.: Ill., Kt. (RPP; 1) – Siehe Nr. 132. 228. 242. 263. 310. 321. 409. 453. 478. 497. 510. 514. 519. 522. 570. 587. 616. 619. 621. 707. 722. 725. 844.

055 **Religion past and present**: encyclopedia of theology and religion (Religion in Geschichte und Gegenwart. 4., adaptierte Aufl. ⟨engl.⟩)/ hrsg. von Hans Dieter Betz ... Bd. 2: **Bia-Chr**/ übers. von Mark E. Biddle ... Leiden: Brill, 2007. CXII, 664 S.: Ill., Kt. (RPP; 2) – Siehe Nr. 211. 370. 406. 416. 425. 456. 558. 600. 624. 673. 687. 692.

056 **Religion und Gewalt**: Konflikte, Rituale, Deutungen (1500-1800)/ hrsg. von Kaspar von Greyerz;

Kim Siebenhüner; in Verbindung mit Christopher Duhamelle ... GÖ: V&R, 2006. 432 S. (Veröffentlichungen des Max-Planck-Instituts für Geschichte; 215) – Siehe LuB 2007, Nr. 072 und LuB 2009, Nr. 337. 542.

057 Séguenny, André: **Teológia és filozófia között:** spiritualisták a 16. században (Zwischen Theologie und Philosophie: Spiritualisten im 16. Jahrhundert)/ übers. von Péter Balázs; Gizella Keserž; Andrea Schaffer. Szeged: Szegedi Tudományegyetem, 2008. 202 S. – Siehe Nr. 532. 567 f. 646. 660-663. 693.

058 **Die Taufe:** Einführung in Geschichte und Praxis/ hrsg. von Christian Lange; Clemens Leonhard; Ralph Olbrich. DA: WB, 2008. XII, 196 S. – Siehe Nr. 260. 262.

059 **Tod und Jenseits in der Schriftkultur der Frühen Neuzeit**/ hrsg. von Marion Kobelt-Groch und Cornelia Niekus Moore. Wiesbaden: Harrassowitz, 2008. 243 S.: Ill. (Wolfenbütteler Forschungen; 119) – Siehe Nr. 258. 493. 675.

060 **Universitäten und Wissenschaften im mitteldeutschen Raum in der Frühen Neuzeit:** Ehrenkolloquium zum 80. Geburtstag von Günter Mühlpfordt/ hrsg. von Karlheinz Blaschke; Detlef Döring. L: Sächsische Akademie der Wissenschaften zu Leipzig; S: Steiner, 2004. 327 S.: Ill. (Quellen und Forschungen zur sächsischen Geschichte; 26) – Siehe Nr. 463. 469. 825.

061 **»Unverzagt und ohne Grauen«:** Paul Gerhardt, der »andere« Luther/ hrsg. von Albrecht Beutel; Winfried Böttler. B: Frank & Timme, 2008. 144 S.: Ill. (Beiträge der Paul-Gerhardt-Gesellschaft; 4) – Siehe Nr. 185. 775. 796.

062 **Wege der Neuzeit:** Festschrift für Heinz Schilling zum 65. Geburtstag/ hrsg. von Stefan Ehrenpreis ... B: Duncker & Humblot, 2007. 656 S.: Ill. (Historische Forschungen; 85) – Siehe Nr. 238. 283. 543. 566. 683. 848.

063 **Wörter – Verbindungen:** Festschrift für Jarmo Korhonen zum 60. Geburtstag/ hrsg. von Ulrich Breuer; Irma Hyvärinen. F; B; Bern; Bruxelles; NY; Oxford; W: Lang, 2006. 516 S.: Ill. – Siehe Nr. 403. 407.

064 **Wohlfahrt und langes Leben:** Luthers Auslegung des 4. Gebots in ihrer aktuellen Bedeutung/ hrsg. von Friedrich-Otto Scharbau. Erlangen: Martin-Luther-Verlag, 2008. 127 S.: Ill. (Veröffentlichungen der Luther-Akademie Sondershausen-Ratzeburg; 5) – Siehe Nr. 197. 365. 468. 902. 937.

065 **Zur Kirche gehört mehr als ein Kruzifix:** Studien zur mitteldeutschen Kirchen- und Frömmigkeitsgeschichte; Festgabe für Gerhard Graf zum 65. Geburtstag/ hrsg. von Michael Beyer; Martin Teubner; Alexander Wieckowski. L: EVA, 2008. 463 S.: Ill. (HCh: Sonderbd.; 13) – Siehe Nr. 16. 83. 433. 439. 721. 782.

A QUELLEN

1 Quellenkunde

1 Arnold, Matthieu: **La correspondance et les propos de table de Martin Luther:** genres mineurs ou sources nouvelles pour la connaissance du Réformateur? Francia 34 (P 2007), 115-127.

2 Eisermann, Falk; Reichert, Volker: **Der wiederentdeckte Reisebericht des Hans von Sternberg.** In: 028, 219-248.

3 Guth, Waltraut: **Bibliotheksgeschichte des Landes Sachsen-Anhalt / Halle (Saale):** Universitäts- und Landesbibliothek Sachsen-Anhalt, 2004. VIII, 237 S. L". (Schriften zum Bibliotheks- und B chereiwesen in Sachsen-Anhalt; 85)

4 **Handbuch der historischen Buchbestände in Deutschland**/ in Zsarb. mit Severin Corsten ... hrsg. von Bernhard Fabian. Bd. 22: **Sachsen-Anhalt**/ hrsg. von Friedhilde Krause; bearb. von Erhardt Mauersberger; Waltraut Guth. Register: Karen Kloth. Hildesheim; ZH; NY: Olms-Weidmann, 2000. 257 S. L".

5 **Handbuch der historischen Buchbestände in Deutschland**/ in Zsarb. mit Severin Corsten ... hrsg. von Bernhard Fabian. Bd. 25: **Gesamtregister:** Sachregister GES-ME/ zsgest. von Karen Kloth; Andre Schüller. Hildesheim; ZH; NY: Olms-Weidmann, 2000. 293 S. L 264 f.

6 Hasse, Hans-Peter: **Inhaltsverzeichnis des Manuskriptbandes MS 896 des Wittenberger Lutherhauses aus dem Nachlass von Nikolaus von Amsdorf.** In: 045, 345-351.

7 Heling-Grewolls, Antje: **Schriftliche Quellen zum Alltagsleben der Familie Luther in Wittenberg.** In: 039, 299-305: Ill.

8 Junghans, Helmar: **Interpunktion und Großschreibung in Texten der Lutherzeit.** LuJ 74 (2007), 153-180.

9 Kopp, Ulrich: **Noch einmal zum Schriftenfälscher Michael Lindener.** In: 04, 323-339: Ill.

10 Kostlán, Antonín: **Bohemikální Alba amicorum**

ve fondech **British Library** (Böhmische Stamm-
bücher im Besitz der British Library). Folia
historica Bohemica 23 (PR: 2008), 91-214.

11 Kühne, Hartmut: **Die Weimarer Amsdorffiana-
Handschriften – ein Inventar.** In: 045, 353-372.

12 Künast, Hans-Jörg: **Die Flugschriftensammlung
des Augsburger Benediktiners Veit Bild aus den
Jahren 1519 bis 1525.** In: 04, 149-178: Ill.

13 Liersch, Helmut: **Martin Luthers Brief an St.
Jacobi:** eine Spurensuche (Briefe [WA Br 5, Nr.
1432]). In: St.-Jakobi-Kirche Goslar: 1073 – 1805
– 2005 = Festschrift zur Wiederbegründung der
Katholischen Kirchengemeinde St. Jakobus der
Ältere vor 200 Jahren/ hrsg. von der Kath. Pfarr-
gemeinde St. Jakobus d. Ä., Goslar. Hildesheim:
Bernward Mediengesellschaft, [2005], 59-71: Faks.
(Hildesheimer Chronik; 15)

14 Ott, Joachim: **Georg Röhrer (1492-1557) und sein
Nachlass in der Thüringer Universitäts- und
Landesbibliothek Jena.** In: 040, 47-57.

15 **Quellenkunde zur deutschen Geschichte der
Neuzeit** von 1500 bis zur Gegenwart/ hrsg. von
Winfried Baumgart. 2., neubearb. und erw. Aufl./
Redaktion: Mathias Friedel. Bd. 1: **Das Zeitalter**

der Glaubensspaltung (**1516-1618**): Reformation
und Konfessionalisierung/ bearb. von Winfried
Dotzauer (1987 und 2004). DA: WB; B: Directmedia [Software], 2005. Bildschirm-S.22-613. L 116 f.
225-243+". (DBWGB; 2)

16 Schirmer, Uwe: **Quellen aus dem Thüringischen
Hauptstaatsarchiv Weimar zur Kirchenpolitik der
ernestinischen Kurfürsten und Herzöge Friedrich
und Johann (1517-1532).** In: 065, 77-87.

17 Schirmer, Uwe: **Unerschlossene Quellen zur
Reformationsgeschichte:** Kirchenrechnungen
aus dem ernestinischen Kursachsen (1514-1547).
In: 048, 107-123.

18 Schneider, Hans: **Neue Quellen zum Konflikt in
der deutschen Reformkongregation der Augustinereremiten zu Beginn des 16. Jahrhunderts.**
Analecta Augustiniana 71 (Roma 2008), 7-37.

19 Seitz, Reinhard: **Ein Sammelband mit überwiegend Basler Lutherdrucken aus dem Besitz von
Tilman Limperger (Telamonius Limpergius).** Zw
34 (2007), 121-141.

20 Treu, Martin: **Urkunde und Reflexion:** Wieder-
entdeckung eines Belegs für Luthers Thesenanschlag. In: 040, 59-67.

2 Wissenschaftliche Ausgaben und Übersetzungen der Werke Luthers sowie der biographischen Quellen

21 [Luther, Martin]: **D. Martin Luthers Werke:** kritische Gesamtausgabe. Bd. 72: **Deutsches Sachregister zur Abteilung Schriften Band 1-60:** O-Ti-
tel/ hrsg. im Auftrag der Heidelberger Akademie
der Wissenschaften von Ulrich Köpf; verf. von
Jochen Berendes ...; Redaktion: Heinz Blanke;
Koordination: Reinhold Rieger. Weimar: Böhlau,
2007. 794 S.

22 [Luther, Martin]: **The bondage of the will** (*De
servo arbitrio* (engl.))/ übers. von J. I. Packer; O.
R. Johnston. Grand Rapids, MI: Revell, 2007. 322
S.

23 [Luther, Martin]: **The bondage of the will:** complete and unabridged (*De servo arbitrio* ⟨engl.⟩)/
hrsg. von Henry Cole; Edward Thomas Vaughan;
Henry Atherton. Greenville, SC: Ambassador
International, 2007. 350 S. (Ambassador classics)

24 Luther, Martin: **Bondage of the will** (*De servo arbitrio* (engl.)). 1. Hendrickson-Ausgabe. Peabody,
MA: Hendrickson, [2008]. 297 S.

25 [Luther, Martin]: **Trois règles de Martin Luther
pour le études de théologie** (*Der erste Teil der
Bücher D. M. Luthers über etliche Epistel der
Apostel. Vorrede Luthers 1539* [Auszug] ⟨franz.⟩)/
übers. von Matthieu Arnold. In: 026, 483-485.

26 Luther, Martin: **Gesammelte Werke**/ hrsg.
von Kurt Aland; mit einer ill. Lebenschronik
und einer Einführung in Werk und Theologie.
CD-ROM-Ausgabe auf der Basis von »Luther
Deutsch« [Ausgabe GÖ 1991]/ Lektorat: Mark
Lehmstedt; biograph. Zeittafel und bibliograph.
Angaben: Gertraud Götz. – Enthält: Heinrich
Bornkamm: **Martin Luther:** Leben und Schriften
(RGG. 3. Aufl. Bd. 4, 480-495); Gerhard Ebeling:
Martin Luther: Theologie (RGG. 3. Aufl. Bd. 4,
495-520). 10 Bde. auf CD-ROM. B: Directmedia,
2008. 1 CD-ROM. (Zeno.org; 39) [Vgl. LuB 2003,
Nr. 34]

27 [Luther, Martin]: **A translation and analysis of
Martin Luther's 1528 catechetical sermons on
the Lord's Supper** (*Katechismuspredigten 1528.
Nr. 923 f. 940* ⟨engl.⟩)/ übers. und komm. von
Aaron Moldenhauer. CJ 33 (2007), 43-60.

28 [Luther, Martin]: **Luther's spirituality**/ hrsg. und
übers. von Philip D. W. Krey; Peter D. S. Krey.
Vorwort: Timothy J. Wengert. NY; Mahwah,
NJ: Paulist, 2007. XXX, 296 S. (The classics of
Western spirituality)

29 [Luther, Martin] Lutero, Martin: **Opere scelte**
(Ausgew. Werke ⟨ital.⟩)/ hrsg. unter Leitung von

Paolo Ricca. Bd. 11: **Alla nobiltà cristiana della nazione tedesca a proposito della correzione e del miglioramento della società cristiana** (1520) (*An den christlichen Adel deutscher Nation von des christlichen Standes Besserung* ⟨ital.⟩)/ hrsg. von Paolo Ricca; übers. von Paolo Tognina. Anhang: La »Donazione di Costantino«; il »Dictatus Papae« di Gregorio VII (»Konstantinische Schenkung; »Dictatus papae« Gregors VII.). Torino: Claudiana, 2008. 317 S.: Ill.

30 **Martin Luther és William Tyndale Pál Rómaiakhoz irt leveléről** (Martin Luther and William Tyndale on Paul's Epistle to the Romans ⟨ungar. und engl.⟩)/ hrsg. und eingel. von András Mikesy; übers. von Szilvia Szita; András Mikesy. Piliscsaba: Pázmány Péter Katolikus Egyetem, 2008. 146 S. (Early Tudor Literature and Religion; 1)

3 Volkstümliche Ausgaben und Übersetzungen der Werke Luthers sowie der biographischen Quellen

a) Auswahl aus dem Gesamtwerk

31 **Ein feste Burg:** Luthers Lieder/ hrsg. von Reinhard Mawick; Einführung: Inge Mager; Ill. von Egbert Herfurth. L: Faber & Faber, 2008. 139 S.: Ill., Noten.

32 **Ein feste Burg:** Luthers Lieder/ hrsg. von Reinhard Mawick; Einführung: Inge Mager; Ill. von Egbert Herfurth. Lizenzausgabe. DA: WB, 2008. 139 S.: Ill., Noten.

33 **Ein feste Burg:** Martin Luther und Gottes Botschaft/ Textzusammenstellung: Walter Pollmann. Birnbach: Verlag am Birnbach, 2007. 24 S.: Ill.

34 [Luther, Martin]: **Collected works of Martin Luther:** Martin Luther's Large catechism. Concerning Christian liberty. The Smalcald articles and Martin Luther's 95 Thesis. [Charleston, SC]: BiblioBazaar, 2007. 248 S.

35 [Luther, Martin]: **Martin Luther's Large catechism and Small catechism** (*Deutsch [Großer] Katechismus . Der Kleine Katechismus* ⟨engl.⟩)/ übers. von F[riedrich] Bente; W[illiam] H. T. Dau; Robert E. Smith. Sioux Falls, SD: NuVision Publications, 2007. 116 S.

36 [Luther, Martin]: **Die 95 Thesen über die Kraft des Ablasses von Dr. Martin Luther:** umrahmt von Chorälen und Liedern mit Texten aus der Feder Martin Luthers (*Disputatio pro declaratione virtutis indulgentiarum; Geistliche Lieder* ⟨neuhochdt.⟩)/ musikal. Idee und Bearbeitungen: Carola Pinder; Produktion: C[arola] Pinder; H[erbert] Peter. s. l.: Edition musicart, 2008. 1 CD & Beil. (Booklet: Text der 95 Thesen). (Edition musicart; 8010-215)

37 Luther, Martin: **Kdybych měl nekonečně světů ...:** výbor z díla I (Wenn ich unendliche Welten hätte ...: Werkauswahl I)/ ausgew. und übers. von Hana Volná; Ondřej Macek. PR: Lutherova společnost, 2008. 234 S.

38 [Luther, Martin]: **Mit Luther durch das Jahr:** Texte des großen Reformators für unsere Zeit/ ausgew., eingel. und komm. von Athina Lexutt. Rheinbach: CMZ, 2003. 383 S.: Ill. [Vgl. LuB 2004, Nr. 85]

39 [Luther, Martin]: **Mit Luther Klartext reden**/ hrsg. von Hans-Joachim Neubauer; Christiane Seiler. Originalausgabe. FR: Herder, 2008. 158 S. (Herder Spektrum; 6035)

40 [Luther, Martin]: **Selected writings of Martin Luther**/ hrsg. von Theodore G. Tappert. Paperbackausgabe der Ausgabe Phil, 1967. Fortress Press 207 Ed. 4 Bde. MP: Fortress, 2007. 1836 S.

41 [Luther, Martin]: **Viisauden lähteillä:** Lutherin seurassa (An der Quelle der Weisheit: mit Luther)/ ges. von Jaakko Mäkeläinen; Bilder von Pirkko Kanervisto. Helsinki: Uusi tie, 2008. 125 S.

42 [Luther, Martin]: **Die Weisheit des Martin Luther**/ hrsg. von Theodor Glaser. [Rosenheim]: Rosenheimer, 2008. 127 S.: Ill. – Bespr.: Junghans, Helmar: LuJ 75 (2008), 215 f.

43 [Luther, Martin]: **»Wir sollen Menschen und nicht Gott sein«:** Luther zum Vergnügen/ hrsg. von Johannes Schilling. S: Reclam, 2008. 155 S.: Ill. (Reclams Universal-Bibliothek; 18579) – Bespr.: Junghans, Helmar: LuJ 75 (2008), 214 f.

44 **Salzburg:** lokalhistorische Texte/ ausgew. und komm. von Andreas Gößner. M: Lindauer, 2008. 112 S.: Ill. (Lindauers lateinische Quellen)

b) Einzelschriften und Teile von ihnen

45 [Luther, Martin]: **Durch Gottes Gnade bin ich wohlauf: Martin Luthers Leben in seinen Briefen** (*Briefe* ⟨hochdt.⟩)/ hrsg. von Reinhard Dithmar. L: EVA, 2008. 223 S.

46 Luther, Martin: **Tohtori Martti Lutherin Iso kate-**

kismus: yksi luterilaisen kirkon tunnustuskirjo-
ista (Doktor Martin Luthers Großer Katechismus
⟨finn.⟩): eine der Bekenntnisschriften der luth.
Kirche. [Lahti]: Luther-kirjat, 2008. 223 S.

47   Luther, Martin: **Mitten wie [wir!] im Leben.**
(*Geistliche Lieder:* Mitten wir im Leben sind
...). In: Zerreiß doch die Wolken: Texte zum
Nachdenken/ hrsg. von Michael Schlagheck ...
FR; BL; W: Herder, 2007, 110 f.

48   Gasser, Christoph: **Vogelfang und Vogelschutz
zur Zeit Martin Luthers** [mit Anhang: *Klage-
schrift der Vögel gegen Wolfgang Sieberger*]. In:
039, 259-266: Ill. L 264 f.

49   [Luther, Martin]: **Luther's Small catechism and
explanation** (*Der Kleine Katechismus* ⟨engl.⟩)/
hrsg. von Hans Andreas Urseth; Harald Ulrik
Sverdrup. MP: Ambassador, 2007. XI, 156 S.: Ill.

50   **Suomen evankelis-luterilaisen kirkon katekis-
mus** (Der Katechismus der Evang.-Luth. Kirche
Finnlands) (*Der Kleine Katechismus* ⟨finn.⟩).
[Helsinki]: Kirjapaja, 2008. 106 S.

51   Luther, Martin: **Lilla katekesen och dess förkla-
ring. Den kristna läran** (*Der kleine Katechismus*
⟨schwed.⟩ und seine Erklärung. Die christliche
Lehre)/ hrsg. von Markku Särelä; Ill: Kimmo
Pälikö; übers. von Johan Lumme. Lahtis: STLK

Finlands konfessionella lutherska kyrka, 2008.
291 S.

52   [Luther, Martin]: **Through the year with Martin Luther:** a selection of sermons celebrating
the feasts and seasons of the Christian year
(*Predigten* ⟨engl.⟩)/ hrsg. von Suzanne Tilton.
Peabody, MA: Hendrickson, 2007. VII, 463 S.

53   [Luther, Martin]: **Radikale Kirchenkritik, radikale Erneuerung:** eine Synodalrede Luthers
aus der Frühzeit der Reformation (*Predigten:*
Sermo praescriptus praeposito ⟨dt.⟩)/ bearb. von
Johannes von L pke. Lu 79 (2008), 2-10.

54   [Luther, Martin]: **Conférence entre Luther et
le diable:** racontée par Luther lui-meme (*Von
der Winkelmesse und Pfaffenweihe* [Auszug]
⟨franz.⟩)/ [übers. von Isidore Liseux; Anmerkungen von Louis-Géraud de Cordemoy; Nicolas
Lenglet Du Fresnoy]. Neuausgabe. Avrillé: du
Sel, 2008. 37 S.: Ill. (Vérité sur l'histoire)

55   [Melanchthon, Philipp]: Melanchthon und Lu-
ther: **Merkmale einer Kirchenreform:** Martin
Luthers Lebensbeschreibung durch Philipp Me-
lanchthon (*Historia de vita et actis ... D. Martini
Lutheri* ⟨lat./dt.⟩)/ hrsg. von Harald Weinacht.
ZH: Theol. Verlag, 2008. 199 S.: Ill.

4   Ausstellungen, Bilder, Bildbiographien, Denkmäler, Lutherstätten

56   **Bugenhagenhaus Lutherstadt Wittenberg**/ hrsg.
von der Wüstenrot Stiftung; Text: Insa Christiane Hennen; Lektorat: Kristina Hasenpflug.
Ludwigsburg: Wüstenrot Stiftung; S: Karl Krä-
mer, 2007. 64 S.: Ill.

57   Dammer, Silvia: **Luthers Hochzeit:** das Buch
zum Fest. Kropstädt: Dammer, 2008. 192 S.: Ill.

58   Dömer, Cornelia: **Mit Martin Luther unterwegs:**
ein biographischer Reisef hrer. Holzgerlingen:
Hänssler, 2008. 150 S.: Ill.

59   Dräger, Ulf: **Die Fundmünzen aus dem Lutherhaus in Wittenberg.** In: 039, 113-117: Ill.

60   Dräger, Ulf: **Die Münzen – eine verlorene Haushaltskasse.** In: 036, 159-168: Ill.

61   Goecke-Seischab, Margarete Luise; Harz, Frieder: **Der Kirchen-Atlas:** Räume entdecken, Stile
erkennen, Symbole und Bilder verstehen; mit
Reise-Tipps. M: Kösel, 2008. 368 S.: Ill.

62   Gutjawr, Mirko: **»Non cultus est, sed memoriae
gratia«:** Hinterlassenschaften Luthers zwischen
Reliquien und Relikten. In: 018, 100-105.

63   Hellmund, Monika: **Pflanzenfunde aus der »Lu-
thergrube«.** In: 036, 187-200: Ill.

64   Hertel, Friederike: **Der Textilfund.** In: 036, 68 f.: Ill.

65   Hoffmann, Claudia: **Lutherzeitliche Ofenkacheln
aus dem Bestand des kulturhistorischen Museums
der Hansestadt Stralsund.** In: 039, 201-208: Ill.

66   Holsing, Henrike: **Luthers Thesenanschlag im
Bild.** In: 040, 141-172.

67   König, Sonja: **Wandbrunnen – Wasserblasen –
Wasserkästen.** In: 039, 101-111: Ill.

68   Krawulsky, Roland: **Wittenberg:** ein Führer durch
die Lutherstadt. 2., überarb. Aufl., 6.-10. Tsd.
Wernigerode: Schmidt-Buch, 2003. 80 S.: Ill.

69   Krawulsky, Roland: **Wittenberg:** ein Führer durch
die Lutherstadt. 3., aktual. Aufl., 11.-15. Tsd.
Wernigerode: Schmidt-Buch, 2006. 80 S.: Ill.

70   Krawulsky, Roland: **Wittenberg:** ein Führer durch
die Lutherstadt. 4., aktual. Aufl., 16.-20. Tsd.
Wernigerode: Schmidt-Buch, 2008. 80 S.: Ill.

71   Lilje, Hanns: **Martin Luther:** mit Selbstzeug-
nissen und Bilddokumenten/ hrsg. von Kurt
Kusenberg; mit 2002 neubearb. Bibliographie
von Helmar Junghans. 27. Aufl. Reinbek bei HH:
Rowohlt, 2008. 151 S.: Ill. (rororo; 50098:rororo-
Bildmonographien)

72   Lück, Heiner: **Universität und Stadt Wittenberg
zur Zeit des Nikolaus von Amsdorf:** ein Rekons-

truktionsversuch möglicher Wahrnehmungen (1502-1524). In: 045, 15-34.

73 **Luthers Schatzkammer:** Kostbarkeiten im Lutherhaus Wittenberg/ hrsg. von Volkmar Joestel im Auftrag der Stiftung Luthergedenkstätten in Sachsen-Anhalt. Dößel: Stekovics, 2008. 192 S.: Ill. – Bespr.: Junghans, Helmar: LuJ 75 (2008), 209-211.

74 Mager, Inge: **Evangelische Glaubensüberzeugung und zeitweilige Toleranz im rekatholisierten Eichsfeld bis zum Beginn des 20. Jahrhunderts.** In: 033, 33-40. L 40.

75 Marchewka, Wolfgang; Schwibb, Michael; Stephainski, Andreas: **Zeit Reise:** 800 Jahre Leben in Wittenberg; Luther; 500 Jahre Reformation. B: Zeit Reise, 2008. 214 S.: Ill. L 38-59+".

76 Matthes, Christian: **Die archäologische Entdeckung des Luthergeburtshauses in Eisleben.** In: 018, 114-119.

77 Matthes, Christian: **Ausgrabungen als stadttopografische Untersuchungen innerhalb und im Umfeld des »Luthergeburtshauses« in Eisleben.** In: 039, 79-90: Ill.

78 Müller, Matthias: **Das Schloß als fürstliches Manifest:** zur Architekturmetaphorik in den wettinischen Residenzschlössern von Meißen und Torgau. In: 025, 395-441. L 436 f.

79 Na[than, Carola]: **Wie aus »Luder« Luther wurde:** das Geburtshaus Martin Luthers in Eisleben. Monumente: Magazin für Denkmalkultur in Deutschland 17 (2007) Heft 5/6, 32 f. – Internetressource: ⟨www.monumente-online.de/07/06/streiflichter/04_Eisleben_Lutherhaus.php

80 **Nationalschätze aus Deutschland:** von Luther zum Bauhaus; anlässlich der Ausstellung »Nationalschätze aus Deutschland: von Luther zum Bauhaus« der Konferenz Nationaler Kultureinrichtungen (KNK) in Kooperation mit der Kunst- und Austellungshalle der Bundesrepublik Deutschland 30. September 2005 bis 8. Januar 2006/ mit Beitr. von Norman Rosenthal ... und Essays von Werner Busch ...; Redaktion: Roland Enke. M; B; LO; NY: Prestel, 2005. 406 S.: Ill. L" [Vgl. LuB 2009, Nr. 99]

81 Roehrer-Ertl, Friedrich-Ulf: **Zur Identifikation und Datierung eines Buchstabens aus der Abfallschüttung.** In: 036, 64-67: Ill.

82 Schlenker, Björn: **Archäologie am Elternhaus Luthers.** In: 036, 17-65. 70-112: Ill.

83 Schmidt, Frank: **Emporenmalerei als neue Bildaufgabe reformatorischen Kirchenbaus.** In: 065, 205-213. L 211.

84 Schmitt, Reinhard; Gutjahr, Mirko: **Das »Schwarze Kloster« in Wittenberg:** Bauforschung und Archäologie im und am Kloster der Augustiner-Eremiten und Wohnhaus Martin Luthers. In: 018, 132-139.

85 Schmitt, Reinhard: **Zur Baugeschichte des Augustiner-Eremitenklosters.** In: 039, 177-191: Ill.

86 Schwabe, Ernst: **Atlas deutsche Geschichte:** Römerzeit bis 1914; 2000 Jahre deutscher Geschichte; in 105 Karten mit Geschichtstabellen und erläuterndem Text. Reprintaufl. der Originalausgabe L, 1916. Früherer Titel: »2000 Jahre deutscher Geschichte«. L: Reprint-Verlag Leipzig, [2008]. 108 S., Kt. L 14 f.

87 Schwartz, Verena: **Die ältere Geschichte des Lutherhauses im Spiegel der Kachelfunde.** In: 039, 209-222: Ill.

88 Schwarz, Hilmar: **Luthers Tintenfleck auf der Wartburg.** Wartburg-Jahrbuch 14 (2005 [gedruckt 2007]), 112-121: Ill.

89 Stahl, Andreas: **Cyriacus Spangenberg als Chronist:** zur Authentizität des Sterbehauses von Martin Luther. In: Historische Bauforschung in Sachsen-Anhalt/ hrsg. vom Landesamt für Denkmalpflege und Archäologie Sachsen-Anhalt; Redaktion: Uwe Steinecke. Petersberg: Imhof, 2007, 294-313. [Arbeitsberichte / Landesamt für Denkmalpflege und Archäologie Sachsen-Anhalt; 6]

90 Stahl, Andreas: **Historische Bauforschung an Luthers Elternhaus:** archivalische Voruntersuchungen und erste Beobachtungen. In: 036, 113-138: Ill.

91 Stahl, Andreas: **Historische Bauforschung an Luthers Elternhaus in Mansfeld.** In: 039, 167-175: Ill.

92 Stahl, Andreas; Schlenker, Björn: **Lutherarchäologie in Mansfeld:** Ausgrabungen und begleitende Bauforschungen am Elternhaus Martin Luthers. In: 018, 120-131.

93 Steffens, Martin: **Luthergedenkstätten im 19. Jahrhundert:** Memoria – Repräsentation – Denkmalpflege. Regensburg: Schnell & Steiner, 2008. 376 S.: Ill., Taf. – Zugl.: B, Freie Univ., Diss., 2006.

94 Steinwachs, Albrecht: **Ich sehe dich mit Freuden an ...:** Bilder aus der Lucas-Cranach-Werkstatt in der Wittenberger Stadtkirche St. Marien. Spröda: Akanthus, 2006. 96 S.: Ill.

95 Stephan, Hans-Georg: **Keramische Funde aus Luthers Elternhaus.** In: 036, 139-158: Ill.

96 Stephan, Hans-Georg: **Lutherarchäologie:** Funde und Befunde aus Mansfeld und Wittenberg; Gedanken und Materialien zur Erforschung der Lebenswelt des Reformators und zur Alltagskul-

tur Mitteldeutschlands im 16.Jh. In: 039, 13-77: Ill.

97 **Stiftung Luthergedenkstätten in Sachsen-Anhalt:** Sendbrief: Zeitschrift für Besucher, Freunde und Förderer/ hrsg. von der Stiftung Luthergendenkstätten in Sachsen-Anhalt; Redaktion: Michael Kühnast. Nr. 9. Wittenberg, 2008. 8 S.: Ill.

98 Treu, Martin: **Luther-Bilder.** In: 018, 94-99.

99 **Von Luther zum Bauhaus:** Nationalschätze aus Deutschland; Auswahl von Highlights der Ausstellung »Nationalschätze aus Deutschland: von Luther zum Bauhaus«, eine Ausstellung der Konferenz Nationaler Kultureinrichtungen (KNK) in Kooperation mit der Kunst- und Ausstellungshalle der Bundesrepublik Deutschland in Bonn, 30. September 2005 - 8. Januar 2006/ Redaktion: Bettina Probst. Text Dt. und Engl. Bonn: Konferenz Nationaler Kultureinrichtungen, 2005. 51 S.: Ill. [Vgl. LuB 2009, Nr. 80]

100 **Zeit-Reise:** 1200 Jahre Leben in Leipzig/ hrsg. von Thomas Seidler; Andreas Stephainski; Armin Kühne. L: Leipziger Verlags- und Druck-Gesellschaft, [2007]. 376 S.: Ill. L". (Leipziger Volkszeitung)

101 **Zichy**/ eingel. und ausgew. von Katalin Gellér. BP: Corvina, 2007. 44 S.: [66] Taf.: Ill. L Taf. 25.

B DARSTELLUNGEN

1 Biographische Darstellungen

a) Das gesamte Leben Luthers

102 Arnold, Matthieu: **Écrire la biographie du Réformateur:** le »Martin Luther« de Volker Leppin (2006). RHPhR 88 (2008), 315-337. [Bespr. zu LuB 2007, Nr. 85]

103 Dieterich, Veit-Jacobus: **Martin Luther:** sein Leben und seine Zeit. Originalausgabe. M: dtv, 2008. 239 S.: Ill. (dtv; 24701: premium)

104 Fausel, Heinrich: **D. Martin Luther:** Leben und Werk 1522-1546. Lizenzausgabe. 2 Bde. in 1 Bd. Holzgerlingen: SCM Hänssler, 2008. 211, 335 S.

105 Febvre, Lucien: **Martin Luther:** un destin/ Nachwort: Robert Mandrou. P: PUF, 2008. 208 S. (Quadrige: Grands textes)

106 Hendrix, Scott: **Martin Luther, reformer.** In: 052, 3-19.

107 Herrmann, Horst: **Martin Luther:** eine Biographie. 4. Aufl. dieser Ausgabe. B: Aufbau Taschenbuch, 2006. 567 S. (AtV; 1933)

108 Junghans, Helmar: **Neue Erkenntnisse und neue Fragen zu Martin Luthers Leben und Umwelt.** In: 018, 142-149.

109 Kaufmann, Thomas: **Lutero** (Martin Luther ⟨ital.⟩)/ übers. von Marco Cupellaro. Bologna: Mulino, 2007. 136 S. (Universale paperbacks il Mulino; 524)

110 Korsch, Dietrich: **Leppins Luther:** eine Buchbesprechung. In: 031, 45-49.

111 Korsch, Dietrich: **Von der Notwendigkeit theologischer Kategorien für die Lutherdeutung:** wie eine Debatte weitergehen könnte. In: 031, 53-55.

112 Leppin, Volker: **Streit um Luther? Gerne!:** eine Antwort. In: 031, 49-52.

113 Lexutt, Athina: **Luther.** Köln; Weimar; W: Böhlau, 2008. 143 S.: Ill. (UTB; 3021: Profile)

114 Richardt, Aimé: **Luther**/ unter Mitarb. von Jean-Gérard Théobald. P: Guibert, 2008. 271 S.: Ill.

115 Stahl, Andreas: **Neue Erkenntnisse zur Biographie Martin Luthers:** Möhra – Eisleben – Mansfeld – Wittenberg. In: 018, 86-93.

116 Tomlin, Graham: **Luther und seine Welt** (Luther and his world ⟨engl.⟩)/ übers. von Gabriele Stein FR; BL; W: Herder, 2007. 190 S.: Ill.

117 Wilson, Derek: **Out of the storm:** the life and legacy of Martin Luther. LO: Hutchinson, 2007. 416 S.: Ill.

118 Wilson, Derek: **Out of the storm:** the life and legacy of Martin Luther. 1. US-amerikan. Ausgabe. NY: St. Martin's, 2007. XIII, 399 S.: Ill.

119 Wilson, Derek: **Out of the storm:** the life and legacy of Martin Luther. Lizenzausgabe der Ausgabe LO. LO: Pimlico, 2008. XIII, 399 S.: Ill. (Pimlico; 810)

b) Einzelne Lebensphasen und Lebensdaten

120 [Bugenhagen, Johannes]: **A newly discovered report of Luther's Reformation breakthrough from Johannes Bugenhagen's 1550 Johna commentary** (Ionas propheta expositus in tertio capite ... [Auszug] ⟨engl.⟩)/ übers. und komm. von Martin Lohrmann. LQ 22 (2008), 324-330.

121 Hamm, Berndt: **Die Einheit der Reformation in ihrer Vielfalt:** das Freiheitspotential der 95 Thesen vom 31. Oktober 1517. In: 024, 29-66.

122 Hamm, Berndt: **Naher Zorn und nahe Gnade:** Luthers frühe Klosterjahre als Beginn seiner reformatorischen Neuorientierung. (2007). In: 053, 103-143.

123 Junghans, Helmar: »**Bibelhumanistische Anstö-ße in Luthers Entwicklung zum Reformator**« [Impulses of biblical humanism in Luther's development towards being a reformer]/ engl. Zusammenfassung: Franz Posset. LuD 16 (2008), 40-42. [Vgl. LuB 2006, Nr. 20979]

124 Junghans, Helmar: **Martin Luther, kirchliche Magnaten und Thesenanschlag:** zur Vorge-schichte von Luthers Widmungsbrief zu den »Resolutiones disputationum de indulgentiarum virtute« an Papst Leo X. In: 040, 33-46.

125 Lemmons, Russel: »**If there is a hell, then Rome stands upon it**«: Martin Luther as travelor and translator. In: Travel and translation in the early modern period/ hrsg. von Carmine G. Di Biase. Amsterdam; NY: Rodopi, 2006, 290 S. [Approaches to translation studies; 26]

126 Leppin, Volker: **Der Thesenanschlag bleibt frag-lich:** Bemerkungen zu einer neuen Diskussion und alten Problemen. LuBu 17 (2008), 40-53.

127 Moeller, Bernd: **Thesenanschläge.** In: 040, 9-31.

128 Nitti, Silvana: **Abituarsi alla libertà:** Lutero alla Wartburg [Gewöhnt werden an Freiheit: Luther auf der Wartburg]/ Einleitung: Adriano Prosperi. Torino: Claudiana, 2008. IX, 278 S.: Ill. [Lutero: Opere scelte, Volume supplementare]

129 Schneider, Hans: **Contentio Staupitii:** der »Staupitzstreit« in der Observanz der deutschen Augustinereremiten 1507-1512. ZKG 117 (2008), 1-44.

130 Schubert, Anselm: **Libertas disputandi:** Luther und die Leipziger Disputation als akademisches Streitgespräch. ZThK 105 (2008), 411-442.

131 Vogel, Lothar: **Zwischen Universität und Seelsor-ge:** Martin Luthers Beweggründe im Ablassstreit. ZKG 117 (2008), 187-212.

132 Zschoch, Hellmut: **Augustinian-hermits** [Au-gustiner-Eremiten ⟨engl.⟩]. In: 054, 503 f.

c) Familie

133 Akerboom, Dick: »**Katharina von Bora und ihr Einfluss auf Martin Luther**« [Katharina von Bora and her influence on Martin Luther]/ engl. Kurzfassung: Rudolf K. Markwald. LuD 16 (2008), 13-19. [Vgl. LuB 2006, Nr. 128 sowie LuB 2003, Nr. 83; 2006, Nr. 127]

134 Degen, Roland: **Leben als Risiko:** Katharina von Bora, die Lutherin. Jahrbuch für Religionspäda-gogik 24 (2008), 184-189.

135 Döhle, Hans-Jürgen: **Schwein, Geflügel und Fisch – bei Luthers zu Tisch.** In: 036, 169-186: Ill.

136 Döhle, Hans-Jürgen: **Tierreste aus Küchenabfäl-len der Familien Hans Luder in Mansfeld und Martin Luther in Wittenberg.** In: 039, 329-335: Ill.

137 Fessner, Michael: **Die Familie Luder in Möhra und Mansfeld:** archivalische Überlieferungen zum Elternhaus von Martin Luther. In: 018, 78-85.

138 Fessner, Michael: **Die Familie Luder und das Berg- und Hüttenwesen.** In: 039, 235-243.

139 Fessner, Michael: **Luthers Speisezettel:** die Versorgung der Grafschaft Mansfeld mit Lebens-mitteln, Gütern und Waren. In: 018, 66-75.

140 Heinrich, Dirk: **Fischkonsum in Luthers Eltern-haus als Spiegel für Fischerei und Fischhandel in der frühen Neuzeit.** In: 039, 337-345: Ill.

141 Hellmund, Monika: **Die Familie Martin Luthers und die Pflanzenwelt.** In: 039, 347-362: Ill.

142 Schlenker, Björn: **Ausgrabungen und Forschungen am Elternhaus Martin Luthers in Mansfeld:** neue Erkenntnisse zu den Lebensverhältnissen des jugendlichen Reformators. In: 039, 91-99: Ill.

143 Sens, Hans-Christoph: **Katharina Luther und Torgau und weitere Beiträge zum Katharina-Lu-ther-Haus.** Torgau: Torgauer Geschichtsverein, 2006. 90 S.: Ill. [Kleine Schriften des Torgauer Geschichtsvereins; 18]

144 Straube, Manfred: **Handel und Verbrauch von Nahrungsmitteln im Umfeld Martin Luthers.** In: 039, 277-281.

145 Wedepohl, Karl Hans; Kronz, Andreas: **Eine stoff-liche Untersuchung von Gläsern aus Luthers Elternhaus in Mansfeld und seinem Wohnhaus in Wittenberg.** In: 039, 323-327: Ill.

146 Westermann, Ekkehard: **Ursachen und Folgen von Besitzwechseln bei Schmelzhütten und Immobilien der Hüttenmeister im Mansfelder Revier in der 1. Hälfte des 16. Jh.** In: 039, 245-251: Ill.

d) Volkstümliche Darstellungen seines Lebens und Werkes, Schulbücher, Lexikonartikel

147 Bagchi, David: **Luther's »Ninety-five theses« and the contemporary criticism of indulgences.** In: Promissory notes on the treasury of merits: indulgences in the late medieval Europe/ hrsg. von R. N. Swanson. Leiden; Boston: Brill, 2006,

331-355: Ill. (Brill's companions to the Christian traditions; 5)

148 Büttgen, Philippe: **Luther (Martin)**. In: 010, 678-680.

149 Gronau, Dietrich: **Martin Luther:** Revolutionär des Glaubens. Lizenzausgabe. Kreuzlingen: Hugendubel, 2006. 202 S. (Focus-Edition Biographien)

150 **Der große Plötz:** die Enzyklopädie der Weltgeschichte. 35., völlig neu bearb. Aufl. GÖ: V&R, 2008. 2128 S.: Ill. L 880-883+".

151 Kalmbach, Sybille: **Bibel dramatisch:** erfahrbare Entwürfe für die Arbeit mit Jugendlichen und Erwachsenen. NK: Aussaat, 2006. 174 S.: Ill. L 140. 158. (Kreativ kompakt)

152 Klein, Günther: **Martin Luther**. In: Giganten: große Wegbereiter der Moderne/ hrsg. von Hans-Christian Ruf. B: List, 2006, 9-74.

153 **Kleines Lexikon zum Christentum**/ erarb. von Sebastian Feydt ... L: EVA, 2007. 168 S.: Ill. L 97+".

154 Lachmann, Rainer; Gutschera, Herbert; Thier-

felder, Jörg: **Kirchengeschichtliche Grundthemen:** historisch – systematisch – didaktisch/ unter Mitarb. von Thomas Breuer ... 2. Aufl. GÖ: V&R, 2003. 360 S.: Ill. (Theologie für Lehrerinnen und Lehrer; 3) – Siehe LuB Nr. 2004, Nr. 047.

155 Naumann, Günter: **Deutsche Geschichte:** das alte Reich 962-1806. Wiesbaden: Marix, 2007. 256 S. L". (Marixwissen)

156 Naumann, Günter: **Deutsche Geschichte in Daten.** Wiesbaden: Marix, 2007. 224 S. L" (Marixwissen)

157 Sunshine, Glenn S.: **Reformation für zwischendurch** (The Reformation for armchair theologians ⟨engl.⟩)/ übers. von Gesine Robinson. GÖ: V&R, 2008. 256 S.: Ill.

158 Tökés, István: **Luther, Márton (1483-1546)** Református szemle 101 (Kolozsvár 2008), 297-304.

159 Ulfig, Alexander: **Große Denker**/ hrsg. von Abraham Melzer. Lizenzausgabe. Köln: Parkland, 2006. 425 S.: Ill. L 245-248.

2 Luthers Theologie und einzelne Seiten seines reformatorischen Wirkens

a) Gesamtdarstellungen seiner Theologie

160 Bayer, Oswald: **Freedom in response:** Lutheran ethics; sources and controversies (Freiheit als Antwort ⟨engl.⟩)/ übers. von Geffrey F. Cayzer. Oxford: Oxford University, 2007. XV, 275 S. (Oxford studies in theological ethics)

161 Bayer, Oswald: **A teologia de Martim Lutero:** uma atualização (Martin Luthers Theologie ⟨portug.⟩)/ übers. von Nélio Schneider. São Paulo: Sinodal, 2007. XVIII, 284 S.: Ill.

162 Bielfeldt, Dennis D.; Mattox, Mickey L.; Hinlicky, Paul R.: **The substance of the faith:** Luther's doctrinal theology for today/ hrsg. und eingef. von Paul R. Hinlicky. MP: Fortress, 2008. VII, 214 S.

163 Brecht, Martin: »**Die Entwicklung der Theologie Luthers aus der Exegese:** vorgefuehrt an der Epistel S. Petri gepredigt und ausgelegt (1522/1523)« [The development of Luther's theology from exegesis, demonstratet in the Epistle of St. Peter, preached and explained 1522/1523]/ engl. Zusammenfassung: Wolf D. Knappe. LuD 16 (2008), 55-60. [Vgl. LuB 2006, Nr. 159]

164 **Grundbegriffe der Theologie**/ hrsg. von Matthias Viertel. M: dtv, 2005. 509 S. L". (dtv; 34256) [Vgl. LuB 2009. Nr 176]

165 Hendrix, Scott H.: **Überlegungen zum Schreiben einer Theologie Luthers.** LuJ 75 (2008), 9-30.

166 Hofmann, Peter: **Katholische Dogmatik.** PB: Schöningh, 2008. 202 S. L". (UTB; 3098)

167 Holm, Bo Kristian: »**Zur Funktion der Lehre bei Luther:** die Lehre als rettendes Gedankenbild gegen Sünde, Tod und Teufel« [Concerning the function of doctrine in Luther: doctrine as saving thought picture against sin, death and devil]/ engl. Zusammenfassung: Rudolf K. Markwald. LuD 16 (2008), 82-87. [Vgl. LuB 2006, Nr. 161]

168 Jung, Martin H.: **Die Reformation:** Theologen, Politiker, Künstler. GÖ: V&R, 2008. 179 S.: Ill.

169 Kolb, Robert; Arand, Charles P.: **The genius of Luther's theology:** a Wittenberg way of thinking for the contemporay church. Grand Rapids, MI: Baker Academic, 2008. 240 S.

170 Lienhard, Marc: **Theologie für die Kirche:** lutherische Perspektiven. Luth. Kirche in der Welt 55 (2008), 15-28.

171 Pesch, Otto Hermann: **Hinführung zu Luther.** 3., aktual. und erw. Neuaufl. Mainz: Matthias Grünewald, 2004. 440 S.

172 Pesch, Otto Hermann: **Zrozumieć Lutra** (Hinführung zu Luther ⟨poln.⟩)/ übers. von Andrzej Marniok; Krzysztof Kowalik. Poznań: W Drodze, 2008. 639 S.

173 Rieger, Hans-Martin: **Theologische Wissenschaft und kirchliche Lehre.** In: 019, 261-284.

318

174 Sommer, Wolfgang; Klahr, Detlef: **Kirchenge-schichtliches Repetitorium:** zwanzig Grund-kapitel der Kirchen-, Dogmen- und Theologie-geschichte; mit Lernfragen auf CD-ROM von Marcel Nieden. 4., Aufl. GÖ: V&R, 2006. 295 S. & Beil. (1 CD-ROM). L 123-147+". (UTB; 1796)

175 Vainio, Olli-Pekka: **Luther.** Helsinki: WSOY, 2008. 138 S.

176 **Wörterbuch Theologie**/ hrsg. von Matthias Viertel. CD-ROM Ausgabe von »Grundbegriffe der Theologie«. B: Directmedia, 2006. 1328 Bild-schirm-S. (Digitale Bibliothek; 148) [Vgl. LuB 2009, Nr. 165]

b) Gott, Schöpfung, Mensch

177 Askani, Hans-Christoph: **Dieu.** In: 026, 429-457.

178 Brandy, Hans Christian: **»Vom Leiden des Men-schen und vom Leiden Gottes«** [The suffering of man and the suffering of God]/ engl. Zusam-menfassung: Wolfgang Vondey. LuD 16 (2008), 107 f. [Vgl. LuB 2007, Nr. 138]

179 Bühler, Pierre; Gounelle, André: **L'être humain et sa connaissance de Dieu.** In: 026, 179-212.

180 Carr, Amy: **A hermeneutics of providence amid affliction:** contributions by Luther and Weil to a cruciform doctrine of providence. Pro ecclesia 16 (Delhi, NY 2007), 278-298.

181 Causse, Jean-Daniel: **Les relations entre croire et penser.** In: 026, 17-47.

182 Danz, Christian: **Wirken Gottes:** zur Geschichte eines theologischen Grundbegriffs. NK: NV, 2007. VIII, 247 S. L 70-86.

183 Gregersen, Niels Henrik: **»Grace in nature and history:** Luther's doctrine of creation revisited«/ Zusammenfassung: Ian Christopher Levy. LuD 16 (2008), 79-81: Ill. [Vgl. LuB 2006, Nr. 182]

184 Grislis, Egil: **Martin Luther's animal farm in Ger-many.** Perichoresis 5 (Oradea 2007), 207-224.

185 Grosse, Sven: **Anfechtung und Verborgenheit Gottes bei Luther und bei Paul Gerhardt.** In: 061, 13-32.

186 Härle, Wilfried: **»Hominem iustificari fide«:** Grundzüge der reformatorischen Anthropologie. In: 023, 338-358.

187 Herms, Eilert: Zur Systematik des Personbe-griffes in reformatorischer Tradition. NZSTh 49 (2007), 377-413.

188 Herzer, Dorothea: **Zurechnung:** Überlegungen zu einem Aspekt des Verantwortungsbegriffs unter besonderer Berücksichtigung von Entwicklungen in Psychotherapie und Theologie. Taunusstein: Driesen, 2007. 187 S. L 117-154. – Zugl.: Marburg, Univ., Diss., 2006.

189 Jüngel, Eberhard: **»Was ist er inwerds?«:** Bemer-kunger. zu einem bemerkenswerten Aufsatz. ZThK 105 (2008), 443-455. [Vgl. unten Nr. 202]

190 Keller, Rudolf: **Vom Wirken des Heiligen Geistes im Verständnis Luthers.** Luth. Kirche in der Welt 54 (2007), 37-56.

191 Leiner, Martin: **Menschenwürde und Reforma-tion.** In: Des Menschen Würde – entdeckt und erfunden im Humanismus der italienischen Renaissance/ hrsg. von Rolf Gröschner ... TÜ: Mohr Siebeck, 2008, 49-62. (Politika; 1)

192 Mann, Jeffrey K.: **Luther and the Holy Spirit:** why pneumatology still matters. CTM 34 (2007), 111-116.

193 Mørstad, Erik M.: **»Denn die Werck (unnd wun-derthatten Christi) hulffen myr nichts«:** der Bruch Martin Luthers mit dem Naturrecht der Kirche und die Folgen daraus. In: Das Naturrecht und Europa/ hrsg. von Tadeusz Guz. F; B; Bern; Bruxelles; NY; Oxford; W: Lang, 2007, 397-426. (Ad fontes; 3)

194 Puskás, Attila: **A teremtés teológiája** (Die Theo-logie der Schöpfung). BP: Szent István Társulat, 2006. 341 S. L 143-145.

195 Saarinen, Risto: **In sinu patris:** the merciful trinity in Luther's exposition of John 1:18. In: Trinitarian theology in the medieval West/ hrsg. von Pekka Kärkkäinen. Helsinki: Luther-Agricola-Society, 2008, 280-298. (Schriften der Luther-Agricola-Gesellschaft; 61)

196 Saarinen, Risto: **Weakness of will in the Renais-sance and the Reformation.** In: Das Problem der Willensschwäche in der mittelalterlichen Philosophie = The problem of weakness of will in medieval philosophy/ hrsg. von Tobias Hoff-mann. Leuven: Peeters, 2006, 331-353. (Recherches de théologie et philosophie médiévales: biblio-theca; 8)

197 Schneider-Flume, Gunda: **Das Verständnis des Alters in der Perspektive der Geschichte Gottes.** In: 064, 89-111.

198 Schwarz, Hans: **Martin Luther's understanding of the person between autonomy and theonomy.** Doon theological journal 4 (Dehradun, Indien 2007) Nr. 2, 153-161.

199 Schwöbel, Christoph: **Gott im Gespräch:** die Gottesfrage im Dialog der Kulturen. NZSTh 49 (2007), 516-533.

200 Seebaß, Gottfried: **Willensfreiheit und Determi-nismus.** Bd. 1: Die Bedeutung des Willensfrei-heitsproblems. B: Akademie, 2007. 236 S.

201 Steiger, Johann Anselm: **Das Lachen Gottes und des Menschen:** die Narretei Gottes, der Vernunft und des Glaubens in der Theologie Martin

Luthers. In: Anthropologie und Medialität des Komischen im 17. Jahrhundert (1580-1730)/ hrsg. von Stefanie Arend. Amsterdam; NY: Rodopi, 2008, 403-427.

202 Stolina, Ralf: »Ökonomische« und »immanente« Trinität?: zur Problematik einer trinitätstheologischen Denkfigur. ZThK 105 (2008), 170-216. [Vgl. oben Nr.189]

203 Strier, Richard: **Martin Luther and the real presence in nature.** Journal of medieval and early modern studies 37 (Durham, NC 2007), 271-303.

204 Szentpétery, Péter: **Omnia sunt facta per ipsum:** Darwin hatása a teremtéshitre: teológiai és emberi kérdések (Darwins Einfluss auf den Schöpfungsglauben: theol. und menschliche Fragen). BP: [Selbstverlag], 2008. 550 S. L 44-46.

205 Wassermann, Emma: **The death of soul in Roman 7:** sin, death, and the law in light of Hellenistic moral psychology. TÜ: Mohr Siebeck, 2008. 171 S. Wissenschaftliche Untersuchungen zum Neuen Testament: Reihe 2; 256. – Zugl.: New Haven, CN, Yale Univ., Diss., 2005.

206 Wendte, Martin: **Entzogenheit als Evangelium:** theologische, schöpfungstheologische, christologische und anthropologische Bemerkungen zur Verborgenheit Gottes. NZSTh 49 (2007), 464-483.

207 Wolff, Jens: **Martin Luthers »innerer Mensch«.** LuJ 75 (2008), 31-66.

208 Žak, Lubomir: **Die Ontologie der menschlichen Person im Denken Martin Luthers.** In: 023, 307-337.

209 Zwanepol, Klaas: **Gekruisigde liefde?:** de houdbaarheid van stelling 28 van Luthers Heidelberger disputatie (Gekreuzigte Liebe?: die Haltbarkeit der 28. Heidelberger These Luthers). LuBu 17 (2008), 19-39.

c) Christus

210 Blocher, Henri: **Luther et Calvin en christologie.** In: 011, 55-85

211 Hauschild, Wolf-Dieter: **Christology II:** history of doctrine; 2. Middle ages to the modern era (Christologie II: dogmengeschichtlich; 2. Mittelalter bis Neuzeit (engl.)). In: 055, 637-641.

212 Hort, Bernard: **Le Christ.** In: 026, 247-278.

213 Johnson, Marcus P.: **Luther and Calvin on union with Christ.** Fides et historia 39 (Terre Haute, IN 2007), 59-77.

214 Kim, Yong Joo: **Crux sola est nostra theologia:** das Kreuz als Schlüsselbegriff der »Theologia crucis« Luthers. F; B; Bern; Bruxelles; NY; Oxford; W: Lang, 2008. XI, 209 S. (EHSch: Reihe

23, Theologie; 863) – Zugl.: B, Humboldt-Univ., Diss., 2007.

215 Madsen, Anna M.: **The theology of the cross in historical perspective.** Eugene, OR: Wipf and Stock: Pickwick, 2007. IX, 269 S. (Distinguished dissertations in Christian theology; 1)

216 Pfleger, Karl: **Krisztus hat merész képviselője** (Die verwegenen Christozentriker (ungar.))/ übers. von Mária Szabó. BP: Kairosz, 2007. 210 S. L 69-93.

217 Rolf, Sibylle: **Crux sola est nostra theologia:** die Bedeutung der Kreuzestheologie für die Theodizeefrage. NZSTh 49 (2007), 223-240.

218 Rosin, Robert: **Reformation Christology:** some Luther starting points. CThQ 71 (2007), 147-168.

219 Schwarz, Reinhard: **Das Heil der christlichen Religion im Verständnis Martin Luthers.** Berliner theol. Zeitschrift 25 (2008), 379-407.

220 Tomlin, Graham: **The power of the cross:** theology and the death of Christ in Paul, Luther and Pascal/ Vorwort von Alister McGrath. Eugene, OR: Wipf & Stock, 2007. 374 S. (Vgl. LuB 2002, Nr. 158; LuB 2008, Nr. 212].

221 Véghelyi, Antal: **Krisztus halálának értelme** (Der Sinn von Christi Tod). In: 032, 141-156.

222 Wernisch, Martin: **Martin Luther:** Kdo pomine jesličky, míří k šípku (Martin Luther: Wer an der Krippe vorbeigeht, geht schief [enthält eine Übers. aus den Reihenpredigten über Joh 14 f]). In: Hledání Ježíšovy tváře: christologická čítanka (Die Suche nach dem Antlitz Jesu: ein christologisches Lesebuch)/ hrsg. von Petr Jandejsek. PR: Jabok, 2008, 46-51.

d) Kirche, Kirchenrecht, Bekenntnisse

223 Arnold, Matthieu: **Lorsque Luther accusa Rome de maintenir l'Église en »captivité babylonienne«.** Religions et histoire 19 (P 2008), 54-57.

224 Avis, Paul: **Beyond the Reformation:** authority, primacy and unity in the conciliar tradition. LO; NY: T&T Clark, 2006. XX, 234 S. L 109-118+'' (T&T Clark: Theology)

225 Avis, Paul: **Beyond the Reformation:** authority, primacy and unity in the conciliar tradition. Paperback-Ausgabe. LO; NY: T&T Clark, 2008. XX, 234 S. L 109-118+''. (T&T Clark: Theology)

226 **Evangelische Bekenntnisse:** Bekenntnisschriften der Reformation und neuere Theologische Erklärungen. 2. Aufl. Teilbd. 1/ im Auftrag der Union Evang. Kirchen in der Evang. Kirche in Deutschland gemeinsam mit Irene Dingel ... hrsg. von Rudolf Mau. Bielefeld: Luther-Verlag, 2008. 355 S.: Faks. [Vgl. LuB 1998, Nr. 231]

227 **Evangelische Bekenntnisse:** Bekenntnisschriften der Reformation und neuere Theologische Erklärungen. Teilbd. 2/ im Auftrag der Union Evang. Kirchen in der Evang. Kirche in Deutschland gemeinsam mit Irene Dingel ... hrsg. von Rudolf Mau. Bielefeld: Luther-Verlag, 2008. 356 S.: Faks. [Vgl. LuB 2002, Nr. 165]

228 Härle, Wilfried: **Apostolicity** (Apostolizität ⟨engl.⟩). In: 054, 339.

229 Härle, Wilfried: **Creatura evangelii:** die Konstitution der Kirche durch Gottes Offenbarung nach lutherischer Lehre. In: 023, 482-502.

230 Hamm, Berndt: **Freiheit vom Papst – Seelsorge am Papst:** Luthers Traktat »Von der Freiheit eines Christenmenschen« und das Widmungsschreiben an Papst Leo X.: eine kompositorische Einheit. LuJ 74 (2007), 113-132: Ill.

231 Hamm, Berndt: **Luther's freedom of a Christian and the pope** (Freiheit vom Papst – Seelsorge am Papst ⟨engl.⟩)/ übers. von Helen Heron; Martin J. Lohrmann. LQ 21 (2007), 249-267.

232 Humbert, Alexandra: **Les 95 thèses de Luther, attaque délibérée contre la papauté et l'unité de la chrétienté?** PL 56 (2008), 217-231.

233 Kaufmann, Thomas: **Das Bekenntnis im Luthertum des konfessionellen Zeitalters.** ZThK 105 (2008), 281-314.

234 Krause, Richard A.: **Remember the Saxon visitation:** devotional modeling for Christian families. Logia: a journal of Lutheran theology 16 (2007) Nr. 4, 21-28.

235 Kühn, Ulrich: **Welche Bedeutung hat das lutherische Bekenntnis heute?** In: 019, 122-140.

236 Leiner, Martin: **L'église dans le monde.** In: 026, 339-372.

237 Leppin, Volker: **Tradition und Traditionskritik bei Luther.** In: 019, 15-30.

238 Moeller, Bernd: **Confessio Augustana – Confessio Tetrapolitana:** die Bekenntnisse von 1530 in ihrem Zusammenhang. In: 062, 57-71.

239 Müller, Gerhard: **Das Kirchenverständnis der lutherischen Reformation.** Luth. Kirche in der Welt 54 (2007), 197-216.

240 Nüssel, Friederike: **Das Konkordienbuch und die Genese einer lutherischen Tradition.** In: 019, 62-83.

241 Oberdorfer, Bernd: **»Ecclesia semper reformanda« – eine Tradition der Traditionsverzehrung?** In: 019, 108-121.

242 Peters, Christian: **Augsburg Confession** (Augsburger Bekenntnis [Confessio Augustana] ⟨engl.⟩). In: 054, 492-494.

243 Plasger, Georg: **Die Confessio Augustana als Grundbekenntnis der Evangelischen Kirche in Deutschland?:** Anmerkungen und Überlegungen aus reformierter Perspektive. ZThK 105 (2008), 315-331.

244 Saler, Robert: **The Lutheran confessional heritage and contemporary hermeneutics.** CTM 34 (2007), 5-21.

245 Schirmer, Uwe: **Reformation und Staatsfinanzen:** vergleichende Anmerkungen zu Sequestration und Säkularisation im ernestinischen und albertinischen Sachsen (1523-1544). In: 07, 179-192.

246 Schlink, Edmund: **Schriften zu Ökumene und Bekenntnis**/ hrsg. von Klaus Engelhardt ... Bd. 4: **Theologie der lutherischen Bekenntnisschriften**/ hrsg. und eingel. von Günther Gassmann. GÖ: V&R, 2008. XIV, 271 S.

247 Steinwachs, Albrecht: **The common chest as a social achievement of the Reformation** (Der Gemeine Kasten: eine oft übersehene Leistung der Reformation ⟨engl.⟩). LQ 22 (2008), 192-195.

248 Theißen, Henning: **Über Kreuz mit der Welt:** der Ort der Kirche bei Luther. Lu 79 (2008), 151-163.

249 Uppala, A. Aijal: **Kirkkokysymys: minkälaista kirkkoa Luther tahtoi** (Die Kirchenfrage: was für eine Kirche wollte Luther). Lahti: Suomen tunnustuksellinen luterilainen kirkko, 2008. 496 S.

250 Véghelyi, Antal: **Luther nézetei az egyházkormányzásról** (Luthers Ansichten vom Kirchenregiment) Keresztyén igazság 64 (BP 2008) Nr. 79, 9-16.

251 Żak, Lubomir: **Die Vermittlung der Offenbarung und die Konstitution der Kirche in der Theologie Luthers.** In: 023, 449-481.

e) Sakramente, Beichte, Ehe

252 Allison, Gregg R.: **A history of the doctrine of the atonement.** Southern Baptist journal of theology 11 (Louisville, KY 2007) Heft 2, 4-19.

253 Botica, Aurelian: **Revisiting Luther's theology of the eucharist.** Perichoresis 5 (Oradea 2007), 97-115.

254 Buitendag, Johan: **Marriage in the theology of Martin Luther – wordly yet sacred:** an option between secularism and clericalism. Hervormde teologiese studies 63 (Pretoria 2007), 445-461.

255 Davis, Thomas J.: **This is my body:** the presence of Christ in Reformation thought. Grand Rapids, MI: Baker, 2008. III, 203 S.: Ill.

256 Haacker, Klaus: **Ist:** zum Sinn der Deuteworte beim Abschiedsmahl Jesu. In: 016, 216-222.

257 Hendel, Kurt K.: **Finitum est capax infiniti:** Luther's radical incarnational perspective. Seminary Ridge review 10 (Gettysburg, PA 2008), 20-35.

258 Kobelt-Groch, Marion: **Selig auch ohne Taufe?:** Gedruckte lutherische Leichenpredigten für ungetauft verstorbene Kinder des 16. und 17. Jahrhunderts. In: 059, 63-78: Ill.

259 Lessing, Reed: **Dying to live:** God`s judgment of Jonah, Jesus, and the baptized. CJ 33 (2007), 9-25.

260 Neijenhuis, Jörg: **Gestalt und Deutung der christlichen Initiation in den reformatorischen Kirchen des 19. und 20. Jahrhunderts in Deutschland.** In: 058, 151-164.

261 Ngien, Dennis: **»Sacramental piety in Luther's Sermon on the ›worthy reception of the sacrament‹, 1521«/** Zusammenfassung: Richard A. Krause. LuD 16 (2008), 99-104. [Vgl. LuB 2007, Nr. 236]

262 Pinggéra, Karl: **Martin Luther und das evangelische Taufverständnis vom 16. bis 18. Jahrhundert.** In: 058, 85-112.

263 Root, Michael: **Absolution I:** dogmatics (Absolution I: dogmatisch ⟨engl.⟩). In: 054, 19.

264 Wandel, Lee Palmer: **The eucharist in the Reformation:** incarnation and liturgy. Cambridge: Cambridge University; 2006. XI, 302 S.

265 Wengert, Timothy J.: **Martin Luther on spousal abuse.** LQ 21 (2007), 337-339.

266 Weyer-Menkhoff, Stephan: **Luthers »Vermahnung zum Sakrament des Leibes und Blutes unseres Herrn« von 1530:** praktische Theologie nach der Reformation. BlPfKG 75 (2008), 319-330 = Ebernburg-Hefte 42 (2008), 7-18.

267 Wieckowski, Alexander: **Evangelische Beichtpraxis in Sachsen und in der Dresdner Frauenkirche.** In: Die Dresdner Frauenkirche: Jahrbuch zu ihrer Geschichte und Gegenwart. Bd. 12/ hrsg. von Heinrich Magirius im Auftrag der Gesellschaft zur Förderung der Frauenkirche Dresden unter Mitw. der Stiftung Frauenkirche Dresden. Regensburg: Schnell + Steiner, 2008, 43-56: Ill.

f) Amt, Seelsorge, Diakonie, Gemeinde, allgemeines Priestertum

268 Arand, Charles P.: **The ministry of the church in light of the two kinds of righteousness.** CJ 33 (2007), 344-356.

269 Cordes, Paul Josef: **Tegyünk jót mindenkivel:** a karitászmunka huszonegy tétele (»Tuet Gutes allen«: 21 Thesen zur Caritas-Arbeit ⟨ungar.⟩)/ übers. von Géza Ifi. BP: Új Ember, 2007. 157 S. L 66-71.

270 Dober, Hans Martin: **Seelsorge bei Luther, Schleiermacher und nach Freud.** L: EVA, 2008. 273 S.

271 Großhans, Hans-Peter: **Instanzen der Lehrbildung und Lehrbeurteilung.** In: 019, 239-260.

272 Leppin, Volker: **Evangelium der Freiheit und allgemeines Priestertum:** Überlegungen zum Zusammenhang von Theologie und Geschichte in der Reformation. Mitteilungen des Konfessionskundlichen Instituts Bensheim 58 (2007), 103-107.

273 Leroux, Neil R.: **Martin Luther as comforter:** writings on death. Leiden; Boston: Brill, 2007. XLIII, 336 S. (Studies in the history of Christian traditions; 133)

274 McLaughlin, R. Emmet: **Luther, spiritualism and the spirit.** In: 050, 28-49.

275 McLaughlin, R. Emmet: **»Luther, spiritualism and the spirit«/** Zusammenfassung: Rebecca E. Moore. LuD 16 (2008), 69-73.

276 Mattson, Daniel L.: **»True theology is practical:** the process behind Luther's pastoral theology«/ Zusammenfassung: James G. Kiecker. LuDology and life 16 (2008), 137-142. [Vgl. LuB 2007, Nr. 268]

277 Ngien, Dennis: **Picture Christ:** Martin Luther's advice on preparing to die. Christianity today 51 (Carol Stream, IL 2007) Nr. 4, 66-69.

278 Reuss, András: **Péteri szolgálat a 3. évezredben:** evangélikus-lutheránus megfontolások (Der Petrusdienst im dritten Jahrtausend: evang.-luth. Überlegungen). LP 83 (2008), 162-167.

279 Reuss, András: **Péteri szolgálat a 3. évezredben:** evangélikus-lutheránus megfontolások (Der Petrusdienst im dritten Jahrtausend: evang.-luth. Überlegungen). In: 049, 183-199.

280 Schürger, Wolfgang: **Amt und Ordination.** DPfBl 106 (2006), 175 f.

281 Siemon-Netto, Uwe: **Work is our mission:** why the godly baker's most significant task is baking good bread. Christianity today 51 (Washington, DC 2007) Nr. 11, 30-32.

282 Wágner, Szilárd: **Még mindig a lelkészi szolgálatról ...:** gondolatok a Lutheránus Világszövetség – Egyházak Közössége lundi állásfoglalásáról: ökumenikus közeledés vagy egy helyben járás? (Noch immer über den Dienst der Geistlichen ...: Gedanken über die Lunder Erklärung der LWB-Kirchengemeinschaft: ökumenische Annäherung oder Nicht-vom-Fleck-kommen?). In: 032, 61-76.

283 Wendebourg, Dorothea: **Martin Luthers frühe Ordination.** In: 062, 97-116.

284 Wengert, Timothy J.: **Priesthood, pastors, bishops:** public ministry for the Reformation and today. MP: Fortress, 2008. VIII, 141 S.

285 Wenz, Armin: **Der Streit um die Frauenordination im Luthertum als paradigmatischer Dogmenkonflikt.** Luth. Beiträge 12 (2007), 103-127.

286 Wenz, Armin: **The argument over women's ordination in Lutheranism as a paradigmatic conflict of dogma** (Der Streit um die Frauenordination im Luthertum als paradigmatischer Dogmenkonflikt ⟨engl.⟩)/ übers. von Holger Sonntag. CThQ 71 (2007), 319-346.

287 Wenz, Gunther: **Az egyetemes egyház egységének szolgálata:** péteri hivatal a 3. évezredben; evangélikus-lutheránus megfontolások (Der Dienst der Einheit der Gesamtkirche: das Petrusamt im dritten Jahrtausend; evang.-luth. Überlegungen)/ übers. von Boglárka Somfai. In: 049, 143-182.

g) Gnade, Glaube, Rechtfertigung, Werke

288 Arand, Charles P.; Biermann, Joel D.: **Why the two kinds of righteousness?** CJ 33 (2007), 116-135.

289 Arnold, Matthieu: **Martin Luther, Theologie der Nächstenliebe.** LuJ 75 (2008), 67-90.

290 Arnold, Matthieu: **Preface [»Justice et grâce«].** In: 029, 11-14.

291 Barth, Hans-Martin: **Freiheit, die ich meine?:** Luthers Verständnis von Freiheit und Gebundenheit. US 62 (2007), 103-115.

292 Bayer, Oswald: **Angeklagt und anerkannt:** religionsphilosophische und dogmatische Aspekte. In: 01, 89-107.

293 Bayer, Oswald: **Ethik der Gabe.** In: 01, 133-154.

294 Birmelé, André: **Le salut:** le péché et la grâce. In: 026, 213-245.

295 Blaser, Klauspeter: **L'Esprit et la sanctification.** In: 026, 279-302.

296 Boer, Theo A.: **Is Luther's ethics Christian ethics?** LQ 21 (2007), 404-421.

297 Brandt, Reinhard: **Lasst ab vom Ablass:** ein evangelisches Plädoyer. GÖ: V&R, 2008. 297 S.

298 Brondos, David A.: **Fortress introduction to salvation and the cross.** MP: Fortress, 2007. XIV, 220 S.: Ill.

299 Brondos, David A.: **Paul, Luther, and the cross:** in Dialog with Karl Donfried. Dialog 46 (Oxford 2007), 174-176. [Vgl. unten Nr. 305]

300 Burger, Christoph: **Nachfolge Christi bei Erasmus und Luther.** LuJ 75 (2008), 91-112.

301 Cary, Phillip: **Sola fide:** Luther and Calvin. CThQ 71 (2007), 265-281.

302 Cary, Phillip: **»Why Luther is not quite Protestant«**/ Zusammenfassung: James G. Kiecker. LuD 16 (2008), 20-27. [Vgl. LuB 2007, Nr. 294]

303 Chung, Paul: **A theology of justification and God's mission.** CTM 34 (2007), 117-127.

304 Dahill, Lisa E.: **Christ in us:** a response to Veli-Matti Kärkkäinen. CTM 34 (2007), 97-100.

305 Donfried, Karl P.: **Paul and the revisionists:** did Luther really get it all wrong? Dialog 46 (Oxford 2007), 31-40. [Vgl. oben Nr. 299]

306 Eberlein, Hermann-Peter: **Luthers Freiheitsverständnis.** Wuppertal: Selbstverlag, 2008. 28 S.

307 **The gospel of justification in Christ:** where does the church stand today?/ hrsg. von Wayne C. Stumme. Grand Rapids, MI: Eerdmans, 2006. X, 182 S. – Bespr.: Mattes, Mark C.: LQ 21 (2007), 108-110.

308 Guyette, Fred: **Lutheran perspectives on mercy.** Logia a journal of Lutheran theology 16 (Fort Wayne, Ind. 2007) Nr. 1, 27-29.

309 Härle, Wilfried: **Das christliche Verständnis von Wahrheit und Gewißheit aus reformatorischer Sicht.** In: 023, 185-213.

310 Herms, Eilert: **Adiaphora** (Adiaphora ⟨engl.⟩). In: 054, 54-56.

311 Herms, Eilert; Schwöbel, Christoph: **Fundament und Wirklichkeit des Glaubens als Begründung eines evangelischen Verständnisses von Lehrverantwortung.** In: 023, 119-155.

312 Holm, Bo Kristian: **»Luther's theology of the gift«**/ Zusammenfassung: Timothy H. Maschke. LuD 16 (2008), 88-90.

313 Holm, Bo Kristian: **Rechtfertigung als gegenseitige Anerkennung bei Luther.** In: 01, 23-42.

314 Iwand, H[ans] J[oachim]: **The righteousness of faith according to Luther:** (introduction and chapter one) (Glaubensgerechtigkeit nach Luthers Lehre [Auszug] ⟨engl.⟩). LQ 21 (2007), 27-58. [Vgl. unten Nr. 866]

315 Iwand, H[ans] J[oachim]: **The righteousness of faith according to Luther:** (chapter two) (Glaubensgerechtigkeit nach Luthers Lehre [Auszug] ⟨engl.⟩). LQ 21 (2007), 211-237. [Vgl. unten Nr. 866]

316 Iwand, H[ans] J[oachim]: **The righteousness of faith according to Luther:** (chapter three) (Glaubensgerechtigkeit nach Luthers Lehre [Auszug] ⟨engl.⟩). LQ 21 (2007), 320-336. [Vgl. unten Nr. 866]

317 Iwand, H[ans] J[oachim]: **The righteousness of faith according to Luther:** (chapter four) (Glaubensgerechtigkeit nach Luthers Lehre [Auszug] ⟨engl.⟩). LQ 21 (2007), 444-459. [Vgl. unten Nr. 866]

318 Kolb, Robert: **Forgiveness liberates and restores:** the freedom of the Christian according to Martin Luther. Word & world 27 (St. Paul, MN 2007), 5-13.

319 Kolb, Robert: **God and his human creatures in Luther's sermons of Genesis:** the reformer's early

use of his distinction of two kinds of righteousness. CJ 33 (2007), 166-184.

320 Kolb, Robert: »**The noblest skill in the Christian church**«: Luther's sermons on the proper distinction of law and gospel. CThQ 71 (2007), 301-318.

321 Lange, Dietz: **Acknowledgement and recognition II**: dogmatics and ethics (Anerkennung II: dogmatisch und ethisch (engl.)). In: 054, 32 f.

322 Lienemann, Wolfgang: **Grundinformation theologische Ethik**. GÖ: V&R, 2008. 319 S. L". (UTB; 3138)

323 Lienhard, Marc: **Justice et grâce dans le »Cours sur l'épître aux Romains« de Luther**. In: 029, 105-123.

324 Link, Christian: **Rechtfertigung**. In: 016, 326-333.

325 Lorizio, Giuseppe: **Überlegungen zu der Beziehung zwischen Offenbarung – Glaube – Vernunft auf der Grundlage der Texte des katholischen Lehramtes**. In: 023, 51-82.

326 Rolf, Sibylle: **Zum Herzen sprechen:** eine Studie zum imputativen Aspekt in Martin Luthers Rechtfertigungslehre und zu seinen Konsequenzen für die Predigt des Evangeliums. L: EVA, 2008. 432 S. (Arbeiten zur systematischen Theologie; 1) – Zugl. HD, Univ., Theol. Fak., Habil., 2007.

327 Roth, Michael: **Lex semper accusat:** lutherische Moralkritik. In: 01, 109-132.

328 Saarnivaara, Uuras: **Pelastus ja pyhitys Lutherin mukaan** (Salvation and sanctification according to Luther (finn.))/ übers. von Risto Soramies. Ryttylä: Uusi tie, 2008. 296 S.

329 Schwöbel, Christoph: **Offenbarung, Glaube und Gewißheit in der reformatorischen Theologie**. In: 023, 214-234.

330 Seifrid, Mark A.: **Ist Gott für uns, wer kann gegen uns sein? (Röm 8,31-39)**: Anklage und Anerkennung in biblischer Perspektive. In: 01, 43-68.

331 Steiger, Johann Anselm: »**Superbia fidei**«: Hochmut des Glaubens und Aufrichtigkeit des Menschen in der Theologie Martin Luthers und das barocke Luthertum. In: Die Kunst der Aufrichtigkeit im 17. Jahrhundert/ hrsg. von Claudia Benthien ... TÜ: Niemeyer, 2006, 19-43. (Frühe Neuzeit; 14)

332 Stümke, Volker: **Das Aufheben eines Strohhalms:** Notizen zu einem Bildwort Luthers. Lu 79 (2008), 11-15.

333 Treu, Martin: »**Wie der Hund auf das Fleisch**«: Theologie und Alltag bei Martin Luther. In: 039, 365-367.

334 Vind, Anna: **Latomus og Luther:** striden om, hvorvidt enhver god gerning er synd; en teologishistorisk afhandling (Latomus und Luther: der

Streit darüber, ob jede gute Tat Sünde ist; eine theologiegeschichtliche Studie). København: Teologiske Fakultet, Københavns Univ., 2007. IX, 361, 9 S. (Ph.d.-afhandling / Det Teologiske Fakultet, Københavns Universitet; 2007, 2) – Copenhagen, Univ., PhD, 2001.

335 Żak, Lubomir: »**Offenbarung und Glaube**« in den **Lehrtexten der Reformation**. In: 023, 83-118.

h) Sozialethik, politische Ethik, Geschichte

336 Arffman, Kaarlo: **Auttamisen vallankumous:** luterilaisuuden yritys ratkaista köyhyyden aiheuttamat ongelmat (Eine Revolution des Helfens: der luth. Versuch, die Probleme der Armut zu lösen). Helsinki: Suomalaisen Kirjallisuuden Seura – Suomen Kirkkohistoriallinen Seura, 2008. 343 S. L 42-104. (Historiallisia tutkimuksia; 236) (Suomen kirkkohistoriallisen seuran toimituksia; 205)

337 Benedict, Philip: **Religion and politics in Europe,** 1500-1700. In: 056, 155-173.

338 Beros, Daniel C.: **Martin Luther:** motives and rules of his ethics/ aus dem Span. übers. von María Eugenia Mendizábal. In: 035, 227-240.

339 Beyer, Michael: **Theologische Grundlagen für Martin Luthers Sozialengagement**. In: 043, 53-72.

340 Birkás, Antal: **Luther és Kálvin jogfilozófiai és politikai filozófiai nézetei:** PhD értekezés tézisei (Law philosophy and political philosophy of Luther and Calvin: propositions of the PhD Thesis (ungar. u. engl.)). Miskolc: [Selbstverlag], 2008. 24 S.

341 Frey, Christiane: **Beruf:** Luther, Weber, Agamben. New German critique 105 (Milwaukee, Wisc. 2008), 35-56.

342 Friedeburg, Robert von: »**Confusing**« around the Magdeburg confession an the making of »**Revolutionary early modern resistance theory**«. ARG 97 (2006), 307-318. [Vgl. LuB 2006, Nr. 956; LuB 2009, Nr. 366]

343 Frohman, Larry: **Poor relief and welfare in Germany from the Reformation to World War I**. Cambridge: Cambridge University, 2008. X, 257 S.: Ill.

344 Guicharrousse, Hubert: **Luther et la légitimité de la guerre:** la ligue de Smalkalde et le droit de résistance. In: 08, 35-48.

345 Hummel, Leonard M.: **Luther, war, and violence:** responses to Joy Schroeder, Gregory Miller and Stanley Hauerwas. Seminary Ridge review 9 (Gettysburg, PA 2007) Nr. 2, 60-67. [Vgl. LuB 2009, Nr. 415. 752. 891]

346 **Jütte, Robert: Die Sorge für Kranke und Gebrech-liche in den Almosen- und Kastenordnungen des 16. Jahrhunderts:** Anspruch und Wirklichkeit. In: 043, 9-21.

347 Junghans, Helmar: **Elemente der Zweireichele-re und der Zweiregimentenlehre Martin Luthers:** eine Einführung. In: 07, 23-40.

348 Kastning, Wieland: **Morgenröte künftigen Le-bens:** das reformatorische Evangelium als Neube-stimmung der Geschichte; Untersuchungen zu Martin Luthers Geschichts- und Wirklichkeits-verständnis. GÖ: V&R, 2008. 458 S. (Forschungen zur systematischen und ökumenischen Theolo-gie; 117) – Zugl.: Göttingen, Univ., Diss., 2003.

349 Klein, Michael: **Geschichtsdenken und Stände-kritik in apokalyptischer Perspektive:** Martin Luthers Meinungs- und Wissensbildung zur »Tür-kenfrage« auf dem Hintergrund der osmanischen Expansion und im Kontext der reformatorischen Bewegung. Internetressource: ⟨http://deposit. fernuni-hagen.de/34/1/Titel_Osmanen.pfd⟩. Ha-gen, 2004. 281 S. – Hagen, FernUniv., Fachbe-reich Kultur- und Sozialwissenschaften, Diss., 2004.

350 Kolb, Robert: **Die Josef-Geschichten als Fürsten-spiegel in der Wittenberger Auslegungstradition:** »Ein verständiger und weiser Mann« (Genesis 41, 33). In: 07, 41-55.

351 Kruse, Jens-Martin: **Martin Luther's distinction between two kingdoms and two goverments in the treatise »Temporal authority, to what extent it should be obeyed«, 1523.** In: 027, 137-153.

352 Laube, Adolf: **Zum Toleranzproblem in der frühen Reformation.** Sitzungsberichte der Leib-niz-Sozietät 84 (2006), 93-106.

353 Lück, Heiner: **Armen- und Fürsorgeordnungen der Reformationszeit:** Anfänge eines neuzeit-lichen Sozialrechts? In: 043, 197-212.

354 MacKenzie, Cameron A.: **The challenge of his-tory:** Luther's two kingdoms theology as a test case. CThQ 71 (2007), 3-28.

355 Malysz, Piotr J.: **Nemo iudex in causa sua as the basis of law, justice, and justification in Luther's thought.** HThR 100 (2007), 363-386.

356 Meireis, Torsten: **Tätigkeit und Erfüllung:** protes-tantische Ethik im Umbruch der Arbeitsgesell-schaft. TÜ: Mohr Siebeck, 2008. 603 S. – Zugl.: MS, Univ., Habil., 2007.

357 Oehmig, Stefan: **Über Arme, Armenfürsorge und Gemeine Kästen mitteldeutscher Städte der frühen Reformationszeit.** In: 043, 73-114. L".

358 Paul, Jean-Marie: **Guerre juste et paix juste:** Saint Augustin et Luther. In: 08, 21-33.

359 Pohlig, Matthias: **Exegese und Historiographie:** lutherische Apokalypsenkommentare als Kir-chengeschichtsschreibung. In: 017, 289-317.

360 Raath, A[ndries] W. G.: **Providence, conscience of liberty and benevolence:** the implications of Luther's and Calvin's views on natural law for fundamental rights. In die Skriflig 41 (Pretoria 2007), 415-442.

361 Schirmer, Uwe: **Alltag, Armut und soziale Not in der ländlichen Gesellschaft:** Beobachtungen aus dem kursächsischen Amt Wittenberg (1485-1547). In: 043, 115-142. L 127 f. 133.

362 Strohm, Christoph: **Widerstandsrecht:** Beobach-tungen zum spannungsvollen Verhältnis von Religion, Moral und Recht. In: 016, 411-421.

363 Stümke, Volker: **Das Friedensverständnis Martin Luthers:** Grundlagen und Anwendungsbereiche seiner politischen Ethik. S: Kohlhammer, 2007. 533 S. (Theologie und Frieden; 34) – Zugl.: Bethel, Kirchl. Hochsch., Habil. 2006/07 unter dem Titel »Mitarbeit am Frieden«.

364 Torvend, Samuel: **Luther and the hungry poor:** gathered fragments. MP: Fortress, 2008. XIII, 177 S.: Ill.

365 Wannenwetsch, Bernd: **Luthers politisches Ver-ständnis der Familie.** In: 064, 68-88.

366 Whitford, David M.: **Rejoinder to Robert von Friedeburg.** ARG 98 (2007), 301-303. [Vgl. LuB 2006, Nr. 956; LuB 2009, Nr. 342]

i) Gottes Wort, Bibel, Predigt, Sprache

367 Àcs, Pál: »**Én fiam vagy, Dávid ...«:** a histori-kus értelmezés korlátai a 2. zsoltár unitárius fordításában (»Du bist mein Sohn, David ...«: die Grenzen der historischen Auslegung in der unitarischen Übersetzung von Psalm 2). ITK 112 (2008), 632-644.

368 Arnold, Matthieu: **Luther et sa Bible.** In: 03, 33-38.

369 Arnold, Matthieu: **Le »sola« scriptura.** In: 03, 59-65.

370 Beutel, Albrecht: **Bible translations II:** Christian translations into European languages since the Middle ages (Bibelübersetzungen II: christliche Übersetzungen in europäische Volkssprachen seit dem Mittelalter ⟨engl.⟩). In: 055, 45-50.

371 Beutel, Albrecht: **Verdanktes Evangelium:** das Leitmotiv in Luthers Predigtwerk. LuJ 74 (2007), 11-28.

372 Birmelé, André: **Les réferences en dogmatique:** l'écriture sainte et les confessions de foi. In: 026, 49-76.

373 Buchholz, Armin: **Schrift Gottes im Lehrstreit:** Luthers Schriftverständnis und Schriftauslegung in seinen drei großen Lehrstreitigkeiten der Jahre

1521-28. Gießen; BL: Brunnen, 2007. VIII, 340 S. (Reihe systematisch-theologische Monographien; 20) – Zugl.: HH, Univ., Diss., 1993. [Vgl. LuB 1995, Nr. 325]

374 Csepregi, András: **A Szentíráshoz kötötten, a Lélek szabadságában** (An die Schrift gebunden, in der Freiheit des Geistes). In: 032, 25-109.

375 Dehsen, Christian D. von: **Matthew 16, the Reformation battleground for ecclesiastical hermeneutics.** Lutheran Forum 41 (NY 2007) Nr. 3, 29-44.

376 **Frühneuhochdeutsches Wörterbuch**/ hrsg. von Ulrich Goebel; Oskar Reichmann ...; begr. von Robert R. Anderson ... Bd. 8, Lfg. 3: **kirmesse-köstlich**/ bearb. von Vibeke Winge. B; NY: de Gruyter, 2008. 973-1484.

377 Grille, Dietrich: **Rhönfränkisch – Luthervaters Muttersprache:** persönliche Erfahrungen mit einer ostfränkischen Ausgleichsmundart. In: 015, 655-664.

378 Hartweg, Frédéric: **»Luther et le livre«** [Luther and the book]/ engl. Zusammenfassung: Wolf D. Knappe. LuD 16 (2008), 33-37: Ill. [Vgl. LuB 2006, Nr. 469]

379 Heen, Erik M.: **The theological interpretation of the Bible.** LQ 21 (2007), 373-403.

380 Hoegen-Rohls, Christina: **Die Kraft der Sprache:** Martin Luthers Bibelübersetzung von den Anfängen bis zur Gegenwart. Jahrbuch für finnisch-deutsche Literaturbeziehungen 39 (Helsinki 2007), 60-80.

381 Hofmann, Frank: »**Christus als Mitte der Schrift:** eine Erinnerung an Martin Luthers Umgang mit der Bibel« [A reminder of Martin Luther's dealing with the bible]/ engl. Zusammenfassung: Rudolf K. Markwald. LuD 16 (2008), 61-64. [Vgl. LuB 2006, Nr. 531]

382 Itkonen-Kaila, Marja: **Michael Agricola als Übersetzer des Neuen Testaments.** Jahrbuch für finnisch-deutsche Literaturbeziehungen 39 (Helsinki 2007), 81-92.

383 Jastrzembski, Volker: **Das Ereignis des Verstehens:** Untersuchungen zur Hermeneutik des Alten Testaments im christlich-jüdischen Dialog. B, 2007. 265 S. L 21. 26. 75. 79. 178. – B, Humboldt-Univ., Theol. Fak., Diss., 2007.

384 Juntunen, Katja: **Der Prediger vom »weißen Berg«:** zur Rezeption der »besseren Gerechtigkeit« aus Mt 5 in Martin Luthers Predigtüberlieferung 1522-1546. [Espoo]: [Katja Juntunen], 2008. 235 S. – Helsinki, Univ., theol. Diss., 2008.

385 Juntunen, Katja: **Der Prediger vom »weißen Berg«:** zur Rezeption der »besseren Gerechtigkeit« aus Mt 5 in Martin Luthers Predigtüberlieferung 1522-1546. Elektronische Ausgabe. Helsinki, 2008. 235 S. – Helsinki, Univ., theol. Diss., 2008.

386 Kammerer, Elsa: **Schnittstelle Bibeldruck:** Entstehung einer Lyoner Bibelreihe im Spannungsfeld der Druckervernetzung und des frühen Humanismus (Lyon-Nürnberg, 1512-1522). In: 017, 225-248: Ill.

387 Kettmann, Gerhard: **Aufbau und Entwicklung der Kursächsischen Kanzleisprache in der Lutherzeit.** (1967). In: 030, 9-15.

388 Kettmann, Gerhard: **Luthersprache – Annotationen zur Begriffsbestimmung.** (1993). In: 030, 143-149.

389 Kettmann, Gerhard: **Studien zum graphematischen Status der Wittenberger Druckersprache in der ersten Hälfte des 16. Jahrhunderts.** (1987). In: 030, 73-85.

390 Kettmann, Gerhard: **Die Wittenberger Drucker in der Reformationszeit und ihr Umgang mit der deutschen Sprache:** sprachliche Probleme der Lutherzeit. (1995). In: 030, 55-66.

391 Kettmann, Gerhard: **Zum Problemkreis »Druckersprachen« in der Frühneuhochdeutschen Forschung.** (1984). In: 030, 67-72.

392 Kettmann, Gerhard: **Zur schreibsprachlichen Überlieferung Wittenbergs in der Lutherzeit:** (Stadt und Schreibsprache im Frühneuhochdeutschen). (1967). In: 030, 17-53.

393 Kettmann, Gerhard: **Zur Soziologie der Wittenberger Schreibsprache in der Lutherzeit.** (1968). In: 030, 123-141.

394 Kodácsy, Tamás: **Miért éppen a beszéd?:** az igehirdetés mint kommunikáció (Warum das Reden?: die Predigt als Kommunikation). In: 032, 247-256.

395 Koller, Werner: **Einführung in die Übersetzungswissenschaft.** 7., aktual. Aufl. HD: Q&M, 2004. 343 S. L 39 f+". (UTB; 819)

396 Kwon, Jin Ho: **Christus pro nobis:** eine Untersuchung zu Luthers Passions- und Osterpredigten bis zum Jahr 1530. B; MS: Lit, 2008. X, 294 S. (Kieler Theologische Reihe; 7) – Zugl.: Kiel, Univ., Diss., 2007.

397 Lexutt, Athina: **Unica regula et norma:** zum Verhältnis von Schrift und Tradition im reformatorischen Verständnis. In: 019, 143-165.

398 Lobenstein-Reichmann, Anja: **Luther als Sprachreformator.** In: 020, 85-94.

399 Luscher, Birgit: **Einführung in das symbolische Denken:** Hermeneutik und elementares Bibelverstehen. B; MS: Lit, 2008. 255 S.: Ill. (Symbol – Mythos – Medien; 15)

400 Maier, Bernhard: **Sternstunden der Religion:** von Augustinus bis Zarathustra. Limitierte Sonder-

ausgabe. M: Beck, 2008. 202 S. L 137-142. (Beck'sche Reihe; 4059)

401 Marissen, Michael: »**Blood, people, and crowds in Matthew, Luther, and Bach**«/ Zusammenfassung: Rebecca E. Moore. LuD 16 (2008), 43-45: Ill. [Vgl. LuB 2006, Nr. 487]

402 Maxfield, John A.: **Luther's lectures on Genesis and the formation of evangelical identity.** Kirksville, MO: Truman State University, 2008. XIV, 242 S.: Ill. (Sixteenth century essays & studies; 80)

403 Mieder, Wolfgang: »**Es ist gut pflugen, wenn der acker gereinigt ist**«: sprichwörtliche Argumentation in Luthers »Sendbrief vom Dolmetschen« (1530). In: 063, 431-446.

404 Nitta, Haruo: **Urbane Eleganz gegen sarkastischen Grobianismus:** ironische Stilmittel in den Streitschriften zwischen Emser und Luther. In: Strukturen und Funktionen in Gegenwart und Geschichte: Festschrift für Franz Simmler zum 65. Geburtstag/ hrsg. von Claudia Wich-Reif. B: Weidler, 2007, 555-569.

405 Oelschläger, Ulrich: **Die Wormser Propheten von 1527:** eine vorlutherische Teilübersetzung der Bibel. BlPfKG 75 (2008), 331-362: Faks. = Ebernburg-Hefte 42 (2008), 19-50: Faks.

406 Otto, Eckart: **Biblical scholarship I:** Old Testament (Bibelwissenschaft I: Altes Testament ⟨engl.⟩). In: 055, 70-78.

407 Piirainen, Ilpo Tapani: **Bibelübersetzungen von Martin Luther und Johann Eck:** ein Beitrag zur Lexik des Frühneuhochdeutschen. In: 063, 447-454.

408 Reventlow, Henning Graf: **Die »Gerechten« und die »Gottlosen«.** In: 016, 136-147.

409 Rieger, Reinhold: **Allegory IV:** church history; 2. Middle ages to modern times (Allegorie/Allegorese IV: kirchengeschichtlich; 2. Mittelalter bis Neuzeit ⟨engl⟩). In: 054, 149.

410 Röhrich, Lutz: **Lexikon der sprichwörtlichen Redensarten.** Elektron. Ausgabe der Ausgabe BL; W, 1994 auf CD-ROM/Lektorat: Mathias Bertram. B: Directmedia, 2004 (c 2000/2004). 7425 Bildschirm-S.: Ill. L".

411 Rössing-Hager, Monika: **Aspekte der Textkonstitution in Luthers Streitschrift »Wider die himmlischen Propheten«.** In: Studien zu Textsorten und Textallianzen um 1500/ hrsg. von Jörg Meier; Ilpo Tapani Piirainen. B: Weidler, 2007, 113-135. (Germanistische Arbeiten zur Sprachgeschichte; 5)

412 Rolf, Sibylle: **Predigen heißt: Die Schüssel vor die Gäste setzen:** Martin Luthers Verständnis von imputatio in seiner Rechtfertigungslehre und seine Predigt der Rechtfertigung. EvTh 68 (2008), 32-49.

413 Schiffner, Kerstin: **Brief/e, neutestamentliche:** eine Entdeckungsreise in Kinder- und Jugendbibeln. In: 016, 46-57. L 49 f.

414 Schreiner, Susan E.: **Martin Luther.** In: The Sermon on the mount through the centuries: from the early church to John Paul II/ hrsg. von Jeffrey P. Greenman ... Grand Rapids, MI: Brazos, 2007, 109-127.

415 Schröder, Joy A.: **Dismembering the adulteress:** sixteenth-century commentary on the narrative of the Levite's concubine (Judges 19-21). Seminary Ridge review 9 (Gettysburg, PA 2007) Nr. 2, 5-24. [Vgl. LuB 2009, Nr. 345]

416 Schwöbel, Christoph: **Bible IV:** dogmatics (Bibel IV: dogmatisch ⟨engl.⟩). In: 055, 13-17.

417 Stolle, Volker: **Die Schlüssel des Himmelreichs:** Luthers Interpretation von Matthäus 16,19 in seiner Auseinandersetzung mit dem Papsttum. NZSTh 49 (2007), 241-281.

418 Stolt, Birgit: **Das Herz »hüpft und springt vor großem Wohlgefallen«:** Emotionen bei Luther im Licht gegenwärtiger Debatten. Studia neophilologica 80 (Oslo 2008), 188-202.

419 Stroh, Wilfried: **Latein ist tot, es lebe Latein!:** kleine Geschichte einer großen Sprache. Lizenzausgabe der Ausgabe B, 2007. F; ZH; W: Büchergilde Gutenberg, 2008. 414 S. L 195-198. 200-205+".

420 Stroh, Wilfried: **Latein ist tot, es lebe Latein!:** kleine Geschichte einer großen Sprache. Ungek. Ausgabe. B: List, 2007. 414 S. L 195-198. 200-205+". (List-Taschenbuch; 60809)

421 **Tanslation – theory and practice:** a historical reader/ hrsg. von Daniel Weissbort und Astradur Eysteinsson. Oxford: Oxford University, 2006. XIV, 649 S.

422 **Les traducteurs dans l'histoire**/ hrsg. von Jean Delisle; Judith Woodsworth. Ottawa: Presses de l'Univ. d'Ottawa, 2007. XXIII, 393 S.: Ill.

423 Walden, Wayne: **Luther:** the one who shaped the canon. Restoration quarterly 49 (Abilene, TX 2007), 1-10.

424 Washof, Wolfram: **Die Bibel auf der Bühne:** Exempelfiguren und protestantische Theologie im lateinischen und deutschen Bibeldrama der Reformationszeit. M: Rhema, 2007. 536 S.: Ill. (Symbolische Kommunikation und gesellschaftliche Wertesysteme; 14)

425 Weder, Hans: **Biblical Scholarship II:** New Testament (Bibelwissenschaft II: Neues Testament ⟨engl.⟩). In: 055, 78-83.

426 Wein, Martin: **Schicksalstage der deutschen Geschichte.** Lizenzausgabe der Ausgabe S, 1993. Erftstadt: Area, 2005. 544 S. L 170-189+".

427 Wels, Volkhard: **Der Begriff der Dichtung vor und nach der Reformation.** In: 044, 81-104.

428 Wengst, Klaus: **Hebräisch für Neutestamentler:** ein Plädoyer. In: 016, 177-187.

429 Westhelle, Vítor: **»Luther on the authority of scripture«**/ Zusammenfassung: Ian Christopher Levy. LuD 16 (2008), 74 f. [Vgl. LuB 2007, Nr. 452]

430 Wilson, H[enry] S.: **»Luther on preaching as God speaking«**/ Zusammenfassung: Karin E. Stetina. LuD 16 (2008), 158-160. [Vgl. LuB 2006, Nr. 519]

431 Wypich, Anita: **Die »Siedelraumthese« von Theodor Frings – ein universelles, ideologie-übergreifendes Erklärungsmodell für die Entstehung des Neuhochdeutschen.** Mitteldeutsches Jahrbuch für Kultur und Geschichte 15 (2008), 39-51.

k) Gottesdienst, Gebet, Spiritualität, Kirchenlied, Musik

432 Akerboom, Dick: **»Ein neues Lied wir heben an«:** über die ersten Märtyrer der Reformation und die Ursprünge des ersten Liedes von Martin Luther (»Ein neues Lied wir heben an«: over de eerste martelaren van de Reformatie en het ontstaan van het eerste lied van Martin Luther ⟨dt.⟩). Luth. Kirche in der Welt 55 (2008), 63-82.

433 Bartmuß, Alexander: **Eine neue Ordnung:** zur Entstehung der »Heinrichsagende« 1539. In: 065, 301-313.

434 Bayer, Oswald: **Aufrücken:** von der der Unverschämtheit des Gebets. In: 016, 27-33.

435 Beyer, Michael: **Martin Luthers Betbüchlein.** LuJ 74 (2007), 29-50.

436 Böttrich, Thomas: **Schuld bekennen – Versöhnung feiern:** die Beichte im lutherischen Gottesdienst. GÖ: V&R, 2008. 319 S. [Arbeiten zur Pastoraltheologie, Liturgik und Hymnologie; 46] – Zugl.: L, Univ., Theol. Fak., Diss., 2004.

437 Braw, Christian: **Luthers Heilstheologie in seinen frühen Liedern.** Diakrisis 29 (2008), 201-211.

438 Brunner, Horst: **»... das Reich muß uns doch bleiben«:** Einführung in Luthers Kirchenlieder. In: Ders.: Annäherungen: Studien zur deutschen Literatur des Mittelalters und der Frühen Neuzeit. B: Erich Schmidt, 2008, 336-349: Faks.

439 Jadatz, Heiko: **Mitteldeutsche Kirchen und deren Ausstattung im Jahrhundert der Reformation:** Befunde in den Akten der evangelischen Kirchenvisitationen. In: 065, 127-139.

440 Junghans, Helmar: **Gott danken, loben und bitten im Alltag bei Martin Luther.** LuJ 74 (2007), 51-68. [Vgl. LuB 2008, Nr. 453]

441 Koch, Ernst: **»Typographus incuriosus?«:** zur Druckgeschichte der »Cantiones ecclesiasticae« von Johann Spangenberg (1545). In: 04, 267-275.

442 McNair, Bruce G.: **»Luther and the pastoral theology of the Lord's prayer«**/ Zusammenfassung: Karin E. Stetina. LuD 16 (2008), 143-146. [Vgl. LuB 2007, Nr. 480]

443 Neef, Friedemann: **»Denn nichts auf Erden kreftiger ist denn die Musica«:** Luther und die Musik. In: Musikkultur in Sachsen-Anhalt seit dem 16. Jahrhundert: Protokoll der wissenschaftlichen Tagung zur regionalen Musikgeschichte am 16. und 17. September 2005 in Salzwedel/ hrsg. von Kathrin Eberl-Ruf ... Halle (Saale): Landesheimatbund Sachsen-Anhalt, 2007, 73-81: Ill. (Beiträge zur Regional- und Landeskultur Sachsen-Anhalts; 42)

444 Ngien, Dennis: **Luther as spiritual adviser:** the interface of theology and piety in Luther's devotional writings. Bletchley: Paternoster, 2007. XXIV, 183 S. (Studies in Christian history and thought)

445 Ngien, Dennis: **»Theology and practice of prayer in Luther's devotional and catechetical writings«**/ Zusammenfassung: Richard A. Krause. LuD 16 (2008), 147-152. [Vgl. LuB 2006, Nr. 567]

446 Ngien, Dennis: **Worship as radical reversal in Martin Luther's »Theologia crucis«.** Reformation: the journal of the Tyndale Society 12 (LO 2007), 1-31.

447 Noll, Mark: **Singing the word of God.** Christian history and biography 95 (Carol Stream, IL 2007), 15-19.

448 Oelke, Harry: **»Erhalt uns, Herr, bei deinem Wort und steur des Papsts und Türken Mord ...«:** ein Kinderlied Luthers im Medienereignis Reformation. LuJ 75 (2008), 141-168.

449 Petzoldt, Martin: **Martin Luthers Vaterunserlied – theologisch und musikalisch betrachtet.** LuJ 74 (2007), 69-90.

450 Ratzmann, Wolfgang: **Danken, loben und bitten in Luthers Deutscher Messe und in heutigen lutherischen Agenden.** LuJ 74 (2007), 91-112.

451 Robinson-Hammerstein, Helga: **Viewing and singing the word of God in Lutheran Germany.** In: Public communication in European reformation: artistic and other media in central Europe 1380-1620/ hrsg. von Milena Bartlová. PR: Artefactum, Institut of Art History, 2007, 159-174: Ill.

452 Schilling, Johannes: **Die erhaltenen Exemplare von Georg Rhaus »Symphoniae iucundae« (1538) und Martin Luthers Vorrede.** In: 04, 251-265: Ill.

453 Schmidt-Lauber, Hans-Christoph: **Altar III:** Christianity; 1. liturgy; b) Protestantism (Altar

III: Christentum; 1. liturgisch; c) evangelisch ⟨engl.⟩). In: 054, 164 f.

454 Schwarz, Hans: »**Martin Luther and music**«/ Zusammenfassung: Wolf D. Knappe. LuD 16 (2008), 152-157. [Vgl. LuB 2007, Nr. 494]

455 Wartenberg, Günther: **Martin Luthers Beten für Freunde und gegen Feinde.** LuJ 75 (2008), 113-124.

456 Werbeck, Walter: **Chorale arrangement** (Choralbearbeitung ⟨engl.⟩). In: 055, 546 f.

l) Katechismus, Konfirmation, Schule, Universität

457 Arnold, Matthieu: **Les catéchismes, une invention de la Réformation?** Annales de l'Est 57 (Nancy 2007) Nr. 1, 93-108. L".

458 Arnold, Matthieu: **Des sept péchés capitaux au décalogue:** les catéchismes de la Réforme. In: Le Décalogue/ hrsg. von Rémi Gounelle; Annie Noblesse-Rocher. P: Cerf, 2008, 68-70. (Cahiers évangile: supplément; 144)

459 Cabanel, Patrick; Encrevé, André: **De Luther à la loi Debré:** protestantisme, école et laïcité. Histoire de l'éducation 110 (P 2006), 5-21.

460 Dingel, Irene: **Eruditio et Pietas:** die Wirkung der Reformation auf Schule und Universität. In: 07, 317-334.

461 Johnson, Richard Olin: **No rest for the Lutherans.** Lutheran Forum 41 (NY 2007) Nr. 3, 16-18.

462 [Mörlin, Joachim]: Joachim **Mörlin on Luther's »Small catechism«.** LQ 21 (2007), 460-463.

463 Mühlpfordt, Günter: **Danksagung und Schlußbetrachtung: mitteldeutsche Universitäten der Frühneuzeit auf dem Weg zur modernen Wissenschaft.** In: 060, 261-327. L 279-283+".

464 Nestingen, James Arne: **Justification by faith in Luther's Small catechism.** Logia: a journal of Lutheran theology 16 (Cresbard, SD 2007) 4, 15-19.

465 Nordling, John G.: **The catechism:** the heart of the Reformation. Logia: a journal of Lutheran theology 16 (Cresbard, SD 2007) Nr. 4, 5-13.

466 Persaud, Winston D.: **Luther's Small and Large catechisms:** defining and confessing Christian faith from the centre in a religiously plural world. Dialog 46 (Oxford 2007), 355-362.

467 Rosin, Robert: **Luther on education.** LQ 21 (2007), 197-210.

468 Thaidigsmann, Edgar: **Achtung und Bildung:** Aspekte einer religionspädagogisch reflektierten Theologie. In: 064, 112-127.

469 Töpfer, Thomas: **Landesherrschaft – fürstliche Autorität – korporative Universitätsautonomie:** die Anfänge der Universität Wittenberg 1502-1525. In: 060, 27-54.

470 von zur Mühlen, Bernt Ture: **Die Bibliothek des Franciscanums in Zerbst.** Mitteldeutsches Jahrbuch für Kultur und Geschichte 15 (2008), 141-145: Ill.

m) Weitere Einzelprobleme

471 Albrecht, Michael J.: **Jsme Žebráci:** Martin Luther o umírání a smrti (We are beggars: Martin Luther on dying and death)/ aus dem Engl. ins Tschech. übers. von Radka Brahová. PR: Lutherova společnost, 2007. 98 S.

472 Angenendt, Arnold: **Toleranz und Gewalt:** das Christentum zwischen Bibel und Schwert. 2., durchges. Aufl. MS: Aschendorff, 2007. 799 S.: Ill.

473 Angenendt, Arnold: **Toleranz und Gewalt:** das Christentum zwischen Bibel und Schwert. 3., durchges. Aufl. MS: Aschendorff, 2007. 799 S.: Ill.

474 Angenendt, Arnold: **Toleranz und Gewalt:** das Christentum zwischen Bibel und Schwert. 4., durchges., Aufl. MS: Aschendorff, 2008. 799 S.: Ill.

475 Birmelé, André: **L'eschatologie:** le choses dernières et avant-dernières. In: 026, 373-399.

476 Carbonnier-Burkard, Marianne: **Pèlerinage et Réforme protestante.** PHPhR 88 (2008), 129-145. L 129: 133-136+".

477 Dalferth, Ingolf U.: **Malum:** theologische Hermeneutik des Bösen. TÜ: Mohr Siebeck, 2008. XV, 593 S.

478 Dörfler-Dierken, Angelika: **Anne, Saint I:** church history (Anna I: kirchengeschichtlich ⟨engl.⟩). In: 054, 246 f.

479 Eire, Carlos M. N.: »**Bite this Satan!**«: the devil in Luther's »Table talk«. In: 050, 70-93.

480 Eire, Carlos M. N.: »**'Bite this Satan!'**: the devil in Luther's »Table talk«/ Zusammenfassung: Richard A. Krause. LuD 16 (2008), 109-115.

481 Friedrich, Markus: **Das Hör-Reich und das Sehe-Reich:** zur Bewertung des Sehens bei Luther und im frühneuzeitlichen Protestantismus. In: Evidentia: Reichweiten visueller Wahrnehmung in der Frühen Neuzeit/ hrsg. von Gabriele Wimböck. MS; B: Lit, 2007, 451-479. (Pluralisierung und Authorität; 9)

482 Gánóczy, Sándor: **Mária Luther, Kálvin és a II. Vatikánum teológiájában** (Maria in der Theologie Luthers, Calvins und des Zweiten Vaticanums). Vigilia 70 (BP 2005), 552-562.

483 Genre, Ermanno: **Pénitence et conversion comme thèmes de la théologie pratique dans les Èglises de la Réforme.** PL 56 (2008), 285-297. L 286-289.

484 Gorski, Horst: **Grundlegender Wandel:** Luthers Marienverehrung, die heutigen Protestanten und die Ökumene. ZZ 8 (2007) Heft 12, 26-29.

485 Harrison, Peter: **Philosophy and the crisis of religion.** In: The Cambridge companion to Renaissance philosophy/ hrsg. von James Hankins. Cambridge: Cambridge University, 2007, 234-249. [Online-Ausgabe unter gleichem Titel]

486 Hendrix, Scott H.; Karant-Nunn, Susan C.: **Introduction:** dimensions of manhood. In: 042, ix-xix.

487 Hendrix, Scott H.: **Masculinity and patriarchy in Reformation Germany.** (1995). In: 042, 71-91.

488 Jarvis, Michael: **The mariology of Martin Luther and its implications for an ecumentical mariology.** The Australian catholic record 84 (Sydney 2007), 305-315.

489 Jones, Ken Sundet: **The apocalyptic Luther/** Zusammenfassung: Ian Christopher Levy. LuD 16 (2008), 38 f. [Vgl. LuB 2007, Nr. 548]

490 Julliard, Catherine: **Le thème du Mal dans le texte de Luther »A la noblesse chrétienne de la nation allemande sur l'amendement de l'état chrétien«.** In: Europäische Begegnungen: Beiträge zur Literaturwissenschaft, Sprache und Philosophie; Festschrift für Joseph Kohen/ hrsg. von Susanne Craemer. Luxembourg: Saint-Paul, [2006], 239-247.

491 Karant-Nunn, Susan C.: **The masculinity of Martin Luther:** theory, practicality, and humor. In: 042, 167-189.

492 Knackmuß, Susanne: **Reformation als »culture clash«:** Geschlechterrollen als Kulturtechnik alt- und neugläubiger Nonnen. In: 022, 174-197.

493 Kolb, Robert: **»Life is king and lord over death«:** Martin Luther's view of death and dying. In: 059, 23-45: Ill.

494 Kühne, Hartmut: **Zwischen Totschlag und Tourismus:** Spuren von Wallfahrt und Pilgerschaft im mitteldeutschen Umfeld Luthers. In: 039, 377-387: Ill.

495 Luscher, Birgit: **Reliquienverehrung als Symbolsystem:** volkskirchliche Praxis und reformatorischer Umbruch; zum Wittenberger Reliquienschatz und zur Transformation des symbolischen Denkens bei Luther. MS: Lit, 2008. 103 S.: Ill., Tab. (Theologie; 86)

496 Matthias, Markus: **Reformation als Reformation des Menschen:** mit welchen Gerechtigkeitskonzeptionen beginnt die Reformation? LuBu 17 (2008), 76-85.

497 Mennecke-Haustein, Ute: **Ars moriendi I:** history (Ars moriendi I: geschichtlich (engl.)). In: 054, 397 f.

498 Pettibone, Dennis L.: **Martin Luther's views on the Antichrist.** Journal of the Adventist Theological Society 18 (Collegedale, TN 2007) Spring, 81-100.

499 Schröder, Richard: **Kreuzzüge und Hexenverfolgungen:** Gewalt in der Christentumsgeschichte. In: Religionen und Gewalt: Konflikt- und Friedenspotentiale in den Weltreligionen / hrsg. von Reinhard Hempelmann; Johannes Kandel. GÖ: V&R, 2006, 329 S. (Kirche und Konfession; 51)

500 Stjerna, Kirsi: **Kenen sana?:** whose word? Seminary Ridge review 9 (Gettysburg, PA 2007), 68-80.

501 Thiel, John: **Time, judgment, and competitive spirituality:** a reading of the development of the doctrine of purgatory. Theological studies 69 (Woodstock, MD 2008), 741-785.

502 Wiesner-Hanks, Merry E.: **»Lustful Luther«:** male libido in the writings of the reformer. In: 042, 190-212

3 Beurteilung der Persönlichkeit und ihres Werkes

503 Brückner, Wolfgang: **Luther, heiliger Mann oder falscher Prophet?:** Legende und Antilegende zwischen 1517 und 1630. In: Mythen Europas: Schlüsselfiguren der Imagination; Renaissance/ hrsg. von Christine Strobl. Regensburg: Pustet, 2006, 37-57: Ill.

504 Goebel, Eckart: **Das Ding (Sublimieren):** Lacans Luther. Komparatistik (2008), 131-144.

505 Nürnberger, Christian: **Das Christentum:** was man wirklich wissen muss. B: Rowohlt Berlin, 2007. 302 S. L 219 f.

506 Nürnberger, Christian: **Das Christentum:** was man wirklich wissen muss. Taschenbuchaus gabe. Reinbek bei HH: Rowohlt-Taschenbuch, 2008. 302 S. L 219 f. (rororo; 62235)

507 Pröhle, Károly: **Luther teológiája és hatása** (Luthers Theologie und Einfluss) (1985). In: Ders.: »Tanítsátok őket ...«. BP: [Selbstverlag], 2007, 85-98.

508 Riswold, Caryn: **Two reformers:** Martin Luther and Mary Daly as political theologians. Eugene, OR: Cascade, 2007. X, 205 S.

509 Slenczka, Notger: **»Neuzeitliche Freiheit oder ursprüngliche Bindung?:** zu einem Paradigmenwechsel in der Reformations- und Lutherdeutung« [Modern freedom or primary bond?:

regarding a paradigm chance in the interpretation of Luther and the Reformation]/ engl.

Zusammenfassung: Wolfgang Vondey. LuD 16 (2003), 125-128. [Vgl. LuB 2006, Nr. 648]

4 Luthers Beziehungen zu früheren Strömungen, Gruppen, Persönlichkeiten und Ereignissen

510 Aubenque, Pierre: **Aristotelianism** (Aristotelismus ⟨engl.⟩). In: 054, 372 f.

511 Basse, Michael: **Von den Reformkonzilien bis zum Vorabend der Reformation.** L: EVA, 2008. 219 S. (Kirchengeschichte in Einzeldarstellungen; II, 2)

512 Bell, Theo M. M. A. C.: **Luther als erfgenaam van de monastieke theologie** (Luthers Aufnehmen monastischer Theologie). LuBu 17 (2008), 6-18.

513 Brondos, David A.: **Did Luther get Paul right?** Dialog 46 (Oxford 2007), 24-30.

514 Burger, Christoph: **Augustinianism** (Augustinismus ⟨engl.⟩). In: 054, 504.

515 Burger, Christoph: **Leben als Mönch und Leben in der »Welt« – monastischer Anspruch und reformatorischer Widerspruch.** In: 053, 7-27.

516 Hultgren, Arland J.: **Flashpoints in interpreting Paul.** Dialog 46 (Oxford 2007), 166-169.

517 Hunsinger, George: **»Aquinas, Luther, and Calvin:** toward a Chalcedonian resolution of the Eucharistic controversies«/ Zusammenfassung: Ian Christopher Levy. LuD 16 (2008), 91 f. [Vgl. LuB 2007, Nr. 594]

518 Hutter, Reinhard: **St. Thomas on grace and free will in the initium fidei:** the surpassing Augustinian synthesis. Nova et vetera 5 (Naples, FL 2007), 521-554.

519 Köpf, Ulrich: **Bernard of Clairvaux** (Bernhard von Clairvaux ⟨engl.⟩). In: 054, 703-705.

520 Köpf, Ulrich: **Wurzeln reformatorischen Denkens in der monastischen Theologie Bernhards von Clairvaux.** In: 053, 29-56.

521 Köpf, Ulrich: **Zisterziensererbe im Protestantismus.** Cistercienser Chronik 114 (Sinzig 2007), 311-328.

522 Leppin, Volker: **Antichrist II:** church history; 1. Early church to the Reformation (Antichrist II: kirchengeschichtlich; 1. Alte Kirche bis Reformation ⟨engl.⟩). In: 054, 264 f.

523 Leppin, Volker: **Humanismus und Mönchtum:** Überlegungen zu ihrer Bedeutung für ein Verständnis der Wittenberger Reformation. In: 053, 79-101.

524 Leppin, Volker: **Ich hab all mein Ding von Doctor Staupitz:** Johannes von Staupitz als geistlicher Begleiter von Luthers reformatorischer Entwicklung. In: Wenn die Seele zu atmen beginnt ...:

geistliche Begleitung in evangelischer Perspektive/ hrsg. von Dorothea Greiner ... L: EVA, 2007, 60-80.

525 Leppin, Volker: **Loi et vangile:** une transformation de la piété mystique, origine d'un principe de la théologie luthérienne/ aus dem Dt. übers. von Matthieu Arnold. RHPhR 88 (2008), 279-293.

526 Leppin, Volker: **Theologie im Mittelalter.** L: EVA, 2007. 181 S. L". (Kirchengeschichte in Einzeldarstellungen; I, 11)

527 Lexutt, Athina; Mantey, Volker; Ortmann, Volkmar: **Einleitung [Reformation und Mönchtum].** In: 053, 1-5.

528 Lund, Eric: **Tauler the mystic's Lutheran admires.** In: 050, 9-27.

529 Monteil, Ariane; Monteil, Michèle: **Luther, lecteur et commentateur de Tauler:** à propos de quelques notes marginales de Martin Luther au sermon »de nativitate domini« de Jean Tauler. RHPhR 88 (2008), 147-171.

530 Pérès, Jacques N.: **»Ils n'étaient que des hommes«:** un jugement de Martin Luther sur les Pères de l'Église. In: 011, 87-94.

531 Saarinen, Risto: **How Luther got Paul right.** Dialog 46 (Oxford 2007), 170-173.

532 Séguenny, André: **Patrarcától Lutherig:** gondolatok a reneszánsz világlátásról (De Pétrarque ... Luther: réflexions sur la vision du monde de la Renaissance ⟨ungar.⟩). In: 057, 7-25.

533 Springer, Carl P. E.: **Martin's Martial:** reconsidering Luther's relationship with the classics. International journal of classical tradition 14 (Boston, MA 2007) Nr. 1/2 (Summer), 23-50.

534 Staats, Reinhart: **Bild Christi im Abendmahl:** patristische Tradition in lutherischer Abendmahlslehre und in lutherischer Naturfrömmigkeit. In: Mystik – Metapher – Bild: Beiträge des VII. Makarios-Symposiums. hrsg. von Martin Tamcke. GÖ: Univ., 2008, 67-82.

535 Volkmar, Christoph: **Zwischen Devotion und Repräsentation:** fürstliche Heiligenverehrung in Mitteldeutschland vor der Reformation. In: 028, 145-173.

536 Wendebourg, Dorothea: **Luther on monasticism.** LQ 19 (2005), 125-152.

537 Wendebourg, Dorothea: **»Luther on monasticism«/** Zusammenfassung: Patricia A. Sullivan. LuD 16 (2008), 129-133: Ill.

538 Wernisch, Martin: **Mystika a reformace:** Theologia Deutsch, text a dějinný kontext (Mystik und Reformation: Theologia Deutsch, Text und geschichtlicher Kontext). Der Franckforter« (Theologia deutsch ⟨tschech.⟩)/ übers. und komm. von Martin Žemla. PR: Vyšerad, 2007. 264 S. L 53-98+".

539 Wicks, Jared: **Luther and »this damned, concei-** ted, rascally heathen« **Aristotle:** an encounter more complicated than many think. Pro ecclesia 16 (Delhi, NY 2007), 90-104.

540 Zimmerling, Peter: **Überlegungen zu »Gottes Nähe unmittelbar erfahren:** Mystik im Mittelalter und bei Martin Luther/ hrsg. von Berndt Hamm; Volker Leppin. Tübingen 2007«. LuJ 75 (2008), 203-208. [Bespr. zu LuB 2008, Nr. 021]

5 Beziehungen zwischen Luther und gleichzeitigen Strömungen, Gruppen, Persönlichkeiten und Ereignissen

a) Allgemein

541 Brady, Thomas A.: **Emergence and consolidation of Protestantism.** In: 052, 20-36.

542 Brady, Thomas A.: **Limits of religious violence in early modern Europe.** In: 056, 125-151.

543 Brady, Thomas A., Jr.: **»We have lost the Reformation«:** Heinz Schilling and the rise of the confessionalization thesis. In: 062, 33-56.

544 Eppehimer, Trevor: **Protestantism.** NY: Marshall Cavendish Benchmark, 2007. 144 S.: Ill. (World religions)

545 Friedeburg, Robert von: **»Officium in rempublicam«:** fürstliche Herrschaft und Territorialstaat in politischen und rechtlichen Reflexionen und Projektionen im Jahrhundert der Reformation. In: 051, 33-69.

546 Gantet, Claire: **Dreams, standards of knowledge and »orthodoxy« in Germany in the sixteenth century.** In: 046, 69-87.

547 Hamm, Berndt: **Die Emergenz der Reformation.** In: 024, 1-27.

548 Head, Randolph C.; Christensen, Daniel: **Orthodoxies and heterodoxies in the early modern German experience:** introduction. In: 046, 1-24.

549 Lemaitre, Nicole: **L'Europe et les réformes au XVIᵉ siècle.** P: Ellipses, 2008. 264 S. (Le monde, une histoire)

550 Lindberg, Carter: **Love:** a brief history through Western Christianity. Malden, MA: Blackwell, 2008. XII, 195 S.

551 MacCulloch, Diarmaid: **Reformation:** Europe's house divided; 1490-1700. LO: Allen Lane, 2003. XXVII, 831 S.: Ill.

552 MacCulloch, Diarmaid: **The Reformation:** Europe's house divided; 1490-1700. 1. amerikan. Aufl. NY: Viking, 2004. XXIV, 792S., [12] Bl.: Ill., Kt.

553 MacCulloch, Diarmaid: **Reformation:** Europe's house divided; 1490-1700. Taschenbuchausgabe. LO: Penguin Books, 2004. XXVII, 831 S.: Ill. (Penguin history)

554 MacCulloch, Diarmaid: **Reformation:** Europe's house divided; 1490-1700. Taschenbuchausgabe. NY: Penguin Books, 2005. XXVII, 831, [24]S.: Ill., Kt. (A Penguin book: history)

555 MacCulloch, Diarmaid: **Die Reformation: 1490-170** (Reformation ⟨dt.⟩)/ übers. von Helke Voß-Becher M: Deutsche Verlags-Anstalt, 2008. XXVII, 1021 S.: Ill., Kt.

556 McGrath, Alister E.: **Christianity's dangerous idea:** the Protestant revolution – a history from the sixteenth century to the twenty-first. NY: HarperOne, 2007. VIII, 552 S.: Ill.

557 Markert, Gerhard: **Menschen um Luther:** eine Geschichte der Reformation in Lebensbildern. Ostfildern: Thorbecke, 2008. 376 S.: Ill.

558 Markschies, Christoph **Christianity II:** church history (Christentum II: kirchengeschichtlich ⟨engl.⟩). In: 055, 577-585.

559 Moeller, Bernd: **Geschichte des Christentums in Grundzügen.** 9., überarb. Aufl. GÖ: V&R, 2008. 436 S. (UTB; 905)

560 Nichols, Stephen J.: **The Reformation:** how a monk and a mallet changed the world. Wheaton, IL: Crossway, 2007. 159 S.: Ill.

561 Noblesse-Rocher, Annie: **Justice et grâce dans les commentaires sur l'épître aux Romains de Jaques Sadolet et de Jean Calvin.** In: 029, 125-146. L".

562 Ocker, Christopher: **Church robbers and reformers in Germany 1525-1547:** confiscation and religious purpose in the Holy Roman Empire. Leiden: Brill, 2006. XX, 338 S.: Ill. (Studies in medieval and reformation traditions; 114)

563 Schmidt, Alexander: **Konfession und nationales Vaterland:** katholische Reaktionen auf den protestantischen Patriotismus im Alten Reich (1520-1620). In: 017, 13-48.

564 Schnyder, Caroline: **Reformation.** S (Hohenheim): Ulmer, 2008. 129 S., Ill. (UTB; 3022: Profile)

565 Schorn-Schütte, Luise: **Eigenlogik oder Verzahnung?**: Religion und Politik im lutherischen Protestantismus des Alten Reiches (16. Jahrhundert). In: 051, 13-31.

566 Seebaß, Gottfried: **Die Reformation als Epoche.** In: 062, 21-32.

567 Séguenny, André: **Eszmék vándorlása:** középkor, reneszánsz, reformáció (Religions en contacts: le problème du transfert des idées; Moyen âge, Renaissance et Réformes protestante et catholique ⟨ungar.⟩). In: 057, 173-191.

568 Séguenny, André: **A hit kérdése a 16. század szellemi áramlataiban** (Das Problem des Glaubens in den verschiedenen geistigen Strömungen des 16. Jh. ⟨ungar.⟩). In: 057, 27-42.

569 Stjerna, Kirsi: **Women and the Reformation.** Bognor Regis, UK: Wiley, 2008. 304 S.

b) Wittenberger Freunde

570 Beyer, Michael: **Amsdorf, Nikolaus von** (Amsdorf, Nikolaus von ⟨engl.⟩). In: 054, 197.

571 Bieber-Wallmann, Anneliese: **Makel des Verrats:** Johannes Bugenhagen, der viele Landeskirchen organisiert hat, starb vor 450 Jahren. ZZ 9 (2008) Heft 4, 52-54: Ill.

572 Büttgen, Philippe: **Melanchthon (Philipp Schwarzerdt dit Philipp).** In: 010, 700-702.

573 DeAngelis, Simone: **Bildungsgedanke und Seelenlehre bei Philipp Melanchthon.** In: Anfänge und Grundlegungen moderner Pädagogik im 16. und 17. Jahrhundert/ hrsg. von Hans-Ulrich Musolff... Köln; Weimar; W: Böhlau, 2003, 95-119. (Beiträge zur historischen Bildungsforschung; 29)

574 DeAngelis, Simone: **Melanchthon in der Frühaufklärung:** Melanchthonrezeption, humanistische Hermeneutik und kopernikanisches Weltbild bei den cartesianischen Theologen um 1650. In: 044, 167-191.

575 Djubo, Boris: **Philipp Melanchthon und die russische Grammatiktradition.** In: 044, 143-166.

576 Gebhardt, Armin: **Philipp Melanchthon:** praeceptor Germaniae; Studie. Marburg: Tectum, 2008. 113 S. L 11-25.

577 Gemeinhardt, Peter: **Traditionsbindung und Traditionskritik bei Melanchthon.** In: 019, 31-61.

578 Grappe, Christian: **Justice et grâce dans l'épître aux Romains: éclairages rhétoriques de Mélanchthon ... l'exégèse récente.** In: 029, 15-44. L 44.

579 **Grenzen überwinden:** die Bedeutung Melanchthons für Europa; von Wittenberg bis Siebenbürgen; internationale Ausstellung der europäischen Melanchthon-Akademie Bretten in Zusammenarbeit mit dem Archiv der Honterus-Gemeinde Kronstadt = **Overcoming borders:** Philipp Melanchthon's significance for Europe; from Wittenberg to Transylvania; international exhibition by the European Melanchthon Academy, Bretten, in cooperation with the archives of the Honterus Congregation of Braşov/ hrsg. von Albert de Lange; Leitung: Günter Frank; Texte: Albert de Lange; Edit Szegedi; theol. Beratung: Michael Beyer; Redaktion: Albert de Lange; Thomas Sindilariu. Bretten: Europäische Melanchthon-Akademie, 2007. 103 S.: Ill.

580 **A határok legyőzése:** Philipp Melanchthon európai jelentősége Wittenbergtől Erdélyig; a Bretteni Melanchthon Akadémia nemzetközi kiállítása (Grenzen überwinden: die Bedeutung Melanchthons für Europa; von Wittenberg bis Siebenbürgen; internationale Ausstellung der europäischen Melanchthon-Akademie Bretten ⟨ungar.⟩)/ hrsg. von Albert de Lange; Günter Frank; Texte: Albert de Lange; Edit Szegedi; Katalin Keveházi; theol. Beratung: Michael Beyer; Redaktion: Botont Szabó; Thomas Sindilariu. Bretten: Europäische Melanchthon-Akademie, 2008. 55 S.: Ill.

581 Gummelt, Volker: **Der Reformator des Nordens:** Johannes Bugenhagen. DPfBl 108 (2008), 213.

582 Heininen, Simo: **Michael Agricola an der Universität Wittenberg.** Jahrbuch für finnisch-deutsche Literaturbeziehungen 39 (Helsinki 2007), 21-40. [Auszug ⟨dt.⟩ aus LuB 2009, Nr. 583]

583 Heininen, Simo: **Mikael Agricola – elämä ja teokset** (Michael Agricola – Leben und Schriften). Helsinki: Edita, 2007. 399 S.: Ill., Kt.

584 Helm, Jürgen: **Wittenberger Anatomie:** Motive und Ausprägungen einer protestantischen Wissenschaft im 16. Jahrhundert. In: 043, 235-248.

585 Herrmann, Klaus: **Melanchthon aus der Sicht des Judentums.** In: 044, 193-228: Ill.

586 Illgner, Christoph: **Nikolaus von Amsdorf »wider den rotten vnnd secten gaist«.** In: 045, 251-279.

587 Koch, Ernst: **Agricola, Johann** (Schneyder, Sneider, Schnitter) (Agricola, [Schneyder, Sneider, Schnitter] Johann ⟨engl.⟩). In: 054, 107.

588 Koch, Hans-Theodor: **Die Wittenberger medizinische Fakultät (1502-1652):** ein biobibliographischer Überblick. In: 043, 289-348. L".

589 Köpf, Ulrich: **Nikolaus von Amsdorf an der Universität Wittenberg:** (mit Abdruck von Disputationsthesen Amsdorfs). In: 045, 35-55.

590 Kohnle, Armin: **Die Frömmigkeit der Wettiner und die Anfänge der Reformation.** LuJ 75 (2008), 125-140.

591 Kuropka, Nicole: **Vor Gott und in der Welt:** Melanchthons Sprachschule für die Gesellschaft. In: 044, 67-79.

592 Leins, Heidemarie; Leins, Rüdiger: **»Ein Monumentalbau von edler Schönheit«:** Baugeschichte des Melanchthonhauses Bretten. In: 044, 13-38: Ill.

593 Leppin, Volker: **Nikolaus von Amsdorf und Johann Friedrich d. Ä.** In: 045, 103-115.

594 Leppin, Volker: **Die Wittenberger Reformation und der Prozess der Transformation kultureller zu institutionellen Polaritäten.** S; L: Hirzel, 2008. 45 S. (Sitzungsberichte der Sächsischen Akademie der Wissenschaften zu Leipzig: Phil.-Hist. Klasse; 140)

595 Lorentzen, Tim: **Johannes Bugenhagen als Reformator der öffentlichen Fürsorge.** TÜ: Mohr Siebeck, 2008. XII, 536 S.: Ill. (Spätmittelalter, Humanismus, Reformation; 44) – Teilw. zugl. M, Univ., Evang.-theol. Fak., Diss., 2007.

596 Melanchthon, Philipp: **Ethicae doctrinae elementa et enarratio Libri quinti ethicorum** = [Grundbegriffe der Ethik und Auslegung des fünften Buches der Nikomachischen Ethik] (⟨lat./dt.⟩)/ hrsg. und eingel. von Günter Frank; unter Mitarb. von Michael Beyer. S-Bad Cannstatt: Frommann-Holzboog, 2008. XLII, 271 S. L XXIII+". (Editionen zur Frühen Neuzeit: lateinisch-deutsche Quelleneditionen; 1)

597 [Melanchthon, Philipp]: **Melanchthon on Christian doctrine:** Loci communes, 1555/ übers. und hrsg. von Clyde L. Manschreck; Einleitung: Hans Engelland. Nachdruck der Ausgabe NY, 1965. Eugene, OR: Wipf and Stock, 2002. LVII, 356 S. (A Library of Protestant thought)

598 [Melanchthon, Philipp]: **Melanchthons Briefwechsel:** kritische und kommentierte Gesamtausgabe/ im Auftrag der Heidelberger Akademie der Wissenschaften hrsg. von Heinz Scheible. Bd. T 9: **Texte 2336-2604 (1540)**/ bearb. von Christine Mundhenk unter Mitw. von Marion Bechtold; Heidi Hein; Simone Kurz; Judith Steiniger. S-Bad Cannstatt: Frommann-Holzboog, 2008. 637 S.

599 Metzler, Regine: **Stephan Roth 1492-1546:** Stadtschreiber in Zwickau und Bildungsbürger der Reformationszeit; Biographie. Edition der Briefe seiner Freunde Franz Pehem, Altenburg, und Nicolaus Günther, Torgau/ hrsg. von Regine Metzler. L: Verlag der Sächsischen Akademie der Wissenschaften zu Leipzig in Kommission bei S: Steiner, 2008. 668 S.: Ill. (Quellen und Forschungen zur sächsischen Geschichte; 32)

600 Müller, Gerhard: **Bugenhagen, Johannes** (Bugenhagen, Johannes ⟨engl.⟩). In: 055, 264.

601 Schäufele, Wolf-Friedrich: **Kirche Christi und Teufelskirche:** Verfall und Kontinuität der Kirche bei Nikolaus Amsdorf. In: 045, 57-90.

602 Scheible, Heinz: **Ein Irrtum Melanchthons:** seine Warnung vor dem Fürstenkrieg 1551/52. In: 07, 233-240

603 Schmalz, Björn: **Georg Spalatin und sein Wirken in Altenburg: (1525-1545).** L, 2006. 223 S.: Ill. – Zugl.: L., Univ., Philos. Fak., MA, 2006.

604 Scholz, Thorsten: **Das Verhältnis zwischen Martin Luther und Philipp Melanchthon anhand ausgewählter Coburg-Briefe.** M: Grin, 2008. 22 S.

605 Schulz, Ronny F.: **Zur Sprache der Flugschrift vom »Bapstesel« und »Munchkalb« (1523) und zu ihrem Verhältnis zur anonym veröffentlichten »Figur des Antichristlichen Bapsts«:** ein Beitrag zur Diskussion der Verfasserschaft Philipp Melanchthons. In: 04, 299-312: Ill.

606 Treu, Martin: **Luthers Universität:** zur Erinnerung an den Studienaufenthalt Michael Agricolas in Wittenberg. Jahrbuch für finnisch-deutsche Literaturbeziehungen 39 (Helsinki 2007], 10-20.

607 Wels, Volkhard: **Die historische Bedeutung von Melanchthons Rhetorik.** In: 044, 229-237.

608 Wengert, Timothy J.: **Georg Major:** an »eyewitness« to the posting of Martin Luther's Ninety-five theses. In: 040, 93-97.

609 Wengert, Timothy J.: **Philip Melanchthon and Augustinus of Hippo.** LQ 22 (2008), 249-267

610 Wollersheim, Heinz-Werner: **»nec ad respublicas gubernandas ...«:** christliche Bildung und staatliche Ordnung bei Philipp Melanchthon. In: 07, 335-353.

c) Altgläubige

611 Bünz, Enno: **Leipzig oder Wittenberg:** Bildung und Konfession im Herzogtum Sachsen 1517-1539. In: 048, 83-94.

612 Cassese, Michele: **La prima controversistica cattolica del cinquecento e la sua concezione della chiesa nella lotta contro Lutero** [Die erste kath. Kontroverse des 16. Jh. und ihr Kirchenverständnis im Kampf gegen Luther] In: Figure moderne della teologia nei secoli XV-XIVV: atti del Convegno Internazionale promosso dall'Istituto di Storia della Teologia di Lugano, Lugano, 30 settembre-1 ottobre 2005/ hrsg. von Inos Biffi. Milano: Jaca, 2007, 87-136.

613 François, Wim: **Vernacular bible reading and censorship in early sixteenth century:** the position of the Louvain theologians. In: 034, 69-96: Ill.

614 Hecht, Christian: **Die Aschaffenburger Gregorsmessen:** Kardinal Albrecht von Brandenburg als

Verteidiger des Meßopfers gegen Luther und Zwingli. In: Der Kardinal. – LuB 2008, Nr. 032 , 80-115: Ill.

615 Jadatz, Heiko: **Religionspolitik und Fürstenpolemik:** der Streit zwischen Herzog Georg von Sachsen und Martin Luther über dessen Brief an Wezeslaus Linck vom 14. Juni 1528. In: 07, 59-72.

616 Jürgensmeier, Friedhelm: **Albert of Brandenburg** (Albrecht of Mainz) (Albrecht von Mainz ⟨engl.⟩). In: 054, 121 f.

617 Kohnle, Armin: **Ein Brief des badischen Kanzlers Hieronymus Vehus an Herzog Georg von Sachsen in der Luthersache (1522).** In: 07, 73-93.

618 Lück, Heiner: **Kardinal Albrecht versus Hans Schenitz:** ein Prozess nach sächsischem Recht 1534/35. LuJ 74 (2007), 133-152: Ill.

619 Müller, Gerhard: **Aleander, Girolamo** (Aleander, Hieronymus ⟨engl.⟩). In: 054, 130.

620 Schlageter, Johannes: **Kaspar Meckenlörs Übersetzung und Bearbeitung von John Fishers »Assertionum Martini Lutheri confutatio«.** Wissenschaft und Weisheit 70 (Kevelaer 2007), 81-119.

621 Selge, Kurt-Victor: **Alvelt, Augustine of** (Alvelt, Augustinus von ⟨engl.⟩). In: 054, 174.

622 Volkmar, Christoph: **Reform statt Reformation:** die Kirchenpolitik Herzog Georgs von Sachsen 1488-1525. TÜ: Mohr Siebeck, 2008. XIV, 701 S.: Tab. (Spätmittelalter und Reformation: N. R.; 41) – Zugl.: L, Univ., Diss., 2006/07.

623 Wallmann, Johannes: **Pietismus-Studien:** gesammelte Aufsätze II. TÜ: Mohr Siebeck, 2008. XIV, 408 S.

624 Wicks, Jared: **Cajetan, Thomas de Vio** (Cajetan, Thomas de Vio ⟨engl.⟩). In: 055, 309.

d) Humanisten

625 Algazi, Gadi: »**Geistesabwesenheit«:** Gelehrte zuhause um 1500. In: Gelehrtenleben: Wissenschaftspraxis in der Neuzeit/ hrsg. von Alf Lüdtke; Reiner Prass. Köln: Böhlau, 2008, 215-234.

626 Arnold, Matthieu: **Reformation und Humanismus im Elsass.** In: 044, 55-65.

627 Flasch, Kurt: **Kampfplätze der Philosophie:** große Kontroversen von Augustin bis Voltaire. F: Klostermann, 2008. 362 S. L 243-274+".

628 Flasch, Kurt: **Kampfplätze der Philosophie:** große Kontroversen von Augustin bis Voltaire. Lizenzausgabe. DA: WB, 2008. 362 S. L 243-274+".

629 Furey, Constance M.: »**Invective and discernment in Martin Luther, D. Erasmus, and Thomas More«/** Zusammenfassung: Rebecca E. Moore. LuD 16 (2008), 28-32. [Vgl. LuB 2007, Nr. 399]

630 Gielis, Marcel: **Leuven theologians as opponents of Erasmus and of humanistic theology.** In: Biblical humanism and scholasticism in the age of Erasmus/ hrsg. von Erika Rummel. Leiden; Boston: Brill, 2008, 197-214. (Brill's companions to the Christian tradition; 9)

631 Herdt, Jennifer A.: »**Virtue's semblance:** Erasmus and Luther on pagan virtue and the Christian life«/ Zusammenfassung: James G. Kiecker. LuD 16 (2008), 116-124. [Vgl. LuB 2007, Nr. 697]

632 Kolb, Robert: »**None of my works is worth anything, except perhaps ›De servo arbitrio ...‹:** Luther on the bondage of human choice« [Bound, choice, election and Wittenberg theological method [Auszug]/ Zusammenfassung: Timothy H. Maschke. LuD 16 (2008), 93-98: Ill. [Vgl. LuB 2006, Nr. 162, S. 11-66]

633 Kroeker, Greta Grace: **Erasmus and the freedom of will.** In: 017, 249-261.

634 McDonald, Grantley: **Laurentius Corvinus and the Epicurean Luther.** LQ 22 (2008), 161-176.

635 Rudersdorf, Manfred: **Luthertum, humanistische Bildung und Territorialstaat:** Anmerkungen zu einem historischen Problemzusammenhang im Reformationsjahrhundert. In: 07, 301-315.

e) Thomas Müntzer und Bauernkrieg

636 Bräuer, Siegfried: **Luthers Reise in das Bauernkriegsgebiet.** In: 02, 299-312.

637 Bräuer, Siegfried: **Das Mansfelder Land.** In: 02, 179-192.

638 Goertz, Hans-Jürgen: **Apokalyptik in Thüringen.** In: 02, 329-346.

639 Graupner, Volker: **Die ernestinischen Fürsten im Thüringer Bauernkrieg.** In: 02, 283-298.

640 Günther, Gerhard: **Flucht, Vertreibung, Verfolgung und Gegenreaktionen.** In: 02, 397-415.

641 Günther, Gerhard: **Die innerstädtische Bewegung in der Reichsstadt Mühlhausen und die Aktionen im Bauernkrieg 1523 bis 1525.** In: 02, 91-111.

642 Jonscher, Reinhard: **Erinnerungsort Bauernkrieg?:** die Erinnerungslandschaft Thüringen und ein unbequemer Gegenstand. In: Couragierte Wissenschaft: eine Festschrift für Jürgen John zum 65. Geburtstag/ hrsg. von Monika Gibas. Jena: Glaux, 2007, 94-113: Ill.

643 Jonscher, Reinhard: **Die Reformation in Thüringen bis zum Vorabend des Bauernkriegs.** In: 02, 31-42.

644 Jonscher, Reinhard: **Zwischen Erinnerung, Verdrängung und Instrumentalisierung:** Bauernkriegserinnerung in Thüringen. In: 02, 467-483.

645 Müller, Thomas T.: **Müntzers Werkzeug oder charismatischer Anführer?** In: 02, 243-259.

646 Séguenny, André: **Thomas Müntzer kora vallási térképén** (Thomas Müntzer auf der religiösen Landkarte seines Zeitalters). In: 057, 71-82.

647 Straube, Manfred: **Reformation, Bauernkrieg und »Klosterstürme«.** In: 02, 381-396.

648 Vogler, Günter: **Bäuerliche und städtische Aufstände zwischen Harz und Thüringer Wald.** In: 02, 65-90.

649 Vogler, Günter: **Thomas Müntzer und die Aufstandsbewegung in Thüringen.** In: 02, 225-242.

650 Vogler, Günter: **Die Tradierung des Müntzerbildes der »Histori Thome Muntzers« durch Johannes Sleidan.** In: 020, 218-226.

651 Wohlfeil, Rainer: **Regenbogenfahne und Regenbogen.** In: 02, 313-328.

652 Zschoch, Hellmut: **Religion, Politik und Gewalt im Bauernkrieg.** In: 021, 87-110.

f) »Schwärmer« und Täufer

653 Bechtoldt, Hans-Joachim: »**Franciscus von Sickingen, ein Feind aller Pfaffen und Geistlichen«:** Sebastian Francks Notizen über Franz von Sickingen in seiner »Chronica« von 1531. BlPfKG 75 (2008), 363-386: Ill.: L 367-369+" = Ebernburg-Hefte 42 (2008), 51-74: Ill.: L 55-57+".

654 Franck, Sebastian: **Sämtliche Werke:** kritische Ausgabe mit Kommentar/ hrsg. von Hans-Gerd Roloff. Berliner Ausgabe. Bd. 1: **Frühe Schriften/** Kommentar von Christoph Dejung. S-Bad Cannstatt: Frommann-Holzboog, 2005. 600 S.

655 Lutterbach, Hubertus: **Das Täuferreich von Münster:** Ursprünge und Merkmale eines religiösen Aufbruchs. MS: Aschendorff, 2008. 208 S.: Ill. – Bespr.: Böcher, Otto: BlPfKG 75 (2008), 430 f = Ebernburg-Hefte 42 (2008), 118 f.

656 McLaughlin, Emmet: **Anabaptists and dissenters.** In: 052, 37-55.

657 Oelschläger, Ulrich: **Die Wormser Propheten von 1527:** eine vorlutherische Teilübersetzung der Bibel. ThZ 64 (2008), 168-198.

658 **Quellen zur Geschichte der Täufer in der Schweiz/** hrsg. von Martin Haas. Bd. 3: **Aargau – Bern – Solothurn.** ZH: Theol. Verlag, 2008. XLVII, 669 S.

659 Schott, Heinz: »**Lutherus medicorum«:** Wege und Irrwege der Paracelsus-Rezeption. In: 043, 273-288.

660 Séguenny, André: **Caspar von Schwenckfeld (1489-1561) krisztológiája:** non aliud sed aliter (La christologie de Caspar Schwenckfeld, 1489-1561: non aliud sed aliter (ungar.)). In: 057, 131-159.

661 Séguenny, André: **Hans Denck pályája** (Hans Dencks Laufbahn). In: 057, 83-105.

662 Séguenny, André: **Jörg Haugk:** felúton humanizmus és spiritualizmus között (Jörg Haugk: entre l'Humanisme et le spiritualisme (ungar.)). In: 057, 55-69.

663 Séguenny, André: **Misztika, lutheranizmus és humanizmus között:** Sebastian Franck (Le spiritualisme de Sebastian Franck: ses rapports avec le mystique, le luthéranisme et l'Humanisme (ungar.)). In: 057, 107-130.

664 Zorzin, Alejandro: **Peter Schöffer d. J. und die Täufer.** In: 04, 179-213.

g) Schweizer und Oberdeutsche

665 Arnold, Matthieu: **De Jean Geiler à Matthieu Zell:** sources et influence de l'anticléricalisme du »Narrenschiff«. In: Sebastian Brant (1457-1521)/ hrsg. von Hans-Gert Roloff; Jean Marie Valentin; Volkhard Wels. B: Weidler, 2008, 37-48. L". (Memoria; 9)

666 Beeke, Joel R.: **Living for God's glory:** an Introduction to Calvinism. Lake Mary, FL: Reformation Trust, 2008. XVI, 416 S.

667 Billings, J. Todd: **Calvin, participation, and the gift:** the activity of believers in union with Christ. NY: Oxford University, 2007. VII, 218 S. (Changing paradigms in historical and systematic theology)

668 Bölcskei, Gusztáv: **Erasmus és Luther hatása Huldrych Zwingli teológiai gondolkodására** (Der Einfluss des Erasmus und Luthers auf Zwinglis theol. Denken). In: 032, 27-32.

669 [Bucer, Martin]: **Correspondance de Martin Bucer.** Bd. 5: **September 1530 - Mai 1531/** hrsg. und bearb. von Reinhold Friedrich; Einleitung von Matthieu Arnold. Leiden: Brill, 2004. LXXI, 448 S. (Bucer, Martin: Opera omnia: series 3, correspondance; 5) (Studies in medieval and Reformation thought; 101)

670 [Bucer, Martin]: **Correspondance de Martin Bucer.** Bd. 7: **Oktober 1531 - März 1532/** hrsg. von Berndt Hamm ...; Einleitung: Matthieu Arnold. Leiden: Brill, 2008. CXXV, 562 S., L XXVII-XXX+". (Bucer, Martin: Opera omnia: series 3, correspondance; 7) (Studies in medieval and Reformation thought; 136)

671 Burnett, Amy Nelson: **Teaching the Reformation:** ministers and their message in Basel, 1529-1629. Oxford; NY: Oxford University, 2006. XII, 448 S.: Ill. (Oxford studies in historical theology) – Bespr.: Friedrich, Markus: ZHF 34 (2007), 712-714; Keßler, Martin: ThZ 64 (2008),

336

206-208; Selderhuis, Herman: ThLZ 133 (2008), 1093 f.

672 Frieß, Peer: **Der Einfluss des Zwinglianismus auf die Reformation der oberschwäbischen Reichsstädte.** Zw 34 (2007), 5-27.

673 Gerrish, B[rian] A.: **Calvin, John** (Calvin, Johannes ⟨engl.⟩). In: 055, 324-336.

674 Gerrish, Brian: **Luther and the reformed eucharist:** What Luther said, or might have said, about Calvin. Seminary Ridge review 10 (Gettysburg, PA 2008) Nr. 2, 5-19.

675 Gordon, Bruce: **Holy and problematic death:** Heinrich Bullinger on Zwingli and Luther. In: 059, 47-61: Ill.

676 Greef, Wulfert de: **The writings of John Calvin:** an introductory guide (Johannes Calvijn: zijn werk en geschriften ⟨engl.⟩)/ Verm. Ausgabe. Louisville, KY; LO: Westminster John Knox, 2008. XVII, 253 S.: Ill.

677 Hesselink, I. John: **Heiliger Geist/** übers. von Ulrike Sawicki. In: 05, 295-307.

678 Hesselink, I. John: **Pneumatologie** (Heiliger Geist ⟨niederl.⟩). In: 06, 337-352.

679 Huizing, Klaas: **Calvin: ... und was vom Reformator übrigbleibt.** F: Hansisches Druck- und Verlags-Haus, 2008. 160 S.: Ill. (Edition Chrismon)

680 Janse, Wim: **Sakramente/** übers. von Ulrike Sawicki. In: 05, 338-349.

681 Janse, Wim: **Sacramenten** (Sakramente). In: 06, 387-398.

682 Janton, Pierre: **Jean Calvin:** ministre de la parole, 1509-1564. P: du Cerf, 2008. 384 S. (Histoire)

683 Kaufmann, Thomas: **Luther und Calvin – eine Reformation.** In: 062, 73-96.

684 Lane, Anthony N. S.: **Was Calvin a crypto-Zwinglian?** In: Adaptations of Calvinism in Reformation Europe: essays in honor of Brian G. Armstrong/ hrsg. von Mack P. Holt. Hampshire; Burlington, VT: Ashgate, 2007, 21-41.

685 Matheson, Peter: **Martin Luther and Argula von Grumbach (1492-1556/7).** LQ 22 (2008), 1-15.

686 Millet, Olivier: **Calvin:** un homme, une œuvre, un auteur. Gollion: Infolio, 2008. 200 S. L". (Illico; 20)

687 Moeller, Bernd: **Bucer, Martin** (Butzer; Nov 11, 1491, Sélestat – Feb 28, 1551, Cambridge) (Bucer [Butzer], Martin ⟨engl.⟩). In: 055, 244 f.

688 Pitkin, Barbara: **Glaube und Rechtfertigung/** übers. von Ulrike Sawicki. In: 05, 284-295.

689 Pitkin, Barbara: **Geloof en rechtvaardiging** (Glaube und Rechtfertigung ⟨niederl.⟩). In: 06, 325-337.

690 Pitkin, Barbara: **The spiritual gospel?:** Christ and human nature in Calvin's commentary on John.

Duch review of church history 85 (Leiden 2005 [2006], 187-204.

691 Reinhardt, Volker: **Die Tyrannei der Tugend:** Calvin und die Reformation in Genf. M: Beck, 2009. 271 S.: Ill.

692 Scheible, Heinz: **Capito, Wolfgang** (Capito, Wolfgang ⟨engl.⟩). In: 055, 385 f.

693 Séguenny, André: **Miért gyűlölte Bucer a spiritualistákat?** (Pourquoi Bucer détestait les Spirituels? ⟨ungar.⟩). In: 057, 161-171.

694 Selderhuis, Herman J.: **Calvin und Wittenberg/** übers. von Ulrike Sawicki. In: 05, 57-63.

695 Selderhuis, Herman J.: **Calvijn en Wittenberg** (Calvin und Wittenberg). In: 06, 81-87.

696 Selderhuis, Herman J.: **Institutio/** übers. von Ulrike Sawicki. In: 05, 197-204.

697 Selderhuis, Herman J.: **Institutie** (Institutio). In: 06, 232-239.

698 Somogyi, Márta: **Az 51. zsoltár magyarázata Katharina Zell meditációja alapján** (Die Auslegung von Ps 51 nach der Meditation von Katharina Zell). ThSz 51 (2008), 155-162.

699 Stephens, Peter: **The sacraments on the confessions of 1536, 1549 and 1566:** Bullinger's understanding in the light of Zwingli's. Zw 33 (2006), 51-76.

700 Strohm, Christoph: **Recht und Kirchenrecht.** In: 05, 392-401.

701 Strohm, Christoph: **Recht en kerkrecht** (Recht und Kirchenrecht ⟨niederl.⟩). In: 06, 443-453.

702 Witte, John, Jr.: **The reformation of rights:** law, religion, and human rights in early modern Calvinism. Cambridge, MA: Cambridge University, 2007. XV, 388 S.: Ill.

703 Zachman, Randall C.: **Communio cum Christo/** übers. von Elisabeth Steinweg-Fleckner. In: 05, 359-366.

704 Zachman, Randall C.: **Communio cum Christo** (Communio cum Christo ⟨niederl.⟩). In: 06, 409-417.

705 [Zwingli, Ulrich]: **Amica exegesis an Martin Luther.** ZH: Literatur-Agentur Danowski, 2007. 18 Bl.

h) Juden

706 Akerboom, Dick: **Luthers houding ten opzichte van de paus als spiegelbeeldvan zijn houding ten opzichte van de Joden** (Luthers Haltung hinsichtlich des Papstes als Spiegelbild seiner Haltung hinsichtlich der Juden). LuBu 17 (2009), 86-95.

707 Dan, Joseph: **Anti-Semitism/Antijudaism V:** the Middle ages and the Early modern period

337

(Antisemitismus/Antijudaismus V: Mittelalter und Frühe Neuzeit ⟨engl.⟩). In: 054, 283-286.

708 Homolka, Walter: **Leo Baeck's criticism on Martin Luther and its purpose in a search for Jewish identity.** In: Leo Baeck – philosophical and rabbinical approaches/ hrsg. von Walter Homolka; Einführung: Thomas Rachel. B: Frank & Timme, 2007, 63-82. (Aus Religion und Recht; 9)

709 Michael, Robert: **Holy hatred**: Christianity, antisemitism, and the holocaust. NY: Palgrave, 2006. 254 S.

710 Pritz, Ray: **»... and the children struggled«:** the church and the Jews through history. Mishkan 50 (Jerusalem 2007), 5-135.

711 Thompson, Mark: **Luther and the Jews.** Reformed theological review 67 (Melbourne 2008), 121-145.

712 Waschke, Ernst-Joachim: **Martin Luther und die Juden oder: von einem Irrweg in der Theologie.** In: Mein Haus wird ein Bethaus für alle Völker genannt werden (Jes 56, 7): Judentum seit der Zeit des zweiten Tempels in Geschichte, Literatur und Kult; Festschrift für Thomas Willi zum 65. Geburtstag/ hrsg. von Julia Männchen in Zsarb. mit Torsten Reiprich. NK: NV, 2007, 371-383.

i) Künstler und Kunst

713 Coelen, Peter van der: **Pictures for the people?:** bible illustration and their audience. In: 034, 185-205: Ill.

714 Dejeumont, Catherine: **Le »Passional Christi et Antichristi« (1521) et la »Vergleichung des Papstes und Jesus (1523) ou: de Luther ... l'homme du commun.** In: 020, 111-119.

715 Koepplin, Dieter: **Cranachs Bilder im theologischen und humanistischen Geiste Luthers und Melanchthons.** In: Cranach der Ältere: Katalog anlässlich der Ausstellung »Cranach der Ältere«, Städel Museum, Frankfurt am Main, 23. November bis 17. Februar 2008, Royal Academy of Arts, London, 8. März bis 8. Juni 2008/ hrsg. von Bodo Brinkmann. Ostfildern: Hatje Cantz, 2007, 63-79: Ill.

716 Marquard, Reiner: **Mathias Grünewalds Tauberbischofsheimer Andachtsbilder in der Kunsthalle Karlsruhe und Martin Luthers »Theologia crucis«.** Zeitschrift für die Geschichte des Oberrheins 156 (2008), 179-194.

717 Michalski, Sergiusz: **Die Bilderfrage um 1500 zwischen Thomismus und Frühhumanismus.** In: Art and the church = Kunst und Kirche: religious art and architecture in the Baltic Region in the 13th-18th centuries; conference dedicated to the centenary of Sten I. Karling in Tallinn, Sept. 6-9, 2006, Institute of Art History, Historian Academy of Arts/ hrsg. von Krista Kodres. Tallinn, Institute of History, 2008, 104-118: Ill.

718 Roch-Lemmer, Irene: **Die Chorgestühlbrüstung in der Annenkirche zu Eisleben:** ein Beitrag zur protestantischen Ikonographie in der zweiten Hälfte des 16. Jahrhunderts. In: 014, 143-164: Ill. L". [Vgl. LuB 2008, Nr. 670]

719 Stolberg, Michael: **Lukas Cranachs »Melancholia«-Darstellungen und die zeitgenössische Medizin.** In: 043, 249-271: Taf.

720 Wandel, Lee Palmer: **Reformation and the visual arts.** In: 052, 371-385.

721 Winter, Christian: **Spes mea Christus:** die Kirche zu Wasewitz bei Wurzen und ihr evangelisches Kanzelgemälde. In: 065, 281-298: Ill. L 291-293.

j) Territorien und Orte innerhalb des Deutschen Reiches

722 Benrath, Gustav Adolf: **Baden** (Baden ⟨engl.⟩). In: 054, 548-550.

723 Breul, Wolfgang: **»Mit gutem Gewissen«:** zum religiösen Hintergrund der Doppelehe Landgraf Philipps von Hessen. ZKG 118 (2007), 149-177.

724 Bünz, Enno: **Kaspar Güttel:** Geistlicher an der Zeitenwende von Spätmittelalter und Reformation. In: 07, 167-178.

725 Ehmer, Hermann: **Alber, Matthäus** (Alber, Matthäus ⟨engl.⟩). In: 054, 121.

726 Kohnle, Armin: **Ottheinrich:** Leben und Wirken eines Reformationsfürsten. In: Kurfürst Ottheinrich und die humanistische Kultur in der Pfalz/ hrsg. von Hans Ammerich; Hartmut Harthausen. Speyer: Pfälzische Gesellschaft zur Förderung der Wissenschaften in Speyer, 2008, 11-29. L".

727 Moeller, Bernd: **Deutschland im Zeitalter der Reformation.** In: 09, 1533-1974 (Bildschirm-)S. (Kleine Vandenhoeck-Reihe; 1432) (Deutsche Geschichte; 4)

728 Naumann, Günter: **Sächsische Geschichte in Daten.** Lizenzausgabe. Wiesbaden: Fourier, 2003. 320 S. L 90-93.

729 Rüttgardt, Antje: **Klosteraustritte in der frühen Reformation:** Studien zu Flugschriften der Jahre 1522-1524. GÜ: GVH, 2007. 378 S. (Quellen und Forschungen zur Reformationsgeschichte; 79) – Zugl.: Kiel, Univ., Diss., 2003/04.

730 Ruf, Susanne: **Das ehemalige Zisterzienserkloster Grünhain im Erzgebirge:** Ergebnisse des »Klosterprojektes« 2001-2003. Arbeits- und

Forschungsberichte zur sächsischen Bodendenk-
malpflege 46 (2004), 325-389: Ill. L 334.

731 Schirmer, Uwe: **Die Hinrichtung einer Zaube-
rin und ihres Gefolges vor Wittenberg im Juni
1540:** die Rekonstruktion des Falls im Lichte
der beginnenden Sozialdisziplinierung. In: 015,
137-151.

732 Schirmer, Uwe: **Untersuchungen zur Herrschafts-
praxis der Kurfürsten und Herzöge von Sachsen:**
Institutionen und Funktionseliten (1485-1513). In:
025, 305-378. L".

733 Schöntube, Ulrich: **Transkonfessionalität und
Konfessionskonformität am Beispiel litera-
rischer Quellen von Emporenbilderzyklen der
Region des Kurfürstentums Brandenburg.** In:
017, 347-374: Ill.

734 Stahl, Andreas: **Die Grafschaft und die Stadt
Mansfeld in der Lutherzeit.** In: 036, 7-16: Ill.,
Kt.

735 Teuber, Stefan W.: **Wohnen und Wohnverhält-
nisse in Einbeck zwischen 1450 und 1550.** In:
039, 119-130: Ill

**k) Länder und Orte außerhalb des
Deutschen Reiches**

736 Arnold, Matthieu: »**Ta théologie … est toute ran-
ce, et puante, et moisie«:** les griefs de Ronsard
contre Luther et la Réformation. PL 56 (2008),
95-113.

737 Balázs, Mihály: **Felekezetiség és fikció:** tanulmányok 16-17. századi irodalmunkról (Konfes-
sionalismus und Fiktion: Studien über die ungarische Literatur im 16. und 17. Jh.). BP: Balassi,
2006. 228 S. (Régi Magyar Könyvtár: tanulmá-
yok; 6)

738 Balázs, Mihály: **Megjegyzések János Zsigmond
valláspolitikájáról** (Bemerkungen zur Religionspolitik des Fürsten Johannes Sigismund). Credo
14 (BP 2008), 67-93.

739 Battafarano, Italo Michele: **Mit Luther oder
Goethe in Italien:** Irritation und Sehnsucht der
Deutschen. Trento: Universit à degli Studi di
Trento, 2007. 165 S. (Testi e richerche die germa-
nistica; 2) (Labirinti; 106)

740 Dejeumont, Catherine; Kemp, William: **John
Frith's »Antithesis of Christes actes compared
to the Popes« (1529) in relation to Heinrich von
Kettenbach's »Vergleyschung«.** Reformation:
the journal of the Tyndale Society 12 (LO 2007),
33-68.

741 Dienes, Dénes: **Sárospatak reformációja** (Die
Reformation in Sárospatak) Egyháztörténeti
szemle 9 (Miskolc 2008) Heft 4, 48-60.

742 Ehmann, Johannes: **Luther, Türken und Islam:**
eine Untersuchung zum Türken- und Islambild
Martin Luthers (1515-1546). GÜ: GVH, 2008. 498
S. (Quellen und Forschungen zur Reformationsgeschichte; 80) – Zugl.: HD, Univ., Habil.-Schr.,
2005.

743 Francisco, Adam S.: **Martin Luther and Islam:** a
study in sixteenth-century polemics and apolo-
getics. Leiden: Brill, 2007. XIII, 260 S. (History of
Christian-Muslim relations; 8) – Zugl.: Oxford,
Univ., Diss.

744 Hein, Markus: **Maria von Habsburg, der ungarische Hof und die Reformation in Ungarn.** In:
041, 261-272.

745 Hubert, Ildikó: **Arcok és művek a magyar múlt-
ból:** tanulmányok (Gesichter und Werke aus der
ungarischen Vergangenheit: Studien). BP, Pápa:
Jókai Mór Városi Könyvtár, 2005. 200 S.

746 Ilič, Luka: **Primus Truber (1508-1586), the Slove-
nian Luther.** LQ 22 (2008), 268-277.

747 Keller, Rudolf: **Maria von Ungarn und Martin
Luther:** Luthers Verbindung zur Königin. In: 041,
273-281.

748 Kreem, Juhan: **Der Deutsche Orden und die
Reformation in Livland.** In: The military orders
and the Reformation: choices, state building, and
the weight of tradition: papers of the Utrecht
conference, 30 September - 2 October 2004/ hrsg.
von Johannes A. Mol. Hilversum: Verloren, 2006,
43-57: Ill.

749 Kritzl, Johannes: »**Adversus turcas et turcarum
deum«:** Beurteilungskriterien des Türkenkriegs
und des Islam in den Werken Martin Luthers.
Bonn: Schirmacher, 2008. 114 S. (Disputationes
religionum orbis: Sectio 0, Orient et occident –
Untersuchungen zur Begegnung von Islam und
Christentum; 4)

750 Krumenacker, Yves: **La généalogie imaginaire de
la Réforme protestante.** Revue historique 638 (P
2006), 259-289.

751 **Lexikon české literatury** (Lexikon der tsche-
chischen Literatur). Bd. 4. Teilbde. 1 f: **S-Ž,** do-
datky k LČL 1-3, A-Ä (S-Ž, mit Nachträgen zum
LČL 1-3, A-Ä)/ bearb. von Luboš Merhaut ... PR:
Academia, 2008. 2400 S. L".

752 Miller, Gregory J.: **Wars of religion and religion
in war:** Luther and the 16th century Islamic
advance into Europe. Seminary Ridge review
9 (Gettysburg, PA 2007) Nr. 2, 38-59. [Vgl. LuB
2009, Nr. 345]

753 Møller Jensen, Janus: **Denmark and the Crusades,
1400-1650.** Leiden [u.a.]: Brill, 2007. XIX, 399 S.:
Ill. (The northern world; 30) – Zugl.: Odense,
Syddank Univ., Diss., 2005.

754 Raeder, Siegfried: **Luthers Verhältnis zum Islam:** Zeitbedingtes und Bedenkenswertes [Luther's relationship with Islam]/ engl. Zusammenfassung: Sibylle G. Krause. LuD 16 (2008), 46-51. [Vgl. LuB 2006, Nr. 1005]

755 Smith, Robert O.: **Luther, the Turks, and Islam.** CTM 34 (2007), 351-364.

756 Tészabó, Júlia: **Karácsony:** magyar hagyományok (Weihnachten: ungarische Traditionen) [BP]: Kossuth, 2007. 175 S.

6 Luthers Wirkung auf spätere Strömungen, Gruppen, Persönlichkeiten und Ereignisse

a) Allgemein

757 Atze, Stefan: **Ethik als Steigerungsform von Theologie?:** systematische Rekonstruktion und Kritik eines Strukturprozesses im neuzeitlichen Protestantismus. B; NY: de Gruyter, 2008. 668 S. (Theologische Bibliothek Töpelmann; 144) – Zugl.: Wien, Univ., Diss., 2006.

758 Bin, Fabrice: **L'influence de la pensée chrétienne sur les systèmes fiscaux d'Europe occidentale.** P: L'Harmattan, 2007. 462 S. (Finances publiques)

759 Bräuer, Siegfried: **Kartographie, Luthermemorie, Sequestration:** die Mansfelder Geschichtskarte von Tilemann Stella / Johannes Mellinger 1571. In: Kirche – Kunst – Kultur: Beiträge aus 800 Jahren Berlin-Brandenburgischer Geschichte; Festschrift für Gerlinde Strohmaier-Wiederanders zum 65. Geburtstag/ hrsg. von Hartmut Kühne. F: Lang, 2008, 215-235: Ill.

760 Cornehl, Peter; Grünberg, Wolfgang: **Protestantismus – eine deutsche Religion?:** die Lutherfeiern 1883 und 1983. In: Politische Erinnerung: Geschichte und kollektive Identität [Peter Reichel zum 65. Geburtstag]/ hrsg. von Harald Schmid; Justyna Krzymianowska. Würzburg: Königshausen & Neumann, 2007, 67-99.

761 Flöter, Jonas: **Religiöse Bildung und Erziehung:** die Landesschule Pforta und das Joachimsthalsche Gymnasium im Kaiserreich und in der Weimarer Republik. In: 07, 355-367.

762 Francisco, Adam S.: **Luther, Lutheranism, and the challenge of Islam.** CThQ 71 (2007), 283-300.

763 Fuchs, Martina: **Der Reichstag der Dohlen:** Luthers Coburg-Aufenthalt 1530 in historischer Belletristik. In: Plus ultra: die Welt der Neuzeit; Festschrift für Alfred Kohler zum 65. Geburtstag/ hrsg. von Friedrich Edelmayer. MS: Aschendorff, 2008, 697-718.

764 Gillespie, Michael Allen: **The theological origins of modernity.** Chicago, IL: Univ. of Chicago, 2008. XIII, 386 S.

765 Grage, Joachim: **Chaotischer Abgrund und erhabene Weite:** das Meer in der skandinavischen Dichtung des 17. und 18. Jahrhunderts. GÖ: V&R, 2000. 331 S. L". (Palaestra; 311) – Zugl.: GÖ, Univ., Diss., 1999.

766 Kampmann, Jürgen: Die **Lutherische Konferenz von Minden-Ravensberg:** Werden und Wandel einer konfessionell prägenden Institution in einer Region der evangelischen Kirche Westfalens – Zu den konfessionellen Prägungen in Westfalen in Vergangenheit und Gegenwart. In: 033, 49-66. L 56f.

767 Kolb, Robert: **The three-hundredth anniversary of Lutheran mission in India.** LQ 21 (2007), 95-101.

768 Kroeschell, Karl; Cordes, Albrecht; Nehlsen-von Stryk, Karin: **Deutsche Rechtsgeschichte.** 9., aktual. Aufl., Neubearb. Bd. 2: **1250-1650.** W: Böhlau, 2008. XV, 367 S.: Ill. (UTB; 2735)

769 Leppin, Volker: **Die Monumentalisierung Luthers:** warum vom Thesenanschlag erzählt wurde – und was davon zu erzählen ist. In: 040, 69-92.

770 Lienhard, Marc: **Deux concepts historiques et théologiques:** Réforme et Réformation; les approches du XVIᵉ et du XXᵉ siècles. In: 020, 95-103.

771 Michel, Stefan: **Gesangbuchfrömmigkeit und regionale Identität:** ihr Zusammenhang und Wandel in den reußischen Herrschaften vom 17. bis zum 20. Jahrhundert. L: EVA, 2007. 309 S.: Ill., Kt. – Zugl.: Neuendettelsau, Augustana-Hochschule, Diss., 2006.

772 Muller, Richard A.: **After Calvin:** studies in the development of a theological tradition. Oxford; NY: Oxford University, 2003. VII, 275 S. L". (Oxford studies in historical theology)

773 Ninness, Richard: **Imperial knights and confessional cooperation in the prince-bishopric of Bamberg (1555-1648).** In: 017, 49-67.

774 Prien, Hans-Jürgen: **Das Christentum in Lateinamerika.** L: EVA, 2007. 448 S. L". (Kirchengeschichte in Einzeldarstellungen; IV, 6)

b) Orthodoxie und Gegenreformation

775 Axmacher, Elke: **Paul Gerhardt und die Tradition.** In: 061, 95-108.

776 Berndorff, Lothar: **Nikolaus von Amsdorf als Argument:** zum Gebrauch protestantischer Schiedsautorität in Publizistik und Kirchenpolitik am Beispiel des Mansfelder Klerus. In: 045, 237-250.

777 Beutel, Albrecht: **Lutherischer Lebenstrost:** Einsichten in Paul Gerhardts Abendlied »Nun ruhen alle Wälder«. ZThK 105 (2008), 217-241.

778 Bok, Vaclav: **Die Bibliotheken von Theobald und Hans Höck von Zweibrücken nach einem Inventar von 1618.** In: 04, 341-356.

779 Bräuer, Siegfried: **Johann Friedrich der Ältere und sein Augsburger Bekenntnis gegen das Interim von 1548.** In: 04, 277-297: Faks.

780 Bräuer, Siegfried: **Nikolaus von Amsdorfs Schrift zum Tod Johann Friedrichs d. Ä.** In: 045, 117-133.

781 Brecht, Martin: **Johann Valentin Andreae 1586-1654:** eine Biographie. Mit einem Essay von Christoph Brecht: **Johann Valentin Andreae:** zum literarischen Profil eines deutschen Schriftstellers im 17. Jahrhundert. GÖ: V&R, 2008. 389 S.: Ill.

782 Bulisch, Jens: **Die evangelischen sorbischen Gottesdienste in der Oberlausitz.** In: 065, 315-336. L 336.

783 Bunners, Christian: **Paul Gerhardt:** Weg – Werk – Wirkung. überarb. und erg. Neuausgabe, 2. Aufl. GÖ: V&R, 2007. 320 S.: Ill.: Noten.

784 Bunners, Christian: **Paul Gerhardt:** Weg – Werk – Wirkung. Überarb. und erg. Neuausgabe, 3. Aufl. GÖ: V&R, 2007. 320 S.: Ill.: Noten.

785 Bunners, Christian: **Paul Gerhardt:** Weg – Werk – Wirkung. Überarb. und erg. Neuausgabe, 4. Aufl. GÖ: V&R, 2007. 320 S.: Ill.: Noten.

786 **Catalogus und Centurien:** interdiszliplinäre Studien zu Matthias Flacius und den Magedburger Centurien/ hrsg. von Arno Mentzel-Reuters; Martina Hartmann. TÜ: Mohr Siebeck, 2008. X, 249 S. (Spätmittelalter, Humanismus, Reformation; 45)

787 Dingel, Irene: **Die Kultivierung des Exulantentums im Luthertum am Beispiel des Nikolaus von Amsdorf.** In: 045, 153-175.

788 François, Wim: **Augustinian Bible exegesis in Louvain:** the case of John Hessels' commentary on 1 John 2,15-18a. Augustiniana 57 (Louvain 2007), 399-424.

789 Freedman, Joseph S.: **The »Melanchthonian encyclopedia«:** [»Judicia florentis scholae Melanchthonis« (1592) / »CRISEIS Melanchthonianae « (1597)] of Gregor Richter (1560-1624). In: 044, 105-141: Faks.

790 Gehrt, Daniel: **Der »Erzbischof« von Thürin-

gen?:** Nikolaus von Amsdorf und die Genese der ernestinischen Landeskirche nach dem Schmalkaldischen Krieg. In: 045, 217-236.

791 Goheen, Katherine R.: **Jesu meine Freude:** a cultural reception analysis of Romans 8. Consensus 32 (Winnipeg, Manitoba 2007), 9-33.

792 Gregory, Brad: **Persecutions and martyrdoms.** In: 052, 261-282.

793 Haemig, Mary Jane: **Paul Gerhardt in Amerika.** In: 047, 245-267.

794 Hasse, Hans-Peter: **Der Hausvater als Katechet:** Beobachtungen zu einem Druckmanuskript Nikolaus von Amsdorfs aus dem Jahre 1562 in seinem handschriftlichen Nachlass. In: 045, 91-102.

795 Heckel, Martin: **Deutschland im konfessionellen Zeitalter.** In: 09, 1975-2554 (Bildschirm-)S. (Kleine Vandenhoeck-Reihe; 1490) (Deutsche Geschichte; 5)

796 Henkys, Jürgen: **Zur Rückbindung der Lieder Paul Gerhardts an Luther und die Bekenntnisschriften:** ausgewählte Beispiele. In: 061, 77-93.

797 Hund, Johannes: **Amsdorfs Testament in seinen theologischen und historischen Zusammenhängen.** In: 045, 325-344.

798 Janse, Wim: **Joachim Westphals sacramentstheologie:** een verdediging van Luthers erfenis (Joachim Westphals Sakramentstheologie: eine Verteidigung von Luthers Erbe). LuBu 17 (2008), 54-75.

799 Janse, Wim: **Joachim Westphal's sacramentology:** (Joachim Westphals sacramentstheologie: een verdediging van Luthers erfenis ⟨engl.⟩). LQ 22 (2008), 54-75.

800 Jürgensen, Werner: **Die Kitzinger »Paul-Eber-Bibel« in ihrer Zeit.** ZBKG 77 (2008), 83-96.

801 Kaufmann, Thomas: **Religious, confessional and cultural conflicts among neighbors:** observations on the sixteenth and seventeenth centuries. In: 046, 91-115.

802 Keil, Siegmar: **Martin Rinckart (1586-1649) und seine Lutherdramen.** Mitteldeutsches Jahrbuch für Kultur und Geschichte 15 (2008), 53-61: Portr.

803 Keil, Siegmar: **Martin Rinckarts Lutherdramen:** eine Bestandsaufnahme. Lu 79 (2009), 95-108: Ill.

804 Kilcrease, Jack D.: **The salvation of the unbaptized in Gerhard and Chemnitz.** Logia: a journal of Lutheran theology 16 (2007) Nr. 4, 29-36.

805 Kohnle, Armin: **Nikolaus von Amsdorf und das Interim.** In: 045, 135-152.

806 Kolb, Robert: **»Bekentnis der reinen lere des Euangelij Vnd Confutatio der jtzigen Schwermer«:** Nikolaus von Amsdorf und die Entfaltung einer neuen Bekenntnisform. In: 045, 307-324.

807 Kordič, Ivan: **Croatian philosophers IV:** Matija Vlačić Ilirik – Mathias Flacius Illyricus (1520-1575). Prolegomena – journal of philosophy 4 (Zagreb 2005), 219-233.

808 Kruse, Joachim: **Herzog Johann Friedrich II. der Mittlere von Sachsen (1529-1995) und das ernestinische Familienepitaph in St. Moritz, Coburg, vollendet 1598:** eine kultur- und kunstgeschichtliche Studie. 2 Teile. Sonderdruck aus dem Jahrbuch der Coburger Landesstiftung. Coburg: Coburger Landesstiftung, 2007/08. 334; 298 S.: Ill. L 135-137+". (Jahrbuch der Coburger Landesstiftung; 52 f)

809 Kühne, Hartmut: **Nikolaus von Amsdorf im Streit zwischen dem Magdeburger Rat und lutherischen Theologen um die Amtsenthebung des Tilemann Heshusius** (mit Abdruck eines Amsdorf-Briefes). In: 045, 281-306.

810 Kümmerle, Julian: **Luthertum, humanistische Bildung und württembergischer Territorialstaat:** die Gelehrtenfamilie Bidembach vom 16. bis zum 18. Jahrhundert. S: Kohlhammer, 2008. 387 S. (Veröffentlichungen der Kommission für geschichtliche Landeskunde in Baden-Württemberg: Reihe B, Forschungen; 170) – Zugl.: TÜ, Univ., Diss., 2006.

811 Lehmann, Hartmut: **Lutheranism in the seventeenth century.** In: 052, 56-72.

812 Lyon, James: **La musique de Johann Sebastian Bach comme source de la prédication luthérienne.** In: Les protestants et la création artistique et littéraire (de réformateurs aux romantiques)/ hrsg. von Alain Joblin. Arras: Artois Presses Université, 2008, 133-145.

813 Mager, Inge: **The reception of the two kingdom idea in Lutheran orthodoxy up to Johann Gerhard.** In: 027, 155-172.

814 Malysz, Piotr J.: **Exchange and ecstasy:** Luther's eucharistic theology in light of radical orthodoxy's critique of gift and sacrifice. Scottish Journal of Theology 60 (Cambridge, UK: 2007), 294-308.

815 Michel, Stefan: **Reformation und konfessionelles Zeitalter im Reussenland.** In: 800 Jahre Christentum im Greizer Land: Einblicke in die reußische Kirchengeschichte/ hrsg. von der Superintendentur Greiz; bearb. von Stefan Michel; Redaktion: Andreas Görbert ... Greiz: Superintendentur, 2009, 33-44. L 37.

816 Rein, Nathan Baruch: **From the history of religions to the history of »religion«:** the late Reformation and the challenge to »sui generis« religion. In: 046, 27-44.

817 Reinis, Austra: **»Admitted to the heavenly school«:** consolation, instruction, and admonition in Aegidius Hunnius's academic funeral sermons. SCJ 38 (2007), 995-1012.

818 Selderhuis, Herman J.: **Luther »totus noster est«:** the reception of Luther's thought at the Heidelberg theological faculty 1583-1622. (2006). In: 053, 173-188.

819 Slenczka, Notger: **Paul Gerhardt und Martin Luther.** In: 047, 141-173.

820 Waschbüsch, Andreas: **Alter Melanchthon:** Muster theologischer Autoritätsstiftung bei Matthias Flacius Illyricus. GÖ: V&R, 2008. 208 S. (Forschungen zur Kirchen- und Dogmengeschichte; 96)

821 Weigel, Valentin: **Seligmachende Erkenntnis Gottes. Unterricht Predigte.** [Anhang:] Bericht vom Glauben/ hrsg. und eingel. von Horst Pfefferl. S-Bad Cannstatt: Frommann-Holzboog, 2008. XLVI, 145 S.: Ill. (Valentin Weigel: Sämtliche Schriften: Neue Edition; 9)

822 Whitford, David Mark: **Tyranny and resistance:** the Magdeburg confession and the Lutheran tradition. StL: Concordia, 2001. 142 S.: Ill.

823 Winter, Christian: **Nikolaus von Amsdorf und Moritz von Sachsen** (mit einer Edition der gegen Moritz gerichteten Schriften Amsdorfs). In: 045, 177-215.

c) Pietismus und Aufklärung

824 Brecht, Martin: **Philipp Jakob Speners Verhältnis zu Martin Luther.** In: Philipp Jakob Spener – Leben, Werk, Bedeutung: Bilanz der Forschung nach 300 Jahren/ hrsg. von Dorothea Wendebourg. Halle: Verlag der Franckeschen Stiftungen; TÜ: Niemeyer, 2007, 187-204. (Hallesche Forschungen; 23)

825 Döring, Detlef: **Die deutsche Gesellschaft zu Leipzig und die von ihr vergebenen Auszeichnungen für Poesie und Beredsamkeit 1728-1738.** In: 060, 187-225. L 214 f.

826 **Geschichte der Evangelisch-methodistischen Kirche:** Weg, Wesen und Auftrag des Methodismus unter besonderer Berücksichtigung der deutschsprachigen Länder Europas/ hrsg. von Karl Steckel; Carl Ernst Sommer. 3. Aufl. GÖ: Edition Ruprecht, 2007. 360 S. (Veröffentlichungen der Evang.-Method. Kirche)

827 Lauster, Jörg: **Krise und Neubegründungen der Schriftautorität seit der Aufklärung.** In: 019, 166-183.

828 Lexutt, Athina: **»Der Mönch braucht keine Gelehrsamkeit«:** Luther zwischen Theologie und Religion in der Beurteilung Johann Salomo

Semlers; ein Beitrag zur Rezeption des Themas »Reformation und Mönchtum« im 18. Jahrhundert. In: 053, 189-212.

829 Mai, Klaus-Rüdiger: **Geheimbünde und Freimaurergesellschaften im Europa der frühen Neuzeit.** In: 015, 243-274.

830 Pugh, Benjamin A.: **A brief history of the blood:** the story of the blood of Christ in transatlantic evangelical devotion. Evangelical review of theology 31 (Exeter 2007), 239-255.

831 Sträter, Udo: **August Hermann Francke und Martin Luther.** Pietismus und Neuzeit 34 (2008), 20-41.

832 Tietz, Claudia: **Johann Winckler (1642-1705):** Anfänge eines lutherischen Pietisten. GÖ: V&R, 2008. 407 S.: Ill. (Arbeiten zur Geschichte des Pietismus; 50) – Zugl.: HH, Univ., Diss., 2004.

833 Wallmann, Johannes: **Pietismus-Studien.** TÜ: Mohr Siebeck, 2008. XIV, 408 S. (Wallmann, Johannes: Gesammelte Aufsätze; 2)

d) 19. und 20. Jahrhundert bis 1917

834 Berner, Christian: **Le chemin vers la vérité et la liberté:** notes sur l'essence de la foi selon Luther' de Feuerbach. Revue germanique internationale 8 (P: 2008), 113-127.

835 Dingel, Irene: **Julius Köstlin.** In: 012, 27-35: Portr.

836 Hamre, James S.: **Ulrik Vilhelm Koren:** »It is written«; »By grace alone«. Concordia Historical Institute quarterly 80 (StL 2007), 138-156.

837 Hoburg, Ralf: **Wicherns theologische Bezugnahme auf Schleiermacher und Luther.** In: Johann Hinrich Wichern – Erbe und Auftrag: Stand und Perspektiven der Forschung / hrsg. von Volker Herrmann ... HD: Winter, 2007, 94-112. (Veröffentlichungen des Diakoniewissenschaftlichen Instituts an der Universität Heidelberg; 30)

838 Huppertz, Hubert: **Ignaz von Döllingers Lutherbild.** Amersfoort: Stichting Oud-Katholiek Seminarie, 2007. 63 S. (Publicatieserie Stichting Oud-Katholiek Seminarie; 2007)

839 Koch, Ernst: **Gustav Kawerau.** In: 012, 36-45: Portr.

840 Koßler, Matthias: **Schopenhauers Ethik zwischen Christentum und Empirie:** ihre Beziehung zu Augustinus und Luther. In: Für einen realen Humanismus: Festschrift zum 75. Geburtstag von Alfred Schmidt / hrsg. von Wolfgang Jordan. F; B; Bern; Bruxelles; NY; Oxford; W: Lang, 2006, 115-127.

841 Kreutziger-Herr, Annette: **Sola Scriptura:** Genesisinterpretation, christliche Anthropologie und Feminismus im viktorianischen Amerika. In: 022, 101-121.

842 Mantey, Volker: **Das Verständnis der Reformation als Epoche bei Ferdinand Christian Baur:** nebst einem Ausblick auf das Verhältnis von Reformation und Mönchtum. In: 053, 213-226.

843 Paulson, Steven D.: **Categorical preaching.** LQ 21 (2007), 268-293.

844 Ruster, Thomas: **Ball, Hugo** (Ball, Hugo ⟨engl.⟩). In: 054, 559 f.

845 Siegwalt, Martin: **Friedrich Weyermüller, chantre du réveil luthérin en Alsace.** PL 56 (2008), 197-216. L 210 f+".

e) 1918 bis 1983

846 Crowe, Benjamin D.: **On the track of the fugitive gods:** Heidegger, Luther, Hölderlin. Journal of religion 87 (Chicago, Ill. 2007), 183-205.

847 Diedrich, Hans-Christian: **»Wohin sollen wir gehen ...«:** der Weg der Christen durch die sowjetische Religionsverfolgung; eine russische Kirchengeschichte des 20. Jahrhunderts in ökumenischer Perspektive. Erlangen, Martin-Luther-Verlag, 2007. 571 S.: Ill. L".

848 Dingel, Irene: **Instrumentalisierung von Geschichte:** Nationalsozialismus und Lutherinterpretation am Beispiel des Erlanger Kirchenhistorikers Hans Preuß. In: 062, 269-284.

849 Fix, Karl-Heinz: **Otto Scheel (1876-1954):** der vergessene zweite bzw. erste Vorsitzende (1918-1946). In: 012, 60-99: Portr.

850 Fuhrmann, Helmut: **Unüberwindliche Ambivalenz:** Thomas Mann und Martin Luther. In: Literatur, Literaturunterricht und die Idee der Humanität: Aufsätze und Vorträge. hrsg. von Helmut Fuhrmann. Würzburg: Königshausen & Neumann, 2007, 47-69.

851 Genton, François: **»... le rustre de Wittenberg n'était pas un pacifiste«:** Luther et le IIIe Reich selon Thomas Mann. In: 08, 273-286.

852 Hinlicky, Paul R.: Luther and Heidegger. LQ 22 (2008). 78-86.

853 Hornig, Gottfried: **Einsprüche:** Gustav Wingrens Systematik und Lutherdeutung. In: 016, 117-123.

854 Kang, An Il: **Von der »Nachfolge« zur »Ethik der Verantwortung«:** die Entwicklung des ethischen Denkens bei Dietrich Bonhoeffer. Bochum, 2008. 231 S. L". ⟨http://222-brs.ruhr-uni-bochum.de/netahtml/HSS/KangAnIl/diss.pdf⟩. – Bochum, Ruhr-Univ., Evang.-Theol. Fak., Diss., 2008.

855 Kaufmann, Thomas: **Heinrich Bornkamm als zweiter und erster Vorsitzender des Vereins für** Reformationsgeschichte (1931-1976). In: 012, 100-158: Portr.

856 Liebenberg, Roland: **Der Gott der feldgrauen Männer:** die theozentrische Erfahrungstheologie von Paul Althaus d. J. im Ersten Weltkrieg. L: EVA, 2008. 585 S. (Arbeiten zur Kirchen- und Theologiegeschichte; 22) – Zugl.: Erlangen-Nürnberg, Univ., Theol. Fak., Diss., 2006.

857 Marga, Amy: **Jesus Christ and the modern sinner:** Karl Barth's retrieval of Luther's substantive christology. CTM 34 (2007), 260-270.

858 Menacher, Mark D.: **Gerhard Ebeling in retrospect.** LQ 21 (2007), 163-196.

859 Moeller, Bernd: **Hans von Schubert (1859-1931):** Vorsitzender des Vereins für Reformationsgeschichte von 1918 bis 1931. In: 012, 46-59: Portr.

860 Nowak, Kurt: **Protestantischer Antisemitismus:** ein deutsch-christliches Manifest aus dem Jahr 1917/ aus dem Nachlass hrsg. von Gisa Bauer. HCh 31 (2007 [gedr. 2008]), 75-89.

861 Pfnür, Vinzenz: **Die Bestreitung des Thesenanschlags durch Erwin Iserloh:** theologiegeschichtlicher Kontext – Auswirkungen auf den katholisch-lutherischen Dialog. In: 040, 111-126.

862 Repgen, Konrad: **Ein profangeschichtlicher Rückblick auf die Iserloh-Debatte.** In: 040, 99-110.

863 Stanley, Timothy: **Heidegger on Luther on Paul.** Dialog 46 (Oxford 2007), 41-45.

864 Sulamaa, Kaarle: **Luther, lotat ja Suomi:** kansallisvaltio luostarina (Luther, Lotta-Svärd Frauen und Finnland: der Nationalstaat als Kloster). Helsinki: Kaarle Sulamaa, 2008. 74 S.

865 Walter, Gregory A.: **Hans Joachim Iwand (1899-1960) and the captivity of thewill.** LQ 21 (2007), 422-443.

866 Walter, Gregory A.: **An introduction to H. J. Iwand's »The righteousness of faith according to Luther«.** LQ 21 (2007), 17-26. [Vgl. oben Nr. 314-317]

7   Luthers Gestalt und Lehre in der Gegenwart

867 Altmann, Walter: **Pastoral letter – county elections 2004, Evangelical Church of the Lutheran Confession in Brazil/** aus dem Portugies. übers. von María Eugenia Mendizábal. In: 035, 51-55.

868 Arand, Charles P.: **A two-dimensional understanding of the church for the twenty-first century.** CJ 33 (2007), 146-165.

869 Bayer, Oswald: **Theses on the doctrine of justification.** LQ 22 (2008), 72-75.

870 Bayer, Oswald: **With Luther in the present.** LQ 21 (2007), 1-16.

871 Beyer, Michael: **In memoriam Günther Wartenberg.** LuJ 74 (2008), 7-10.

872 Brandt, Reinhard: **»Reformator ohne Hammer«:** zur öffentlichen Aufmerksamkeit für die Bestreitung des Thesenanschlags. In: 040, 127-140.

873 Breidert, Martin: **Gerechter Krieg gegen Terror und Gewalt:** eine rechtsethische Argumentationsfigur am Beispiel des Afghanistan-Krieges. In: 021, 69-86.

874 Briskina-Müller, Anna: **»Apophatische« Ökumenik? oder: warum wir uns immer noch nicht verstehen …** US 62 (2007), 35-51.

875 Bühler, Pierre: **L'ancrage de la dogmatique dans la réalité.** In: 026, 77-98.

876 Bühler, Pierre: **Les assertions de la foi et leurs articulations.** In: 026, 99-123.

877 Bühler, Pierre: **Pistes de travail pour une relecture active.** In: 026, 461-485.

878 Chia, Roland: **Protestant reflections on Pope Benedict XVI's faith, reason and the university.** Dialog 46 (Oxford 2007), 66-77.

879 Chung, Paul: **Christian faith and Buddhist enlightenment:** for mutual learning and renewal. Studies in interreligious dialogue 17 (Louvain 2007) Nr. 2, 205-220.

880 Chung, Paul: **Lutheran theology in engagement with world religions.** Dialog 46 (Oxford 2007), 335-343.

881 Collange, Jean-François: **Actualité de la Réformation:** réflexions sur la grâce, la foi et le salut. In: 020, 104-110.

882 Daunis, Roberto: **Über Rom zu Luther:** Autobiographisches und Theologisches einer Priesterkonversion. Aachen: Shaker, 2003. 213 S. – Bespr.: Völkers, Klaus: DPfBl 108 (2008), 385 f.

883 Dorgerloh, Stephan: **Von freien Christen und mündigen Bürgern.** In: 013, 15 f.

884 Fabiny, Tibor: **Hívő megértés:** válogatott egyházi publicisztika (Gläubiges Verstehen: ausgewählte kirchliche Publizistik). BP: Hermeneutikai Kutatóközpont, 2008. 200 S.

885 Fazakas, Sándor: **»És igyekezzetek a városnak jólétén …«:** az egyház és a teológia közéleti felelőssége korunk társadalmában (»Suchet der Stadt Bestes …«: die öffentliche Verantwortung der Kirche in der heutigen Gesellschaft). In: 032, 329-340.

886 Fleinert-Jensen, Flemming: **Le langage de la justification.** In: 011, 41-53.

887 **Fragen nach dem einen Gott:** die Monotheismusdebatte im Kontext/ hrsg. von Gesine Palmer. TÜ: Mohr, 2007. X, 401 S. (Religion und Aufklärung; 14)

888 Gisel, Pierre: **Comment construire une théologie?**: essai typologique. In: 026, 125-176.

889 Grözinger, Albrecht: **Homiletik.** GÜ: GVH, 2007. (Lehrbuch Praktische Theologie; 2)

890 Harmati, Béla: **Reuss András köszöntése 70. születésnapján** (Grußworte an András Reuss zum 70. Geburtstag). In: 032, 175-187.

891 Hauerwas, Stanley: **Why war is a moral necessity for America or how realistic is realism?** Seminary Ridge review 9 (2007) Nr. 2, 25-37. [Vgl. LuB 2009, Nr. 345]

892 Hein, Markus: **In memoriam Günther Wartenberg (1943-2007).** HCh 31 (2007 [gedr. 2008]), 9-12: Portr.

893 Henson, Mark S.: **»Wo stehen wir als Menschheit 500 Jahre nach Luthers Ankunft?«:** Predigt zu Römerbrief 14, 17-19; Markus 12, 28-34. In: 013, 7-9.

894 Huber, Wolfgang: **Die Bedeutung der Reformation – 500 Jahre danach:** Festrede zur Eröffnung der Lutherdekade in der Schlosskirche zu Wittenberg. In: 013, 10-14.

895 Huber, Wolfgang: **Luther brachte Wind der Freiheit in die Welt.** In: 013, 2. 18.

896 Jörns, Klaus-Peter: **Lebensgaben Gottes feiern:** Abschied vom Sühneopfermahl; eine neue Liturgie. GÜ: GVH, 2007. 256 S.

897 Kleinig, John: **Grace upon grace:** spirituality for today. StL: Concordia, 2008. 287 S.

898 Klessmann, Michael: **Seelsorge:** Begleitung, Begegnung, Lebensdeutung im Horizont des christlichen Glaubens. NK: NV, 2008. XIII, 499 S.: Ill.

899 Krüger, Jürgen; Meyer-Blanck, Michael: **Evangelisch in Rom:** der etwas andere Reiseführer. GÖ: V&R, 2008. 240 S.: Ill.

900 Kühn, Christoph: **Von der Wittenberger Reformation zu den Ökumenischen Pilgerwegen:** evangelische Erfahrung und Kritik des Pilgerns im Horizont von Konfessionalisierung und Ökumene. In: 028, 291-

901 Lai, Alan Ka Lun: **Enliven the spirit of Reformation.** Consensus 32 (Winnipeg, Manitoba 2007), 141-144.

902 Landmesser, Christof: **Individualität und Sozialität:** Perspektiven biblischer Theologie zur Intergenerationalität. In: 064, 45-67.

903 Ludwig, Frieder: **Jonah's mission:** intercultural and interreligious perspectives. Word & world 27 (St. Paul, MN 2007), 185-194.

904 **The Lutheran handbook II:** here we stand/ hrsg. von Barbara S. Wilson; Arlene Flancher. MP: Augsburg Fortress, 2007. 304 S.: Ill. [enthält: Luthers Kleinen Katechismus ⟨engl.⟩]

905 Meyer, Harding: **The papal office:** a subject for Lutheran theology? Theology digest 52 (StL 2007), 225-230.

906 **Miteinander feiern – voneinander wissen:** Feste im Kirchenjahr/ hrsg. von Helmut Hanisch; Dieter Reiher im Auftrag des Instituts für Diasporawissenschaft, Leipzig; unter Mitarb. von Sara Bodó/Ungarn ... GÖ: V&R, 2008. 105 S.: Ill. L 77-88.

907 Morgenthaler, Christoph: **Systemische Seelsorge:** Impulse der Familien- und Systemtherapie für die kirchliche Praxis. 4. Aufl. S: Kohlhammer, 2005. 304 S.: Ill.

908 Olson, Roger E.: **Deification in contemporary theology.** Theology today 64 (Princeton, NJ 2007), 186-200.

909 Reglitz, Ellen; Wagemann, Jutta: **Martin Luther Superstar:** die evangelische Kirche feierte in Wittenberg die Eröffnung der Lutherdekade. In: 013, 17.

910 Rieth, Ricardo W.: **In memoriam Joachim Fischer.** LuJ 75 (2008), 7 f.

911 Rittgers, Ronald K.: **Anxious penitents and the appeal of the Reformation:** Ozment and the historiography of confession. In: 050, 50-69.

912 Sahayadoss, Santhosh J.: **The social thought of Martin Luther and its relevance for the Indian society.** Doon theological journal 4 (Dehradun, Indien 2007) Nr. 1, 37-54.

913 Schäuble, Wolfgang: **Erinnerung und Gegenwart:** Luther im 21. Jahrhundert. In: 013, 4-6.

914 Schild, Basil: **»God like Whitefella more better I reckon«.** In: Identity, survival, witnes: reconfiguring theological agendas/ hrsg. von Karen Bloomquist. Geneva: Lutheran World Federation, [2008], 51-57. (Theology in the life of the church; 3)

915 Scholz, Stefan: **Ideologien des Verstehens:** eine Diskurskritik der neutestamentlichen Hermeneutiken von Klaus Berger, Elisabeth Schüssler Fiorenza, Peter Stuhlmacher und Hans Weder. TÜ; BL: Francke, 2008. 396 S. L''. – Zugl.: Erlangen-Nürnberg, Univ., Theol. Fak., Diss., 2006.

916 Stahl, Rainer: **Martin Luther für uns heute.** Erlangen: Martin-Luther-Verlag, 2008. 70 S.: Ill.

917 Sweeney, Douglas A.: **On the vocation of historians to the priesthood of believers:** faithful practices in service of the guild. Fides et historia 39 (Terre Haute, IN 2007), 1-13.

918 Thomsen, Mark: **A book worth discussing:** Vitor Westhelle's The scandalous God; the use and abuse of the cross. CTM 34 (2007), 282-286.

919 Tietz, Christiane: **Martin Luther im interkulturellen Kontext.** Nordhausen: Bautz, 2008. 106 S.: Ill. (Interkulturelle Bibliothek; 110)

920 Wefers, Sabine: **Eine Frage der Authentizität.** In: 040, 199-201.

921 Welker, Michael: **Die Botschaft der Reformation – heute.** In: 024, 67-90.

922 Werbick, Jürgen: »**Zur Freiheit hat uns Christus befreit**« (Gal 5,1): was Luthers Widerspruch gegen Erasmus einer theologischen Theorie der Freiheit heute zu denken gibt. In: Freiheit Gottes und der Menschen: Festschrift für Thomas Pröpper/ hrsg. von Michael Böhnke. Regensburg: Pustet, 2006, 41-69.

923 Westhelle, Vítor: **Use and abuses of the cross:** the Reformation then and now. Trinity Seminary review 28 (Columbus, Ohio 2007), 83-93.

924 Whitford, David M.: **Verbum domini manet in aeternum:** finding perspective for our calling in the history of the church. Journal of Theology 111 (Dayton, OH 2007), 53-58.

8 Romane, Schauspiele, Filme, Varia

925 Dapper, Alexandra: **Zu Tisch bei Martin Luther/** hrsg. von Harald Meller. Halle (Saale): Landesamt für Denkmalpflege und Archäologie Sachsen-Anhalt, Landesmuseum für Vorgeschichte, 2008. 134 S.: Ill.

926 Dapper, Alexandra: **Zu Tisch bei Martin Luther/** hrsg. von Harald Meller. S: Theiss, 2008. 134 S.: Ill.

927 **Erinnerungen an Martin Luther/** ausgew. und neu erzählt von Manfred Lemmer. Sandersdorf: Renneritz, 2008. 143 S.: Ill.

928 Fabiny, Tamás: **Luther a filmvásznon – egykor és most** (Luther auf der Leinwand – damals und jetzt). Confessio 29 (BP 2005) Heft 1, 117-119.

929 Ilič, Luka: **Lutheran reformer on Euro coin.** LQ 21 (2007), 340 f.

930 Koch, Ursula: **Rosen im Schnee:** Katharina Luther, geborene von Bora; eine Frau wagt ihr Leben. 12. Aufl. Gießen: Brunnen, 2007. 199 S.

931 Küstenmacher, Werner Tiki: **Der Anschlag in** Wittenberg und andere Rätsel- und Gaukelspiel samt einer himmlischen Vorrede von Doktor Martinus Luther. 3. Aufl. M-Neuhausen: Claudius, 2004. 46 S.: Ill.

932 [Luther, Martin]: **Luther kurz & knackig:** seine originellsten Sprüche/ zsgst. von Gundula Dittrich; mit Ill. von Mathias Wedel. 2. Aufl. L: EVA, 2008. 55 S.: Ill.

933 **Lutherleben:** [das Church-night-Buch]/ hrsg. von Thomas Hofmann-Dietrich; Reinhold Krebs. S: Buch + Musik, 2007. 166 S.: Ill., Noten.

934 Rödding, Gerhard: **Luther und Calvin:** Briefe, die nie geschrieben wurden. NK: Aussaat, 2008. 142 S.

935 Wipfler, Esther P.: **Luthers 95 Thesen im bewegten Bild:** ein Beispiel für die Schriftlichkeit im Film. In: 040, 173-197.

936 Wolf, Manfred: **Eine Frage noch, Herr Luther ...:** Interview mit einem Ketzer. 2. Aufl. L: EVA, 2006. 144 S.

C FORSCHUNGSBERICHTE, SAMMELBESPRECHUNGEN, BIBLIOGRAPHIEN

937 Austad, Torleiv: **75 Jahre Luther-Akademie:** Geschichte und Aufgaben. In: 064, 26-44.

938 Barth, Hans-Martin: **Die Theologie Martin Luthers im globalen Kontext:** Lutherforschung auf dem Weg zum Jahr 2017. MD 59 (2008), 3-8.

939 Bayer, Helmut: **Raum- und zeitabhängige Religionsentwicklungen im deutschsprachigen Europa als Forschungsfeld der Territorialkirchengeschichte:** zu einer vorläufigen Konzeption eines Atlas. In: 033, 157-162.

940 **Bibliographie Albert Greiner.** In: 011, 177-184.

941 **Bibliographie de Frédéric Hartweg.** In: 020, 477-492.

942 Briskina, Anna: **An orthodox view of Finnish Luther research.** LQ 22 (2008), 16-39.

943 Bünz, Enno: »**Vorreformation**«: ein Forschungskonzept zwischen Landesgeschichte und regionaler Kirchengeschichte, Mittelalter- und Frühneuzeitforschung. In: 033, 13-32.

944 Csepregi, Zoltán: **Von der Lutherstatue bis zum Lutherfilm:** ein Vierteljahrhundert Lutherrezeption in Ungarn (1983-2008). LuJ 75 (2008), 169-202.

945 Csepregi, Zoltán: **A Luther-szobortól a Lutherfilmig:** a hazai Luther-recepció utolsó negyedszázada (1983-2008) (Von der Lutherstatue bis zum Lutherfilm: ein Vierteljahrhundert Lutherrezeption in Ungarn (ungar.)). In: 032, 157-174.

946 **Deutscher Humanismus 1480-1520:** Verfasserlexikon/ hrsg. von Franz-Josef Worstbrock. Bd. 1, Lfg. 3: **Engelbrecht, Philipp - Gratius, Ortwinus.** B; NY: de Gruyter, 2007. 160 S.

947 **Deutscher Humanismus 1480-1520:** Verfasserlexikon/ hrsg. von Franz-Josef Worstbrock. Bd. 1, Lfg. 4: **Gresemund, Dietrich - Kruyshaer, Johannes.** B; NY: de Gruyter, 2008. IV, 193 S.

948 Dingel, Irene: **Die Quellen und Forschungen zur Reformationsgeschichte.** In: 012, 274-283.

949 Fabiny, Tibor: **Az amerikai Luther-kutatás** (Die Lutherforschung in Amerika). In: 032, 188-197.

950 Fries, Patrick: **»Damit es recht und christlich eingeweihet und gesegnet werde ...«:** Luther, Foucault und der Blick auf »andere« Räume in Torgau und anderswo. Lu 79 (2008), 164-185.

951 Junghans, Helmar: **Fünfzig Jahre »Lutherjahrbuch« aus Leipzig.** LuJ 74 (2007), 181-198.

952 Junghans, Helmar: **Martin Luther und die Welt der Reformation.** LuJ 75 (2008), 209-218.

953 Karkkainen, Veli-Matti: **Drinking from the same wells with Orthodox and Catholics:** insights from the Finnish interpretation of Luther's theology. CTM 34 (2007), 85-96.

954 Leppin, Volker: **Luther resarch in Germany:** the presence and absence of theology. Dialog: a journal of theology 47 (2008), 105-113.

955 **Liste der im Archiv für Reformationsgeschichte von 1903 bis 2006 erschienenen Aufsätze.** In: 012, 284-415.

956 **Lutherbibliographie 2007/** mit ... bearb. von Helmar Junghans; Michael Beyer; Cornelia Schnapka-Bartmuß. LuJ 74 (2007 [gedr. 2008]), 209-276.

957 **Lutherbibliographie 2008/** mit ... bearb. von Helmar Junghans; Michael Beyer; Alexander Bartmuß; Cornelia Schnapka-Bartmuß. LuJ 75 (2008), 233-288.

958 **Luther-Nachrichten.** Lu 79 (2008), 68.

959 **Materialien** [Verein für Reformationsgeschichte, Quellen]. In: 012, 159-273.

960 Nestingen, James Arne: **Logia forum:** short studies and commentary. Logia: a journal of Lutheran theology 16 (2007) Nr. 4, 63-68.

961 Ortmann, Volkmar: **Luther und das Mönchtum als Thema der Lutherforschung im 20. Jahrhundert.** In: 053, 227-239.

962 Parish, Helen L.: **New perspectives on the Reformation.** Journal of religious history. 32 (Oxford 2008), 96-108.

963 **Religion in Geschichte und Gegenwart:** Handwörterbuch für Theologie und Religionswissenschaft. 4., völlig neu bearb. Aufl./ hrsg. von Hans Dieter Betz ... **Register/** Redaktion: Brigitte Schäfer ... TÜ: Mohr Siebeck, 2007. 1919 Sp. L 1114-1116.

964 Roob, Helmut: **Laudatio** [Helmut Claus]. In: 04, 11-13.

965 Saarinen, Risto: **Partizipation als Gabe:** zwanzig Jahre neue finnische Lutherforschung. Ökumenische Rundschau 57 (2008), 131-143.

966 Schorn-Schütte, Luise: **Der Verein für Reformationsgeschichte 1883-2008:** 125 Jahre Vereins- und Forschungsgeschichte; eine Einleitung. In: 012, 11-26.

967 Schultheis, Saskia: **Bibliographie** [Reformation und Mönchtum]. In: 053, 265-274.

968 Seebaß, Gottfried: **Zur Wiederaufnahme der Edition der Evangelischen Kirchenordnungen des XVI. Jahrhunderts.** Zeitschrift für Württembergische Landesgeschichte 66 (2007), 137-146.

969 **Verzeichnis der Schriften von Helmut Claus/** zsgest. von Elisabeth Rimpler. In: 04, 459-464.

NACHTRÄGLICHE BESPRECHUNGEN

LuB 1997

1244 Horkel, Wilhelm. – Haigis, Peter: DPfBl 108 (2008), 225.

LuB 1999

1069 Hofmann, Frank. – Mahlmann, Theodor: ZKG 118 (2007), 131-133.

LuB 2003

057 Theologen des 16. Jh. – Arnold, Claus: ThRe 103 (2007), 478 f.

LuB 2004

240 Kärkkäinen, Pekka. – Dieter, Theodor: ThRe 104

(2008). 225-227; Plathow, Michael: MD 58 (2007), 60f.

856 Ehrenpreis, Stefan. – Wolf, Hubert: ThRe 103 (2007), 52.

1120 Jadatz, Heiko. – Rhein, Stefan: ThLZ 133 (2008), 1097 f.

LuB 2005

054 Reformer als Ketzer. – Ohst, Martin: ThR 73 (2008), 477-480.

154 Schwanke, Johannes. – Walter, Gregory: LQ 21 (2007), 482-484.

279 Asendorf, Ulrich. – Bienert, Wolfgang A.: ZKG 118 (2007), 261-264.

428 Parsons, Michael. – Mattox, Mickey L.: LQ 21 (2009), 369-371.

549 Töpfer, Thomas.– Junghans, Helmar: LuJ 74
   (2007), 206-208.
834 Hamm, Berndt. – Junghans, Helmar: LuJ 74
   (2007), 204-206.

LuB 2006

023 Glaube und Macht. – Gotthard, Axel: ZHF 34
   (2007), 337-339.
031 Das Jahrhundert der Reformation ... – M[ark-
   schies], Ch[ristoph]: ThLZ 133 (2008), 824.
049 Luther Handbuch. – Hendrix, Scott H.: LuJ 74
   (2007), 199-201; Müller, Gerhard: ThLZ 132 (2007),
   1085-1087; Simon, Wolfgang: ZBKG 77 (2008), 339-
   342.
052 Luthers Erfurter Kloster.– M[arkschies], Ch[ris-
   toph: ThLZ 133 (2008), 1103.
162 Kolb, Robert. – Kern, Udo: ZKG 117 (2008), 411-
   413.
179 Forde, Gerhard O. – Erwin, R. Guy: LQ 21 (2007),
   351 f.
410 Estes, James Martin. – Scheible, Heinz: ZKG 118
   (2007), 264 f.
422 Mantey, Volker. – Schuster, Susanne: ThRe 104
   (2008), 297 f.
492 Mikoteit, Matthias. – Spehr, Christopher: ThRe
   103 (2007), 62 f.
579 Russell, William R. –Schmidt, Timothy A. M.:
   LQ 21 (2007), 113-114.
720 Schorn-Schütte, Luise. – Junghans, Helmar: Mitteldeutsches Jahrbuch für Kultur und Geschichte
   15 (2008), 313 f.

LuB 2007

06 Bildung und Konfession. – Kolb, Robert: LQ 21
   (2007), 473-475.
064 Die Patristik ... – Junghans, Helmar: LuJ 74 (2007),
   203 f.
079 Smolinsky, Heribert. – Köpf, Ulrich: Zeitschrift
   für Württembergische Landesgeschichte 67 (2008),
   596-598.
10 Luther, Martin.– Junghans, Helmar: LuJ 74 (2007),
   199.
85 Leppin, Volker. – Siehe LuB 2009, Nr. 102. 110 f;
   Windhorst, Christof: ThR 73 (2008), 237-246.
316 Holm, Bo Kristian. – Hoping, Helmut: ThLZ 133
   (2008), 964 f.
338 Suda, Max Josef. – Grundmann, Christoffer H.:
   LQ 21 (2007), 244-246.
630 Mörke, Olaf. – Schyder, Caroline: ZKG 117 (2008),
   277 f.
662 Melanchthons Briefwechsel T7. – Benrath, Gustav Adolf: BlPfKG 75 (2008), 428-430 = Ebernburg-

Hefte 42 (2008), 116-118; Junghans, Helmar: LuJ
   74 (2007), 202 f.
982 Kaufmann, Thomas. – Holzem, Andreas: ThRe
   104 (2008), 471-474.
1298 Luther, Martin. – Junghans, Helmar: LuJ 75
   (2008), 213 f.

LuB 2008

012 Creator est Creatura. – Rolf, Sibylle: Lu 79 (2008),
   56 f.
021 Gottes Nähe ... – Basse, Michael: Lu 79 (2008),
   57 f; Zimmerling, Peter: LuJ 75 (2008), 203-208.
050 M. Luther und Eisleben. – Leppin, Volker: ThLZ
   133 (2008), 537-539.
073 Was tun?. – Rolf, Sibylle: ThLZ 133 (2008), 98-
   100.
5 Luther, Martin. – Junghans, Helmar: LuJ 75
   (2008), 209.
108 M. Luther. – Boerke, Christa: LuBu 17 (2008),
   96-98.
145 Paulson, Steven D. – Breitling, Felix: ZBKG 77
   (2008), 338 f.
156 Leiner, Hanns. – Schlichting, Wolfhart: DPfBl
   108 (2008), 337.
179 Jenson, Matt. – Kleffmann, Tom: ThLZ 133
   (2008), 965-968.
237 Schütte, Heinz. – Knoche, Hansjügen: Diakrisis
   28 (2007), 173-175.
284 Krarup, Martin. – Brecht, Martin: ThLZ 133
   (2008), 539-541.
288 Reinis, Austra. – Gößner, Andreas: ZBKG 77
   (2008), 337 f.
388 Frühneuhochdt. Wörterbuch 6 III. – Junghans,
   Helmar: LuJ 75 (2008), 216-218.
498 Gritsch, Eric W. – Lohrmann, Martin J.: LQ 21
   (2007), 471 f.
584 Melanchthons Briefwechsel T4 I. – Daugirdas,
   Kęstutis: BlPfKG 75 (2008), 425-428 = Ebernburg-
   Hefte 42 (2008), 113-116; Junghans, Helmar: LuJ
   75 (2008), 211 f.
585 Melanchthons Briefwechsel T4 II. – Daugirdas,
   Kęstutis: BlPfKG 75 (2008), 425-428 = Ebernburg-
   Hefte 42 (2008), 113-116; Junghans, Helmar: LuJ
   75 (2008), 211 f.
586 Melanchthons Briefwechsel T4 8. – Benrath,
   Gustav Adolf: BlPfKG 75 (2008), 428-430 = Ebernburg-Hefte 42 (2008), 116-118; Junghans, Helmar:
   LuJ 75 (2008), 211-213.
665 Litz, Gudrun. – Schröder, Tilman: Zeitschrift für
   Württembergische Landesgeschichte 67 (2008),
   598-600.
669 Reinitzer, Heimo. – Zschoch, Hellmut: Lu 79
   (2008), 61-63.